LONDON
CONFESSION OF FAITH
REVISED

LONDON
CONFESSION OF FAITH
REVISED

INDEPENDENT HUGUENOT PRESS

INDEPENDENT HUGUENOT PRESS

londonconfessionrevised@gmail.com

Second *London Confession* first published 1677

First IHP *Revised* edition 2017

ISBN-13: 978-0-9979680-1-9 (hardback)

ISBN-13: 978-0-9979680-0-2 (paperback)

PUBLISHER'S NOTE

The base text used for this edition of the London Confession *Revised* is a copy of the original edition of 1677, from McGlothlin, *Baptist Confessions of Faith*, 220-274. The base text used for the catechisms and addenda is the Free Presbyterian Publications 1994 edition of the *Westminster Confession of Faith.*

The primary comparison texts used are the *Second London Confession* of 1688, from Underhill, *Confessions of Faith and other public documents illustrative of the history of the Baptist Churches of England in the 17th century*, 169-246, and the *Westminster Confession* Critical Text produced by S. W. Carruthers. The primary Scripture proof comparison text used is *The Westminster Confession of Faith and Catechisms as adopted by The Orthodox Presbyterian Church*, published by the Committee on Christian Education, 2005.

CONTENTS

TO THE
JUDICIOUS AND IMPARTIAL
READER

Courteous Reader,

It has now been many years since divers of our faithful brethren "with other sober Christians then living and walking in the way of the Lord that we professe" did conceive themselves to be:

> under a necessity of Publishing a *Confession of our Faith*, for the information, and satisfaction of those, that did not thoroughly understand what our principles were, or had entertained prejudices against our Profession, by reason of the strange representation of them, by some men of note, who had taken very wrong measures, and accordingly led others into misapprehensions, of us, and them: and this was first put forth about the year, 1643, in the name of seven Congregations then gathered in *London;* since which time, diverse impressions thereof have been dispersed abroad, and our end proposed, in good measure answered, inasmuch as many (and some of those men eminent, both for piety and learning) were thereby satisfied, that we were no way guilty of those Heterodoxies and fundamental errors, which had too frequently been charged upon us without ground, or occasion given on our part. And forasmuch, as that *Confession* is not now commonly to be had; and also that many others have since embraced the same truth which is owned therein; it was judged necessary by us to joyn together in giving a testimony to the world; of our firm adhering to those wholesome Principles, by the publication of this which is now in your hand.

And as it was the method of those Particular Baptists of London and the vicinity, put forth about the year 1677, to express their sentiments in a way that not only gave a full account of things believed among them, but also fixed their method on the one adopted by the Westminster Assembly and "those of the Congregational way;" it is our design to readily conform to the same order in the present Confession. For those mighty Puritans who assembled at Westminster, Savoy, and in London, were of as godly, judicious divines, as the world ever knew! Therefore, care has been diligently taken to compare all three 17th-century confessions to preserve the doctrines, words and terms, the sense, and agreement, insofar as they are agreeable to the word of God. It is hoped that the reader discovers straightaway the conformity to the thought flow of the originals; and the sequence, words, and phrases that were common in the 17th-century were assiduously chosen, except where it was impossible to do so. We desire as they did to manifest our consent and solidarity with them:

> in all the fundamental articles of the Christian religion, as also with many others whose orthodox confessions have been published to the World, on the behalf of the protestants in divers nations and cities; and also to convince all that we have no itch to clog religion with new words, but to readily acquiesce in that form of sound words which hath been, in consent with the holy scriptures, used by others before us; hereby declaring before God, angels, and men, our hearty agreement with them, in that wholesome protestant doctrine

It remains grievous that there is and shall be those things wherein we differ from others, especially among those of the Protestant Doctrine. It has been our aim to walk in like manner as our Puritan fathers, both in circumspection and method; and so hope to "have also observed those rules of modesty and humility as will render our freedom in this [work] inoffensive, even to those whose sentiments are different from ours." Further, we maintain that contention is as distant from our design as it was from our forebears, with whom we heartily consent the freedom of conscience to display our heart to the sons of God, and that none would take offense from it:

> And oh that other contentions being laid asleep, the only care and contention of all upon whom the name of our blessed Redeemer is called, might for the future be, to walk humbly with their God, and in the exercise of all Love and Meekness towards each other, to perfect holyness in the fear of the Lord, each one endeavouring to have his conversation such as becometh the Gospel; and also, suitable to his place and capacity, vigorously to promote in others the practice of true Religion and undefiled in the sight of God and our Father. And that in this backsliding day, we might not spend our breath in fruitless complaints of the evils of others; but may every one begin at home, to reform in the first place our own hearts, and wayes; and then to quicken all that we may have influence upon, to the same work; that if the will of God were so,

> none might deceive themselves, by resting in, and trusting to, a form of Godliness, without the power of it, and inward experience of the efficacy of those truths that are professed by them.

And finally, the "decay of Religion" persists in our day the same as it did theirs: the egregious neglect "of the worship of God in Families, by those to whom the charge and conduct of them is committed" and the unspeakable decay of the power of godliness. We have, therefore, added a Larger Catechism, hitherto unknown to the Baptists, to expand and fully articulate the statements in the Confession and to increase knowledge among the people of God. A Shorter Catechism has been added which is meant to be useful in the training of children, new converts, and as many as are of weaker capacity. Both the London Larger and Shorter Catechisms were revised in the same manner as the Confession in order to preserve uniformity and agreement, and that both would be agreeable to the word of God, and in nothing contrary to the received doctrine. All three treatises taken together are meant to form the London Standards, and it is here presented for consideration. Let the "Epistle to the Reader" affixed to the Westminster Confession of Faith speak thus: "It is ordinary in these days for men to speak evil of things they know not; but if any are possessed with mean thoughts of these treatises, we shall only give the same counsel to them that Philip gives Nathanael, *Come and see*, John i. 46."

We must take our leave and conclude with a most earnest petition to almighty God, that He would pour out those measures of His Holy Spirit upon us so that our words would not be "enticing words of man's wisdom, but in demonstration of the Spirit and of power: that [our] faith should not stand in the wisdom of men, but in the power of God," and that His "name may in all things be glorified, through Jesus Christ our Lord, *Amen*."

TO THE
JUDICIOUS AND IMPARTIAL
READER.

Courteous Reader,–It is now many years since divers of us (with other sober Christians then living and walking in the way of the Lord that we professe) did conceive our selves to be under a necessity of Publishing a *Confession of our Faith*, for the information, and satisfaction of those, that did not thoroughly understand what our principles were, or had entertained prejudices against our Profession, by reason of the strange representation of them, by some men of note, who had taken very wrong measures, and accordingly led others into misapprehensions, of us, and them: and this was first put forth about the year, 1643, in the name of seven Congregations then gathered in *London;* since which time, diverse impressions thereof have been dispersed abroad, and our end proposed, in good measure answered, inasmuch as many (and some of those men eminent, both for piety and learning) were thereby satisfied, that we were no way guilty of those Heterodoxies and fundamental errors, which had too frequently been charged upon us without ground, or occasion given on our part. And forasmuch, as that *Confession* is not now commonly to be had; and also that many others have since embraced the same truth which is owned therein; it was judged necessary by us to joyn together in giving a testimony to the world; of our firm adhering to those wholesome Principles, by the publication of this which is now in your hand.

And forasmuch as our method, and manner of expressing our sentiments in this doth vary from the former (although the substance of the matter is the same) we shall freely impart to you the reason and occasion thereof. One thing that greatly prevailed with us to undertake this work, was (not only to give a full account of ourselves to those Christians that differ from us about the subject of baptism, but also) the profit that might from thence arise unto those that have any account of our labours, in their instruction and establishment in the great truths of the gospel; in the clear understanding and steady belief of which our comfortable walking with God, and fruitfulness before him in all our ways is most nearly concerned. And therefore we did conclude it necessary to express ourselves the more fully and distinctly, and also to fix on such a method as might be most comprehensive of those things which we designed to explain our sense and belief of; and finding no defect in this regard in that fixed on by the Assembly, and after them by those of the Congregational way, we did readily conclude it best to retain the same order in our present Confession. And also when we observed that those last mentioned did, in their Confession (for reasons which seemed of weight both to themselves and others), choose not only to express their mind in words concurrent with the former in sense, concerning all those articles wherein they were agreed, but also for the most part without any variation of the terms, we did in like manner conclude it best to follow their example, in making use of the very same words with them both, in those articles (which are very many) wherein our faith and doctrine is the same with theirs. And this we did, the more abundantly to manifest our consent with both, in all the fundamental articles of the Christian religion, as also with many others whose orthodox confessions have been published to the World, on the behalf of the protestants in divers nations and cities; and also to convince all that we have no itch to clog religion with new words, but to readily acquiesce in that form of sound words which hath been, in consent with the holy scriptures, used by others before us; hereby declaring before God, angels, and men, our hearty agreement with them, in that wholesome protestant doctrine, which, with so clear evidence of scriptures they have asserted. Some things, indeed, are in some places added, some terms omitted, and some few changed; but these alterations are of that nature, as that we need not doubt any charge or suspicion of unsoundness in the faith, from any of our brethren upon the account of them.

In those things wherein we differ from others, we have expressed ourselves with all candour and plainness, that none might entertain Jealousy of aught secretly lodged in our breasts, that we would not the world should be acquainted with; yet we hope we have also observed those rules of modesty and humility as will render our freedom in this respect inoffensive, even to those whose sentiments are different from ours.

We have also taken care to affix texts of scripture in the margin, for the confirmation of each article in our Confession; in which work we have studiously endeavored to select such as are most clear and pertinent for the proof of what is asserted by us; and our earnest desire is, that all into whose hands this may come would follow that (never enough commended) example of the noble Bereans, who searched the scriptures daily that they might find out whether the things preached to them were so or not.

There is one thing more which we sincerely profess, and earnestly desire credence in, viz., that contention is most remote from our design in all that we have done in this matter; and we hope the liberty of an ingenuous unfolding our principles and opening our hearts unto our brethren, with the scripture-grounds on which our faith and practice leans, will by none of them be either denied to us, or taken ill from us. Our whole design is accomplished if we may obtain that justice, as to be measured in our principles and practice and the judgement of both by others, according to what we have now published; which the Lord (whose eyes are as a flame of fire) knoweth to be the doctrine, which with our hearts we most firmly believe, and sincerely indeavour to conform our lives to. And oh that other contentions being laid asleep, the only care and contention of all upon whom the name of our blessed Redeemer is called, might for the future be, to walk humbly with their God, and in the exercise of all Love and Meekness towards each other, to perfect holyness in the fear of the Lord, each one endeavouring to have his conversation such as becometh the Gospel; and also, suitable to his place and capacity, vigorously to promote in others the practice of true Religion and undefiled in the sight of God and our Father. And that in this backsliding day, we might not spend our breath in fruitless complaints of the evils of others; but may every one begin at home, to reform in the first place our own hearts, and wayes; and then to quicken all that we may have influence upon, to the same work; that if the will of God were so, none might deceive themselves, by resting in, and trusting to, a form of Godliness, without the power of it, and inward experience of the efficacy of those truths that are professed by them.

And verily there is one spring and cause of the decay of Religion in our day, which we cannot but touch upon, and earnestly urge a redress of; and that is the neglect of the worship of God in Families, by those to whom the charge and conduct of them is committed. May not the grosse ignorance, and instability of many; with the prophaneness of others, be justly charged upon their Parents and Masters, who have not trained them up in the way wherein they ought to walk when they were young; but have neglected those frequent and solemn commands which the Lord hath laid upon them so to catechise, and instruct them, that their tender years might be seasoned with the knowledge of the truth of God as revealed in the Scriptures; and also by their own omission of Prayer, and other duties of Religion in their families, together with the ill example of their loose conversation, have inured them first to a neglect, and then contempt of all Piety and Religion? we know this will not excuse the blindness, or wickedness of any; but certainly it will fall heavy upon those that have been thus the occasion thereof; they indeed dye in their sins; but will not their blood be required of those under whose care they were, who yet permitted them to go on without *warning*, yea led them into the paths of destruction? and will not the diligence of Christians with respect to the discharge of these duties, in ages past, rise up in judgment against, and condemn many of those who would be esteemed such now?

We shall conclude with our earnest prayer, that the God of all grace, will pour out those measures of his holy Spirit upon us, that the profession of truth may be accompanyed with the sound belief, and diligent practise of it by us; that his name may in all things be glorified, through Jesus Christ our Lord, *Amen*.

THE CONFESSION OF FAITH REVISED

Thirty-Two Articles of Christian Faith and Practice

CHAPTER 1

Of the Holy Scriptures

1. The Holy Scripture is the only sufficient, certain, and infallible rule of all saving knowledge, faith, and obedience;[1] although the light of nature, and the works of creation and providence do so far manifest the goodness, wisdom and power of God, as to leave men inexcusable;[2] yet are they not sufficient to give that knowledge of God and His will, which is necessary unto salvation.[3] Therefore it pleased the Lord at sundry times, and in divers manners, to reveal Himself, and to declare that His will unto His church;[4] and afterward for the better preserving, and propagating of the truth, and for the more sure establishment and comfort of the church against the corruption of the flesh, and the malice of Satan, and of the world, to commit the same wholly

---

[1] **2 Tim. 3:15-17:** ... and that from childhood you have known the Holy Scriptures, which are able to make you wise for salvation through faith which is in Christ Jesus. All Scripture is given by inspiration of God, and is profitable for doctrine, for reproof, for correction, for instruction in righteousness, that the man of God may be complete, thoroughly equipped for every good work. **Isa. 8:20:** To the law and to the testimony! If they do not speak according to this word, it is because there is no light in them. **Luke 16:29:** Abraham said to him, 'They have Moses and the prophets; let them hear them.' **Eph. 2:20:** ... having been built on the foundation of the apostles and prophets, Jesus Christ Himself being the chief cornerstone.

[2] **Rom. 1:19-21:** ... because what may be known of God is manifest in them, for God has shown it to them. For since the creation of the world His invisible attributes are clearly seen, being understood by the things that are made, even His eternal power and Godhead, so that they are without excuse, because, although they knew God, they did not glorify Him as God, nor were thankful, but became futile in their thoughts, and their foolish hearts were darkened. **Rom. 2:14-15:** ... for when Gentiles, who do not have the law, by nature do the things in the law, these, although not having the law, are a law to themselves. **Ps. 19:1-4:** The heavens declare the glory of God; And the firmament shows His handiwork. Day unto day utters speech, And night unto night reveals knowledge. There is no speech nor language Where their voice is not heard. Their line has gone out through all the earth, And their words to the end of the world. In them He has set a tabernacle for the sun. **See Rom. 1:32-2:1.**

[3] **John 17:3:** And this is eternal life, that they may know You, the only true God, and Jesus Christ whom You have sent. **1 Cor. 1:21:** For since, in the wisdom of God, the world through wisdom did not know God, it pleased God through the foolishness of the message preached to save those who believe. **1 Cor. 2:13-14:** These things we also speak, not in words which man's wisdom teaches but which the Holy Spirit teaches, comparing spiritual things with spiritual. But the natural man does not receive the things of the Spirit of God, for they are foolishness to him; nor can he know them, because they are spiritually discerned.

[4] **Heb. 1:1-2:** God, who at various times and in various ways spoke in time past to the fathers by the prophets, has in these last days spoken to us by His Son, whom He has appointed heir of all things, through whom also He made the worlds.

unto writing;[5] which maketh the Holy Scriptures to be most necessary,[6] those former ways of God's revealing His will unto His people being now ceased.[7]

2. Under the name of Holy Scripture, or the word of God written; are now contained all the books of the Old and New Testament, which are these:

OF THE OLD TESTAMENT: Genesis, Exodus, Leviticus, Numbers, Deuteronomy, Joshua, Judges, Ruth, 1 Samuel, 2 Samuel, 1 Kings, 2 Kings, 1 Chronicles, 2 Chronicles, Ezra, Nehemiah, Esther, Job, Psalms, Proverbs, Ecclesiastes, The Song of Solomon, Isaiah, Jeremiah, Lamentations, Ezekiel, Daniel, Hosea, Joel, Amos, Obadiah, Jonah, Micah, Nahum, Habakkuk, Zephaniah, Haggai, Zechariah, Malachi.

OF THE NEW TESTAMENT: Matthew, Mark, Luke, John, The Acts of the Apostles, Paul's Epistle to the Romans, 1 Corinthians, 2 Corinthians, Galatians, Ephesians, Philippians, Colossians, 1 Thessalonians, 2 Thessalonians, 1 Timothy, 2 Timothy, to Titus,

---

[5] **Luke 1:3-4:** ... it seemed good to me also, having had perfect understanding of all things from the very first, to write to you an orderly account, most excellent Theophilus, that you may know the certainty of those things in which you were instructed. **Prov. 22:19-21:** So that your trust may be in the LORD; I have instructed you today, even you. Have I not written to you excellent things Of counsels and knowledge, That I may make you know the certainty of the words of truth, That you may answer words of truth To those who send to you? **Rom. 15:4:** For whatever things were written before were written for our learning, that we through the patience and comfort of the Scriptures might have hope. **Matt. 4:4, 7, 10:** But He answered and said, "It is written, 'Man shall not live by bread alone, but by every word that proceeds from the mouth of God.'" ... Jesus said to him, "It is written again, 'You shall not tempt the LORD your God.'" ... Then Jesus said to him, "Away with you, Satan! For it is written, 'You shall worship the LORD your God, and Him only you shall serve.'" **Isa. 8:20:** To the law and to the testimony! If they do not speak according to this word, it is because there is no light in them.

[6] **2 Tim. 3:15:** ... and that from childhood you have known the Holy Scriptures, which are able to make you wise for salvation through faith which is in Christ Jesus. **2 Pet. 1:19-20:** And so we have the prophetic word confirmed, which you do well to heed as a light that shines in a dark place, until the day dawns and the morning star rises in your hearts; knowing this first, that no prophecy of Scripture is of any private interpretation.

[7] **John 20:31:** ... but these are written that you may believe that Jesus is the Christ, the Son of God, and that believing you may have life in His name. **1 Cor. 14:37:** If anyone thinks himself to be a prophet or spiritual, let him acknowledge that the things which I write to you are the commandments of the Lord. **1 John 5:13:** These things I have written to you who believe in the name of the Son of God, that you may know that you have eternal life, and that you may continue to believe in the name of the Son of God. **Heb. 1:1-2:** God, who at various times and in various ways spoke in time past to the fathers by the prophets, has in these last days spoken to us by His Son, whom He has appointed heir of all things, through whom also He made the worlds. **Heb. 2:2-4:** For if the word spoken through angels proved steadfast, and every transgression and disobedience received a just reward, how shall we escape if we neglect so great a salvation, which at the first began to be spoken by the Lord, and was confirmed to us by those who heard Him, God also bearing witness both with signs and wonders, with various miracles, and gifts of the Holy Spirit, according to His own will?

to Philemon, The Epistle to the Hebrews, The Epistle of James, The First and Second Epistles of Peter, The First, Second, and Third Epistles of John, The Epistle of Jude, The Revelation.

All of which are given by the entire, full, and absolute inspiration of God,[8] that extendeth even unto every word used and every doctrine declared,[9] to be the enduring rule of faith and life.[10]

3. The books commonly called Apocrypha not being of divine inspiration, are no part of the canon (or rule) of the Scripture,[11] and therefore are of no authority to the church of God, nor to be any otherwise approved or made use of, than other human writings.[12]

4. The authority of the Holy Scripture for which it ought to be believed dependeth not upon the testimony of any man, or church; but wholly upon God (who is truth itself) the author

---

[8] **2 Tim. 3:15-16:** ... and that from childhood you have known the Holy Scriptures, which are able to make you wise for salvation through faith which is in Christ Jesus. All Scripture is given by inspiration of God, and is profitable for doctrine, for reproof, for correction, for instruction in righteousness. **2 Pet. 1:21:** ... for prophecy never came by the will of man, but holy men of God spoke as they were moved by the Holy Spirit.

[9] **1 Cor. 2:12-13:** Now we have received, not the spirit of the world, but the Spirit who is from God, that we might know the things that have been freely given to us by God. These things we also speak, not in words which man's wisdom teaches but which the Holy Spirit teaches, comparing spiritual things with spiritual. **Deut. 18:18:** I will raise up for them a Prophet like you from among their brethren, and will put My words in His mouth, and He shall speak to them all that I command Him. **Zech. 7:12:** Yes, they made their hearts like flint, refusing to hear the law and the words which the LORD of hosts had sent by His Spirit through the former prophets. Thus great wrath came from the LORD of hosts. **Matt. 4:4, 7, 10:** But He answered and said, "It is written, 'Man shall not live by bread alone, but by every word that proceeds from the mouth of God.'" ... Jesus said to him, "It is written again, 'You shall not tempt the LORD your God.'" ... Then Jesus said to him, "Away with you, Satan! For it is written, 'You shall worship the LORD your God, and Him only you shall serve.'"

[10] **Ps. 119:160:** The entirety of Your word is truth, And every one of Your righteous judgments endures forever. **1 Pet. 1:23-25:** ... having been born again, not of corruptible seed but incorruptible, through the word of God which lives and abides forever, because "All flesh is as grass, And all the glory of man as the flower of the grass. The grass withers, And its flower falls away, But the word of the LORD endures forever." Now this is the word which by the gospel was preached to you. **John 10:34-35:** Jesus answered them, "Is it not written in your law, 'I said, "You are gods"'? If He called them gods, to whom the word of God came (and the Scripture cannot be broken). **Matt. 5:18:** For assuredly, I say to you, till heaven and earth pass away, one jot or one tittle will by no means pass from the law till all is fulfilled.

[11] **Luke 24:27, 44:** And beginning at Moses and all the Prophets, He expounded to them in all the Scriptures the things concerning Himself.... Then He said to them, "These are the words which I spoke to you while I was still with you, that all things must be fulfilled which were written in the Law of Moses and the Prophets and the Psalms concerning Me." **Rom. 3:2:** Much in every way! Chiefly because to them were committed the oracles of God.

[12] **Rev. 22:18-19:** For I testify to everyone who hears the words of the prophecy of this book: If anyone adds to these things, God will add to him the plagues that are written in this book; and if anyone takes away from the words of the book of this prophecy, God shall take away his part from the Book of Life, from the holy city, and from the things which are written in this book.

thereof; therefore it is to be received, because it is the word of God.[13]

5. We may be moved and induced by the testimony of the church of God, to an high and reverent esteem of the Holy Scriptures;[14] and the heavenliness of the matter, the efficacy of the doctrine, and the majesty of the style, the consent of all the parts, the scope of the whole (which is to give all glory to God), the full discovery it makes of the only way of man's salvation, and many other incomparable excellencies, and entire perfections thereof, are arguments whereby it doth abundantly evidence itself to be the word of God; yet, notwithstanding; our full persuasion, and assurance of the infallible truth, and divine authority thereof, is from the inward work of the Holy Spirit, bearing witness by and with the word in our hearts.[15]

---

[13] **2 Pet. 1:19-21:** And so we have the prophetic word confirmed, which you do well to heed as a light that shines in a dark place, until the day dawns and the morning star rises in your hearts; knowing this first, that no prophecy of Scripture is of any private interpretation, for prophecy never came by the will of man, but holy men of God spoke as they were moved by the Holy Spirit. **2 Tim. 3:16:** All Scripture is given by inspiration of God, and is profitable for doctrine, for reproof, for correction, for instruction in righteousness. **1 Thess. 2:13:** For this reason we also thank God without ceasing, because when you received the word of God which you heard from us, you welcomed it not as the word of men, but as it is in truth, the word of God, which also effectively works in you who believe. **1 John 5:9:** If we receive the witness of men, the witness of God is greater; for this is the witness of God which He has testified of His Son. **Rev. 1:1-2:** The Revelation of Jesus Christ, which God gave Him to show His servants—things which must shortly take place. And He sent and signified it by His angel to His servant John, who bore witness to the word of God, and to the testimony of Jesus Christ, to all things that he saw.

[14] **2 Tim. 3:14-15:** But you must continue in the things which you have learned and been assured of, knowing from whom you have learned them, and that from childhood you have known the Holy Scriptures, which are able to make you wise for salvation through faith which is in Christ Jesus.

[15] **John 16:13-14:** However, when He, the Spirit of truth, has come, He will guide you into all truth; for He will not speak on His own authority, but whatever He hears He will speak; and He will tell you things to come. He will glorify Me, for He will take of what is Mine and declare it to you. **1 Cor. 2:9-16:** But as it is written: "Eye has not seen, nor ear heard, Nor have entered into the heart of man The things which God has prepared for those who love Him." But God has revealed them to us through His Spirit. For the Spirit searches all things, yes, the deep things of God. For what man knows the things of a man except the spirit of the man which is in him? Even so no one knows the things of God except the Spirit of God. Now we have received, not the spirit of the world, but the Spirit who is from God, that we might know the things that have been freely given to us by God. These things we also speak, not in words which man's wisdom teaches but which the Holy Spirit teaches, comparing spiritual things with spiritual. But the natural man does not receive the things of the Spirit of God, for they are foolishness to him; nor can he know them, because they are spiritually discerned. But he who is spiritual judges all things, yet he himself is rightly judged by no one. For "who has known the mind of the Lord that he may instruct Him?" But we have the mind of Christ. **Heb. 4:12:** For the word of God is living and powerful, and sharper than any two-edged sword, piercing even to the division of soul and spirit, and of joints and marrow, and is a discerner of the thoughts and intents of the heart. **Isa. 55:11:** So shall My word be that goes forth from My mouth; It shall not return to Me void, But it shall accomplish what I please, And it shall prosper in the thing for which I sent it. **See Rom. 11:36. Ps. 19:7-11:** The law of the LORD is perfect, converting the soul; The testimony of the Lord is sure, making wise the simple; The statutes of the LORD are right, rejoicing the heart; The commandment of the LORD is pure, enlightening the eyes; The fear of the LORD is clean, enduring forever; The judgments of the LORD are true and righteous altogether. More to be desired are they than gold, Yea, than much fine gold; Sweeter also than honey and the honeycomb. Moreover by them Your servant is warned, And in keeping them there is great reward. **1 Cor. 2:4-5:** And my speech and my preaching were not with persuasive words of

6. The whole counsel of God concerning all things necessary for His own glory, man's salvation, faith and life, is either expressly set down or necessarily contained in the Holy Scripture, that, by good and necessary consequence, may be deduced from it; unto which nothing at any time is to be added, whether by new revelation of the Spirit, or traditions of men.[16] Nevertheless, we acknowledge the inward illumination of the Spirit of God, to be necessary for the saving understanding of such things as are revealed in the word,[17] and that there are some circumstances concerning the worship of God, and government of the church common to human actions and societies; which are to be ordered by the light of nature, and Christian prudence according to the general rules of the word, which are always to be observed.[18]

---

human wisdom, but in demonstration of the Spirit and of power, that your faith should not be in the wisdom of men but in the power of God. **1 Thess. 1:5:** For our gospel did not come to you in word only, but also in power, and in the Holy Spirit and in much assurance, as you know what kind of men we were among you for your sake. **1 John 2:20, 27:** But you have an anointing from the Holy One, and you know all things. I have not written to you because you do not know the truth, but because you know it, and that no lie is of the truth.... But the anointing which you have received from Him abides in you, and you do not need that anyone teach you; but as the same anointing teaches you concerning all things, and is true, and is not a lie, and just as it has taught you, you will abide in Him.

[16] **2 Tim. 3:15-17:** ... and that from childhood you have known the Holy Scriptures, which are able to make you wise for salvation through faith which is in Christ Jesus. All Scripture is given by inspiration of God, and is profitable for doctrine, for reproof, for correction, for instruction in righteousness, that the man of God may be complete, thoroughly equipped for every good work. **Gal. 1:8-9:** But even if we, or an angel from heaven, preach any other gospel to you than what we have preached to you, let him be accursed. As we have said before, so now I say again, if anyone preaches any other gospel to you than what you have received, let him be accursed.

[17] **John 6:45:** It is written in the prophets, 'And they shall all be taught by God.' Therefore everyone who has heard and learned from the Father comes to Me. **1 Cor. 2:9-15:** But as it is written: "Eye has not seen, nor ear heard, Nor have entered into the heart of man The things which God has prepared for those who love Him." But God has revealed *them* to us through His Spirit. For the Spirit searches all things, yes, the deep things of God. For what man knows the things of a man except the spirit of the man which is in him? Even so no one knows the things of God except the Spirit of God. Now we have received, not the spirit of the world, but the Spirit who is from God, that we might know the things that have been freely given to us by God. These things we also speak, not in words which man's wisdom teaches but which the Holy Spirit teaches, comparing spiritual things with spiritual. But the natural man does not receive the things of the Spirit of God, for they are foolishness to him; nor can he know *them,* because they are spiritually discerned. But he who is spiritual judges all things, yet he himself is *rightly* judged by no one. **Eph. 1:18:** ... the eyes of your understanding being enlightened; that you may know what is the hope of His calling, what are the riches of the glory of His inheritance in the saints. **See 2 Cor. 4:6.**

[18] **1 Cor. 11:13-14:** Judge among yourselves. Is it proper for a woman to pray to God with her head uncovered? Does not even nature itself teach you that if a man has long hair, it is a dishonor to him? **1 Cor. 14:26, 40:** How is it then, brethren? Whenever you come together, each of you has a psalm, has a teaching, has a tongue, has a revelation, has an interpretation. Let all things be done for edification.... Let all things be done decently and in order.

7. All things in Scripture are not alike plain in themselves, nor alike clear unto all;[19] yet those things which are necessary to be known, believed, and observed for salvation, are so clearly propounded, and opened in some place of Scripture or other, that not only the learned, but the unlearned, in a due use of ordinary means, may attain to a sufficient understanding of them,[20] although the inspiration of God be not limited only to the doctrines of the gospel but extendeth unto all matters declared in Scripture which cannot err.[21]

8. The Old Testament in Hebrew (which was the native language of the people of God of old),[22] and the New Testament in Greek (which at the time of the writing of it was most generally known to the nations), being immediately inspired by God, and by His singular care and providence kept pure in all ages, are therefore authentic;[23] so as in all controversies of religion, the church is finally to appeal unto them.[24] But because these original tongues are not known to all the people of God, who have a right unto, and interest in the Scriptures, and are commanded in the fear of God to read and search them,[25] therefore they are to be

---

[19] **2 Pet. 3:16:** ... as also in all his epistles, speaking in them of these things, in which are some things hard to understand, which untaught and unstable *people* twist to their own destruction, as *they do* also the rest of the Scriptures.

[20] **Ps. 19:7:** The law of the LORD *is* perfect, converting the soul; The testimony of the LORD *is* sure, making wise the simple. **Ps. 119:105, 130:** Your word *is* a lamp to my feet And a light to my path.... The entrance of Your words gives light; It gives understanding to the simple. **Deut. 29:29:** The secret *things belong* to the LORD our God, but those *things which are* revealed *belong* to us and to our children forever, that *we* may do all the words of this law. **Deut. 30:10-14:** ... if you obey the voice of the LORD your God, to keep His commandments and His statutes which are written in this Book of the Law, *and* if you turn to the LORD your God with all your heart and with all your soul. "For this commandment which I command you today *is* not *too* mysterious for you, nor *is* it far off. It *is* not in heaven, that you should say, 'Who will ascend into heaven for us and bring it to us, that we may hear it and do it?' Nor *is* it beyond the sea, that you should say, 'Who will go over the sea for us and bring it to us, that we may hear it and do it?' But the word *is* very near you, in your mouth and in your heart, that you may do it." **Acts 17:11:** These were more fair-minded than those in Thessalonica, in that they received the word with all readiness, and searched the Scriptures daily *to find out* whether these things were so.

[21] **Ps. 12:6:** The words of the LORD *are* pure words, *Like* silver tried in a furnace of earth, Purified seven times. **Ps. 119:142, 151:** Your righteousness *is* an everlasting righteousness, And Your law *is* truth.... You *are* near, O LORD, And all Your commandments *are* truth. **John 17:17:** Sanctify them by Your truth. Your word is truth. **Prov. 30:5-6:** Every word of God *is* pure; He *is* a shield to those who put their trust in Him. Do not add to His words, Lest He rebuke you, and you be found a liar.

[22] **Rom. 3:2:** Much in every way! Chiefly because to them were committed the oracles of God.

[23] **Matt. 5:18:** For assuredly, I say to you, till heaven and earth pass away, one jot or one tittle will by no means pass from the law till all is fulfilled. **Ps. 119:89:** Forever, O LORD, Your word is settled in heaven.

[24] **Isa. 8:20:** To the law and to the testimony! If they do not speak according to this word, it is because there is no light in them. **Acts 15:15:** And with this the words of the prophets agree, just as it is written.... **See Luke 16:31.**

[25] **John 5:39:** You search the Scriptures, for in them you think you have eternal life; and these are they which testify of Me. **Acts 17:11:** These were more fair-minded than those in Thessalonica, in

translated into the vulgar language of every nation, unto which they come,[26] that the word of God dwelling plentifully in all, they may worship Him in an acceptable manner, and through patience and comfort of the Scriptures may have hope.[27]

9. The infallible rule of interpretation of Scripture is the Scripture itself: And therefore when there is a question about the true and full sense of any Scripture (which is not manifold, but one) it must be searched by other places that speak more clearly.[28]

10. The supreme judge by which all controversies of religion are to be determined, and all decrees of councils, opinions of ancient writers, doctrines of men, and private spirits, are to be examined, and in whose sentence we are to rest, can be no other but the Holy Scripture delivered by the Spirit, into which Scripture so delivered, our faith is finally resolved.[29]

---

that they received the word with all readiness, and searched the Scriptures daily *to find out* whether these things were so. **Rev. 1:3:** Blessed *is* he who reads and those who hear the words of this prophecy, and keep those things which are written in it; for the time *is* near. **See 2 Tim. 3:14-15.**

[26] **1 Cor. 14:6, 9, 11-12, 24, 28:** But now, brethren, if I come to you speaking with tongues, what shall I profit you unless I speak to you either by revelation, by knowledge, by prophesying, or by teaching? ... So likewise you, unless you utter by the tongue words easy to understand, how will it be known what is spoken? For you will be speaking into the air.... Therefore, if I do not know the meaning of the language, I shall be a foreigner to him who speaks, and he who speaks *will be* a foreigner to me. Even so you, since you are zealous for spiritual *gifts, let it be* for the edification of the church *that* you seek to excel.... But if all prophesy, and an unbeliever or an uninformed person comes in, he is convinced by all, he is convicted by all.... But if there is no interpreter, let him keep silent in church, and let him speak to himself and to God. **See Mark 15:34.**

[27] **Col. 3:16:** Let the word of Christ dwell in you richly in all wisdom, teaching and admonishing one another in psalms and hymns and spiritual songs, singing with grace in your hearts to the Lord. **See Ex. 20:4-6; Matt. 15:7-9. Rom. 15:4:** For whatever things were written before were written for our learning, that we through the patience and comfort of the Scriptures might have hope.

[28] **Acts 15:15-16:** And with this the words of the prophets agree, just as it is written: 'After this I will return And will rebuild the tabernacle of David, which has fallen own; I will rebuild its ruins, And I will set it up.' **John 5:46:** For if you believed Moses, you would believe Me; for he wrote about Me. **John 10:34-36:** Jesus answered them, "Is it not written in your law, 'I said, "You are gods"'? If He called them gods, to whom the word of God came (and the Scripture cannot be broken), do you say of Him whom the Father sanctified and sent into the world, 'You are blaspheming,' because I said, 'I am the Son of God'?" **See 2 Pet. 1:20-21.**

[29] **Matt. 22:29, 31:** Jesus answered and said to them, "You are mistaken, not knowing the Scriptures nor the power of God.... But concerning the resurrection of the dead, have you not read what was spoken to you by God...." **Eph. 2:20:** ... having been built on the foundation of the apostles and prophets, Jesus Christ Himself being the chief cornerstone. **Acts 17:11:** These were more fair-minded than those in Thessalonica, in that they received the word with all readiness, and searched the Scriptures daily *to find out* whether these things were so. **Acts 28:23-25:** So when they had appointed him a day, many came to him at *his* lodging, to whom he explained and solemnly testified of the kingdom of God, persuading them concerning Jesus from both the Law of Moses and the Prophets, from morning till evening. And some were persuaded by the things which were spoken, and some disbelieved. So when they did not agree among themselves, they departed after Paul had said one word: "The Holy Spirit spoke rightly through Isaiah the prophet to our fathers." **See 1 John 4:1-6.**

CHAPTER 2

Of God and the Holy Trinity

1. The Lord our God is but one only[1] living, and true God;[2] whose subsistence is in and of Himself,[3] infinite in being, and perfection,[4] whose essence cannot be comprehended by any but Himself;[5] a most pure Spirit,[6] invisible,[7] without body, parts,[8] or passions,[9] who only hath immortality, dwelling in the light, which no man can approach unto,[10] who is immutable,[11] immense,[12] eternal,[13] incomprehensible,[14] almighty,[15] every way

---

[1] **1 Cor. 8:4, 6:** Therefore concerning the eating of things offered to idols, we know that an idol *is* nothing in the world, and that *there is* no other God but one.... yet for us *there is* one God, the Father, of whom *are* all things, and we for Him; and one Lord Jesus Christ, through whom *are* all things, and through whom we *live.* **Deut. 6:4:** Hear, O Israel: The LORD our God, the LORD *is* one! **Isa. 48:12:** Listen to Me, O Jacob, And Israel, My called: I *am* He, I *am* the First, I *am* also the Last. **See Gal. 3:20.**

[2] **1 Thess. 1:9:** For they themselves declare concerning us what manner of entry we had to you, and how you turned to God from idols to serve the living and true God. **Jer. 10:10:** But the LORD *is* the true God; He *is* the living God and the everlasting King. At His wrath the earth will tremble, And the nations will not be able to endure His indignation.

[3] **Ex. 3:14:** And God said to Moses, "I AM WHO I AM." And He said, "Thus you shall say to the children of Israel, 'I AM has sent me to you.'"

[4] **Job 11:7-9:** Can you search out the deep things of God? Can you find out the limits of the Almighty? *They are* higher than heaven—what can you do? Deeper than Sheol—what can you know? Their measure *is* longer than the earth And broader than the sea. **Job 26:14:** Indeed these *are* the mere edges of His ways, And how small a whisper we hear of Him! But the thunder of His power who can understand? **See Ps. 139:6.**

[5] **Matt. 11:27:** All things have been delivered to Me by My Father, and no one knows the Son except the Father. Nor does anyone know the Father except the Son, and *the one* to whom the Son wills to reveal *Him.* **Col. 2:3:** ... in whom are hidden all the treasures of wisdom and knowledge.

[6] **John 4:24:** God *is* Spirit, and those who worship Him must worship in spirit and truth.

[7] **1 Tim. 1:17:** Now to the King eternal, immortal, invisible, to God who alone is wise, *be* honor and glory forever and ever. Amen. **See John 1:18.**

[8] **Deut. 4:15-16:** Take careful heed to yourselves, for you saw no form when the LORD spoke to you at Horeb out of the midst of the fire, lest you act corruptly and make for yourselves a carved image in the form of any figure: the likeness of male or female. **Cf. John 4:24 with Luke 24:39.**

[9] **Acts 14:11, 15:** Now when the people saw what Paul had done, they raised their voices, saying in the Lycaonian *language,* "The gods have come down to us in the likeness of men!" ... and saying, "Men, why are you doing these things? We also are men with the same nature as you, and preach to you that you should turn from these useless things to the living God, who made the heaven, the earth, the sea, and all things that are in them."

[10] **1 Tim. 6:16:** ... who alone has immortality, dwelling in unapproachable light, whom no man has seen or can see, to whom *be* honor and everlasting power. Amen.

[11] **James 1:17:** Every good gift and every perfect gift is from above, and comes down from the Father of lights, with whom there is no variation or shadow of turning. **Mal. 3:6:** For I *am* the LORD, I do not change; Therefore you are not consumed, O sons of Jacob.

[12] **1 Kings 8:27:** But will God indeed dwell on the earth? Behold, heaven and the heaven of heavens cannot contain You. How much less this temple which I have built! **Jer. 23:23-24:** "*Am* I a God near at hand," says the LORD, "And not a God afar off? Can anyone hide himself in secret places, So I shall not see him?" says the LORD; "Do I not fill heaven and earth?" says the LORD.

[13] **Ps. 90:2:** Before the mountains were brought forth, Or ever You had formed the earth and the world, Even from everlasting to everlasting, You *are* God. **See 1 Tim. 1:17.**

[14] **Ps. 145:3:** Great *is* the LORD, and greatly to be praised; And His greatness *is* unsearchable. **See Rom. 11:34.**

[15] **Gen. 17:1:** When Abram was ninety-nine years old, the LORD appeared to Abram and said to him, "I *am* Almighty God; walk before Me and be blameless."

infinite,[16] most holy,[17] most wise,[18] most free,[19] most absolute,[20] working all things according to the counsel of His own immutable, and most righteous will,[21] for His own glory,[22] most loving,[23] gracious, merciful, long-suffering, abundant in goodness and truth, forgiving iniquity, transgression and sin,[24] the rewarder of them that diligently seek Him,[25] and withal most just, and terrible in His judgments,[26] hating all sin,[27] and who will by no means clear the guilty.[28]

2. God having all life,[29] glory,[30] goodness,[31] blessedness,[32] in and of Himself: is alone in, and unto Himself all-sufficient, not

---

[16] **Ps. 145:7:** They shall utter the memory of Your great goodness, And shall sing of Your righteousness.

[17] **Isa. 6:3:** And one cried to another and said: "Holy, holy, holy *is* the LORD of hosts; The whole earth *is* full of His glory!" **See Rev. 4:8.**

[18] **Rom. 16:27:** ... to God, alone wise, *be* glory through Jesus Christ forever. Amen.

[19] **Ps. 115:3:** But our God *is* in heaven; He does whatever He pleases. **Isa. 46:10:** Declaring the end from the beginning, And from ancient times *things* that are not *yet* done, Saying, 'My counsel shall stand, And I will do all My pleasure.' **See Isa. 14:24.**

[20] **Isa. 45:5-6:** I *am* the LORD, and *there is* no other; *There is* no God besides Me. I will gird you, though you have not known Me, That they may know from the rising of the sun to its setting That *there is* none besides Me. **See Ex. 3:14.**

[21] **Eph. 1:11:** In Him also we have obtained an inheritance, being predestined according to the purpose of Him who works all things according to the counsel of His will.

[22] **Prov. 16:4:** The LORD has made all for Himself, Yes, even the wicked for the day of doom. **Rom. 11:36:** For of Him and through Him and to Him *are* all things, to whom *be* glory forever. Amen. **See Rev. 4:11.**

[23] **1 John 4:8:** He who does not love does not know God, for God is love. **See 1 John 4:16; John 3:16.**

[24] **Ex. 34:6-7:** And the LORD passed before him and proclaimed, "The LORD, the LORD God, merciful and gracious, longsuffering, and abounding in goodness and truth, keeping mercy for thousands, forgiving iniquity and transgression and sin, by no means clearing *the guilty,* visiting the iniquity of the fathers upon the children and the children's children to the third and the fourth generation."

[25] **Heb. 11:6:** But without faith *it is* impossible to please *Him,* for he who comes to God must believe that He is, and *that* He is a rewarder of those who diligently seek Him.

[26] **Neh. 9:32-33:** Now therefore, our God, The great, the mighty, and awesome God, Who keeps covenant and mercy: Do not let all the trouble seem small before You That has come upon us, Our kings and our princes, Our priests and our prophets, Our fathers and on all Your people, From the days of the kings of Assyria until this day. However You *are* just in all that has befallen us; For You have dealt faithfully, But we have done wickedly. **See Heb. 10:28-31.**

[27] **Hab. 1:13:** *You are* of purer eyes than to behold evil, And cannot look on wickedness. Why do You look on those who deal treacherously, *And* hold Your tongue when the wicked devours A *person* more righteous than he? **Rom. 1:18:** For the wrath of God is revealed from heaven against all ungodliness and unrighteousness of men, who suppress the truth in unrighteousness. **Ps. 5:5-6:** The boastful shall not stand in Your sight; You hate all workers of iniquity. You shall destroy those who speak falsehood; The LORD abhors the bloodthirsty and deceitful man. **See Ps. 11:5.**

[28] **Ex. 34:7:** ... keeping mercy for thousands, forgiving iniquity and transgression and sin, by no means clearing *the guilty,* visiting the iniquity of the fathers upon the children and the children's children to the third and the fourth generation. **Nah. 1:2-3:** God *is* jealous, and the LORD avenges; The LORD avenges and *is* furious. The LORD will take vengeance on His adversaries, And He reserves *wrath* for His enemies; The LORD *is* slow to anger and great in power, And will not at all acquit *the wicked.* The LORD has His way In the whirlwind and in the storm, And the clouds *are* the dust of His feet.

[29] **Jer. 10:10:** But the LORD *is* the true God; He *is* the living God and the everlasting King. At His wrath the earth will tremble, And the nations will not be able to endure His indignation. **John 5:26:** For as the Father has life in Himself, so He has granted the Son to have life in Himself.

standing in need of any creature which He hath made,[33] nor deriving any glory from them,[34] but only manifesting His own glory in, by, unto, and upon them, He is the alone fountain of all being, of whom, through whom, and to whom are all things,[35] and He hath most sovereign dominion over all creatures, to do by them, for them, and upon them, whatsoever Himself pleaseth;[36] in His sight all things are open and manifest,[37] His knowledge is infinite, infallible, and independent upon the creature,[38] so as nothing is to Him contingent, or uncertain;[39] He is most holy in all His counsels, in all His works, and in all His commands;[40] to Him is due from angels and men, whatsoever worship, service, or obedience as creatures they owe unto the Creator, and whatever He is further pleased to require of them.[41]

---

[30] **Ps. 148:13:** Let them praise the name of the LORD, For His name alone is exalted; His glory *is* above the earth and heaven. **Acts 7:2:** And he said, "Brethren and fathers, listen: The God of glory appeared to our father Abraham when he was in Mesopotamia, before he dwelt in Haran."

[31] **Ps. 119:68:** I keep Your precepts and Your testimonies, For all my ways *are* before You.

[32] **1 Tim. 6:15:** ... which He will manifest in His own time, *He who is* the blessed and only Potentate, the King of kings and Lord of lords. **See Rom. 9:5.**

[33] **Acts 17:24-25:** God, who made the world and everything in it, since He is Lord of heaven and earth, does not dwell in temples made with hands. **Job. 22:2-3:** Can a man be profitable to God, Though he who is wise may be profitable to himself? *Is it* any pleasure to the Almighty that you are righteous? Or *is it* gain *to Him* that you make your ways blameless?

[34] **Luke 17:10:** So likewise you, when you have done all those things which you are commanded, say, 'We are unprofitable servants. We have done what was our duty to do.'

[35] **Rom. 11:34-36:** "For who has known the mind of the LORD? Or who has become His counselor?" "Or who has first given to Him And it shall be repaid to him?" For of Him and through Him and to Him *are* all things, to whom *be* glory forever. Amen.

[36] **Rev. 4:11:** "You are worthy, O Lord, To receive glory and honor and power; For You created all things, And by Your will they exist and were created." **Dan. 4:25, 34-35:** They shall drive you from men, your dwelling shall be with the beasts of the field, and they shall make you eat grass like oxen. They shall wet you with the dew of heaven, and seven times shall pass over you, till you know that the Most High rules in the kingdom of men, and gives it to whomever He chooses.... And at the end of the time I, Nebuchadnezzar, lifted my eyes to heaven, and my understanding returned to me; and I blessed the Most High and praised and honored Him who lives forever: For His dominion *is* an everlasting dominion, And His kingdom *is* from generation to generation. All the inhabitants of the earth *are* reputed as nothing; He does according to His will in the army of heaven And *among* the inhabitants of the earth. No one can restrain His hand Or say to Him, "What have You done?" **See 1 Tim. 6:15.**

[37] **Heb. 4:13:** And there is no creature hidden from His sight, but all things *are* naked and open to the eyes of Him to whom we *must give* account.

[38] **Rom. 11:33-34:** Oh, the depth of the riches both of the wisdom and knowledge of God! How unsearchable *are* His judgments and His ways past finding out! "For who has known the mind of the LORD? Or who has become His counselor?" **Ps. 147:5:** Great *is* our Lord, and mighty in power; His understanding *is* infinite.

[39] **Ezek. 11:5:** Then the Spirit of the LORD fell upon me, and said to me, "Speak! 'Thus says the LORD: "Thus you have said, O house of Israel; for I know the things that come into your mind."'" **Acts 15:18:** Known to God from eternity are all His works.

[40] **Ps. 145:17:** The LORD *is* righteous in all His ways, Gracious in all His works. **Rom. 7:12:** Therefore the law *is* holy, and the commandment holy and just and good.

[41] **Rev. 5:12-14:** ... saying with a loud voice: "Worthy is the Lamb who was slain To receive power and riches and wisdom, And strength and honor and glory and blessing!" And every creature which is in heaven and on the earth and under the earth and such as are in the sea, and all that are in

3. In this divine and infinite Being there are three subsistences, the Father, the Word or Son, and Holy Spirit,[42] of one substance, power, and eternity, each having the whole divine essence, yet the essence undivided,[43] the Father is of none, neither begotten nor proceeding, the Son is eternally begotten of the Father,[44] the Holy Spirit proceeding from the Father and the Son,[45] all infinite, without beginning, therefore but one God, who is not to be divided in nature and being; but distinguished by several peculiar, relative properties, and personal relations; which doctrine of the Trinity is the foundation of all our communion with God, and comfortable dependence on Him.

---

them, I heard saying: "Blessing and honor and glory and power *Be* to Him who sits on the throne, And to the Lamb, forever and ever!"

[42] **Matt. 3:16-17:** When He had been baptized, Jesus came up immediately from the water; and behold, the heavens were opened to Him, and He saw the Spirit of God descending like a dove and alighting upon Him. And suddenly a voice *came* from heaven, saying, "This is My beloved Son, in whom I am well pleased." **Matt. 28:19:** Go therefore and make disciples of all the nations, baptizing them in the name of the Father and of the Son and of the Holy Spirit. **2 Cor. 13:14:** All the saints greet you. The grace of the Lord Jesus Christ, and the love of God, and the communion of the Holy Spirit *be* with you all. Amen. **See Eph. 2:18.**

[43] **Ex. 3:14:** And God said to Moses, "I AM WHO I AM." And He said, "Thus you shall say to the children of Israel, 'I AM has sent me to you.'" **John 14:11:** Believe Me that I *am* in the Father and the Father in Me, or else believe Me for the sake of the works themselves. **1 Cor. 8:6:** ... yet for us *there is* one God, the Father, of whom *are* all things, and we for Him; and one Lord Jesus Christ, through whom *are* all things, and through whom we *live.* **Ps. 139:7-10:** Where can I go from Your Spirit? Or where can I flee from Your presence? If I ascend into heaven, You *are* there; If I make my bed in hell, behold, You *are there. If* I take the wings of the morning, *And* dwell in the uttermost parts of the sea, Even there Your hand shall lead me, And Your right hand shall hold me.

[44] **John 1:14, 18:** And the Word became flesh and dwelt among us, and we beheld His glory, the glory as of the only begotten of the Father, full of grace and truth.... No one has seen God at any time. The only begotten Son, who is in the bosom of the Father, He has declared *Him.* **See Heb. 1:2-3; Col. 1:15.**

[45] **John 15:26:** But when the Helper comes, whom I shall send to you from the Father, the Spirit of truth who proceeds from the Father, He will testify of Me. **Gal. 4:6:** And because you are sons, God has sent forth the Spirit of His Son into your hearts, crying out, "Abba, Father!"

CHAPTER 3

Of God's Decree

1. God hath decreed in Himself from all eternity, by the most wise and holy counsel of His own will, freely and unchangeably, all things whatsoever come to pass;[1] yet so as thereby is God neither the author of sin, nor hath fellowship with any therein,[2] nor is violence offered to the will of the creature, nor yet is the liberty, or contingency of second causes taken away, but rather established,[3] in which appears His wisdom in disposing all things, and power, and faithfulness in accomplishing His decree.[4]

2. Although God knoweth whatsoever may, or can come to pass upon all supposed conditions;[5] yet hath He not decreed anything, because He foresaw it as future, or as that which would come to pass upon such conditions.[6]

---

[1] **Isa. 46:10:** Declaring the end from the beginning, And from ancient times *things* that are not *yet* done, Saying, 'My counsel shall stand, And I will do all My pleasure.' **Eph. 1:11:** In Him also we have obtained an inheritance, being predestined according to the purpose of Him who works all things according to the counsel of His will. **Heb. 6:17:** Thus God, determining to show more abundantly to the heirs of promise the immutability of His counsel, confirmed *it* by an oath. **Rom. 9:15, 18:** For He says to Moses, "I will have mercy on whomever I will have mercy, and I will have compassion on whomever I will have compassion." ... Therefore He has mercy on whom He wills, and whom He wills He hardens.

[2] **Ps. 5:4:** For You *are* not a God who takes pleasure in wickedness, Nor shall evil dwell with You. **James 1:13, 17:** Let no one say when he is tempted, "I am tempted by God"; for God cannot be tempted by evil, nor does He Himself tempt anyone... Every good gift and every perfect gift is from above, and comes down from the Father of lights, with whom there is no variation or shadow of turning. **1 John 1:5:** This is the message which we have heard from Him and declare to you, that God is light and in Him is no darkness at all. **See Hab. 1:13.**

[3] **Acts 2:23:** Him, being delivered by the determined purpose and foreknowledge of God, you have taken by lawless hands, have crucified, and put to death. **Acts 4:27-28:** "For truly against Your holy Servant Jesus, whom You anointed, both Herod and Pontius Pilate, with the Gentiles and the people of Israel, were gathered together to do whatever Your hand and Your purpose determined before to be done. **John 19:11:** Jesus answered, "You could have no power at all against Me unless it had been given you from above. Therefore the one who delivered Me to you has the greater sin." **Prov. 16:33:** The lot is cast into the lap, But its every decision *is* from the LORD.

[4] **Num. 23:19:** God *is* not a man, that He should lie, Nor a son of man, that He should repent. Has He said, and will He not do? Or has He spoken, and will He not make it good? **Eph. 1:3-5:** Blessed *be* the God and Father of our Lord Jesus Christ, who has blessed us with every spiritual blessing in the heavenly *places* in Christ, just as He chose us in Him before the foundation of the world, that we should be holy and without blame before Him in love, having predestined us to adoption as sons by Jesus Christ to Himself, according to the good pleasure of His will.

[5] **1 Sam. 23:11-12:** "Will the men of Keilah deliver me into his hand? Will Saul come down, as Your servant has heard? O LORD God of Israel, I pray, tell Your servant." And the LORD said, "He will come down." Then David said, "Will the men of Keilah deliver me and my men into the hand of Saul?" And the LORD said, "They will deliver *you.*" **Acts 15:18:** Known to God from eternity are all His works.

[6] **Rom. 9:11-18:** (for *the children* not yet being born, nor having done any good or evil, that the purpose of God according to election might stand, not of works but of Him who calls), it was said to her, "The older shall serve the younger." As it is written, "Jacob I have loved, but Esau I have hated." What shall we say then? *Is there* unrighteousness with God? Certainly not! For He says to Moses, "I will have mercy on whomever I will have mercy, and I will have compassion on whomever I will have compassion." So then *it is* not of him who wills, nor of him who runs, but of God who

3. By the decree of God, for the manifestation of His glory some men and angels are predestinated, or foreordained to eternal life,[7] through Jesus Christ, to the praise of His glorious grace;[8] others being left to act in their sin to their just condemnation, God was pleased, according to the unsearchable counsel of His own will, whereby He extendeth or withholdeth mercy, as He pleaseth, for the glory of His sovereign power over His creatures, to pass by and to ordain them to dishonour and wrath for their sin, to the praise of His glorious justice.[9]

4. These angels and men thus predestinated, and foreordained, are particularly, and unchangeably designed, and their number

---

shows mercy. For the Scripture says to the Pharaoh, "For this very purpose I have raised you up, that I may show My power in you, and that My name may be declared in all the earth." Therefore He has mercy on whom He wills, and whom He wills He hardens.

[7] **1 Tim. 5:21:** I charge *you* before God and the Lord Jesus Christ and the elect angels that you observe these things without prejudice, doing nothing with partiality. **Matt. 25:31-34:** When the Son of Man comes in His glory, and all the holy angels with Him, then He will sit on the throne of His glory. All the nations will be gathered before Him, and He will separate them one from another, as a shepherd divides *his* sheep from the goats. And He will set the sheep on His right hand, but the goats on the left. Then the King will say to those on His right hand, 'Come, you blessed of My Father, inherit the kingdom prepared for you from the foundation of the world.'

[8] **Eph. 1:5-6:** ... having predestined us to adoption as sons by Jesus Christ to Himself, according to the good pleasure of His will, to the praise of the glory of His grace, by which He made us accepted in the Beloved.

[9] **Rom. 9:6-24:** But it is not that the word of God has taken no effect. For they *are* not all Israel who *are* of Israel, nor *are they* all children because they are the seed of Abraham; but, "In Isaac your seed shall be called." That is, those who *are* the children of the flesh, these *are* not the children of God; but the children of the promise are counted as the seed. For this *is* the word of promise: "At this time I will come and Sarah shall have a son." And not only *this,* but when Rebecca also had conceived by one man, *even* by our father Isaac (for *the children* not yet being born, nor having done any good or evil, that the purpose of God according to election might stand, not of works but of Him who calls), it was said to her, "The older shall serve the younger." As it is written, "Jacob I have loved, but Esau I have hated." What shall we say then? *Is there* unrighteousness with God? Certainly not! For He says to Moses, "I will have mercy on whomever I will have mercy, and I will have compassion on whomever I will have compassion." So then *it is* not of him who wills, nor of him who runs, but of God who shows mercy. For the Scripture says to the Pharaoh, "For this very purpose I have raised you up, that I may show My power in you, and that My name may be declared in all the earth." Therefore He has mercy on whom He wills, and whom He wills He hardens. You will say to me then, "Why does He still find fault? For who has resisted His will?" But indeed, O man, who are you to reply against God? Will the thing formed say to him who formed *it,* "Why have you made me like this?" Does not the potter have power over the clay, from the same lump to make one vessel for honor and another for dishonor? *What* if God, wanting to show *His* wrath and to make His power known, endured with much longsuffering the vessels of wrath prepared for destruction, and that He might make known the riches of His glory on the vessels of mercy, which He had prepared beforehand for glory, even us whom He called, not of the Jews only, but also of the Gentiles? **Jude 4:** For certain men have crept in unnoticed, who long ago were marked out for this condemnation, ungodly men, who turn the grace of our God into lewdness and deny the only Lord God and our Lord Jesus Christ. **1 Pet. 2:8:** and "A stone of stumbling And a rock of offense." They stumble, being disobedient to the word, to which they also were appointed. **2 Tim. 2:19-20:** Nevertheless the solid foundation of God stands, having this seal: "The Lord knows those who are His," and, "Let everyone who names the name of Christ depart from iniquity." But in a great house there are not only vessels of gold and silver, but also of wood and clay, some for honor and some for dishonor. **Matt. 11:26:** Even so, Father, for so it seemed good in Your sight.

so certain, and definite, that it cannot be either increased, or diminished.[10]

5. Those of mankind that are predestinated to life, God, before the foundation of the world was laid, according to His eternal and immutable purpose, and the secret counsel and good pleasure of His will, hath chosen in Christ unto everlasting glory,[11] out of His mere free grace and love; without any other thing in the creature as a condition or cause moving Him thereunto.[12]

6. As God hath appointed the elect unto glory, so He hath by the eternal and most free purpose of His will, foreordained all the means thereunto,[13] wherefore they who are elected, being fallen

---

[10] **2 Tim. 2:19:** Nevertheless the solid foundation of God stands, having this seal: "The Lord knows those who are His," and, "Let everyone who names the name of Christ depart from iniquity." **John 13:18:** I do not speak concerning all of you. I know whom I have chosen; but that the Scripture may be fulfilled, 'He who eats bread with Me has lifted up his heel against Me.' **See John 10:14-16, 27-28; 17:2, 6, 9-12.**

[11] **Eph. 1:3-12:** Blessed *be* the God and Father of our Lord Jesus Christ, who has blessed us with every spiritual blessing in the heavenly *places* in Christ, just as He chose us in Him before the foundation of the world, that we should be holy and without blame before Him in love, having predestined us to adoption as sons by Jesus Christ to Himself, according to the good pleasure of His will, to the praise of the glory of His grace, by which He made us accepted in the Beloved. In Him we have redemption through His blood, the forgiveness of sins, according to the riches of His grace which He made to abound toward us in all wisdom and prudence, having made known to us the mystery of His will, according to His good pleasure which He purposed in Himself, that in the dispensation of the fullness of the times He might gather together in one all things in Christ, both which are in heaven and which are on earth—in Him. In Him also we have obtained an inheritance, being predestined according to the purpose of Him who works all things according to the counsel of His will, that we who first trusted in Christ should be to the praise of His glory. **Rom. 8:30:** Moreover whom He predestined, these He also called; whom He called, these He also justified; and whom He justified, these He also glorified. **2 Tim. 1:9:** ... who has saved us and called *us* with a holy calling, not according to our works, but according to His own purpose and grace which was given to us in Christ Jesus before time began. **1 Thess. 5:9:** For God did not appoint us to wrath, but to obtain salvation through our Lord Jesus Christ.

[12] **Rom. 9:11, 13, 15-16:** (for *the children* not yet being born, nor having done any good or evil, that the purpose of God according to election might stand, not of works but of Him who calls) ... As it is written, "Jacob I have loved, but Esau I have hated." ... For He says to Moses, "I will have mercy on whomever I will have mercy, and I will have compassion on whomever I will have compassion." So then *it is* not of him who wills, nor of him who runs, but of God who shows mercy. **Eph. 2:4-10:** But God, who is rich in mercy, because of His great love with which He loved us, even when we were dead in trespasses, made us alive together with Christ (by grace you have been saved), and raised *us* up together, and made *us* sit together in the heavenly *places* in Christ Jesus, that in the ages to come He might show the exceeding riches of His grace in *His* kindness toward us in Christ Jesus. For by grace you have been saved through faith, and that not of yourselves; *it is* the gift of God, not of works, lest anyone should boast. For we are His workmanship, created in Christ Jesus for good works, which God prepared beforehand that we should walk in them. **See Eph. 1:5, 9, 11.**

[13] **1 Pet. 1:2:** ... elect according to the foreknowledge of God the Father, in sanctification of the Spirit, for obedience and sprinkling of the blood of Jesus Christ: Grace to you and peace be multiplied. **Eph. 2:10:** For we are His workmanship, created in Christ Jesus for good works, which God prepared beforehand that we should walk in them. **2 Thess. 2:13:** But we are bound to give thanks to God always for you, brethren beloved by the Lord, because God from the beginning chose you for salvation through sanctification by the Spirit and belief in the truth.

in Adam, are redeemed by Christ,[14] are effectually called unto faith in Christ, by His Spirit working in due season, are justified, adopted, sanctified,[15] and kept by His power through faith unto salvation;[16] neither are any other redeemed by Christ, or effectually called, justified, adopted, sanctified, and saved, but the elect only.[17]

7. The doctrine of this high mystery of predestination, is to be handled with special prudence, and care;[18] that men attending the will of God revealed in His word, and yielding obedience thereunto, may from the certainty of their effectual vocation, be assured of their eternal election;[19] so shall this doctrine afford matter of praise, reverence, and admiration of God,[20] and of

---

[14] **1 Thess. 5:9-10:** For God did not appoint us to wrath, but to obtain salvation through our Lord Jesus Christ, who died for us, that whether we wake or sleep, we should live together with Him. **Titus 2:14:** ... who gave Himself for us, that He might redeem us from every lawless deed and purify for Himself *His* own special people, zealous for good works.

[15] **Rom. 8:30:** Moreover whom He predestined, these He also called; whom He called, these He also justified; and whom He justified, these He also glorified. **2 Thess. 2:13:** But we are bound to give thanks to God always for you, brethren beloved by the Lord, because God from the beginning chose you for salvation through sanctification by the Spirit and belief in the truth. **See Eph. 1:5.**

[16] **1 Pet. 1:5:** ... who are kept by the power of God through faith for salvation ready to be revealed in the last time.

[17] **John 6:64:** "But there are some of you who do not believe." For Jesus knew from the beginning who they were who did not believe, and who would betray Him. **John 10:26:** But you do not believe, because you are not of My sheep, as I said to you. **John 17:9:** "I pray for them. I do not pray for the world but for those whom You have given Me, for they are Yours. **Rom. 8:28-39:** And we know that all things work together for good to those who love God, to those who are the called according to *His* purpose. For whom He foreknew, He also predestined *to be* conformed to the image of His Son, that He might be the firstborn among many brethren. Moreover whom He predestined, these He also called; whom He called, these He also justified; and whom He justified, these He also glorified. What then shall we say to these things? If God *is* for us, who *can be* against us? He who did not spare His own Son, but delivered Him up for us all, how shall He not with Him also freely give us all things? Who shall bring a charge against God's elect? *It is* God who justifies. Who *is* he who condemns? *It is* Christ who died, and furthermore is also risen, who is even at the right hand of God, who also makes intercession for us. Who shall separate us from the love of Christ? *Shall* tribulation, or distress, or persecution, or famine, or nakedness, or peril, or sword? As it is written: "For Your sake we are killed all day long; We are accounted as sheep for the slaughter." Yet in all these things we are more than conquerors through Him who loved us. For I am persuaded that neither death nor life, nor angels nor principalities nor powers, nor things present nor things to come, nor height nor depth, nor any other created thing, shall be able to separate us from the love of God which is in Christ Jesus our Lord. **See John 8:47; 1 John 2:19.**

[18] **Rom. 9:20:** But indeed, O man, who are you to reply against God? Will the thing formed say to him who formed *it*, "Why have you made me like this?" **Rom. 11:33:** Oh, the depth of the riches both of the wisdom and knowledge of God! How unsearchable *are* His judgments and His ways past finding out! **Deut. 29:29:** The secret *things belong* to the LORD our God, but those *things which are* revealed *belong* to us and to our children forever, that we may do all the words of this law.

[19] **1 Thess. 1:4-5:** ... knowing, beloved brethren, your election by God. For our gospel did not come to you in word only, but also in power, and in the Holy Spirit and in much assurance, as you know what kind of men we were among you for your sake. **2 Pet. 1:10:** Therefore, brethren, be even more diligent to make your call and election sure, for if you do these things you will never stumble.

[20] **Eph. 1:6:** ... to the praise of the glory of His grace, by which He made us accepted in the Beloved. **Rom. 11:33:** Oh, the depth of the riches both of the wisdom and knowledge of God! How unsearchable *are* His judgments and His ways past finding out!

humility, diligence, and abundant consolation, to all that sincerely obey the gospel.[21]

---

[21] **Rom. 11:5-6, 20:** Even so then, at this present time there is a remnant according to the election of grace. And if by grace, then *it is* no longer of works; otherwise grace is no longer grace. But if *it is* of works, it is no longer grace; otherwise work is no longer work.... Well *said.* Because of unbelief they were broken off, and you stand by faith. Do not be haughty, but fear. **Luke 10:20:** Nevertheless do not rejoice in this, that the spirits are subject to you, but rather rejoice because your names are written in heaven. **2 Pet. 1:10:** Therefore, brethren, be even more diligent to make your call and election sure, for if you do these things you will never stumble. **Rom. 8:33:** Who shall bring a charge against God's elect? *It is* God who justifies.

CHAPTER 4
Of Creation

1. In the beginning it pleased God the Father, Son, and Holy Spirit,[1] for the manifestation of the glory of His eternal power, wisdom, and goodness,[2] to create or make the world, and all things therein, whether visible or invisible,[3] in the space of six days, and all very good.[4]

2. After God had made all other creatures, He created man, male and female,[5] with reasonable and immortal souls,[6] rendering them fit unto that life to God for which they were created; being made after the image of God, in knowledge, righteousness, and true holiness;[7] having the law of God written in their hearts,[8] and power to fulfill it;[9] and yet under a possibility of transgressing,

---

[1] **Gen. 1:2:** The earth was without form, and void; and darkness *was* on the face of the deep. And the Spirit of God was hovering over the face of the waters. **John 1:2-3:** He was in the beginning with God. All things were made through Him, and without Him nothing was made that was made. **Heb. 1:2:** ... has in these last days spoken to us by *His* Son, whom He has appointed heir of all things, through whom also He made the worlds. **Job 33:4:** The Spirit of God has made me, And the breath of the Almighty gives me life. **Job 26:13:** By His Spirit He adorned the heavens; His hand pierced the fleeing serpent.

[2] **Rom. 1:20:** For since the creation of the world His invisible *attributes* are clearly seen, being understood by the things that are made, *even* His eternal power and Godhead, so that they are without excuse. **Jer. 10:12:** He has made the earth by His power, He has established the world by His wisdom, And has stretched out the heavens at His discretion. **Ps. 33:5:** He loves righteousness and justice; The earth is full of the goodness of the LORD. **Ps. 104:24:** O LORD, how manifold are Your works! In wisdom You have made them all. The earth is full of Your possessions.

[3] **Col. 1:16:** For by Him all things were created that are in heaven and that are on earth, visible and invisible, whether thrones or dominions or principalities or powers. All things were created through Him and for Him.

[4] **Ex. 20:11:** For *in* six days the LORD made the heavens and the earth, the sea, and all that *is* in them, and rested the seventh day. Therefore the LORD blessed the Sabbath day and hallowed it. **Gen. 1:31:** Then God saw everything that He had made, and indeed it was very good. So the evening and the morning were the sixth day.

[5] **Gen. 1:27:** So God created man in His *own* image; in the image of God He created him; male and female He created them.

[6] **Gen. 2:7:** And the LORD God formed man *of* the dust of the ground, and breathed into his nostrils the breath of life; and man became a living being. **Eccl. 12:7:** Then the dust will return to the earth as it was, And the spirit will return to God who gave it.

[7] **Gen. 1:26:** Then God said, "Let Us make man in Our image, according to Our likeness; let them have dominion over the fish of the sea, over the birds of the air, and over the cattle, over all the earth and over every creeping thing that creeps on the earth." **Col. 3:10:** ... and have put on the new *man* who is renewed in knowledge according to the image of Him who created him. **Eph. 4:24:** ... and that you put on the new man which was created according to God, in true righteousness and holiness.

[8] **Rom. 2:14-15:** ... for when Gentiles, who do not have the law, by nature do the things in the law, these, although not having the law, are a law to themselves, who show the work of the law written in their hearts, their conscience also bearing witness, and between themselves *their* thoughts accusing or else excusing *them*).

[9] **Gen. 2:17:** ... but of the tree of the knowledge of good and evil you shall not eat, for in the day that you eat of it you shall surely die. **Eccl. 7:29:** Truly, this only I have found: That God made man upright, But they have sought out many schemes.

being left to the liberty of their own will, which was subject to change.[10]

3. Besides the law written in their hearts, they received a command not to eat of the tree of knowledge of good and evil;[11] which whilst they kept, they were happy in their communion with God,[12] and had dominion over the creatures.[13]

---

[10] **Gen. 3:6, 17:** So when the woman saw that the tree *was* good for food, that it *was* pleasant to the eyes, and a tree desirable to make *one* wise, she took of its fruit and ate. She also gave to her husband with her, and he ate.... Then to Adam He said, "Because you have heeded the voice of your wife, and have eaten from the tree of which I commanded you, saying, 'You shall not eat of it': Cursed *is* the ground for your sake; In toil you shall eat *of* it All the days of your life."

[11] **Gen. 2:17:** ... but of the tree of the knowledge of good and evil you shall not eat, for in the day that you eat of it you shall surely die. **Gen. 3:11:** And He said, "Who told you that you *were* naked? Have you eaten from the tree of which I commanded you that you should not eat?"

[12] **Gen. 1:29:** And God said, "See, I have given you every herb *that* yields seed which *is* on the face of all the earth, and every tree whose fruit yields seed; to you it shall be for food." **Gen. 2:** And the LORD God formed man *of* the dust of the ground, and breathed into his nostrils the breath of life; and man became a living being. The LORD God planted a garden eastward in Eden, and there He put the man whom He had formed. And out of the ground the LORD God made every tree grow that is pleasant to the sight and good for food.... Now a river went out of Eden to water the garden, and from there it parted and became four riverheads.... where *there is* gold. And the gold of that land *is* good. Bdellium and the onyx stone *are* there.... Then the LORD God took the man and put him in the garden of Eden to tend and keep it.... And the LORD God said, "*It is* not good that man should be alone; I will make him a helper comparable to him." Out of the ground the LORD God formed every beast of the field and every bird of the air, and brought *them* to Adam to see what he would call them. And whatever Adam called each living creature, that *was* its name. So Adam gave names to all cattle, to the birds of the air, and to every beast of the field. But for Adam there was not found a helper comparable to him. And the LORD God caused a deep sleep to fall on Adam, and he slept; and He took one of his ribs, and closed up the flesh in its place. Then the rib which the LORD God had taken from man He made into a woman, and He brought her to the man. And Adam said: "This *is* now bone of my bones And flesh of my flesh; She shall be called Woman, Because she was taken out of Man." Therefore a man shall leave his father and mother and be joined to his wife, and they shall become one flesh.

[13] **Gen. 1:26, 28:** Then God said, "Let Us make man in Our image, according to Our likeness; let them have dominion over the fish of the sea, over the birds of the air, and over the cattle, over all the earth and over every creeping thing that creeps on the earth." ... Then God blessed them, and God said to them, "Be fruitful and multiply; fill the earth and subdue it; have dominion over the fish of the sea, over the birds of the air, and over every living thing that moves on the earth." **See Gen. 1:29-30; Ps. 8:6-8.**

CHAPTER 5

Of Divine Providence

1. God, the good Creator of all things, in His infinite power, and wisdom, doth uphold,[1] direct, dispose, and govern all creatures, and things,[2] from the greatest even to the least,[3] by His most wise and holy providence,[4] to the end for the which they were created;[5] according unto His infallible foreknowledge,[6] and the

---

[1] **Neh. 9:6:** You alone *are* the LORD; You have made heaven, The heaven of heavens, with all their host, The earth and everything on it, The seas and all that is in them, And You preserve them all. The host of heaven worships You. **Ps. 145:14-16:** The LORD upholds all who fall, And raises up all *who are* bowed down. The eyes of all look expectantly to You, And You give them their food in due season. You open Your hand And satisfy the desire of every living thing. **Heb. 1:3**: ... who being the brightness of *His* glory and the express image of His person, and upholding all things by the word of His power, when He had by Himself purged our sins, sat down at the right hand of the Majesty on high.

[2] **Dan. 4:34-35:** And at the end of the time I, Nebuchadnezzar, lifted my eyes to heaven, and my understanding returned to me; and I blessed the Most High and praised and honored Him who lives forever: For His dominion *is* an everlasting dominion, And His kingdom *is* from generation to generation. All the inhabitants of the earth *are* reputed as nothing; He does according to His will in the army of heaven And *among* the inhabitants of the earth. No one can restrain His hand Or say to Him, "What have You done?" **Acts 17:25-28:** Nor is He worshiped with men's hands, as though He needed anything, since He gives to all life, breath, and all things. And He has made from one blood every nation of men to dwell on all the face of the earth, and has determined their preappointed times and the boundaries of their dwellings, so that they should seek the Lord, in the hope that they might grope for Him and find Him, though He is not far from each one of us; for in Him we live and move and have our being, as also some of your own poets have said, 'For we are also His offspring.' **Job 38-41:** Then the LORD answered Job out of the whirlwind, and said: ... "Where were you when I laid the foundations of the earth? Tell *Me*, if you have understanding.... "Or *who* shut in the sea with doors, When it burst forth *and* issued from the womb.... Have the gates of death been revealed to you? Or have you seen the doors of the shadow of death.... "Can you bind the cluster of the Pleiades, Or loose the belt of Orion.... "Have you given the horse strength? Have you clothed his neck with thunder.... Have you an arm like God? Or can you thunder with a voice like His? Then adorn yourself *with* majesty and splendor, And array yourself with glory and beauty.... "Can you draw out Leviathan with a hook, Or *snare* his tongue with a line *which* you lower...." **Isa. 46:10-11:** Declaring the end from the beginning, And from ancient times *things* that are not *yet* done, Saying, 'My counsel shall stand, And I will do all My pleasure,' Calling a bird of prey from the east, The man who executes My counsel, from a far country. Indeed I have spoken *it*; I will also bring it to pass. I have purposed *it*; I will also do it. **Ps. 135:6:** Whatever the LORD pleases He does, In heaven and in earth, In the seas and in all deep places.

[3] **Matt. 10:29-31:** Are not two sparrows sold for a copper coin? And not one of them falls to the ground apart from your Father's will. But the very hairs of your head are all numbered. Do not fear therefore; you are of more value than many sparrows. **See Matt. 6:26-32.**

[4] **Prov. 15:3:** The eyes of the LORD *are* in every place, Keeping watch on the evil and the good. **2 Chron. 16:9:** For the eyes of the LORD run to and fro throughout the whole earth, to show Himself strong on behalf of *those* whose heart *is* loyal to Him. In this you have done foolishly; therefore from now on you shall have wars. **Ps. 104:24:** O LORD, how manifold are Your works! In wisdom You have made them all. The earth is full of Your possessions. **Ps. 145:17:** The LORD *is* righteous in all His ways, Gracious in all His works.

[5] **Col. 1:16:** For by Him all things were created that are in heaven and that are on earth, visible and invisible, whether thrones or dominions or principalities or powers. All things were created through Him and for Him. **Acts 17:24-28:** God, who made the world and everything in it, since He is Lord of heaven and earth, does not dwell in temples made with hands. Nor is He worshiped with men's hands, as though He needed anything, since He gives to all life, breath, and all things. And He has made from one blood every nation of men to dwell on all the face of the earth, and has determined their preappointed times and the boundaries of their dwellings, so that they should seek the Lord, in the hope that they might grope for Him and find Him, though He is not far from each one of us; for in Him we live and move and have our being, as also some of your own poets have said, 'For we are also His offspring.'

free and immutable counsel of His own will;[7] to the praise of the glory of His wisdom, power, justice, infinite goodness and mercy.[8]

2. Although in relation to the foreknowledge and decree of God, the first cause, all things come to pass immutably and infallibly;[9] so that there is not anything, befalls any by chance, or without His providence;[10] yet by the same providence He ordereth them to fall out, according to the nature of second causes, either necessarily, freely, or contingently.[11]

3. God in His ordinary providence maketh use of means;[12] yet is free to work, without,[13] above,[14] and against them at His pleasure.[15]

---

[6] **Acts 15:18:** And He is the head of the body, the church, who is the beginning, the firstborn from the dead, that in all things He may have the preeminence. **Isa. 42:9:** Behold, the former things have come to pass, And new things I declare; Before they spring forth I tell you of them. **Ezek. 11:5:** Then the Spirit of the LORD fell upon me, and said to me, "Speak! 'Thus says the LORD: "Thus you have said, O house of Israel; for I know the things that come into your mind."'"

[7] **Eph. 1:11:** In Him also we have obtained an inheritance, being predestined according to the purpose of Him who works all things according to the counsel of His will. **Ps. 33:10-11:** The LORD brings the counsel of the nations to nothing; He makes the plans of the peoples of no effect. The counsel of the LORD stands forever, The plans of His heart to all generations.

[8] **Isa. 63:14:** As a beast goes down into the valley, *And* the Spirit of the LORD causes him to rest, So You lead Your people, To make Yourself a glorious name. **Eph. 3:10:** ... to the intent that now the manifold wisdom of God might be made known by the church to the principalities and powers in the heavenly *places*. **Rom. 9:17:** For the Scripture says to the Pharaoh, "For this very purpose I have raised you up, that I may show My power in you, and that My name may be declared in all the earth." **Gen. 45:7:** And God sent me before you to preserve a posterity for you in the earth, and to save your lives by a great deliverance. **Ps. 145:7:** They shall utter the memory of Your great goodness, And shall sing of Your righteousness.

[9] **Acts 2:23:** Him, being delivered by the determined purpose and foreknowledge of God, you have taken by lawless hands, have crucified, and put to death. **See Isa. 14:24, 27.**

[10] **Prov. 16:33:** The lot is cast into the lap, But its every decision *is* from the LORD.

[11] **Gen. 8:22:** While the earth remains, Seedtime and harvest, Cold and heat, Winter and summer, And day and night Shall not cease." **Jer. 31:35:** Thus says the LORD, Who gives the sun for a light by day, The ordinances of the moon and the stars for a light by night, Who disturbs the sea, And its waves roar (The LORD of hosts *is* His name). **Isa. 10:6-7:** I will send him against an ungodly nation, And against the people of My wrath I will give him charge, To seize the spoil, to take the prey, And to tread them down like the mire of the streets. Yet he does not mean so, Nor does his heart think so; But *it is* in his heart to destroy, And cut off not a few nations. **See Ex. 21:13 and Deut. 19:5; 1 Kings 22:28-34.**

[12] **Acts 27:24, 31, 44:** ... saying, 'Do not be afraid, Paul; you must be brought before Caesar; and indeed God has granted you all those who sail with you.' ... Paul said to the centurion and the soldiers, "Unless these men stay in the ship, you cannot be saved." ... and the rest, some on boards and some on *parts* of the ship. And so it was that they all escaped safely to land. **Isa. 55:10-11:** For as the rain comes down, and the snow from heaven, And do not return there, But water the earth, And make it bring forth and bud, That it may give seed to the sower And bread to the eater, So shall My word be that goes forth from My mouth; It shall not return to Me void, But it shall accomplish what I please, And it shall prosper *in the thing* for which I sent it.

[13] **Hos. 1:7:** Yet I will have mercy on the house of Judah, Will save them by the LORD their God, And will not save them by bow, Nor by sword or battle, By horses or horsemen. **Matt. 4:4:** But He answered and said, "It is written, 'Man shall not live by bread alone, but by every word that proceeds from the mouth of God.'" **Job 34:20:** In a moment they die, in the middle of the night; The people are shaken and pass away; The mighty are taken away without a hand.

4. The almighty power, unsearchable wisdom, and infinite goodness of God, so far manifest themselves in His providence, that His determinate counsel extendeth itself even to the first fall, and all other sinful actions both of angels, and men;[16] (and that not by a bare permission)[17] which also He most wisely and powerfully boundeth,[18] and otherwise ordereth, and governeth, in a manifold dispensation to His most holy ends:[19] yet so, as the sinfulness of their acts proceedeth only from the creatures, and not from God; who being most holy and righteous, neither is nor can be, the author or approver of sin.[20]

---

[14] **Rom. 4:19-21:** And not being weak in faith, he did not consider his own body, already dead (since he was about a hundred years old), and the deadness of Sarah's womb. He did not waver at the promise of God through unbelief, but was strengthened in faith, giving glory to God, and being fully convinced that what He had promised He was also able to perform. And therefore "it was accounted to him for righteousness."

[15] **2 Kings 6:6:** So the man of God said, "Where did it fall?" And he showed him the place. So he cut off a stick, and threw *it* in there; and he made the iron float. **Dan. 3:27:** And the satraps, administrators, governors, and the king's counselors gathered together, and they saw these men on whose bodies the fire had no power; the hair of their head was not singed nor were their garments affected, and the smell of fire was not on them.

[16] **Isa. 45:7:** I form the light and create darkness, I make peace and create calamity; I, the LORD, do all these *things.* **Rom. 11:32-34:** For God has committed them all to disobedience, that He might have mercy on all. Oh, the depth of the riches both of the wisdom and knowledge of God! How unsearchable *are* His judgments and His ways past finding out! "For who has known the mind of the LORD? Or who has become His counselor?" **2 Sam. 16:10:** But the king said, "What have I to do with you, you sons of Zeruiah? So let him curse, because the LORD has said to him, 'Curse David.' Who then shall say, 'Why have you done so?'" **2 Sam. 24:1:** Again the anger of the LORD was aroused against Israel, and He moved David against them to say, "Go, number Israel and Judah." **1 Chron. 21:1:** Now Satan stood up against Israel, and moved David to number Israel. **Acts 2:23:** Him, being delivered by the determined purpose and foreknowledge of God, you have taken by lawless hands, have crucified, and put to death. **Acts 4:27-28:** For truly against Your holy Servant Jesus, whom You anointed, both Herod and Pontius Pilate, with the Gentiles and the people of Israel, were gathered together to do whatever Your hand and Your purpose determined before to be done. **See 1 Kings 22:22-23; 1 Chron. 10:4, 13-14.**

[17] **John 12:40:** He has blinded their eyes and hardened their hearts, Lest they should see with *their* eyes, Lest they should understand with *their* hearts and turn, So that I should heal them. **2 Thess. 2:11:** And for this reason God will send them strong delusion, that they should believe the lie.

[18] **2 Kings 19:28:** Because your rage against Me and your tumult Therefore I will put My hook in your nose And My bridle in your lips, And I will turn you back By the way which you came. **Ps. 76:10:** Surely the wrath of man shall praise You; With the remainder of wrath You shall gird Yourself.

[19] **Gen. 50:20:** But as for you, you meant evil against me; *but* God meant it for good, in order to bring it about as *it is* this day, to save many people alive. **Isa. 10:6-7, 12:** I will send him against an ungodly nation, And against the people of My wrath I will give him charge, To seize the spoil, to take the prey, And to tread them down like the mire of the streets. Yet he does not mean so, Nor does his heart think so; But *it is* in his heart to destroy, And cut off not a few nations.... Therefore it shall come to pass, when the Lord has performed all His work on Mount Zion and on Jerusalem, *that He will say,* "I will punish the fruit of the arrogant heart of the king of Assyria, and the glory of his haughty looks."

[20] **James 1:13-14, 17:** Let no one say when he is tempted, "I am tempted by God"; for God cannot be tempted by evil, nor does He Himself tempt anyone. But each one is tempted when he is drawn away by his own desires and enticed.... Every good gift and every perfect gift is from above, and comes down from the Father of lights, with whom there is no variation or shadow of turning. **Ps. 50:21:** These *things* you have done, and I kept silent; You thought that I was altogether like you; *But* I will rebuke you, And set *them* in order before your eyes. **1 John 2:16:** For all that *is* in the

5. The most wise, righteous, and gracious God, doth oftentimes, leave for a season His own children to manifold temptations, and the corruptions of their own heart, to chastise them for their former sins, or to discover unto them the hidden strength of corruption, and deceitfulness of their hearts, that they may be humbled;[21] and to raise them to a more close, and constant dependence for their support, upon Himself; and to make them more watchful against all future occasions of sin, and for other just and holy ends.[22] So that whatsoever befalls any of His elect is by His appointment, for His glory, and their good.[23]

6. As for those wicked and ungodly men, whom God as the righteous judge, for former sin doth blind and harden;[24] from them He not only withholdeth His grace, whereby they might have been enlightened in their understanding, and wrought upon their hearts:[25] But sometimes also withdraweth the gifts which

---

world—the lust of the flesh, the lust of the eyes, and the pride of life—is not of the Father but is of the world.

[21] **2 Chron. 32:25-26, 31:** But Hezekiah did not repay according to the favor *shown* him, for his heart was lifted up; therefore wrath was looming over him and over Judah and Jerusalem. Then Hezekiah humbled himself for the pride of his heart, he and the inhabitants of Jerusalem, so that the wrath of the LORD did not come upon them in the days of Hezekiah.... However, *regarding* the ambassadors of the princes of Babylon, whom they sent to him to inquire about the wonder that was *done* in the land, God withdrew from him, in order to test him, that He might know all *that was* in his heart. **Deut. 8:2-3, 5:** And you shall remember that the LORD your God led you all the way these forty years in the wilderness, to humble you *and* test you, to know what *was* in your heart, whether you would keep His commandments or not. So He humbled you, allowed you to hunger, and fed you with manna which you did not know nor did your fathers know, that He might make you know that man shall not live by bread alone; but man lives by every *word* that proceeds from the mouth of the LORD.... You should know in your heart that as a man chastens his son, *so* the LORD your God chastens you. **Luke 22:31-32:** And the Lord said, "Simon, Simon! Indeed, Satan has asked for you, that he may sift *you* as wheat. But I have prayed for you, that your faith should not fail; and when you have returned to *Me,* strengthen your brethren." **2 Sam. 24:1:** Again the anger of the LORD was aroused against Israel, and He moved David against them to say, "Go, number Israel and Judah."

[22] **2 Cor. 12:7-9:** And lest I should be exalted above measure by the abundance of the revelations, a thorn in the flesh was given to me, a messenger of Satan to buffet me, lest I be exalted above measure. Concerning this thing I pleaded with the Lord three times that it might depart from me. And He said to me, "My grace is sufficient for you, for My strength is made perfect in weakness." Therefore most gladly I will rather boast in my infirmities, that the power of Christ may rest upon me. **See Ps. 73:1-28; 77:1-12; Mark 14:66-72; John 21:15-19.**

[23] **Rom. 8:28:** And we know that all things work together for good to those who love God, to those who are the called according to *His* purpose.

[24] **Rom. 1:24, 26, 28:** Therefore God also gave them up to uncleanness, in the lusts of their hearts, to dishonor their bodies among themselves ... For this reason God gave them up to vile passions. For even their women exchanged the natural use for what is against nature.... And even as they did not like to retain God in *their* knowledge, God gave them over to a debased mind, to do those things which are not fitting. **Rom. 11:7-8:** What then? Israel has not obtained what it seeks; but the elect have obtained it, and the rest were blinded. Just as it is written: "God has given them a spirit of stupor, Eyes that they should not see And ears that they should not hear, To this very day."

[25] **Deut. 29:4:** Yet the LORD has not given you a heart to perceive and eyes to see and ears to hear, to this *very* day. **Mark 4:11-12:** And He said to them, "To you it has been given to know the mystery of the kingdom of God; but to those who are outside, all things come in parables, so that

they had,[26] and exposeth them to such objects as their corruption makes occasion of sin;[27] and withal gives them over to their own lusts, the temptations of the world, and the power of Satan,[28] whereby it comes to pass, that they harden themselves, even under those means which God useth for the softening of others.[29]

7. As the providence of God doth in general reach to all creatures, so after a most special manner it taketh care of His church, and disposeth of all things to the good thereof.[30]

'Seeing they may see and not perceive, And hearing they may hear and not understand; Lest they should turn, And *their* sins be forgiven them.'"

[26] **Matt. 13:12:** For whoever has, to him more will be given, and he will have abundance; but whoever does not have, even what he has will be taken away from him. **Matt: 25:29:** 'For to everyone who has, more will be given, and he will have abundance; but from him who does not have, even what he has will be taken away. **See Acts 13:10-11.**

[27] **Gen. 4:8:** Now Cain talked with Abel his brother; and it came to pass, when they were in the field, that Cain rose up against Abel his brother and killed him. **Deut. 2:30:** "But Sihon king of Heshbon would not let us pass through, for the LORD your God hardened his spirit and made his heart obstinate, that He might deliver him into your hand, as *it is* this day. **2 Kings 8:12-13:** And Hazael said, "Why is my lord weeping?" He answered, "Because I know the evil that you will do to the children of Israel: Their strongholds you will set on fire, and their young men you will kill with the sword; and you will dash their children, and rip open their women with child." So Hazael said, "But what *is* your servant—a dog, that he should do this gross thing?" And Elisha answered, "The LORD has shown me that you *will become* king over Syria." **See Matt. 26:14-16.**

[28] **Ps. 109:6:** Set a wicked man over him, And let an accuser stand at his right hand. **Ps. 81:11-12:** "But My people would not heed My voice, And Israel would *have* none of Me. So I gave them over to their own stubborn heart, To walk in their own counsels. **Luke 22:3:** Then Satan entered Judas, surnamed Iscariot, who was numbered among the twelve. **2 Thess. 2:10-12:** ... and with all unrighteous deception among those who perish, because they did not receive the love of the truth, that they might be saved. And for this reason God will send them strong delusion, that they should believe the lie, that they all may be condemned who did not believe the truth but had pleasure in unrighteousness.

[29] **Ex. 8:15, 32:** But when Pharaoh saw that there was relief, he hardened his heart and did not heed them, as the LORD had said.... But Pharaoh hardened his heart at this time also; neither would he let the people go. **Isa. 6:9-10:** And He said, "Go, and tell this people: 'Keep on hearing, but do not understand; Keep on seeing, but do not perceive.' Make the heart of this people dull, And their ears heavy, And shut their eyes; Lest they see with their eyes, And hear with their ears, And understand with their heart, And return and be healed." **Isa. 8:14:** He will be as a sanctuary, But a stone of stumbling and a rock of offense To both the houses of Israel, As a trap and a snare to the inhabitants of Jerusalem. **2 Cor. 2:15-16:** For we are to God the fragrance of Christ among those who are being saved and among those who are perishing. To the one *we are* the aroma of death *leading* to death, and to the other the aroma of life *leading* to life. And who *is* sufficient for these things? **1 Pet. 2:7-8:** Therefore, to you who believe, *He is* precious; but to those who are disobedient, "The stone which the builders rejected Has become the chief cornerstone," and "A stone of stumbling And a rock of offense." **See Ex. 7:3; Acts 28:26-27.**

[30] **1 Tim. 4:10:** For to this *end* we both labor and suffer reproach, because we trust in the living God, who is *the* Savior of all men, especially of those who believe. **Amos 9:8-9:** "Behold, the eyes of the Lord God *are* on the sinful kingdom, And I will destroy it from the face of the earth; Yet I will not utterly destroy the house of Jacob," Says the LORD. "For surely I will command, And will sift the house of Israel among all nations, As *grain* is sifted in a sieve; Yet not the smallest grain shall fall to the ground." **Matt. 16:18:** And I also say to you that you are Peter, and on this rock I will build My church, and the gates of Hades shall not prevail against it. **Rom. 8:28:** And we know that all things work together for good to those who love God, to those who are the called according to *His* purpose. **Isa. 43:3-5:** For I *am* the LORD your God, The Holy One of Israel, your Savior; I gave Egypt for your ransom, Ethiopia and Seba in your place. Since you were precious in My sight, You have been honored, And I have loved you; Therefore I will give men for you, And people for your life. Fear not, for I *am* with you; I will bring your descendants from the east, And gather you from the west.

CHAPTER 6

Of the Fall of Man, of Sin, and of the Punishment thereof

1. Although God created man upright, and perfect,[1] and gave him a righteous law, which had been unto life had he kept it, and threatened death upon the breach thereof;[2] yet he did not long abide in this honour; Satan using the subtlety of the serpent to subdue Eve, then by her seducing Adam, who without any compulsion, did willfully transgress the law of their creation, and the command given unto them, in eating the forbidden fruit;[3] which God was pleased according to His wise and holy counsel to permit, having purposed to order it, to His own glory.[4]

---

[1] **Eccl. 7:29:** Truly, this only I have found: That God made man upright, But they have sought out many schemes. **Gen. 1:26-27:** Then God said, "Let Us make man in Our image, according to Our likeness; let them have dominion over the fish of the sea, over the birds of the air, and over the cattle, over all the earth and over every creeping thing that creeps on the earth." So God created man in His *own* image; in the image of God He created him; male and female He created them.

[2] **Gen. 2:16-17:** And the LORD God commanded the man, saying, "Of every tree of the garden you may freely eat; but of the tree of the knowledge of good and evil you shall not eat, for in the day that you eat of it you shall surely die." **James 2:10:** For whoever shall keep the whole law, and yet stumble in one *point,* he is guilty of all.

[3] **Gen. 3:6-8, 13:** So when the woman saw that the tree *was* good for food, that it *was* pleasant to the eyes, and a tree desirable to make *one* wise, she took of its fruit and ate. She also gave to her husband with her, and he ate. Then the eyes of both of them were opened, and they knew that they *were* naked; and they sewed fig leaves together and made themselves coverings. And they heard the sound of the LORD God walking in the garden in the cool of the day, and Adam and his wife hid themselves from the presence of the LORD God among the trees of the garden.... And the LORD God said to the woman, "What *is* this you have done?" The woman said, "The serpent deceived me, and I ate." **Eccl. 7:29:** Truly, this only I have found: That God made man upright, But they have sought out many schemes. **2 Cor. 11:3:** But I fear, lest somehow, as the serpent deceived Eve by his craftiness, so your minds may be corrupted from the simplicity that is in Christ.

[4] **Isa. 45:7:** I form the light and create darkness, I make peace and create calamity; I, the LORD, do all these *things.'* **Rom. 11:32-34:** For God has committed them all to disobedience, that He might have mercy on all. Oh, the depth of the riches both of the wisdom and knowledge of God! How unsearchable *are* His judgments and His ways past finding out! "For who has known the mind of the LORD? Or who has become His counselor?" **2 Sam. 16:10:** But the king said, "What have I to do with you, you sons of Zeruiah? So let him curse, because the LORD has said to him, 'Curse David.' Who then shall say, 'Why have you done so?'" **2 Sam. 24:1:** Again the anger of the LORD was aroused against Israel, and He moved David against them to say, "Go, number Israel and Judah." **1 Chron. 21:1:** Now Satan stood up against Israel, and moved David to number Israel. **Acts 2:23:** Him, being delivered by the determined purpose and foreknowledge of God, you have taken by lawless hands, have crucified, and put to death. **Acts 4:27-28:** For truly against Your holy Servant Jesus, whom You anointed, both Herod and Pontius Pilate, with the Gentiles and the people of Israel, were gathered together to do whatever Your hand and Your purpose determined before to be done. **Gen. 50:20:** But as for you, you meant evil against me; *but* God meant it for good, in order to bring it about as *it is* this day, to save many people alive. **Isa. 10:6-7, 12:** I will send him against an ungodly nation, And against the people of My wrath I will give him charge, To seize the spoil, to take the prey, And to tread them down like the mire of the streets. Yet he does not mean so, Nor does his heart think so; But *it is* in his heart to destroy, And cut off not a few nations.... Therefore it shall come to pass, when the Lord has performed all His work on Mount Zion and on Jerusalem, *that He will say,* "I will punish the fruit of the arrogant heart of the king of Assyria, and the glory of his haughty looks."

2. Our first parents by this sin, fell from their original righteousness and communion with God,[5] and we in them, whereby death came upon all; all becoming dead in sin,[6] and wholly defiled, in all the faculties, and parts, of soul, and body.[7]

3. They being the root, and by God's appointment, standing in the room, and stead of all mankind; the guilt of the sin was imputed,[8] and corrupted nature conveyed, to all their posterity descending from them by ordinary generation,[9] being now conceived in sin,

---

[5] **Gen. 3:6-8:** So when the woman saw that the tree *was* good for food, that it *was* pleasant to the eyes, and a tree desirable to make *one* wise, she took of its fruit and ate. She also gave to her husband with her, and he ate. Then the eyes of both of them were opened, and they knew that they *were* naked; and they sewed fig leaves together and made themselves coverings. And they heard the sound of the LORD God walking in the garden in the cool of the day, and Adam and his wife hid themselves from the presence of the LORD God among the trees of the garden. **Rom. 3:23:** ... for all have sinned and fall short of the glory of God.

[6] **Rom. 5:12:** Therefore, just as through one man sin entered the world, and death through sin, and thus death spread to all men, because all sinned. **Eph. 2:1-3:** And you *He made alive,* who were dead in trespasses and sins, in which you once walked according to the course of this world, according to the prince of the power of the air, the spirit who now works in the sons of disobedience, among whom also we all once conducted ourselves in the lusts of our flesh, fulfilling the desires of the flesh and of the mind, and were by nature children of wrath, just as the others. **See Gen. 2:17.**

[7] **Tit. 1:15:** To the pure all things are pure, but to those who are defiled and unbelieving nothing is pure; but even their mind and conscience are defiled. **Gen. 6:5:** Then the LORD saw that the wickedness of man *was* great in the earth, and *that* every intent of the thoughts of his heart *was* only evil continually. **Jer. 17:9:** The heart *is* deceitful above all *things,* And desperately wicked; Who can know it? **Rom. 3:10-19:** As it is written: "There is none righteous, no, not one; There is none who understands; There is none who seeks after God. They have all turned aside; They have together become unprofitable; There is none who does good, no, not one." "Their throat *is* an open tomb; With their tongues they have practiced deceit"; "The poison of asps *is* under their lips"; "Whose mouth *is* full of cursing and bitterness." "Their feet *are* swift to shed blood; Destruction and misery *are* in their ways; And the way of peace they have not known." "There is no fear of God before their eyes." Now we know that whatever the law says, it says to those who are under the law, that every mouth may be stopped, and all the world may become guilty before God.

[8] **Rom. 5:12-19:** Therefore, just as through one man sin entered the world, and death through sin, and thus death spread to all men, because all sinned—(For until the law sin was in the world, but sin is not imputed when there is no law. Nevertheless death reigned from Adam to Moses, even over those who had not sinned according to the likeness of the transgression of Adam, who is a type of Him who was to come. But the free gift *is* not like the offense. For if by the one man's offense many died, much more the grace of God and the gift by the grace of the one Man, Jesus Christ, abounded to many. And the gift *is* not like *that which came* through the one who sinned. For the judgment *which came* from one *offense resulted* in condemnation, but the free gift *which came* from many offenses *resulted* in justification. For if by the one man's offense death reigned through the one, much more those who receive abundance of grace and of the gift of righteousness will reign in life through the One, Jesus Christ.) Therefore, as through one man's offense *judgment came* to all men, resulting in condemnation, even so through one Man's righteous act *the free gift came* to all men, resulting in justification of life. For as by one man's disobedience many were made sinners, so also by one Man's obedience many will be made righteous. **1 Cor. 15:21-22, 45, 49:** For since by man *came* death, by Man also *came* the resurrection of the dead. For as in Adam all die, even so in Christ all shall be made alive.... And so it is written, "The first man Adam became a living being." The last Adam *became* a life-giving spirit.... And as we have borne the image of the *man* of dust, we shall also bear the image of the heavenly *Man.* Acts 17:26: And He has made from one blood every nation of men to dwell on all the face of the earth, and has determined their preappointed times and the boundaries of their dwellings.

[9] **Ps. 51:5:** Behold, I was brought forth in iniquity, And in sin my mother conceived me. **John 3:6:** That which is born of the flesh is flesh, and that which is born of the Spirit is spirit. **Gen. 5:3:** And Adam lived one hundred and thirty years, and begot *a son* in his own likeness, after his image, and named him Seth. **Job 14:4:** Who can bring a clean *thing* out of an unclean? No one! **Job 15:14:** What *is* man, that he could be pure? And *he who is* born of a woman, that he could be righteous?

and by nature children of wrath,[10] the servants of sin, the subjects of death[11] and all other miseries, spiritual,[12] temporal[13] and eternal,[14] unless the Lord Jesus set them free.[15]

4. From this original corruption, whereby we are utterly indisposed, disabled, and made opposite to all good,[16] and wholly inclined to all evil,[17] do proceed all actual transgressions.[18]

5. This corruption of nature, during this life, doth remain in those that are regenerated:[19] and although it be through Christ pardoned, and mortified, yet both itself, and the first motions thereof, are truly and properly sin.[20]

---

[10] **Eph. 2:3:** ... among whom also we all once conducted ourselves in the lusts of our flesh, fulfilling the desires of the flesh and of the mind, and were by nature children of wrath, just as the others.

[11] **Rom. 6:20:** For when you were slaves of sin, you were free in regard to righteousness. **Rom. 5:12:** Therefore, just as through one man sin entered the world, and death through sin, and thus death spread to all men, because all sinned.

[12] **Eph. 4:18:** ... having their understanding darkened, being alienated from the life of God, because of the ignorance that is in them, because of the blindness of their heart.

[13] **Rom. 8:20:** For the creation was subjected to futility, not willingly, but because of Him who subjected *it* in hope. **Lam. 3:39:** Why should a living man complain, A man for the punishment of his sins?

[14] **Matt. 25:41:** Then He will also say to those on the left hand, 'Depart from Me, you cursed, into the everlasting fire prepared for the devil and his angels.' **2 Thess. 1:9:** These shall be punished with everlasting destruction from the presence of the Lord and from the glory of His power.

[15] **Heb. 2:14:** Inasmuch then as the children have partaken of flesh and blood, He Himself likewise shared in the same, that through death He might destroy him who had the power of death, that is, the devil. **1 Thess. 1:10:** ... and to wait for His Son from heaven, whom He raised from the dead, *even* Jesus who delivers us from the wrath to come.

[16] **Rom. 5:6:** For when we were still without strength, in due time Christ died for the ungodly. **Rom. 7:18:** For I know that in me (that is, in my flesh) nothing good dwells; for to will is present with me, but *how* to perform what is good I do not find. **Rom. 8:7:** Because the carnal mind *is* enmity against God; for it is not subject to the law of God, nor indeed can be. **Col. 1:21:** And you, who once were alienated and enemies in your mind by wicked works, yet now He has reconciled.

[17] **Gen. 8:21:** And the LORD smelled a soothing aroma. Then the LORD said in His heart, "I will never again curse the ground for man's sake, although the imagination of man's heart *is* evil from his youth; nor will I again destroy every living thing as I have done." **See Gen. 6:5; Rom. 3:10-12.**

[18] **James 1:14-15:** But each one is tempted when he is drawn away by his own desires and enticed. Then, when desire has conceived, it gives birth to sin; and sin, when it is full-grown, brings forth death. **Matt. 15:19:** For out of the heart proceed evil thoughts, murders, adulteries, fornications, thefts, false witness, blasphemies. **Eph. 2:2-3:** ... in which you once walked according to the course of this world, according to the prince of the power of the air, the spirit who now works in the sons of disobedience, among whom also we all once conducted ourselves in the lusts of our flesh, fulfilling the desires of the flesh and of the mind, and were by nature children of wrath, just as the others.

[19] **Prov. 20:9:** Who can say, "I have made my heart clean, I am pure from my sin"? **Rom. 7:14, 17-18, 21-23:** For we know that the law is spiritual, but I am carnal, sold under sin.... But now, *it is* no longer I who do it, but sin that dwells in me. For I know that in me (that is, in my flesh) nothing good dwells; for to will is present with me, but *how* to perform what is good I do not find.... I find then a law, that evil is present with me, the one who wills to do good. For I delight in the law of God according to the inward man. But I see another law in my members, warring against the law of my mind, and bringing me into captivity to the law of sin which is in my members. **Eccl. 7:20:** For *there is* not a just man on earth who does good And does not sin. 1 John 1:8, 10: If we say that we have no sin, we deceive ourselves, and the truth is not in us.... If we say that we have not sinned, we make Him a liar, and His word is not in us.

[20] **Rom. 7:7-8, 24-25:** What shall we say then? *Is* the law sin? Certainly not! On the contrary, I would not have known sin except through the law. For I would not have known covetousness unless

the law had said, "You shall not covet." But sin, taking opportunity by the commandment, produced in me all *manner of evil* desire. For apart from the law sin *was* dead.... O wretched man that I am! Who will deliver me from this body of death? I thank God—through Jesus Christ our Lord! So then, with the mind I myself serve the law of God, but with the flesh the law of sin. **Gal. 5:17:** For the flesh lusts against the Spirit, and the Spirit against the flesh; and these are contrary to one another, so that you do not do the things that you wish.

CHAPTER 7
Of God's Covenant

1. The distance between God and the creature is so great,[1] that although reasonable creatures do owe obedience unto Him as their Creator, yet they could never have attained the hope of life and eternal rest, but by some voluntary condescension on God's part,[2] which He hath been pleased to express, by way of covenant, the solemn promissory oath of God.[3]

---

[1] **Isa. 40:13-17:** Who has directed the Spirit of the LORD, Or *as* His counselor has taught Him? With whom did He take counsel, and *who* instructed Him, And taught Him in the path of justice? Who taught Him knowledge, And showed Him the way of understanding? Behold, the nations *are* as a drop in a bucket, And are counted as the small dust on the scales; Look, He lifts up the isles as a very little thing. And Lebanon *is* not sufficient to burn, Nor its beasts sufficient for a burnt offering. All nations before Him *are* as nothing, And they are counted by Him less than nothing and worthless. **Job 9:32-33:** "For *He is* not a man, as I *am, That* I may answer Him, *And that* we should go to court together. Nor is there any mediator between us, *Who* may lay his hand on us both. **Ps. 113:5-6:** Who *is* like the LORD our God, Who dwells on high, Who humbles Himself to behold *The things that are* in the heavens and in the earth?

[2] **Luke 17:10:** So likewise you, when you have done all those things which you are commanded, say, 'We are unprofitable servants. We have done what was our duty to do.' **Job 22:2-3:** Can a man be profitable to God, Though he who is wise may be profitable to himself? *Is it* any pleasure to the Almighty that you are righteous? Or *is it* gain *to Him* that you make your ways blameless? **Job 35:7-8:** If you are righteous, what do you give Him? Or what does He receive from your hand? Your wickedness affects a man such as you, And your righteousness a son of man. **Acts 17:24-25:** God, who made the world and everything in it, since He is Lord of heaven and earth, does not dwell in temples made with hands. Nor is He worshiped with men's hands, as though He needed anything, since He gives to all life, breath, and all things. **Gen. 2:1-3, 17:** Thus the heavens and the earth, and all the host of them, were finished. And on the seventh day God ended His work which He had done, and He rested on the seventh day from all His work which He had done. Then God blessed the seventh day and sanctified it, because in it He rested from all His work which God had created and made.... "but of the tree of the knowledge of good and evil you shall not eat, for in the day that you eat of it you shall surely die."

[3] **Heb. 6:13-18:** For when God made a promise to Abraham, because He could swear by no one greater, He swore by Himself, saying, "Surely blessing I will bless you, and multiplying I will multiply you." And so, after he had patiently endured, he obtained the promise. For men indeed swear by the greater, and an oath for confirmation *is* for them an end of all dispute. Thus God, determining to show more abundantly to the heirs of promise the immutability of His counsel, confirmed *it* by an oath, that by two immutable things, in which it *is* impossible for God to lie, we might have strong consolation, who have fled for refuge to lay hold of the hope set before *us.* **Gen. 9:8-17:** Then God spoke to Noah and to his sons with him, saying: "And as for Me, behold, I establish My covenant with you and with your descendants after you, and with every living creature that *is* with you: the birds, the cattle, and every beast of the earth with you, of all that go out of the ark, every beast of the earth. Thus I establish My covenant with you: Never again shall all flesh be cut off by the waters of the flood; never again shall there be a flood to destroy the earth." And God said: "This *is* the sign of the covenant which I make between Me and you, and every living creature that *is* with you, for perpetual generations: I set My rainbow in the cloud, and it shall be for the sign of the covenant between Me and the earth. It shall be, when I bring a cloud over the earth, that the rainbow shall be seen in the cloud; and I will remember My covenant which *is* between Me and you and every living creature of all flesh; the waters shall never again become a flood to destroy all flesh. The rainbow shall be in the cloud, and I will look on it to remember the everlasting covenant between God and every living creature of all flesh that *is* on the earth." And God said to Noah, "This *is* the sign of the covenant which I have established between Me and all flesh that *is* on the earth." **Isa. 54:9-10:** "For the mountains shall depart And the hills be removed, But My kindness shall not depart from you, Nor shall My covenant of peace be removed," Says the LORD, who has mercy on you.

2. Moreover man having brought himself under the curse of the law by his fall,[4] it pleased the Lord to make a pledge of the Seed which should bruise the serpent's head, wherein the gospel, as to the substance of it, was revealed, and is therein effectual for the conversion and salvation of the elect,[5] according to the doctrine of the covenant of grace by which He freely offereth unto sinners life and salvation by Jesus Christ.[6]

3. This doctrine is revealed in the gospel; first of all to Adam in the promise of salvation by the Seed of the woman,[7] and afterwards by farther steps, until the full discovery thereof was completed in the New Covenant;[8] and it is founded in that eternal

---

[4] **Gen. 2:17:** ... but of the tree of the knowledge of good and evil you shall not eat, for in the day that you eat of it you shall surely die. **Gen. 3:6:** So when the woman saw that the tree *was* good for food, that it *was* pleasant to the eyes, and a tree desirable to make *one* wise, she took of its fruit and ate. She also gave to her husband with her, and he ate. **Gal. 3:10:** For as many as are of the works of the law are under the curse; for it is written, "Cursed *is* everyone who does not continue in all things which are written in the book of the law, to do them."

[5] **Gen. 3:15:** And I will put enmity Between you and the woman, And between your seed and her Seed; He shall bruise your head, And you shall bruise His heel. **Rom. 3:20-22:** Therefore by the deeds of the law no flesh will be justified in His sight, for by the law *is* the knowledge of sin. But now the righteousness of God apart from the law is revealed, being witnessed by the Law and the Prophets, even the righteousness of God, through faith in Jesus Christ, to all and on all who believe. For there is no difference. **Isa. 53:10-11:** Yet it pleased the LORD to bruise Him; He has put *Him* to grief. When You make His soul an offering for sin, He shall see *His* seed, He shall prolong *His* days, And the pleasure of the LORD shall prosper in His hand. He shall see the labor of His soul, *and* be satisfied. By His knowledge My righteous Servant shall justify many, For He shall bear their iniquities. **Eph. 2:12-13:** ... that at that time you were without Christ, being aliens from the commonwealth of Israel and strangers from the covenants of promise, having no hope and without God in the world. But now in Christ Jesus you who once were far off have been brought near by the blood of Christ. **Rom. 8:28-30:** And we know that all things work together for good to those who love God, to those who are the called according to *His* purpose. For whom He foreknew, He also predestined *to be* conformed to the image of His Son, that He might be the firstborn among many brethren. Moreover whom He predestined, these He also called; whom He called, these He also justified; and whom He justified, these He also glorified.

[6] **Isa. 45:22:** Look to Me, and be saved, All you ends of the earth! For I *am* God, and *there is* no other. **Rom. 10:6, 9:** But the righteousness of faith speaks in this way, "Do not say in your heart, 'Who will ascend into heaven?'" (that is, to bring Christ down *from above*) ... that if you confess with your mouth the Lord Jesus and believe in your heart that God has raised Him from the dead, you will be saved. **Mark 16:15-16:** And He said to them, "Go into all the world and preach the gospel to every creature. He who believes and is baptized will be saved; but he who does not believe will be condemned." **Rev. 22:17:** And the Spirit and the bride say, "Come!" And let him who hears say, "Come!" And let him who thirsts come. Whoever desires, let him take the water of life freely.

[7] **Gen. 3:15:** And I will put enmity Between you and the woman, And between your seed and her Seed; He shall bruise your head, And you shall bruise His heel.

[8] **Rom. 16:25-26:** Now to Him who is able to establish you according to my gospel and the preaching of Jesus Christ, according to the revelation of the mystery kept secret since the world began but now made manifest, and by the prophetic Scriptures made known to all nations, according to the commandment of the everlasting God, for obedience to the faith. **Eph. 3:1-6:** For this reason I, Paul, the prisoner of Christ Jesus for you Gentiles—if indeed you have heard of the dispensation of the grace of God which was given to me for you, how that by revelation He made known to me the mystery (as I have briefly written already, by which, when you read, you may understand my knowledge in the mystery of Christ), which in other ages was not made known to the sons of men, as it has now been revealed by the Spirit to His holy apostles and prophets: that the Gentiles should be fellow heirs, of the same body, and partakers of His promise in Christ through the gospel. **Heb. 1:1-3:** God, who at various times and in various ways spoke in time past to the fathers by the prophets, has in these last days spoken to us by *His* Son, whom He has appointed heir of all things, through whom also He made the worlds; who being the brightness of *His* glory and

purpose and secret counsel, that was between the Father, the Son, and Holy Spirit, about the redemption of the elect;[9] and it is alone by the grace of this promise, that all of the posterity of fallen Adam, that ever were saved, did obtain life and a blessed immortality; man being now utterly incapable of acceptance with God upon those terms, on which Adam stood in his state of innocency.[10]

4. This covenant of grace is frequently set forth in the Scripture as the foundation upon which the gospel reveals Christ and the redemption of His elect:[11] under the law it is held forth to the

---

the express image of His person, and upholding all things by the word of His power, when He had by Himself purged our sins, sat down at the right hand of the Majesty on high.

[9] **Eph. 1:3-11:** Blessed *be* the God and Father of our Lord Jesus Christ, who has blessed us with every spiritual blessing in the heavenly *places* in Christ, just as He chose us in Him before the foundation of the world, that we should be holy and without blame before Him in love, having predestined us to adoption as sons by Jesus Christ to Himself, according to the good pleasure of His will, to the praise of the glory of His grace, by which He made us accepted in the Beloved. In Him we have redemption through His blood, the forgiveness of sins, according to the riches of His grace which He made to abound toward us in all wisdom and prudence, having made known to us the mystery of His will, according to His good pleasure which He purposed in Himself, that in the dispensation of the fullness of the times He might gather together in one all things in Christ, both which are in heaven and which are on earth—in Him. In Him also we have obtained an inheritance, being predestined according to the purpose of Him who works all things according to the counsel of His will. **1 Pet. 1:19-20:** ... but with the precious blood of Christ, as of a lamb without blemish and without spot. He indeed was foreordained before the foundation of the world, but was manifest in these last times for you. **Titus 3:5-6:** ... not by works of righteousness which we have done, but according to His mercy He saved us, through the washing of regeneration and renewing of the Holy Spirit, whom He poured out on us abundantly through Jesus Christ our Savior. **2 Tim. 1:9-10:** ... who has saved us and called *us* with a holy calling, not according to our works, but according to His own purpose and grace which was given to us in Christ Jesus before time began, but has now been revealed by the appearing of our Savior Jesus Christ, *who* has abolished death and brought life and immortality to light through the gospel. **Tit. 1:2:** ... in hope of eternal life which God, who cannot lie, promised before time began.

[10] **Heb. 11:6, 13:** But without faith *it is* impossible to please *Him,* for he who comes to God must believe that He is, and *that* He is a rewarder of those who diligently seek Him.... These all died in faith, not having received the promises, but having seen them afar off were assured of them, embraced *them* and confessed that they were strangers and pilgrims on the earth. **See Rom. 4. Acts 4:12:** Nor is there salvation in any other, for there is no other name under heaven given among men by which we must be saved. **John 8:56:** Your father Abraham rejoiced to see My day, and he saw *it* and was glad.

[11] **Gen. 4:25:** And Adam knew his wife again, and she bore a son and named him Seth, "For God has appointed another seed for me instead of Abel, whom Cain killed." **Gen. 6:18:** But I will establish My covenant with you; and you shall go into the ark—you, your sons, your wife, and your sons' wives with you. **Gen. 22:15-18:** Then the Angel of the LORD called to Abraham a second time out of heaven, and said: "By Myself I have sworn, says the LORD, because you have done this thing, and have not withheld your son, your only *son*—blessing I will bless you, and multiplying I will multiply your descendants as the stars of the heaven and as the sand which *is* on the seashore; and your descendants shall possess the gate of their enemies. In your seed all the nations of the earth shall be blessed, because you have obeyed My voice." **2 Sam. 7:12-16:** When your days are fulfilled and you rest with your fathers, I will set up your seed after you, who will come from your body, and I will establish his kingdom. He shall build a house for My name, and I will establish the throne of his kingdom forever. I will be his Father, and he shall be My son. If he commits iniquity, I will chasten him with the rod of men and with the blows of the sons of men. But My mercy shall not depart from him, as I took *it* from Saul, whom I removed from before you. And your house and your kingdom shall be established forever before you. Your throne shall be established forever. **Matt. 1:20-21:** But while he thought about these things, behold, an angel of the Lord appeared to him in a dream, saying, "Joseph, son of David, do not be afraid to take to you Mary your wife, for that which is conceived in her is of the Holy Spirit. And she will bring forth a Son, and you shall call His

people of the Jews through the covenants of promise, all fore-signifying Christ to come,[12] which were for that time sufficient

---

name Jesus, for He will save His people from their sins." **Luke 1:30-33:** Then the angel said to her, "Do not be afraid, Mary, for you have found favor with God. And behold, you will conceive in your womb and bring forth a Son, and shall call His name Jesus. He will be great, and will be called the Son of the Highest; and the Lord God will give Him the throne of His father David. And He will reign over the house of Jacob forever, and of His kingdom there will be no end." **Luke 2:25-38:** And behold, there was a man in Jerusalem whose name *was* Simeon, and this man *was* just and devout, waiting for the Consolation of Israel, and the Holy Spirit was upon him. And it had been revealed to him by the Holy Spirit that he would not see death before he had seen the Lord's Christ. So he came by the Spirit into the temple. And when the parents brought in the Child Jesus, to do for Him according to the custom of the law, he took Him up in his arms and blessed God and said: "Lord, now You are letting Your servant depart in peace, According to Your word; For my eyes have seen Your salvation Which You have prepared before the face of all peoples, A light to *bring* revelation to the Gentiles, And the glory of Your people Israel." And Joseph and His mother marveled at those things which were spoken of Him. Then Simeon blessed them, and said to Mary His mother, "Behold, this *Child* is destined for the fall and rising of many in Israel, and for a sign which will be spoken against (yes, a sword will pierce through your own soul also), that the thoughts of many hearts may be revealed." Now there was one, Anna, a prophetess, the daughter of Phanuel, of the tribe of Asher. She was of a great age, and had lived with a husband seven years from her virginity; and this woman *was* a widow of about eighty-four years, who did not depart from the temple, but served *God* with fastings and prayers night and day. And coming in that instant she gave thanks to the Lord, and spoke of Him to all those who looked for redemption in Jerusalem. **Rev. 1:1-3:** The Revelation of Jesus Christ, which God gave Him to show His servants—things which must shortly take place. And He sent and signified *it* by His angel to His servant John, who bore witness to the word of God, and to the testimony of Jesus Christ, to all things that he saw. Blessed *is* he who reads and those who hear the words of this prophecy, and keep those things which are written in it; for the time *is* near. **Rev. 12:1-12:** Now a great sign appeared in heaven: a woman clothed with the sun, with the moon under her feet, and on her head a garland of twelve stars. Then being with child, she cried out in labor and in pain to give birth. And another sign appeared in heaven: behold, a great, fiery red dragon having seven heads and ten horns, and seven diadems on his heads. His tail drew a third of the stars of heaven and threw them to the earth. And the dragon stood before the woman who was ready to give birth, to devour her Child as soon as it was born. She bore a male Child who was to rule all nations with a rod of iron. And her Child was caught up to God and His throne. Then the woman fled into the wilderness, where she has a place prepared by God, that they should feed her there one thousand two hundred and sixty days. And war broke out in heaven: Michael and his angels fought with the dragon; and the dragon and his angels fought, but they did not prevail, nor was a place found for them in heaven any longer. So the great dragon was cast out, that serpent of old, called the Devil and Satan, who deceives the whole world; he was cast to the earth, and his angels were cast out with him. Then I heard a loud voice saying in heaven, "Now salvation, and strength, and the kingdom of our God, and the power of His Christ have come, for the accuser of our brethren, who accused them before our God day and night, has been cast down. And they overcame him by the blood of the Lamb and by the word of their testimony, and they did not love their lives to the death. Therefore rejoice, O heavens, and you who dwell in them! Woe to the inhabitants of the earth and the sea! For the devil has come down to you, having great wrath, because he knows that he has a short time." **Rev. 20:1-6:** Then I saw an angel coming down from heaven, having the key to the bottomless pit and a great chain in his hand. He laid hold of the dragon, that serpent of old, who is *the* Devil and Satan, and bound him for a thousand years; and he cast him into the bottomless pit, and shut him up, and set a seal on him, so that he should deceive the nations no more till the thousand years were finished. But after these things he must be released for a little while. And I saw thrones, and they sat on them, and judgment was committed to them. Then *I saw* the souls of those who had been beheaded for their witness to Jesus and for the word of God, who had not worshiped the beast or his image, and had not received *his* mark on their foreheads or on their hands. And they lived and reigned with Christ for a thousand years. But the rest of the dead did not live again until the thousand years were finished. This *is* the first resurrection. Blessed and holy *is* he who has part in the first resurrection. Over such the second death has no power, but they shall be priests of God and of Christ, and shall reign with Him a thousand years. **Gal. 4:4-5:** But when the fullness of the time had come, God sent forth His Son, born of a woman, born under the law, to redeem those who were under the law, that we might receive the adoption as sons. **Ps. 2:7-12:** "I will declare the decree: The LORD has said to Me, 'You *are* My Son, Today I have begotten You. Ask of Me, and I will give *You* The nations *for* Your inheritance, And the ends of the earth *for* Your possession. You shall break them with a rod of iron; You shall dash them to pieces like a potter's vessel.'" Now therefore, be wise, O kings; Be instructed, you judges of the earth. Serve the LORD with fear, And rejoice with trembling. Kiss the Son, lest He be angry, And you perish *in* the way, When His wrath is kindled but a little. Blessed *are* all those who put their trust in Him.

and efficacious, through the operation of the Spirit, to instruct and build up the elect in faith in the promised Messiah, by whom they had full remission of sins, and eternal salvation.[13]

5. Under the gospel, when Christ the substance was fully revealed,[14] the covenant of grace is held forth in all fullness, evidence, and spiritual efficacy, to all nations, both Jews and

---

[12] **Heb. 8-10:** Now this is the main point of the things we are saying: We have such a High Priest, who is seated at the right hand of the throne of the Majesty in the heavens, a Minister of the sanctuary and of the true tabernacle which the Lord erected, and not man.... For if He were on earth, He would not be a priest, since there are priests who offer the gifts according to the law; who serve the copy and shadow of the heavenly things, as Moses was divinely instructed when he was about to make the tabernacle. For He said, "See that you make all things according to the pattern shown you on the mountain." But now He has obtained a more excellent ministry, inasmuch as He is also Mediator of a better covenant, which was established on better promises.... But Christ came as High Priest of the good things to come, with the greater and more perfect tabernacle not made with hands, that is, not of this creation. Not with the blood of goats and calves, but with His own blood He entered the Most Holy Place once for all, having obtained eternal redemption.... For Christ has not entered the holy places made with hands, which are copies of the true, but into heaven itself, now to appear in the presence of God for us ... For the law, having a shadow of the good things to come, and not the very image of the things, can never with these same sacrifices, which they offer continually year by year, make those who approach perfect..... **Rom. 4:11:** And he received the sign of circumcision, a seal of the righteousness of the faith which *he had while still* uncircumcised, that he might be the father of all those who believe, though they are uncircumcised, that righteousness might be imputed to them also. **Col. 2:11-12:** In Him you were also circumcised with the circumcision made without hands, by putting off the body of the sins of the flesh, by the circumcision of Christ, buried with Him in baptism, in which you also were raised with *Him* through faith in the working of God, who raised Him from the dead. **1 Cor. 5:7:** Therefore purge out the old leaven, that you may be a new lump, since you truly are unleavened. For indeed Christ, our Passover, was sacrificed for us.

[13] **1 Cor. 10:1-4:** Moreover, brethren, I do not want you to be unaware that all our fathers were under the cloud, all passed through the sea, all were baptized into Moses in the cloud and in the sea, all ate the same spiritual food, and all drank the same spiritual drink. For they drank of that spiritual Rock that followed them, and that Rock was Christ. **Heb. 11:13:** These all died in faith, not having received the promises, but having seen them afar off were assured of them, embraced *them* and confessed that they were strangers and pilgrims on the earth. **John 8:56:** Your father Abraham rejoiced to see My day, and he saw *it* and was glad. **Gal. 3:7-9, 14:** Therefore know that *only* those who are of faith are sons of Abraham. And the Scripture, foreseeing that God would justify the Gentiles by faith, preached the gospel to Abraham beforehand, *saying,* "In you all the nations shall be blessed." So then those who *are* of faith are blessed with believing Abraham.... that the blessing of Abraham might come upon the Gentiles in Christ Jesus, that we might receive the promise of the Spirit through faith. **Ps. 32:1-2, 5:** Blessed *is he whose* transgression *is* forgiven, *Whose* sin *is* covered. Blessed *is* the man to whom the LORD does not impute iniquity, And in whose spirit *there is* no deceit.... I acknowledged my sin to You, And my iniquity I have not hidden. I said, "I will confess my transgressions to the LORD," And You forgave the iniquity of my sin. *Selah.*

[14] **Heb. 12:22-28:** But you have come to Mount Zion and to the city of the living God, the heavenly Jerusalem, to an innumerable company of angels, to the general assembly and church of the firstborn *who are* registered in heaven, to God the Judge of all, to the spirits of just men made perfect, to Jesus the Mediator of the new covenant, and to the blood of sprinkling that speaks better things than *that of* Abel. See that you do not refuse Him who speaks. For if they did not escape who refused Him who spoke on earth, much more *shall we not escape* if we turn away from Him who *speaks* from heaven, whose voice then shook the earth; but now He has promised, saying, "Yet once more I shake not only the earth, but also heaven." Now this, "Yet once more," indicates the removal of those things that are being shaken, as of things that are made, that the things which cannot be shaken may remain. Therefore, since we are receiving a kingdom which cannot be shaken, let us have grace, by which we may serve God acceptably with reverence and godly fear. For our God *is* a consuming fire. **Jer. 31:33-34:** But this *is* the covenant that I will make with the house of Israel after those days, says the LORD: I will put My law in their minds, and write it on their hearts; and I will be their God, and they shall be My people. No more shall every man teach his neighbor, and every man his brother, saying, 'Know the LORD,' for they all shall know Me, from the least of them to the greatest of them, says the LORD. For I will forgive their iniquity, and their sin I will remember no more.

Gentiles.[15] There are not, therefore, two covenants of grace differing in substance, but one and the same under various dispensations,[16] to wit, according to redemption, the Old and New Covenants.[17]

---

[15] **2 Cor. 3:9-11:** For if the ministry of condemnation *had* glory, the ministry of righteousness exceeds much more in glory. For even what was made glorious had no glory in this respect, because of the glory that excels. For if what is passing away *was* glorious, what remains *is* much more glorious. **Matt. 28:19:** Go therefore and make disciples of all the nations, baptizing them in the name of the Father and of the Son and of the Holy Spirit. **Eph. 2:15-19:** ... having abolished in His flesh the enmity, *that is,* the law of commandments *contained* in ordinances, so as to create in Himself one new man *from* the two, *thus* making peace, and that He might reconcile them both to God in one body through the cross, thereby putting to death the enmity. And He came and preached peace to you who were afar off and to those who were near. For through Him we both have access by one Spirit to the Father. Now, therefore, you are no longer strangers and foreigners, but fellow citizens with the saints and members of the household of God.

[16] **Gal. 3:8-9, 14, 16:** And the Scripture, foreseeing that God would justify the Gentiles by faith, preached the gospel to Abraham beforehand, *saying,* "In you all the nations shall be blessed." So then those who *are* of faith are blessed with believing Abraham.... that the blessing of Abraham might come upon the Gentiles in Christ Jesus, that we might receive the promise of the Spirit through faith.... Now to Abraham and his Seed were the promises made. He does not say, "And to seeds," as of many, but as of one, "And to your Seed," who is Christ. **Rom. 3:21-23, 30:** But now the righteousness of God apart from the law is revealed, being witnessed by the Law and the Prophets, even the righteousness of God, through faith in Jesus Christ, to all and on all who believe. For there is no difference; for all have sinned and fall short of the glory of God ... since *there is* one God who will justify the circumcised by faith and the uncircumcised through faith. **Rom. 4:3, 6-8, 16-17, 23-24:** For what does the Scripture say? "Abraham believed God, and it was accounted to him for righteousness." ... just as David also describes the blessedness of the man to whom God imputes righteousness apart from works: "Blessed *are those* whose lawless deeds are forgiven, And whose sins are covered; Blessed *is the* man to whom the LORD shall not impute sin." ... Therefore *it is* of faith that *it might be* according to grace, so that the promise might be sure to all the seed, not only to those who are of the law, but also to those who are of the faith of Abraham, who is the father of us all (as it is written, "I have made you a father of many nations") in the presence of Him whom he believed—God, who gives life to the dead and calls those things which do not exist as though they did ... Now it was not written for his sake alone that it was imputed to him, but also for us. It shall be imputed to us who believe in Him who raised up Jesus our Lord from the dead. **See Gen. 15:6. Ps. 32:1-2:** Blessed *is he whose* transgression *is* forgiven, *Whose* sin *is* covered. Blessed *is* the man to whom the LORD does not impute iniquity, And in whose spirit *there is* no deceit. **Heb. 4:2:** For indeed the gospel was preached to us as well as to them; but the word which they heard did not profit them, not being mixed with faith in those who heard *it.* **See Rom. 10:6-10; 1 Cor. 10:3-4. Acts 15:10-17:** Now therefore, why do you test God by putting a yoke on the neck of the disciples which neither our fathers nor we were able to bear? But we believe that through the grace of the Lord Jesus Christ we shall be saved in the same manner as they." Then all the multitude kept silent and listened to Barnabas and Paul declaring how many miracles and wonders God had worked through them among the Gentiles. And after they had become silent, James answered, saying, "Men *and* brethren, listen to me: Simon has declared how God at the first visited the Gentiles to take out of them a people for His name. And with this the words of the prophets agree, just as it is written: 'After this I will return And will rebuild the tabernacle of David, which has fallen down; I will rebuild its ruins, And I will set it up; So that the rest of mankind may seek the LORD, Even all the Gentiles who are called by My name, Says the LORD who does all these things.'"

[17] **Heb. 8:7-13:** For if that first *covenant* had been faultless, then no place would have been sought for a second. Because finding fault with them, He says: "Behold, the days are coming, says the LORD, when I will make a new covenant with the house of Israel and with the house of Judah—not according to the covenant that I made with their fathers in the day when I took them by the hand to lead them out of the land of Egypt; because they did not continue in My covenant, and I disregarded them, says the LORD. For this *is* the covenant that I will make with the house of Israel after those days, says the LORD: I will put My laws in their mind and write them on their hearts; and I will be their God, and they shall be My people. None of them shall teach his neighbor, and none his brother, saying, 'Know the LORD,' for all shall know Me, from the least of them to the greatest of them. For I will be merciful to their unrighteousness, and their sins and their lawless deeds I will remember no more." In that He says, "A new *covenant,*" He has made the first obsolete. Now what is becoming

obsolete and growing old is ready to vanish away. **Heb. 10:9:** ... then He said, "Behold, I have come to do Your will, O God." He takes away the first that He may establish the second.

CHAPTER 8
Of Christ the Mediator

1. It pleased God in His eternal purpose, to choose and ordain the Lord Jesus His only begotten Son, according to the covenant made between them both when He sat down on the right hand of the Majesty on high,[1] to be the Mediator between God and man;[2] the Prophet,[3] Priest[4] and King;[5] Head and saviour of His church,[6] the heir of all things,[7] and judge of the world:[8] Unto whom He did from all eternity give a people to be His seed,[9] and to be by Him in time redeemed, called, justified, sanctified, and glorified.[10]

2. The Son of God, the second person in the Holy Trinity, being very and eternal God,[11] the brightness of the Father's glory, of

---

[1] **Ps. 110:4:** The LORD has sworn And will not relent, "You *are* a priest forever According to the order of Melchizedek." **Heb. 7:28:** For the law appoints as high priests men who have weakness, but the word of the oath, which came after the law, *appoints* the Son who has been perfected forever.

[2] **Isa. 42:1:** Behold! My Servant whom I uphold, My Elect One *in whom* My soul delights! I have put My Spirit upon Him; He will bring forth justice to the Gentiles. **1 Pet. 1:19-20:** ... but with the precious blood of Christ, as of a lamb without blemish and without spot. He indeed was foreordained before the foundation of the world, but was manifest in these last times for you. **John 3:16:** ... because it is written, "Be holy, for I am holy." **1 Tim. 2:5:** For *there is* one God and one Mediator between God and men, *the* Man Christ Jesus.

[3] **Acts 3:20, 22:** and that He may send Jesus Christ, who was preached to you before ... For Moses truly said to the fathers, 'The LORD your God will raise up for you a Prophet like me from your brethren. Him you shall hear in all things, whatever He says to you.' **See Deut. 18:15.**

[4] **Heb. 5:5-6:** So also Christ did not glorify Himself to become High Priest, but *it was* He who said to Him: "You are My Son, Today I have begotten You." As *He* also *says* in another *place:* "You *are* a priest forever According to the order of Melchizedek."

[5] **Ps. 2:6:** "Yet I have set My King On My holy hill of Zion." **Luke 1:33:** And He will reign over the house of Jacob forever, and of His kingdom there will be no end. **See Isa. 9:5–6; Acts 2:29–36; Col. 1:13.**

[6] **Eph. 1:23:** ... which is His body, the fullness of Him who fills all in all. **Eph. 5:23:** For the husband is head of the wife, as also Christ is head of the church; and He is the Savior of the body.

[7] **Heb. 1:2:** ... has in these last days spoken to us by *His* Son, whom He has appointed heir of all things, through whom also He made the worlds.

[8] **Acts 17:31:** ... because He has appointed a day on which He will judge the world in righteousness by the Man whom He has ordained. He has given assurance of this to all by raising Him from the dead."

[9] **Isa. 53:10:** Yet it pleased the LORD to bruise Him; He has put *Him* to grief. When You make His soul an offering for sin, He shall see *His* seed, He shall prolong *His* days, And the pleasure of the LORD shall prosper in His hand. **John 17:6:** I have manifested Your name to the men whom You have given Me out of the world. They were Yours, You gave them to Me, and they have kept Your word. **Ps. 22:30:** A posterity shall serve Him. It will be recounted of the Lord to the *next* generation.

[10] **1 Tim. 2:6:** ... who gave Himself a ransom for all, to be testified in due time. **Isa. 55:4-5:** Indeed I have given him *as* a witness to the people, A leader and commander for the people. Surely you shall call a nation you do not know, And nations *who* do not know you shall run to you, Because of the LORD your God, And the Holy One of Israel; For He has glorified you. **Rom. 8:30:** Moreover whom He predestined, these He also called; whom He called, these He also justified; and whom He justified, these He also glorified. **1 Cor. 1:30:** But of Him you are in Christ Jesus, who became for us wisdom from God—and righteousness and sanctification and redemption.

[11] **John 1:1, 14:** In the beginning was the Word, and the Word was with God, and the Word was God.... And the Word became flesh and dwelt among us, and we beheld His glory, the glory as of the only begotten of the Father, full of grace and truth. **1 John 5:20:** And we know that the Son of

one substance and equal with Him: who made the world,[12] who upholdeth and governeth all things He hath made:[13] did when the fullness of time was come take upon Him man's nature,[14] with all the essential properties, and common infirmities thereof, yet without sin:[15] being conceived by the Holy Spirit in the womb of the virgin Mary, the Holy Spirit coming down upon her, and the power of the Most High overshadowing her, and so was made of a woman,[16] of the tribe of Judah, of the seed of Abraham, and David according to the Scriptures:[17] So that two whole, perfect, and distinct natures, were inseparably joined together in one person: without conversion, composition, or confusion:[18] which person is very God, and very man; yet one Christ, the only Mediator between God and man.[19]

God has come and has given us an understanding, that we may know Him who is true; and we are in Him who is true, in His Son Jesus Christ. This is the true God and eternal life. **Heb. 1:8-9:** But to the Son *He says:* "Your throne, O God, *is* forever and ever; A scepter of righteousness *is* the scepter of Your kingdom. You have loved righteousness and hated lawlessness; Therefore God, Your God, has anointed You With the oil of gladness more than Your companions."

[12] **Phil. 2:6:** ... who, being in the form of God, did not consider it robbery to be equal with God.

[13] **Heb. 1:3:** ... who being the brightness of *His* glory and the express image of His person, and upholding all things by the word of His power, when He had by Himself purged our sins, sat down at the right hand of the Majesty on high.

[14] **Gal. 4:4:** But when the fullness of the time had come, God sent forth His Son, born of a woman, born under the law. **Rom. 8:3:** For what the law could not do in that it was weak through the flesh, God *did* by sending His own Son in the likeness of sinful flesh, on account of sin: He condemned sin in the flesh.

[15] **Heb. 2:14-17:** Inasmuch then as the children have partaken of flesh and blood, He Himself likewise shared in the same, that through death He might destroy him who had the power of death, that is, the devil, and release those who through fear of death were all their lifetime subject to bondage. For indeed He does not give aid to angels, but He does give aid to the seed of Abraham. Therefore, in all things He had to be made like *His* brethren, that He might be a merciful and faithful High Priest in things *pertaining* to God, to make propitiation for the sins of the people. **Heb. 4:15:** For we do not have a High Priest who cannot sympathize with our weaknesses, but was in all *points* tempted as *we are, yet* without sin.

[16] **Luke 1:27, 31, 35:** ... to a virgin betrothed to a man whose name was Joseph, of the house of David. The virgin's name *was* Mary.... And behold, you will conceive in your womb and bring forth a Son, and shall call His name JESUS.... And the angel answered and said to her, "*The* Holy Spirit will come upon you, and the power of the Highest will overshadow you; therefore, also, that Holy One who is to be born will be called the Son of God." **Gal. 4:4:** But when the fullness of the time had come, God sent forth His Son, born of a woman, born under the law. **See Matt. 1:18, 20-21.**

[17] **Heb. 7:14:** For *it is* evident that our Lord arose from Judah, of which tribe Moses spoke nothing concerning priesthood. **Rev. 5:5:** But one of the elders said to me, "Do not weep. Behold, the Lion of the tribe of Judah, the Root of David, has prevailed to open the scroll and to loose its seven seals." **Gal. 3:16:** Now to Abraham and his Seed were the promises made. He does not say, "And to seeds," as of many, but as of one, "And to your Seed," who is Christ. **Rom. 1:3:** ... concerning His Son Jesus Christ our Lord, who was born of the seed of David according to the flesh.

[18] **Matt. 16:16:** Simon Peter answered and said, "You are the Christ, the Son of the living God." **Col. 2:9:** For in Him dwells all the fullness of the Godhead bodily. **Rom. 9:5:** ... of whom *are* the fathers and from whom, according to the flesh, Christ *came,* who is over all, *the* eternally blessed God. Amen. **1 Tim. 3:16:** And without controversy great is the mystery of godliness: God was manifested in the flesh, Justified in the Spirit, Seen by angels, Preached among the Gentiles, Believed on in the world, Received up in glory.

[19] **Rom. 1:3-4:** ... concerning His Son Jesus Christ our Lord, who was born of the seed of David according to the flesh, *and* declared *to be* the Son of God with power according to the Spirit of

3. The Lord Jesus in His human nature thus united to the divine, in the person of the Son, was sanctified, anointed with the Holy Spirit, above measure;[20] having in Him all the treasures of wisdom and knowledge;[21] in whom it pleased the Father that all fullness should dwell:[22] To the end that being holy, harmless, undefiled, and full of grace, and truth,[23] He might be thoroughly furnished to execute the office of a Mediator, and surety;[24] which office He took not upon Himself, but was thereunto called by His Father;[25] who also put all power and judgement in His hand, and gave Him commandment to execute the same.[26]

4. This office the Lord Jesus did most willingly undertake,[27] which that He might discharge He was made under the law,[28] and

---

holiness, by the resurrection from the dead. **1 Tim. 2:5:** For *there is* one God and one Mediator between God and men, *the* Man Christ Jesus.

[20] **Ps. 45:7:** You love righteousness and hate wickedness; Therefore God, Your God, has anointed You With the oil of gladness more than Your companions. **Acts 10:38:** ... how God anointed Jesus of Nazareth with the Holy Spirit and with power, who went about doing good and healing all who were oppressed by the devil, for God was with Him. **John 3:34:** For He whom God has sent speaks the words of God, for God does not give the Spirit by measure. **See Isa. 61:1; Luke 4:18; Heb. 1:8-9.**

[21] **Col. 2:3:** ... in whom are hidden all the treasures of wisdom and knowledge.

[22] **Col. 1:19:** For it pleased *the Father that* in Him all the fullness should dwell.

[23] **Heb. 7:26:** For such a High Priest was fitting for us, *who is* holy, harmless, undefiled, separate from sinners, and has become higher than the heavens. **John 1:14:** And the Word became flesh and dwelt among us, and we beheld His glory, the glory as of the only begotten of the Father, full of grace and truth.

[24] **Heb. 12:24:** ... to Jesus the Mediator of the new covenant, and to the blood of sprinkling that speaks better things than *that of* Abel. **Heb. 7:22:** ... by so much more Jesus has become a surety of a better covenant.

[25] **Heb. 5:4-5:** And no man takes this honor to himself, but he who is called by God, just as Aaron *was.*

[26] **John 5:22, 27:** For the Father judges no one, but has committed all judgment to the Son ... and has given Him authority to execute judgment also, because He is the Son of Man. **Matt. 28:18:** And Jesus came and spoke to them, saying, "All authority has been given to Me in heaven and on earth." **Acts 2:36:** "Therefore let all the house of Israel know assuredly that God has made this Jesus, whom you crucified, both Lord and Christ."

[27] **Ps. 40:7-8:** Then I said, "Behold, I come; In the scroll of the book *it is* written of me. I delight to do Your will, O my God, And Your law *is* within my heart." **Heb. 10:5-11:** Therefore, when He came into the world, He said: "Sacrifice and offering You did not desire, But a body You have prepared for Me. In burnt offerings and *sacrifices* for sin You had no pleasure. Then I said, 'Behold, I have come—In the volume of the book it is written of Me—To do Your will, O God.'" Previously saying, "Sacrifice and offering, burnt offerings, and *offerings* for sin You did not desire, nor had pleasure *in them*" (which are offered according to the law), then He said, "Behold, I have come to do Your will, O God." He takes away the first that He may establish the second. By that will we have been sanctified through the offering of the body of Jesus Christ once *for all.* And every priest stands ministering daily and offering repeatedly the same sacrifices, which can never take away sins. **John 4:34:** Jesus said to them, "My food is to do the will of Him who sent Me, and to finish His work." **John 10:18:** No one takes it from Me, but I lay it down of Myself. I have power to lay it down, and I have power to take it again. This command I have received from My Father. **Phil. 2:8:** And being found in appearance as a man, He humbled Himself and became obedient to *the point of* death, even the death of the cross.

[28] **Gal. 4:4:** But when the fullness of the time had come, God sent forth His Son, born of a woman, born under the law.

did perfectly fulfill it,[29] and underwent the punishment due to us, which we should have borne and suffered, being made sin and a curse for us:[30] enduring most grievous sorrows in His soul;[31] and most painful sufferings in His body;[32] was crucified, and died,[33] and remained in the state of the dead; yet saw no corruption:[34]

---

[29] **Matt. 3:15:** But Jesus answered and said to him, "Permit *it to be so* now, for thus it is fitting for us to fulfill all righteousness." Then he allowed Him. **Matt. 5:17:** Do not think that I came to destroy the Law or the Prophets. I did not come to destroy but to fulfill. **Heb. 5:8-9:** ... though He was a Son, *yet* He learned obedience by the things which He suffered. And having been perfected, He became the author of eternal salvation to all who obey Him.

[30] **Gal. 3:13:** Christ has redeemed us from the curse of the law, having become a curse for us (for it is written, "Cursed *is* everyone who hangs on a tree."). **Isa. 53:6:** All we like sheep have gone astray; We have turned, every one, to his own way; And the LORD has laid on Him the iniquity of us all. **1 Pet. 3:18:** For Christ also suffered once for sins, the just for the unjust, that He might bring us to God, being put to death in the flesh but made alive by the Spirit. **2 Cor. 5:21:** For He made Him who knew no sin *to be* sin for us, that we might become the righteousness of God in Him.

[31] **Matt. 26:37-38:** And He took with Him Peter and the two sons of Zebedee, and He began to be sorrowful and deeply distressed. Then He said to them, "My soul is exceedingly sorrowful, even to death. Stay here and watch with Me." **Luke 22:44:** And being in agony, He prayed more earnestly. Then His sweat became like great drops of blood falling down to the ground. **Matt. 27:46:** And about the ninth hour Jesus cried out with a loud voice, saying, "Eli, Eli, lama sabachthani?" that is, "My God, My God, why have You forsaken Me?"

[32] **Matt. 26:67-68:** Then they spat in His face and beat Him; and others struck *Him* with the palms of their hands, saying, "Prophesy to us, Christ! Who is the one who struck You?" **Matt. 27:27-50:** Then the soldiers of the governor took Jesus into the Praetorium and gathered the whole garrison around Him. And they stripped Him and put a scarlet robe on Him. When they had twisted a crown of thorns, they put *it* on His head, and a reed in His right hand. And they bowed the knee before Him and mocked Him, saying, "Hail, King of the Jews!" Then they spat on Him, and took the reed and struck Him on the head. And when they had mocked Him, they took the robe off Him, put His *own* clothes on Him, and led Him away to be crucified. Now as they came out, they found a man of Cyrene, Simon by name. Him they compelled to bear His cross. And when they had come to a place called Golgotha, that is to say, Place of a Skull, they gave Him sour wine mingled with gall to drink. But when He had tasted *it,* He would not drink. Then they crucified Him, and divided His garments, casting lots, that it might be fulfilled which was spoken by the prophet: "They divided My garments among them, And for My clothing they cast lots." Sitting down, they kept watch over Him there. And they put up over His head the accusation written against Him: THIS IS JESUS THE KING OF THE JEWS. Then two robbers were crucified with Him, one on the right and another on the left. And those who passed by blasphemed Him, wagging their heads and saying, "You who destroy the temple and build *it* in three days, save Yourself! If You are the Son of God, come down from the cross." Likewise the chief priests also, mocking with the scribes and elders, said, "He saved others; Himself He cannot save. If He is the King of Israel, let Him now come down from the cross, and we will believe Him. He trusted in God; let Him deliver Him now if He will have Him; for He said, 'I am the Son of God.'" Even the robbers who were crucified with Him reviled Him with the same thing. Now from the sixth hour until the ninth hour there was darkness over all the land. And about the ninth hour Jesus cried out with a loud voice, saying, "Eli, Eli, lama sabachthani?" that is, "My God, My God, why have You forsaken Me?" Some of those who stood there, when they heard *that,* said, "This Man is calling for Elijah!" Immediately one of them ran and took a sponge, filled *it* with sour wine and put *it* on a reed, and offered it to Him to drink. The rest said, "Let Him alone; let us see if Elijah will come to save Him." And Jesus cried out again with a loud voice, and yielded up His spirit.

[33] **Mark 15:24, 37:** And when they crucified Him, they divided His garments, casting lots for them *to determine* what every man should take.... And Jesus cried out with a loud voice, and breathed His last. **Phil. 2:8:** And being found in appearance as a man, He humbled Himself and became obedient to *the point of* death, even the death of the cross.

[34] **Matt. 27:60:** ... and laid it in his new tomb which he had hewn out of the rock; and he rolled a large stone against the door of the tomb, and departed. **Acts 2:24, 27:** whom God raised up, having loosed the pains of death, because it was not possible that He should be held by it.... For You will not leave my soul in Hades,
Nor will You allow Your Holy One to see corruption. **Acts 13:29, 37:** Now when they had fulfilled all that was written concerning Him, they took *Him* down from the tree and laid *Him* in a tomb.... but He whom God raised up saw no corruption. **Rom. 6:9:** ... knowing that Christ, having been raised from the dead, dies no more. Death no longer has dominion over Him.

on the third day He arose from the dead,[35] with the same body in which He suffered;[36] with which He also ascended into heaven: and there sitteth at the right hand of His Father,[37] making intercession;[38] and shall return to judge men and angels, at the end of the world.[39]

5. The Lord Jesus by His perfect obedience and sacrifice of Himself, which He through the eternal Spirit once offered up unto God, hath fully satisfied the justice of God,[40] procured reconciliation, and purchased an everlasting inheritance in the

---

[35] **1 Cor. 15:3-4:** For I delivered to you first of all that which I also received: that Christ died for our sins according to the Scriptures, and that He was buried, and that He rose again the third day according to the Scriptures.

[36] **Luke 24:39:** Behold My hands and My feet, that it is I Myself. Handle Me and see, for a spirit does not have flesh and bones as you see I have. **John 20:25, 27:** The other disciples therefore said to him, "We have seen the Lord." So he said to them, "Unless I see in His hands the print of the nails, and put my finger into the print of the nails, and put my hand into His side, I will not believe." ... Then He said to Thomas, "Reach your finger here, and look at My hands; and reach your hand *here,* and put *it* into My side. Do not be unbelieving, but believing."

[37] **Luke 24:50-51:** And He led them out as far as Bethany, and He lifted up His hands and blessed them. Now it came to pass, while He blessed them, that He was parted from them and carried up into heaven. **1 Pet. 3:22:** ... who has gone into heaven and is at the right hand of God, angels and authorities and powers having been made subject to Him. **Mark 16:19:** So then, after the Lord had spoken to them, He was received up into heaven, and sat down at the right hand of God. **Acts 1:9-11:** Now when He had spoken these things, while they watched, He was taken up, and a cloud received Him out of their sight. And while they looked steadfastly toward heaven as He went up, behold, two men stood by them in white apparel, who also said, "Men of Galilee, why do you stand gazing up into heaven? This *same* Jesus, who was taken up from you into heaven, will so come in like manner as you saw Him go into heaven."

[38] **Rom. 8:34:** Who *is* he who condemns? *It is* Christ who died, and furthermore is also risen, who is even at the right hand of God, who also makes intercession for us. **Heb. 7:25:** Therefore He is also able to save to the uttermost those who come to God through Him, since He always lives to make intercession for them. **Heb. 9:24:** For Christ has not entered the holy places made with hands, *which are* copies of the true, but into heaven itself, now to appear in the presence of God for us.

[39] **Acts 1:11:** ... who also said, "Men of Galilee, why do you stand gazing up into heaven? This *same* Jesus, who was taken up from you into heaven, will so come in like manner as you saw Him go into heaven." **Acts 10:42:** And He commanded us to preach to the people, and to testify that it is He who was ordained by God *to be* Judge of the living and the dead. **John 5:28-29:** Do not marvel at this; for the hour is coming in which all who are in the graves will hear His voice and come forth—those who have done good, to the resurrection of life, and those who have done evil, to the resurrection of condemnation. **Rom. 14:10:** But why do you judge your brother? Or why do you show contempt for your brother? For we shall all stand before the judgment seat of Christ. **Matt. 13:40-42:** Therefore as the tares are gathered and burned in the fire, so it will be at the end of this age. The Son of Man will send out His angels, and they will gather out of His kingdom all things that offend, and those who practice lawlessness, and will cast them into the furnace of fire. There will be wailing and gnashing of teeth. **Jude 6:** And the angels who did not keep their proper domain, but left their own abode, He has reserved in everlasting chains under darkness for the judgment of the great day. **See 2 Pet. 2:4.**

[40] **Heb. 9:14:** ... how much more shall the blood of Christ, who through the eternal Spirit offered Himself without spot to God, cleanse your conscience from dead works to serve the living God? **Heb. 10:14:** For by one offering He has perfected forever those who are being sanctified. **Eph. 5:2:** And walk in love, as Christ also has loved us and given Himself for us, an offering and a sacrifice to God for a sweet-smelling aroma. **Rom. 3:25-26:** ... whom God set forth *as* a propitiation by His blood, through faith, to demonstrate His righteousness, because in His forbearance God had passed over the sins that were previously committed, to demonstrate at the present time His righteousness, that He might be just and the justifier of the one who has faith in Jesus. **Rom. 5:19:** For as by one man's disobedience many were made sinners, so also by one Man's obedience many will be made righteous.

kingdom of heaven, for all those whom the Father hath given unto Him.[41]

6. Although the price of redemption was not actually paid by Christ, till after His incarnation, yet the virtue, efficacy, and benefit thereof were communicated to the elect in all ages successively, from the beginning of the world,[42] in and by those promises, types, and sacrifices, wherein He was revealed,[43] and signified to be the Seed of the woman, which should bruise the serpent's head;[44] and the Lamb slain from the foundation of the world:[45] being the same yesterday, and today, and forever.[46]

7. Christ in the work of mediation acteth according to both natures, by each nature doing that which is proper to itself;[47] yet by reason of the unity of the person, that which is proper to one

---

[41] **Dan. 9:24:** Seventy weeks are determined For your people and for your holy city, To finish the transgression, To make an end of sins, To make reconciliation for iniquity, To bring in everlasting righteousness, To seal up vision and prophecy, And to anoint the Most Holy. **2 Cor. 5:18:** Now all things *are* of God, who has reconciled us to Himself through Jesus Christ, and has given us the ministry of reconciliation. **Col. 1:20:** ... and by Him to reconcile all things to Himself, by Him, whether things on earth or things in heaven, having made peace through the blood of His cross. **Eph. 1:11, 14:** In Him also we have obtained an inheritance, being predestined according to the purpose of Him who works all things according to the purpose of Him who works all things according to the counsel of His will ... who is the guarantee of our inheritance until the redemption of the purchased possession, to the praise of His glory. **John 17:2:** ... as You have given Him authority over all flesh, that He should give eternal life to as many as You have given Him. **Heb. 9:12, 15:** Not with the blood of goats and calves, but with His own blood He entered the Most Holy Place once for all, having obtained eternal redemption.... And for this reason He is the Mediator of the new covenant, by means of death, for the redemption of the transgressions under the first covenant, that those who are called may receive the promise of the eternal inheritance.

[42] **1 Cor. 10:4:** ... and all drank the same spiritual drink. For they drank of that spiritual Rock that followed them, and that Rock was Christ. **Heb. 4:2:** For indeed the gospel was preached to us as well as to them; but the word which they heard did not profit them, not being mixed with faith in those who heard *it*. **1 Pet. 1:10-11:** Of this salvation the prophets have inquired and searched carefully, who prophesied of the grace *that would come* to you, searching what, or what manner of time, the Spirit of Christ who was in them was indicating when He testified beforehand the sufferings of Christ and the glories that would follow.

[43] **Heb. 13:11-13:** For the bodies of those animals, whose blood is brought into the sanctuary by the high priest for sin, are burned outside the camp. Therefore Jesus also, that He might sanctify the people with His own blood, suffered outside the gate. Therefore let us go forth to Him, outside the camp, bearing His reproach. **Gal. 3:24-25:** Therefore the law was our tutor *to bring us* to Christ, that we might be justified by faith. But after faith has come, we are no longer under a tutor.

[44] **Gen. 3:15:** And I will put enmity Between you and the woman, And between your seed and her Seed; He shall bruise your head, And you shall bruise His heel.

[45] **Rev. 13:8:** All who dwell on the earth will worship him, whose names have not been written in the Book of Life of the Lamb slain from the foundation of the world.

[46] **Heb. 13:8:** Jesus Christ *is* the same yesterday, today, and forever.

[47] **John 10:17-18:** "Therefore My Father loves Me, because I lay down My life that I may take it again. No one takes it from Me, but I lay it down of Myself. I have power to lay it down, and I have power to take it again. This command I have received from My Father." **1 Pet. 3:18:** For Christ also suffered once for sins, the just for the unjust, that He might bring us to God, being put to death in the flesh but made alive by the Spirit. **Heb. 1:3:** ... who being the brightness of *His* glory and the express image of His person, and upholding all things by the word of His power, when He had by Himself purged our sins, sat down at the right hand of the Majesty on high. **See Heb. 9:14.**

nature, is sometimes in Scripture attributed to the person denominated by the other nature.[48]

8. To all those for whom Christ hath obtained eternal redemption, He doth certainly, and effectually apply, and communicate the same;[49] making intercession for them,[50] uniting them to Himself by His Spirit,[51] revealing unto them, in and by the word, the mystery of salvation;[52] persuading them to believe, and obey; governing their hearts by His word and Spirit,[53] and overcoming all their enemies by His almighty power, and wisdom; in such manner, and ways as are most consonant to His wonderful, and unsearchable dispensation;[54] and all of free, and

---

[48] **Acts 20:28:** Therefore take heed to yourselves and to all the flock, among which the Holy Spirit has made you overseers, to shepherd the church of God which He purchased with His own blood. **Luke 1:43:** But why *is* this *granted* to me, that the mother of my Lord should come to me? **John 3:13:** No one has ascended to heaven but He who came down from heaven, *that is,* the Son of Man who is in heaven. **See Rom. 9:5.**

[49] **John 6:37, 39:** All that the Father gives Me will come to Me, and the one who comes to Me I will by no means cast out.... This is the will of the Father who sent Me, that of all He has given Me I should lose nothing, but should raise it up at the last day. **John 10:15-16, 27-28:** As the Father knows Me, even so I know the Father; and I lay down My life for the sheep. And other sheep I have which are not of this fold; them also I must bring, and they will hear My voice; and there will be one flock *and* one shepherd.... My sheep hear My voice, and I know them, and they follow Me. And I give them eternal life, and they shall never perish; neither shall anyone snatch them out of My hand.

[50] **1 John 2:1:** My little children, these things I write to you, so that you may not sin. And if anyone sins, we have an Advocate with the Father, Jesus Christ the righteous. **Rom. 8:34:** Who *is* he who condemns? *It is* Christ who died, and furthermore is also risen, who is even at the right hand of God, who also makes intercession for us.

[51] **1 Cor. 6:17:** But he who is joined to the Lord is one spirit *with Him.* **Gal. 3:27:** For as many of you as were baptized into Christ have put on Christ.

[52] **John 15:5:** I am the vine, you *are* the branches. He who abides in Me, and I in him, bears much fruit; for without Me you can do nothing. **John 17:6:** I have manifested Your name to the men whom You have given Me out of the world. They were Yours, You gave them to Me, and they have kept Your word. **Eph. 1:9:** ... having made known to us the mystery of His will, according to His good pleasure which He purposed in Himself. **1 John 5:20:** And we know that the Son of God has come and has given us an understanding, that we may know Him who is true; and we are in Him who is true, in His Son Jesus Christ. This is the true God and eternal life.

[53] **John 14:26:** But the Helper, the Holy Spirit, whom the Father will send in My name, He will teach you all things, and bring to your remembrance all things that I said to you. **2 Cor. 4:13:** And since we have the same spirit of faith, according to what is written, "I believed and therefore I spoke," we also believe and therefore speak. **Rom. 8:9, 14:** But you are not in the flesh but in the Spirit, if indeed the Spirit of God dwells in you. Now if anyone does not have the Spirit of Christ, he is not His.... For as many as are led by the Spirit of God, these are sons of God. **Rom. 15:18-19:** For I will not dare to speak of any of those things which Christ has not accomplished through me, in word and deed, to make the Gentiles obedient—in mighty signs and wonders, by the power of the Spirit of God, so that from Jerusalem and round about to Illyricum I have fully preached the gospel of Christ. **John 17:17:** Sanctify them by Your truth. Your word is truth.

[54] **Ps. 110:1:** The LORD said to my Lord, "Sit at My right hand, Till I make Your enemies Your footstool." **1 Cor. 15:25-26:** For He must reign till He has put all enemies under His feet. The last enemy *that* will be destroyed *is* death. **Col. 2:15:** Having disarmed principalities and powers, He made a public spectacle of them, triumphing over them in it. **Luke 10:19:** Behold, I give you the authority to trample on serpents and scorpions, and over all the power of the enemy, and nothing shall by any means hurt you.

absolute grace,[55] without any condition foreseen in them, to procure it.[56]

9. This office of Mediator between God and man, is proper only to Christ, who is the Prophet, Priest, and King of the church of God; and may not be either in whole, or any part thereof transferred from Him to any other.[57]

10. This number and order of offices is necessary; for in respect of our ignorance, we stand in need of His prophetical office;[58] and in respect of our alienation from God, and imperfection of the best of our services, we need His priestly office, to reconcile us, and present us acceptable unto God:[59] and in respect of our averseness, and utter inability to return to God,[60] and for our rescue, and security from our spiritual adversaries,[61] we need His kingly office, to convince, subdue, draw, uphold, deliver, and preserve us to His heavenly kingdom.[62]

---

[55] **Eph. 2:8:** For by grace you have been saved through faith, and that not of yourselves; *it is* the gift of God.

[56] **Rom. 9:11, 17-24:** ... (for *the children* not yet being born, nor having done any good or evil, that the purpose of God according to election might stand, not of works but of Him who calls) ... For the Scripture says to the Pharaoh, "For this very purpose I have raised you up, that I may show My power in you, and that My name may be declared in all the earth." Therefore He has mercy on whom He wills, and whom He wills He hardens. You will say to me then, "Why does He still find fault? For who has resisted His will?" But indeed, O man, who are you to reply against God? Will the thing formed say to him who formed *it*, "Why have you made me like this?" Does not the potter have power over the clay, from the same lump to make one vessel for honor and another for dishonor? *What* if God, wanting to show *His* wrath and to make His power known, endured with much longsuffering the vessels of wrath prepared for destruction, and that He might make known the riches of His glory on the vessels of mercy, which He had prepared beforehand for glory, even us whom He called, not of the Jews only, but also of the Gentiles?

[57] **1 Tim. 2:5:** For *there is* one God and one Mediator between God and men, *the* Man Christ Jesus.

[58] **John 1:18:** No one has seen God at any time. The only begotten Son, who is in the bosom of the Father, He has declared *Him.*

[59] **Col. 1:21:** And you, who once were alienated and enemies in your mind by wicked works, yet now He has reconciled. **Gal. 5:17:** For the flesh lusts against the Spirit, and the Spirit against the flesh; and these are contrary to one another, so that you do not do the things that you wish.

[60] **Matt. 23:37:** O Jerusalem, Jerusalem, the one who kills the prophets and stones those who are sent to her! How often I wanted to gather your children together, as a hen gathers her chicks under *her* wings, but you were not willing! **1 Cor. 2:14:** But the natural man does not receive the things of the Spirit of God, for they are foolishness to him; nor can he know *them,* because they are spiritually discerned. **Eph. 2:1:** And you *He made alive,* who were dead in trespasses and sins.

[61] **Luke 1:71, 74:** That we should be saved from our enemies And from the hand of all who hate us ... To grant us that we, Being delivered from the hand of our enemies, Might serve Him without fear. **Eph. 2:2:** in which you once walked according to the course of this world, according to the prince of the power of the air, the spirit who now works in the sons of disobedience.

[62] **John 16:8:** And when He has come, He will convict the world of sin, and of righteousness, and of judgment. **Ps. 110:3:** Your people *shall be* volunteers In the day of Your power; In the beauties of holiness, from the womb of the morning, You have the dew of Your youth. **John 6:44:** No one can come to Me unless the Father who sent Me draws him; and I will raise him up at the last day. **Isa. 41:10:** Fear not, for I *am* with you; Be not dismayed, for I *am* your God. I will strengthen you, Yes, I will help you, I will uphold you with My righteous right hand. **2 Cor. 1:10:** ... who delivered us from so great a death, and does deliver us; in whom we trust that He will still deliver *us.* **2 Tim.**

4:18: And the Lord will deliver me from every evil work and preserve *me* for His heavenly kingdom. To Him *be* glory forever and ever. Amen!

CHAPTER 9
Of Free Will

1. God hath endued the will of man, with that natural liberty, and power of acting upon choice; that it is neither forced, nor by any necessity of nature determined to do good or evil.[1]

2. Man in his state of innocency, had freedom, and power, to will, and to do that which was good, and well-pleasing to God;[2] but yet was mutable, so that he might fall from it.[3]

3. Man by his fall into a state of sin hath wholly lost all ability of will, to any spiritual good accompanying salvation;[4] so as a natural man, being altogether averse from that good,[5] and dead in sin,[6] is not able, by his own strength, to convert himself; or to prepare himself thereunto.[7]

---

[1] **Matt. 17:12:** But I say to you that Elijah has come already, and they did not know him but did to him whatever they wished. Likewise the Son of Man is also about to suffer at their hands. **James 1:13, 14:** Let no one say when he is tempted, "I am tempted by God"; for God cannot be tempted by evil, nor does He Himself tempt anyone. But each one is tempted when he is drawn away by his own desires and enticed. **Deut. 30:19:** I call heaven and earth as witnesses today against you, *that* I have set before you life and death, blessing and cursing; therefore choose life, that both you and your descendants may live. **Isa. 7:11-12:** "Ask a sign for yourself from the LORD your God; ask it either in the depth or in the height above." But Ahaz said, "I will not ask, nor will I test the LORD!" **John 5:40:** But you are not willing to come to Me that you may have life. **James 4:7:** Therefore submit to God. Resist the devil and he will flee from you.

[2] **Eccl. 7:29:** Truly, this only I have found: That God made man upright, But they have sought out many schemes. **Gen. 1:26, 31:** Then God said, "Let Us make man in Our image, according to Our likeness; let them have dominion over the fish of the sea, over the birds of the air, and over the cattle, over all the earth and over every creeping thing that creeps on the earth." ... Then God saw everything that He had made, and indeed *it was* very good. So the evening and the morning were the sixth day. **Col. 3:10:** ... and have put on the new *man* who is renewed in knowledge according to the image of Him who created him.

[3] **Gen. 2:16-17:** And the LORD God commanded the man, saying, "Of every tree of the garden you may freely eat; but of the tree of the knowledge of good and evil you shall not eat, for in the day that you eat of it you shall surely die." **Gen. 3:6, 17:** So when the woman saw that the tree *was* good for food, that it *was* pleasant to the eyes, and a tree desirable to make *one* wise, she took of its fruit and ate. She also gave to her husband with her, and he ate.... Then to Adam He said, "Because you have heeded the voice of your wife, and have eaten from the tree of which I commanded you, saying, 'You shall not eat of it': Cursed *is* the ground for your sake; In toil you shall eat *of* it All the days of your life."

[4] **Rom. 5:6:** For when we were still without strength, in due time Christ died for the ungodly. **Rom. 8:7-8:** Because the carnal mind *is* enmity against God; for it is not subject to the law of God, nor indeed can be. So then, those who are in the flesh cannot please God. **John 6:44, 65:** No one can come to Me unless the Father who sent Me draws him; and I will raise him up at the last day.... And He said, "Therefore I have said to you that no one can come to Me unless it has been granted to him by My Father." **John 15:5:** I am the vine, you *are* the branches. He who abides in Me, and I in him, bears much fruit; for without Me you can do nothing.

[5] **Rom. 3:9-10, 12, 23:** What then? Are we better *than they?* Not at all. For we have previously charged both Jews and Greeks that they are all under sin. As it is written: "There is none righteous, no, not one ... They have all turned aside; They have together become unprofitable; There is none who does good, no, not one." ... for all have sinned and fall short of the glory of God.

[6] **Eph. 2:1, 5:** And you *He made alive,* who were dead in trespasses and sins ... even when we were dead in trespasses, made us alive together with Christ (by grace you have been saved). **Col. 2:13:**

4. When God converts a sinner, and translates him into the state of grace, He freeth him from his natural bondage under sin,[8] and by His grace alone, enables him freely to will, and to do that which is spiritually good;[9] yet so as that by reason of his remaining corruptions he doth not perfectly nor only will that which is good; but doth also will that which is evil.[10]

5. This will of man is made perfectly, and immutably free to good alone, in the state of glory only.[11]

And you, being dead in your trespasses and the uncircumcision of your flesh, He has made alive together with Him, having forgiven you all trespasses.

[7] **John 3:3, 5-6:** Jesus answered and said to him, "Most assuredly, I say to you, unless one is born again, he cannot see the kingdom of God." ... Jesus answered, "Most assuredly, I say to you, unless one is born of water and the Spirit, he cannot enter the kingdom of God. That which is born of the flesh is flesh, and that which is born of the Spirit is spirit. **John 6:44, 65:** No one can come to Me unless the Father who sent Me draws him; and I will raise him up at the last day.... And He said, "Therefore I have said to you that no one can come to Me unless it has been granted to him by My Father." **1 Cor. 2:14:** But the natural man does not receive the things of the Spirit of God, for they are foolishness to him; nor can he know *them,* because they are spiritually discerned. **Tit. 3:3-5:** For we ourselves were also once foolish, disobedient, deceived, serving various lusts and pleasures, living in malice and envy, hateful and hating one another. But when the kindness and the love of God our Savior toward man appeared, not by works of righteousness which we have done, but according to His mercy He saved us, through the washing of regeneration and renewing of the Holy Spirit.

[8] **Col. 1:13:** He has delivered us from the power of darkness and conveyed *us* into the kingdom of the Son of His love. **John 8:34, 36:** Jesus answered them, "Most assuredly, I say to you, whoever commits sin is a slave of sin.... Therefore if the Son makes you free, you shall be free indeed." **Rom. 6:6-7:** ... knowing this, that our old man was crucified with *Him,* that the body of sin might be done away with, that we should no longer be slaves of sin. For he who has died has been freed from sin.

[9] **Phil. 2:13:** ... for it is God who works in you both to will and to do for *His* good pleasure. **Rom. 6:14, 17-19, 22:** For sin shall not have dominion over you, for you are not under law but under grace.... But God be thanked that *though* you were slaves of sin, yet you obeyed from the heart that form of doctrine to which you were delivered. And having been set free from sin, you became slaves of righteousness. I speak in human *terms* because of the weakness of your flesh. For just as you presented your members *as* slaves of uncleanness, and of lawlessness *leading* to *more* lawlessness, so now present your members *as* slaves *of* righteousness for holiness.... But now having been set free from sin, and having become slaves of God, you have your fruit to holiness, and the end, everlasting life.

[10] **Gal. 5:17:** For the flesh lusts against the Spirit, and the Spirit against the flesh; and these are contrary to one another, so that you do not do the things that you wish. **Rom. 7:14-25:** For we know that the law is spiritual, but I am carnal, sold under sin. For what I am doing, I do not understand. For what I will to do, that I do not practice; but what I hate, that I do. If, then, I do what I will not to do, I agree with the law that *it is* good. But now, *it is* no longer I who do it, but sin that dwells in me. For I know that in me (that is, in my flesh) nothing good dwells; for to will is present with me, but *how* to perform what is good I do not find. For the good that I will *to do,* I do not do; but the evil I will not *to do,* that I practice. Now if I do what I will not *to do,* it is no longer I who do it, but sin that dwells in me. I find then a law, that evil is present with me, the one who wills to do good. For I delight in the law of God according to the inward man. But I see another law in my members, warring against the law of my mind, and bringing me into captivity to the law of sin which is in my members. O wretched man that I am! Who will deliver me from this body of death? I thank God—through Jesus Christ our Lord! So then, with the mind I myself serve the law of God, but with the flesh the law of sin. **1 John 1:8, 10:** If we say that we have no sin, we deceive ourselves, and the truth is not in us.... If we say that we have not sinned, we make Him a liar, and His word is not in us.

[11] **Eph. 4:13:** ... till we all come to the unity of the faith and of the knowledge of the Son of God, to a perfect man, to the measure of the stature of the fullness of Christ. **Heb. 12:23:** ... to the general assembly and church of the firstborn *who are* registered in heaven, to God the Judge of all, to the spirits of just men made perfect. **1 John 3:2:** Beloved, now we are children of God; and it has not yet been revealed what we shall be, but we know that when He is revealed, we shall be like Him, for

we shall see Him as He is. **Jude 24:** Now to Him who is able to keep you from stumbling, And to present you faultless Before the presence of His glory with exceeding joy. **Rev. 21:27:** But there shall by no means enter it anything that defiles, or causes an abomination or a lie, but only those who are written in the Lamb's Book of Life.

CHAPTER 10
Of Effectual Calling

1. Those whom God hath predestinated unto life, He is pleased, in His appointed, and accepted time, effectually to call[1] by His word, and Spirit,[2] out of that state of sin, and death, in which they are by nature, to grace and salvation by Jesus Christ;[3] enlightening their minds, spiritually, and savingly to understand the things of God;[4] taking away their heart of stone, and giving unto them an heart of flesh;[5] renewing their wills, and by His almighty power determining them to that which is good,[6] and effectually drawing

---

[1] **Acts 13:48:** Now when the Gentiles heard this, they were glad and glorified the word of the Lord. And as many as had been appointed to eternal life believed. **Rom. 8:28, 30:** And we know that all things work together for good to those who love God, to those who are the called according to *His* purpose.... Moreover whom He predestined, these He also called; whom He called, these He also justified; and whom He justified, these He also glorified. **Rom. 11:7:** What then? Israel has not obtained what it seeks; but the elect have obtained it, and the rest were blinded. **Eph. 1:5, 11:** ... having predestined us to adoption as sons by Jesus Christ to Himself, according to the good pleasure of His will ... In Him also we have obtained an inheritance, being predestined according to the purpose of Him who works all things according to the counsel of His will. **2 Tim. 1:9-10:** ... who has saved us and called *us* with a holy calling, not according to our works, but according to His own purpose and grace which was given to us in Christ Jesus before time began, but has now been revealed by the appearing of our Savior Jesus Christ, *who* has abolished death and brought life and immortality to light through the gospel.

[2] **2 Thess. 2:13-14:** But we are bound to give thanks to God always for you, brethren beloved by the Lord, because God from the beginning chose you for salvation through sanctification by the Spirit and belief in the truth, to which He called you by our gospel, for the obtaining of the glory of our Lord Jesus Christ. **James 1:18:** Of His own will He brought us forth by the word of truth, that we might be a kind of firstfruits of His creatures. **2 Cor. 3:3, 6:** ... clearly you are an epistle of Christ, ministered by us, written not with ink but by the Spirit of the living God, not on tablets of stone but on tablets of flesh, *that is,* of the heart.... who also made us sufficient as ministers of the new covenant, not of the letter but of the Spirit; for the letter kills, but the Spirit gives life. **1 Cor. 2:12:** Now we have received, not the spirit of the world, but the Spirit who is from God, that we might know the things that have been freely given to us by God.

[3] **2 Tim. 1:9-10:** ... who has saved us and called *us* with a holy calling, not according to our works, but according to His own purpose and grace which was given to us in Christ Jesus before time began, but has now been revealed by the appearing of our Savior Jesus Christ, *who* has abolished death and brought life and immortality to light through the gospel. **1 Pet. 2:9:** But you *are* a chosen generation, a royal priesthood, a holy nation, His own special people, that you may proclaim the praises of Him who called you out of darkness into His marvelous light. **Rom. 8:2:** For the law of the Spirit of life in Christ Jesus has made me free from the law of sin and death. **Eph. 2:1-1:** And you *He made alive,* who were dead in trespasses and sins.

[4] **Acts 26:18:** ... to open their eyes, *in order* to turn *them* from darkness to light, and *from* the power of Satan to God, that they may receive forgiveness of sins and an inheritance among those who are sanctified by faith in Me. **1 Cor. 2:10, 12:** But God has revealed *them* to us through His Spirit. For the Spirit searches all things, yes, the deep things of God.... Now we have received, not the spirit of the world, but the Spirit who is from God, that we might know the things that have been freely given to us by God. **Eph. 1:17-18:** ... that the God of our Lord Jesus Christ, the Father of glory, may give to you the spirit of wisdom and revelation in the knowledge of Him, the eyes of your understanding being enlightened; that you may know what is the hope of His calling, what are the riches of the glory of His inheritance in the saints. **2 Cor. 4:6:** For it is the God who commanded light to shine out of darkness, who has shone in our hearts to *give* the light of the knowledge of the glory of God in the face of Jesus Christ.

[5] **Ezek. 36:26:** I will give you a new heart and put a new spirit within you; I will take the heart of stone out of your flesh and give you a heart of flesh.

[6] **Ezek. 11:19:** Then I will give them one heart, and I will put a new spirit within them, and take the stony heart out of their flesh, and give them a heart of flesh. **Ezek. 36:27:** I will put My Spirit within you and cause you to walk in My statutes, and you will keep My judgments and do *them.*

them to Jesus Christ;[7] yet so as they come most freely, being made willing by His grace.[8]

2. This effectual call is of God's free, and special grace alone not from anything at all foreseen in man,[9] nor from any power, or agency in the creature, co-working with His special grace, the creature being wholly passive therein,[10] being dead in sins and trespasses,[11] until being quickened and renewed by the Holy Spirit,[12] he is thereby enabled to answer this call, and to embrace

---

Deut. 30:6: And the LORD your God will circumcise your heart and the heart of your descendants, to love the LORD your God with all your heart and with all your soul, that you may live. **John 3:5:** Jesus answered, "Most assuredly, I say to you, unless one is born of water and the Spirit, he cannot enter the kingdom of God." **Titus 3:5:** ... not by works of righteousness which we have done, but according to His mercy He saved us, through the washing of regeneration and renewing of the Holy Spirit. **1 Pet. 1:23:** ... having been born again, not of corruptible seed but incorruptible, through the word of God which lives and abides forever. **Eph. 1:19:** ... and what *is* the exceeding greatness of His power toward us who believe, according to the working of His mighty power.

[7] **John 6:44-45:** No one can come to Me unless the Father who sent Me draws him; and I will raise him up at the last day. It is written in the prophets, 'And they shall all be taught by God.' Therefore everyone who has heard and learned from the Father comes to Me. **Acts 16:14:** Now a certain woman named Lydia heard *us.* She was a seller of purple from the city of Thyatira, who worshiped God. The Lord opened her heart to heed the things spoken by Paul.

[8] **Ps. 110:3:** Your people *shall be* volunteers In the day of Your power; In the beauties of holiness, from the womb of the morning, You have the dew of Your youth. **John 6:37:** All that the Father gives Me will come to Me, and the one who comes to Me I will by no means cast out. **Matt. 11:28:** Come to Me, all *you* who labor and are heavy laden, and I will give you rest. **Rev. 22:17:** And the Spirit and the bride say, "Come!" And let him who hears say, "Come!" And let him who thirsts come. Whoever desires, let him take the water of life freely. **Rom. 6:16-18:** Do you not know that to whom you present yourselves slaves to obey, you are that one's slaves whom you obey, whether of sin *leading* to death, or of obedience *leading* to righteousness? But God be thanked that *though* you were slaves of sin, yet you obeyed from the heart that form of doctrine to which you were delivered. And having been set free from sin, you became slaves of righteousness. **Eph. 2:8:** For by grace you have been saved through faith, and that not of yourselves; *it is* the gift of God. **Phil. 1:29:** For to you it has been granted on behalf of Christ, not only to believe in Him, but also to suffer for His sake, having the same conflict which you saw in me and now hear *is* in me. **Song 1:4:** Draw me away! We will run after you. The king has brought me into his chambers. We will be glad and rejoice in you. We will remember your love more than wine. Rightly do they love you.

[9] **2 Tim. 1:9:** ... who has saved us and called *us* with a holy calling, not according to our works, but according to His own purpose and grace which was given to us in Christ Jesus before time began. **Eph. 2:8-9:** For by grace you have been saved through faith, and that not of yourselves; *it is* the gift of God, not of works, lest anyone should boast. **Rom. 9:11:** ... (for *the children* not yet being born, nor having done any good or evil, that the purpose of God according to election might stand, not of works but of Him who calls).

[10] **1 Cor. 2:14:** But the natural man does not receive the things of the Spirit of God, for they are foolishness to him; nor can he know *them,* because they are spiritually discerned. **Rom. 8:7-9:** Because the carnal mind *is* enmity against God; for it is not subject to the law of God, nor indeed can be. So then, those who are in the flesh cannot please God. But you are not in the flesh but in the Spirit, if indeed the Spirit of God dwells in you. Now if anyone does not have the Spirit of Christ, he is not His.

[11] **Eph. 2:5:** ... even when we were dead in trespasses, made us alive together with Christ (by grace you have been saved).

[12] **John 5:25:** Most assuredly, I say to you, the hour is coming, and now is, when the dead will hear the voice of the Son of God; and those who hear will live. **Titus 3:4-5:** But when the kindness and the love of God our Savior toward man appeared, not by works of righteousness which we have done, but according to His mercy He saved us, through the washing of regeneration and renewing of the Holy Spirit.

the grace offered and conveyed in it;[13] and that by no less power, than that which raised up Christ from the dead.[14]

3. Others not elected, although they may be called by the ministry of the word,[15] and may have some common operations of the Spirit,[16] yet not being effectually drawn by the Father, they neither will nor can truly come to Christ; and therefore cannot be saved:[17] much less can men that receive not the Christian religion be saved; be they never so diligent to frame their lives according to the light of nature, and the law of that religion they do profess.[18]

---

[13] **John 6:37:** All that the Father gives Me will come to Me, and the one who comes to Me I will by no means cast out. **Ezek 36:27:** I will put My Spirit within you and cause you to walk in My statutes, and you will keep My judgments and do *them.* **1 John 5:1:** Whoever believes that Jesus is the Christ is born of God, and everyone who loves Him who begot also loves him who is begotten of Him. **Cf. 1 John 3:9.**

[14] **Rom. 8:11:** But if the Spirit of Him who raised Jesus from the dead dwells in you, He who raised Christ from the dead will also give life to your mortal bodies through His Spirit who dwells in you. **Eph. 1:19-20:** ... and what *is* the exceeding greatness of His power toward us who believe, according to the working of His mighty power which He worked in Christ when He raised Him from the dead and seated *Him* at His right hand in the heavenly *places*.

[15] **Matt. 13:14-15:** And in them the prophecy of Isaiah is fulfilled, which says: 'Hearing you will hear and shall not understand, And seeing you will see and not perceive; For the hearts of this people have grown dull. *Their* ears are hard of hearing, And their eyes they have closed, Lest they should see with *their* eyes and hear with *their* ears, Lest they should understand with *their* hearts and turn, So that I should heal them.' **Matt. 22:14:** "For many are called, but few *are* chosen." **Acts 28:24:** And some were persuaded by the things which were spoken, and some disbelieved. **Cf. Acts 13:48.**

[16] **Matt. 7:22:** Many will say to Me in that day, 'Lord, Lord, have we not prophesied in Your name, cast out demons in Your name, and done many wonders in Your name?' **Matt. 13:20-21:** But he who received the seed on stony places, this is he who hears the word and immediately receives it with joy; yet he has no root in himself, but endures only for a while. For when tribulation or persecution arises because of the word, immediately he stumbles. **Heb. 6:4-5:** For *it is* impossible for those who were once enlightened, and have tasted the heavenly gift, and have become partakers of the Holy Spirit, and have tasted the good word of God and the powers of the age to come.

[17] **John 6:37, 44-45, 64-66:** "All that the Father gives Me will come to Me, and the one who comes to Me I will by no means cast out.... No one can come to Me unless the Father who sent Me draws him; and I will raise him up at the last day. It is written in the prophets, 'And they shall all be taught by God.' Therefore everyone who has heard and learned from the Father comes to Me.... But there are some of you who do not believe." For Jesus knew from the beginning who they were who did not believe, and who would betray Him. And He said, "Therefore I have said to you that no one can come to Me unless it has been granted to him by My Father." From that *time* many of His disciples went back and walked with Him no more. **John 8:24:** Therefore I said to you that you will die in your sins; for if you do not believe that I am *He,* you will die in your sins. **Cf. John 17:12.**

[18] **Acts 4:12:** Nor is there salvation in any other, for there is no other name under heaven given among men by which we must be saved. **1 John 4:2-3:** By this you know the Spirit of God: Every spirit that confesses that Jesus Christ has come in the flesh is of God, and every spirit that does not confess that Jesus Christ has come in the flesh is not of God. And this is the *spirit* of the Antichrist, which you have heard was coming, and is now already in the world. **2 John 9:** Whoever transgresses and does not abide in the doctrine of Christ does not have God. He who abides in the doctrine of Christ has both the Father and the Son. **John 4:22:** You worship what you do not know; we know what we worship, for salvation is of the Jews. **John 14:6:** Jesus said to him, "I am the way, the truth, and the life. No one comes to the Father except through Me." **John 17:3:** And this is eternal life, that they may know You, the only true God, and Jesus Christ whom You have sent. **Eph. 2:12-13:** ... that at that time you were without Christ, being aliens from the commonwealth of Israel and strangers from the covenants of promise, having no hope and without God in the world. But now in Christ Jesus you who once were far off have been brought near by the blood of Christ. **Rom. 10:13-17:** For "whoever calls on the name of the LORD shall be saved." How then shall they

call on Him in whom they have not believed? And how shall they believe in Him of whom they have not heard? And how shall they hear without a preacher? And how shall they preach unless they are sent? As it is written: "How beautiful are the feet of those who preach the gospel of peace, Who bring glad tidings of good things!" But they have not all obeyed the gospel. For Isaiah says, "LORD, who has believed our report?" So then faith *comes* by hearing, and hearing by the word of God.

CHAPTER 11
Of Justification

1. Those whom God effectually calleth, He also freely justifieth,[1] not by infusing righteousness into them, but by pardoning their sins,[2] and by accounting, and accepting their persons as righteous;[3] not for anything wrought in them, or done by them,[4] but for Christ's sake alone,[5] not by imputing faith itself, the act of believing, or any other evangelical obedience to them, as their righteousness;[6] but by imputing Christ's active obedience unto

---

[1] **Rom. 3:24:** ... being justified freely by His grace through the redemption that is in Christ Jesus. **Rom. 8:30:** Moreover whom He predestined, these He also called; whom He called, these He also justified; and whom He justified, these He also glorified.

[2] **Mic. 7:18:** Who *is* a God like You, Pardoning iniquity And passing over the transgression of the remnant of His heritage? He does not retain His anger forever, Because He delights *in* mercy. **Rom. 4:7-8:** "Blessed *are those* whose lawless deeds are forgiven, And whose sins are covered; Blessed *is the* man to whom the LORD shall not impute sin." **Eph. 1:7:** In Him we have redemption through His blood, the forgiveness of sins, according to the riches of His grace. **2 Cor. 5:19:** ... that is, that God was in Christ reconciling the world to Himself, not imputing their trespasses to them, and has committed to us the word of reconciliation.

[3] **Rom. 3:22:** even the righteousness of God, through faith in Jesus Christ, to all and on all who believe. For there is no difference. **Rom. 4:22-25:** And therefore "it was accounted to him for righteousness." Now it was not written for his sake alone that it was imputed to him, but also for us. It shall be imputed to us who believe in Him who raised up Jesus our Lord from the dead, who was delivered up because of our offenses, and was raised because of our justification. **2 Cor. 5:21:** For He made Him who knew no sin *to be* sin for us, that we might become the righteousness of God in Him.

[4] **Titus 3:5:** ... not by works of righteousness which we have done, but according to His mercy He saved us, through the washing of regeneration and renewing of the Holy Spirit. **Eph. 2:9:** ... not of works, lest anyone should boast. **2 Tim. 1:9:** ... who has saved us and called *us* with a holy calling, not according to our works, but according to His own purpose and grace which was given to us in Christ Jesus before time began. **Rom. 3:10; 20:** As it is written: There is none righteous, no, not one.... Therefore by the deeds of the law no flesh will be justified in His sight, for by the law *is* the knowledge of sin. **Rom. 4:4-6:** Now to him who works, the wages are not counted as grace but as debt. But to him who does not work but believes on Him who justifies the ungodly, his faith is accounted for righteousness, just as David also describes the blessedness of the man to whom God imputes righteousness apart from works. **Rom. 9:16:** So then *it is* not of him who wills, nor of him who runs, but of God who shows mercy. **Luke 18:26-27:** And those who heard it said, "Who then can be saved?" But He said, "The things which are impossible with men are possible with God."

[5] **Phil. 1:29:** For to you it has been granted on behalf of Christ, not only to believe in Him, but also to suffer for His sake. **1 Cor. 3:11:** For no other foundation can anyone lay than that which is laid, which is Jesus Christ. **1 Cor. 1:30-31:** But of Him you are in Christ Jesus, who became for us wisdom from God—and righteousness and sanctification and redemption—that, as it is written, "He who glories, let him glory in the LORD." **Eph. 2:20:** ... having been built on the foundation of the apostles and prophets, Jesus Christ Himself being the chief corner*stone.* **2 Tim. 2:10:** Therefore I endure all things for the sake of the elect, that they also may obtain the salvation which is in Christ Jesus with eternal glory.

[6] **Rom. 3:21-22:** But now the righteousness of God apart from the law is revealed, being witnessed by the Law and the Prophets, even the righteousness of God, through faith in Jesus Christ, to all and on all who believe. For there is no difference. **Rom. 4:5-6, 10:** But to him who does not work but believes on Him who justifies the ungodly, his faith is accounted for righteousness, just as David also describes the blessedness of the man to whom God imputes righteousness apart from works.... How then was it accounted? While he was circumcised, or uncircumcised? Not while circumcised, but while uncircumcised. **Rom. 10:10:** For with the heart one believes unto righteousness, and with the mouth confession is made unto salvation. **2 Cor. 5:21:** For He made Him who knew no sin *to be* sin for us, that we might become the righteousness of God in Him. **Phil. 3:9:** ... and be found in Him,

the whole law,[7] and passive obedience in His death,[8] for their whole and sole righteousness, they receiving, and resting on Him, and and His righteousness, by faith;[9] which faith they have not of themselves, it is the gift of God.[10]

2. Faith thus receiving and resting on Christ, and His righteousness, is the alone instrument of justification:[11] yet it is not alone in the person justified, but is ever accompanied with all other saving graces,[12] and is no dead faith, but worketh by love.[13]

---

not having my own righteousness, which *is* from the law, but that which *is* through faith in Christ, the righteousness which is from God by faith.

[7] **Rom. 5:18-19:** Therefore, as through one man's offense *judgment came* to all men, resulting in condemnation, even so through one Man's righteous act *the free gift came* to all men, resulting in justification of life. For as by one man's disobedience many were made sinners, so also by one Man's obedience many will be made righteous. **Gal. 4:4-5:** But when the fullness of the time had come, God sent forth His Son, born of a woman, born under the law, to redeem those who were under the law, that we might receive the adoption as sons. **Heb. 10:7-9:** Then I said, 'Behold, I have come—In the volume of the book it is written of Me—To do Your will, O God.' Previously saying, "Sacrifice and offering, burnt offerings, and *offerings* for sin You did not desire, nor had pleasure *in them*" (which are offered according to the law), then He said, "Behold, I have come to do Your will, O God." He takes away the first that He may establish the second. **Matt. 3:15:** But Jesus answered and said to him, "Permit *it to be so* now, for thus it is fitting for us to fulfill all righteousness." Then he allowed Him. **Matt. 5:17-18:** Do not think that I came to destroy the Law or the Prophets. I did not come to destroy but to fulfill. For assuredly, I say to you, till heaven and earth pass away, one jot or one tittle will by no means pass from the law till all is fulfilled. **John 15:10:** If you keep My commandments, you will abide in My love, just as I have kept My Father's commandments and abide in His love.

[8] **Isa. 53:6:** All we like sheep have gone astray; We have turned, every one, to his own way; And the LORD has laid on Him the iniquity of us all. **Rom. 4:25:** ... who was delivered up because of our offenses, and was raised because of our justification. **1 Pet. 2:24:** ... who Himself bore our sins in His own body on the tree, that we, having died to sins, might live for righteousness—by whose stripes you were healed. **1 Pet. 3:18:** For Christ also suffered once for sins, the just for the unjust, that He might bring us to God, being put to death in the flesh but made alive by the Spirit. **1 John 2:2:** And He Himself is the propitiation for our sins, and not for ours only but also for the whole world.

[9] **Rom. 5:21:** ... so that as sin reigned in death, even so grace might reign through righteousness to eternal life through Jesus Christ our Lord. **Rom. 10:4:** For Christ *is* the end of the law for righteousness to everyone who believes. **Phil. 3:9:** ... and be found in Him, not having my own righteousness, which *is* from the law, but that which *is* through faith in Christ, the righteousness which is from God by faith.

[10] **Eph. 2:8:** For by grace you have been saved through faith, and that not of yourselves; *it is* the gift of God. **John 5:44:** How can you believe, who receive honor from one another, and do not seek the honor that *comes* from the only God? **James 2:19:** You believe that there is one God. You do well. Even the demons believe—and tremble! **Rom. 5:17:** For if by the one man's offense death reigned through the one, much more those who receive abundance of grace and of the gift of righteousness will reign in life through the One, Jesus Christ.)

[11] **Rom. 3:28:** Therefore we conclude that a man is justified by faith apart from the deeds of the law. **Rom. 5:1:** Therefore, having been justified by faith, we have peace with God through our Lord Jesus Christ. **John 1:12:** But as many as received Him, to them He gave the right to become children of God, to those who believe in His name. **John 3:18, 36:** "He who believes in Him is not condemned; but he who does not believe is condemned already, because he has not believed in the name of the only begotten Son of God.... He who believes in the Son has everlasting life; and he who does not believe the Son shall not see life, but the wrath of God abides on him." **Gal. 2:16:** ... knowing that a man is not justified by the works of the law but by faith in Jesus Christ, even we have believed in Christ Jesus, that we might be justified by faith in Christ and not by the works of the law; for by the works of the law no flesh shall be justified.

[12] **Rom. 5:1:** Therefore, having been justified by faith, we have peace with God through our Lord Jesus Christ. **Rom. 8:30:** Moreover whom He predestined, these He also called; whom He called, these He also justified; and whom He justified, these He also glorified. **Rom. 14:17:** ... for the kingdom of God is not eating and drinking, but righteousness and peace and joy in the Holy Spirit. **1**

3. Christ by His obedience, and death, did fully discharge the debt of all those that are justified;[14] and did by the sacrifice of Himself, in the blood of His cross,[15] undergoing in their stead, the penalty due unto them:[16] make a proper, real, and full satisfaction to God's

---

Cor. 1:30: But of Him you are in Christ Jesus, who became for us wisdom from God—and righteousness and sanctification and redemption. **1 Cor. 6:11:** And such were some of you. But you were washed, but you were sanctified, but you were justified in the name of the Lord Jesus and by the Spirit of our God. **Eph. 1:5:** ... having predestined us to adoption as sons by Jesus Christ to Himself, according to the good pleasure of His will. **2 Pet. 3:18:** ... but grow in the grace and knowledge of our Lord and Savior Jesus Christ. To Him *be* the glory both now and forever. Amen. **1 Pet. 1:5:** ... who are kept by the power of God through faith for salvation ready to be revealed in the last time.

[13] **Gal. 5:6:** For in Christ Jesus neither circumcision nor uncircumcision avails anything, but faith working through love. **Rom. 2:6-7, 10, 13:** ... who "will render to each one according to his deeds": eternal life to those who by patient continuance in doing good seek for glory, honor, and immortality ... but glory, honor, and peace to everyone who works what is good, to the Jew first and also to the Greek.... for not the hearers of the law *are* just in the sight of God, but the doers of the law will be justified. **James 2:18-26:** But someone will say, "You have faith, and I have works." Show me your faith without your works, and I will show you my faith by my works. You believe that there is one God. You do well. Even the demons believe—and tremble! But do you want to know, O foolish man, that faith without works is dead? Was not Abraham our father justified by works when he offered Isaac his son on the altar? Do you see that faith was working together with his works, and by works faith was made perfect? And the Scripture was fulfilled which says, "Abraham believed God, and it was accounted to him for righteousness." And he was called the friend of God. You see then that a man is justified by works, and not by faith only. Likewise, was not Rahab the harlot also justified by works when she received the messengers and sent *them* out another way? For as the body without the spirit is dead, so faith without works is dead also.

[14] **Col. 2:13-15:** And you, being dead in your trespasses and the uncircumcision of your flesh, He has made alive together with Him, having forgiven you all trespasses, having wiped out the handwriting of requirements that was against us, which was contrary to us. And He has taken it out of the way, having nailed it to the cross. Having disarmed principalities and powers, He made a public spectacle of them, triumphing over them in it. **Eph. 2:14-16:** For He Himself is our peace, who has made both one, and has broken down the middle wall of separation, having abolished in His flesh the enmity, *that is,* the law of commandments *contained* in ordinances, so as to create in Himself one new man *from* the two, *thus* making peace, and that He might reconcile them both to God in one body through the cross, thereby putting to death the enmity. **Gal. 3:13:** Christ has redeemed us from the curse of the law, having become a curse for us (for it is written, "Cursed *is* everyone who hangs on a tree"). **Heb. 1:3:** ... who being the brightness of *His* glory and the express image of His person, and upholding all things by the word of His power, when He had by Himself purged our sins, sat down at the right hand of the Majesty on high.

[15] **1 Pet. 2:24:** ... who Himself bore our sins in His own body on the tree, that we, having died to sins, might live for righteousness—by whose stripes you were healed. **Col. 1:20:** ... and by Him to reconcile all things to Himself, by Him, whether things on earth or things in heaven, having made peace through the blood of His cross. **Heb. 10:10-12:** By that will we have been sanctified through the offering of the body of Jesus Christ once *for all.* And every priest stands ministering daily and offering repeatedly the same sacrifices, which can never take away sins. But this Man, after He had offered one sacrifice for sins forever, sat down at the right hand of God. **Eph. 2:13:** But now in Christ Jesus you who once were far off have been brought near by the blood of Christ.

[16] **Rom. 5:6-8:** For when we were still without strength, in due time Christ died for the ungodly. For scarcely for a righteous man will one die; yet perhaps for a good man someone would even dare to die. But God demonstrates His own love toward us, in that while we were still sinners, Christ died for us. **Isa. 53:4-6, 12:** Surely He has borne our griefs And carried our sorrows; Yet we esteemed Him stricken, Smitten by God, and afflicted. But He *was* wounded for our transgressions, *He was* bruised for our iniquities; The chastisement for our peace *was* upon Him, And by His stripes we are healed. All we like sheep have gone astray; We have turned, every one, to his own way; And the LORD has laid on Him the iniquity of us all.... Therefore I will divide Him a portion with the great, And He shall divide the spoil with the strong, Because He poured out His soul unto death, And He was numbered with the transgressors, And He bore the sin of many, And made intercession for the transgressors. **Mark 10:45:** For even the Son of Man did not come to be served, but to serve, and to give His life a ransom for many. **2 Cor. 5:21:** For He made Him who knew no sin *to be* sin for us, that we might become the righteousness of God in Him.

justice in their behalf:[17] yet inasmuch as He was given by the Father for them, and His obedience and satisfaction accepted in their stead,[18] and both freely, not for anything in them; their justification is only of free grace,[19] that both the exact justice and rich grace of God, might be glorified in the justification of sinners.[20]

4. God did from all eternity decree to justify all the elect,[21] and Christ did in the fullness of time die for their sins, and rise again for their justification;[22] nevertheless they are not justified

---

[17] **Rom. 3:25:** ... whom God set forth *as* a propitiation by His blood, through faith, to demonstrate His righteousness, because in His forbearance God had passed over the sins that were previously committed. **Rom. 5:9-11:** Much more then, having now been justified by His blood, we shall be saved from wrath through Him. For if when we were enemies we were reconciled to God through the death of His Son, much more, having been reconciled, we shall be saved by His life. And not only *that,* but we also rejoice in God through our Lord Jesus Christ, through whom we have now received the reconciliation. **1 John 2:2:** And He Himself is the propitiation for our sins, and not for ours only but also for the whole world. **1 John 4:10:** In this is love, not that we loved God, but that He loved us and sent His Son *to be* the propitiation for our sins.

[18] **Rom. 8:32:** He who did not spare His own Son, but delivered Him up for us all, how shall He not with Him also freely give us all things? **2 Cor. 5:21:** For He made Him who knew no sin *to be* sin for us, that we might become the righteousness of God in Him. **Eph. 5:2:** And walk in love, as Christ also has loved us and given Himself for us, an offering and a sacrifice to God for a sweet-smelling aroma. **Phil. 2:6-9:** ... who, being in the form of God, did not consider it robbery to be equal with God, but made Himself of no reputation, taking the form of a bondservant, *and* coming in the likeness of men. And being found in appearance as a man, He humbled Himself and became obedient to *the point of* death, even the death of the cross. Therefore God also has highly exalted Him and given Him the name which is above every name. **Isa. 53:10-11:** Yet it pleased the LORD to bruise Him; He has put *Him* to grief. When You make His soul an offering for sin, He shall see *His* seed, He shall prolong *His* days, And the pleasure of the LORD shall prosper in His hand. He shall see the labor of His soul, *and* be satisfied. By His knowledge My righteous Servant shall justify many, For He shall bear their iniquities.

[19] **Rom. 3:24:** ... being justified freely by His grace through the redemption that is in Christ Jesus. **Eph. 1:7:** In Him we have redemption through His blood, the forgiveness of sins, according to the riches of His grace. **Eph. 2:8:** For by grace you have been saved through faith, and that not of yourselves; *it is* the gift of God.

[20] **Rom. 3:26:** ... to demonstrate at the present time His righteousness, that He might be just and the justifier of the one who has faith in Jesus. **Eph. 1:6:** ... to the praise of the glory of His grace, by which He made us accepted in the Beloved. **Eph. 2:7:** ... that in the ages to come He might show the exceeding riches of His grace in *His* kindness toward us in Christ Jesus. **Isa. 45:21:** Tell and bring forth *your case;* Yes, let them take counsel together. Who has declared this from ancient time? *Who* has told it from that time? *Have* not I, the LORD? And *there is* no other God besides Me, A just God and a Savior; *There is* none besides Me.

[21] **Rom. 8:29-30:** For whom He foreknew, He also predestined *to be* conformed to the image of His Son, that He might be the firstborn among many brethren. Moreover whom He predestined, these He also called; whom He called, these He also justified; and whom He justified, these He also glorified. **Gal. 3:8:** And the Scripture, foreseeing that God would justify the Gentiles by faith, preached the gospel to Abraham beforehand, *saying,* "In you all the nations shall be blessed." **1 Pet. 1:2, 19-20:** ... elect according to the foreknowledge of God the Father, in sanctification of the Spirit, for obedience and sprinkling of the blood of Jesus Christ: Grace to you and peace be multiplied.... but with the precious blood of Christ, as of a lamb without blemish and without spot. He indeed was foreordained before the foundation of the world, but was manifest in these last times for you who through Him believe in God, who raised Him from the dead and gave Him glory, so that your faith and hope are in God.

[22] **Gal. 4:4:** But when the fullness of the time had come, God sent forth His Son, born of a woman, born under the law. **1 Tim. 2:6:** ... who gave Himself a ransom for all, to be testified in due time. **Rom. 4:25:** ... who was delivered up because of our offenses, and was raised because of our justification.

personally, until the Holy Spirit, doth in due time actually apply Christ unto them.[23]

5. God doth continue to forgive the sins of those that are justified,[24] and although they can never fall from the state of justification;[25] yet they may by their sins fall under God's fatherly displeasure; and in that condition, they have not usually the light of His countenance restored unto them, until they humble themselves, confess their sins, beg pardon, and renew their faith, and repentance.[26]

---

[23] **Eph. 2:3:** ... among whom also we all once conducted ourselves in the lusts of our flesh, fulfilling the desires of the flesh and of the mind, and were by nature children of wrath, just as the others. **Titus 3:3-7:** For we ourselves were also once foolish, disobedient, deceived, serving various lusts and pleasures, living in malice and envy, hateful and hating one another. But when the kindness and the love of God our Savior toward man appeared, not by works of righteousness which we have done, but according to His mercy He saved us, through the washing of regeneration and renewing of the Holy Spirit, whom He poured out on us abundantly through Jesus Christ our Savior, that having been justified by His grace we should become heirs according to the hope of eternal life. **Col. 1:21-22:** And you, who once were alienated and enemies in your mind by wicked works, yet now He has reconciled in the body of His flesh through death, to present you holy, and blameless, and above reproach in His sight. **Cf. Gal. 2:16.**

[24] **Matt. 6:12:** And forgive us our debts, As we forgive our debtors. **1 John 1:7, 9:** But if we walk in the light as He is in the light, we have fellowship with one another, and the blood of Jesus Christ His Son cleanses us from all sin.... If we confess our sins, He is faithful and just to forgive us *our* sins and to cleanse us from all unrighteousness. **1 John 2:1-2:** My little children, these things I write to you, so that you may not sin. And if anyone sins, we have an Advocate with the Father, Jesus Christ the righteous. And He Himself is the propitiation for our sins, and not for ours only but also for the whole world.

[25] **John 10:28:** And I give them eternal life, and they shall never perish; neither shall anyone snatch them out of My hand. **Rom. 5:1-5:** Therefore, having been justified by faith, we have peace with God through our Lord Jesus Christ, through whom also we have access by faith into this grace in which we stand, and rejoice in hope of the glory of God. And not only *that,* but we also glory in tribulations, knowing that tribulation produces perseverance; and perseverance, character; and character, hope. Now hope does not disappoint, because the love of God has been poured out in our hearts by the Holy Spirit who was given to us. **Rom. 8:30-39:** Moreover whom He predestined, these He also called; whom He called, these He also justified; and whom He justified, these He also glorified. What then shall we say to these things? If God *is* for us, who *can be* against us? He who did not spare His own Son, but delivered Him up for us all, how shall He not with Him also freely give us all things? Who shall bring a charge against God's elect? *It is* God who justifies. Who *is* he who condemns? *It is* Christ who died, and furthermore is also risen, who is even at the right hand of God, who also makes intercession for us. Who shall separate us from the love of Christ? *Shall* tribulation, or distress, or persecution, or famine, or nakedness, or peril, or sword? As it is written: "For Your sake we are killed all day long; We are accounted as sheep for the slaughter." Yet in all these things we are more than conquerors through Him who loved us. For I am persuaded that neither death nor life, nor angels nor principalities nor powers, nor things present nor things to come, nor height nor depth, nor any other created thing, shall be able to separate us from the love of God which is in Christ Jesus our Lord. **Heb. 10:14:** For by one offering He has perfected forever those who are being sanctified. **Cf. Luke 22:32.**

[26] **Ps. 89:30-33:** If his sons forsake My law And do not walk in My judgments, If they break My statutes And do not keep My commandments, Then I will punish their transgression with the rod, And their iniquity with stripes. Nevertheless My lovingkindness I will not utterly take from him, Nor allow My faithfulness to fail. **Ps. 32:5:** I acknowledged my sin to You, And my iniquity I have not hidden. I said, "I will confess my transgressions to the LORD," And You forgave the iniquity of my sin. *Selah*. **Ps. 51:** Have mercy upon me, O God, According to Your lovingkindness;
According to the multitude of Your tender mercies, Blot out my transgressions. Wash me thoroughly from my iniquity, And cleanse me from my sin. For I acknowledge my transgressions, And my sin *is* always before me.... Create in me a clean heart, O God, And renew a steadfast spirit within me.... Restore to me the joy of Your salvation, And uphold me *by Your* generous Spirit.... **Matt. 26:75:** And Peter remembered the word of Jesus who had said to him, "Before the rooster crows, you will

6. The justification of believers under the Old Covenant was in all these respects, one and the same with the justification of believers under the New Covenant.[27]

---

deny Me three times." So he went out and wept bitterly. **Luke 1:20:** But behold, you will be mute and not able to speak until the day these things take place, because you did not believe my words which will be fulfilled in their own time. **1 Cor. 11:30, 32:** For this reason many *are* weak and sick among you, and many sleep.... But when we are judged, we are chastened by the Lord, that we may not be condemned with the world.

[27] **Gal. 3:9, 13-14:** So then those who *are* of faith are blessed with believing Abraham.... Christ has redeemed us from the curse of the law, having become a curse for us (for it is written, "Cursed *is* everyone who hangs on a tree"), that the blessing of Abraham might come upon the Gentiles in Christ Jesus, that we might receive the promise of the Spirit through faith. **Rom. 4:6-8, 22-24:** ... just as David also describes the blessedness of the man to whom God imputes righteousness apart from works: "Blessed *are those* whose lawless deeds are forgiven, And whose sins are covered; Blessed *is the* man to whom the LORD shall not impute sin." ... And therefore "it was accounted to him for righteousness." Now it was not written for his sake alone that it was imputed to him, but also for us. It shall be imputed to us who believe in Him who raised up Jesus our Lord from the dead. **Rom. 10:6-13:** But the righteousness of faith speaks in this way, "Do not say in your heart, 'Who will ascend into heaven?'" (that is, to bring Christ down *from above*) or, "'Who will descend into the abyss?'" (that is, to bring Christ up from the dead). But what does it say? "The word is near you, in your mouth and in your heart" (that is, the word of faith which we preach): that if you confess with your mouth the Lord Jesus and believe in your heart that God has raised Him from the dead, you will be saved. For with the heart one believes unto righteousness, and with the mouth confession is made unto salvation. For the Scripture says, "Whoever believes on Him will not be put to shame." For there is no distinction between Jew and Greek, for the same Lord over all is rich to all who call upon Him. For "whoever calls on the name of the LORD shall be saved." **Heb. 13:8:** Jesus Christ *is* the same yesterday, today, and forever.

CHAPTER 12
Of Adoption

All those that are justified, God vouchsafed, in, and for the sake of His only Son Jesus Christ, to make partakers of the grace of adoption;[1] by which they are taken into the number, and enjoy the liberties, and privileges of children of God;[2] have His name put upon them,[3] receive the spirit of adoption,[4] have access to the throne of grace with boldness,[5] are enabled to cry Abba Father,[6] are pitied,[7] protected,[8] provided for,[9] and chastened by Him, as by a Father;[10] yet never cast off;[11] but sealed to the day of redemption,[12] and inherit the promises,[13] as heirs, of everlasting salvation.[14]

---

[1] **Eph. 1:5:** ... having predestined us to adoption as sons by Jesus Christ to Himself, according to the good pleasure of His will. **Gal. 4:4-5:** But when the fullness of the time had come, God sent forth His Son, born of a woman, born under the law, to redeem those who were under the law, that we might receive the adoption as sons.

[2] **John 1:12:** But as many as received Him, to them He gave the right to become children of God, to those who believe in His name. **Rom. 8:17:** ... and if children, then heirs—heirs of God and joint heirs with Christ, if indeed we suffer with *Him,* that we may also be glorified together.

[3] **Amos 9:12:** "That they may possess the remnant of Edom, And all the Gentiles who are called by My name," Says the LORD who does this thing. **Acts 15:17:** So that the rest of mankind may seek the LORD, Even all the Gentiles who are called by My name, Says the LORD who does all these things.' **2 Cor. 6:18:** "I will be a Father to you, And you shall be My sons and daughters, Says the LORD Almighty." **Rev. 3:12:** He who overcomes, I will make him a pillar in the temple of My God, and he shall go out no more. I will write on him the name of My God and the name of the city of My God, the New Jerusalem, which comes down out of heaven from My God. And *I will write on him* My new name.

[4] **Rom. 8:15:** For as many as are led by the Spirit of God, these are sons of God. For you did not receive the spirit of bondage again to fear, but you received the Spirit of adoption by whom we cry out, "Abba, Father."

[5] **Eph. 2:18:** For through Him we both have access by one Spirit to the Father. **Eph. 3:12:** ... in whom we have boldness and access with confidence through faith in Him.

[6] **Rom. 8:15:** For you did not receive the spirit of bondage again to fear, but you received the Spirit of adoption by whom we cry out, "Abba, Father." **See Rom. 8:16. Gal. 4:6:** And because you are sons, God has sent forth the Spirit of His Son into your hearts, crying out, "Abba, Father!"

[7] **Ps. 103:13:** As a father pities *his* children, *So* the LORD pities those who fear Him.

[8] **Prov. 14:26:** In the fear of the LORD *there is* strong confidence, And His children will have a place of refuge.

[9] **Matt. 6:30, 32:** Now if God so clothes the grass of the field, which today is, and tomorrow is thrown into the oven, *will He* not much more *clothe* you, O you of little faith?... For after all these things the Gentiles seek. For your heavenly Father knows that you need all these things. **1 Pet. 5:7:** ... casting all your care upon Him, for He cares for you.

[10] **Heb. 12:6:** For whom the LORD loves He chastens, And scourges every son whom He receives.

[11] **Isa. 54:8-9:** "With a little wrath I hid My face from you for a moment; But with everlasting kindness I will have mercy on you," Says the LORD, your Redeemer. "For this *is* like the waters of Noah to Me; For as I have sworn That the waters of Noah would no longer cover the earth, So have I sworn That I would not be angry with you, nor rebuke you." **Lam. 3:31-32:** For the Lord will not cast off forever. Though He causes grief, Yet He will show compassion According to the multitude of His mercies. **See Ps. 89:30–35.**

[12] **Eph. 4:30:** And do not grieve the Holy Spirit of God, by whom you were sealed for the day of redemption.

[13] **Heb. 6:12:** ... that you do not become sluggish, but imitate those who through faith and patience inherit the promises.

[14] **1 Pet. 1:3-4:** Blessed *be* the God and Father of our Lord Jesus Christ, who according to His abundant mercy has begotten us again to a living hope through the resurrection of Jesus Christ from

the dead, to an inheritance incorruptible and undefiled and that does not fade away, reserved in heaven for you. **Heb. 1:14:** Are they not all ministering spirits sent forth to minister for those who will inherit salvation?

CHAPTER 13
Of Sanctification

1. They who are united to Christ, effectually called, and regenerated, having a new heart, and a new spirit created in them, through the virtue of Christ's death, and resurrection; are also further sanctified, really, and personally, through the same virtue,[1] by His word and Spirit dwelling in them;[2] the dominion of the whole body of sin is destroyed,[3] and the several lusts thereof, are more and more weakened, and mortified;[4] and they more and more quickened, and strengthened in all saving

---

[1] **1 Thess. 5:23-24:** Now may the God of peace Himself sanctify you completely; and may your whole spirit, soul, and body be preserved blameless at the coming of our Lord Jesus Christ. He who calls you *is* faithful, who also will do *it.* **2 Thess. 2:13-14:** But we are bound to give thanks to God always for you, brethren beloved by the Lord, because God from the beginning chose you for salvation through sanctification by the Spirit and belief in the truth, to which He called you by our gospel, for the obtaining of the glory of our Lord Jesus Christ. **Ezek. 36:22-28:** Therefore say to the house of Israel, 'Thus says the Lord God: "I do not do *this* for your sake, O house of Israel, but for My holy name's sake, which you have profaned among the nations wherever you went. And I will sanctify My great name, which has been profaned among the nations, which you have profaned in their midst; and the nations shall know that I *am* the LORD," says the Lord God, "when I am hallowed in you before their eyes. For I will take you from among the nations, gather you out of all countries, and bring you into your own land. Then I will sprinkle clean water on you, and you shall be clean; I will cleanse you from all your filthiness and from all your idols. I will give you a new heart and put a new spirit within you; I will take the heart of stone out of your flesh and give you a heart of flesh. I will put My Spirit within you and cause you to walk in My statutes, and you will keep My judgments and do *them.* Then you shall dwell in the land that I gave to your fathers; you shall be My people, and I will be your God."' **Titus 3:5:** ... not by works of righteousness which we have done, but according to His mercy He saved us, through the washing of regeneration and renewing of the Holy Spirit. **Acts 20:32:** So now, brethren, I commend you to God and to the word of His grace, which is able to build you up and give you an inheritance among all those who are sanctified. **Phil. 3:10:** ... that I may know Him and the power of His resurrection, and the fellowship of His sufferings, being conformed to His death. **Rom. 6:5-6:** For if we have been united together in the likeness of His death, certainly we also shall be *in the likeness* of *His* resurrection, knowing this, that our old man was crucified with *Him,* that the body of sin might be done away with, that we should no longer be slaves of sin. **Heb. 2:11, 14-15, 18:** For both He who sanctifies and those who are being sanctified *are* all of one, for which reason He is not ashamed to call them brethren ... Inasmuch then as the children have partaken of flesh and blood, He Himself likewise shared in the same, that through death He might destroy him who had the power of death, that is, the devil, and release those who through fear of death were all their lifetime subject to bondage.... For in that He Himself has suffered, being tempted, He is able to aid those who are tempted.

[2] **John 17:17, 19:** Sanctify them by Your truth. Your word is truth.... And for their sakes I sanctify Myself, that they also may be sanctified by the truth. **Eph. 5:26:** ... that He might sanctify and cleanse her with the washing of water by the word. **Rom. 8:13-14:** For if you live according to the flesh you will die; but if by the Spirit you put to death the deeds of the body, you will live. For as many as are led by the Spirit of God, these are sons of God. **2 Thess. 2:13:** But we are bound to give thanks to God always for you, brethren beloved by the Lord, because God from the beginning chose you for salvation through sanctification by the Spirit and belief in the truth.

[3] **Rom. 6:6, 14:** ... knowing this, that our old man was crucified with *Him,* that the body of sin might be done away with, that we should no longer be slaves of sin.... For sin shall not have dominion over you, for you are not under law but under grace.

[4] **Gal. 5:24:** And those *who are* Christ's have crucified the flesh with its passions and desires. **Rom. 8:13:** For if you live according to the flesh you will die; but if by the Spirit you put to death the deeds of the body, you will live.

graces,[5] to the practice of all true holiness, without which no man shall see the Lord.[6]

2. This sanctification is throughout, in the whole man,[7] yet imperfect in this life; there abideth still some remnants of corruption in every part,[8] whence ariseth a continual, and irreconcilable war; the flesh lusting against the Spirit, and the Spirit against the flesh.[9]

3. In which war, although the remaining corruption for a time may much prevail;[10] yet through the continual supply of strength from the sanctifying Spirit of Christ the regenerate part doth overcome;[11] and so the saints grow in grace,[12] perfecting holiness

---

[5] **Col. 1:10-11:** ... that you may walk worthy of the Lord, fully pleasing *Him,* being fruitful in every good work and increasing in the knowledge of God; strengthened with all might, according to His glorious power, for all patience and longsuffering with joy. **Eph. 3:16-19:** ... that He would grant you, according to the riches of His glory, to be strengthened with might through His Spirit in the inner man, that Christ may dwell in your hearts through faith; that you, being rooted and grounded in love, may be able to comprehend with all the saints what *is* the width and length and depth and height—to know the love of Christ which passes knowledge; that you may be filled with all the fullness of God.

[6] **2 Cor. 7:1:** Therefore, having these promises, beloved, let us cleanse ourselves from all filthiness of the flesh and spirit, perfecting holiness in the fear of God. **Col. 1:28:** Him we preach, warning every man and teaching every man in all wisdom, that we may present every man perfect in Christ Jesus. **Col. 4:12:** Epaphras, who is *one* of you, a bondservant of Christ, greets you, always laboring fervently for you in prayers, that you may stand perfect and complete in all the will of God. **Heb. 12:14:** Pursue peace with all *people,* and holiness, without which no one will see the Lord.

[7] **1 Thess. 5:23:** Now may the God of peace Himself sanctify you completely; and may your whole spirit, soul, and body be preserved blameless at the coming of our Lord Jesus Christ. **Rom. 12:1-2:** I beseech you therefore, brethren, by the mercies of God, that you present your bodies a living sacrifice, holy, acceptable to God, *which is* your reasonable service. And do not be conformed to this world, but be transformed by the renewing of your mind, that you may prove what *is* that good and acceptable and perfect will of God.

[8] **1 John 1:8-10:** If we say that we have no sin, we deceive ourselves, and the truth is not in us. If we confess our sins, He is faithful and just to forgive us *our* sins and to cleanse us from all unrighteousness. If we say that we have not sinned, we make Him a liar, and His word is not in us. **Rom. 7:14-25:** For we know that the law is spiritual, but I am carnal, sold under sin. For what I am doing, I do not understand. For what I will to do, that I do not practice; but what I hate, that I do. If, then, I do what I will not to do, I agree with the law that *it is* good. But now, *it is* no longer I who do it, but sin that dwells in me. For I know that in me (that is, in my flesh) nothing good dwells; for to will is present with me, but *how* to perform what is good I do not find. For the good that I will *to do,* I do not do; but the evil I will not *to do,* that I practice. Now if I do what I will not *to do,* it is no longer I who do it, but sin that dwells in me. I find then a law, that evil is present with me, the one who wills to do good. For I delight in the law of God according to the inward man. But I see another law in my members, warring against the law of my mind, and bringing me into captivity to the law of sin which is in my members. O wretched man that I am! Who will deliver me from this body of death? I thank God—through Jesus Christ our Lord! So then, with the mind I myself serve the law of God, but with the flesh the law of sin. **Phil. 3:12:** Not that I have already attained, or am already perfected; but I press on, that I may lay hold of that for which Christ Jesus has also laid hold of me.

[9] **Gal. 5:17:** For the flesh lusts against the Spirit, and the Spirit against the flesh; and these are contrary to one another, so that you do not do the things that you wish. **1 Pet. 2:11:** Beloved, I beg *you* as sojourners and pilgrims, abstain from fleshly lusts which war against the soul.

[10] **Rom. 7:23:** But I see another law in my members, warring against the law of my mind, and bringing me into captivity to the law of sin which is in my members.

[11] **Rom. 6:14:** For sin shall not have dominion over you, for you are not under law but under grace. **1 John 5:4:** For whatever is born of God overcomes the world. And this is the victory that has overcome the world—our faith. **Eph. 4:15-16:** ... but, speaking the truth in love, may grow up in all

in the fear of God,[13] pressing after an heavenly life,[14] in evangelical obedience to all the commands which Christ as Head and King, in His word hath prescribed to them.[15]

---

things into Him who is the head—Christ—from whom the whole body, joined and knit together by what every joint supplies, according to the effective working by which every part does its share, causes growth of the body for the edifying of itself in love. **See Rom. 8:2.**

[12] **2 Pet. 3:18:** ... but grow in the grace and knowledge of our Lord and Savior Jesus Christ. To Him *be* the glory both now and forever. Amen. **2 Cor. 3:18:** But we all, with unveiled face, beholding as in a mirror the glory of the Lord, are being transformed into the same image from glory to glory, just as by the Spirit of the Lord.

[13] **2 Cor. 7:1:** Therefore, having these promises, beloved, let us cleanse ourselves from all filthiness of the flesh and spirit, perfecting holiness in the fear of God.

[14] **Phil. 3:14:** I press toward the goal for the prize of the upward call of God in Christ Jesus. Luke 6:16: Judas *the son* of James, and Judas Iscariot who also became a traitor. **1 Cor. 9:24:** Do you not know that those who run in a race all run, but one receives the prize? Run in such a way that you may obtain *it*.

[15] **John 14:15, 21, 23:** "If you love Me, keep My commandments.... He who has My commandments and keeps them, it is he who loves Me. And he who loves Me will be loved by My Father, and I will love him and manifest Myself to him." ... Jesus answered and said to him, "If anyone loves Me, he will keep My word; and My Father will love him, and We will come to him and make Our home with him." **Matt. 28:20:** ... teaching them to observe all things that I have commanded you; and lo, I am with you always, *even* to the end of the age. Amen. **Rev. 14:12:** Here is the patience of the saints; here *are* those who keep the commandments of God and the faith of Jesus.

CHAPTER 14
Of Saving Faith

1. The grace of faith, whereby the elect are enabled to believe to the saving of their souls,[1] is the work of the Spirit of Christ in their hearts;[2] and is ordinarily wrought by the ministry of the word;[3] by which also, and by the administration of baptism, and the Lord's Supper, prayer and other means appointed of God, it is increased, and strengthened.[4]

---

[1] **Titus 1:1:** Paul, a bondservant of God and an apostle of Jesus Christ, according to the faith of God's elect and the acknowledgment of the truth which accords with godliness. **Heb. 10:39:** But we are not of those who draw back to perdition, but of those who believe to the saving of the soul.

[2] **1 Cor. 12:3:** Therefore I make known to you that no one speaking by the Spirit of God calls Jesus accursed, and no one can say that Jesus is Lord except by the Holy Spirit. **John 3:5:** Jesus answered, "Most assuredly, I say to you, unless one is born of water and the Spirit, he cannot enter the kingdom of God." **John 6:44-45, 65:** No one can come to Me unless the Father who sent Me draws him; and I will raise him up at the last day. It is written in the prophets, 'And they shall all be taught by God.' Therefore everyone who has heard and learned from the Father comes to Me.... And He said, "Therefore I have said to you that no one can come to Me unless it has been granted to him by My Father." **Titus 3:5:** ... not by works of righteousness which we have done, but according to His mercy He saved us, through the washing of regeneration and renewing of the Holy Spirit. **Eph. 2:8:** For by grace you have been saved through faith, and that not of yourselves; *it is* the gift of God. **Phil. 1:29:** For to you it has been granted on behalf of Christ, not only to believe in Him, but also to suffer for His sake. **2 Pet. 1:1:** Simon Peter, a bondservant and apostle of Jesus Christ, To those who have obtained like precious faith with us by the righteousness of our God and Savior Jesus Christ. **See 1 Pet. 1:2.**

[3] **Matt. 28:19-20:** Go therefore and make disciples of all the nations, baptizing them in the name of the Father and of the Son and of the Holy Spirit, teaching them to observe all things that I have commanded you; and lo, I am with you always, *even* to the end of the age. Amen. **Rom. 10:14, 17:** How then shall they call on Him in whom they have not believed? And how shall they believe in Him of whom they have not heard? And how shall they hear without a preacher?... So then faith *comes* by hearing, and hearing by the word of God. **1 Cor. 1:21:** For since, in the wisdom of God, the world through wisdom did not know God, it pleased God through the foolishness of the message preached to save those who believe.

[4] **Luke 17:5:** And the apostles said to the Lord, "Increase our faith." **1 Pet. 2:2:** ... as newborn babes, desire the pure milk of the word, that you may grow thereby. **Acts 20:32:** So now, brethren, I commend you to God and to the word of His grace, which is able to build you up and give you an inheritance among all those who are sanctified. **Rom. 1:16-17:** For I am not ashamed of the gospel of Christ, for it is the power of God to salvation for everyone who believes, for the Jew first and also for the Greek. For in it the righteousness of God is revealed from faith to faith; as it is written, "The just shall live by faith." **Matt. 28:19:** Go therefore and make disciples of all the nations, baptizing them in the name of the Father and of the Son and of the Holy Spirit. **See Acts 2:38. 1 Cor. 11:23-29:** For I received from the Lord that which I also delivered to you: that the Lord Jesus on the *same* night in which He was betrayed took bread; and when He had given thanks, He broke *it* and said, "Take, eat; this is My body which is broken for you; do this in remembrance of Me." In the same manner *He* also *took* the cup after supper, saying, "This cup is the new covenant in My blood. This do, as often as you drink *it*, in remembrance of Me." For as often as you eat this bread and drink this cup, you proclaim the Lord's death till He comes. Therefore whoever eats this bread or drinks *this* cup of the Lord in an unworthy manner will be guilty of the body and blood of the Lord. But let a man examine himself, and so let him eat of the bread and drink of the cup. For he who eats and drinks in an unworthy manner eats and drinks judgment to himself, not discerning the Lord's body. **Phil. 4:6-7:** Be anxious for nothing, but in everything by prayer and supplication, with thanksgiving, let your requests be made known to God; and the peace of God, which surpasses all understanding, will guard your hearts and minds through Christ Jesus.

2. By this faith a Christian believeth to be true, whatsoever is revealed in the word, for the authority of God Himself;[5] and also apprehendeth an excellency therein, above all other writings; and all things in the world: as it bears forth the glory of God in His attributes,[6] the excellency of Christ in His nature and offices;[7] and the power and fullness of the Holy Spirit in His workings, and operations;[8] and so is enabled to cast his soul upon the truth thus believed;[9] and also acteth differently, upon that which each particular passage thereof containeth; yielding obedience to the commands,[10] trembling at the threatenings,[11] and embracing the

---

[5] **Acts 24:14:** But this I confess to you, that according to the Way which they call a sect, so I worship the God of my fathers, believing all things which are written in the Law and in the Prophets. **2 Pet. 1:20-21:** ... knowing this first, that no prophecy of Scripture is of any private interpretation, for prophecy never came by the will of man, but holy men of God spoke *as they were* moved by the Holy Spirit. **John 4:42:** Then they said to the woman, "Now we believe, not because of what you said, for we ourselves have heard *Him* and we know that this is indeed the Christ, the Savior of the world." **1 Thess. 2:13:** For this reason we also thank God without ceasing, because when you received the word of God which you heard from us, you welcomed *it* not *as* the word of men, but as it is in truth, the word of God, which also effectively works in you who believe. **1 John 5:9-10:** If we receive the witness of men, the witness of God is greater; for this is the witness of God which He has testified of His Son. He who believes in the Son of God has the witness in himself; he who does not believe God has made Him a liar, because he has not believed the testimony that God has given of His Son.

[6] **2 Pet. 1:3:** ... as His divine power has given to us all things that *pertain* to life and godliness, through the knowledge of Him who called us by glory and virtue. **Ps. 19:7-10:** The law of the LORD *is* perfect, converting the soul; The testimony of the LORD *is* sure, making wise the simple; The statutes of the LORD *are* right, rejoicing the heart; The commandment of the LORD *is* pure, enlightening the eyes; The fear of the LORD *is* clean, enduring forever; The judgments of the LORD *are* true *and* righteous altogether. More to be desired *are they* than gold, Yea, than much fine gold; Sweeter also than honey and the honeycomb. **Ps. 119:72:** The law of Your mouth *is* better to me Than thousands of *coins of* gold and silver.

[7] **Phil. 3:8:** Yet indeed I also count all things loss for the excellence of the knowledge of Christ Jesus my Lord, for whom I have suffered the loss of all things, and count them as rubbish, that I may gain Christ. **Eph. 4:13:** ... till we all come to the unity of the faith and of the knowledge of the Son of God, to a perfect man, to the measure of the stature of the fullness of Christ. **John 17:3:** And this is eternal life, that they may know You, the only true God, and Jesus Christ whom You have sent.

[8] **John 14:26:** But the Helper, the Holy Spirit, whom the Father will send in My name, He will teach you all things, and bring to your remembrance all things that I said to you. **1 Cor. 1:10-11:** Now I plead with you, brethren, by the name of our Lord Jesus Christ, that you all speak the same thing, and *that* there be no divisions among you, but *that* you be perfectly joined together in the same mind and in the same judgment. For it has been declared to me concerning you, my brethren, by those of Chloe's *household,* that there are contentions among you. **1 Cor. 2:4:** And my speech and my preaching *were* not with persuasive words of human wisdom, but in demonstration of the Spirit and of power. **Rom. 8:26:** Likewise the Spirit also helps in our weaknesses. For we do not know what we should pray for as we ought, but the Spirit Himself makes intercession for us with groanings which cannot be uttered. **Eph. 5:18:** And do not be drunk with wine, in which is dissipation; but be filled with the Spirit.

[9] **1 John 3:19:** And by this we know that we are of the truth, and shall assure our hearts before Him. **2 Tim. 1:12:** For this reason I also suffer these things; nevertheless I am not ashamed, for I know whom I have believed and am persuaded that He is able to keep what I have committed to Him until that Day. **Ps. 37:5:** Commit your way to the LORD, Trust also in Him, And He shall bring *it* to pass.

[10] **Ps. 119:10-11, 48, 97-98, 167-168:** With my whole heart I have sought You; Oh, let me not wander from Your commandments! Your word I have hidden in my heart, That I might not sin against You.... My hands also I will lift up to Your commandments, Which I love, And I will meditate on Your statutes.... Oh, how I love Your law! It *is* my meditation all the day. You, through Your commandments, make me wiser than my enemies; For they *are* ever with me.... My soul keeps Your testimonies, And I love them exceedingly. I keep Your precepts and Your testimonies, For all my

promises of God, for this life, and that which is to come:[12] But the principal acts of saving faith, have immediate relation to Christ, accepting, receiving, and resting upon Him alone, for justification, sanctification, and eternal life,[13] by virtue of the covenant of grace.[14]

3. This faith although it be different in degrees, and may be weak, or strong;[15] yet it is in the least degree of it, different in the kind, or nature of it (as is all other saving grace) from the faith, and common grace of temporary believers;[16] and therefore though it

---

ways *are* before You. **John 14:15:** If you love Me, keep My commandments. **John 15:14:** You are My friends if you do whatever I command you.

[11] **Ezra 9:4:** Then everyone who trembled at the words of the God of Israel assembled to me, because of the transgression of those who had been carried away captive, and I sat astonished until the evening sacrifice. **Isa. 66:2:** "For all those *things* My hand has made, And all those *things* exist," Says the LORD. "But on this *one* will I look: On *him who is* poor and of a contrite spirit, And who trembles at My word." **Heb. 4:1:** Therefore, since a promise remains of entering His rest, let us fear lest any of you seem to have come short of it.

[12] **Heb. 11:13:** These all died in faith, not having received the promises, but having seen them afar off were assured of them, embraced *them* and confessed that they were strangers and pilgrims on the earth. **1 Tim. 4:8:** For bodily exercise profits a little, but godliness is profitable for all things, having promise of the life that now is and of that which is to come.

[13] **John 1:12:** But as many as received Him, to them He gave the right to become children of God, to those who believe in His name. **Acts 16:31:** So they said, "Believe on the Lord Jesus Christ, and you will be saved, you and your household." **Gal. 2:20:** I have been crucified with Christ; it is no longer I who live, but Christ lives in me; and the *life* which I now live in the flesh I live by faith in the Son of God, who loved me and gave Himself for me. **Acts 15:11:** But we believe that through the grace of the Lord Jesus Christ we shall be saved in the same manner as they.

[14] **2 Tim. 1:9-10:** ... who has saved us and called *us* with a holy calling, not according to our works, but according to His own purpose and grace which was given to us in Christ Jesus before time began, but has now been revealed by the appearing of our Savior Jesus Christ, *who* has abolished death and brought life and immortality to light through the gospel. **Rom. 5:6-11:** For when we were still without strength, in due time Christ died for the ungodly. For scarcely for a righteous man will one die; yet perhaps for a good man someone would even dare to die. But God demonstrates His own love toward us, in that while we were still sinners, Christ died for us. Much more then, having now been justified by His blood, we shall be saved from wrath through Him. For if when we were enemies we were reconciled to God through the death of His Son, much more, having been reconciled, we shall be saved by His life. And not only *that,* but we also rejoice in God through our Lord Jesus Christ, through whom we have now received the reconciliation.

[15] **Heb. 5:13-14:** For everyone who partakes *only* of milk *is* unskilled in the word of righteousness, for he is a babe. But solid food belongs to those who are of full age, *that is,* those who by reason of use have their senses exercised to discern both good and evil. **Matt. 6:30:** Now if God so clothes the grass of the field, which today is, and tomorrow is thrown into the oven, *will He* not much more *clothe* you, O you of little faith? **Matt. 8:10:** When Jesus heard *it,* He marveled, and said to those who followed, "Assuredly, I say to you, I have not found such great faith, not even in Israel!" **Rom. 14:1-2:** Receive one who is weak in the faith, *but* not to disputes over doubtful things. For one believes he may eat all things, but he who is weak eats *only* vegetables. **Rom. 4:19-20:** And not being weak in faith, he did not consider his own body, already dead (since he was about a hundred years old), and the deadness of Sarah's womb. He did not waver at the promise of God through unbelief, but was strengthened in faith, giving glory to God.

[16] **Luke 8:11-15:** Now the parable is this: The seed is the word of God. Those by the wayside are the ones who hear; then the devil comes and takes away the word out of their hearts, lest they should believe and be saved. But the ones on the rock *are those* who, when they hear, receive the word with joy; and these have no root, who believe for a while and in time of temptation fall away. Now the ones *that* fell among thorns are those who, when they have heard, go out and are choked with cares, riches, and pleasures of life, and bring no fruit to maturity. But the ones *that* fell on the good ground are those who, having heard the word with a noble and good heart, keep *it* and bear fruit with patience. **2 Pet. 1:1:** Simon Peter, a bondservant and apostle of Jesus Christ, To those who have obtained like precious faith with us by the righteousness of our God and Savior Jesus

may be many times assailed, and weakened; yet it gets the victory;[17] growing up in many, to the attainment of a full assurance through Christ,[18] who is both the author and finisher of our faith.[19]

Christ. **Acts 26:27-28:** "King Agrippa, do you believe the prophets? I know that you do believe." Then Agrippa said to Paul, "You almost persuade me to become a Christian." **James 2:18-26:** But someone will say, "You have faith, and I have works." Show me your faith without your works, and I will show you my faith by my works. You believe that there is one God. You do well. Even the demons believe—and tremble! But do you want to know, O foolish man, that faith without works is dead? Was not Abraham our father justified by works when he offered Isaac his son on the altar? Do you see that faith was working together with his works, and by works faith was made perfect? And the Scripture was fulfilled which says, "Abraham believed God, and it was accounted to him for righteousness." And he was called the friend of God. You see then that a man is justified by works, and not by faith only. Likewise, was not Rahab the harlot also justified by works when she received the messengers and sent *them* out another way? For as the body without the spirit is dead, so faith without works is dead also.

[17] **Luke 22:31-32:** And the Lord said, "Simon, Simon! Indeed, Satan has asked for you, that he may sift *you* as wheat. But I have prayed for you, that your faith should not fail; and when you have returned to *Me,* strengthen your brethren." **Eph. 6:16:** ... above all, taking the shield of faith with which you will be able to quench all the fiery darts of the wicked one. **1 John 5:4-5:** For whatever is born of God overcomes the world. And this is the victory that has overcome the world—our faith. Who is he who overcomes the world, but he who believes that Jesus is the Son of God?

[18] **Heb. 6:11-12:** And we desire that each one of you show the same diligence to the full assurance of hope until the end, that you do not become sluggish, but imitate those who through faith and patience inherit the promises. **Heb. 10:22:** ... let us draw near with a true heart in full assurance of faith, having our hearts sprinkled from an evil conscience and our bodies washed with pure water. **Col. 2:2:** ... that their hearts may be encouraged, being knit together in love, and *attaining* to all riches of the full assurance of understanding, to the knowledge of the mystery of God, both of the Father and of Christ.

[19] **Heb. 12:2:** ... looking unto Jesus, the author and finisher of *our* faith, who for the joy that was set before Him endured the cross, despising the shame, and has sat down at the right hand of the throne of God.

CHAPTER 15
Of Repentance unto Life and Salvation

1. Saving repentance is an evangelical grace,[1] whereby a person, being by the Holy Spirit made sensible of the manifold evils of his sin,[2] doth, by faith in Christ,[3] humble himself for it, with godly sorrow, detestation of it, and self-abhorrencey;[4] praying for pardon, and strength of grace,[5] with a purpose and endeavour by

---

[1] **Acts 5:31:** Him God has exalted to His right hand *to be* Prince and Savior, to give repentance to Israel and forgiveness of sins. **Acts 11:18:** When they heard these things they became silent; and they glorified God, saying, "Then God has also granted to the Gentiles repentance to life." **2 Tim. 2:25:** ... in humility correcting those who are in opposition, if God perhaps will grant them repentance, so that they may know the truth.

[2] **John 16:8-11:** And when He has come, He will convict the world of sin, and of righteousness, and of judgment: of sin, because they do not believe in Me; of righteousness, because I go to My Father and you see Me no more; of judgment, because the ruler of this world is judged. **Ezek. 6:9:** Then those of you who escape will remember Me among the nations where they are carried captive, because I was crushed by their adulterous heart which has departed from Me, and by their eyes which play the harlot after their idols; they will loathe themselves for the evils which they committed in all their abominations. **Ezek. 20:43:** And there you shall remember your ways and all your doings with which you were defiled; and you shall loathe yourselves in your own sight because of all the evils that you have committed. **Ezek. 36:31:** Then you will remember your evil ways and your deeds that *were* not good; and you will loathe yourselves in your own sight, for your iniquities and your abominations.

[3] **Mark 1:14-15:** Now after John was put in prison, Jesus came to Galilee, preaching the gospel of the kingdom of God, and saying, "The time is fulfilled, and the kingdom of God is at hand. Repent, and believe in the gospel." **Acts 2:38:** Then Peter said to them, "Repent, and let every one of you be baptized in the name of Jesus Christ for the remission of sins; and you shall receive the gift of the Holy Spirit." **Zech. 12:10:** And I will pour on the house of David and on the inhabitants of Jerusalem the Spirit of grace and supplication; then they will look on Me whom they pierced. Yes, they will mourn for Him as one mourns for *his* only *son,* and grieve for Him as one grieves for a firstborn.

[4] **Job 42:6:** Therefore I abhor *myself,* And repent in dust and ashes. **Ps. 32:5:** I acknowledged my sin to You, And my iniquity I have not hidden. I said, "I will confess my transgressions to the LORD," And You forgave the iniquity of my sin. *Selah*. **Ps. 51:3-4:** For I acknowledge my transgressions, And my sin *is* always before me. Against You, You only, have I sinned, And done *this* evil in Your sight—That You may be found just when You speak, *And* blameless when You judge. **Jer. 31:18-19:** I have surely heard Ephraim bemoaning himself: 'You have chastised me, and I was chastised, Like an untrained bull; Restore me, and I will return, For You *are* the LORD my God. Surely, after my turning, I repented; And after I was instructed, I struck myself on the thigh; I was ashamed, yes, even humiliated, Because I bore the reproach of my youth.' **2 Cor. 7:11:** For observe this very thing, that you sorrowed in a godly manner: What diligence it produced in you, *what clearing of yourselves, what* indignation, *what* fear, *what* vehement desire, *what* zeal, *what* vindication! In all *things* you proved yourselves to be clear in this matter.

[5] **Ps. 51:1-2:** Have mercy upon me, O God, According to Your lovingkindness; According to the multitude of Your tender mercies, Blot out my transgressions. Wash me thoroughly from my iniquity, And cleanse me from my sin. **Ps. 7:17:** I will praise the LORD according to His righteousness, And will sing praise to the name of the LORD Most High. **Ps. 143:1-7:** Hear my prayer, O LORD, Give ear to my supplications! In Your faithfulness answer me, *And* in Your righteousness. Do not enter into judgment with Your servant, For in Your sight no one living is righteous. For the enemy has persecuted my soul; He has crushed my life to the ground; He has made me dwell in darkness, Like those who have long been dead. Therefore my spirit is overwhelmed within me; My heart within me is distressed. I remember the days of old; I meditate on all Your works; I muse on the work of Your hands. I spread out my hands to You; My soul *longs* for You like a thirsty land. *Selah*. Answer me speedily, O LORD; My spirit fails! Do not hide Your face from me, Lest I be like those who go down into the pit.

supplies of the Spirit, to walk before God unto all well-pleasing in all things.[6]

2. Such of the elect as are converted at riper years, having sometime lived in the state of nature, and therein served divers lusts and pleasures, God in their effectual calling giveth them repentance unto life.[7]

---

[6] **Ps. 143:8-10:** Cause me to hear Your lovingkindness in the morning, For in You do I trust; Cause me to know the way in which I should walk, For I lift up my soul to You. Deliver me, O LORD, from my enemies; In You I take shelter. Teach me to do Your will, For You *are* my God; Your Spirit *is* good. Lead me in the land of uprightness. **Ps. 119:6, 57-64, 106:** Then I would not be ashamed, When I look into all Your commandments.... *You are* my portion, O LORD; I have said that I would keep Your words. I entreated Your favor with *my* whole heart; Be merciful to me according to Your word. I thought about my ways, And turned my feet to Your testimonies. I made haste, and did not delay To keep Your commandments. The cords of the wicked have bound me, *But* I have not forgotten Your law. At midnight I will rise to give thanks to You, Because of Your righteous judgments. I *am* a companion of all who fear You, And of those who keep Your precepts. The earth, O LORD, is full of Your mercy; Teach me Your statutes.... I have sworn and confirmed That I will keep Your righteous judgments. **Luke 1:6:** And they were both righteous before God, walking in all the commandments and ordinances of the Lord blameless. **Luke 15:17-18:** But when he came to himself, he said, 'How many of my father's hired servants have bread enough and to spare, and I perish with hunger! I will arise and go to my father, and will say to him, "Father, I have sinned against heaven and before you."'

[7] **Luke 15:11-24:** Then He said: "A certain man had two sons. And the younger of them said to *his* father, 'Father, give me the portion of goods that falls *to me.*' So he divided to them *his* livelihood. And not many days after, the younger son gathered all together, journeyed to a far country, and there wasted his possessions with prodigal living. But when he had spent all, there arose a severe famine in that land, and he began to be in want. Then he went and joined himself to a citizen of that country, and he sent him into his fields to feed swine. And he would gladly have filled his stomach with the pods that the swine ate, and no one gave him *anything.* But when he came to himself, he said, 'How many of my father's hired servants have bread enough and to spare, and I perish with hunger! I will arise and go to my father, and will say to him, "Father, I have sinned against heaven and before you, and I am no longer worthy to be called your son. Make me like one of your hired servants."' And he arose and came to his father. But when he was still a great way off, his father saw him and had compassion, and ran and fell on his neck and kissed him. And the son said to him, 'Father, I have sinned against heaven and in your sight, and am no longer worthy to be called your son.' But the father said to his servants, 'Bring out the best robe and put *it* on him, and put a ring on his hand and sandals on *his* feet. And bring the fatted calf here and kill *it,* and let us eat and be merry; for this my son was dead and is alive again; he was lost and is found.' And they began to be merry." **Luke 23:39-43:** Then one of the criminals who were hanged blasphemed Him, saying, "If You are the Christ, save Yourself and us." But the other, answering, rebuked him, saying, "Do you not even fear God, seeing you are under the same condemnation? And we indeed justly, for we receive the due reward of our deeds; but this Man has done nothing wrong." Then he said to Jesus, "Lord, remember me when You come into Your kingdom." And Jesus said to him, "Assuredly, I say to you, today you will be with Me in Paradise." **Acts 16:29-30:** Then he called for a light, ran in, and fell down trembling before Paul and Silas. And he brought them out and said, "Sirs, what must I do to be saved?" **1 Cor. 6:9-11:** Do you not know that the unrighteous will not inherit the kingdom of God? Do not be deceived. Neither fornicators, nor idolaters, nor adulterers, nor homosexuals, nor sodomites, nor thieves, nor covetous, nor drunkards, nor revilers, nor extortioners will inherit the kingdom of God. And such were some of you. But you were washed, but you were sanctified, but you were justified in the name of the Lord Jesus and by the Spirit of our God. **Titus 3:2-5:** ... to speak evil of no one, to be peaceable, gentle, showing all humility to all men. For we ourselves were also once foolish, disobedient, deceived, serving various lusts and pleasures, living in malice and envy, hateful and hating one another. But when the kindness and the love of God our Savior toward man appeared, not by works of righteousness which we have done, but according to His mercy He saved us, through the washing of regeneration and renewing of the Holy Spirit.

3. Whereas there is none that doth good, and sinneth not;[8] and the best of men may, through the power, and deceitfulness of their corruption dwelling in them,[9] with the prevalency of temptation,[10] fall into great sins, and provocations;[11] God hath in the covenant of grace, mercifully provided that believers so sinning, and falling, be renewed through repentance unto salvation.[12]

4. As repentance is to be continued through the whole course of our lives, upon the account of the body of death, and the motions

---

[8] **Eccl. 7:20:** For *there is* not a just man on earth who does good And does not sin. Rom. 3:10-18: As it is written: "There is none righteous, no, not one; There is none who understands; There is none who seeks after God. They have all turned aside; They have together become unprofitable; There is none who does good, no, not one." "Their throat *is* an open tomb; With their tongues they have practiced deceit"; "The poison of asps *is* under their lips"; "Whose mouth *is* full of cursing and bitterness." "Their feet *are* swift to shed blood; Destruction and misery *are* in their ways; And the way of peace they have not known." "There is no fear of God before their eyes."

[9] **Rom. 7:13-25:** Has then what is good become death to me? Certainly not! But sin, that it might appear sin, was producing death in me through what is good, so that sin through the commandment might become exceedingly sinful. For we know that the law is spiritual, but I am carnal, sold under sin. For what I am doing, I do not understand. For what I will to do, that I do not practice; but what I hate, that I do. If, then, I do what I will not to do, I agree with the law that *it is* good. But now, *it is* no longer I who do it, but sin that dwells in me. For I know that in me (that is, in my flesh) nothing good dwells; for to will is present with me, but *how* to perform what is good I do not find. For the good that I will *to do,* I do not do; but the evil I will not *to do,* that I practice. Now if I do what I will not *to do,* it is no longer I who do it, but sin that dwells in me. I find then a law, that evil is present with me, the one who wills to do good. For I delight in the law of God according to the inward man. But I see another law in my members, warring against the law of my mind, and bringing me into captivity to the law of sin which is in my members. O wretched man that I am! Who will deliver me from this body of death? I thank God—through Jesus Christ our Lord! So then, with the mind I myself serve the law of God, but with the flesh the law of sin.

[10] **1 Cor. 10:13:** No temptation has overtaken you except such as is common to man; but God *is* faithful, who will not allow you to be tempted beyond what you are able, but with the temptation will also make the way of escape, that you may be able to bear *it.* **James 1:12-15:** Blessed *is* the man who endures temptation; for when he has been approved, he will receive the crown of life which the Lord has promised to those who love Him. Let no one say when he is tempted, "I am tempted by God"; for God cannot be tempted by evil, nor does He Himself tempt anyone. But each one is tempted when he is drawn away by his own desires and enticed. Then, when desire has conceived, it gives birth to sin; and sin, when it is full-grown, brings forth death.

[11] **Ps. 51:1:** Have mercy upon me, O God, According to Your lovingkindness; According to the multitude of Your tender mercies, Blot out my transgressions. **1 Cor. 5:1-2:** It is actually reported *that there is* sexual immorality among you, and such sexual immorality as is not even named among the Gentiles—that a man has his father's wife! And you are puffed up, and have not rather mourned, that he who has done this deed might be taken away from among you. **Gal. 6:1:** Brethren, if a man is overtaken in any trespass, you who *are* spiritual restore such a one in a spirit of gentleness, considering yourself lest you also be tempted.

[12] **2 Cor. 7:10:** For godly sorrow produces repentance *leading* to salvation, not to be regretted; but the sorrow of the world produces death. **2 Sam. 12:13:** So David said to Nathan, "I have sinned against the LORD." And Nathan said to David, "The LORD also has put away your sin; you shall not die." **Luke 18:13:** And the tax collector, standing afar off, would not so much as raise *his* eyes to heaven, but beat his breast, saying, 'God, be merciful to me a sinner!' **Luke 22:31-32:** And the Lord said, "Simon, Simon! Indeed, Satan has asked for you, that he may sift *you* as wheat. But I have prayed for you, that your faith should not fail; and when you have returned to *Me,* strengthen your brethren." **Prov. 24:16:** For a righteous *man* may fall seven times And rise again, But the wicked shall fall by calamity.

thereof;[13] so it is every man's duty, to repent of his particular known sins, particularly.[14]

5. Such is the provision which God hath made through Christ in the covenant of grace, for the preservation of believers unto salvation, that although there is no sin so small, but it deserves damnation;[15] yet there is no sin so great, that it shall bring damnation upon those who truly repent;[16] which makes the constant preaching of repentance necessary.[17]

---

[13] **1 John 1:8-10:** If we say that we have no sin, we deceive ourselves, and the truth is not in us. If we confess our sins, He is faithful and just to forgive us *our* sins and to cleanse us from all unrighteousness. If we say that we have not sinned, we make Him a liar, and His word is not in us. **Prov. 28:13:** He who covers his sins will not prosper, But whoever confesses and forsakes *them* will have mercy. **Mark 11:25:** "And whenever you stand praying, if you have anything against anyone, forgive him, that your Father in heaven may also forgive you your trespasses. **Rev. 2:5:** Remember therefore from where you have fallen; repent and do the first works, or else I will come to you quickly and remove your lampstand from its place—unless you repent.

[14] **Ps. 32:5:** I acknowledged my sin to You, And my iniquity I have not hidden. I said, "I will confess my transgressions to the LORD," And You forgave the iniquity of my in. *Selah*. **Ps. 51:1-4, 14:** Have mercy upon me, O God, According to Your lovingkindness; According to the multitude of Your tender mercies, Blot out my transgressions. Wash me thoroughly from my iniquity, And cleanse me from my sin. For I acknowledge my transgressions, And my sin *is* always before me. Against You, You only, have I sinned, And done *this* evil in Your sight—That You may be found just when You speak, *And* blameless when You judge.... Deliver me from the guilt of bloodshed, O God, The God of my salvation, *And* my tongue shall sing aloud of Your righteousness. **Ezra 10:1:** Now while Ezra was praying, and while he was confessing, weeping, and bowing down before the house of God, a very large assembly of men, women, and children gathered to him from Israel; for the people wept very bitterly. **Lev. 26:40-42:** *But* if they confess their iniquity and the iniquity of their fathers, with their unfaithfulness in which they were unfaithful to Me, and that they also have walked contrary to Me, and *that* I also have walked contrary to them and have brought them into the land of their enemies; if their uncircumcised hearts are humbled, and they accept their guilt—then I will remember My covenant with Jacob, and My covenant with Isaac and My covenant with Abraham I will remember; I will remember the land.

[15] **Gen. 2:17:** ... but of the tree of the knowledge of good and evil you shall not eat, for in the day that you eat of it you shall surely die. **Rom. 5:12:** Therefore, just as through one man sin entered the world, and death through sin, and thus death spread to all men, because all sinned. **James 1:15:** Then, when desire has conceived, it gives birth to sin; and sin, when it is full-grown, brings forth death. **James 2:10:** For whoever shall keep the whole law, and yet stumble in one *point,* he is guilty of all.

[16] **Mark 3:28:** Assuredly, I say to you, all sins will be forgiven the sons of men, and whatever blasphemies they may utter. **Titus 2:14:** ... who gave Himself for us, that He might redeem us from every lawless deed and purify for Himself *His* own special people, zealous for good works. **Isa. 1:16, 18:** "Wash yourselves, make yourselves clean; Put away the evil of your doings from before My eyes. Cease to do evil ... Come now, and let us reason together," Says the LORD, "Though your sins are like scarlet, They shall be as white as snow; Though they are red like crimson, They shall be as wool." **Isa. 55:7:** Let the wicked forsake his way, And the unrighteous man his thoughts; Let him return to the LORD, And He will have mercy on him; And to our God, For He will abundantly pardon.

[17] **Luke 24:46-47:** Then He said to them, "Thus it is written, and thus it was necessary for the Christ to suffer and to rise from the dead the third day, and that repentance and remission of sins should be preached in His name to all nations, beginning at Jerusalem." **Acts 2:36-38:** "Therefore let all the house of Israel know assuredly that God has made this Jesus, whom you crucified, both Lord and Christ." Now when they heard *this,* they were cut to the heart, and said to Peter and the rest of the apostles, "Men *and* brethren, what shall we do?" Then Peter said to them, "Repent, and let every one of you be baptized in the name of Jesus Christ for the remission of sins; and you shall receive the gift of the Holy Spirit." **Acts 10:43:** To Him all the prophets witness that, through His name, whoever believes in Him will receive remission of sins. **Acts 17:30:** Truly, these times of ignorance God overlooked, but now commands all men everywhere to repent. **Acts 26:16-18:** But rise and stand on your feet; for I have appeared to you for this purpose, to make you a minister and a witness both of the things which you have seen and of the things which I will yet reveal to you. I will deliver you from the *Jewish* people, as well as *from* the Gentiles, to whom I now send you, to

open their eyes, *in order* to turn *them* from darkness to light, and *from* the power of Satan to God, that they may receive forgiveness of sins and an inheritance among those who are sanctified by faith in Me.

CHAPTER 16
Of Good Works

1. Good works are only such as God hath commanded in His holy word;[1] and not such as without the warrant thereof, are devised by men, out of blind zeal, or upon any pretence of good intentions.[2]

2. These good works, done in obedience to God's commandments, are the fruits, and evidences of a true, and lively faith;[3] and by them believers manifest their thankfulness,[4] strengthen their assurance,[5] edify their brethren,[6] adorn the

---

[1] **Mic. 6:8:** He has shown you, O man, what *is* good; And what does the LORD require of you But to do justly, To love mercy, And to walk humbly with your God? **Heb. 13:21:** ... make you complete in every good work to do His will, working in you what is well pleasing in His sight, through Jesus Christ, to whom *be* glory forever and ever. Amen.

[2] **Matt. 15:9:** And in vain they worship Me, Teaching *as* doctrines the commandments of men. **Isa. 29:13:** Therefore the Lord said: "Inasmuch as these people draw near with their mouths And honor Me with their lips, But have removed their hearts far from Me, And their fear toward Me is taught by the commandment of men." **1 Pet. 1:18:** ... knowing that you were not redeemed with corruptible things, *like* silver or gold, from your aimless conduct *received* by tradition from your fathers. **John 16:2:** They will put you out of the synagogues; yes, the time is coming that whoever kills you will think that he offers God service. **Rom. 10:2:** For I bear them witness that they have a zeal for God, but not according to knowledge. **1 Sam. 15:21-23:** But the people took of the plunder, sheep and oxen, the best of the things which should have been utterly destroyed, to sacrifice to the LORD your God in Gilgal. So Samuel said: "Has the LORD *as great* delight in burnt offerings and sacrifices, As in obeying the voice of the LORD? Behold, to obey is better than sacrifice, *And* to heed than the fat of rams. For rebellion *is as* the sin of witchcraft, And stubbornness *is as* iniquity and idolatry. Because you have rejected the word of the LORD, He also has rejected you from *being* king." **Deut. 10:12-13:** And now, Israel, what does the LORD your God require of you, but to fear the LORD your God, to walk in all His ways and to love Him, to serve the LORD your God with all your heart and with all your soul, *and* to keep the commandments of the LORD and His statutes which I command you today for your good? **Col. 2:16-17, 20-23:** So let no one judge you in food or in drink, or regarding a festival or a new moon or sabbaths, which are a shadow of things to come, but the substance is of Christ.... Therefore, if you died with Christ from the basic principles of the world, why, as *though* living in the world, do you subject yourselves to regulations—"Do not touch, do not taste, do not handle," which all concern things which perish with the using—according to the commandments and doctrines of men? These things indeed have an appearance of wisdom in self-imposed religion, *false* humility, and neglect of the body, *but are* of no value against the indulgence of the flesh.

[3] **James 2:18, 22:** But someone will say, "You have faith, and I have works." Show me your faith without your works, and I will show you my faith by my works.... Do you see that faith was working together with his works, and by works faith was made perfect?

[4] **Ps. 116:12-14:** What shall I render to the LORD *For* all His benefits toward me? I will take up the cup of salvation, And call upon the name of the LORD. I will pay my vows to the LORD Now in the presence of all His people. **Col. 3:15-17:** And let the peace of God rule in your hearts, to which also you were called in one body; and be thankful. Let the word of Christ dwell in you richly in all wisdom, teaching and admonishing one another in psalms and hymns and spiritual songs, singing with grace in your hearts to the Lord. And whatever you do in word or deed, *do* all in the name of the Lord Jesus, giving thanks to God the Father through Him. **1 Pet. 2:9:** But you *are* a chosen generation, a royal priesthood, a holy nation, His own special people, that you may proclaim the praises of Him who called you out of darkness into His marvelous light.

[5] **1 John 2:3, 5:** Now by this we know that we know Him, if we keep His commandments.... But whoever keeps His word, truly the love of God is perfected in him. By this we know that we are in Him. **2 Pet. 1:5-11:** But also for this very reason, giving all diligence, add to your faith virtue, to virtue knowledge, to knowledge self-control, to self-control perseverance, to perseverance godliness, to godliness brotherly kindness, and to brotherly kindness love. For if these things are yours and abound, *you* will be neither barren nor unfruitful in the knowledge of our Lord Jesus

profession of the gospel,[7] stop the mouths of the adversaries,[8] and glorify God,[9] whose workmanship they are, created in Christ Jesus thereunto,[10] that having their fruit unto holiness, they may have the end eternal life.[11]

3. Their ability to do good works, is not at all of themselves; but wholly from the Spirit of Christ;[12] and that they may be enabled thereunto, besides the graces they have already received, there is necessary an actual influence of the same Holy Spirit, to work in

---

Christ. For he who lacks these things is shortsighted, even to blindness, and has forgotten that he was cleansed from his old sins. Therefore, brethren, be even more diligent to make your call and election sure, for if you do these things you will never stumble; for so an entrance will be supplied to you abundantly into the everlasting kingdom of our Lord and Savior Jesus Christ.

[6] **2 Cor. 9:2:** ... for I know your willingness, about which I boast of you to the Macedonians, that Achaia was ready a year ago; and your zeal has stirred up the majority. **Matt. 5:16:** Let your light so shine before men, that they may see your good works and glorify your Father in heaven. **1 Tim. 4:12:** Let no one despise your youth, but be an example to the believers in word, in conduct, in love, in spirit, in faith, in purity.

[7] **Titus 2:5, 9-12:** ... *to be* discreet, chaste, homemakers, good, obedient to their own husbands, that the word of God may not be blasphemed.... *Exhort* bondservants to be obedient to their own masters, to be well pleasing in all *things,* not answering back, not pilfering, but showing all good fidelity, that they may adorn the doctrine of God our Savior in all things. For the grace of God that brings salvation has appeared to all men, teaching us that, denying ungodliness and worldly lusts, we should live soberly, righteously, and godly in the present age. **1 Tim. 6:1:** Let as many bondservants as are under the yoke count their own masters worthy of all honor, so that the name of God and *His* doctrine may not be blasphemed.

[8] **1 Pet. 2:15:** For this is the will of God, that by doing good you may put to silence the ignorance of foolish men.

[9] **1 Pet. 2:12:** ... having your conduct honorable among the Gentiles, that when they speak against you as evildoers, they may, by *your* good works which they observe, glorify God in the day of visitation. **Phil. 1:11:** ... being filled with the fruits of righteousness which *are* by Jesus Christ, to the glory and praise of God. **John 15:8:** By this My Father is glorified, that you bear much fruit; so you will be My disciples.

[10] **Eph. 2:10:** For we are His workmanship, created in Christ Jesus for good works, which God prepared beforehand that we should walk in them.

[11] **Rom. 6:22:** But now having been set free from sin, and having become slaves of God, you have your fruit to holiness, and the end, everlasting life.

[12] **John 15:4-6:** Abide in Me, and I in you. As the branch cannot bear fruit of itself, unless it abides in the vine, neither can you, unless you abide in Me. "I am the vine, you *are* the branches. He who abides in Me, and I in him, bears much fruit; for without Me you can do nothing. If anyone does not abide in Me, he is cast out as a branch and is withered; and they gather them and throw *them* into the fire, and they are burned. **Rom. 8:4-14:** ... that the righteous requirement of the law might be fulfilled in us who do not walk according to the flesh but according to the Spirit. For those who live according to the flesh set their minds on the things of the flesh, but those *who live* according to the Spirit, the things of the Spirit. For to be carnally minded *is* death, but to be spiritually minded *is* life and peace. Because the carnal mind *is* enmity against God; for it is not subject to the law of God, nor indeed can be. So then, those who are in the flesh cannot please God. But you are not in the flesh but in the Spirit, if indeed the Spirit of God dwells in you. Now if anyone does not have the Spirit of Christ, he is not His. And if Christ *is* in you, the body *is* dead because of sin, but the Spirit *is* life because of righteousness. But if the Spirit of Him who raised Jesus from the dead dwells in you, He who raised Christ from the dead will also give life to your mortal bodies through His Spirit who dwells in you. Therefore, brethren, we are debtors—not to the flesh, to live according to the flesh. For if you live according to the flesh you will die; but if by the Spirit you put to death the deeds of the body, you will live. For as many as are led by the Spirit of God, these are sons of God. **Ezek. 36:26-27:** I will give you a new heart and put a new spirit within you; I will take the heart of stone out of your flesh and give you a heart of flesh. I will put My Spirit within you and cause you to walk in My statutes, and you will keep My judgments and do *them.*

them to will, and to do, of His good pleasure;[13] yet are they not hereupon to grow negligent, as if they were not bound to perform any duty, unless upon a special motion of the Spirit; but they ought to be diligent in stirring up the grace of God that is in them.[14]

4. They who in their obedience attain to the greatest height which is possible in this life, are so far from being able to supererogate, and to do more than God requires, as that they fall short of much which in duty they are bound to do.[15]

5. We cannot by our best works merit pardon of sin or eternal life at the hand of God,[16] by reason of the great disproportion

---

[13] **Phil. 2:13:** ... for it is God who works in you both to will and to do for *His* good pleasure. **Phil. 4:13:** I can do all things through Christ who strengthens me. **2 Cor. 3:5:** Not that we are sufficient of ourselves to think of anything as *being* from ourselves, but our sufficiency *is* from God. **Eph. 3:16:** ... that He would grant you, according to the riches of His glory, to be strengthened with might through His Spirit in the inner man.

[14] **Phil. 2:12:** Therefore, my beloved, as you have always obeyed, not as in my presence only, but now much more in my absence, work out your own salvation with fear and trembling. **Heb. 6:11-12:** And we desire that each one of you show the same diligence to the full assurance of hope until the end, that you do not become sluggish, but imitate those who through faith and patience inherit the promises. **2 Pet. 1:3, 5, 10-11:** ... as His divine power has given to us all things that *pertain* to life and godliness, through the knowledge of Him who called us by glory and virtue ... But also for this very reason, giving all diligence, add to your faith virtue, to virtue knowledge ... Therefore, brethren, be even more diligent to make your call and election sure, for if you do these things you will never stumble; for so an entrance will be supplied to you abundantly into the everlasting kingdom of our Lord and Savior Jesus Christ. **Isa. 64:7:** And *there is* no one who calls on Your name, Who stirs himself up to take hold of You; For You have hidden Your face from us, And have consumed us because of our iniquities. **2 Tim. 1:6:** Therefore I remind you to stir up the gift of God which is in you through the laying on of my hands. **Acts 26:6-7:** And now I stand and am judged for the hope of the promise made by God to our fathers. To this *promise* our twelve tribes, earnestly serving *God* night and day, hope to attain. For this hope's sake, King Agrippa, I am accused by the Jews. **Jude 20-21:** But you, beloved, building yourselves up on your most holy faith, praying in the Holy Spirit, keep yourselves in the love of God, looking for the mercy of our Lord Jesus Christ unto eternal life.

[15] **Luke 17:10:** So likewise you, when you have done all those things which you are commanded, say, 'We are unprofitable servants. We have done what was our duty to do. **Neh. 13:22:** And I commanded the Levites that they should cleanse themselves, and that they should go and guard the gates, to sanctify the Sabbath day. Remember me, O my God, *concerning* this also, and spare me according to the greatness of Your mercy! **Rom. 8:21-25:** ... because the creation itself also will be delivered from the bondage of corruption into the glorious liberty of the children of God. For we know that the whole creation groans and labors with birth pangs together until now. Not only *that,* but we also who have the firstfruits of the Spirit, even we ourselves groan within ourselves, eagerly waiting for the adoption, the redemption of our body. For we were saved in this hope, but hope that is seen is not hope; for why does one still hope for what he sees? But if we hope for what we do not see, we eagerly wait for *it* with perseverance. **Gal. 5:17:** For the flesh lusts against the Spirit, and the Spirit against the flesh; and these are contrary to one another, so that you do not do the things that you wish. **Job 9:2-3:** "Truly I know *it is* so, But how can a man be righteous before God? If one wished to contend with Him, He could not answer Him one time out of a thousand.

[16] **Rom. 3:20:** Therefore by the deeds of the law no flesh will be justified in His sight, for by the law *is* the knowledge of sin. **Rom. 4:1-6:** What then shall we say that Abraham our father has found according to the flesh? For if Abraham was justified by works, he has *something* to boast about, but not before God. For what does the Scripture say? "Abraham believed God, and it was accounted to him for righteousness." Now to him who works, the wages are not counted as grace but as debt. But to him who does not work but believes on Him who justifies the ungodly, his faith is accounted for

that is between them and the glory to come;[17] and the infinite distance that is between us and God,[18] whom by them we can neither profit, nor satisfy for the debt of our former sins;[19] but when we have done all we can, we have done but our duty, and are unprofitable servants;[20] and because as they are good they proceed from His Spirit,[21] and as they are wrought by us they are defiled and mixed with so much weakness and imperfection[22] that they cannot endure the severity of God's judgment.[23]

6. Yet notwithstanding the persons of believers being accepted through Christ their good works also are accepted in Him;[24] not

---

righteousness, just as David also describes the blessedness of the man to whom God imputes righteousness apart from works.

[17] **Rom. 8:18, 22-24:** For I consider that the sufferings of this present time are not worthy *to be compared* with the glory which shall be revealed in us.... For we know that the whole creation groans and labors with birth pangs together until now. Not only *that,* but we also who have the firstfruits of the Spirit, even we ourselves groan within ourselves, eagerly waiting for the adoption, the redemption of our body. For we were saved in this hope, but hope that is seen is not hope; for why does one still hope for what he sees?

[18] **Isa. 40:13-17:** Who has directed the Spirit of the LORD, Or *as* His counselor has taught Him? With whom did He take counsel, and *who* instructed Him, And taught Him in the path of justice? Who taught Him knowledge, And showed Him the way of understanding? Behold, the nations *are* as a drop in a bucket, And are counted as the small dust on the scales; Look, He lifts up the isles as a very little thing. And Lebanon *is* not sufficient to burn, Nor its beasts sufficient for a burnt offering. All nations before Him *are* as nothing, And they are counted by Him less than nothing and worthless. **Job 9:32-33:** For *He is* not a man, as I *am, That* I may answer Him, *And that* we should go to court together. Nor is there any mediator between us, *Who* may lay his hand on us both.

[19] **Eph. 2:8-9:** For by grace you have been saved through faith, and that not of yourselves; *it is* the gift of God, not of works, lest anyone should boast. **Titus 3:5-7:** not by works of righteousness which we have done, but according to His mercy He saved us, through the washing of regeneration and renewing of the Holy Spirit, whom He poured out on us abundantly through Jesus Christ our Savior, that having been justified by His grace we should become heirs according to the hope of eternal life. **Ps. 16:2:** *O my soul,* you have said to the LORD, "You *are* my Lord, My goodness is nothing apart from You." **Job 22:2-3:** "Can a man be profitable to God, Though he who is wise may be profitable to himself? *Is it* any pleasure to the Almighty that you are righteous? Or *is it* gain *to Him* that you make your ways blameless? **Job 35:7-8:** If you are righteous, what do you give Him? Or what does He receive from your hand? Your wickedness affects a man such as you, And your righteousness a son of man.

[20] **Luke 17:10:** So likewise you, when you have done all those things which you are commanded, say, 'We are unprofitable servants. We have done what was our duty to do.'

[21] **Rom. 8:13-14:** For if you live according to the flesh you will die; but if by the Spirit you put to death the deeds of the body, you will live. For as many as are led by the Spirit of God, these are sons of God. **Gal. 5:22-23:** But the fruit of the Spirit is love, joy, peace, longsuffering, kindness, goodness, faithfulness, gentleness, self-control. Against such there is no law.

[22] **Isa. 64:6:** But we are all like an unclean *thing,* And all our righteousnesses *are* like filthy rags; We all fade as a leaf, And our iniquities, like the wind, Have taken us away. **Gal. 5:17:** For the flesh lusts against the Spirit, and the Spirit against the flesh; and these are contrary to one another, so that you do not do the things that you wish. **Rom. 7:15, 18:** For what I am doing, I do not understand. For what I will to do, that I do not practice; but what I hate, that I do.... For I know that in me (that is, in my flesh) nothing good dwells; for to will is present with me, but *how* to perform what is good I do not find.

[23] **Ps. 76:7:** You, Yourself, *are* to be feared; And who may stand in Your presence When once You are angry? **Ps. 130:3:** If You, LORD, should mark iniquities, O Lord, who could stand? **Ps. 143:2:** Do not enter into judgment with Your servant, For in Your sight no one living is righteous. **Rev. 6:17:** For the great day of His wrath has come, and who is able to stand? **Ezra. 9:15:** O LORD God of Israel, You *are* righteous, for we are left as a remnant, as *it is* this day. Here we *are* before You, in our guilt, though no one can stand before You because of this!

[24] **Eph. 1:6:** ... to the praise of the glory of His grace, by which He made us accepted in the Beloved. **1 Pet. 2:5:** ... you also, as living stones, are being built up a spiritual house, a holy

as though they were in this life wholly unblameable and unreprovable in God's sight;[25] but that He looking upon them in His Son is pleased to accept and reward that which is sincere although accompanied with many weaknesses and imperfections.[26]

7. Works done by unregenerate men, although for the matter of them they may be things which God commands, and of good use, both to themselves and others;[27] yet because they proceed not from a heart purified by faith,[28] nor are done in a right manner according to the word,[29] nor to a right end the glory of God;[30]

---

priesthood, to offer up spiritual sacrifices acceptable to God through Jesus Christ. **See Ex. 28:38; Gen. 4:4; Heb. 11:4.**

[25] **Job 9:20:** Though I were righteous, my own mouth would condemn me; Though I *were* blameless, it would prove me perverse. **Ps. 143:2:** Do not enter into judgment with Your servant, For in Your sight no one living is righteous. **1 John 1:8:** If we say that we have no sin, we deceive ourselves, and the truth is not in us.

[26] **Heb. 13:20-21:** Now may the God of peace who brought up our Lord Jesus from the dead, that great Shepherd of the sheep, through the blood of the everlasting covenant, make you complete in every good work to do His will, working in you what is well pleasing in His sight, through Jesus Christ, to whom *be* glory forever and ever. Amen. **Heb. 6:10:** For God *is* not unjust to forget your work and labor of love which you have shown toward His name, *in that* you have ministered to the saints, and do minister. **2 Cor. 8:12:** For if there is first a willing mind, *it is* accepted according to what one has, *and* not according to what he does not have. **Matt. 25:21, 23:** His lord said to him, 'Well *done,* good and faithful servant; you were faithful over a few things, I will make you ruler over many things. Enter into the joy of your lord.' ... His lord said to him, 'Well *done,* good and faithful servant; you have been faithful over a few things, I will make you ruler over many things. Enter into the joy of your lord.' **1 Cor. 3:14:** If anyone's work which he has built on *it* endures, he will receive a reward. **1 Cor. 4:5:** Therefore judge nothing before the time, until the Lord comes, who will both bring to light the hidden things of darkness and reveal the counsels of the hearts. Then each one's praise will come from God.

[27] **2 Kings 10:30-31:** And the LORD said to Jehu, "Because you have done well in doing *what is* right in My sight, *and* have done to the house of Ahab all that *was* in My heart, your sons shall sit on the throne of Israel to the fourth *generation.*" But Jehu took no heed to walk in the law of the LORD God of Israel with all his heart; for he did not depart from the sins of Jeroboam, who had made Israel sin. **1 Kings 21:27, 29:** So it was, when Ahab heard those words, that he tore his clothes and put sackcloth on his body, and fasted and lay in sackcloth, and went about mourning.... "See how Ahab has humbled himself before Me? Because he has humbled himself before Me, I will not bring the calamity in his days. In the days of his son I will bring the calamity on his house." **Luke 6:32-34:** But if you love those who love you, what credit is that to you? For even sinners love those who love them. And if you do good to those who do good to you, what credit is that to you? For even sinners do the same. And if you lend *to those* from whom you hope to receive back, what credit is that to you? For even sinners lend to sinners to receive as much back. **Luke 18:2-7:** ... saying: "There was in a certain city a judge who did not fear God nor regard man. Now there was a widow in that city; and she came to him, saying, 'Get justice for me from my adversary.' And he would not for a while; but afterward he said within himself, 'Though I do not fear God nor regard man, yet because this widow troubles me I will avenge her, lest by her continual coming she weary me.'" Then the Lord said, "Hear what the unjust judge said. And shall God not avenge His own elect who cry out day and night to Him, though He bears long with them?" **See Rom. 13:4.**

[28] **Gen. 4:5:** ... but He did not respect Cain and his offering. And Cain was very angry, and his countenance fell. **Heb. 11:4, 6:** By faith Abel offered to God a more excellent sacrifice than Cain, through which he obtained witness that he was righteous, God testifying of his gifts; and through it he being dead still speaks.... But without faith *it is* impossible to please *Him,* for he who comes to God must believe that He is, and *that* He is a rewarder of those who diligently seek Him.

[29] **1 Cor. 13:1-3:** Though I speak with the tongues of men and of angels, but have not love, I have become sounding brass or a clanging cymbal. And though I have *the gift of* prophecy, and understand all mysteries and all knowledge, and though I have all faith, so that I could remove mountains, but have not love, I am nothing. And though I bestow all my goods to feed *the poor,*

they are therefore sinful and cannot please God; nor make a man meet to receive grace from God;[31] and yet their neglect of them is more sinful and displeasing to God.[32]

---

and though I give my body to be burned, but have not love, it profits me nothing. **Isa. 1:12:** When you come to appear before Me, Who has required this from your hand, To trample My courts?

[30] **Matt. 6:2, 5, 16:** Therefore, when you do a charitable deed, do not sound a trumpet before you as the hypocrites do in the synagogues and in the streets, that they may have glory from men. Assuredly, I say to you, they have their reward.... And when you pray, you shall not be like the hypocrites. For they love to pray standing in the synagogues and on the corners of the streets, that they may be seen by men. Assuredly, I say to you, they have their reward.... Moreover, when you fast, do not be like the hypocrites, with a sad countenance. For they disfigure their faces that they may appear to men to be fasting. Assuredly, I say to you, they have their reward. **1 Cor. 10:31:** Therefore, whether you eat or drink, or whatever you do, do all to the glory of God.

[31] **Prov. 21:27:** The sacrifice of the wicked *is* an abomination; How much more *when* he brings it with wicked intent! **Hag. 2:14:** Then Haggai answered and said, 'So is this people, and so is this nation before Me,' says the LORD, 'and so is every work of their hands; and what they offer there is unclean.' **Titus 1:15:** To the pure all things are pure, but to those who are defiled and unbelieving nothing is pure; but even their mind and conscience are defiled. **Titus 3:5:** ... not by works of righteousness which we have done, but according to His mercy He saved us, through the washing of regeneration and renewing of the Holy Spirit. **Amos 5:21-22:** I hate, I despise your feast days, And I do not savor your sacred assemblies. Though you offer Me burnt offerings and your grain offerings, I will not accept *them,* Nor will I regard your fattened peace offerings. **Mark 7:6-7:** He answered and said to them, "Well did Isaiah prophesy of you hypocrites, as it is written: 'This people honors Me with *their* lips, But their heart is far from Me. And in vain they worship Me, Teaching *as* doctrines the commandments of men.'" **Hos. 1:4:** Then the LORD said to him: "Call his name Jezreel, For in a little *while* I will avenge the bloodshed of Jezreel on the house of Jehu, And bring an end to the kingdom of the house of Israel." **Rom. 9:16:** So then *it is* not of him who wills, nor of him who runs, but of God who shows mercy.

[32] **Job 21:14-15:** Yet they say to God, 'Depart from us, For we do not desire the knowledge of Your ways. Who *is* the Almighty, that we should serve Him? And what profit do we have if we pray to Him?' **Ps. 14:4:** Have all the workers of iniquity no knowledge, Who eat up my people *as* they eat bread, And do not call on the LORD? **Ps. 36:3:** The words of his mouth *are* wickedness and deceit; He has ceased to be wise *and* to do good. **Matt. 25:41-45:** Then He will also say to those on the left hand, 'Depart from Me, you cursed, into the everlasting fire prepared for the devil and his angels: for I was hungry and you gave Me no food; I was thirsty and you gave Me no drink; I was a stranger and you did not take Me in, naked and you did not clothe Me, sick and in prison and you did not visit Me.' Then they also will answer Him, saying, 'Lord, when did we see You hungry or thirsty or a stranger or naked or sick or in prison, and did not minister to You?' Then He will answer them, saying, 'Assuredly, I say to you, inasmuch as you did not do *it* to one of the least of these, you did not do *it* to Me.' **Matt. 23:23:** Woe to you, scribes and Pharisees, hypocrites! For you pay tithe of mint and anise and cummin, and have neglected the weightier *matters* of the law: justice and mercy and faith. These you ought to have done, without leaving the others undone. **See Rom. 1:21-32.**

CHAPTER 17

Of the Perseverance of the Saints

1. Those whom God hath accepted in the beloved, effectually called and sanctified by His Spirit, and given the precious faith of His elect unto, can neither totally nor finally fall from the state of grace; but shall certainly persevere therein to the end and be eternally saved,[1] seeing the gifts and callings of God are without repentance,[2] (whence He still begets and nourisheth in them faith, repentance, love, joy, hope, and all the graces of the Spirit unto immortality)[3] and though many storms and floods arise and beat against them, yet they shall never be able to take them off that foundation and rock which by faith they are fastened upon:[4]

---

[1] **John 10:28-29:** And I give them eternal life, and they shall never perish; neither shall anyone snatch them out of My hand. My Father, who has given *them* to Me, is greater than all; and no one is able to snatch *them* out of My Father's hand. **Phil. 1:6:** ... being confident of this very thing, that He who has begun a good work in you will complete *it* until the day of Jesus Christ. **2 Pet. 1:10:** Therefore, brethren, be even more diligent to make your call and election sure, for if you do these things you will never stumble. **Rom. 8:28-30:** And we know that all things work together for good to those who love God, to those who are the called according to *His* purpose. For whom He foreknew, He also predestined *to be* conformed to the image of His Son, that He might be the firstborn among many brethren. Moreover whom He predestined, these He also called; whom He called, these He also justified; and whom He justified, these He also glorified. **1 John 3:9:** Whoever has been born of God does not sin, for His seed remains in him; and he cannot sin, because he has been born of God. **1 John 5:18:** We know that whoever is born of God does not sin; but he who has been born of God keeps himself, and the wicked one does not touch him. **1 Pet. 1:5, 9:** ... who are kept by the power of God through faith for salvation ready to be revealed in the last time ... receiving the end of your faith—the salvation of *your* souls. **2 Tim. 2:19:** Nevertheless the solid foundation of God stands, having this seal: "The Lord knows those who are His," and, "Let everyone who names the name of Christ depart from iniquity." **1 John 2:19:** They went out from us, but they were not of us; for if they had been of us, they would have continued with us; but *they went out* that they might be made manifest, that none of them were of us.

[2] **Rom. 11:29:** For the gifts and the calling of God *are* irrevocable.

[3] **Gal. 5:22-25:** But the fruit of the Spirit is love, joy, peace, longsuffering, kindness, goodness, faithfulness, gentleness, self-control. Against such there is no law. And those *who are* Christ's have crucified the flesh with its passions and desires. If we live in the Spirit, let us also walk in the Spirit. **Eph. 5:9:** ... for the fruit of the Spirit *is* in all goodness, righteousness, and truth. **Col. 3:12-16:** Therefore, as *the* elect of God, holy and beloved, put on tender mercies, kindness, humility, meekness, longsuffering; bearing with one another, and forgiving one another, if anyone has a complaint against another; even as Christ forgave you, so you also *must do*. But above all these things put on love, which is the bond of perfection. And let the peace of God rule in your hearts, to which also you were called in one body; and be thankful. Let the word of Christ dwell in you richly in all wisdom, teaching and admonishing one another in psalms and hymns and spiritual songs, singing with grace in your hearts to the Lord.

[4] **Matt. 7:24-25:** Therefore whoever hears these sayings of Mine, and does them, I will liken him to a wise man who built his house on the rock: and the rain descended, the floods came, and the winds blew and beat on that house; and it did not fall, for it was founded on the rock. **John 16:33:** These things I have spoken to you, that in Me you may have peace. In the world you will have tribulation; but be of good cheer, I have overcome the world. **Rom. 5:1-11:** Therefore, having been justified by faith, we have peace with God through our Lord Jesus Christ, through whom also we have access by faith into this grace in which we stand, and rejoice in hope of the glory of God. And not only *that,* but we also glory in tribulations, knowing that tribulation produces perseverance; and perseverance, character; and character, hope. Now hope does not disappoint, because the love of God has been poured out in our hearts by the Holy Spirit who was given to us. For when we were still without strength, in due time Christ died for the ungodly. For scarcely for a righteous man will one die; yet perhaps for a good man someone would even dare to die. But God demonstrates His own love

notwithstanding through unbelief and the temptations of Satan the sensible sight of the light and love of God, may for a time be clouded, and obscured from them,[5] yet He is still the same, and they shall be sure to be kept by the power of God unto salvation,[6] where they shall enjoy their purchased possession, they being engraven upon the palms of His hands, and their names having been written in the book of life from all eternity.[7]

2. This perseverance of the saints depends not upon their own free will;[8] but upon the immutability of the decree of election,[9] flowing from the free and unchangeable love of God the Father;[10]

---

toward us, in that while we were still sinners, Christ died for us. Much more then, having now been justified by His blood, we shall be saved from wrath through Him. For if when we were enemies we were reconciled to God through the death of His Son, much more, having been reconciled, we shall be saved by His life. And not only *that,* but we also rejoice in God through our Lord Jesus Christ, through whom we have now received the reconciliation. **1 Pet. 1:6-7:** In this you greatly rejoice, though now for a little while, if need be, you have been grieved by various trials, that the genuineness of your faith, *being* much more precious than gold that perishes, though it is tested by fire, may be found to praise, honor, and glory at the revelation of Jesus Christ. **Col. 1:23:** ... if indeed you continue in the faith, grounded and steadfast, and are not moved away from the hope of the gospel which you heard, which was preached to every creature under heaven, of which I, Paul, became a minister. **Ps. 62:2, 6-7:** He only *is* my rock and my salvation; *He is* my defense; I shall not be greatly moved.... He only *is* my rock and my salvation; *He is* my defense; I shall not be moved. In God *is* my salvation and my glory; The rock of my strength, *And* my refuge, *is* in God.

[5] **Ps. 51:12:** Restore to me the joy of Your salvation, And uphold me *by Your* generous Spirit. **Luke 22:31, 57-62:** And the Lord said, "Simon, Simon! Indeed, Satan has asked for you, that he may sift *you* as wheat.... But he denied Him, saying, "Woman, I do not know Him." And after a little while another saw him and said, "You also are of them." But Peter said, "Man, I am not!" Then after about an hour had passed, another confidently affirmed, saying, "Surely this *fellow* also was with Him, for he is a Galilean." But Peter said, "Man, I do not know what you are saying!" Immediately, while he was still speaking, the rooster crowed. And the Lord turned and looked at Peter. Then Peter remembered the word of the Lord, how He had said to him, "Before the rooster crows, you will deny Me three times." So Peter went out and wept bitterly. **Job 29:2-6:** Oh, that I were as *in* months past, As *in* the days *when* God watched over me; When His lamp shone upon my head, *And when* by His light I walked *through* darkness; Just as I was in the days of my prime, When the friendly counsel of God *was* over my tent; When the Almighty *was* yet with me, *When* my children *were* around me; When my steps were bathed with cream, And the rock poured out rivers of oil for me!

[6] **Mal. 3:6:** For I *am* the LORD, I do not change; Therefore you are not consumed, O sons of Jacob. **1 Pet. 1:5:** ... who are kept by the power of God through faith for salvation ready to be revealed in the last time. **Luke 22:31-32:** And the Lord said, "Simon, Simon! Indeed, Satan has asked for you, that he may sift *you* as wheat. But I have prayed for you, that your faith should not fail; and when you have returned to *Me,* strengthen your brethren."

[7] **Eph. 1:14:** ... who is the guarantee of our inheritance until the redemption of the purchased possession, to the praise of His glory. **Isa. 49:15-16:** Can a woman forget her nursing child, And not have compassion on the son of her womb? Surely they may forget, Yet I will not forget you. See, I have inscribed you on the palms *of My hands;* Your walls *are* continually before Me. **Rev. 13:8:** All who dwell on the earth will worship him, whose names have not been written in the Book of Life of the Lamb slain from the foundation of the world. **Phil. 4:3:** And I urge you also, true companion, help these women who labored with me in the gospel, with Clement also, and the rest of my fellow workers, whose names *are* in the Book of Life.

[8] **Phil. 2:13:** ... for it is God who works in you both to will and to do for *His* good pleasure. **Rom. 9:16:** So then *it is* not of him who wills, nor of him who runs, but of God who shows mercy.

[9] **Rom. 8:30:** Moreover whom He predestined, these He also called; whom He called, these He also justified; and whom He justified, these He also glorified. **Rom. 9:11, 16:** ... for *the children* not yet being born, nor having done any good or evil, that the purpose of God according to election might stand, not of works but of Him who calls ... So then *it is* not of him who wills, nor of him who runs, but of God who shows mercy.

[10] **Ps. 89:3-4, 28-33:** I have made a covenant with My chosen, I have sworn to My servant David: 'Your seed I will establish forever, And build up your throne to all generations.' *Selah*.... My mercy I

upon the efficacy of the merit and intercession of Jesus Christ and union with Him,[11] the oath of God,[12] the abiding of His Spirit and the seed of God within them,[13] and the nature of the covenant of grace[14] from all which ariseth also the certainty and infallibility thereof.[15]

---

will keep for him forever, And My covenant shall stand firm with him. His seed also I will make *to endure* forever, And his throne as the days of heaven. If his sons forsake My law And do not walk in My judgments, If they break My statutes And do not keep My commandments, Then I will punish their transgression with the rod, And their iniquity with stripes. Nevertheless My lovingkindness I will not utterly take from him, Nor allow My faithfulness to fail. **2 Tim. 2:18-19:** ... who have strayed concerning the truth, saying that the resurrection is already past; and they overthrow the faith of some. Nevertheless the solid foundation of God stands, having this seal: "The Lord knows those who are His," and, "Let everyone who names the name of Christ depart from iniquity." **Jer. 31:3:** The LORD has appeared of old to me, *saying:* "Yes, I have loved you with an everlasting love; Therefore with lovingkindness I have drawn you."

[11] **Heb. 10:10, 14:** By that will we have been sanctified through the offering of the body of Jesus Christ once *for all*.... For by one offering He has perfected forever those who are being sanctified. **Heb. 13:20-21:** Now may the God of peace who brought up our Lord Jesus from the dead, that great Shepherd of the sheep, through the blood of the everlasting covenant, make you complete in every good work to do His will, working in you what is well pleasing in His sight, through Jesus Christ, to whom *be* glory forever and ever. Amen. **Heb. 9:12-15:** Not with the blood of goats and calves, but with His own blood He entered the Most Holy Place once for all, having obtained eternal redemption. For if the blood of bulls and goats and the ashes of a heifer, sprinkling the unclean, sanctifies for the purifying of the flesh, how much more shall the blood of Christ, who through the eternal Spirit offered Himself without spot to God, cleanse your conscience from dead works to serve the living God? And for this reason He is the Mediator of the new covenant, by means of death, for the redemption of the transgressions under the first covenant, that those who are called may receive the promise of the eternal inheritance. **Luke 22:32:** But I have prayed for you, that your faith should not fail; and when you have returned to *Me,* strengthen your brethren. **Heb. 7:25:** Therefore He is also able to save to the uttermost those who come to God through Him, since He always lives to make intercession for them. **Rom. 8:33-39:** Who shall bring a charge against God's elect? *It is* God who justifies. Who *is* he who condemns? *It is* Christ who died, and furthermore is also risen, who is even at the right hand of God, who also makes intercession for us. Who shall separate us from the love of Christ? *Shall* tribulation, or distress, or persecution, or famine, or nakedness, or peril, or sword? As it is written: "For Your sake we are killed all day long; We are accounted as sheep for the slaughter." Yet in all these things we are more than conquerors through Him who loved us. For I am persuaded that neither death nor life, nor angels nor principalities nor powers, nor things present nor things to come, nor height nor depth, nor any other created thing, shall be able to separate us from the love of God which is in Christ Jesus our Lord. **John 17:11, 24:** Now I am no longer in the world, but these are in the world, and I come to You. Holy Father, keep through Your name those whom You have given Me, that they may be one as We *are*.... "Father, I desire that they also whom You gave Me may be with Me where I am, that they may behold My glory which You have given Me; for You loved Me before the foundation of the world.

[12] **Heb. 6:13-18:** For when God made a promise to Abraham, because He could swear by no one greater, He swore by Himself, saying, "Surely blessing I will bless you, and multiplying I will multiply you." And so, after he had patiently endured, he obtained the promise. For men indeed swear by the greater, and an oath for confirmation *is* for them an end of all dispute. Thus God, determining to show more abundantly to the heirs of promise the immutability of His counsel, confirmed *it* by an oath, that by two immutable things, in which it *is* impossible for God to lie, we might have strong consolation, who have fled for refuge to lay hold of the hope set before *us.*

[13] **John 14:16-17:** And I will pray the Father, and He will give you another Helper, that He may abide with you forever—the Spirit of truth, whom the world cannot receive, because it neither sees Him nor knows Him; but you know Him, for He dwells with you and will be in you. **1 John 2:27:** But the anointing which you have received from Him abides in you, and you do not need that anyone teach you; but as the same anointing teaches you concerning all things, and is true, and is not a lie, and just as it has taught you, you will abide in Him. **1 John 3:9:** Whoever has been born of God does not sin, for His seed remains in him; and he cannot sin, because he has been born of God.

[14] **Jer. 31:31-34:** Behold, the days are coming, says the LORD, when I will make a new covenant with the house of Israel and with the house of Judah—not according to the covenant that I made with their fathers in the day *that* I took them by the hand to lead them out of the land of Egypt, My covenant which they broke, though I was a husband to them, says the LORD. But this *is* the covenant that I will make with the house of Israel after those days, says the LORD: I will put My law in their minds, and write it on their hearts; and I will be their God, and they shall be My people. No

3. And though they may, through the temptation of Satan and of the world, the prevalency of corruption remaining in them, and the neglect of the means of their preservation fall into grievous sins,[16] and for a time continue therein;[17] whereby they incur God's displeasure,[18] and grieve His Holy Spirit,[19] come to have

---

more shall every man teach his neighbor, and every man his brother, saying, 'Know the LORD,' for they all shall know Me, from the least of them to the greatest of them, says the LORD. For I will forgive their iniquity, and their sin I will remember no more. **Jer. 32:40:** And I will make an everlasting covenant with them, that I will not turn away from doing them good; but I will put My fear in their hearts so that they will not depart from Me. **Gal. 3:15-18:** Brethren, I speak in the manner of men: Though *it is* only a man's covenant, yet *if it is* confirmed, no one annuls or adds to it. Now to Abraham and his Seed were the promises made. He does not say, "And to seeds," as of many, but as of one, "And to your Seed," who is Christ. And this I say, *that* the law, which was four hundred and thirty years later, cannot annul the covenant that was confirmed before by God in Christ, that it should make the promise of no effect. For if the inheritance *is* of the law, *it is* no longer of promise; but God gave *it* to Abraham by promise. **Isa. 53:10-11:** Yet it pleased the LORD to bruise Him; He has put *Him* to grief. When You make His soul an offering for sin, He shall see *His* seed, He shall prolong *His* days, And the pleasure of the LORD shall prosper in His hand. He shall see the labor of His soul, *and* be satisfied. By His knowledge My righteous Servant shall justify many, For He shall bear their iniquities. **Isa. 59:20-21:** "The Redeemer will come to Zion, And to those who turn from transgression in Jacob," Says the LORD. "As for Me," says the LORD, "this *is* My covenant with them: My Spirit who *is* upon you, and My words which I have put in your mouth, shall not depart from your mouth, nor from the mouth of your descendants, nor from the mouth of your descendants' descendants," says the LORD, "from this time and forevermore."

[15] **John 6:38-40:** For I have come down from heaven, not to do My own will, but the will of Him who sent Me. This is the will of the Father who sent Me, that of all He has given Me I should lose nothing, but should raise it up at the last day. And this is the will of Him who sent Me, that everyone who sees the Son and believes in Him may have everlasting life; and I will raise him up at the last day. **John 10:28:** And I give them eternal life, and they shall never perish; neither shall anyone snatch them out of My hand. **2 Thess. 3:3:** But the Lord is faithful, who will establish you and guard *you* from the evil one. **1 John 2:19:** They went out from us, but they were not of us; for if they had been of us, they would have continued with us; but *they went out* that they might be made manifest, that none of them were of us.

[16] **Ex. 32:21:** And Moses said to Aaron, "What did this people do to you that you have brought *so* great a sin upon them?" **Jonah 1:3, 10:** But Jonah arose to flee to Tarshish from the presence of the LORD. He went down to Joppa, and found a ship going to Tarshish; so he paid the fare, and went down into it, to go with them to Tarshish from the presence of the LORD.... Then the men were exceedingly afraid, and said to him, "Why have you done this?" For the men knew that he fled from the presence of the LORD, because he had told them. **Ps. 51:14:** Deliver me from the guilt of bloodshed, O God, The God of my salvation, *And* my tongue shall sing aloud of Your righteousness. **Matt. 26:70, 72, 74:** But he denied it before *them* all, saying, "I do not know what you are saying." ... But again he denied with an oath, "I do not know the Man!" ... Then he began to curse and swear, *saying,* "I do not know the Man!" Immediately a rooster crowed. **Heb. 12:1:** Therefore we also, since we are surrounded by so great a cloud of witnesses, let us lay aside every weight, and the sin which so easily ensnares *us,* and let us run with endurance the race that is set before us.

[17] **2 Sam. 12:9-13:** Why have you despised the commandment of the LORD, to do evil in His sight? You have killed Uriah the Hittite with the sword; you have taken his wife *to be* your wife, and have killed him with the sword of the people of Ammon. Now therefore, the sword shall never depart from your house, because you have despised Me, and have taken the wife of Uriah the Hittite to be your wife. Thus says the LORD: 'Behold, I will raise up adversity against you from your own house; and I will take your wives before your eyes and give *them* to your neighbor, and he shall lie with your wives in the sight of this sun. For you did *it* secretly, but I will do this thing before all Israel, before the sun.' So David said to Nathan, "I have sinned against the LORD." And Nathan said to David, "The LORD also has put away your sin; you shall not die." **Gal. 2:11-14:** Now when Peter had come to Antioch, I withstood him to his face, because he was to be blamed; for before certain men came from James, he would eat with the Gentiles; but when they came, he withdrew and separated himself, fearing those who were of the circumcision. And the rest of the Jews also played the hypocrite with him, so that even Barnabas was carried away with their hypocrisy. But when I saw that they were not straightforward about the truth of the gospel, I said to Peter before *them* all, "If you, being a Jew, live in the manner of Gentiles and not as the Jews, why do you compel Gentiles to live as Jews?"

[18] **Num. 20:12:** Then the LORD spoke to Moses and Aaron, "Because you did not believe Me, to hallow Me in the eyes of the children of Israel, therefore you shall not bring this assembly into the

their graces and comforts impaired[20] have their hearts hardened,[21] and their consciences wounded,[22] hurt, and scandalize others,[23] and bring temporal judgments upon themselves:[24] yet they shall renew their repentance and be preserved through faith in Christ Jesus to the end.[25]

---

land which I have given them." **2 Sam. 11:27:** And when her mourning was over, David sent and brought her to his house, and she became his wife and bore him a son. But the thing that David had done displeased the LORD. **Isa. 64:7, 9:** And *there is* no one who calls on Your name, Who stirs himself up to take hold of You; For You have hidden Your face from us, And have consumed us because of our iniquities.... Do not be furious, O LORD, Nor remember iniquity forever; Indeed, please look—we all *are* Your people!

[19] **Eph. 4:30:** And do not grieve the Holy Spirit of God, by whom you were sealed for the day of redemption.

[20] **Ps. 51:8, 10, 12:** Make me hear joy and gladness, *That* the bones You have broken may rejoice.... Create in me a clean heart, O God, And renew a steadfast spirit within me.... Restore to me the joy of Your salvation, And uphold me *by Your* generous Spirit. **Matt. 26:75:** And Peter remembered the word of Jesus who had said to him, "Before the rooster crows, you will deny Me three times." So he went out and wept bitterly.

[21] **Isa. 63:17:** O LORD, why have You made us stray from Your ways, *And* hardened our heart from Your fear? Return for Your servants' sake, The tribes of Your inheritance.

[22] **Ps. 32:3-4:** When I kept silent, my bones grew old Through my groaning all the day long. For day and night Your hand was heavy upon me; My vitality was turned into the drought of summer. *Selah*. **Ps. 51:8:** Make me hear joy and gladness,
That the bones You have broken may rejoice.

[23] **Gen. 12:10-20:** Now there was a famine in the land, and Abram went down to Egypt to dwell there, for the famine *was* severe in the land. And it came to pass, when he was close to entering Egypt, that he said to Sarai his wife, "Indeed I know that you *are* a woman of beautiful countenance. Therefore it will happen, when the Egyptians see you, that they will say, 'This *is* his wife'; and they will kill me, but they will let you live. Please say you *are* my sister, that it may be well with me for your sake, and that I may live because of you." So it was, when Abram came into Egypt, that the Egyptians saw the woman, that she *was* very beautiful. The princes of Pharaoh also saw her and commended her to Pharaoh. And the woman was taken to Pharaoh's house. He treated Abram well for her sake. He had sheep, oxen, male donkeys, male and female servants, female donkeys, and camels. But the LORD plagued Pharaoh and his house with great plagues because of Sarai, Abram's wife. And Pharaoh called Abram and said, "What *is* this you have done to me? Why did you not tell me that she *was* your wife? Why did you say, 'She *is* my sister'? I might have taken her as my wife. Now therefore, here is your wife; take *her* and go your way." So Pharaoh commanded *his* men concerning him; and they sent him away, with his wife and all that he had. **2 Sam. 12:14:** However, because by this deed you have given great occasion to the enemies of the LORD to blaspheme, the child also *who is* born to you shall surely die." **Gal. 2:13:** And the rest of the Jews also played the hypocrite with him, so that even Barnabas was carried away with their hypocrisy.

[24] **Ps. 89:31-32:** If they break My statutes And do not keep My commandments, Then I will punish their transgression with the rod, And their iniquity with stripes. **1 Cor. 11:32:** But when we are judged, we are chastened by the Lord, that we may not be condemned with the world.

[25] **Ps. 32:5:** I acknowledged my sin to You, And my iniquity I have not hidden. I said, "I will confess my transgressions to the LORD," And You forgave the iniquity of my sin. *Selah*. **Prov. 28:13:** He who covers his sins will not prosper, But whoever confesses and forsakes *them* will have mercy. **1 Thess. 5:23:** Now may the God of peace Himself sanctify you completely; and may your whole spirit, soul, and body be preserved blameless at the coming of our Lord Jesus Christ. **Jude 1:1:** Jude, a bondservant of Jesus Christ, and brother of James, To those who are called, sanctified by God the Father, and preserved in Jesus Christ. **1 John 1:5-10:** This is the message which we have heard from Him and declare to you, that God is light and in Him is no darkness at all. If we say that we have fellowship with Him, and walk in darkness, we lie and do not practice the truth. But if we walk in the light as He is in the light, we have fellowship with one another, and the blood of Jesus Christ His Son cleanses us from all sin. If we say that we have no sin, we deceive ourselves, and the truth is not in us. If we confess our sins, He is faithful and just to forgive us *our* sins and to cleanse us from all unrighteousness. If we say that we have not sinned, we make Him a liar, and His word is not in us.

CHAPTER 18

Of the Assurance of Grace and Salvation

1. Although temporary believers, and other unregenerate men, may vainly deceive themselves with false hopes, and carnal presumptions, of being in the favour of God, and state of salvation,[1] which hope of theirs shall perish;[2] yet such as truly believe in the Lord Jesus, and love Him in sincerity, endeavouring to walk in all good conscience before Him, may in this life be certainly assured that they are in the state of grace;[3] and may rejoice in the hope of the glory of God which hope shall never make them ashamed.[4]

2. This certainty is not a bare conjectural and probable persuasion, grounded upon a fallible hope;[5] but an infallible assurance of faith, founded on the blood and righteousness of Christ revealed in the gospel;[6] and also upon the inward evidence of those graces of the Spirit unto which promises are

---

[1] **Job 8:13-14:** So *are* the paths of all who forget God; And the hope of the hypocrite shall perish, Whose confidence shall be cut off, And whose trust *is* a spider's web. **Mic. 3:11:** Her heads judge for a bribe, Her priests teach for pay, And her prophets divine for money. Yet they lean on the LORD, and say, "Is not the LORD among us? No harm can come upon us." **Deut. 29:19:** ... and so it may not happen, when he hears the words of this curse, that he blesses himself in his heart, saying, 'I shall have peace, even though I follow the dictates of my heart'—as though the drunkard could be included with the sober. **John 8:41:** You do the deeds of your father. Then they said to Him, "We were not born of fornication; we have one Father—God."

[2] **Amos 9:10:** All the sinners of My people shall die by the sword, Who say, 'The calamity shall not overtake nor confront us.' **Matt. 7:22-23:** Many will say to Me in that day, 'Lord, Lord, have we not prophesied in Your name, cast out demons in Your name, and done many wonders in Your name?' And then I will declare to them, 'I never knew you; depart from Me, you who practice lawlessness!'

[3] **1 John 2:3:** Now by this we know that we know Him, if we keep His commandments. **1 John 3:14, 18-19, 21, 24:** We know that we have passed from death to life, because we love the brethren. He who does not love *his* brother abides in death.... My little children, let us not love in word or in tongue, but in deed and in truth. And by this we know that we are of the truth, and shall assure our hearts before Him.... Beloved, if our heart does not condemn us, we have confidence toward God.... Now he who keeps His commandments abides in Him, and He in him. And by this we know that He abides in us, by the Spirit whom He has given us. **1 John 5:13:** These things I have written to you who believe in the name of the Son of God, that you may know that you have eternal life, and that you may *continue to* believe in the name of the Son of God.

[4] **Rom. 5:2, 5:** ... through whom also we have access by faith into this grace in which we stand, and rejoice in hope of the glory of God.... Now hope does not disappoint, because the love of God has been poured out in our hearts by the Holy Spirit who was given to us.

[5] **Heb. 6:11, 19:** And we desire that each one of you show the same diligence to the full assurance of hope until the end ... This *hope* we have as an anchor of the soul, both sure and steadfast, and which enters the *Presence* behind the veil.

[6] **Heb. 6:17-18:** Thus God, determining to show more abundantly to the heirs of promise the immutability of His counsel, confirmed *it* by an oath, that by two immutable things, in which it *is* impossible for God to lie, we might have strong consolation, who have fled for refuge to lay hold of the hope set before *us*. **Heb. 10:14, 19:** For by one offering He has perfected forever those who are being sanctified.... Therefore, brethren, having boldness to enter the Holiest by the blood of Jesus. **Matt. 16:16-17:** Simon Peter answered and said, "You are the Christ, the Son of the living God." Jesus answered and said to him, "Blessed are you, Simon Bar-Jonah, for flesh and blood has not revealed *this* to you, but My Father who is in heaven."

made,[7] and on the testimony of the Spirit of adoption, witnessing with our spirits that we are the children of God;[8] and as a fruit thereof keeping the heart both humble and holy.[9]

3. This infallible assurance doth not so belong to the essence of faith, but that a true believer, may wait long and conflict with many difficulties before he be partaker of it;[10] yet being enabled by the Spirit to know the things which are freely given him of God, he may without extraordinary revelation in the right use of means attain thereunto:[11] and therefore it is the duty of every

---

[7] **2 Pet. 1:4-11:** ... by which have been given to us exceedingly great and precious promises, that through these you may be partakers of the divine nature, having escaped the corruption *that is* in the world through lust. But also for this very reason, giving all diligence, add to your faith virtue, to virtue knowledge, to knowledge self-control, to self-control perseverance, to perseverance godliness, to godliness brotherly kindness, and to brotherly kindness love. For if these things are yours and abound, *you* will be neither barren nor unfruitful in the knowledge of our Lord Jesus Christ. For he who lacks these things is shortsighted, even to blindness, and has forgotten that he was cleansed from his old sins. Therefore, brethren, be even more diligent to make your call and election sure, for if you do these things you will never stumble; for so an entrance will be supplied to you abundantly into the everlasting kingdom of our Lord and Savior Jesus Christ. **1 John 2:3**: Now by this we know that we know Him, if we keep His commandments. **1 John 3:14:** We know that we have passed from death to life, because we love the brethren. He who does not love *his* brother abides in death. **2 Cor. 1:12:** For our boasting is this: the testimony of our conscience that we conducted ourselves in the world in simplicity and godly sincerity, not with fleshly wisdom but by the grace of God, and more abundantly toward you.

[8] **Rom. 8:15-16:** For you did not receive the spirit of bondage again to fear, but you received the Spirit of adoption by whom we cry out, "Abba, Father." The Spirit Himself bears witness with our spirit that we are children of God. **1 John 3:1-3:** Behold what manner of love the Father has bestowed on us, that we should be called children of God! Therefore the world does not know us, because it did not know Him. Beloved, now we are children of God; and it has not yet been revealed what we shall be, but we know that when He is revealed, we shall be like Him, for we shall see Him as He is. And everyone who has this hope in Him purifies himself, just as He is pure.

[9] **Matt. 5:9:** Blessed *are* the peacemakers, For they shall be called sons of God. **Rom. 8:23:** Not only *that,* but we also who have the firstfruits of the Spirit, even we ourselves groan within ourselves, eagerly waiting for the adoption, the redemption of our body. **Luke 6:35-36:** But love your enemies, do good, and lend, hoping for nothing in return; and your reward will be great, and you will be sons of the Most High. For He is kind to the unthankful and evil. Therefore be merciful, just as your Father also is merciful.

[10] **Isa. 50:10:** Who among you fears the LORD? Who obeys the voice of His Servant? Who walks in darkness And has no light? Let him trust in the name of the LORD And rely upon his God. **Ps. 88:** O LORD, God of my salvation, I have cried out day and night before You. Let my prayer come before You; Incline Your ear to my cry. For my soul is full of troubles, And my life draws near to the grave.... You have laid me in the lowest pit, In darkness, in the depths. Your wrath lies heavy upon me, And You have afflicted *me* with all Your waves.... My eye wastes away because of affliction. LORD, I have called daily upon You; I have stretched out my hands to You. Will You work wonders for the dead? Shall the dead arise *and* praise You?... But to You I have cried out, O LORD, And in the morning my prayer comes before You. LORD, why do You cast off my soul? *Why* do You hide Your face from me? I *have been* afflicted and ready to die from *my* youth; I suffer Your terrors; I am distraught. **Ps. 77:1-12:** I cried out to God with my voice—To God with my voice; And He gave ear to me. In the day of my trouble I sought the Lord ... Will the Lord cast off forever? And will He be favorable no more? Has His mercy ceased forever? Has *His* promise failed forevermore? Has God forgotten to be gracious? Has He in anger shut up His tender mercies? *Selah*. And I said, "This *is* my anguish; *But I will remember* the years of the right hand of the Most High." I will remember the works of the LORD; Surely I will remember Your wonders of old. I will also meditate on all Your work, And talk of Your deeds.

[11] **1 Cor. 2:12:** Now we have received, not the spirit of the world, but the Spirit who is from God, that we might know the things that have been freely given to us by God. **1 John 4:13:** By this we know that we abide in Him, and He in us, because He has given us of His Spirit. **Heb. 6:11-12:** And we desire that each one of you show the same diligence to the full assurance of hope until the end,

one, to give all diligence to make their calling and election sure,[12] that thereby his heart may be enlarged in peace and joy in the Holy Spirit, in love and thankfulness to God, and in strength and cheerfulness in the duties of obedience, the proper fruits of this assurance;[13] so far is it from inclining men to looseness.[14]

4. True believers may have the assurance of their salvation divers ways shaken, diminished, and intermitted; as by negligence in preserving of it, by falling into some special sin, which woundeth the conscience, and grieveth the Spirit, by some sudden or vehement temptation, by God's withdrawing the light

---

that you do not become sluggish, but imitate those who through faith and patience inherit the promises. **Eph. 3:17-18:** ... that Christ may dwell in your hearts through faith; that you, being rooted and grounded in love, may be able to comprehend with all the saints what *is* the width and length and depth and height.

[12] **2 Pet. 1:10:** Therefore, brethren, be even more diligent to make your call and election sure, for if you do these things you will never stumble. **2 Pet. 3:17:** You therefore, beloved, since you know *this* beforehand, beware lest you also fall from your own steadfastness, being led away with the error of the wicked. **Heb. 2:1-4:** Therefore we must give the more earnest heed to the things we have heard, lest we drift away. For if the word spoken through angels proved steadfast, and every transgression and disobedience received a just reward, how shall we escape if we neglect so great a salvation, which at the first began to be spoken by the Lord, and was confirmed to us by those who heard *Him,* God also bearing witness both with signs and wonders, with various miracles, and gifts of the Holy Spirit, according to His own will? **Heb. 3:12-14:** Beware, brethren, lest there be in any of you an evil heart of unbelief in departing from the living God; but exhort one another daily, while it is called "Today," lest any of you be hardened through the deceitfulness of sin. For we have become partakers of Christ if we hold the beginning of our confidence steadfast to the end.

[13] **Rom. 5:1-2, 5:** Therefore, having been justified by faith, we have peace with God through our Lord Jesus Christ, through whom also we have access by faith into this grace in which we stand, and rejoice in hope of the glory of God.... Now hope does not disappoint, because the love of God has been poured out in our hearts by the Holy Spirit who was given to us. **Rom. 14:17:** ... for the kingdom of God is not eating and drinking, but righteousness and peace and joy in the Holy Spirit. **Rom. 15:13:** Now may the God of hope fill you with all joy and peace in believing, that you may abound in hope by the power of the Holy Spirit. **Eph. 1:3-4:** Blessed *be* the God and Father of our Lord Jesus Christ, who has blessed us with every spiritual blessing in the heavenly *places* in Christ, just as He chose us in Him before the foundation of the world, that we should be holy and without blame before Him in love. **Ps. 4:6-7:** *There are* many who say, "Who will show us *any* good?" LORD, lift up the light of Your countenance upon us. You have put gladness in my heart, More than in the season that their grain and wine increased. **Ps. 119:32:** I will run the course of Your commandments, For You shall enlarge my heart.

[14] **1 John 1:6-7:** If we say that we have fellowship with Him, and walk in darkness, we lie and do not practice the truth. But if we walk in the light as He is in the light, we have fellowship with one another, and the blood of Jesus Christ His Son cleanses us from all sin. **1 John 2:1-2:** My little children, these things I write to you, so that you may not sin. And if anyone sins, we have an Advocate with the Father, Jesus Christ the righteous. And He Himself is the propitiation for our sins, and not for ours only but also for the whole world. **1 John 3:2-3:** Beloved, now we are children of God; and it has not yet been revealed what we shall be, but we know that when He is revealed, we shall be like Him, for we shall see Him as He is. And everyone who has this hope in Him purifies himself, just as He is pure. **Rom. 6:1-2:** What shall we say then? Shall we continue in sin that grace may abound? Certainly not! How shall we who died to sin live any longer in it? **Rom. 8:1, 12:** *There is* therefore now no condemnation to those who are in Christ Jesus, who do not walk according to the flesh, but according to the Spirit.... Therefore, brethren, we are debtors—not to the flesh, to live according to the flesh. **Titus 2:11-12, 14:** For the grace of God that brings salvation has appeared to all men, teaching us that, denying ungodliness and worldly lusts, we should live soberly, righteously, and godly in the present age ... who gave Himself for us, that He might redeem us from every lawless deed and purify for Himself *His* own special people, zealous for good works. **2 Cor. 7:1:** Therefore, having these promises, beloved, let us cleanse ourselves from all filthiness of the flesh and spirit, perfecting holiness in the fear of God.

of His countenance, and suffering even such as fear Him to walk in darkness and to have no light;[15] yet are they never destitute of the seed of God, and life of faith, that love of Christ, and the brethren, that sincerity of heart, and conscience of duty, out of which by the operation of the Spirit, this assurance may in due time be revived:[16] and by the which in the meantime they are preserved from utter despair.[17]

---

[15] **Song 5:2-3, 6:** I sleep, but my heart is awake; *It is* the voice of my beloved! He knocks, *saying,* "Open for me, my sister, my love, My dove, my perfect one; For my head is covered with dew, My locks with the drops of the night." I have taken off my robe; How can I put it on *again?* I have washed my feet; How can I defile them?... I opened for my beloved, But my beloved had turned away *and* was gone. My heart leaped up when he spoke. I sought him, but I could not find him; I called him, but he gave me no answer. **Ps. 51:8, 12, 14:** Make me hear joy and gladness, *That* the bones You have broken may rejoice.... Restore to me the joy of Your salvation, And uphold me *by Your* generous Spirit.... Deliver me from the guilt of bloodshed, O God, The God of my salvation, *And* my tongue shall sing aloud of Your righteousness. **Eph. 4:30-31:** And do not grieve the Holy Spirit of God, by whom you were sealed for the day of redemption. Let all bitterness, wrath, anger, clamor, and evil speaking be put away from you, with all malice. **Ps. 31:22:** For I said in my haste, "I am cut off from before Your eyes"; Nevertheless You heard the voice of my supplications When I cried out to You. **Ps. 77:1-10:** I cried out to God with my voice—To God with my voice; And He gave ear to me. In the day of my trouble I sought the Lord; My hand was stretched out in the night without ceasing; My soul refused to be comforted. I remembered God, and was troubled; I complained, and my spirit was overwhelmed. *Selah.* You hold my eyelids *open;* I am so troubled that I cannot speak. I have considered the days of old, The years of ancient times. I call to remembrance my song in the night; I meditate within my heart, And my spirit makes diligent search. Will the Lord cast off forever? And will He be favorable no more? Has His mercy ceased forever? Has *His* promise failed forevermore? Has God forgotten to be gracious? Has He in anger shut up His tender mercies? *Selah.* And I said, "This *is* my anguish; *But I will remember* the years of the right hand of the Most High." **Cf. Matt. 26:69-72 and Luke 22:31-34.**

[16] **1 John 3:9:** Whoever has been born of God does not sin, for His seed remains in him; and he cannot sin, because he has been born of God. **Luke 22:32:** But I have prayed for you, that your faith should not fail; and when you have returned to *Me,* strengthen your brethren." **Ps. 51:8, 12:** Make me hear joy and gladness, *That* the bones You have broken may rejoice.... Restore to me the joy of Your salvation, And uphold me *by Your* generous Spirit. **See Ps. 73:15.**

[17] **Mic. 7:7-9:** Therefore I will look to the LORD; I will wait for the God of my salvation; My God will hear me. Do not rejoice over me, my enemy; When I fall, I will arise; When I sit in darkness, The LORD *will be* a light to me. I will bear the indignation of the LORD, Because I have sinned against Him, Until He pleads my case And executes justice for me. He will bring me forth to the light; I will see His righteousness. **Jer. 32:40:** And I will make an everlasting covenant with them, that I will not turn away from doing them good; but I will put My fear in their hearts so that they will not depart from Me. **Isa. 54:7-14:** "For a mere moment I have forsaken you, But with great mercies I will gather you. With a little wrath I hid My face from you for a moment; But with everlasting kindness I will have mercy on you," Says the LORD, your Redeemer. "For this *is* like the waters of Noah to Me; For as I have sworn That the waters of Noah would no longer cover the earth, So have I sworn That I would not be angry with you, nor rebuke you. For the mountains shall depart And the hills be removed, But My kindness shall not depart from you, Nor shall My covenant of peace be removed," Says the LORD, who has mercy on you. O you afflicted one, Tossed with tempest, *and* not comforted, Behold, I will lay your stones with colorful gems, And lay your foundations with sapphires. I will make your pinnacles of rubies, Your gates of crystal, And all your walls of precious stones. All your children *shall be* taught by the LORD, And great *shall be* the peace of your children. In righteousness you shall be established; You shall be far from oppression, for you shall not fear; And from terror, for it shall not come near you. **2 Cor. 4:8-10:** *We are* hard-pressed on every side, yet not crushed; *we are* perplexed, but not in despair; persecuted, but not forsaken; struck down, but not destroyed—always carrying about in the body the dying of the Lord Jesus, that the life of Jesus also may be manifested in our body.

CHAPTER 19
Of the Law of God

1. God gave to Adam a law of universal obedience, written in his heart,[1] and a particular precept of not eating the fruit of the tree of knowledge of good and evil;[2] by which He bound him, and all his posterity to personal, entire, exact, and perpetual obedience; promised[3] continual life upon the fulfilling,[4] and threatened death upon the breach of it,[5] and endued him with power and ability to keep it.[6]

---

[1] **Gen. 1:27:** So God created man in His *own* image; in the image of God He created him; male and female He created them. **Eccl. 7:29:** Truly, this only I have found: That God made man upright, But they have sought out many schemes. **Rom. 2:14-15:** ... for when Gentiles, who do not have the law, by nature do the things in the law, these, although not having the law, are a law to themselves, who show the work of the law written in their hearts, their conscience also bearing witness, and between themselves *their* thoughts accusing or else excusing *them*.

[2] **Gen. 2:16-17:** And the LORD God commanded the man, saying, "Of every tree of the garden you may freely eat; but of the tree of the knowledge of good and evil you shall not eat, for in the day that you eat of it you shall surely die."

[3] **Rom. 10:5:** For Moses writes about the righteousness which is of the law, "The man who does those things shall live by them." **Rom. 5:12-21:** Therefore, just as through one man sin entered the world, and death through sin, and thus death spread to all men, because all sinned—(For until the law sin was in the world, but sin is not imputed when there is no law. Nevertheless death reigned from Adam to Moses, even over those who had not sinned according to the likeness of the transgression of Adam, who is a type of Him who was to come. But the free gift *is* not like the offense. For if by the one man's offense many died, much more the grace of God and the gift by the grace of the one Man, Jesus Christ, abounded to many. And the gift *is* not like *that which came* through the one who sinned. For the judgment *which came* from one *offense resulted* in condemnation, but the free gift *which came* from many offenses *resulted* in justification. For if by the one man's offense death reigned through the one, much more those who receive abundance of grace and of the gift of righteousness will reign in life through the One, Jesus Christ.) Therefore, as through one man's offense *judgment came* to all men, resulting in condemnation, even so through one Man's righteous act *the free gift came* to all men, resulting in justification of life. For as by one man's disobedience many were made sinners, so also by one Man's obedience many will be made righteous. Moreover the law entered that the offense might abound. But where sin abounded, grace abounded much more, so that as sin reigned in death, even so grace might reign through righteousness to eternal life through Jesus Christ our Lord.

[4] **Gen. 2:16:** And the LORD God commanded the man, saying, "Of every tree of the garden you may freely eat. **Gen. 1:28:** Then God blessed them, and God said to them, "Be fruitful and multiply; fill the earth and subdue it; have dominion over the fish of the sea, over the birds of the air, and over every living thing that moves on the earth." **Gen. 2:1-3:** Thus the heavens and the earth, and all the host of them, were finished. And on the seventh day God ended His work which He had done, and He rested on the seventh day from all His work which He had done. Then God blessed the seventh day and sanctified it, because in it He rested from all His work which God had created and made. **Gen. 3:22:** Then the LORD God said, "Behold, the man has become like one of Us, to know good and evil. And now, lest he put out his hand and take also of the tree of life, and eat, and live forever"—

[5] **Gen. 2:17:** ... but of the tree of the knowledge of good and evil you shall not eat, for in the day that you eat of it you shall surely die.

[6] **Gen. 1:26:** Then God said, "Let Us make man in Our image, according to Our likeness; let them have dominion over the fish of the sea, over the birds of the air, and over the cattle, over all the earth and over every creeping thing that creeps on the earth." **Eccl. 7:29:** Truly, this only I have found: That God made man upright, But they have sought out many schemes.

2. The same law that was first written in the heart of man, continued to be a perfect rule of righteousness after the fall;[7] and was delivered by God upon Mount Sinai, in ten commandments and written in two tables;[8] the four first containing our duty towards God,[9] and the other six our duty to man.[10]

3. Besides this law commonly called moral, God was pleased to give to the people of Israel ceremonial laws, containing several typical ordinances, partly of worship, prefiguring Christ, His

---

[7] **James 1:25:** But he who looks into the perfect law of liberty and continues *in it,* and is not a forgetful hearer but a doer of the work, this one will be blessed in what he does. **James 2:8-12:** If you really fulfill *the* royal law according to the Scripture, "You shall love your neighbor as yourself," you do well; but if you show partiality, you commit sin, and are convicted by the law as transgressors. For whoever shall keep the whole law, and yet stumble in one *point,* he is guilty of all. For He who said, "Do not commit adultery," also said, "Do not murder." Now if you do not commit adultery, but you do murder, you have become a transgressor of the law. So speak and so do as those who will be judged by the law of liberty. **Rom. 2:14-15:** ... for when Gentiles, who do not have the law, by nature do the things in the law, these, although not having the law, are a law to themselves, who show the work of the law written in their hearts, their conscience also bearing witness, and between themselves *their* thoughts accusing or else excusing *them.* **Rom. 3:19:** Now we know that whatever the law says, it says to those who are under the law, that every mouth may be stopped, and all the world may become guilty before God. **Deut. 5:32:** Therefore you shall be careful to do as the LORD your God has commanded you; you shall not turn aside to the right hand or to the left.

[8] **Ex. 32:15-16:** And Moses turned and went down from the mountain, and the two tablets of the Testimony *were* in his hand. The tablets *were* written on both sides; on the one *side* and on the other they were written. Now the tablets *were* the work of God, and the writing *was* the writing of God engraved on the tablets. **Ex. 34:4, 28:** So he cut two tablets of stone like the first *ones.* Then Moses rose early in the morning and went up Mount Sinai, as the LORD had commanded him; and he took in his hand the two tablets of stone.... So he was there with the LORD forty days and forty nights; he neither ate bread nor drank water. And He wrote on the tablets the words of the covenant, the Ten Commandments. **Deut. 10:4:** And He wrote on the tablets according to the first writing, the Ten Commandments, which the LORD had spoken to you in the mountain from the midst of the fire in the day of the assembly; and the LORD gave them to me.

[9] **Ex. 20:3-11:** "You shall have no other gods before Me. "You shall not make for yourself a carved image—any likeness *of anything* that *is* in heaven above, or that *is* in the earth beneath, or that *is* in the water under the earth; you shall not bow down to them nor serve them. For I, the LORD your God, *am* a jealous God, visiting the iniquity of the fathers upon the children to the third and fourth *generations* of those who hate Me, but showing mercy to thousands, to those who love Me and keep My commandments. "You shall not take the name of the LORD your God in vain, for the LORD will not hold *him* guiltless who takes His name in vain. "Remember the Sabbath day, to keep it holy. Six days you shall labor and do all your work, but the seventh day *is* the Sabbath of the LORD your God. *In it* you shall do no work: you, nor your son, nor your daughter, nor your male servant, nor your female servant, nor your cattle, nor your stranger who *is* within your gates. For *in* six days the LORD made the heavens and the earth, the sea, and all that *is* in them, and rested the seventh day. Therefore the LORD blessed the Sabbath day and hallowed it." **Matt. 22:37-38:** Jesus said to him, "'You shall love the LORD your God with all your heart, with all your soul, and with all your mind.' This is *the* first and great commandment."

[10] **Ex. 20:12-17:** "Honor your father and your mother, that your days may be long upon the land which the LORD your God is giving you. "You shall not murder. "You shall not commit adultery. "You shall not steal. "You shall not bear false witness against your neighbor. "You shall not covet your neighbor's house; you shall not covet your neighbor's wife, nor his male servant, nor his female servant, nor his ox, nor his donkey, nor anything that *is* your neighbor's." **Matt. 22:39-40:** And *the* second *is* like it: 'You shall love your neighbor as yourself.' On these two commandments hang all the Law and the Prophets." **Rom. 13:8-9:** Owe no one anything except to love one another, for he who loves another has fulfilled the law. For the commandments, "You shall not commit adultery," "You shall not murder," "You shall not steal," "You shall not bear false witness," "You shall not covet," and if *there is* any other commandment, are *all* summed up in this saying, namely, "You shall love your neighbor as yourself." **James 2:8:** If you really fulfill *the* royal law according to the Scripture, "You shall love your neighbor as yourself," you do well.

graces, actions, sufferings, and benefits;[11] and partly holding forth divers instructions of moral duties,[12] all which ceremonial laws being appointed only to the time of reformation, are by Jesus Christ the true Messiah and only Lawgiver, who was furnished with power from the Father, for that end, abrogated and taken away.[13]

---

[11] **Heb. 10:1:** For the law, having a shadow of the good things to come, *and* not the very image of the things, can never with these same sacrifices, which they offer continually year by year, make those who approach perfect. **Gal. 4:1-3:** Now I say *that* the heir, as long as he is a child, does not differ at all from a slave, though he is master of all, but is under guardians and stewards until the time appointed by the father. Even so we, when we were children, were in bondage under the elements of the world. **Col. 2:17:** ... which are a shadow of things to come, but the substance is of Christ. **Heb. 9:** Then indeed, even the first *covenant* had ordinances of divine service and the earthly sanctuary. For a tabernacle was prepared: the first *part,* in which *was* the lampstand, the table, and the showbread, which is called the sanctuary; and behind the second veil, the part of the tabernacle which is called the Holiest of All ... Now when these things had been thus prepared, the priests always went into the first part of the tabernacle, performing the services. But into the second part the high priest *went* alone once a year, not without blood, which he offered for himself and *for* the people's sins *committed* in ignorance; the Holy Spirit indicating this, that the way into the Holiest of All was not yet made manifest while the first tabernacle was still standing. It *was* symbolic for the present time in which both gifts and sacrifices are offered which cannot make him who performed the service perfect in regard to the conscience—*concerned* only with foods and drinks, various washings, and fleshly ordinances imposed until the time of reformation. But Christ came *as* High Priest of the good things to come, with the greater and more perfect tabernacle not made with hands, that is, not of this creation. Not with the blood of goats and calves, but with His own blood He entered the Most Holy Place once for all, having obtained eternal redemption.... Therefore *it was* necessary that the copies of the things in the heavens should be purified with these, but the heavenly things themselves with better sacrifices than these. For Christ has not entered the holy places made with hands, *which are* copies of the true, but into heaven itself, now to appear in the presence of God for us.

[12] **Lev. 19:9-10, 19, 23, 27:** 'When you reap the harvest of your land, you shall not wholly reap the corners of your field, nor shall you gather the gleanings of your harvest. And you shall not glean your vineyard, nor shall you gather *every* grape of your vineyard; you shall leave them for the poor and the stranger: I *am* the LORD your God.... 'You shall keep My statutes. You shall not let your livestock breed with another kind. You shall not sow your field with mixed seed. Nor shall a garment of mixed linen and wool come upon you.... 'When you come into the land, and have planted all kinds of trees for food, then you shall count their fruit as uncircumcised. Three years it shall be as uncircumcised to you. *It* shall not be eaten.... You shall not shave around the sides of your head, nor shall you disfigure the edges of your beard.' **Deut. 24:19-21:** When you reap your harvest in your field, and forget a sheaf in the field, you shall not go back to get it; it shall be for the stranger, the fatherless, and the widow, that the LORD your God may bless you in all the work of your hands. When you beat your olive trees, you shall not go over the boughs again; it shall be for the stranger, the fatherless, and the widow. When you gather the grapes of your vineyard, you shall not glean *it* afterward; it shall be for the stranger, the fatherless, and the widow. **See 1 Cor. 5:7; 2 Cor. 6:17; Jude 23.**

[13] **Col. 2:14, 16-17:** ... having wiped out the handwriting of requirements that was against us, which was contrary to us. And He has taken it out of the way, having nailed it to the cross.... So let no one judge you in food or in drink, or regarding a festival or a new moon or sabbaths, which are a shadow of things to come, but the substance is of Christ. **Dan. 9:27:** Then he shall confirm a covenant with many for one week; But in the middle of the week He shall bring an end to sacrifice and offering. And on the wing of abominations shall be one who makes desolate, Even until the consummation, which is determined, Is poured out on the desolate. **Eph. 2:14-16:** For He Himself is our peace, who has made both one, and has broken down the middle wall of separation, having abolished in His flesh the enmity, *that is,* the law of commandments *contained* in ordinances, so as to create in Himself one new man *from* the two, *thus* making peace, and that He might reconcile them both to God in one body through the cross, thereby putting to death the enmity. **Heb. 9:10:** ... *concerned* only with foods and drinks, various washings, and fleshly ordinances imposed until the time of reformation. **Acts 10:9-16:** The next day, as they went on their journey and drew near the city, Peter went up on the housetop to pray, about the sixth hour. Then he became very hungry and wanted to eat; but while they made ready, he fell into a trance and saw heaven opened and an object like a great sheet bound at the four corners, descending to him and let down to the earth. In it were all kinds of four-footed animals of the earth, wild beasts, creeping things, and birds of the

4. To them also He gave sundry judicial laws,[14] which expired together with the state of that people, not obliging any now by virtue of that institution; their general equity only, being of moral use.[15]

---

air. And a voice came to him, "Rise, Peter; kill and eat." But Peter said, "Not so, Lord! For I have never eaten anything common or unclean." And a voice *spoke* to him again the second time, "What God has cleansed you must not call common." This was done three times. And the object was taken up into heaven again. **Acts 11:2-10:** And when Peter came up to Jerusalem, those of the circumcision contended with him, saying, "You went in to uncircumcised men and ate with them!" But Peter explained *it* to them in order from the beginning, saying: "I was in the city of Joppa praying; and in a trance I saw a vision, an object descending like a great sheet, let down from heaven by four corners; and it came to me. When I observed it intently and considered, I saw four-footed animals of the earth, wild beasts, creeping things, and birds of the air. And I heard a voice saying to me, 'Rise, Peter; kill and eat.' But I said, 'Not so, Lord! For nothing common or unclean has at any time entered my mouth.' But the voice answered me again from heaven, 'What God has cleansed you must not call common.' Now this was done three times, and all were drawn up again into heaven."

[14] **Ex. 21:1-23:19:** Now these *are* the judgments which you shall set before them: If you buy a Hebrew servant, he shall serve six years; and in the seventh he shall go out free and pay nothing.... He who strikes a man so that he dies shall surely be put to death.... And he who curses his father or his mother shall surely be put to death.... If an ox gores a man or a woman to death, then the ox shall surely be stoned, and its flesh shall not be eaten; but the owner of the ox *shall be* acquitted.... If a man steals an ox or a sheep, and slaughters it or sells it, he shall restore five oxen for an ox and four sheep for a sheep.... If a man entices a virgin who is not betrothed, and lies with her, he shall surely pay the bride-price for her *to be* his wife.... "You shall not permit a sorceress to live.... "You shall not afflict any widow or fatherless child.... "And you shall be holy men to Me: you shall not eat meat torn *by beasts* in the field; you shall throw it to the dogs. "You shall not circulate a false report. Do not put your hand with the wicked to be an unrighteous witness.... "Three times you shall keep a feast to Me in the year ... The first of the firstfruits of your land you shall bring into the house of the LORD your God. You shall not boil a young goat in its mother's milk." **1 Cor. 9:8-10:** Do I say these things as a *mere* man? Or does not the law say the same also? For it is written in the law of Moses, "You shall not muzzle an ox while it treads out the grain." Is it oxen God is concerned about? Or does He say *it* altogether for our sakes? For our sakes, no doubt, *this* is written, that he who plows should plow in hope, and he who threshes in hope should be partaker of his hope.

[15] **Gen. 49:10:** The scepter shall not depart from Judah, Nor a lawgiver from between his feet, Until Shiloh comes; And to Him *shall be* the obedience of the people. **Luke 21:20-24:** But when you see Jerusalem surrounded by armies, then know that its desolation is near. Then let those who are in Judea flee to the mountains, let those who are in the midst of her depart, and let not those who are in the country enter her. For these are the days of vengeance, that all things which are written may be fulfilled. But woe to those who are pregnant and to those who are nursing babies in those days! For there will be great distress in the land and wrath upon this people. And they will fall by the edge of the sword, and be led away captive into all nations. And Jerusalem will be trampled by Gentiles until the times of the Gentiles are fulfilled. **2 Cor. 3:8-11:** ... how will the ministry of the Spirit not be more glorious? For if the ministry of condemnation *had* glory, the ministry of righteousness exceeds much more in glory. For even what was made glorious had no glory in this respect, because of the glory that excels. For if what is passing away *was* glorious, what remains *is* much more glorious. **Heb. 3:1-6:** Therefore, holy brethren, partakers of the heavenly calling, consider the Apostle and High Priest of our confession, Christ Jesus, who was faithful to Him who appointed Him, as Moses also *was faithful* in all His house. For this One has been counted worthy of more glory than Moses, inasmuch as He who built the house has more honor than the house. For every house is built by someone, but He who built all things *is* God. And Moses indeed *was* faithful in all His house as a servant, for a testimony of those things which would be spoken *afterward,* but Christ as a Son over His own house, whose house we are if we hold fast the confidence and the rejoicing of the hope firm to the end. **Col. 2:16-23:** So let no one judge you in food or in drink, or regarding a festival or a new moon or sabbaths, which are a shadow of things to come, but the substance is of Christ. Let no one cheat you of your reward, taking delight in *false* humility and worship of angels, intruding into those things which he has not seen, vainly puffed up by his fleshly mind, and not holding fast to the Head, from whom all the body, nourished and knit together by joints and ligaments, grows with the increase *that is* from God. Therefore, if you died with Christ from the basic principles of the world, why, as *though* living in the world, do you subject yourselves to regulations—"Do not touch, do not taste, do not handle," which all concern things which perish with the using—according to the

5. The moral law doth forever bind all, as well justified persons as others, to the obedience thereof,[16] and that not only in regard of the matter contained in it, but also in respect of the authority of God the Creator, who gave it:[17] neither doth Christ in the gospel any way dissolve, but much strengthen this obligation.[18]

6. Although true believers be not under the law, as a covenant of works, to be thereby justified or condemned;[19] yet it is of great

---

commandments and doctrines of men? These things indeed have an appearance of wisdom in self-imposed religion, *false* humility, and neglect of the body, *but are* of no value against the indulgence of the flesh.

[16] **Rom. 13:8-10:** Owe no one anything except to love one another, for he who loves another has fulfilled the law. For the commandments, "You shall not commit adultery," "You shall not murder," "You shall not steal," "You shall not bear false witness," "You shall not covet," and if *there is* any other commandment, are *all* summed up in this saying, namely, "You shall love your neighbor as yourself." Love does no harm to a neighbor; therefore love *is* the fulfillment of the law. **Rom. 3:31:** Do we then make void the law through faith? Certainly not! On the contrary, we establish the law. **Rom. 7:25:** I thank God—through Jesus Christ our Lord! So then, with the mind I myself serve the law of God, but with the flesh the law of sin. **1 Cor. 9:21:** ... to those *who are* without law, as without law (not being without law toward God, but under law toward Christ), that I might win those *who are* without law. **Gal. 5:14:** For all the law is fulfilled in one word, *even* in this: "You shall love your neighbor as yourself." **Eph. 6:2-3:** "Honor your father and mother," which is the first commandment with promise: "that it may be well with you and you may live long on the earth." **1 John 2:3-4, 7:** Now by this we know that we know Him, if we keep His commandments. He who says, "I know Him," and does not keep His commandments, is a liar, and the truth is not in him.... Brethren, I write no new commandment to you, but an old commandment which you have had from the beginning. The old commandment is the word which you heard from the beginning. **Cf. Rom. 3:20; Rom. 7:7-8 and 1 John 3:4 with Rom. 6:15.**

[17] **Deut. 6:4-5:** Hear, O Israel: The LORD our God, the LORD *is* one! You shall love the LORD your God with all your heart, with all your soul, and with all your strength. **Ex. 20:11:** For *in* six days the LORD made the heavens and the earth, the sea, and all that *is* in them, and rested the seventh day. Therefore the LORD blessed the Sabbath day and hallowed it. **Rom. 3:19:** Now we know that whatever the law says, it says to those who are under the law, that every mouth may be stopped, and all the world may become guilty before God. **James 2:8-12:** If you really fulfill *the* royal law according to the Scripture, "You shall love your neighbor as yourself," you do well; but if you show partiality, you commit sin, and are convicted by the law as transgressors. For whoever shall keep the whole law, and yet stumble in one *point,* he is guilty of all. For He who said, "Do not commit adultery," also said, "Do not murder." Now if you do not commit adultery, but you do murder, you have become a transgressor of the law. So speak and so do as those who will be judged by the law of liberty. **Matt. 19:4-6:** And He answered and said to them, "Have you not read that He who made *them* at the beginning 'made them male and female,' and said, 'For this reason a man shall leave his father and mother and be joined to his wife, and the two shall become one flesh'? So then, they are no longer two but one flesh. Therefore what God has joined together, let not man separate." **Gen. 17:1:** When Abram was ninety-nine years old, the LORD appeared to Abram and said to him, "I *am* Almighty God; walk before Me and be blameless."

[18] **Matt. 5:17-19:** Do not think that I came to destroy the Law or the Prophets. I did not come to destroy but to fulfill. For assuredly, I say to you, till heaven and earth pass away, one jot or one tittle will by no means pass from the law till all is fulfilled. Whoever therefore breaks one of the least of these commandments, and teaches men so, shall be called least in the kingdom of heaven; but whoever does and teaches *them,* he shall be called great in the kingdom of heaven. **Rom. 3:31:** Do we then make void the law through faith? Certainly not! On the contrary, we establish the law. **1 Cor. 9:21:** ... to those *who are* without law, as without law (not being without law toward God, but under law toward Christ), that I might win those *who are* without law. **Luke 16:17-18:** And it is easier for heaven and earth to pass away than for one tittle of the law to fail. "Whoever divorces his wife and marries another commits adultery; and whoever marries her who is divorced from *her* husband commits adultery.

[19] **Rom. 6:14:** For sin shall not have dominion over you, for you are not under law but under grace. **Rom. 7:4:** Therefore, my brethren, you also have become dead to the law through the body of Christ, that you may be married to another—to Him who was raised from the dead, that we should bear fruit to God. **Gal. 2:16:** ... knowing that a man is not justified by the works of the law but by faith in Jesus Christ, even we have believed in Christ Jesus, that we might be justified by faith in

use to them as well as to others: in that, as a rule of life, informing them of the will of God, and their duty, it directs and binds them, to walk accordingly[20] discovering also the sinful pollutions of their natures, hearts and lives;[21] so as examining themselves thereby, they may come to further conviction of, humiliation for, and hatred against sin;[22] together with a clearer sight of the need they have of Christ and the perfection of His obedience:[23] it is likewise of use to the regenerate to restrain

---

Christ and not by the works of the law; for by the works of the law no flesh shall be justified. **Gal. 3:13:** ... knowing that a man is not justified by the works of the law but by faith in Jesus Christ, even we have believed in Christ Jesus, that we might be justified by faith in Christ and not by the works of the law; for by the works of the law no flesh shall be justified. **Gal. 4:4-5:** But when the fullness of the time had come, God sent forth His Son, born of a woman, born under the law, to redeem those who were under the law, that we might receive the adoption as sons. **Acts 13:38-39:** Therefore let it be known to you, brethren, that through this Man is preached to you the forgiveness of sins; and by Him everyone who believes is justified from all things from which you could not be justified by the law of Moses. **Rom. 8:1, 33:** *There is* therefore now no condemnation to those who are in Christ Jesus, who do not walk according to the flesh, but according to the Spirit.... Who shall bring a charge against God's elect? *It is* God who justifies. **Rom. 10:4:** For Christ *is* the end of the law for righteousness to everyone who believes.

[20] **Rom. 7:12, 22, 25:** Therefore the law *is* holy, and the commandment holy and just and good.... For I delight in the law of God according to the inward man.... I thank God—through Jesus Christ our Lord! So then, with the mind I myself serve the law of God, but with the flesh the law of sin. **Ps. 119:1-6:** Blessed *are* the undefiled in the way, Who walk in the law of the LORD! Blessed *are* those who keep His testimonies, Who seek Him with the whole heart! They also do no iniquity; They walk in His ways. You have commanded *us* To keep Your precepts diligently. Oh, that my ways were directed To keep Your statutes! Then I would not be ashamed, When I look into all Your commandments. **1 Cor. 7:19:** Circumcision is nothing and uncircumcision is nothing, but keeping the commandments of God *is what matters.* **Gal. 5:14-23:** For all the law is fulfilled in one word, *even* in this: "You shall love your neighbor as yourself." But if you bite and devour one another, beware lest you be consumed by one another! I say then: Walk in the Spirit, and you shall not fulfill the lust of the flesh. For the flesh lusts against the Spirit, and the Spirit against the flesh; and these are contrary to one another, so that you do not do the things that you wish. But if you are led by the Spirit, you are not under the law. Now the works of the flesh are evident, which are: adultery, fornication, uncleanness, lewdness, idolatry, sorcery, hatred, contentions, jealousies, outbursts of wrath, selfish ambitions, dissensions, heresies, envy, murders, drunkenness, revelries, and the like; of which I tell you beforehand, just as I also told *you* in time past, that those who practice such things will not inherit the kingdom of God. But the fruit of the Spirit is love, joy, peace, longsuffering, kindness, goodness, faithfulness, gentleness, self-control. Against such there is no law.

[21] **Rom. 7:7, 13:** What shall we say then? *Is* the law sin? Certainly not! On the contrary, I would not have known sin except through the law. For I would not have known covetousness unless the law had said, "You shall not covet." ... Has then what is good become death to me? Certainly not! But sin, that it might appear sin, was producing death in me through what is good, so that sin through the commandment might become exceedingly sinful. **Rom. 3:20:** Therefore by the deeds of the law no flesh will be justified in His sight, for by the law *is* the knowledge of sin.

[22] **James 1:23-25:** For if anyone is a hearer of the word and not a doer, he is like a man observing his natural face in a mirror; for he observes himself, goes away, and immediately forgets what kind of man he was. But he who looks into the perfect law of liberty and continues *in it,* and is not a forgetful hearer but a doer of the work, this one will be blessed in what he does. **Rom. 7:9, 14, 24:** I was alive once without the law, but when the commandment came, sin revived and I died.... For we know that the law is spiritual, but I am carnal, sold under sin.... O wretched man that I am! Who will deliver me from this body of death?

[23] **Gal. 3:24:** Therefore the law was our tutor *to bring us* to Christ, that we might be justified by faith. **Rom. 7:24-25:** O wretched man that I am! Who will deliver me from this body of death? I thank God—through Jesus Christ our Lord! **Rom. 8:3-4:** For what the law could not do in that it was weak through the flesh, God *did* by sending His own Son in the likeness of sinful flesh, on account of sin: He condemned sin in the flesh, that the righteous requirement of the law might be fulfilled in us who do not walk according to the flesh but according to the Spirit.

their corruptions, in that it forbids sin;[24] and the threatenings of it serve to show what even their sins deserve; and what afflictions in this life they may expect for them, although freed from the curse and unallayed rigour thereof.[25] The promises of it likewise show them God's approbation of obedience, and what blessings they may expect upon the performance thereof,[26] though not as due to them by the law as a covenant of works;[27] so as man's doing good and refraining from evil, because the law

---

[24] **James 2:11-12:** For He who said, "Do not commit adultery," also said, "Do not murder." Now if you do not commit adultery, but you do murder, you have become a transgressor of the law. So speak and so do as those who will be judged by the law of liberty. **Ps. 119:101, 104, 128:** I have restrained my feet from every evil way, That I may keep Your word.... Through Your precepts I get understanding; Therefore I hate every false way.... Therefore all *Your* precepts *concerning* all *things* I consider *to be* right; I hate every false way.

[25] **Ezra 9:13-14:** And after all that has come upon us for our evil deeds and for our great guilt, since You our God have punished us less than our iniquities *deserve,* and have given us *such* deliverance as this, should we again break Your commandments, and join in marriage with the people *committing* these abominations? Would You not be angry with us until You had consumed *us,* so that *there would be* no remnant or survivor? **Ps. 89:30-34:** "If his sons forsake My law And do not walk in My judgments, If they break My statutes And do not keep My commandments, Then I will punish their transgression with the rod, And their iniquity with stripes. Nevertheless My lovingkindness I will not utterly take from him, Nor allow My faithfulness to fail. My covenant I will not break, Nor alter the word that has gone out of My lips. **Gal. 3:13:** Christ has redeemed us from the curse of the law, having become a curse for us (for it is written, "Cursed *is* everyone who hangs on a tree").

[26] **Ex. 19:5-6:** Now therefore, if you will indeed obey My voice and keep My covenant, then you shall be a special treasure to Me above all people; for all the earth *is* Mine. And you shall be to Me a kingdom of priests and a holy nation. These *are* the words which you shall speak to the children of Israel. **Deut. 5:33:** You shall walk in all the ways which the LORD your God has commanded you, that you may live and *that it may be* well with you, and *that* you may prolong *your* days in the land which you shall possess. **Lev. 18:5:** You shall therefore keep My statutes and My judgments, which if a man does, he shall live by them: I *am* the LORD. **Matt. 19:17:** So He said to him, "Why do you call Me good? No one *is* good but One, *that is,* God. But if you want to enter into life, keep the commandments." **Lev. 26:1-13:** 'You shall not make idols for yourselves; neither a carved image nor a *sacred* pillar shall you rear up for yourselves; nor shall you set up an engraved stone in your land, to bow down to it; for I *am* the LORD your God. You shall keep My Sabbaths and reverence My sanctuary: I *am* the LORD. 'If you walk in My statutes and keep My commandments, and perform them, then I will give you rain in its season, the land shall yield its produce, and the trees of the field shall yield their fruit. Your threshing shall last till the time of vintage, and the vintage shall last till the time of sowing; you shall eat your bread to the full, and dwell in your land safely. I will give peace in the land, and you shall lie down, and none will make *you* afraid; I will rid the land of evil beasts, and the sword will not go through your land. You will chase your enemies, and they shall fall by the sword before you. Five of you shall chase a hundred, and a hundred of you shall put ten thousand to flight; your enemies shall fall by the sword before you. 'For I will look on you favorably and make you fruitful, multiply you and confirm My covenant with you. You shall eat the old harvest, and clear out the old because of the new. I will set My tabernacle among you, and My soul shall not abhor you. I will walk among you and be your God, and you shall be My people. I *am* the LORD your God, who brought you out of the land of Egypt, that *you* should not be their slaves; I have broken the bands of your yoke and made you walk upright.' **2 Cor. 6:16:** And what agreement has the temple of God with idols? For you are the temple of the living God. As God has said: "I will dwell in them And walk among them. I will be their God, And they shall be My people." **Eph. 6:2-3:** "Honor your father and mother," which is the first commandment with promise: "that it may be well with you and you may live long on the earth." **Ps. 19:11:** Moreover by them Your servant is warned, *And* in keeping them *there is* great reward. **Ps. 37:11:** But the meek shall inherit the earth, And shall delight themselves in the abundance of peace. **Matt. 5:5:** Blessed *are* the meek, For they shall inherit the earth.

[27] **Gal. 2:16:** ... knowing that a man is not justified by the works of the law but by faith in Jesus Christ, even we have believed in Christ Jesus, that we might be justified by faith in Christ and not by the works of the law; for by the works of the law no flesh shall be justified. **Luke 17:10:** So likewise you, when you have done all those things which you are commanded, say, 'We are unprofitable servants. We have done what was our duty to do.'

encourageth to the one and deterreth from the other, is no evidence of his being under the law and not under grace.[28]

7. Neither are the aforementioned uses of the law contrary to the grace of the gospel; but do sweetly comply with it;[29] the Spirit of Christ subduing and enabling the will of man, to do that freely and cheerfully, which the will of God revealed in the law, requireth to be done.[30]

[28] **Rom. 6:12-15:** Therefore do not let sin reign in your mortal body, that you should obey it in its lusts. And do not present your members *as* instruments of unrighteousness to sin, but present yourselves to God as being alive from the dead, and your members *as* instruments of righteousness to God. For sin shall not have dominion over you, for you are not under law but under grace. What then? Shall we sin because we are not under law but under grace? Certainly not! **1 Pet. 3:8-13:** Finally, all *of you be* of one mind, having compassion for one another; love as brothers, *be* tenderhearted, *be* courteous; not returning evil for evil or reviling for reviling, but on the contrary blessing, knowing that you were called to this, that you may inherit a blessing. For "He who would love life And see good days, Let him refrain his tongue from evil, And his lips from speaking deceit. Let him turn away from evil and do good; Let him seek peace and pursue it. For the eyes of the LORD *are* on the righteous, And His ears *are open* to their prayers; But the face of the LORD *is* against those who do evil." And who *is* he who will harm you if you become followers of what is good? **Cf. Ps. 34:12-16:** Who *is* the man *who* desires life, And loves *many* days, that he may see good? Keep your tongue from evil, And your lips from speaking deceit. Depart from evil and do good; Seek peace and pursue it. The eyes of the LORD *are* on the righteous, And His ears *are open* to their cry. The face of the LORD *is* against those who do evil, To cut off the remembrance of them from the earth. **Heb. 12:28-29:** Therefore, since we are receiving a kingdom which cannot be shaken, let us have grace, by which we may serve God acceptably with reverence and godly fear. For our God *is* a consuming fire.

[29] **Rom. 3:31:** Do we then make void the law through faith? Certainly not! On the contrary, we establish the law. **Gal. 3:21:** *Is* the law then against the promises of God? Certainly not! For if there had been a law given which could have given life, truly righteousness would have been by the law. **Titus 2:11-14:** For the grace of God that brings salvation has appeared to all men, teaching us that, denying ungodliness and worldly lusts, we should live soberly, righteously, and godly in the present age, looking for the blessed hope and glorious appearing of our great God and Savior Jesus Christ, who gave Himself for us, that He might redeem us from every lawless deed and purify for Himself *His* own special people, zealous for good works.

[30] **Ezek. 36:27:** I will put My Spirit within you and cause you to walk in My statutes, and you will keep My judgments and do *them*. **Heb. 8:10:** For this *is* the covenant that I will make with the house of Israel after those days, says the LORD: I will put My laws in their mind and write them on their hearts; and I will be their God, and they shall be My people. **Cf. Jer. 31:33:** But this *is* the covenant that I will make with the house of Israel after those days, says the LORD: I will put My law in their minds, and write it on their hearts; and I will be their God, and they shall be My people. **Ps. 119:35, 47:** Make me walk in the path of Your commandments, For I delight in it.... And I will delight myself in Your commandments, Which I love. **Rom. 7:22:** For I delight in the law of God according to the inward man.

CHAPTER 20

Of the Gospel, and of the Extent of the Grace thereof

1. The divine pledge, communion, and righteous law of God being broken by sin (commonly called the covenant of works),[1] and made unprofitable unto life;[2] God was pleased to give forth the promise of Christ, the Seed of the woman,[3] as the means of calling the elect, and begetting in them faith and repentance;[4] in this promise, the gospel, as to the substance of it, was revealed, and is therein effectual, for the conversion and salvation of sinners.[5]

---

[1] **Gen. 3:1-7:** Now the serpent was more cunning than any beast of the field which the LORD God had made. And he said to the woman, "Has God indeed said, 'You shall not eat of every tree of the garden'?" And the woman said to the serpent, "We may eat the fruit of the trees of the garden; but of the fruit of the tree which *is* in the midst of the garden, God has said, 'You shall not eat it, nor shall you touch it, lest you die.'" Then the serpent said to the woman, "You will not surely die. For God knows that in the day you eat of it your eyes will be opened, and you will be like God, knowing good and evil." So when the woman saw that the tree *was* good for food, that it *was* pleasant to the eyes, and a tree desirable to make *one* wise, she took of its fruit and ate. She also gave to her husband with her, and he ate. Then the eyes of both of them were opened, and they knew that they *were* naked; and they sewed fig leaves together and made themselves coverings.

[2] **Gal. 3:21:** *Is* the law then against the promises of God? Certainly not! For if there had been a law given which could have given life, truly righteousness would have been by the law. **Rom. 3:20-21:** Therefore by the deeds of the law no flesh will be justified in His sight, for by the law *is* the knowledge of sin. But now the righteousness of God apart from the law is revealed, being witnessed by the Law and the Prophets. **Gen. 3:22-24:** Then the LORD God said, "Behold, the man has become like one of Us, to know good and evil. And now, lest he put out his hand and take also of the tree of life, and eat, and live forever"— therefore the LORD God sent him out of the garden of Eden to till the ground from which he was taken. So He drove out the man; and He placed cherubim at the east of the garden of Eden, and a flaming sword which turned every way, to guard the way to the tree of life.

[3] **Gen. 3:15:** And I will put enmity Between you and the woman, And between your seed and her Seed; He shall bruise your head, And you shall bruise His heel.

[4] **2 Thess. 2:13-14:** But we are bound to give thanks to God always for you, brethren beloved by the Lord, because God from the beginning chose you for salvation through sanctification by the Spirit and belief in the truth, to which He called you by our gospel, for the obtaining of the glory of our Lord Jesus Christ. **Eph. 2:4-10:** But God, who is rich in mercy, because of His great love with which He loved us, even when we were dead in trespasses, made us alive together with Christ (by grace you have been saved), and raised *us* up together, and made *us* sit together in the heavenly *places* in Christ Jesus, that in the ages to come He might show the exceeding riches of His grace in *His* kindness toward us in Christ Jesus. For by grace you have been saved through faith, and that not of yourselves; *it is* the gift of God, not of works, lest anyone should boast. For we are His workmanship, created in Christ Jesus for good works, which God prepared beforehand that we should walk in them. **Rom. 5:6-11:** For when we were still without strength, in due time Christ died for the ungodly. For scarcely for a righteous man will one die; yet perhaps for a good man someone would even dare to die. But God demonstrates His own love toward us, in that while we were still sinners, Christ died for us. Much more then, having now been justified by His blood, we shall be saved from wrath through Him. For if when we were enemies we were reconciled to God through the death of His Son, much more, having been reconciled, we shall be saved by His life. And not only *that,* but we also rejoice in God through our Lord Jesus Christ, through whom we have now received the reconciliation. **Acts 20:20-21:** ... how I kept back nothing that was helpful, but proclaimed it to you, and taught you publicly and from house to house, testifying to Jews, and also to Greeks, repentance toward God and faith toward our Lord Jesus Christ.

[5] **Gal. 3:19:** What purpose then *does* the law *serve?* It was added because of transgressions, till the Seed should come to whom the promise was made; *and it was* appointed through angels by the hand of a mediator. **Heb. 11:13-16:** These all died in faith, not having received the promises, but having seen them afar off were assured of them, embraced *them* and confessed that they were strangers and pilgrims on the earth. For those who say such things declare plainly that they seek a homeland. And truly if they had called to mind that *country* from which they had come out, they would have had opportunity to return. But now they desire a better, that is, a heavenly *country.*

2. This promise of Christ, and salvation by Him, is revealed only by the word of God;[6] neither do the works of creation, or providence, with the light of nature, make discovery of Christ, or of grace by Him; so much as in a general, or obscure way;[7] much less that men destitute of the revelation of Him by the promise, or gospel; should be enabled thereby, to attain saving faith, or repentance.[8]

3. The revelation of the gospel unto sinners, made in divers times, and by sundry parts; with the addition of promises, and precepts for the obedience required therein, as to the nations,

---

Therefore God is not ashamed to be called their God, for He has prepared a city for them. **Eph. 2:12:** ... that at that time you were without Christ, being aliens from the commonwealth of Israel and strangers from the covenants of promise, having no hope and without God in the world. **Rom. 1:1-4:** Paul, a bondservant of Jesus Christ, called *to be* an apostle, separated to the gospel of God which He promised before through His prophets in the Holy Scriptures, concerning His Son Jesus Christ our Lord, who was born of the seed of David according to the flesh, *and* declared *to be* the Son of God with power according to the Spirit of holiness, by the resurrection from the dead.

[6] **Rom. 1:1-2, 16-17:** Paul, a bondservant of Jesus Christ, called *to be* an apostle, separated to the gospel of God which He promised before through His prophets in the Holy Scriptures ... For I am not ashamed of the gospel of Christ, for it is the power of God to salvation for everyone who believes, for the Jew first and also for the Greek. For in it the righteousness of God is revealed from faith to faith; as it is written, "The just shall live by faith." **Rom. 10:14-15, 17:** How then shall they call on Him in whom they have not believed? And how shall they believe in Him of whom they have not heard? And how shall they hear without a preacher? And how shall they preach unless they are sent? As it is written: "How beautiful are the feet of those who preach the gospel of peace, Who bring glad tidings of good things!" ... So then faith *comes* by hearing, and hearing by the word of God. **Rom. 16:25-27:** Now to Him who is able to establish you according to my gospel and the preaching of Jesus Christ, according to the revelation of the mystery kept secret since the world began but now made manifest, and by the prophetic Scriptures made known to all nations, according to the commandment of the everlasting God, for obedience to the faith—to God, alone wise, *be* glory through Jesus Christ forever. Amen.

[7] **Ps. 19:1-4:** The heavens declare the glory of God; And the firmament shows His handiwork. Day unto day utters speech, And night unto night reveals knowledge. *There is* no speech nor language *Where* their voice is not heard. Their line has gone out through all the earth, And their words to the end of the world. In them He has set a tabernacle for the sun. **Rom. 1:18-23:** For the wrath of God is revealed from heaven against all ungodliness and unrighteousness of men, who suppress the truth in unrighteousness, because what may be known of God is manifest in them, for God has shown *it* to them. For since the creation of the world His invisible *attributes* are clearly seen, being understood by the things that are made, *even* His eternal power and Godhead, so that they are without excuse, because, although they knew God, they did not glorify *Him* as God, nor were thankful, but became futile in their thoughts, and their foolish hearts were darkened. Professing to be wise, they became fools, and changed the glory of the incorruptible God into an image made like corruptible man—and birds and four-footed animals and creeping things.

[8] **Rom. 10:14-15, 17:** How then shall they call on Him in whom they have not believed? And how shall they believe in Him of whom they have not heard? And how shall they hear without a preacher? And how shall they preach unless they are sent? As it is written: "How beautiful are the feet of those who preach the gospel of peace, Who bring glad tidings of good things!" ... So then faith *comes* by hearing, and hearing by the word of God. **Acts 4:12:** Nor is there salvation in any other, for there is no other name under heaven given among men by which we must be saved. **John 3:18:** He who believes in Him is not condemned; but he who does not believe is condemned already, because he has not believed in the name of the only begotten Son of God. **John 14:6:** Jesus said to him, I am the way, the truth, and the life. No one comes to the Father except through Me. **Matt. 28:19-20:** Go therefore and make disciples of all the nations, baptizing them in the name of the Father and of the Son and of the Holy Spirit, teaching them to observe all things that I have commanded you; and lo, I am with you always, *even* to the end of the age." Amen.

and persons, to whom it is granted,[9] is merely of the sovereign will and good pleasure of God;[10] not being annexed by virtue of any promise, to the due improvement of men's natural abilities, by virtue of common light received without it; which none ever did make, or can so do:[11] and therefore in all ages the preaching of the gospel hath been granted unto persons and nations, as to the extent, or straitening of it, in great variety, according to the counsel of the will of God.[12]

---

[9] **Rom. 16:25-27:** Now to Him who is able to establish you according to my gospel and the preaching of Jesus Christ, according to the revelation of the mystery kept secret since the world began but now made manifest, and by the prophetic Scriptures made known to all nations, according to the commandment of the everlasting God, for obedience to the faith— to God, alone wise, *be* glory through Jesus Christ forever. Amen. **Eph. 3:1-7:** For this reason I, Paul, the prisoner of Christ Jesus for you Gentiles— if indeed you have heard of the dispensation of the grace of God which was given to me for you, how that by revelation He made known to me the mystery (as I have briefly written already, by which, when you read, you may understand my knowledge in the mystery of Christ), which in other ages was not made known to the sons of men, as it has now been revealed by the Spirit to His holy apostles and prophets: that the Gentiles should be fellow heirs, of the same body, and partakers of His promise in Christ through the gospel, of which I became a minister according to the gift of the grace of God given to me by the effective working of His power. **Heb. 1:1-4:** God, who at various times and in various ways spoke in time past to the fathers by the prophets, has in these last days spoken to us by *His* Son, whom He has appointed heir of all things, through whom also He made the worlds; who being the brightness of *His* glory and the express image of His person, and upholding all things by the word of His power, when He had by Himself purged our sins, sat down at the right hand of the Majesty on high, having become so much better than the angels, as He has by inheritance obtained a more excellent name than they. **Isa. 6:9-10:** And He said, "Go, and tell this people: 'Keep on hearing, but do not understand; Keep on seeing, but do not perceive.' "Make the heart of this people dull, And their ears heavy, And shut their eyes; Lest they see with their eyes, And hear with their ears, And understand with their heart, And return and be healed."

[10] **John 6:44, 65:** No one can come to Me unless the Father who sent Me draws him; and I will raise him up at the last day.... And He said, "Therefore I have said to you that no one can come to Me unless it has been granted to him by My Father." **John 15:6:** If anyone does not abide in Me, he is cast out as a branch and is withered; and they gather them and throw *them* into the fire, and they are burned. **Acts 13:48:** Now when the Gentiles heard this, they were glad and glorified the word of the Lord. And as many as had been appointed to eternal life believed. **Titus 3:5:** ... not by works of righteousness which we have done, but according to His mercy He saved us, through the washing of regeneration and renewing of the Holy Spirit.

[11] **Rom. 3:10-12:** As it is written: "There is none righteous, no, not one; There is none who understands; There is none who seeks after God. They have all turned aside; They have together become unprofitable; There is none who does good, no, not one." **Rom. 8:7-8:** Because the carnal mind *is* enmity against God; for it is not subject to the law of God, nor indeed can be. So then, those who are in the flesh cannot please God.

[12] **Rom. 11:28-36:** Concerning the gospel *they are* enemies for your sake, but concerning the election *they are* beloved for the sake of the fathers. For the gifts and the calling of God *are* irrevocable. For as you were once disobedient to God, yet have now obtained mercy through their disobedience, even so these also have now been disobedient, that through the mercy shown you they also may obtain mercy. For God has committed them all to disobedience, that He might have mercy on all. Oh, the depth of the riches both of the wisdom and knowledge of God! How unsearchable *are* His judgments and His ways past finding out! "For who has known the mind of the LORD? Or who has become His counselor?" "Or who has first given to Him And it shall be repaid to him?" For of Him and through Him and to Him *are* all things, to whom *be* glory forever. Amen. **1 Cor. 1:30-31:** But of Him you are in Christ Jesus, who became for us wisdom from God—and righteousness and sanctification and redemption—that, as it is written, "He who glories, let him glory in the LORD." **Isa. 6:8:** Also I heard the voice of the Lord, saying: "Whom shall I send, And who will go for Us?" Then I said, "Here *am* I! Send me." **Acts 16:7:** After they had come to Mysia, they tried to go into Bithynia, but the Spirit did not permit them.

4. Although the gospel be the only outward means, of revealing Christ, and saving grace; and is, as such, abundantly sufficient thereunto;[13] yet that men who are dead in trespasses, may be born again, quickened or regenerated; there is moreover necessary, an effectual, insuperable work of the Holy Spirit, upon the whole soul, for the producing in them a new spiritual life; without which no other means will effect their conversion unto God.[14]

---

[13] **Rom. 1:16-17:** For I am not ashamed of the gospel of Christ, for it is the power of God to salvation for everyone who believes, for the Jew first and also for the Greek. For in it the righteousness of God is revealed from faith to faith; as it is written, "The just shall live by faith."

[14] **Titus 3:5:** ... not by works of righteousness which we have done, but according to His mercy He saved us, through the washing of regeneration and renewing of the Holy Spirit. **1 Cor. 2:14:** But the natural man does not receive the things of the Spirit of God, for they are foolishness to him; nor can he know *them,* because they are spiritually discerned. **Eph. 1:17-20:** ... that the God of our Lord Jesus Christ, the Father of glory, may give to you the spirit of wisdom and revelation in the knowledge of Him, the eyes of your understanding being enlightened; that you may know what is the hope of His calling, what are the riches of the glory of His inheritance in the saints, and what *is* the exceeding greatness of His power toward us who believe, according to the working of His mighty power which He worked in Christ when He raised Him from the dead and seated *Him* at His right hand in the heavenly *places.* **John 6:44:** No one can come to Me unless the Father who sent Me draws him; and I will raise him up at the last day. **2 Cor. 4:4, 6:** ... whose minds the god of this age has blinded, who do not believe, lest the light of the gospel of the glory of Christ, who is the image of God, should shine on them.... For it is the God who commanded light to shine out of darkness, who has shone in our hearts to *give* the light of the knowledge of the glory of God in the face of Jesus Christ.

CHAPTER 21

Of Christian Liberty and Liberty of Conscience

1. The liberty which Christ hath purchased for believers under the gospel, consists in their freedom from the guilt of sin, the condemning wrath of God, the rigour and curse of the law;[1] and in their being delivered from this present evil world, bondage to Satan, and dominion of sin;[2] from the evil of afflictions; the fear, and sting of death, the victory of the grave, and everlasting damnation;[3] as also in their free access to God;[4] and their yielding obedience unto Him not out of a slavish fear, but a child-like love, and willing mind.[5] All which were common also to believers under the law for the substance of them;[6] but under the

---

[1] **Titus 2:14:** ... who gave Himself for us, that He might redeem us from every lawless deed and purify for Himself *His* own special people, zealous for good works. **1 Thess. 1:10:** ... and to wait for His Son from heaven, whom He raised from the dead, *even* Jesus who delivers us from the wrath to come. **Gal. 3:13:** Christ has redeemed us from the curse of the law, having become a curse for us (for it is written, "Cursed *is* everyone who hangs on a tree").

[2] **Gal. 1:4:** ... who gave Himself for our sins, that He might deliver us from this present evil age, according to the will of our God and Father. **Col. 1:13:** He has delivered us from the power of darkness and conveyed *us* into the kingdom of the Son of His love. **Acts 26:18:** ... to open their eyes, *in order* to turn *them* from darkness to light, and *from* the power of Satan to God, that they may receive forgiveness of sins and an inheritance among those who are sanctified by faith in Me. **Rom. 6:14:** For sin shall not have dominion over you, for you are not under law but under grace. **Rom. 8:3:** For what the law could not do in that it was weak through the flesh, God *did* by sending His own Son in the likeness of sinful flesh, on account of sin: He condemned sin in the flesh.

[3] **Rom. 8:28:** And we know that all things work together for good to those who love God, to those who are the called according to *His* purpose. **Ps. 119:71:** *It is* good for me that I have been afflicted, That I may learn Your statutes. **2 Cor. 4:15-18:** For all things *are* for your sakes, that grace, having spread through the many, may cause thanksgiving to abound to the glory of God. **1 Cor. 15:54-57:** So when this corruptible has put on incorruption, and this mortal has put on immortality, then shall be brought to pass the saying that is written: "Death is swallowed up in victory." "O Death, where *is* your sting? O Hades, where *is* your victory?" The sting of death *is* sin, and the strength of sin *is* the law. But thanks *be* to God, who gives us the victory through our Lord Jesus Christ. **Rom. 5:9:** Much more then, having now been justified by His blood, we shall be saved from wrath through Him. **Rom. 8:1:** *There is* therefore now no condemnation to those who are in Christ Jesus, who do not walk according to the flesh, but according to the Spirit. **See 1 Thess. 1:10.**

[4] **Rom. 5:1-2:** Therefore, having been justified by faith, we have peace with God through our Lord Jesus Christ, through whom also we have access by faith into this grace in which we stand, and rejoice in hope of the glory of God.

[5] **Rom. 8:14-15:** For as many as are led by the Spirit of God, these are sons of God. For you did not receive the spirit of bondage again to fear, but you received the Spirit of adoption by whom we cry out, "Abba, Father." **Gal. 4:6:** And because you are sons, God has sent forth the Spirit of His Son into your hearts, crying out, "Abba, Father!" **1 John 4:18:** There is no fear in love; but perfect love casts out fear, because fear involves torment. But he who fears has not been made perfect in love.

[6] **Gal. 3:8-9, 14:** And the Scripture, foreseeing that God would justify the Gentiles by faith, preached the gospel to Abraham beforehand, *saying,* "In you all the nations shall be blessed." So then those who *are* of faith are blessed with believing Abraham.... that the blessing of Abraham might come upon the Gentiles in Christ Jesus, that we might receive the promise of the Spirit through faith. **Rom. 4:6-8:** ... just as David also describes the blessedness of the man to whom God imputes righteousness apart from works: "Blessed *are those* whose lawless deeds are forgiven, And whose sins are covered; Blessed *is the* man to whom the LORD shall not impute sin." **1 Cor. 10:3-4:** ... all ate the same spiritual food, and all drank the same spiritual drink. For they drank of that spiritual Rock that followed them, and that Rock was Christ. **Heb. 11:** Now faith is the substance of things hoped for, the evidence of things not seen. For by it the elders obtained a *good* testimony....

New Covenant, the liberty of Christians is further enlarged in their freedom from the yoke of the ceremonial law, to which the people of the Jews were subjected;[7] and in greater boldness of access to the throne of grace;[8] and in fuller communications of the free Spirit of God, than believers under the law did ordinarily partake of.[9]

2. God alone is Lord of the conscience,[10] and hath left it free from the doctrines and commandments of men which are in anything

---

By faith Abel offered to God a more excellent sacrifice than Cain, through which he obtained witness that he was righteous, God testifying of his gifts; and through it he being dead still speaks.... By faith Noah, being divinely warned of things not yet seen, moved with godly fear, prepared an ark for the saving of his household, by which he condemned the world and became heir of the righteousness which is according to faith. By faith Abraham obeyed when he was called to go out to the place which he would receive as an inheritance. And he went out, not knowing where he was going.... By faith Moses, when he was born, was hidden three months by his parents, because they saw *he was* a beautiful child; and they were not afraid of the king's command. By faith Moses, when he became of age, refused to be called the son of Pharaoh's daughter, choosing rather to suffer affliction with the people of God than to enjoy the passing pleasures of sin, esteeming the reproach of Christ greater riches than the treasures in Egypt; for he looked to the reward.... And all these, having obtained a good testimony through faith, did not receive the promise, God having provided something better for us, that they should not be made perfect apart from us.

[7] **Gal. 4:1-7:** Now I say *that* the heir, as long as he is a child, does not differ at all from a slave, though he is master of all, but is under guardians and stewards until the time appointed by the father. Even so we, when we were children, were in bondage under the elements of the world. But when the fullness of the time had come, God sent forth His Son, born of a woman, born under the law, to redeem those who were under the law, that we might receive the adoption as sons. And because you are sons, God has sent forth the Spirit of His Son into your hearts, crying out, "Abba, Father!" Therefore you are no longer a slave but a son, and if a son, then an heir of God through Christ. **Gal. 5:1:** Stand fast therefore in the liberty by which Christ has made us free, and do not be entangled again with a yoke of bondage. **Acts 15:10-11:** Now therefore, why do you test God by putting a yoke on the neck of the disciples which neither our fathers nor we were able to bear? But we believe that through the grace of the Lord Jesus Christ we shall be saved in the same manner as they."

[8] **Heb. 4:14-16:** Seeing then that we have a great High Priest who has passed through the heavens, Jesus the Son of God, let us hold fast *our* confession. For we do not have a High Priest who cannot sympathize with our weaknesses, but was in all *points* tempted as *we are, yet* without sin. Let us therefore come boldly to the throne of grace, that we may obtain mercy and find grace to help in time of need. **Heb. 10:19-22:** Therefore, brethren, having boldness to enter the Holiest by the blood of Jesus, by a new and living way which He consecrated for us, through the veil, that is, His flesh, and *having* a High Priest over the house of God, let us draw near with a true heart in full assurance of faith, having our hearts sprinkled from an evil conscience and our bodies washed with pure water.

[9] **John 7:38-39:** He who believes in Me, as the Scripture has said, out of his heart will flow rivers of living water." But this He spoke concerning the Spirit, whom those believing in Him would receive; for the Holy Spirit was not yet *given,* because Jesus was not yet glorified. **Acts 2:17-18:** 'And it shall come to pass in the last days, says God, That I will pour out of My Spirit on all flesh; Your sons and your daughters shall prophesy, Your young men shall see visions, Your old men shall dream dreams. And on My menservants and on My maidservants I will pour out My Spirit in those days; And they shall prophesy. **2 Cor. 3:8, 13, 17-18:** ... how will the ministry of the Spirit not be more glorious?... unlike Moses, *who* put a veil over his face so that the children of Israel could not look steadily at the end of what was passing away.... Now the Lord is the Spirit; and where the Spirit of the Lord *is*, there *is* liberty. But we all, with unveiled face, beholding as in a mirror the glory of the Lord, are being transformed into the same image from glory to glory, just as by the Spirit of the Lord. **See Jer. 31:31-34.**

[10] **James 4:12:** There is one Lawgiver, who is able to save and to destroy. Who are you to judge another? **Rom. 14:4, 10:** Who are you to judge another's servant? To his own master he stands or falls. Indeed, he will be made to stand, for God is able to make him stand.... But why do you judge your brother? Or why do you show contempt for your brother? For we shall all stand before the

contrary to His word, or not contained in it.[11] So that to believe such doctrines, or obey such commands out of conscience, is to betray true liberty of conscience;[12] and the requiring of an implicit faith, and absolute and blind obedience, is to destroy liberty of conscience, and reason also.[13]

3. They who upon pretence of Christian liberty do practice any sin, or cherish any sinful lust; as they do thereby pervert the main design of the grace of the gospel to their own destruction; so they wholly destroy the end of Christian liberty, which is, that being delivered out of the hands of all our enemies we might

---

judgment seat of Christ. **1 Cor. 10:29:** "Conscience," I say, not your own, but that of the other. For why is my liberty judged by another *man's* conscience?

[11] **Acts 4:19:** But Peter and John answered and said to them, "Whether it is right in the sight of God to listen to you more than to God, you judge." **Acts 5:29:** But Peter and the *other* apostles answered and said: "We ought to obey God rather than men." **1 Cor. 7:22-23:** For he who is called in the Lord *while* a slave is the Lord's freedman. Likewise he who is called *while* free is Christ's slave. You were bought at a price; do not become slaves of men. **Matt. 15:1-6, 9:** Then the scribes and Pharisees who were from Jerusalem came to Jesus, saying, "Why do Your disciples transgress the tradition of the elders? For they do not wash their hands when they eat bread." He answered and said to them, "Why do you also transgress the commandment of God because of your tradition? For God commanded, saying, 'Honor your father and your mother'; and, 'He who curses father or mother, let him be put to death.' But you say, 'Whoever says to his father or mother, "Whatever profit you might have received from me *is* a gift *to God*"—then he need not honor his father or mother.' Thus you have made the commandment of God of no effect by your tradition.... And in vain they worship Me, Teaching *as* doctrines the commandments of men.' **Matt. 23:8-10:** But you, do not be called 'Rabbi'; for One is your Teacher, the Christ, and you are all brethren. Do not call anyone on earth your father; for One is your Father, He who is in heaven. And do not be called teachers; for One is your Teacher, the Christ. **2 Cor. 1:24:** Not that we have dominion over your faith, but are fellow workers for your joy; for by faith you stand.

[12] **Col. 2:20-23:** Therefore, if you died with Christ from the basic principles of the world, why, as *though* living in the world, do you subject yourselves to regulations— "Do not touch, do not taste, do not handle," which all concern things which perish with the using—according to the commandments and doctrines of men? These things indeed have an appearance of wisdom in self-imposed religion, *false* humility, and neglect of the body, *but are* of no value against the indulgence of the flesh. **Gal. 1:10:** For do I now persuade men, or God? Or do I seek to please men? For if I still pleased men, I would not be a bondservant of Christ. **Gal. 2:4-5:** And *this occurred* because of false brethren secretly brought in (who came in by stealth to spy out our liberty which we have in Christ Jesus, that they might bring us into bondage), to whom we did not yield submission even for an hour, that the truth of the gospel might continue with you. **Gal. 4:9-10:** But now after you have known God, or rather are known by God, how *is it that* you turn again to the weak and beggarly elements, to which you desire again to be in bondage? You observe days and months and seasons and years. **Gal. 5:1:** Stand fast therefore in the liberty by which Christ has made us free, and do not be entangled again with a yoke of bondage.

[13] **Rom. 10:17:** So then faith *comes* by hearing, and hearing by the word of God. **Isa. 8:20:** To the law and to the testimony! If they do not speak according to this word, *it is* because *there is* no light in them. **Acts 17:11:** These were more fair-minded than those in Thessalonica, in that they received the word with all readiness, and searched the Scriptures daily *to find out* whether these things were so. **John 4:22:** You worship what you do not know; we know what we worship, for salvation is of the Jews. **Rev. 13:12, 16-17:** And he exercises all the authority of the first beast in his presence, and causes the earth and those who dwell in it to worship the first beast, whose deadly wound was healed.... He causes all, both small and great, rich and poor, free and slave, to receive a mark on their right hand or on their foreheads, and that no one may buy or sell except one who has the mark or the name of the beast, or the number of his name. **Jer. 8:9:** The wise men are ashamed, They are dismayed and taken. Behold, they have rejected the word of the LORD; So what wisdom do they have? **1 Pet. 3:15:** But sanctify the Lord God in your hearts, and always *be* ready to *give* a defense to everyone who asks you a reason for the hope that is in you, with meekness and fear.

serve the Lord without fear in holiness, and righteousness before Him, all the days of our life.[14]

[14] **Gal. 5:13:** For you, brethren, have been called to liberty; only do not *use* liberty as an opportunity for the flesh, but through love serve one another. **1 Pet. 2:16:** ... as free, yet not using liberty as a cloak for vice, but as bondservants of God. **2 Pet. 2:18-21:** For when they speak great swelling *words* of emptiness, they allure through the lusts of the flesh, through lewdness, the ones who have actually escaped from those who live in error. While they promise them liberty, they themselves are slaves of corruption; for by whom a person is overcome, by him also he is brought into bondage. For if, after they have escaped the pollutions of the world through the knowledge of the Lord and Savior Jesus Christ, they are again entangled in them and overcome, the latter end is worse for them than the beginning. For it would have been better for them not to have known the way of righteousness, than having known *it,* to turn from the holy commandment delivered to them. **Rom. 6:15:** What then? Shall we sin because we are not under law but under grace? Certainly not! **John 8:34:** Jesus answered them, "Most assuredly, I say to you, whoever commits sin is a slave of sin." **Luke 1:74-75:** To grant us that we, Being delivered from the hand of our enemies, Might serve Him without fear, In holiness and righteousness before Him all the days of our life.

CHAPTER 22

Of Religious Worship, and the Sabbath Day

1. The light of nature shews that there is a God, who hath lordship, and sovereignty over all; is just, good, and doth good unto all; and is therefore to be feared, loved, praised, called upon, trusted in, and served, with all the heart, and all the soul, and with all the might.[1] But the acceptable way of worshipping the true God, is instituted by Himself; and so limited by His own revealed will, that He may not be worshipped according to the imaginations, and devices of men, or the suggestions of Satan, under any visible representations, or any other way, not prescribed in the Holy Scriptures.[2]

---

[1] **Rom. 1:20:** For since the creation of the world His invisible *attributes* are clearly seen, being understood by the things that are made, *even* His eternal power and Godhead, so that they are without excuse. **Ps. 19:1-4:** The heavens declare the glory of God; And the firmament shows His handiwork. Day unto day utters speech, And night unto night reveals knowledge. *There is* no speech nor language *Where* their voice is not heard. Their line has gone out through all the earth, And their words to the end of the world. In them He has set a tabernacle for the sun. **Ps. 50:6:** Let the heavens declare His righteousness, For God Himself *is* Judge. *Selah.* **Jer. 10:7:** Who would not fear You, O King of the nations? For this is Your rightful due. For among all the wise *men* of the nations, And in all their kingdoms, *There is* none like You. **Ps. 97:6:** The heavens declare His righteousness, And all the peoples see His glory. **Ps. 145:9-12:** The LORD *is* good to all, And His tender mercies *are* over all His works. All Your works shall praise You, O LORD, And Your saints shall bless You. They shall speak of the glory of Your kingdom, And talk of Your power, To make known to the sons of men His mighty acts, And the glorious majesty of His kingdom. **Acts 14:17:** Nevertheless He did not leave Himself without witness, in that He did good, gave us rain from heaven and fruitful seasons, filling our hearts with food and gladness. **Ps. 104:** Bless the LORD, O my soul! O LORD my God, You are very great: You are clothed with honor and majesty ... *You who* laid the foundations of the earth, So *that* it should not be moved forever ... He causes the grass to grow for the cattle, And vegetation for the service of man, That he may bring forth food from the earth ... O LORD, how manifold are Your works! In wisdom You have made them all. The earth is full of Your possessions.... May the glory of the LORD endure forever; May the LORD rejoice in His works. He looks on the earth, and it trembles; He touches the hills, and they smoke. I will sing to the LORD as long as I live; I will sing praise to my God while I have my being. May my meditation be sweet to Him; I will be glad in the LORD.... **Ps. 86:8-10:** Among the gods *there is* none like You, O Lord; Nor *are there any works* like Your works. All nations whom You have made Shall come and worship before You, O Lord, And shall glorify Your name. For You *are* great, and do wondrous things; You alone *are* God. **Ps. 95:1-6:** Oh come, let us sing to the LORD! Let us shout joyfully to the Rock of our salvation. Let us come before His presence with thanksgiving; Let us shout joyfully to Him with psalms. For the LORD *is* the great God, And the great King above all gods. In His hand *are* the deep places of the earth; The heights of the hills *are* His also. The sea *is* His, for He made it; And His hands formed the dry *land.* Oh come, let us worship and bow down; Let us kneel before the LORD our Maker. **Ps. 89:5-7:** And the heavens will praise Your wonders, O LORD; Your faithfulness also in the assembly of the saints. For who in the heavens can be compared to the LORD? *Who* among the sons of the mighty can be likened to the LORD? God is greatly to be feared in the assembly of the saints, And to be held in reverence by all *those* around Him. **Deut. 6:4-5:** Hear, O Israel: The LORD our God, the LORD *is* one! You shall love the LORD your God with all your heart, with all your soul, and with all your strength. **Mark 12:33:** And to love Him with all the heart, with all the understanding, with all the soul, and with all the strength, and to love one's neighbor as oneself, is more than all the whole burnt offerings and sacrifices.

[2] **Deut. 12:32:** Whatever I command you, be careful to observe it; you shall not add to it nor take away from it. **Matt. 15:9:** And in vain they worship Me, Teaching *as* doctrines the commandments of men. **Acts 17:23-25:** ... for as I was passing through and considering the objects of your worship, I even found an altar with this inscription: TO THE UNKNOWN GOD. Therefore, the One whom you worship without knowing, Him I proclaim to you: "God, who made the world and everything in it, since He is Lord of heaven and earth, does not dwell in temples made with hands.

2. Religious worship is to be given to God the Father, Son and Holy Spirit, and to Him alone;[3] not to angels, saints, or any other creatures;[4] and since the fall, not without a Mediator, nor in the mediation of any other but Christ alone.[5]

Nor is He worshiped with men's hands, as though He needed anything, since He gives to all life, breath, and all things. **Matt. 4:9-10:** And he said to Him, "All these things I will give You if You will fall down and worship me." Then Jesus said to him, "Away with you, Satan! For it is written, 'You shall worship the LORD your God, and Him only you shall serve.'" **Deut. 4:15-20:** Take careful heed to yourselves, for you saw no form when the LORD spoke to you at Horeb out of the midst of the fire, lest you act corruptly and make for yourselves a carved image in the form of any figure: the likeness of male or female, the likeness of any animal that *is* on the earth or the likeness of any winged bird that flies in the air, the likeness of anything that creeps on the ground or the likeness of any fish that *is* in the water beneath the earth. And *take heed,* lest you lift your eyes to heaven, and *when* you see the sun, the moon, and the stars, all the host of heaven, you feel driven to worship them and serve them, which the LORD your God has given to all the peoples under the whole heaven as a heritage. But the LORD has taken you and brought you out of the iron furnace, out of Egypt, to be His people, an inheritance, as you are this day. **Ex. 20:4-6:** You shall not make for yourself a carved image—any likeness *of anything* that *is* in heaven above, or that *is* in the earth beneath, or that *is* in the water under the earth; you shall not bow down to them nor serve them. For I, the LORD your God, *am* a jealous God, visiting the iniquity of the fathers upon the children to the third and fourth *generations* of those who hate Me, but showing mercy to thousands, to those who love Me and keep My commandments. **John 4:23-24:** But the hour is coming, and now is, when the true worshipers will worship the Father in spirit and truth; for the Father is seeking such to worship Him. God *is* Spirit, and those who worship Him must worship in spirit and truth. **Col. 2:18-23:** Let no one cheat you of your reward, taking delight in *false* humility and worship of angels, intruding into those things which he has not seen, vainly puffed up by his fleshly mind, and not holding fast to the Head, from whom all the body, nourished and knit together by joints and ligaments, grows with the increase *that is* from God. Therefore, if you died with Christ from the basic principles of the world, why, as *though* living in the world, do you subject yourselves to regulations—"Do not touch, do not taste, do not handle," which all concern things which perish with the using—according to the commandments and doctrines of men? These things indeed have an appearance of wisdom in self-imposed religion, *false* humility, and neglect of the body, *but are* of no value against the indulgence of the flesh.

[3] **Matt. 4:9-10:** And he said to Him, "All these things I will give You if You will fall down and worship me." Then Jesus said to him, "Away with you, Satan! For it is written, 'You shall worship the LORD your God, and Him only you shall serve.'" **John 5:23:** ... that all should honor the Son just as they honor the Father. He who does not honor the Son does not honor the Father who sent Him. **Matt. 28:19:** Go therefore and make disciples of all the nations, baptizing them in the name of the Father and of the Son and of the Holy Spirit. **2 Cor. 13:14:** The grace of the Lord Jesus Christ, and the love of God, and the communion of the Holy Spirit *be* with you all. Amen. **Eph. 3:14:** For this reason I bow my knees to the Father of our Lord Jesus Christ. **Rev. 5:11-14:** Then I looked, and I heard the voice of many angels around the throne, the living creatures, and the elders; and the number of them was ten thousand times ten thousand, and thousands of thousands, saying with a loud voice: "Worthy is the Lamb who was slain To receive power and riches and wisdom, And strength and honor and glory and blessing!" And every creature which is in heaven and on the earth and under the earth and such as are in the sea, and all that are in them, I heard saying: "Blessing and honor and glory and power *Be* to Him who sits on the throne, And to the Lamb, forever and ever!" Then the four living creatures said, "Amen!" And the twenty-four elders fell down and worshiped Him who lives forever and ever. **Acts 10:25-26:** As Peter was coming in, Cornelius met him and fell down at his feet and worshiped *him.* But Peter lifted him up, saying, "Stand up; I myself am also a man."

[4] **Rom. 1:25:** ... who exchanged the truth of God for the lie, and worshiped and served the creature rather than the Creator, who is blessed forever. Amen. **Col. 2:18:** Let no one cheat you of your reward, taking delight in *false* humility and worship of angels, intruding into those things which he has not seen, vainly puffed up by his fleshly mind. **Rev. 19:10:** And I fell at his feet to worship him. But he said to me, "See *that you do* not *do that!* I am your fellow servant, and of your brethren who have the testimony of Jesus. Worship God! For the testimony of Jesus is the spirit of prophecy."

[5] **John 14:6:** Jesus said to him, "I am the way, the truth, and the life. No one comes to the Father except through Me." **1 Tim. 2:5:** For *there is* one God and one Mediator between God and men, *the* Man Christ Jesus. **Eph. 2:18:** For through Him we both have access by one Spirit to the Father. **Col.**

3. Prayer with thanksgiving, being one special part of natural worship,[6] is by God required of all men.[7] But that it may be accepted, it is to be made in the name of the Son,[8] by the help of the Spirit,[9] according to His will;[10] with understanding, reverence, humility, fervency, faith, love, and perseverance;[11] and when with others, in a known tongue.[12]

4. Prayer is to be made for things lawful,[13] and for all sorts of men living, or that shall live hereafter;[14] but not for the dead,[15]

3:17: And whatever you do in word or deed, *do* all in the name of the Lord Jesus, giving thanks to God the Father through Him.

[6] **Phil. 4:6:** Be anxious for nothing, but in everything by prayer and supplication, with thanksgiving, let your requests be made known to God. **1 Tim. 2:1:** Therefore I exhort first of all that supplications, prayers, intercessions, *and* giving of thanks be made for all men. **Col. 4:2:** Continue earnestly in prayer, being vigilant in it with thanksgiving.

[7] **Ps. 65:2:** O You who hear prayer, To You all flesh will come. **Ps. 67:3:** Let the peoples praise You, O God; Let all the peoples praise You. **Ps. 96:7-8:** Give to the LORD, O families of the peoples, Give to the LORD glory and strength. Give to the LORD the glory *due* His name; Bring an offering, and come into His courts. **Ps. 148:11-13:** Kings of the earth and all peoples; Princes and all judges of the earth; Both young men and maidens; Old men and children. Let them praise the name of the LORD, For His name alone is exalted; His glory *is* above the earth and heaven. **Isa. 55:6-7:** Seek the LORD while He may be found, Call upon Him while He is near. Let the wicked forsake his way, And the unrighteous man his thoughts; Let him return to the LORD, And He will have mercy on him; And to our God, For He will abundantly pardon.

[8] **John 14:13-14:** And whatever you ask in My name, that I will do, that the Father may be glorified in the Son. If you ask anything in My name, I will do *it.* **1 Pet. 2:5:** ... you also, as living stones, are being built up a spiritual house, a holy priesthood, to offer up spiritual sacrifices acceptable to God through Jesus Christ.

[9] **Rom. 8:26:** Likewise the Spirit also helps in our weaknesses. For we do not know what we should pray for as we ought, but the Spirit Himself makes intercession for us with groanings which cannot be uttered. **Eph. 6:18:** ... praying always with all prayer and supplication in the Spirit, being watchful to this end with all perseverance and supplication for all the saints.

[10] **1 John 5:14:** Now this is the confidence that we have in Him, that if we ask anything according to His will, He hears us.

[11] **Ps. 47:7:** For God *is* the King of all the earth; Sing praises with understanding. **Eccl. 5:1-2:** Walk prudently when you go to the house of God; and draw near to hear rather than to give the sacrifice of fools, for they do not know that they do evil. Do not be rash with your mouth, And let not your heart utter anything hastily before God. For God *is* in heaven, and you on earth; Therefore let your words be few. **Heb. 12:28:** Therefore, since we are receiving a kingdom which cannot be shaken, let us have grace, by which we may serve God acceptably with reverence and godly fear. **Gen. 18:27:** Then Abraham answered and said, "Indeed now, I who *am but* dust and ashes have taken it upon myself to speak to the Lord." **James 5:16:** Confess *your* trespasses to one another, and pray for one another, that you may be healed. The effective, fervent prayer of a righteous man avails much. **James 1:6-7:** But let him ask in faith, with no doubting, for he who doubts is like a wave of the sea driven and tossed by the wind. For let not that man suppose that he will receive anything from the Lord. **Mark 11:24:** Therefore I say to you, whatever things you ask when you pray, believe that you receive *them,* and you will have *them.* **Matt. 6:12, 14-15:** And forgive us our debts, As we forgive our debtors.... For if you forgive men their trespasses, your heavenly Father will also forgive you. But if you do not forgive men their trespasses, neither will your Father forgive your trespasses. **Col. 4:2:** Continue earnestly in prayer, being vigilant in it with thanksgiving. **Eph. 6:18:** ... praying always with all prayer and supplication in the Spirit, being watchful to this end with all perseverance and supplication for all the saints.

[12] **1 Cor. 14:14-17:** For if I pray in a tongue, my spirit prays, but my understanding is unfruitful. What is *the conclusion* then? I will pray with the spirit, and I will also pray with the understanding. I will sing with the spirit, and I will also sing with the understanding. Otherwise, if you bless with the spirit, how will he who occupies the place of the uninformed say "Amen" at your giving of thanks, since he does not understand what you say? For you indeed give thanks well, but the other is not edified.

[13] **1 John 5:14, 16:** Now this is the confidence that we have in Him, that if we ask anything according to His will, He hears us.... If anyone sees his brother sinning a sin *which does* not *lead* to

nor for those of whom it may be known that they have sinned the sin unto death.[16]

5. The reading of the Scriptures,[17] preaching,[18] and hearing the word of God,[19] teaching and admonishing one another in psalms, hymns and spiritual songs, singing with grace in our hearts to the

---

death, he will ask, and He will give him life for those who commit sin not *leading* to death. There is sin *leading* to death. I do not say that he should pray about that. **John 15:7:** If you abide in Me, and My words abide in you, you will ask what you desire, and it shall be done for you.

[14] **1 Tim. 2:1-2:** Therefore I exhort first of all that supplications, prayers, intercessions, *and* giving of thanks be made for all men, for kings and all who are in authority, that we may lead a quiet and peaceable life in all godliness and reverence. **John 17:20:** I do not pray for these alone, but also for those who will believe in Me through their word. **2 Sam. 7:29:** Now therefore, let it please You to bless the house of Your servant, that it may continue before You forever; for You, O Lord God, have spoken *it,* and with Your blessing let the house of Your servant be blessed forever. **2 Chron. 6:14-42:** ... and he said: "LORD God of Israel, *there is* no God in heaven or on earth like You, who keep *Your* covenant and mercy with Your servants who walk before You with all their hearts.... Therefore, LORD God of Israel, now keep what You promised Your servant David my father, saying, 'You shall not fail to have a man sit before Me on the throne of Israel, only if your sons take heed to their way, that they walk in My law as you have walked before Me.' ... And may You hear the supplications of Your servant and of Your people Israel, when they pray toward this place. Hear from heaven Your dwelling place, and when You hear, forgive.... Moreover, concerning a foreigner, who is not of Your people Israel, but has come from a far country for the sake of Your great name and Your mighty hand and Your outstretched arm, when they come and pray in this temple; then hear from heaven Your dwelling place, and do according to all for which the foreigner calls to You, that all peoples of the earth may know Your name and fear You, as *do* Your people Israel, and that they may know that this temple which I have built is called by Your name....

[15] **Luke 16:25-26:** But Abraham said, 'Son, remember that in your lifetime you received your good things, and likewise Lazarus evil things; but now he is comforted and you are tormented. And besides all this, between us and you there is a great gulf fixed, so that those who want to pass from here to you cannot, nor can those from there pass to us.' **Isa. 57:1-2:** The righteous perishes, And no man takes *it* to heart; Merciful men *are* taken away, While no one considers That the righteous is taken away from evil. He shall enter into peace; They shall rest in their beds, *Each one* walking *in* his uprightness. **Ps. 73:24:** You will guide me with Your counsel, And afterward receive me *to* glory. **2 Cor. 5:8, 10:** We are confident, yes, well pleased rather to be absent from the body and to be present with the Lord.... For we must all appear before the judgment seat of Christ, that each one may receive the things *done* in the body, according to what he has done, whether good or bad. **Phil. 1:21-24:** For to me, to live *is* Christ, and to die *is* gain. But if *I* live on in the flesh, this *will mean* fruit from *my* labor; yet what I shall choose I cannot tell. For I am hard-pressed between the two, having a desire to depart and be with Christ, *which is* far better. Nevertheless to remain in the flesh *is* more needful for you. **Rev. 14:13:** Then I heard a voice from heaven saying to me, "Write: 'Blessed *are* the dead who die in the Lord from now on.'" "Yes," says the Spirit, "that they may rest from their labors, and their works follow them."

[16] **1 John 5:16:** If anyone sees his brother sinning a sin *which does* not *lead* to death, he will ask, and He will give him life for those who commit sin not *leading* to death. There is sin *leading* to death. I do not say that he should pray about that.

[17] **1 Tim. 4:13:** Till I come, give attention to reading, to exhortation, to doctrine. **Acts 15:21:** For Moses has had throughout many generations those who preach him in every city, being read in the synagogues every Sabbath. **Col. 4:16:** Now when this epistle is read among you, see that it is read also in the church of the Laodiceans, and that you likewise read the *epistle* from Laodicea. **1 Thess. 5:27:** I charge you by the Lord that this epistle be read to all the holy brethren. **Rev. 1:3:** Blessed *is* he who reads and those who hear the words of this prophecy, and keep those things which are written in it; for the time *is* near.

[18] **2 Tim. 4:2:** Preach the word! Be ready in season *and* out of season. Convince, rebuke, exhort, with all longsuffering and teaching. **Acts 5:42:** And daily in the temple, and in every house, they did not cease teaching and preaching Jesus *as* the Christ.

[19] **James 1:22:** But be doers of the word, and not hearers only, deceiving yourselves. **Acts 10:33:** So I sent to you immediately, and you have done well to come. Now therefore, we are all present before God, to hear all the things commanded you by God. **Matt. 13:19:** When anyone hears the word of the kingdom, and does not understand *it,* then the wicked *one* comes and snatches away what was sown in his heart. This is he who received seed by the wayside.

Lord;[20] as also the administration of baptism, and the Lord's Supper are all parts of religious worship of God,[21] to be performed in obedience to Him, with understanding, faith, reverence, and godly fear;[22] moreover solemn humiliation,[23] with fastings;[24] and thanksgiving upon special occasions,[25] ought to be used in an holy and religious manner.[26]

---

[20] **Col. 3:16:** Let the word of Christ dwell in you richly in all wisdom, teaching and admonishing one another in psalms and hymns and spiritual songs, singing with grace in your hearts to the Lord. **Eph. 5:19:** ... speaking to one another in psalms and hymns and spiritual songs, singing and making melody in your heart to the Lord. **James 5:13:** Is anyone among you suffering? Let him pray. Is anyone cheerful? Let him sing psalms. **1 Cor. 14:15:** What is *the conclusion* then? I will pray with the spirit, and I will also pray with the understanding. I will sing with the spirit, and I will also sing with the understanding.

[21] **Matt. 28:19:** Go therefore and make disciples of all the nations, baptizing them in the name of the Father and of the Son and of the Holy Spirit. **1 Cor.11:23-29:** For I received from the Lord that which I also delivered to you: that the Lord Jesus on the *same* night in which He was betrayed took bread; and when He had given thanks, He broke *it* and said, "Take, eat; this is My body which is broken for you; do this in remembrance of Me." In the same manner *He* also *took* the cup after supper, saying, "This cup is the new covenant in My blood. This do, as often as you drink *it,* in remembrance of Me." For as often as you eat this bread and drink this cup, you proclaim the Lord's death till He comes. Therefore whoever eats this bread or drinks *this* cup of the Lord in an unworthy manner will be guilty of the body and blood of the Lord. But let a man examine himself, and so let him eat of the bread and drink of the cup. For he who eats and drinks in an unworthy manner eats and drinks judgment to himself, not discerning the Lord's body. **Acts 2:42:** And they continued steadfastly in the apostles' doctrine and fellowship, in the breaking of bread, and in prayers.

[22] **Heb. 4:2:** For indeed the gospel was preached to us as well as to them; but the word which they heard did not profit them, not being mixed with faith in those who heard *it.* **Isa. 66:2:** "For all those *things* My hand has made, And all those *things* exist," Says the LORD. "But on this *one* will I look: On *him who is* poor and of a contrite spirit, And who trembles at My word."

[23] **Est. 4:16:** Go, gather all the Jews who are present in Shushan, and fast for me; neither eat nor drink for three days, night or day. My maids and I will fast likewise. And so I will go to the king, which *is* against the law; and if I perish, I perish!

[24] **Joel 2:12:** "Now, therefore," says the LORD, "Turn to Me with all your heart, With fasting, with weeping, and with mourning." **Matt. 9:15:** And Jesus said to them, "Can the friends of the bridegroom mourn as long as the bridegroom is with them? But the days will come when the bridegroom will be taken away from them, and then they will fast." **Acts 14:23:** So when they had appointed elders in every church, and prayed with fasting, they commended them to the Lord in whom they had believed.

[25] **Ex. 15:1-21:** Then Moses and the children of Israel sang this song to the LORD, and spoke, saying: "I will sing to the LORD, For He has triumphed gloriously! The horse and its rider He has thrown into the sea! The LORD *is* my strength and song, And He has become my salvation; He *is* my God, and I will praise Him; My father's God, and I will exalt Him. The LORD *is* a man of war; The LORD *is* His name. Pharaoh's chariots and his army He has cast into the sea; His chosen captains also are drowned in the Red Sea.... Then Miriam the prophetess, the sister of Aaron, took the timbrel in her hand; and all the women went out after her with timbrels and with dances. And Miriam answered them: "Sing to the LORD, For He has triumphed gloriously! The horse and its rider He has thrown into the sea!" **Ps. 107:** Oh, give thanks to the LORD, for *He is* good! For His mercy *endures* forever. Let the redeemed of the LORD say *so,* Whom He has redeemed from the hand of the enemy, And gathered out of the lands, From the east and from the west, From the north and from the south.... Then they cried out to the LORD in their trouble, *And* He saved them out of their distresses.... Oh, that *men* would give thanks to the LORD *for* His goodness, And *for* His wonderful works to the children of men.... **Neh. 12:27-43:** Now at the dedication of the wall of Jerusalem they sought out the Levites in all their places, to bring them to Jerusalem to celebrate the dedication with gladness, both with thanksgivings and singing, *with* cymbals and stringed instruments and harps. And the sons of the singers gathered together from the countryside around Jerusalem, from the villages of the Netophathites.... So the two thanksgiving choirs stood in the house of God, likewise I and the half of the rulers with me ... Also that day they offered great sacrifices, and rejoiced, for God had made them rejoice with great joy; the women and the children also rejoiced, so that the joy of Jerusalem was heard afar off. **Est. 9:20-22:** And Mordecai wrote these things and sent letters to all the Jews, near and far, who *were* in all the provinces of King Ahasuerus, to establish among them that they should celebrate yearly the fourteenth and fifteenth days of the month of Adar, as the days on which the Jews had rest from their enemies, as the month which was

6. Neither prayer, nor any other part of religious worship, is now under the gospel tied unto, or made more acceptable by, any place in which it is performed, or towards which it is directed;[27] but God is to be worshipped everywhere[28] in spirit, and in truth;[29] as in private families[30] daily,[31] and in secret each one by himself,[32] so more solemnly in the public assemblies, which are not carelessly, nor willfully, to be neglected, or forsaken, when God by His word, or providence calleth thereunto.[33]

---

turned from sorrow to joy for them, and from mourning to a holiday; that they should make them days of feasting and joy, of sending presents to one another and gifts to the poor.

[26] **Heb. 12:28:** Therefore, since we are receiving a kingdom which cannot be shaken, let us have grace, by which we may serve God acceptably with reverence and godly fear.

[27] **John 4:21:** Jesus said to her, "Woman, believe Me, the hour is coming when you will neither on this mountain, nor in Jerusalem, worship the Father.

[28] **Mal. 1:11:** "For from the rising of the sun, even to its going down, My name *shall be* great among the Gentiles; In every place incense *shall be* offered to My name, And a pure offering; For My name shall be great among the nations," Says the LORD of hosts. **1 Tim. 2:8:** I desire therefore that the men pray everywhere, lifting up holy hands, without wrath and doubting.

[29] **John 4:23-24:** But the hour is coming, and now is, when the true worshipers will worship the Father in spirit and truth; for the Father is seeking such to worship Him. God *is* Spirit, and those who worship Him must worship in spirit and truth.

[30] **Jer. 10:25:** Pour out Your fury on the Gentiles, who do not know You, And on the families who do not call on Your name; For they have eaten up Jacob, Devoured him and consumed him, And made his dwelling place desolate. **Deut. 6:6-7:** And these words which I command you today shall be in your heart. You shall teach them diligently to your children, and shall talk of them when you sit in your house, when you walk by the way, when you lie down, and when you rise up. **Job 1:5:** So it was, when the days of feasting had run their course, that Job would send and sanctify them, and he would rise early in the morning and offer burnt offerings *according to* the number of them all. For Job said, "It may be that my sons have sinned and cursed God in their hearts." Thus Job did regularly. **2 Sam. 6:18, 20:** And when David had finished offering burnt offerings and peace offerings, he blessed the people in the name of the LORD of hosts.... Then David returned to bless his household. And Michal the daughter of Saul came out to meet David, and said, "How glorious was the king of Israel today, uncovering himself today in the eyes of the maids of his servants, as one of the base fellows shamelessly uncovers himself!"

[31] **Matt. 6:11:** Give us this day our daily bread. **Ps. 55:17:** Evening and morning and at noon I will pray, and cry aloud, And He shall hear my voice. **See Job 1:5.**

[32] **Matt. 6:6, 16-18:** But you, when you pray, go into your room, and when you have shut your door, pray to your Father who *is* in the secret *place;* and your Father who sees in secret will reward you openly.... Moreover, when you fast, do not be like the hypocrites, with a sad countenance. For they disfigure their faces that they may appear to men to be fasting. Assuredly, I say to you, they have their reward. But you, when you fast, anoint your head and wash your face, so that you do not appear to men to be fasting, but to your Father who *is* in the secret *place;* and your Father who sees in secret will reward you openly. **Neh. 1:4-11:** So it was, when I heard these words, that I sat down and wept, and mourned *for many* days; I was fasting and praying before the God of heaven. And I said ... O Lord, I pray, please let Your ear be attentive to the prayer of Your servant, and to the prayer of Your servants who desire to fear Your name; and let Your servant prosper this day, I pray, and grant him mercy in the sight of this man." For I was the king's cupbearer. **Dan. 9:3-4:** Then I set my face toward the Lord God to make request by prayer and supplications, with fasting, sackcloth, and ashes. And I prayed to the LORD my God, and made confession, and said, "O Lord, great and awesome God, who keeps His covenant and mercy with those who love Him, and with those who keep His commandments."

[33] **Isa. 56:6-7:** Also the sons of the foreigner Who join themselves to the LORD, to serve Him, And to love the name of the LORD, to be His servants—Everyone who keeps from defiling the Sabbath, And holds fast My covenant—Even them I will bring to My holy mountain, And make them joyful in My house of prayer. Their burnt offerings and their sacrifices *Will be* accepted on My altar; For My house shall be called a house of prayer for all nations. **Heb. 10:25:** ... not forsaking the assembling of ourselves together, as *is* the manner of some, but exhorting *one another,* and so much the more as you see the Day approaching. **Ps. 100:4:** Enter into His gates with thanksgiving, *And* into His courts with praise. Be thankful to Him, *and* bless His name. **Ps. 122:1:** I was glad when they said to me, "Let us go into the house of the LORD." **Ps. 84:** How lovely *is* Your tabernacle, O LORD of hosts! My soul longs, yes, even faints For the courts of the LORD; My heart and my flesh cry out for

7. As it is of the law of nature, that in general a proportion of time by God's appointment, be set apart for the worship of God; so by His word, in a positive moral, and perpetual commandment, binding all men, in all ages, He hath particularly appointed one day in seven for a Sabbath to be kept holy unto Him,[34] which from the beginning of the world to the resurrection of Christ, was the last day of the week; and from the resurrection of Christ, was changed into the first day of the week[35] which is called the Lord's Day;[36] and is to be continued to the end of the world, as the Christian Sabbath;[37] the observation of the last day of the week being abolished.

---

the living God.... For a day in Your courts *is* better than a thousand. I would rather be a doorkeeper in the house of my God Than dwell in the tents of wickedness.... O LORD of hosts, Blessed *is* the man who trusts in You! **Luke 4:16:** So He came to Nazareth, where He had been brought up. And as His custom was, He went into the synagogue on the Sabbath day, and stood up to read. **Acts 13:42, 44:** So when the Jews went out of the synagogue, the Gentiles begged that these words might be preached to them the next Sabbath.... On the next Sabbath almost the whole city came together to hear the word of God. **Acts 2:42:** And they continued steadfastly in the apostles' doctrine and fellowship, in the breaking of bread, and in prayers.

[34] **Ex. 20:8-11:** Remember the Sabbath day, to keep it holy. Six days you shall labor and do all your work, but the seventh day *is* the Sabbath of the LORD your God. *In it* you shall do no work: you, nor your son, nor your daughter, nor your male servant, nor your female servant, nor your cattle, nor your stranger who *is* within your gates. For *in* six days the LORD made the heavens and the earth, the sea, and all that *is* in them, and rested the seventh day. Therefore the LORD blessed the Sabbath day and hallowed it. **Isa. 56:2-7:** Blessed *is* the man *who* does this, And the son of man *who* lays hold on it; Who keeps from defiling the Sabbath, And keeps his hand from doing any evil. Do not let the son of the foreigner Who has joined himself to the LORD Speak, saying, "The LORD has utterly separated me from His people"; Nor let the eunuch say, "Here I am, a dry tree." For thus says the LORD: "To the eunuchs who keep My Sabbaths, And choose what pleases Me, And hold fast My covenant, Even to them I will give in My house And within My walls a place and a name Better than that of sons and daughters; I will give them an everlasting name That shall not be cut off. "Also the sons of the foreigner Who join themselves to the LORD, to serve Him, And to love the name of the LORD, to be His servants—Everyone who keeps from defiling the Sabbath, And holds fast My covenant—Even them I will bring to My holy mountain, And make them joyful in My house of prayer. Their burnt offerings and their sacrifices *Will be* accepted on My altar; For My house shall be called a house of prayer for all nations."

[35] **Gen. 2:2-3:** And on the seventh day God ended His work which He had done, and He rested on the seventh day from all His work which He had done. Then God blessed the seventh day and sanctified it, because in it He rested from all His work which God had created and made. **1 Cor. 16:1-2:** Now concerning the collection for the saints, as I have given orders to the churches of Galatia, so you must do also: On the first *day* of the week let each one of you lay something aside, storing up as he may prosper, that there be no collections when I come. **Acts 20:7:** Now on the first *day* of the week, when the disciples came together to break bread, Paul, ready to depart the next day, spoke to them and continued his message until midnight.

[36] **Rev. 1:10:** I was in the Spirit on the Lord's Day, and I heard behind me a loud voice, as of a trumpet.

[37] **Matt.5:17-18:** Do not think that I came to destroy the Law or the Prophets. I did not come to destroy but to fulfill. For assuredly, I say to you, till heaven and earth pass away, one jot or one tittle will by no means pass from the law till all is fulfilled. **Mark 2:27-28:** And He said to them, "The Sabbath was made for man, and not man for the Sabbath. Therefore the Son of Man is also Lord of the Sabbath." **Rom. 13:8-10:** Owe no one anything except to love one another, for he who loves another has fulfilled the law. For the commandments, "You shall not commit adultery," "You shall not murder," "You shall not steal," "You shall not bear false witness," "You shall not covet," and if *there is* any other commandment, are *all* summed up in this saying, namely, "You shall love your neighbor as yourself." Love does no harm to a neighbor; therefore love *is* the fulfillment of the law. **James 2:8-12:** If you really fulfill *the* royal law according to the Scripture, "You shall love your neighbor as yourself," you do well; but if you show partiality, you commit sin, and are convicted by the law as transgressors. For whoever shall keep the whole law, and yet stumble in one *point,* he is guilty of all. For He who said, "Do not commit adultery," also said, "Do not murder." Now if you do

8. The Sabbath is then kept holy unto the Lord, when men after a due preparing of their hearts, and ordering their common affairs aforehand, do not only observe an holy rest all the day, from their own works, words, and thoughts, about their worldly employment, and recreations,[38] but also are taken up the whole time in the public and private exercises of His worship, and in the duties of necessity and mercy.[39]

---

not commit adultery, but you do murder, you have become a transgressor of the law. So speak and so do as those who will be judged by the law of liberty.

[38] **Ex. 20:8:** Remember the Sabbath day, to keep it holy. **Ex. 16:23-30:** Then he said to them, "This *is what* the LORD has said: 'Tomorrow *is* a Sabbath rest, a holy Sabbath to the LORD. Bake what you will bake *today,* and boil what you will boil; and lay up for yourselves all that remains, to be kept until morning.'" So they laid it up till morning, as Moses commanded; and it did not stink, nor were there any worms in it. Then Moses said, "Eat that today, for today *is* a Sabbath to the LORD; today you will not find it in the field. Six days you shall gather it, but on the seventh day, the Sabbath, there will be none." Now it happened *that some* of the people went out on the seventh day to gather, but they found none. And the LORD said to Moses, "How long do you refuse to keep My commandments and My laws? See! For the LORD has given you the Sabbath; therefore He gives you on the sixth day bread for two days. Let every man remain in his place; let no man go out of his place on the seventh day." So the people rested on the seventh day. **Ex. 31:15-17:** Work shall be done for six days, but the seventh *is* the Sabbath of rest, holy to the LORD. Whoever does *any* work on the Sabbath day, he shall surely be put to death. Therefore the children of Israel shall keep the Sabbath, to observe the Sabbath throughout their generations *as* a perpetual covenant. It *is* a sign between Me and the children of Israel forever; for *in* six days the LORD made the heavens and the earth, and on the seventh day He rested and was refreshed. **Is. 58:13-14:** If you turn away your foot from the Sabbath, *From* doing your pleasure on My holy day, And call the Sabbath a delight, The holy *day* of the LORD honorable, And shall honor Him, not doing your own ways, Nor finding your own pleasure, Nor speaking *your own* words, Then you shall delight yourself in the LORD; And I will cause you to ride on the high hills of the earth, And feed you with the heritage of Jacob your father. The mouth of the LORD has spoken. **Neh. 13:15-22:** In those days I saw *people* in Judah treading wine presses on the Sabbath, and bringing in sheaves, and loading donkeys with wine, grapes, figs, and all *kinds of* burdens, which they brought into Jerusalem on the Sabbath day. And I warned *them* about the day on which they were selling provisions. Men of Tyre dwelt there also, who brought in fish and all kinds of goods, and sold *them* on the Sabbath to the children of Judah, and in Jerusalem. Then I contended with the nobles of Judah, and said to them, "What evil thing *is* this that you do, by which you profane the Sabbath day? Did not your fathers do thus, and did not our God bring all this disaster on us and on this city? Yet you bring added wrath on Israel by profaning the Sabbath." So it was, at the gates of Jerusalem, as it began to be dark before the Sabbath, that I commanded the gates to be shut, and charged that they must not be opened till after the Sabbath. Then I posted *some* of my servants at the gates, *so that* no burdens would be brought in on the Sabbath day. Now the merchants and sellers of all kinds of wares lodged outside Jerusalem once or twice. Then I warned them, and said to them, "Why do you spend the night around the wall? If you do *so* again, I will lay hands on you!" From that time on they came no *more* on the Sabbath. And I commanded the Levites that they should cleanse themselves, and that they should go and guard the gates, to sanctify the Sabbath day. Remember me, O my God, *concerning* this also, and spare me according to the greatness of Your mercy!

[39] **Isa. 58:13-14:** If you turn away your foot from the Sabbath, *From* doing your pleasure on My holy day, And call the Sabbath a delight, The holy *day* of the LORD honorable, And shall honor Him, not doing your own ways, Nor finding your own pleasure, Nor speaking *your own* words, Then you shall delight yourself in the LORD; And I will cause you to ride on the high hills of the earth, And feed you with the heritage of Jacob your father. The mouth of the LORD has spoken. **Luke 4:16:** So He came to Nazareth, where He had been brought up. And as His custom was, He went into the synagogue on the Sabbath day, and stood up to read. **Matt. 12:1-13:** At that time Jesus went through the grainfields on the Sabbath. And His disciples were hungry, and began to pluck heads of grain and to eat. And when the Pharisees saw *it,* they said to Him, "Look, Your disciples are doing what is not lawful to do on the Sabbath!" But He said to them, "Have you not read what David did when he was hungry, he and those who were with him: how he entered the house of God and ate the showbread which was not lawful for him to eat, nor for those who were with him, but only for the priests? Or have you not read in the law that on the Sabbath the priests in the temple profane the Sabbath, and are blameless? Yet I say to you that in this place there is *One* greater than the temple. But if you had known what *this* means, 'I desire mercy and not sacrifice,' you would not have condemned the guiltless. For the Son of Man is Lord even of the Sabbath." Now when He had

departed from there, He went into their synagogue. And behold, there was a man who had a withered hand. And they asked Him, saying, "Is it lawful to heal on the Sabbath?"—that they might accuse Him. Then He said to them, "What man is there among you who has one sheep, and if it falls into a pit on the Sabbath, will not lay hold of it and lift *it* out? Of how much more value then is a man than a sheep? Therefore it is lawful to do good on the Sabbath." Then He said to the man, "Stretch out your hand." And he stretched *it* out, and it was restored as whole as the other. **Mark 3:1-5:** And He entered the synagogue again, and a man was there who had a withered hand. So they watched Him closely, whether He would heal him on the Sabbath, so that they might accuse Him. And He said to the man who had the withered hand, "Step forward." Then He said to them, "Is it lawful on the Sabbath to do good or to do evil, to save life or to kill?" But they kept silent. And when He had looked around at them with anger, being grieved by the hardness of their hearts, He said to the man, "Stretch out your hand." And he stretched *it* out, and his hand was restored as whole as the other.

CHAPTER 23

Of Lawful Oaths and Vows

1. A lawful oath is a part of religious worship,[1] wherein the person swearing in truth, righteousness, and judgement, solemnly calleth God to witness what he sweareth; and to judge him according to the truth or falseness thereof.[2]

2. The name of God only is that by which men ought to swear; and therein it is to be used, with all holy fear and reverence,[3] therefore to swear vainly or rashly by that glorious, and dreadful name; or to swear at all by any other thing, is sinful and to be abhorred;[4] yet as in matter of weight and moment for confirmation of truth, and ending all strife, an oath is warranted by the word of God;[5] so a lawful oath being imposed, by lawful authority, in such matters, ought to be taken.[6]

---

[1] **Deut. 10:20:** You shall fear the LORD your God; you shall serve Him, and to Him you shall hold fast, and take oaths in His name. **Isa. 45:23:** I have sworn by Myself; The word has gone out of My mouth *in* righteousness, And shall not return, That to Me every knee shall bow, Every tongue shall take an oath. **Rom. 14:11:** For it is written: "*As* I live, says the LORD, Every knee shall bow to Me, And every tongue shall confess to God." **Phil. 2:10-11:** ... that at the name of Jesus every knee should bow, of those in heaven, and of those on earth, and of those under the earth, and *that* every tongue should confess that Jesus Christ *is* Lord, to the glory of God the Father.

[2] **Ex. 20:7:** You shall not take the name of the LORD your God in vain, for the LORD will not hold *him* guiltless who takes His name in vain. **Lev. 19:12:** And you shall not swear by My name falsely, nor shall you profane the name of your God: I *am* the LORD. **Rom. 1:9:** For God is my witness, whom I serve with my spirit in the gospel of His Son, that without ceasing I make mention of you always in my prayers. **2 Cor. 1:23:** Moreover I call God as witness against my soul, that to spare you I came no more to Corinth. **2 Cor. 11:31**: The God and Father of our Lord Jesus Christ, who is blessed forever, knows that I am not lying. **Gal. 1:20:** Now *concerning* the things which I write to you, indeed, before God, I do not lie. **2 Chron. 6:22-23:** If anyone sins against his neighbor, and is forced to take an oath, and comes *and* takes an oath before Your altar in this temple, then hear from heaven, and act, and judge Your servants, bringing retribution on the wicked by bringing his way on his own head, and justifying the righteous by giving him according to his righteousness.

[3] **Deut. 6:13:** You shall fear the LORD your God and serve Him, and shall take oaths in His name. **Josh. 23:7:** ... *and* lest you go among these nations, these who remain among you. You shall not make mention of the name of their gods, nor cause *anyone* to swear *by them;* you shall not serve them nor bow down to them.

[4] **Ex. 20:7:** You shall not take the name of the LORD your God in vain, for the LORD will not hold *him* guiltless who takes His name in vain. **Jer. 5:7:** How shall I pardon you for this? Your children have forsaken Me And sworn by *those that are* not gods. When I had fed them to the full, Then they committed adultery And assembled themselves by troops in the harlots' houses. **Matt. 5:33-37:** Again you have heard that it was said to those of old, 'You shall not swear falsely, but shall perform your oaths to the Lord.' But I say to you, do not swear at all: neither by heaven, for it is God's throne; nor by the earth, for it is His footstool; nor by Jerusalem, for it is the city of the great King. Nor shall you swear by your head, because you cannot make one hair white or black. But let your 'Yes' be 'Yes,' and your 'No,' 'No.' For whatever is more than these is from the evil one. **James 5:12:** But above all, my brethren, do not swear, either by heaven or by earth or with any other oath. But let your "Yes" be "Yes," and *your* "No," "No," lest you fall into judgment.

[5] **Heb. 6:16:** For men indeed swear by the greater, and an oath for confirmation *is* for them an end of all dispute. **2 Cor. 1:23:** Moreover I call God as witness against my soul, that to spare you I came no more to Corinth. **Isa. 65:16:** So that he who blesses himself in the earth Shall bless himself in the God of truth; And he who swears in the earth Shall swear by the God of truth; Because the former troubles are forgotten, And because they are hidden from My eyes.

3. Whosoever taketh an oath warranted by the word of God, ought duly to consider the weightiness of so solemn an act; and therein to avouch nothing, but what he knoweth to be the truth;[7] for that by rash, false, and vain oaths the Lord is provoked, and for them this land mourns.[8] Neither may any man bind himself by oath to anything but what is good and just, and what he believeth so to be, and what he is able and resolved to perform.[9]

4. An oath is to be taken in the plain, and common sense of the words; without equivocation, or mental reservation.[10] It cannot oblige to sin, but in anything not sinful, being taken, it binds to performance, although to a man's own hurt.[11] Nor is it to be violated, although made to heretics, or infidels.[12]

---

[6] **1 Kings 8:31:** When anyone sins against his neighbor, and is forced to take an oath, and comes *and* takes an oath before Your altar in this temple. **Neh. 13:25:** So I contended with them and cursed them, struck some of them and pulled out their hair, and made them swear by God, *saying,* "You shall not give your daughters as wives to their sons, nor take their daughters for your sons or yourselves." **Ezra 10:5:** Then Ezra arose, and made the leaders of the priests, the Levites, and all Israel swear an oath that they would do according to this word. So they swore an oath.

[7] **Ex. 20:7:** You shall not take the name of the LORD your God in vain, for the LORD will not hold *him* guiltless who takes His name in vain. **Lev. 19:12:** And you shall not swear by My name falsely, nor shall you profane the name of your God: I *am* the LORD. **Jer. 4:2:** And you shall swear, 'The LORD lives,' In truth, in judgment, and in righteousness; The nations shall bless themselves in Him, And in Him they shall glory.

[8] **Jer. 23:10:** For the land is full of adulterers; For because of a curse the land mourns. The pleasant places of the wilderness are dried up. Their course of life is evil, And their might *is* not right.

[9] **Gen. 24:2-9:** So Abraham said to the oldest servant of his house, who ruled over all that he had, "Please, put your hand under my thigh, and I will make you swear by the LORD, the God of heaven and the God of the earth, that you will not take a wife for my son from the daughters of the Canaanites, among whom I dwell; but you shall go to my country and to my family, and take a wife for my son Isaac." And the servant said to him, "Perhaps the woman will not be willing to follow me to this land. Must I take your son back to the land from which you came?" But Abraham said to him, "Beware that you do not take my son back there. The LORD God of heaven, who took me from my father's house and from the land of my family, and who spoke to me and swore to me, saying, 'To your descendants I give this land,' He will send His angel before you, and you shall take a wife for my son from there. And if the woman is not willing to follow you, then you will be released from this oath; only do not take my son back there." So the servant put his hand under the thigh of Abraham his master, and swore to him concerning this matter. **Neh. 5:12-13:** So they said, "We will restore *it,* and will require nothing from them; we will do as you say." Then I called the priests, and required an oath from them that they would do according to this promise. Then I shook out the fold of my garment and said, "So may God shake out each man from his house, and from his property, who does not perform this promise. Even thus may he be shaken out and emptied." And all the assembly said, "Amen!" and praised the LORD. Then the people did according to this promise. **Eccl. 5:2, 5:** Do not be rash with your mouth, And let not your heart utter anything hastily before God. For God *is* in heaven, and you on earth; Therefore let your words be few.... Better not to vow than to vow and not pay.

[10] **Jer. 4:2:** And you shall swear, 'The LORD lives,' In truth, in judgment, and in righteousness; The nations shall bless themselves in Him, And in Him they shall glory. **Ps. 24:4:** He who has clean hands and a pure heart, Who has not lifted up his soul to an idol, Nor sworn deceitfully.

[11] **1 Sam. 25:22, 32–34:** May God do so, and more also, to the enemies of David, if I leave one male of all who *belong* to him by morning light.... Then David said to Abigail: "Blessed *is* the LORD God of Israel, who sent you this day to meet me! And blessed *is* your advice and blessed *are* you, because you have kept me this day from coming to bloodshed and from avenging myself with my own hand. For indeed, *as* the LORD God of Israel lives, who has kept me back from hurting you, unless you had hurried and come to meet me, surely by morning light no males would have been left to Nabal!" **Ps. 15:4:** In whose eyes a vile person is despised, But he honors those who fear the LORD; He *who* swears to his own hurt and does not change.

5. A vow, which is not to be made to any creature, but to God alone,[13] is to be made and performed with all religious care, and faithfulness;[14] but popish monastical vows, of perpetual single life, professed poverty, and regular obedience, are so far from being degrees of higher perfection, that they are superstitious, and sinful snares, in which no Christian may entangle himself.[15]

---

[12] **Ezek. 17:16–19:** '*As* I live,' says the Lord God, 'surely in the place *where* the king *dwells* who made him king, whose oath he despised and whose covenant he broke—with him in the midst of Babylon he shall die. Nor will Pharaoh with *his* mighty army and great company do anything in the war, when they heap up a siege mound and build a wall to cut off many persons. Since he despised the oath by breaking the covenant, and in fact gave his hand and still did all these *things,* he shall not escape.' Therefore thus says the Lord God: "*As* I live, surely My oath which he despised, and My covenant which he broke, I will recompense on his own head." **Josh. 9:18–19:** But the children of Israel did not attack them, because the rulers of the congregation had sworn to them by the LORD God of Israel. And all the congregation complained against the rulers. Then all the rulers said to all the congregation, "We have sworn to them by the LORD God of Israel; now therefore, we may not touch them." **2 Sam. 21:1:** Now there was a famine in the days of David for three years, year after year; and David inquired of the LORD. And the LORD answered, "*It is* because of Saul and *his* bloodthirsty house, because he killed the Gibeonites."

[13] **Ps. 50:14:** Offer to God thanksgiving, And pay your vows to the Most High. **Ps. 76:11:** Make vows to the LORD your God, and pay *them;* Let all who are around Him bring presents to Him who ought to be feared. **Ps. 116:14:** I will pay my vows to the LORD Now in the presence of all His people.

[14] **Num. 30:2:** If a man makes a vow to the LORD, or swears an oath to bind himself by some agreement, he shall not break his word; he shall do according to all that proceeds out of his mouth. **Isa. 19:21:** Then the LORD will be known to Egypt, and the Egyptians will know the LORD in that day, and will make sacrifice and offering; yes, they will make a vow to the LORD and perform *it.* **Eccl. 5:4-6:** When you make a vow to God, do not delay to pay it; For *He has* no pleasure in fools. Pay what you have vowed—Better not to vow than to vow and not pay. Do not let your mouth cause your flesh to sin, nor say before the messenger *of God* that it *was* an error. Why should God be angry at your excuse and destroy the work of your hands? **Ps. 61:8:** So I will sing praise to Your name forever, That I may daily perform my vows. **Ps. 66:13-14:** I will go into Your house with burnt offerings; I will pay You my vows, Which my lips have uttered And my mouth has spoken when I was in trouble.

[15] **Matt. 19:11-12:** But He said to them, "All cannot accept this saying, but only *those* to whom it has been given: For there are eunuchs who were born thus from *their* mother's womb, and there are eunuchs who were made eunuchs by men, and there are eunuchs who have made themselves eunuchs for the kingdom of heaven's sake. He who is able to accept *it,* let him accept *it.*" **1 Cor. 7:2, 9:** Nevertheless, because of sexual immorality, let each man have his own wife, and let each woman have her own husband.... but if they cannot exercise self-control, let them marry. For it is better to marry than to burn *with passion.* **Heb. 13:4:** Marriage *is* honorable among all, and the bed undefiled; but fornicators and adulterers God will judge. **Eph. 4:28:** Let him who stole steal no longer, but rather let him labor, working with *his* hands what is good, that he may have something to give him who has need. **1 Thess. 4:11-12:** ... that you also aspire to lead a quiet life, to mind your own business, and to work with your own hands, as we commanded you, that you may walk properly toward those who are outside, and *that* you may lack nothing. **1 Cor. 7:23:** You were bought at a price; do not become slaves of men.

CHAPTER 24
Of the Civil Magistrate

1. God the supreme Lord, and King of all the world, hath ordained civil magistrates to be under Him, over the people, for His own glory, and the public good; and to this end hath armed them with the power of the sword, for defence and encouragement of them that do good, and for the punishment of evil doers.[1]

2. It is lawful for Christians to accept, and execute the office of a magistrate, when called thereunto;[2] in the management whereof,

---

[1] **Rom. 13:1-4:** Let every soul be subject to the governing authorities. For there is no authority except from God, and the authorities that exist are appointed by God. Therefore whoever resists the authority resists the ordinance of God, and those who resist will bring judgment on themselves. For rulers are not a terror to good works, but to evil. Do you want to be unafraid of the authority? Do what is good, and you will have praise from the same. For he is God's minister to you for good. But if you do evil, be afraid; for he does not bear the sword in vain; for he is God's minister, an avenger to *execute* wrath on him who practices evil. **1 Pet. 2:13-14:** Therefore submit yourselves to every ordinance of man for the Lord's sake, whether to the king as supreme, or to governors, as to those who are sent by him for the punishment of evildoers and *for the* praise of those who do good.

[2] **Gen. 41:39-43:** Then Pharaoh said to Joseph, "Inasmuch as God has shown you all this, *there is* no one as discerning and wise as you. You shall be over my house, and all my people shall be ruled according to your word; only in regard to the throne will I be greater than you." And Pharaoh said to Joseph, "See, I have set you over all the land of Egypt." Then Pharaoh took his signet ring off his hand and put it on Joseph's hand; and he clothed him in garments of fine linen and put a gold chain around his neck. And he had him ride in the second chariot which he had; and they cried out before him, "Bow the knee!" So he set him over all the land of Egypt. **Neh. 12:26:** These *lived* in the days of Joiakim the son of Jeshua, the son of Jozadak, and in the days of Nehemiah the governor, and of Ezra the priest, the scribe. **Neh. 13:15-31:** In those days I saw *people* in Judah treading wine presses on the Sabbath, and bringing in sheaves, and loading donkeys with wine, grapes, figs, and all *kinds of* burdens, which they brought into Jerusalem on the Sabbath day. And I warned *them* about the day on which they were selling provisions. Men of Tyre dwelt there also, who brought in fish and all kinds of goods, and sold *them* on the Sabbath to the children of Judah, and in Jerusalem. Then I contended with the nobles of Judah, and said to them, "What evil thing *is* this that you do, by which you profane the Sabbath day? Did not your fathers do thus, and did not our God bring all this disaster on us and on this city? Yet you bring added wrath on Israel by profaning the Sabbath." So it was, at the gates of Jerusalem, as it began to be dark before the Sabbath, that I commanded the gates to be shut, and charged that they must not be opened till after the Sabbath. Then I posted *some* of my servants at the gates, *so that* no burdens would be brought in on the Sabbath day. Now the merchants and sellers of all kinds of wares lodged outside Jerusalem once or twice. Then I warned them, and said to them, "Why do you spend the night around the wall? If you do *so* again, I will lay hands on you!" From that time on they came no *more* on the Sabbath. And I commanded the Levites that they should cleanse themselves, and that they should go and guard the gates, to sanctify the Sabbath day. Remember me, O my God, *concerning* this also, and spare me according to the greatness of Your mercy! In those days I also saw Jews *who* had married women of Ashdod, Ammon, *and* Moab. And half of their children spoke the language of Ashdod, and could not speak the language of Judah, but spoke according to the language of one or the other people. So I contended with them and cursed them, struck some of them and pulled out their hair, and made them swear by God, *saying,* "You shall not give your daughters as wives to their sons, nor take their daughters for your sons or yourselves. Did not Solomon king of Israel sin by these things? Yet among many nations there was no king like him, who was beloved of his God; and God made him king over all Israel. Nevertheless pagan women caused even him to sin. Should we then hear of your doing all this great evil, transgressing against our God by marrying pagan women?" And *one* of the sons of Joiada, the son of Eliashib the high priest, *was* a son-in-law of Sanballat the Horonite; therefore I drove him from me. Remember them, O my God, because they have defiled the priesthood and the covenant of the priesthood and the Levites. Thus I cleansed them of everything

as they ought especially to maintain justice, and peace, according to the wholesome laws of each kingdom, and commonwealth:[3] so for that end they may lawfully now under the New Covenant wage war upon just and necessary occasions.[4]

3. Civil magistrates being set up by God, for the ends aforesaid; subjection in all lawful things commanded by them, ought to be yielded by us, in the Lord; not only for wrath but for conscience' sake;[5] and we ought to make supplications and prayers for kings, and all that are in authority, that under them we may live a quiet and peaceable life, in all godliness and honesty.[6]

---

pagan. I also assigned duties to the priests and the Levites, each to his service, and *to bringing* the wood offering and the firstfruits at appointed times. Remember me, O my God, for good! **Dan. 2:48-49:** Then the king promoted Daniel and gave him many great gifts; and he made him ruler over the whole province of Babylon, and chief administrator over all the wise *men* of Babylon. Also Daniel petitioned the king, and he set Shadrach, Meshach, and Abed-Nego over the affairs of the province of Babylon; but Daniel *sat* in the gate of the king. **Prov. 8:15-16:** By me kings reign, And rulers decree justice. By me princes rule, and nobles, All the judges of the earth. **Rom. 13:1-4:** Let every soul be subject to the governing authorities. For there is no authority except from God, and the authorities that exist are appointed by God. Therefore whoever resists the authority resists the ordinance of God, and those who resist will bring judgment on themselves. For rulers are not a terror to good works, but to evil. Do you want to be unafraid of the authority? Do what is good, and you will have praise from the same. For he is God's minister to you for good. But if you do evil, be afraid; for he does not bear the sword in vain; for he is God's minister, an avenger to *execute* wrath on him who practices evil.

[3] **Ps. 2:10-12:** Now therefore, be wise, O kings; Be instructed, you judges of the earth. Serve the LORD with fear, And rejoice with trembling. Kiss the Son, lest He be angry, And you perish *in* the way, When His wrath is kindled but a little. Blessed *are* all those who put their trust in Him. **1 Tim. 2:2:** ... for kings and all who are in authority, that we may lead a quiet and peaceable life in all godliness and reverence. **2 Sam. 23:3:** The God of Israel said, The Rock of Israel spoke to me: 'He who rules over men *must be* just, Ruling in the fear of God. **Ps. 82:3-4:** Defend the poor and fatherless; Do justice to the afflicted and needy. Deliver the poor and needy; Free *them* from the hand of the wicked. **1 Pet. 2:13:** Therefore submit yourselves to every ordinance of man for the Lord's sake, whether to the king as supreme.

[4] **Luke 3:14:** Likewise the soldiers asked him, saying, "And what shall we do?" So he said to them, "Do not intimidate anyone or accuse falsely, and be content with your wages." **Rom. 13:4:** For he is God's minister to you for good. But if you do evil, be afraid; for he does not bear the sword in vain; for he is God's minister, an avenger to *execute* wrath on him who practices evil. **Matt. 8:9-10:** For I also am a man under authority, having soldiers under me. And I say to this *one,* 'Go,' and he goes; and to another, 'Come,' and he comes; and to my servant, 'Do this,' and he does *it.*" When Jesus heard *it,* He marveled, and said to those who followed, "Assuredly, I say to you, I have not found such great faith, not even in Israel! **Acts 10:1-2:** There was a certain man in Caesarea called Cornelius, a centurion of what was called the Italian Regiment, a devout *man* and one who feared God with all his household, who gave alms generously to the people, and prayed to God always.

[5] **Rom. 13:5-7:** Therefore *you* must be subject, not only because of wrath but also for conscience' sake. For because of this you also pay taxes, for they are God's ministers attending continually to this very thing. Render therefore to all their due: taxes to whom taxes *are due,* customs to whom customs, fear to whom fear, honor to whom honor. **Titus 3:1:** Remind them to be subject to rulers and authorities, to obey, to be ready for every good work. **1 Pet. 2:17:** Honor all *people.* Love the brotherhood. Fear God. Honor the king. **Matt. 22:21:** They said to Him, "Caesar's." And He said to them, "Render therefore to Caesar the things that are Caesar's, and to God the things that are God's."

[6] **1 Tim. 2:1-3:** Therefore I exhort first of all that supplications, prayers, intercessions, *and* giving of thanks be made for all men, for kings and all who are in authority, that we may lead a quiet and

peaceable life in all godliness and reverence. For this *is* good and acceptable in the sight of God our Savior.

CHAPTER 25
Of Marriage

1. Marriage, which was instituted by God, is to be between one man and one woman,[1] according to a covenant made between them both;[2] neither is it lawful for any man to have more than one wife, nor for any woman to have more than one husband at the same time.[3]

2. Marriage was ordained for the mutual help of husband and wife,[4] for the increase of mankind, with a legitimate issue,[5] and for preventing of uncleanness.[6]

3. It is lawful for all sorts of people to marry, who are able with judgement to give their consent;[7] yet it is the duty of Christians

---

[1] **Gen. 2:18, 24:** And the LORD God said, "*It is* not good that man should be alone; I will make him a helper comparable to him." ... Therefore a man shall leave his father and mother and be joined to his wife, and they shall become one flesh. **Matt. 19:4-6:** And He answered and said to them, "Have you not read that He who made *them* at the beginning 'made them male and female,' and said, 'For this reason a man shall leave his father and mother and be joined to his wife, and the two shall become one flesh'? So then, they are no longer two but one flesh. Therefore what God has joined together, let not man separate."

[2] **Mal. 2:14-15:** Yet you say, "For what reason?" Because the LORD has been witness Between you and the wife of your youth, With whom you have dealt treacherously; Yet she is your companion And your wife by covenant. But did He not make *them* one, Having a remnant of the Spirit? And why one? He seeks godly offspring. Therefore take heed to your spirit, And let none deal treacherously with the wife of his youth. **Jer. 31:32:** ... not according to the covenant that I made with their fathers in the day *that* I took them by the hand to lead them out of the land of Egypt, My covenant which they broke, though I was a husband to them, says the LORD. **Ezek. 16:8:** "When I passed by you again and looked upon you, indeed your time *was* the time of love; so I spread My wing over you and covered your nakedness. Yes, I swore an oath to you and entered into a covenant with you, and you became Mine," says the Lord God. **See Deut. 22:22-29.**

[3] **Rom. 7:3:** So then if, while *her* husband lives, she marries another man, she will be called an adulteress; but if her husband dies, she is free from that law, so that she is no adulteress, though she has married another man. **1 Tim. 3:2:** A bishop then must be blameless, the husband of one wife, temperate, sober-minded, of good behavior, hospitable, able to teach.

[4] **Gen. 2:18:** And the LORD God said, "*It is* not good that man should be alone; I will make him a helper comparable to him." **Eph. 5:28:** So husbands ought to love their own wives as their own bodies; he who loves his wife loves himself. **1 Pet. 3:7:** Husbands, likewise, dwell with *them* with understanding, giving honor to the wife, as to the weaker vessel, and as *being* heirs together of the grace of life, that your prayers may not be hindered.

[5] **Gen. 1:28:** Then God blessed them, and God said to them, "Be fruitful and multiply; fill the earth and subdue it; have dominion over the fish of the sea, over the birds of the air, and over every living thing that moves on the earth." **Gen. 9:1:** So God blessed Noah and his sons, and said to them: "Be fruitful and multiply, and fill the earth. **Mal. 2:15:** But did He not make *them* one, Having a remnant of the Spirit? And why one? He seeks godly offspring. Therefore take heed to your spirit, And let none deal treacherously with the wife of his youth.

[6] **1 Cor. 7:2, 9:** Nevertheless, because of sexual immorality, let each man have his own wife, and let each woman have her own husband.... but if they cannot exercise self-control, let them marry. For it is better to marry than to burn *with passion.*

[7] **Heb. 13:4:** Marriage *is* honorable among all, and the bed undefiled; but fornicators and adulterers God will judge. **1 Tim. 4:3:** ... forbidding to marry, *and commanding* to abstain from foods which God created to be received with thanksgiving by those who believe and know the truth. **1 Cor. 7:36-38:** But if any man thinks he is behaving improperly toward his virgin, if she is past the flower of youth, and thus it must be, let him do what he wishes. He does not sin; let them marry.

to marry only in the Lord,[8] and therefore such as profess the true religion, should not marry with infidels, or idolaters; neither should such as are godly be unequally yoked, by marrying with such as are wicked, in their life, or maintain damnable heresy.[9]

4. Marriage ought not to be within the degrees of consanguinity, or affinity forbidden in the word;[10] nor can such incestuous marriage ever be made lawful, by any law of man or consent of parties, so as those persons may live together as man and wife.[11]

Nevertheless he who stands steadfast in his heart, having no necessity, but has power over his own will, and has so determined in his heart that he will keep his virgin, does well. So then he who gives *her* in marriage does well, but he who does not give *her* in marriage does better. **Gen. 24:57-58:** So they said, "We will call the young woman and ask her personally." Then they called Rebekah and said to her, "Will you go with this man?" And she said, "I will go."

[8] **1 Cor. 7:39:** A wife is bound by law as long as her husband lives; but if her husband dies, she is at liberty to be married to whom she wishes, only in the Lord.

[9] **Gen. 34:14:** And they said to them, "We cannot do this thing, to give our sister to one who is uncircumcised, for that *would be* a reproach to us." **Ex. 34:16:** ... and you take of his daughters for your sons, and his daughters play the harlot with their gods and make your sons play the harlot with their gods. **2 Cor. 6:14:** Do not be unequally yoked together with unbelievers. For what fellowship has righteousness with lawlessness? And what communion has light with darkness? **See Deut. 7:3-4; 1 Kings 11:4; Neh.13:25-27; Mal. 2:11-12.**

[10] **Lev. 18:6-17, 24-30:** 'None of you shall approach anyone who is near of kin to him, to uncover his nakedness: I *am* the LORD. The nakedness of your father or the nakedness of your mother you shall not uncover. She *is* your mother; you shall not uncover her nakedness. The nakedness of your father's wife you shall not uncover; it *is* your father's nakedness. The nakedness of your sister, the daughter of your father, or the daughter of your mother, *whether* born at home or elsewhere, their nakedness you shall not uncover. The nakedness of your son's daughter or your daughter's daughter, their nakedness you shall not uncover; for theirs *is* your own nakedness. The nakedness of your father's wife's daughter, begotten by your father—she *is* your sister—you shall not uncover her nakedness. You shall not uncover the nakedness of your father's sister; she *is* near of kin to your father. You shall not uncover the nakedness of your mother's sister, for she *is* near of kin to your mother. You shall not uncover the nakedness of your father's brother. You shall not approach his wife; she *is* your aunt. You shall not uncover the nakedness of your daughter-in-law—she *is* your son's wife—you shall not uncover her nakedness. You shall not uncover the nakedness of your brother's wife; it *is* your brother's nakedness. You shall not uncover the nakedness of a woman and her daughter, nor shall you take her son's daughter or her daughter's daughter, to uncover her nakedness. They *are* near of kin to her. It *is* wickedness.... 'Do not defile yourselves with any of these things; for by all these the nations are defiled, which I am casting out before you. For the land is defiled; therefore I visit the punishment of its iniquity upon it, and the land vomits out its inhabitants. You shall therefore keep My statutes and My judgments, and shall not commit *any* of these abominations, *either* any of your own nation or any stranger who dwells among you (for all these abominations the men of the land have done, who *were* before you, and thus the land is defiled), lest the land vomit you out also when you defile it, as it vomited out the nations that *were* before you. For whoever commits any of these abominations, the persons who commit *them* shall be cut off from among their people. 'Therefore you shall keep My ordinance, so that *you* do not commit *any* of these abominable customs which were committed before you, and that you do not defile yourselves by them: I *am* the LORD your God.' **Lev. 20:19:** You shall not uncover the nakedness of your mother's sister nor of your father's sister, for that would uncover his near of kin. They shall bear their guilt. **1 Cor. 5:1:** t is actually reported *that there is* sexual immorality among you, and such sexual immorality as is not even named among the Gentiles—that a man has his father's wife! **Amos 2:7:** They pant after the dust of the earth *which is* on the head of the poor, And pervert the way of the humble. A man and his father go in to the *same* girl, To defile My holy name.

[11] **Mark 6:18:** Because John had said to Herod, "It is not lawful for you to have your brother's wife." **Lev. 18:24-28:** Do not defile yourselves with any of these things; for by all these the nations are defiled, which I am casting out before you. For the land is defiled; therefore I visit the punishment of its iniquity upon it, and the land vomits out its inhabitants. You shall therefore keep My statutes and My judgments, and shall not commit *any* of these abominations, *either* any of your own nation or any stranger who dwells among you (for all these abominations the men of the land have done,

5. Adultery or fornication committed after a contract, being detected before marriage, giveth just occasion to the innocent party to dissolve that contract.[12] In the case of adultery after marriage, it is lawful for the innocent party to sue out a divorce:[13] and, after the divorce, to marry another, as if the offending party were dead.[14]

6. Although the corruption of man be such as is apt to study arguments unduly to put asunder those whom God hath joined together in marriage: yet nothing but adultery, or such willful desertion as can no way be remedied by the Church or civil magistrate, is cause sufficient of dissolving the bond of marriage:[15] wherein, a public and orderly course of proceeding is to be observed; and the persons concerned in it not left to their own wills and discretion, in their own case.[16]

---

who *were* before you, and thus the land is defiled), lest the land vomit you out also when you defile it, as it vomited out the nations that *were* before you.

[12] **Matt. 1:18-20:** Now the birth of Jesus Christ was as follows: After His mother Mary was betrothed to Joseph, before they came together, she was found with child of the Holy Spirit. Then Joseph her husband, being a just *man,* and not wanting to make her a public example, was minded to put her away secretly. But while he thought about these things, behold, an angel of the Lord appeared to him in a dream, saying, "Joseph, son of David, do not be afraid to take to you Mary your wife, for that which is conceived in her is of the Holy Spirit." **See Deut. 22:23-24.**

[13] **Matt. 5:31-32:** Furthermore it has been said, 'Whoever divorces his wife, let him give her a certificate of divorce.' But I say to you that whoever divorces his wife for any reason except sexual immorality causes her to commit adultery; and whoever marries a woman who is divorced commits adultery.

[14] **Matt. 19:9:** And I say to you, whoever divorces his wife, except for sexual immorality, and marries another, commits adultery; and whoever marries her who is divorced commits adultery. **Rom. 7:2-3:** For the woman who has a husband is bound by the law to *her* husband as long as he lives. But if the husband dies, she is released from the law of *her* husband. So then if, while *her* husband lives, she marries another man, she will be called an adulteress; but if her husband dies, she is free from that law, so that she is no adulteress, though she has married another man.

[15] **Matt. 19:8-9:** He said to them, "Moses, because of the hardness of your hearts, permitted you to divorce your wives, but from the beginning it was not so. And I say to you, whoever divorces his wife, except for sexual immorality, and marries another, commits adultery; and whoever marries her who is divorced commits adultery." **1 Cor. 7:15:** But if the unbeliever departs, let him depart; a brother or a sister is not under bondage in such *cases.* But God has called us to peace. **Matt. 19:6:** So then, they are no longer two but one flesh. Therefore what God has joined together, let not man separate.

[16] **Deut. 24:1-4:** When a man takes a wife and marries her, and it happens that she finds no favor in his eyes because he has found some uncleanness in her, and he writes her a certificate of divorce, puts *it* in her hand, and sends her out of his house, when she has departed from his house, and goes and becomes another man's *wife, if* the latter husband detests her and writes her a certificate of divorce, puts *it* in her hand, and sends her out of his house, or if the latter husband dies who took her as his wife, *then* her former husband who divorced her must not take her back to be his wife after she has been defiled; for that *is* an abomination before the LORD, and you shall not bring sin on the land which the LORD your God is giving you *as* an inheritance.

CHAPTER 26
Of the Church

1. The catholic or universal church, which (with respect to the internal work of the Spirit and truth of grace) may be called invisible, consists of the whole number of the elect, that have been, are, or shall be gathered into one, under Christ the Head thereof; and is the spouse, the body, the fullness of Him that filleth all in all.[1]

2. All persons throughout the world, professing the faith of the gospel, and obedience unto God by Christ, according unto it; not destroying their own profession by any errors everting the foundation, or unholiness of conversation, are and may be called visible saints;[2] and of such ought all particular congregations to be constituted.[3]

---

[1] **Heb. 12:23:** ... to the general assembly and church of the firstborn *who are* registered in heaven, to God the Judge of all, to the spirits of just men made perfect. **Eph. 1:10, 22-23:** ... that in the dispensation of the fullness of the times He might gather together in one all things in Christ, both which are in heaven and which are on earth—in Him.... And He put all *things* under His feet, and gave Him *to be* head over all *things* to the church, which is His body, the fullness of Him who fills all in all. **Eph. 5:23, 27, 32:** For the husband is head of the wife, as also Christ is head of the church; and He is the Savior of the body.... that He might present her to Himself a glorious church, not having spot or wrinkle or any such thing, but that she should be holy and without blemish.... This is a great mystery, but I speak concerning Christ and the church. **Col. 1:18:** And He is the head of the body, the church, who is the beginning, the firstborn from the dead, that in all things He may have the preeminence.

[2] **1 Cor. 1:2:** To the church of God which is at Corinth, to those who are sanctified in Christ Jesus, called *to be* saints, with all who in every place call on the name of Jesus Christ our Lord, both theirs and ours. **1 Cor. 5:1-9:** It is actually reported *that there is* sexual immorality among you, and such sexual immorality as is not even named among the Gentiles—that a man has his father's wife! And you are puffed up, and have not rather mourned, that he who has done this deed might be taken away from among you. For I indeed, as absent in body but present in spirit, have already judged (as though I were present) him who has so done this deed. In the name of our Lord Jesus Christ, when you are gathered together, along with my spirit, with the power of our Lord Jesus Christ, deliver such a one to Satan for the destruction of the flesh, that his spirit may be saved in the day of the Lord Jesus. Your glorying *is* not good. Do you not know that a little leaven leavens the whole lump? Therefore purge out the old leaven, that you may be a new lump, since you truly are unleavened. For indeed Christ, our Passover, was sacrificed for us. Therefore let us keep the feast, not with old leaven, nor with the leaven of malice and wickedness, but with the unleavened *bread* of sincerity and truth. I wrote to you in my epistle not to keep company with sexually immoral people. **Acts 11:26:** And when he had found him, he brought him to Antioch. So it was that for a whole year they assembled with the church and taught a great many people. And the disciples were first called Christians in Antioch.

[3] **Rom. 1:7:** To all who are in Rome, beloved of God, called *to be* saints: Grace to you and peace from God our Father and the Lord Jesus Christ. **Eph. 1:20-22:** ... which He worked in Christ when He raised Him from the dead and seated *Him* at His right hand in the heavenly *places,* far above all principality and power and might and dominion, and every name that is named, not only in this age but also in that which is to come. And He put all *things* under His feet, and gave Him *to be* head over all *things* to the church.

3. The purest churches under heaven are subject to mixture, and error;[4] and some have so degenerated as to become no churches of Christ, but synagogues of Satan;[5] nevertheless Christ always hath had, and ever shall have a kingdom, in this world, to the end thereof, of such as believe in Him, and make profession of His name.[6]

---

[4] **1 Cor. 13:12:** For now we see in a mirror, dimly, but then face to face. Now I know in part, but then I shall know just as I also am known. **Rev. 2-3:** To the angel of the church of Ephesus write ... I know your works, your labor, your patience, and that you cannot bear those who are evil. And you have tested those who say they are apostles and are not, and have found them liars ... Nevertheless I have *this* against you, that you have left your first love.... And to the angel of the church in Smyrna write ... I know your works, tribulation, and poverty (but you are rich) ... And to the angel of the church in Pergamos write ... I have a few things against you, because you have there those who hold the doctrine of Balaam.... And to the angel of the church in Thyatira write ... I have a few things against you, because you allow that woman Jezebel, who calls herself a prophetess, to teach and seduce My servants to commit sexual immorality and eat things sacrificed to idols.... And to the angel of the church in Sardis write ... Remember therefore how you have received and heard; hold fast and repent.... And to the angel of the church in Philadelphia write ... I know your works.... you have a little strength, have kept My word, and have not denied My name.... And to the angel of the church of the Laodiceans write ... I know your works, that you are neither cold nor hot.... **Matt. 13:24-30, 47:** Another parable He put forth to them, saying: "The kingdom of heaven is like a man who sowed good seed in his field; but while men slept, his enemy came and sowed tares among the wheat and went his way. But when the grain had sprouted and produced a crop, then the tares also appeared. So the servants of the owner came and said to him, 'Sir, did you not sow good seed in your field? How then does it have tares?' He said to them, 'An enemy has done this.' The servants said to him, 'Do you want us then to go and gather them up?' But he said, 'No, lest while you gather up the tares you also uproot the wheat with them. Let both grow together until the harvest, and at the time of harvest I will say to the reapers, "First gather together the tares and bind them in bundles to burn them, but gather the wheat into my barn."'" ... Again, the kingdom of heaven is like a dragnet that was cast into the sea and gathered some of every kind.

[5] **Rev. 2:9:** I know your works, tribulation, and poverty (but you are rich); and *I know* the blasphemy of those who say they are Jews and are not, but *are* a synagogue of Satan. **Rev. 3:9:** Indeed I will make *those* of the synagogue of Satan, who say they are Jews and are not, but lie—indeed I will make them come and worship before your feet, and to know that I have loved you. **Rom. 11:18-22:** ... do not boast against the branches. But if you do boast, *remember that* you do not support the root, but the root *supports* you. You will say then, "Branches were broken off that I might be grafted in." Well *said*. Because of unbelief they were broken off, and you stand by faith. Do not be haughty, but fear. For if God did not spare the natural branches, He may not spare you either. Therefore consider the goodness and severity of God: on those who fell, severity; but toward you, goodness, if you continue in *His* goodness. Otherwise you also will be cut off. **2 Cor. 11:13-15:** For such *are* false apostles, deceitful workers, transforming themselves into apostles of Christ. And no wonder! For Satan himself transforms himself into an angel of light. Therefore it is no great thing if his ministers also transform themselves into ministers of righteousness, whose end will be according to their works. **2 Thess. 2:11-12:** And for this reason God will send them strong delusion, that they should believe the lie, that they all may be condemned who did not believe the truth but had pleasure in unrighteousness.

[6] **Matt. 16:18:** And I also say to you that you are Peter, and on this rock I will build My church, and the gates of Hades shall not prevail against it. **Ps. 72:17:** His name shall endure forever; His name shall continue as long as the sun. And *men* shall be blessed in Him; All nations shall call Him blessed. **Ps. 102:28:** The children of Your servants will continue, And their descendants will be established before You. **Matt. 28:19-20:** Go therefore and make disciples of all the nations, baptizing them in the name of the Father and of the Son and of the Holy Spirit, teaching them to observe all things that I have commanded you; and lo, I am with you always, *even* to the end of the age." Amen. **1 Cor. 15:51-52:** Behold, I tell you a mystery: We shall not all sleep, but we shall all be changed—in a moment, in the twinkling of an eye, at the last trumpet. For the trumpet will sound, and the dead will be raised incorruptible, and we shall be changed. **1 Thess. 4:17:** Then we who are alive *and* remain shall be caught up together with them in the clouds to meet the Lord in the air. And thus we shall always be with the Lord.

4. The Lord Jesus Christ is the Head of the church, in whom by the appointment of the Father, all power for the calling, institution, order, or government of the church, is invested in a supreme and sovereign manner,[7] neither can the Pope of Rome in any sense be head thereof.[8]

5. In the execution of this power wherewith He is so entrusted, the Lord Jesus calleth out of the world unto Himself, through the ministry of His word, by His Spirit, those that are given unto Him by His Father;[9] that they may walk before Him in all the ways of obedience, which He prescribeth to them in His word.[10] Those thus called He commandeth to walk together in particular societies, or churches, for their mutual edification; and the due performance of that public worship, which He requireth of them in the world.[11]

---

[7] **Col. 1:18:** And He is the head of the body, the church, who is the beginning, the firstborn from the dead, that in all things He may have the preeminence. **Eph. 1:22:** And He put all *things* under His feet, and gave Him *to be* head over all *things* to the church. **Matt. 28:18-20:** And Jesus came and spoke to them, saying, "All authority has been given to Me in heaven and on earth. Go therefore and make disciples of all the nations, baptizing them in the name of the Father and of the Son and of the Holy Spirit, teaching them to observe all things that I have commanded you; and lo, I am with you always, *even* to the end of the age." Amen.

[8] **Matt. 23:8-10:** But you, do not be called 'Rabbi'; for One is your Teacher, the Christ, and you are all brethren. Do not call anyone on earth your father; for One is your Father, He who is in heaven. And do not be called teachers; for One is your Teacher, the Christ. **1 Pet. 5:2-4:** Shepherd the flock of God which is among you, serving as overseers, not by compulsion but willingly, not for dishonest gain but eagerly; nor as being lords over those entrusted to you, but being examples to the flock; and when the Chief Shepherd appears, you will receive the crown of glory that does not fade away.

[9] **John 10:16:** And other sheep I have which are not of this fold; them also I must bring, and they will hear My voice; and there will be one flock *and* one shepherd. **John 12:32:** And I, if I am lifted up from the earth, will draw all *peoples* to Myself. **John 17:2:** ... as You have given Him authority over all flesh, that He should give eternal life to as many as You have given Him. **Acts 5:31-32:** Him God has exalted to His right hand *to be* Prince and Savior, to give repentance to Israel and forgiveness of sins. And we are His witnesses to these things, and *so* also *is* the Holy Spirit whom God has given to those who obey Him.

[10] **Matt. 28:20:** teaching them to observe all things that I have commanded you; and lo, I am with you always, *even* to the end of the age. Amen. **Rom. 2:6-7, 10:** ... who "will render to each one according to his deeds": eternal life to those who by patient continuance in doing good seek for glory, honor, and immortality ... but glory, honor, and peace to everyone who works what is good, to the Jew first and also to the Greek. **Luke 1:6:** And they were both righteous before God, walking in all the commandments and ordinances of the Lord blameless. **1 Tim. 3:14:** These things I write to you, though I hope to come to you shortly.

[11] **Matt. 18:15-20:** "Moreover if your brother sins against you, go and tell him his fault between you and him alone. If he hears you, you have gained your brother. But if he will not hear, take with you one or two more, that 'by the mouth of two or three witnesses every word may be established.' And if he refuses to hear them, tell *it* to the church. But if he refuses even to hear the church, let him be to you like a heathen and a tax collector. "Assuredly, I say to you, whatever you bind on earth will be bound in heaven, and whatever you loose on earth will be loosed in heaven. "Again I say to you that if two of you agree on earth concerning anything that they ask, it will be done for them by My Father in heaven. For where two or three are gathered together in My name, I am there in the midst of them." **Acts 14:21-23:** And when they had preached the gospel to that city and made many disciples, they returned to Lystra, Iconium, and Antioch, strengthening the souls of the disciples, exhorting *them* to continue in the faith, and *saying,* "We must through many tribulations enter the kingdom of God." So when they had appointed elders in every church, and prayed with fasting, they commended them to the Lord in whom they had believed." **Titus 1:5:** For this reason I left you in Crete, that you should set in order the things that are lacking, and appoint elders in every

6. The members of these churches are saints by calling, visibly manifesting and evidencing (in and by their profession and walking) their obedience unto that call of Christ;[12] and do willingly consent to walk together according to the appointment of Christ, giving up themselves, to the Lord and one to another by the will of God, in professed subjection to the ordinances of the gospel.[13]

7. To each of these churches thus gathered, according to His mind, declared in His word, He hath given all that power and authority, which is any way needful for their carrying on that order in worship, and discipline, which He hath instituted for them to observe; with commands, and rules for the due and right exerting, and executing of that power.[14]

8. A particular church gathered, and completely organized, according to the mind of Christ, consists of officers, and members; and the officers appointed by Christ to be chosen and set apart by the church (so called and gathered) for the peculiar administration of ordinances, and execution of power, or duty,

---

city as I commanded you. **1 Tim. 3:14-15:** These things I write to you, though I hope to come to you shortly; but if I am delayed, *I write* so that you may know how you ought to conduct yourself in the house of God, which is the church of the living God, the pillar and ground of the truth.

[12] **Rom. 1:7:** To all who are in Rome, beloved of God, called *to be* saints: Grace to you and peace from God our Father and the Lord Jesus Christ. **1 Cor. 1:2:** To the church of God which is at Corinth, to those who are sanctified in Christ Jesus, called *to be* saints, with all who in every place call on the name of Jesus Christ our Lord, both theirs and ours. **Acts 2:41-47:** Then those who gladly received his word were baptized; and that day about three thousand souls were added *to them.* And they continued steadfastly in the apostles' doctrine and fellowship, in the breaking of bread, and in prayers. Then fear came upon every soul, and many wonders and signs were done through the apostles. Now all who believed were together, and had all things in common, and sold their possessions and goods, and divided them among all, as anyone had need. So continuing daily with one accord in the temple, and breaking bread from house to house, they ate their food with gladness and simplicity of heart, praising God and having favor with all the people. And the Lord added to the church daily those who were being saved.

[13] **Acts 2:41-42:** Then those who gladly received his word were baptized; and that day about three thousand souls were added *to them.* And they continued steadfastly in the apostles' doctrine and fellowship, in the breaking of bread, and in prayers. **Acts 5:13-14:** Yet none of the rest dared join them, but the people esteemed them highly. And believers were increasingly added to the Lord, multitudes of both men and women. **2 Cor. 9:13:** ... while, through the proof of this ministry, they glorify God for the obedience of your confession to the gospel of Christ, and for *your* liberal sharing with them and all *men.*

[14] **Matt. 18:17-18:** And if he refuses to hear them, tell *it* to the church. But if he refuses even to hear the church, let him be to you like a heathen and a tax collector. Assuredly, I say to you, whatever you bind on earth will be bound in heaven, and whatever you loose on earth will be loosed in heaven. **1 Cor. 5:4-5, 13:** In the name of our Lord Jesus Christ, when you are gathered together, along with my spirit, with the power of our Lord Jesus Christ, deliver such a one to Satan for the destruction of the flesh, that his spirit may be saved in the day of the Lord Jesus. But those who are outside God judges. Therefore "put away from yourselves the evil person."

which He intrusts them with, or calls them to, to be continued to the end of the world, are bishops or elders and deacons.[15]

9. The way appointed by Christ for the calling of any person, fitted, and gifted by the Holy Spirit, unto the office of bishop, or elder, in a church,[16] is, that He be chosen thereunto by the common suffrage of the church itself;[17] and solemnly set apart by fasting and prayer, with imposition of hands of the eldership of the church, if there be any before constituted therein;[18] and of a deacon that he be chosen by the like suffrage, and set apart by prayer, and the like imposition of hands.[19]

---

[15] **1 Cor. 12:28:** And God has appointed these in the church: first apostles, second prophets, third teachers, after that miracles, then gifts of healings, helps, administrations, varieties of tongues. **Eph. 4:11-13:** And He Himself gave some *to be* apostles, some prophets, some evangelists, and some pastors and teachers, for the equipping of the saints for the work of ministry, for the edifying of the body of Christ, till we all come to the unity of the faith and of the knowledge of the Son of God, to a perfect man, to the measure of the stature of the fullness of Christ. **Acts 20:17, 28:** From Miletus he sent to Ephesus and called for the elders of the church.... Therefore take heed to yourselves and to all the flock, among which the Holy Spirit has made you overseers, to shepherd the church of God which He purchased with His own blood. **Phil. 1:1:** Paul and Timothy, bondservants of Jesus Christ, To all the saints in Christ Jesus who are in Philippi, with the bishops and deacons.

[16] **1 Tim. 3:1-7:** This *is* a faithful saying: If a man desires the position of a bishop, he desires a good work. A bishop then must be blameless, the husband of one wife, temperate, sober-minded, of good behavior, hospitable, able to teach; not given to wine, not violent, not greedy for money, but gentle, not quarrelsome, not covetous; one who rules his own house well, having *his* children in submission with all reverence (for if a man does not know how to rule his own house, how will he take care of the church of God?); not a novice, lest being puffed up with pride he fall into the *same* condemnation as the devil. Moreover he must have a good testimony among those who are outside, lest he fall into reproach and the snare of the devil. **Titus 1:6-9:** ... if a man is blameless, the husband of one wife, having faithful children not accused of dissipation or insubordination. For a bishop must be blameless, as a steward of God, not self-willed, not quick-tempered, not given to wine, not violent, not greedy for money, but hospitable, a lover of what is good, sober-minded, just, holy, self-controlled, holding fast the faithful word as he has been taught, that he may be able, by sound doctrine, both to exhort and convict those who contradict. **Eph. 4:11.** And He Himself gave some *to be* apostles, some prophets, some evangelists, and some pastors and teachers.

[17] **Acts 6:1-7:** Now in those days, when *the number of* the disciples was multiplying, there arose a complaint against the Hebrews by the Hellenists, because their widows were neglected in the daily distribution. Then the twelve summoned the multitude of the disciples and said, "It is not desirable that we should leave the word of God and serve tables. Therefore, brethren, seek out from among you seven men of *good* reputation, full of the Holy Spirit and wisdom, whom we may appoint over this business; but we will give ourselves continually to prayer and to the ministry of the word." And the saying pleased the whole multitude. And they chose Stephen, a man full of faith and the Holy Spirit, and Philip, Prochorus, Nicanor, Timon, Parmenas, and Nicolas, a proselyte from Antioch, whom they set before the apostles; and when they had prayed, they laid hands on them. Then the word of God spread, and the number of the disciples multiplied greatly in Jerusalem, and a great many of the priests were obedient to the faith. **Acts 14:23:** So when they had appointed elders in every church, and prayed with fasting, they commended them to the Lord in whom they had believed.

[18] **1 Tim. 4:14:** Do not neglect the gift that is in you, which was given to you by prophecy with the laying on of the hands of the eldership. **1 Tim. 5:22:** Do not lay hands on anyone hastily, nor share in other people's sins; keep yourself pure.

[19] **Acts 6:3, 5, 6:** Therefore, brethren, seek out from among you seven men of *good* reputation, full of the Holy Spirit and wisdom, whom we may appoint over this business ... And the saying pleased the whole multitude. And they chose Stephen, a man full of faith and the Holy Spirit, and Philip,

10. The work of pastors being constantly to attend the service of Christ, in His churches, in the ministry of the word, and prayer, with watching for their souls, as they that must give an account to Him;[20] it is incumbent on the churches to whom they minister, not only to give them all due respect, but also to communicate to them of all their good things according to their ability,[21] so as they may have a comfortable supply, without being themselves entangled in secular affairs;[22] and may also be capable of exercising hospitality towards others;[23] and this is required by the law of nature, and by the express order of our Lord Jesus, who hath ordained that they that preach the gospel, should live of the gospel.[24]

Prochorus, Nicanor, Timon, Parmenas, and Nicolas, a proselyte from Antioch ... whom they set before the apostles; and when they had prayed, they laid hands on them.

[20] **Acts 6:4:** ... but we will give ourselves continually to prayer and to the ministry of the word. **Heb. 13:17:** Obey those who rule over you, and be submissive, for they watch out for your souls, as those who must give account. Let them do so with joy and not with grief, for that would be unprofitable for you. **1 Pet. 5:1-4:** The elders who are among you I exhort, I who am a fellow elder and a witness of the sufferings of Christ, and also a partaker of the glory that will be revealed: Shepherd the flock of God which is among you, serving as overseers, not by compulsion but willingly, not for dishonest gain but eagerly; nor as being lords over those entrusted to you, but being examples to the flock; and when the Chief Shepherd appears, you will receive the crown of glory that does not fade away.

[21] **1 Tim. 5:17-18:** Let the elders who rule well be counted worthy of double honor, especially those who labor in the word and doctrine. For the Scripture says, "You shall not muzzle an ox while it treads out the grain," and, "The laborer *is* worthy of his wages." **Gal. 6:6-7:** Let him who is taught the word share in all good things with him who teaches. Do not be deceived, God is not mocked; for whatever a man sows, that he will also reap. **1 Cor. 9:6-14:** Or *is it* only Barnabas and I *who* have no right to refrain from working? Who ever goes to war at his own expense? Who plants a vineyard and does not eat of its fruit? Or who tends a flock and does not drink of the milk of the flock? Do I say these things as a *mere* man? Or does not the law say the same also? For it is written in the law of Moses, "You shall not muzzle an ox while it treads out the grain." Is it oxen God is concerned about? Or does He say *it* altogether for our sakes? For our sakes, no doubt, *this* is written, that he who plows should plow in hope, and he who threshes in hope should be partaker of his hope. If we have sown spiritual things for you, *is it* a great thing if we reap your material things? If others are partakers of *this* right over you, *are* we not even more? Nevertheless we have not used this right, but endure all things lest we hinder the gospel of Christ. Do you not know that those who minister the holy things eat *of the things* of the temple, and those who serve at the altar partake of *the offerings of* the altar? Even so the Lord has commanded that those who preach the gospel should live from the gospel.

[22] **2 Tim. 2:4:** No one engaged in warfare entangles himself with the affairs of *this* life, that he may please him who enlisted him as a soldier.

[23] **1 Tim. 3:2:** A bishop then must be blameless, the husband of one wife, temperate, sober-minded, of good behavior, hospitable, able to teach.

[24] **1 Cor. 9:6-14:** Or *is it* only Barnabas and I *who* have no right to refrain from working? Who ever goes to war at his own expense? Who plants a vineyard and does not eat of its fruit? Or who tends a flock and does not drink of the milk of the flock? Do I say these things as a *mere* man? Or does not the law say the same also? For it is written in the law of Moses, "You shall not muzzle an ox while it treads out the grain." Is it oxen God is concerned about? Or does He say *it* altogether for our sakes? For our sakes, no doubt, *this* is written, that he who plows should plow in hope, and he who threshes in hope should be partaker of his hope. If we have sown spiritual things for you, *is it* a great thing if we reap your material things? If others are partakers of *this* right over you, *are* we not even more? Nevertheless we have not used this right, but endure all things lest we hinder the gospel of Christ. Do you not know that those who minister the holy things eat *of the things* of the temple, and those who serve at the altar partake of *the offerings of* the altar? Even so the Lord has commanded that those who preach the gospel should live from the gospel. **1 Tim. 5:17-18:** Let the elders who rule well be counted worthy of double honor, especially those who labor in the word and

11. Although it be incumbent on the bishops or pastors of the churches to be instant in preaching the word, by way of office; yet the work of preaching the word, is not so peculiarly confined to them; but that others also gifted, and fitted by the Holy Spirit for it, and approved, and called by the church, may and ought to perform it.[25]

12. As all believers are bound to join themselves to particular churches, when and where they have opportunity so to do; so all that are admitted unto the privileges of a church, are also under the censures and government thereof, according to the rule of Christ.[26]

13. No church members upon any offence taken by them, having performed their duty required of them towards the person they are offended at, ought to disturb any church order, or absent themselves from the assemblies of the church, or administration of any ordinances, upon the account of such offence at any of their fellow members; but to wait upon Christ, in the further proceeding of the church.[27]

---

doctrine. For the Scripture says, "You shall not muzzle an ox while it treads out the grain," and, "The laborer *is* worthy of his wages."

[25] **Acts 6:5:** And the saying pleased the whole multitude. And they chose Stephen, a man full of faith and the Holy Spirit, and Philip, Prochorus, Nicanor, Timon, Parmenas, and Nicolas, a proselyte from Antioch. **Acts 8:5-6, 12:** Then Philip went down to the city of Samaria and preached Christ to them. And the multitudes with one accord heeded the things spoken by Philip, hearing and seeing the miracles which he did.... But when they believed Philip as he preached the things concerning the kingdom of God and the name of Jesus Christ, both men and women were baptized. **Acts 11:19-21:** Now those who were scattered after the persecution that arose over Stephen traveled as far as Phoenicia, Cyprus, and Antioch, preaching the word to no one but the Jews only. But some of them were men from Cyprus and Cyrene, who, when they had come to Antioch, spoke to the Hellenists, preaching the Lord Jesus. And the hand of the Lord was with them, and a great number believed and turned to the Lord. **1 Pet. 4:10-11:** As each one has received a gift, minister it to one another, as good stewards of the manifold grace of God. If anyone speaks, *let him speak* as the oracles of God. If anyone ministers, *let him do it* as with the ability which God supplies, that in all things God may be glorified through Jesus Christ, to whom belong the glory and the dominion forever and ever. Amen.

[26] **1 Thess. 5:14:** Now we exhort you, brethren, warn those who are unruly, comfort the fainthearted, uphold the weak, be patient with all. **2 Thess. 3:6, 14-15:** But we command you, brethren, in the name of our Lord Jesus Christ, that you withdraw from every brother who walks disorderly and not according to the tradition which he received from us.... And if anyone does not obey our word in this epistle, note that person and do not keep company with him, that he may be ashamed. Yet do not count *him* as an enemy, but admonish *him* as a brother. **Heb. 13:17:** Obey those who rule over you, and be submissive, for they watch out for your souls, as those who must give account. Let them do so with joy and not with grief, for that would be unprofitable for you.

[27] **Matt. 18:15-22:** "Moreover if your brother sins against you, go and tell him his fault between you and him alone. If he hears you, you have gained your brother. But if he will not hear, take with you one or two more, that 'by the mouth of two or three witnesses every word may be established.' And if he refuses to hear them, tell *it* to the church. But if he refuses even to hear the church, let him be to you like a heathen and a tax collector. "Assuredly, I say to you, whatever you bind on earth will be bound in heaven, and whatever you loose on earth will be loosed in heaven. "Again I say to you that if two of you agree on earth concerning anything that they ask, it will be done for

14. As each church, and all the members of it, are bound to pray continually, for the good and prosperity of all the churches of Christ, in all places; and upon all occasions to further it (every one within the bounds of their places, and callings, in the exercise of their gifts and graces)[28] so the churches (when planted by the providence of God so as they may enjoy opportunity and advantage for it) ought to hold communion amongst themselves for their peace, increase of love, and mutual edification.[29]

---

them by My Father in heaven. For where two or three are gathered together in My name, I am there in the midst of them." Then Peter came to Him and said, "Lord, how often shall my brother sin against me, and I forgive him? Up to seven times?" Jesus said to him, "I do not say to you, up to seven times, but up to seventy times seven." **Eph. 4:1-6:** I, therefore, the prisoner of the Lord, beseech you to walk worthy of the calling with which you were called, with all lowliness and gentleness, with longsuffering, bearing with one another in love, endeavoring to keep the unity of the Spirit in the bond of peace. *There is* one body and one Spirit, just as you were called in one hope of your calling; one Lord, one faith, one baptism; one God and Father of all, who *is* above all, and through all, and in you all. **Col. 3:12-15:** Therefore, as *the* elect of God, holy and beloved, put on tender mercies, kindness, humility, meekness, longsuffering; bearing with one another, and forgiving one another, if anyone has a complaint against another; even as Christ forgave you, so you also *must do.* But above all these things put on love, which is the bond of perfection. And let the peace of God rule in your hearts, to which also you were called in one body; and be thankful.

[28] **Eph. 6:18:** ... praying always with all prayer and supplication in the Spirit, being watchful to this end with all perseverance and supplication for all the saints. **Ps. 122:6:** Pray for the peace of Jerusalem: "May they prosper who love you." **Col. 3:15:** And let the peace of God rule in your hearts, to which also you were called in one body; and be thankful. **Col. 4:3:** ... meanwhile praying also for us, that God would open to us a door for the word, to speak the mystery of Christ, for which I am also in chains. **James 5:16:** Confess *your* trespasses to one another, and pray for one another, that you may be healed. The effective, fervent prayer of a righteous man avails much. **Matt. 9:38:** Therefore pray the Lord of the harvest to send out laborers into His harvest. **2 Thess. 2:16-17:** Now may our Lord Jesus Christ Himself, and our God and Father, who has loved us and given *us* everlasting consolation and good hope by grace, comfort your hearts and establish you in every good word and work. **2 Thess. 1:11:** Therefore we also pray always for you that our God would count you worthy of *this* calling, and fulfill all the good pleasure of *His* goodness and the work of faith with power. **2 Thess. 3:1:** Finally, brethren, pray for us, that the word of the Lord may run *swiftly* and be glorified, just as *it is* with you. **Acts 4:29-30:** Now, Lord, look on their threats, and grant to Your servants that with all boldness they may speak Your word, by stretching out Your hand to heal, and that signs and wonders may be done through the name of Your holy Servant Jesus. **Eph. 3:14-20:** For this reason I bow my knees to the Father of our Lord Jesus Christ, from whom the whole family in heaven and earth is named, that He would grant you, according to the riches of His glory, to be strengthened with might through His Spirit in the inner man, that Christ may dwell in your hearts through faith; that you, being rooted and grounded in love, may be able to comprehend with all the saints what *is* the width and length and depth and height—to know the love of Christ which passes knowledge; that you may be filled with all the fullness of God. Now to Him who is able to do exceedingly abundantly above all that we ask or think, according to the power that works in us. **Eph. 6:18-20:** ... praying always with all prayer and supplication in the Spirit, being watchful to this end with all perseverance and supplication for all the saints—and for me, that utterance may be given to me, that I may open my mouth boldly to make known the mystery of the gospel, for which I am an ambassador in chains; that in it I may speak boldly, as I ought to speak. **Rom. 15:29-30, 32:** But I know that when I come to you, I shall come in the fullness of the blessing of the gospel of Christ. Now I beg you, brethren, through the Lord Jesus Christ, and through the love of the Spirit, that you strive together with me in prayers to God for me ... that I may come to you with joy by the will of God, and may be refreshed together with you.

[29] **Rom. 16:1-3:** I commend to you Phoebe our sister, who is a servant of the church in Cenchrea, that you may receive her in the Lord in a manner worthy of the saints, and assist her in whatever business she has need of you; for indeed she has been a helper of many and of myself also. Greet Priscilla and Aquila, my fellow workers in Christ Jesus. **3 John 8-10:** We therefore ought to receive such, that we may become fellow workers for the truth. I wrote to the church, but Diotrephes, who loves to have the preeminence among them, does not receive us. Therefore, if I come, I will call to mind his deeds which he does, prating against us with malicious words. And not content with that,

15. In cases of difficulties or differences, either in point of doctrine, or administration; wherein either the churches in general are concerned, or any one church in their peace, union, and edification; or any member, or members, of any church are injured, in or by any proceedings in censures not agreeable to truth, and order: it is according to the mind of Christ, that many churches holding communion together, do, by their messengers meet to consider, and give their advice in, or about that matter in difference, to be reported to all the churches concerned;[30] howbeit these messengers assembled, are not entrusted with any church-power properly so called; or with any jurisdiction over the churches themselves, to exercise any censures either over any churches, or persons: or to impose their determination on the churches, or officers.[31]

---

he himself does not receive the brethren, and forbids those who wish to, putting *them* out of the church. **2 Cor. 9:12-15:** For the administration of this service not only supplies the needs of the saints, but also is abounding through many thanksgivings to God, while, through the proof of this ministry, they glorify God for the obedience of your confession to the gospel of Christ, and for *your* liberal sharing with them and all *men,* and by their prayer for you, who long for you because of the exceeding grace of God in you. Thanks *be* to God for His indescribable gift! **Acts 2:42:** And they continued steadfastly in the apostles' doctrine and fellowship, in the breaking of bread, and in prayers. **1 Cor. 12:12-13:** For as the body is one and has many members, but all the members of that one body, being many, are one body, so also *is* Christ. For by one Spirit we were all baptized into one body—whether Jews or Greeks, whether slaves or free—and have all been made to drink into one Spirit.

[30] **Acts 15:2, 4, 6, 22-23, 25:** Therefore, when Paul and Barnabas had no small dissension and dispute with them, they determined that Paul and Barnabas and certain others of them should go up to Jerusalem, to the apostles and elders, about this question.... And when they had come to Jerusalem, they were received by the church and the apostles and the elders; and they reported all things that God had done with them.... Now the apostles and elders came together to consider this matter.... Then it pleased the apostles and elders, with the whole church, to send chosen men of their own company to Antioch with Paul and Barnabas, *namely,* Judas who was also named Barsabas, and Silas, leading men among the brethren. They wrote this *letter* by them: The apostles, the elders, and the brethren, To the brethren who are of the Gentiles in Antioch, Syria, and Cilicia: Greetings.... it seemed good to us, being assembled with one accord, to send chosen men to you with our beloved Barnabas and Paul.

[31] **2 Cor. 1:24:** Not that we have dominion over your faith, but are fellow workers for your joy; for by faith you stand. **1 John 4:1:** Beloved, do not believe every spirit, but test the spirits, whether they are of God; because many false prophets have gone out into the world. **1 Cor. 7:25, 36, 40:** Now concerning virgins: I have no commandment from the Lord; yet I give judgment as one whom the Lord in His mercy has made trustworthy.... But if any man thinks he is behaving improperly toward his virgin, if she is past the flower of youth, and thus it must be, let him do what he wishes. He does not sin; let them marry.... But she is happier if she remains as she is, according to my judgment—and I think I also have the Spirit of God.

CHAPTER 27
Of the Communion of Saints

1. All saints that are united to Jesus Christ their Head, by His Spirit, and faith; although they are not made thereby one person with Him, have fellowship in His graces, sufferings, death, resurrection, and glory;[1] and, being united to one another in love, they have communion in each other's gifts, and graces;[2] and are obliged to the performance of such duties, public and private, in an orderly way, as do conduce to their mutual good, both in the inward and outward man.[3]

2. Saints by profession are bound to maintain an holy fellowship and communion in the worship of God, and in performing such other spiritual services, as tend to their mutual edification;[4] as

---

[1] **1 John 1:3:** ... that which we have seen and heard we declare to you, that you also may have fellowship with us; and truly our fellowship *is* with the Father and with His Son Jesus Christ. **Eph. 3:16-18:** ... that He would grant you, according to the riches of His glory, to be strengthened with might through His Spirit in the inner man, that Christ may dwell in your hearts through faith; that you, being rooted and grounded in love, may be able to comprehend with all the saints what *is* the width and length and depth and height. **John 1:16:** And of His fullness we have all received, and grace for grace. **Eph. 2:5-6:** ... even when we were dead in trespasses, made us alive together with Christ (by grace you have been saved), and raised *us* up together, and made *us* sit together in the heavenly *places* in Christ Jesus. **Phil. 3:10:** ... that I may know Him and the power of His resurrection, and the fellowship of His sufferings, being conformed to His death. **Rom. 6:5-6:** For if we have been united together in the likeness of His death, certainly we also shall be *in the likeness* of *His* resurrection, knowing this, that our old man was crucified with *Him,* that the body of sin might be done away with, that we should no longer be slaves of sin. **Rom. 8:17:** ... and if children, then heirs—heirs of God and joint heirs with Christ, if indeed we suffer with *Him,* that we may also be glorified together. **2 Tim. 2:12:** If we endure, We shall also reign with *Him.* If we deny *Him,* He also will deny us.

[2] **Eph. 4:15-16:** ... but, speaking the truth in love, may grow up in all things into Him who is the head—Christ—from whom the whole body, joined and knit together by what every joint supplies, according to the effective working by which every part does its share, causes growth of the body for the edifying of itself in love. **1 Cor. 12:7, 12:** But the manifestation of the Spirit is given to each one for the profit *of all* ... For as the body is one and has many members, but all the members of that one body, being many, are one body, so also *is* Christ. **1 Cor. 3:21-23:** Therefore let no one boast in men. For all things are yours: whether Paul or Apollos or Cephas, or the world or life or death, or things present or things to come—all are yours. And you *are* Christ's, and Christ *is* God's. **Col. 2:19:** ... and not holding fast to the Head, from whom all the body, nourished and knit together by joints and ligaments, grows with the increase *that is* from God.

[3] **1 Thess. 5:11, 14:** Therefore comfort each other and edify one another, just as you also are doing.... Now we exhort you, brethren, warn those who are unruly, comfort the fainthearted, uphold the weak, be patient with all. **Rom. 1:11-12, 14:** For I long to see you, that I may impart to you some spiritual gift, so that you may be established—that is, that I may be encouraged together with you by the mutual faith both of you and me.... I am a debtor both to Greeks and to barbarians, both to wise and to unwise. **1 John 3:16-18:** By this we know love, because He laid down His life for us. And we also ought to lay down *our* lives for the brethren. But whoever has this world's goods, and sees his brother in need, and shuts up his heart from him, how does the love of God abide in him? My little children, let us not love in word or in tongue, but in deed and in truth. **Gal. 6:10:** Therefore, as we have opportunity, let us do good to all, especially to those who are of the household of faith.

[4] **Heb. 10:24-25:** And let us consider one another in order to stir up love and good works, not forsaking the assembling of ourselves together, as *is* the manner of some, but exhorting *one another,* and so much the more as you see the Day approaching. **Heb. 3:12-13:** Beware, brethren,

also in relieving each other in outward things according to their several abilities, and necessities;[5] which communion, according to the rule of the gospel, though especially to be exercised by them, in the relations wherein they stand, whether in families,[6] or churches;[7] yet as God offereth opportunity is to be extended to all the household of faith, even all those who in every place call upon the name of the Lord Jesus; nevertheless their communion one with another as saints, doth not take away or infringe the title or propriety, which each man hath in his goods and possessions.[8]

---

lest there be in any of you an evil heart of unbelief in departing from the living God; but exhort one another daily, while it is called "Today," lest any of you be hardened through the deceitfulness of sin. **Acts 2:42, 46:** And they continued steadfastly in the apostles' doctrine and fellowship, in the breaking of bread, and in prayers.... So continuing daily with one accord in the temple, and breaking bread from house to house, they ate their food with gladness and simplicity of heart. **Isa. 2:3:** Many people shall come and say, "Come, and let us go up to the mountain of the LORD, To the house of the God of Jacob; He will teach us His ways, And we shall walk in His paths." For out of Zion shall go forth the law, And the word of the LORD from Jerusalem. **1 Cor. 11:20:** Therefore when you come together in one place, it is not to eat the Lord's Supper.

[5] **1 John 3:17:** But whoever has this world's goods, and sees his brother in need, and shuts up his heart from him, how does the love of God abide in him? **2 Cor. 8-9:** Moreover, brethren, we make known to you the grace of God bestowed on the churches of Macedonia: that in a great trial of affliction the abundance of their joy and their deep poverty abounded in the riches of their liberality.... But as you abound in everything—in faith, in speech, in knowledge, in all diligence, and in your love for us—*see* that you abound in this grace also.... For *I do* not mean that others should be eased and you burdened; but by an equality, *that* now at this time your abundance *may supply* their lack, that their abundance also may *supply* your lack—that there may be equality.... For the administration of this service not only supplies the needs of the saints, but also is abounding through many thanksgivings to God, while, through the proof of this ministry, they glorify God for the obedience of your confession to the gospel of Christ, and for *your* liberal sharing with them and all *men.* **Acts 11:29-30:** Then the disciples, each according to his ability, determined to send relief to the brethren dwelling in Judea. This they also did, and sent it to the elders by the hands of Barnabas and Saul. **Acts 2:44-45:** Now all who believed were together, and had all things in common, and sold their possessions and goods, and divided them among all, as anyone had need.

[6] **Eph. 6:4:** And you, fathers, do not provoke your children to wrath, but bring them up in the training and admonition of the Lord.

[7] **1 Cor. 12:14-27:** For in fact the body is not one member but many. If the foot should say, "Because I am not a hand, I am not of the body," is it therefore not of the body? And if the ear should say, "Because I am not an eye, I am not of the body," is it therefore not of the body? If the whole body *were* an eye, where *would be* the hearing? If the whole *were* hearing, where *would be* the smelling? But now God has set the members, each one of them, in the body just as He pleased. And if they were all one member, where *would* the body *be?* But now indeed *there are* many members, yet one body. And the eye cannot say to the hand, "I have no need of you"; nor again the head to the feet, "I have no need of you." No, much rather, those members of the body which seem to be weaker are necessary. And those *members* of the body which we think to be less honorable, on these we bestow greater honor; and our unpresentable *parts* have greater modesty, but our presentable *parts* have no need. But God composed the body, having given greater honor to that *part* which lacks it, that there should be no schism in the body, but *that* the members should have the same care for one another. And if one member suffers, all the members suffer with *it;* or if one member is honored, all the members rejoice with *it.* Now you are the body of Christ, and members individually.

[8] **Ex. 20:15:** You shall not steal. **Acts 5:4:** While it remained, was it not your own? And after it was sold, was it not in your own control? Why have you conceived this thing in your heart? You have not lied to men but to God. **Eph. 4:28:** Let him who stole steal no longer, but rather let him labor, working with *his* hands what is good, that he may have something to give him who has need.

CHAPTER 28
Of Baptism and the Lord's Supper

1. Baptism and the Lord's Supper are ordinances of positive, and sovereign institution; appointed by the Lord Jesus the only Lawgiver,[1] to be continued in His church to the end of the world.[2]

2. These holy appointments are to be administered by those only, who are qualified and thereunto called, which are the elders of the church, according to the commission of Christ.[3]

---

[1] **Matt. 28:19-20:** Go therefore and make disciples of all the nations, baptizing them in the name of the Father and of the Son and of the Holy Spirit, teaching them to observe all things that I have commanded you; and lo, I am with you always, *even* to the end of the age. Amen. **1 Cor. 11:24-25:** ... and when He had given thanks, He broke *it* and said, "Take, eat; this is My body which is broken for you; do this in remembrance of Me." In the same manner *He* also *took* the cup after supper, saying, "This cup is the new covenant in My blood. This do, as often as you drink *it,* in remembrance of Me."

[2] **Matt. 28:18-20:** And Jesus came and spoke to them, saying, "All authority has been given to Me in heaven and on earth. Go therefore and make disciples of all the nations, baptizing them in the name of the Father and of the Son and of the Holy Spirit, teaching them to observe all things that I have commanded you; and lo, I am with you always, *even* to the end of the age." Amen. **1 Cor. 11:26:** For as often as you eat this bread and drink this cup, you proclaim the Lord's death till He comes. **Eph. 4:5-6:** ... one Lord, one faith, one baptism; one God and Father of all, who *is* above all, and through all, and in you all. **1 Pet. 3:21:** There is also an antitype which now saves us—baptism (not the removal of the filth of the flesh, but the answer of a good conscience toward God), through the resurrection of Jesus Christ.

[3] **Matt. 28:19:** Go therefore and make disciples of all the nations, baptizing them in the name of the Father and of the Son and of the Holy Spirit. **1 Cor. 11:20, 23:** Therefore when you come together in one place, it is not to eat the Lord's Supper.... For I received from the Lord that which I also delivered to you: that the Lord Jesus on the *same* night in which He was betrayed took bread. **1 Cor. 4:1:** Let a man so consider us, as servants of Christ and stewards of the mysteries of God. **Eph. 4:11-12:** And He Himself gave some *to be* apostles, some prophets, some evangelists, and some pastors and teachers, for the equipping of the saints for the work of ministry, for the edifying of the body of Christ.

CHAPTER 29
Of Baptism

1. Baptism is an ordinance of the New Covenant, ordained by Jesus Christ,[1] to be a covenant transaction unto the party baptized, a sign of His fellowship with him, in His death, and resurrection;[2] of his being engrafted into Him;[3] of remission of sins;[4] and of his giving up unto God through Jesus Christ, to live and walk in newness of life.[5]

2. Those who do actually profess repentance towards God, faith in, and obedience, to our Lord Jesus, are the only proper subjects of this ordinance.[6]

3. The outward element to be used in this ordinance is water, wherein the party is to be baptized, in the name of the Father, and of the Son, and of the Holy Spirit.[7]

---

[1] **Matt. 28:19:** Go therefore and make disciples of all the nations, baptizing them in the name of the Father and of the Son and of the Holy Spirit.

[2] **Rom. 6:3-5:** Or do you not know that as many of us as were baptized into Christ Jesus were baptized into His death? Therefore we were buried with Him through baptism into death, that just as Christ was raised from the dead by the glory of the Father, even so we also should walk in newness of life. For if we have been united together in the likeness of His death, certainly we also shall be *in the likeness* of *His* resurrection. **Col. 2:12:** ... buried with Him in baptism, in which you also were raised with *Him* through faith in the working of God, who raised Him from the dead.

[3] **Gal. 3:27:** For as many of you as were baptized into Christ have put on Christ.

[4] **Mark 1:4:** John came baptizing in the wilderness and preaching a baptism of repentance for the remission of sins. **Acts 2:38:** Then Peter said to them, "Repent, and let every one of you be baptized in the name of Jesus Christ for the remission of sins; and you shall receive the gift of the Holy Spirit." **Acts 22:16:** And now why are you waiting? Arise and be baptized, and wash away your sins, calling on the name of the Lord.

[5] **Rom. 6:3-4:** Or do you not know that as many of us as were baptized into Christ Jesus were baptized into His death? Therefore we were buried with Him through baptism into death, that just as Christ was raised from the dead by the glory of the Father, even so we also should walk in newness of life.

[6] **Mark 16:15-16:** And He said to them, "Go into all the world and preach the gospel to every creature. He who believes and is baptized will be saved; but he who does not believe will be condemned." **Acts 2:41:** Then those who gladly received his word were baptized; and that day about three thousand souls were added *to them.* **Acts 8:12, 36-37:** But when they believed Philip as he preached the things concerning the kingdom of God and the name of Jesus Christ, both men and women were baptized.... Now as they went down the road, they came to some water. And the eunuch said, "See, *here is* water. What hinders me from being baptized?" Then Philip said, "If you believe with all your heart, you may." And he answered and said, "I believe that Jesus Christ is the Son of God." **Acts 16:14-15:** Now a certain woman named Lydia heard *us.* She was a seller of purple from the city of Thyatira, who worshiped God. The Lord opened her heart to heed the things spoken by Paul. And when she and her household were baptized, she begged *us,* saying, "If you have judged me to be faithful to the Lord, come to my house and stay." So she persuaded us. **1 Pet. 3:21:** There is also an antitype which now saves us—baptism (not the removal of the filth of the flesh, but the answer of a good conscience toward God), through the resurrection of Jesus Christ. **Phil. 3:3:** For we are the circumcision, who worship God in the Spirit, rejoice in Christ Jesus, and have no confidence in the flesh.

[7] **Acts 10:47:** Can anyone forbid water, that these should not be baptized who have received the Holy Spirit just as we *have?* **Acts 8:36, 38:** Now as they went down the road, they came to some water. And the eunuch said, "See, *here is* water. What hinders me from being baptized?" ... So he

4. Immersion, or dipping of the person in water, is necessary to the due administration of this ordinance.[8]

---

commanded the chariot to stand still. And both Philip and the eunuch went down into the water, and he baptized him. **Matt. 28:19:** Go therefore and make disciples of all the nations, baptizing them in the name of the Father and of the Son and of the Holy Spirit.

[8] **2 Kings 5:10, 14:** And Elisha sent a messenger to him, saying, "Go and wash in the Jordan seven times, and your flesh shall be restored to you, and *you shall* be clean." ... So he went down and dipped seven times in the Jordan, according to the saying of the man of God; and his flesh was restored like the flesh of a little child, and he was clean. **Matt. 3:16:** When He had been baptized, Jesus came up immediately from the water; and behold, the heavens were opened to Him, and He saw the Spirit of God descending like a dove and alighting upon Him. **John 3:23:** Now John also was baptizing in Aenon near Salim, because there was much water there. And they came and were baptized. **Acts 8:36, 38:** Now as they went down the road, they came to some water. And the eunuch said, "See, *here is* water. What hinders me from being baptized?" ... So he commanded the chariot to stand still. And both Philip and the eunuch went down into the water, and he baptized him.

CHAPTER 30
Of the Lord's Supper

1. The Supper of the Lord Jesus, was instituted by Him, the same night wherein He was betrayed,[1] to be observed in His churches[2] unto the end of the world,[3] for the perpetual remembrance, and shewing forth the sacrifice of Himself in His death,[4] confirmation

---

[1] **1 Cor. 11:23:** For I received from the Lord that which I also delivered to you: that the Lord Jesus on the *same* night in which He was betrayed took bread. **Matt. 26:20-26:** When evening had come, He sat down with the twelve. Now as they were eating, He said, "Assuredly, I say to you, one of you will betray Me." And they were exceedingly sorrowful, and each of them began to say to Him, "Lord, is it I?" He answered and said, "He who dipped *his* hand with Me in the dish will betray Me. The Son of Man indeed goes just as it is written of Him, but woe to that man by whom the Son of Man is betrayed! It would have been good for that man if he had not been born." Then Judas, who was betraying Him, answered and said, "Rabbi, is it I?" He said to him, "You have said it." And as they were eating, Jesus took bread, blessed and broke *it,* and gave *it* to the disciples and said, "Take, eat; this is My body." **Mark 14:17-22:** In the evening He came with the twelve. Now as they sat and ate, Jesus said, "Assuredly, I say to you, one of you who eats with Me will betray Me." And they began to be sorrowful, and to say to Him one by one, "*Is* it I?" And another *said,* "*Is* it I?" He answered and said to them, "*It is* one of the twelve, who dips with Me in the dish. The Son of Man indeed goes just as it is written of Him, but woe to that man by whom the Son of Man is betrayed! It would have been good for that man if he had never been born." And as they were eating, Jesus took bread, blessed and broke *it,* and gave *it* to them and said, "Take, eat; this is My body." **Luke 22:19-23:** And He took bread, gave thanks and broke *it,* and gave *it* to them, saying, "This is My body which is given for you; do this in remembrance of Me." Likewise He also *took* the cup after supper, saying, "This cup *is* the new covenant in My blood, which is shed for you. But behold, the hand of My betrayer *is* with Me on the table. And truly the Son of Man goes as it has been determined, but woe to that man by whom He is betrayed!" Then they began to question among themselves, which of them it was who would do this thing.

[2] **Acts 2:41-42:** Then those who gladly received his word were baptized; and that day about three thousand souls were added *to them.* And they continued steadfastly in the apostles' doctrine and fellowship, in the breaking of bread, and in prayers. **Acts 20:7:** Now on the first *day* of the week, when the disciples came together to break bread, Paul, ready to depart the next day, spoke to them and continued his message until midnight. **1 Cor. 11:17-22, 33-34:** Now in giving these instructions I do not praise *you,* since you come together not for the better but for the worse. For first of all, when you come together as a church, I hear that there are divisions among you, and in part I believe it. For there must also be factions among you, that those who are approved may be recognized among you. Therefore when you come together in one place, it is not to eat the Lord's Supper. For in eating, each one takes his own supper ahead of *others;* and one is hungry and another is drunk. What! Do you not have houses to eat and drink in? Or do you despise the church of God and shame those who have nothing? What shall I say to you? Shall I praise you in this? I do not praise *you....* Therefore, my brethren, when you come together to eat, wait for one another. But if anyone is hungry, let him eat at home, lest you come together for judgment. And the rest I will set in order when I come.

[3] **Mark 14:24-25:** And He said to them, "This is My blood of the new covenant, which is shed for many. Assuredly, I say to you, I will no longer drink of the fruit of the vine until that day when I drink it new in the kingdom of God." **Luke 22:17-22:** Then He took the cup, and gave thanks, and said, "Take this and divide *it* among yourselves; for I say to you, I will not drink of the fruit of the vine until the kingdom of God comes." And He took bread, gave thanks and broke *it,* and gave *it* to them, saying, "This is My body which is given for you; do this in remembrance of Me." Likewise He also *took* the cup after supper, saying, "This cup *is* the new covenant in My blood, which is shed for you. But behold, the hand of My betrayer *is* with Me on the table. And truly the Son of Man goes as it has been determined, but woe to that man by whom He is betrayed!" **1 Cor. 11:24-26:** ... and when He had given thanks, He broke *it* and said, "Take, eat; this is My body which is broken for you; do this in remembrance of Me." In the same manner *He* also *took* the cup after supper, saying, "This cup is the new covenant in My blood. This do, as often as you drink *it,* in remembrance of Me." For as often as you eat this bread and drink this cup, you proclaim the Lord's death till He comes.

[4] **1 Cor. 11:24-26:** ... and when He had given thanks, He broke *it* and said, "Take, eat; this is My body which is broken for you; do this in remembrance of Me." In the same manner *He* also *took* the cup after supper, saying, "This cup is the new covenant in My blood. This do, as often as you drink *it,* in remembrance of Me." For as often as you eat this bread and drink this cup, you proclaim the

of the faith of believers in all the benefits thereof,[5] their spiritual nourishment, and growth in Him,[6] their further engagement in, and to, all duties which they owe unto Him;[7] and to be a bond and pledge of their communion with Him, and with each other.[8]

2. In this ordinance Christ is not offered up to His Father, nor any real sacrifice made at all, for remission of sin of the quick or dead;[9] but only a memorial of that one offering up of Himself, by Himself, upon the cross, once for all; and a spiritual oblation of all possible praise unto God for the same;[10] so that the popish

---

Lord's death till He comes. **Matt. 26:27-28:** Then He took the cup, and gave thanks, and gave *it* to them, saying, "Drink from it, all of you. For this is My blood of the new covenant, which is shed for many for the remission of sins." **Luke 22:19-20:** And He took bread, gave thanks and broke *it,* and gave *it* to them, saying, "This is My body which is given for you; do this in remembrance of Me." Likewise He also *took* the cup after supper, saying, "This cup *is* the new covenant in My blood, which is shed for you."

[5] **Rom. 4:11:** And he received the sign of circumcision, a seal of the righteousness of the faith which *he had while still* uncircumcised, that he might be the father of all those who believe, though they are uncircumcised, that righteousness might be imputed to them also.

[6] **John 6:29, 35, 47-58:** Jesus answered and said to them, "This is the work of God, that you believe in Him whom He sent." ... And Jesus said to them, "I am the bread of life. He who comes to Me shall never hunger, and he who believes in Me shall never thirst.... Most assuredly, I say to you, he who believes in Me has everlasting life. I am the bread of life. Your fathers ate the manna in the wilderness, and are dead. This is the bread which comes down from heaven, that one may eat of it and not die. I am the living bread which came down from heaven. If anyone eats of this bread, he will live forever; and the bread that I shall give is My flesh, which I shall give for the life of the world." The Jews therefore quarreled among themselves, saying, "How can this Man give us *His* flesh to eat?" Then Jesus said to them, "Most assuredly, I say to you, unless you eat the flesh of the Son of Man and drink His blood, you have no life in you. Whoever eats My flesh and drinks My blood has eternal life, and I will raise him up at the last day. For My flesh is food indeed, and My blood is drink indeed. He who eats My flesh and drinks My blood abides in Me, and I in him. As the living Father sent Me, and I live because of the Father, so he who feeds on Me will live because of Me. This is the bread which came down from heaven—not as your fathers ate the manna, and are dead. He who eats this bread will live forever."

[7] **1 Cor.11:25:** In the same manner *He* also *took* the cup after supper, saying, "This cup is the new covenant in My blood. This do, as often as you drink *it,* in remembrance of Me."

[8] **1 Cor. 10:16-17:** The cup of blessing which we bless, is it not the communion of the blood of Christ? The bread which we break, is it not the communion of the body of Christ? For we, *though* many, are one bread *and* one body; for we all partake of that one bread.

[9] **Heb. 9:22, 25-26, 28:** And according to the law almost all things are purified with blood, and without shedding of blood there is no remission.... not that He should offer Himself often, as the high priest enters the Most Holy Place every year with blood of another—He then would have had to suffer often since the foundation of the world; but now, once at the end of the ages, He has appeared to put away sin by the sacrifice of Himself.... so Christ was offered once to bear the sins of many. To those who eagerly wait for Him He will appear a second time, apart from sin, for salvation. **Heb. 10:10-14:** By that will we have been sanctified through the offering of the body of Jesus Christ once *for all.* And every priest stands ministering daily and offering repeatedly the same sacrifices, which can never take away sins. But this Man, after He had offered one sacrifice for sins forever, sat down at the right hand of God, from that time waiting till His enemies are made His footstool. For by one offering He has perfected forever those who are being sanctified.

[10] **1 Cor. 11:24-26:** ... and when He had given thanks, He broke *it* and said, "Take, eat; this is My body which is broken for you; do this in remembrance of Me." In the same manner *He* also *took* the cup after supper, saying, "This cup is the new covenant in My blood. This do, as often as you drink *it,* in remembrance of Me." For as often as you eat this bread and drink this cup, you proclaim the Lord's death till He comes. **Matt. 26:26-27:** And as they were eating, Jesus took bread, blessed and broke *it,* and gave *it* to the disciples and said, "Take, eat; this is My body." Then He took the cup, and gave thanks, and gave *it* to them, saying, "Drink from it, all of you." **Luke 22:19-20:** And He took bread, gave thanks and broke *it,* and gave *it* to them, saying, "This is My body which is

sacrifice of the mass (as they call it) is most abominable, injurious to Christ's own only sacrifice, the alone propitiation for all the sins of the elect.[11]

3. The Lord Jesus hath in this ordinance, appointed His ministers to pray, and bless the elements of bread and wine, and thereby to set them apart from a common to an holy use, and to take and break the bread; to take the cup, and (they communicating also themselves) to give both to the communicants;[12] but to none who cannot be present in the congregation to observe it.[13]

4. The denial of the cup to the people,[14] worshipping the elements, the lifting them up, or carrying them about for adoration, and reserving them for any pretended religious use,

---

given for you; do this in remembrance of Me." Likewise He also *took* the cup after supper, saying, "This cup *is* the new covenant in My blood, which is shed for you."

[11] **Heb. 7:23-24, 27:** Also there were many priests, because they were prevented by death from continuing. But He, because He continues forever, has an unchangeable priesthood.... who does not need daily, as those high priests, to offer up sacrifices, first for His own sins and then for the people's, for this He did once for all when He offered up Himself. **Heb. 10:11-12, 14, 18:** And every priest stands ministering daily and offering repeatedly the same sacrifices, which can never take away sins. But this Man, after He had offered one sacrifice for sins forever, sat down at the right hand of God ... For by one offering He has perfected forever those who are being sanctified.... Now where there is remission of these, *there is* no longer an offering for sin.

[12] **Matt. 26:26-28:** And as they were eating, Jesus took bread, blessed and broke *it,* and gave *it* to the disciples and said, "Take, eat; this is My body." Then He took the cup, and gave thanks, and gave *it* to them, saying, "Drink from it, all of you. For this is My blood of the new covenant, which is shed for many for the remission of sins. **Mark 14:22-24:** And as they were eating, Jesus took bread, blessed and broke *it,* and gave *it* to them and said, "Take, eat; this is My body." Then He took the cup, and when He had given thanks He gave *it* to them, and they all drank from it. And He said to them, "This is My blood of the new covenant, which is shed for many." **Luke 22:19-20:** And He took bread, gave thanks and broke *it,* and gave *it* to them, saying, "This is My body which is given for you; do this in remembrance of Me." Likewise He also *took* the cup after supper, saying, "This cup *is* the new covenant in My blood, which is shed for you." **1 Cor. 10:16-17:** The cup of blessing which we bless, is it not the communion of the blood of Christ? The bread which we break, is it not the communion of the body of Christ? For we, *though* many, are one bread *and* one body; for we all partake of that one bread. **1 Cor. 11:23-27:** For I received from the Lord that which I also delivered to you: that the Lord Jesus on the *same* night in which He was betrayed took bread; and when He had given thanks, He broke *it* and said, "Take, eat; this is My body which is broken for you; do this in remembrance of Me." In the same manner *He* also *took* the cup after supper, saying, "This cup is the new covenant in My blood. This do, as often as you drink *it,* in remembrance of Me." For as often as you eat this bread and drink this cup, you proclaim the Lord's death till He comes. Therefore whoever eats this bread or drinks *this* cup of the Lord in an unworthy manner will be guilty of the body and blood of the Lord.

[13] **Acts 20:7:** Now on the first *day* of the week, when the disciples came together to break bread, Paul, ready to depart the next day, spoke to them and continued his message until midnight. **1 Cor. 11:20:** Therefore when you come together in one place, it is not to eat the Lord's Supper.

[14] **Matt. 26:27-28:** Then He took the cup, and gave thanks, and gave *it* to them, saying, "Drink from it, all of you. For this is My blood of the new covenant, which is shed for many for the remission of sins." **Mark 14:23:** Then He took the cup, and when He had given thanks He gave *it* to them, and they all drank from it. **1 Cor. 11:25-29:** In the same manner *He* also *took* the cup after supper, saying, "This cup is the new covenant in My blood. This do, as often as you drink *it,* in remembrance of Me." For as often as you eat this bread and drink this cup, you proclaim the Lord's death till He comes. Therefore whoever eats this bread or drinks *this* cup of the Lord in an unworthy manner will be guilty of the body and blood of the Lord. But let a man examine himself, and so let him eat of the bread and drink of the cup. For he who eats and drinks in an unworthy manner eats and drinks judgment to himself, not discerning the Lord's body.

are all contrary to the nature of this ordinance, and to the institution of Christ.[15]

5. The outward elements in this ordinance, duly set apart to the uses ordained by Christ, have such relation to Him crucified, as that truly, although in terms used figuratively, they are sometimes called by the names of the things they represent, to wit, the body and blood of Christ;[16] albeit in substance, and nature, they still remain truly, and only bread, and wine, as they were before,[17] and are the clear token of the New Covenant.[18]

6. That doctrine which maintains a change of the substance of bread and wine, into the substance of Christ's body and blood (commonly called transubstantiation) by consecration of a priest, or by any other way, is repugnant not to Scripture alone, but even to common sense and reason; overthroweth the nature of the ordinance, and hath been and is the cause of manifold superstitions, yea, of gross idolatries.[19]

---

[15] **Ex. 20:4-5:** You shall not make for yourself a carved image—any likeness *of anything* that *is* in heaven above, or that *is* in the earth beneath, or that *is* in the water under the earth; you shall not bow down to them nor serve them. For I, the LORD your God, *am* a jealous God, visiting the iniquity of the fathers upon the children to the third and fourth *generations* of those who hate Me. **Matt. 15:9:** And in vain they worship Me, Teaching *as* doctrines the commandments of men.

[16] **Matt. 26:26-28:** And as they were eating, Jesus took bread, blessed and broke *it*, and gave *it* to the disciples and said, "Take, eat; this is My body." Then He took the cup, and gave thanks, and gave *it* to them, saying, "Drink from it, all of you. For this is My blood of the new covenant, which is shed for many for the remission of sins. **1 Cor. 11:27:** Therefore whoever eats this bread or drinks *this* cup of the Lord in an unworthy manner will be guilty of the body and blood of the Lord.

[17] **1 Cor. 11:26-28:** For as often as you eat this bread and drink this cup, you proclaim the Lord's death till He comes. Therefore whoever eats this bread or drinks *this* cup of the Lord in an unworthy manner will be guilty of the body and blood of the Lord. But let a man examine himself, and so let him eat of the bread and drink of the cup. **Matt. 26:29:** But I say to you, I will not drink of this fruit of the vine from now on until that day when I drink it new with you in My Father's kingdom.

[18] **Luke 22:19-20:** And He took bread, gave thanks and broke *it*, and gave *it* to them, saying, "This is My body which is given for you; do this in remembrance of Me." Likewise He also *took* the cup after supper, saying, "This cup *is* the new covenant in My blood, which is shed for you." **1 Cor. 11:23-26:** For I received from the Lord that which I also delivered to you: that the Lord Jesus on the *same* night in which He was betrayed took bread; and when He had given thanks, He broke *it* and said, "Take, eat; this is My body which is broken for you; do this in remembrance of Me." In the same manner *He* also *took* the cup after supper, saying, "This cup is the new covenant in My blood. This do, as often as you drink *it*, in remembrance of Me." For as often as you eat this bread and drink this cup, you proclaim the Lord's death till He comes.

[19] **Acts 3:21:** ... whom heaven must receive until the times of restoration of all things, which God has spoken by the mouth of all His holy prophets since the world began. **Luke 24:6, 39:** He is not here, but is risen! Remember how He spoke to you when He was still in Galilee ... Behold My hands and My feet, that it is I Myself. Handle Me and see, for a spirit does not have flesh and bones as you see I have. **1 Cor. 11:24-26:** ... and when He had given thanks, He broke *it* and said, "Take, eat; this is My body which is broken for you; do this in remembrance of Me." In the same manner *He* also *took* the cup after supper, saying, "This cup is the new covenant in My blood. This do, as often

7. Worthy receivers, outwardly partaking of the visible elements in this ordinance,[20] do then also inwardly by faith, really and indeed, yet not carnally, and corporally, but spiritually receive, and feed upon Christ crucified, and all the benefits of His death: the body and blood of Christ, being then not corporally, or carnally, but spiritually present to the faith of believers, in that ordinance, as the elements themselves are to their outward senses.[21]

8. All ignorant and ungodly persons, as they are unfit to enjoy communion with Christ; so are they unworthy of the Lord's table; and cannot without great sin against Him, while they remain such, partake of these holy mysteries, or be admitted thereunto:[22] yea whosoever shall receive unworthily are guilty of the body and blood of the Lord, eating and drinking judgement to themselves.[23]

---

as you drink *it,* in remembrance of Me." For as often as you eat this bread and drink this cup, you proclaim the Lord's death till He comes.

[20] **1 Cor. 11:28:** But let a man examine himself, and so let him eat of the bread and drink of the cup.

[21] **1 Cor. 10:16, 3-4:** The cup of blessing which we bless, is it not the communion of the blood of Christ? The bread which we break, is it not the communion of the body of Christ?... all ate the same spiritual food, and all drank the same spiritual drink. For they drank of that spiritual Rock that followed them, and that Rock was Christ.

[22] **2 Cor. 6:14-16:** Do not be unequally yoked together with unbelievers. For what fellowship has righteousness with lawlessness? And what communion has light with darkness? And what accord has Christ with Belial? Or what part has a believer with an unbeliever? And what agreement has the temple of God with idols? For you are the temple of the living God. As God has said: "I will dwell in them And walk among them. I will be their God, And they shall be My people." **1 Cor. 10:21:** You cannot drink the cup of the Lord and the cup of demons; you cannot partake of the Lord's table and of the table of demons. **1 Cor. 5:6-7, 13:** Your glorying *is* not good. Do you not know that a little leaven leavens the whole lump? Therefore purge out the old leaven, that you may be a new lump, since you truly are unleavened. For indeed Christ, our Passover, was sacrificed for us.... But those who are outside God judges. Therefore "put away from yourselves the evil person." **2 Thess. 3:6, 14-15:** But we command you, brethren, in the name of our Lord Jesus Christ, that you withdraw from every brother who walks disorderly and not according to the tradition which he received from us.... And if anyone does not obey our word in this epistle, note that person and do not keep company with him, that he may be ashamed. Yet do not count *him* as an enemy, but admonish *him* as a brother. **Matt. 7:6:** "Do not give what is holy to the dogs; nor cast your pearls before swine, lest they trample them under their feet, and turn and tear you in pieces.

[23] **1 Cor. 11:27-29:** Therefore whoever eats this bread or drinks *this* cup of the Lord in an unworthy manner will be guilty of the body and blood of the Lord. But let a man examine himself, and so let him eat of the bread and drink of the cup. For he who eats and drinks in an unworthy manner eats and drinks judgment to himself, not discerning the Lord's body.

CHAPTER 31

Of the State of Man after Death, and of the Resurrection of the Dead

1. The bodies of men after death return to dust, and see corruption;[1] but their souls (which neither die nor sleep) having an immortal subsistence, immediately return to God who gave them;[2] the souls of the righteous being then made perfect in holiness, are received into paradise where they are with Christ, and behold the face of God, in light and glory; waiting for the full redemption of their bodies;[3] and the souls of the wicked, are cast into hell; where they remain in torment and utter darkness, reserved to the judgement of the great day;[4] besides these two places for souls separated from their bodies, the Scripture acknowledgeth none.

2. At the last day such of the saints as are found alive shall not sleep but be changed;[5] and all the dead shall be raised up with

---

[1] **Gen. 3:19:** In the sweat of your face you shall eat bread Till you return to the ground, For out of it you were taken; For dust you *are,* And to dust you shall return. **Acts 13:36:** For David, after he had served his own generation by the will of God, fell asleep, was buried with his fathers, and saw corruption.

[2] **Eccl. 12:7:** Then the dust will return to the earth as it was, And the spirit will return to God who gave it. **Luke 23:43:** And Jesus said to him, "Assuredly, I say to you, today you will be with Me in Paradise."

[3] **2 Cor. 5:1, 6, 8:** For we know that if our earthly house, *this* tent, is destroyed, we have a building from God, a house not made with hands, eternal in the heavens.... So *we are* always confident, knowing that while we are at home in the body we are absent from the Lord.... We are confident, yes, well pleased rather to be absent from the body and to be present with the Lord. **Phil. 1:23:** For I am hard-pressed between the two, having a desire to depart and be with Christ, *which is* far better. **Heb. 12:23:** ... to the general assembly and church of the firstborn *who are* registered in heaven, to God the Judge of all, to the spirits of just men made perfect. **Acts 3:21:** ... whom heaven must receive until the times of restoration of all things, which God has spoken by the mouth of all His holy prophets since the world began. **Eph. 4:10:** He who descended is also the One who ascended far above all the heavens, that He might fill all things. **Rom. 8:23:** Not only *that,* but we also who have the firstfruits of the Spirit, even we ourselves groan within ourselves, eagerly waiting for the adoption, the redemption of our body.

[4] **Jude 6:7:** And the angels who did not keep their proper domain, but left their own abode, He has reserved in everlasting chains under darkness for the judgment of the great day. **1 Pet. 3:19:** ... by whom also He went and preached to the spirits in prison. **Luke 16:23-24:** And being in torments in Hades, he lifted up his eyes and saw Abraham afar off, and Lazarus in his bosom. "Then he cried and said, 'Father Abraham, have mercy on me, and send Lazarus that he may dip the tip of his finger in water and cool my tongue; for I am tormented in this flame.'" **Acts 1:25:** ... to take part in this ministry and apostleship from which Judas by transgression fell, that he might go to his own place.

[5] **1 Cor. 15:51-52:** Behold, I tell you a mystery: We shall not all sleep, but we shall all be changed—in a moment, in the twinkling of an eye, at the last trumpet. For the trumpet will sound, and the dead will be raised incorruptible, and we shall be changed. **1 Thess. 4:17:** Then we who are alive *and* remain shall be caught up together with them in the clouds to meet the Lord in the air. And thus we shall always be with the Lord.

the selfsame bodies, and none other; although with different qualities, which shall be united again to their souls forever.[6]

3. The bodies of the unjust shall by the power of Christ, be raised to dishonour; the bodies of the just by His Spirit unto honour, and be made conformable to His own glorious body.[7]

---

[6] **Job 19:26-27:** And after my skin is destroyed, this *I know,* That in my flesh I shall see God, Whom I shall see for myself, And my eyes shall behold, and not another. *How* my heart yearns within me! **1 Cor. 15:42-44:** So also *is* the resurrection of the dead. *The body* is sown in corruption, it is raised in incorruption. It is sown in dishonor, it is raised in glory. It is sown in weakness, it is raised in power. It is sown a natural body, it is raised a spiritual body. There is a natural body, and there is a spiritual body. **John 5:25-29:** Most assuredly, I say to you, the hour is coming, and now is, when the dead will hear the voice of the Son of God; and those who hear will live. For as the Father has life in Himself, so He has granted the Son to have life in Himself, and has given Him authority to execute judgment also, because He is the Son of Man. Do not marvel at this; for the hour is coming in which all who are in the graves will hear His voice and come forth—those who have done good, to the resurrection of life, and those who have done evil, to the resurrection of condemnation. **Acts 24:15:** I have hope in God, which they themselves also accept, that there will be a resurrection of *the* dead, both of *the* just and *the* unjust. **Dan. 12:2:** And many of those who sleep in the dust of the earth shall awake, Some to everlasting life, Some to shame *and* everlasting contempt.

[7] **Acts 24:15:** I have hope in God, which they themselves also accept, that there will be a resurrection of *the* dead, both of *the* just and *the* unjust. **John 5:25-29:** Most assuredly, I say to you, the hour is coming, and now is, when the dead will hear the voice of the Son of God; and those who hear will live. For as the Father has life in Himself, so He has granted the Son to have life in Himself, and has given Him authority to execute judgment also, because He is the Son of Man. Do not marvel at this; for the hour is coming in which all who are in the graves will hear His voice and come forth—those who have done good, to the resurrection of life, and those who have done evil, to the resurrection of condemnation. **1 Cor. 15:43:** It is sown in dishonor, it is raised in glory. It is sown in weakness, it is raised in power. **Phil. 3:21:** ... who will transform our lowly body that it may be conformed to His glorious body, according to the working by which He is able even to subdue all things to Himself.

CHAPTER 32
Of the Last Judgment

1. God hath appointed a day wherein He will judge the world in righteousness, by Jesus Christ;[1] to whom all power and judgement is given of the Father;[2] in which day not only the apostate angels shall be judged;[3] but likewise all persons that have lived upon the earth, shall appear before the tribunal of Christ; to give an account of their thoughts, words, and deeds, and to receive according to what they have done in the body, whether good or evil.[4]

2. The end of God's appointing this day, is for the manifestation of the glory of His mercy, in the eternal salvation of the elect; and of His justice in the eternal damnation of the reprobate, who are wicked and disobedient; for then shall the righteous go into everlasting life, and receive that fullness of joy, and glory, with everlasting reward, in the presence of the Lord: but the wicked who know not God, and obey not the gospel of Jesus Christ, shall be cast into eternal torments, and punished with everlasting destruction, from the presence of the Lord, and from the glory of His power.[5]

---

[1] **Acts 17:31:** ... because He has appointed a day on which He will judge the world in righteousness by the Man whom He has ordained. He has given assurance of this to all by raising Him from the dead.

[2] **John 5:22, 27:** For the Father judges no one, but has committed all judgment to the Son ... and has given Him authority to execute judgment also, because He is the Son of Man.

[3] **Jude 6:** And the angels who did not keep their proper domain, but left their own abode, He has reserved in everlasting chains under darkness for the judgment of the great day. **2 Pet. 2:4:** For if God did not spare the angels who sinned, but cast *them* down to hell and delivered *them* into chains of darkness, to be reserved for judgment.

[4] **2 Cor. 5:10:** For we must all appear before the judgment seat of Christ, that each one may receive the things *done* in the body, according to what he has done, whether good or bad. **Eccl. 12:14:** For God will bring every work into judgment, Including every secret thing, Whether good or evil. **Matt. 12:36-37:** But I say to you that for every idle word men may speak, they will give account of it in the day of judgment. For by your words you will be justified, and by your words you will be condemned. **Rom. 2:16:** ... in the day when God will judge the secrets of men by Jesus Christ, according to my gospel. **Rom. 14:10, 12:** But why do you judge your brother? Or why do you show contempt for your brother? For we shall all stand before the judgment seat of Christ.... So then each of us shall give account of himself to God.

[5] **Matt. 25:31-46:** "When the Son of Man comes in His glory, and all the holy angels with Him, then He will sit on the throne of His glory. All the nations will be gathered before Him, and He will separate them one from another, as a shepherd divides *his* sheep from the goats. And He will set the sheep on His right hand, but the goats on the left. Then the King will say to those on His right hand, 'Come, you blessed of My Father, inherit the kingdom prepared for you from the foundation of the world: for I was hungry and you gave Me food; I was thirsty and you gave Me drink; I was a stranger and you took Me in; I *was* naked and you clothed Me; I was sick and you visited Me; I was in prison and you came to Me.' "Then the righteous will answer Him, saying, 'Lord, when did we see You hungry and feed *You,* or thirsty and give *You* drink? When did we see You a stranger and take *You* in, or naked and clothe *You?* Or when did we see You sick, or in prison, and come to You?' And

3. As Christ would have us to be certainly persuaded that there shall be a day of judgement, both to deter all men from sin, and for the greater consolation of the godly, in their adversity;[6] so will He have that day unknown to men, that they may shake off all carnal security, and be always watchful, because they know not at what hour, the Lord will come; and may ever be prepared to say, *Come Lord Jesus, come quickly, Amen.*[7]

---

the King will answer and say to them, 'Assuredly, I say to you, inasmuch as you did *it* to one of the least of these My brethren, you did *it* to Me.' "Then He will also say to those on the left hand, 'Depart from Me, you cursed, into the everlasting fire prepared for the devil and his angels: for I was hungry and you gave Me no food; I was thirsty and you gave Me no drink; I was a stranger and you did not take Me in, naked and you did not clothe Me, sick and in prison and you did not visit Me.' "Then they also will answer Him, saying, 'Lord, when did we see You hungry or thirsty or a stranger or naked or sick or in prison, and did not minister to You?' Then He will answer them, saying, 'Assuredly, I say to you, inasmuch as you did not do *it* to one of the least of these, you did not do *it* to Me.' And these will go away into everlasting punishment, but the righteous into eternal life." **Rom. 2:5-6:** But in accordance with your hardness and your impenitent heart you are treasuring up for yourself wrath in the day of wrath and revelation of the righteous judgment of God, who "will render to each one according to his deeds." **Rom. 9:22-23:** *What* if God, wanting to show *His* wrath and to make His power known, endured with much longsuffering the vessels of wrath prepared for destruction, and that He might make known the riches of His glory on the vessels of mercy, which He had prepared beforehand for glory. **Matt. 25:21:** His lord said to him, 'Well *done,* good and faithful servant; you were faithful over a few things, I will make you ruler over many things. Enter into the joy of your lord.' **Acts 3:19:** Repent therefore and be converted, that your sins may be blotted out, so that times of refreshing may come from the presence of the Lord. **2 Thess. 1:7-10:** ... and to *give* you who are troubled rest with us when the Lord Jesus is revealed from heaven with His mighty angels, in flaming fire taking vengeance on those who do not know God, and on those who do not obey the gospel of our Lord Jesus Christ. These shall be punished with everlasting destruction from the presence of the Lord and from the glory of His power, when He comes, in that Day, to be glorified in His saints and to be admired among all those who believe, because our testimony among you was believed. **Mark 9:4:** And Elijah appeared to them with Moses, and they were talking with Jesus.

[6] **2 Pet. 3:11, 14:** Therefore, since all these things will be dissolved, what manner *of persons* ought you to be in holy conduct and godliness ... Therefore, beloved, looking forward to these things, be diligent to be found by Him in peace, without spot and blameless. **2 Cor. 5:10-11:** For we must all appear before the judgment seat of Christ, that each one may receive the things *done* in the body, according to what he has done, whether good or bad. Knowing, therefore, the terror of the Lord, we persuade men; but we are well known to God, and I also trust are well known in your consciences. **2 Thess. 1:5-7:** ... *which is* manifest evidence of the righteous judgment of God, that you may be counted worthy of the kingdom of God, for which you also suffer; since *it is* a righteous thing with God to repay with tribulation those who trouble you, and to *give* you who are troubled rest with us when the Lord Jesus is revealed from heaven with His mighty angels. **Luke 21:27-28:** Then they will see the Son of Man coming in a cloud with power and great glory. Now when these things begin to happen, look up and lift up your heads, because your redemption draws near. **Rom. 8:23-25:** Not only *that,* but we also who have the firstfruits of the Spirit, even we ourselves groan within ourselves, eagerly waiting for the adoption, the redemption of our body. For we were saved in this hope, but hope that is seen is not hope; for why does one still hope for what he sees? But if we hope for what we do not see, we eagerly wait for *it* with perseverance.

[7] **Matt. 24:36, 42-44:** But of that day and hour no one knows, not even the angels of heaven, but My Father only.... Watch therefore, for you do not know what hour your Lord is coming. But know this, that if the master of the house had known what hour the thief would come, he would have watched and not allowed his house to be broken into. Therefore you also be ready, for the Son of Man is coming at an hour you do not expect. **Rev. 22:20:** He who testifies to these things says, "Surely I am coming quickly." Amen. Even so, come, Lord Jesus!

THE

LARGER CATECHISM

TO BE A DIRECTORY FOR CATECHISING SUCH AS HAVE MADE SOME PROFICIENCY IN THE KNOWLEDGE OF THE GOUNDS OF RELIGION,

WITH

THE PROOFS FROM THE SCRIPTURE

THE LARGER CATECHISM

Q. 1. *What is the chief and highest end of man?*

A. Man's chief and highest end is to glorify God,[1] and fully to enjoy Him forever.[2]

1 **Matt. 22:37-40:** Jesus said to him, "'You shall love the LORD your God with all your heart, with all your soul, and with all your mind.' This is *the* first and great commandment. And *the* second *is* like it: 'You shall love your neighbor as yourself.' On these two commandments hang all the Law and the Prophets." **Rom. 11:36:** For of Him and through Him and to Him *are* all things, to whom *be* glory forever. Amen. **1 Cor. 6:20:** For you were bought at a price; therefore glorify God in your body and in your spirit, which are God's. **1 Cor. 10:31:** Therefore, whether you eat or drink, or whatever you do, do all to the glory of God. **Ps. 86:9, 12:** All nations whom You have made Shall come and worship before You, O Lord, And shall glorify Your name.... I will praise You, O Lord my God, with all my heart, And I will glorify Your name forevermore.

2 **Ps. 73:24-28:** You will guide me with Your counsel, And afterward receive me to glory. Whom have I in heaven but You? And there is none upon earth that I desire besides You. My flesh and my heart fail; But God is the strength of my heart and my portion forever. For indeed, those who are far from You shall perish; You have destroyed all those who desert You for harlotry. But it is good for me to draw near to God; I have put my trust in the Lord GOD, That I may declare all Your works. **John 17:21-23: ...** that they all may be one, as You, Father, are in Me, and I in You; that they also may be one in Us, that the world may believe that You sent Me. And the glory which You gave Me I have given them, that they may be one just as We are one: I in them, and You in Me; that they may be made perfect in one, and that the world may know that You have sent Me, and have loved them as You have loved Me. **Ps. 16:5-11:** O LORD, *You are* the portion of my inheritance and my cup; You maintain my lot. The lines have fallen to me in pleasant *places;* Yes, I have a good inheritance. I will bless the LORD who has given me counsel; My heart also instructs me in the night seasons. I have set the LORD always before me; Because *He is* at my right hand I shall not be moved. Therefore my heart is glad, and my glory rejoices; My flesh also will rest in hope. For You will not leave my soul in Sheol, Nor will You allow Your Holy One to see corruption. You will show me the path of life; In Your presence *is* fullness of joy; At Your right hand *are* pleasures forevermore. **Rev. 21:3-4:** And I heard a loud voice from heaven saying, "Behold, the tabernacle of God *is* with men, and He will dwell with them, and they shall be His people. God Himself will be with them *and be* their God. And God will wipe away every tear from their eyes; there shall be no more death, nor sorrow, nor crying. There shall be no more pain, for the former things have passed away."

Q. 2. *How doth it appear that there is a God?*

A. The very light of nature in man, and the works of God, declare plainly that there is a God;[1] but His word and Spirit only do sufficiently and effectually reveal Him unto men for their salvation.[2]

1 **Rom. 1:19-20:** ... because what may be known of God is manifest in them, for God has shown it to them. For since the creation of the world His invisible attributes are clearly seen, being understood by the things that are made, even His eternal power and Godhead, so that they are without excuse. **Acts 17:28:** ... for in Him we live and move and have our being, as also some of your own poets have said, 'For we are also His offspring.' **See Ps. 19:1-3.**

2 **1 Cor. 2:9-10:** But as it is written: "Eye has not seen, nor ear heard, Nor have entered into the heart of man The things which God has prepared for those who love Him." But God has revealed them to us through His Spirit. For the Spirit searches all things, yes, the deep things of God. **1 Cor. 1:20-21:** Where is the wise? Where is the scribe? Where is the disputer of this age? Has not God made foolish the wisdom of this world? For since, in the wisdom of God, the world through wisdom

did not know God, it pleased God through the foolishness of the message preached to save those who believe. **2 Tim. 3:15-17:** ... and that from childhood you have known the Holy Scriptures, which are able to make you wise for salvation through faith which is in Christ Jesus. All Scripture *is* given by inspiration of God, and *is* profitable for doctrine, for reproof, for correction, for instruction in righteousness, that the man of God may be complete, thoroughly equipped for every good work. **See Isa. 59:21.**

Q. 3. *What is the word of God?*

A. The Holy Scriptures of the Old and New Testament are the word of God,[1] the only rule of faith and obedience.[2]

[1] **2 Tim. 3:16-17:** All Scripture *is* given by inspiration of God, and *is* profitable for doctrine, for reproof, for correction, for instruction in righteousness, that the man of God may be complete, thoroughly equipped for every good work. **2 Peter 1:19-21:** And so we have the prophetic word confirmed, which you do well to heed as a light that shines in a dark place, until the day dawns and the morning star rises in your hearts; knowing this first, that no prophecy of Scripture is of any private interpretation, for prophecy never came by the will of man, but holy men of God spoke as they were moved by the Holy Spirit. **2 Peter 3:2, 15-16:** ... that you may be mindful of the words which were spoken before by the holy prophets, and of the commandment of us, the apostles of the Lord and Savior ... and consider that the longsuffering of our Lord is salvation—as also our beloved brother Paul, according to the wisdom given to him, has written to you, as also in all his epistles, speaking in them of these things, in which are some things hard to understand, which untaught and unstable people twist to their own destruction, as they do also the rest of the Scriptures. **Matt. 19:4-5:** And He answered and said to them, "Have you not read that He who made *them* at the beginning 'made them male and female,' and said, 'For this reason a man shall leave his father and mother and be joined to his wife, and the two shall become one flesh'? **Cf. Gen. 2:24:** Therefore a man shall leave his father and mother and be joined to his wife, and they shall become one flesh.

[2] **Deut. 4:2:** You shall not add to the word which I command you, nor take from it, that you may keep the commandments of the LORD your God which I command you. **Eph. 2:20:** ... having been built on the foundation of the apostles and prophets, Jesus Christ Himself being the chief corner*stone*. **Rev. 22:18-19:** For I testify to everyone who hears the words of the prophecy of this book: If anyone adds to these things, God will add to him the plagues that are written in this book; and if anyone takes away from the words of the book of this prophecy, God shall take away his part from the Book of Life, from the holy city, and *from* the things which are written in this book. **Isa. 8:20:** To the law and to the testimony! If they do not speak according to this word, *it is* because *there is* no light in them. **Luke 16:29, 31:** Abraham said to him, 'They have Moses and the prophets; let them hear them.' ... But he said to him, 'If they do not hear Moses and the prophets, neither will they be persuaded though one rise from the dead.' **Gal. 1:8-9:** But even if we, or an angel from heaven, preach any other gospel to you than what we have preached to you, let him be accursed. As we have said before, so now I say again, if anyone preaches any other gospel to you than what you have received, let him be accursed. **2 Tim. 3:15-16:** ... and that from childhood you have known the Holy Scriptures, which are able to make you wise for salvation through faith which is in Christ Jesus. All Scripture is given by inspiration of God, and is profitable for doctrine, for reproof, for correction, for instruction in righteousness.

Q. 4. *How doth it appear that the Scriptures are the word of God?*

A. The Scriptures manifest themselves to be the word of God, by their majesty[1] and purity;[2] by the consent of all the parts,[3] and the scope of the whole, which is to give all glory to God;[4] by their light and power to convince and convert sinners, to comfort and build up believers unto salvation:[5] but the Spirit of God bearing witness by and with the Scriptures in the heart of man, is alone able fully to persuade it that they are the very word of God.[6]

1
Hos. 8:12: I have written for him the great things of My law, But they were considered a strange thing. **1 Cor. 2:6-7, 13:** However, we speak wisdom among those who are mature, yet not the wisdom of this age, nor of the rulers of this age, who are coming to nothing. But we speak the wisdom of God in a mystery, the hidden wisdom which God ordained before the ages for our glory ... These things we also speak, not in words which man's wisdom teaches but which the Holy Spirit teaches, comparing spiritual things with spiritual. **Ps. 119:18, 129:** Open my eyes, that I may see Wondrous things from Your law.... Your testimonies are wonderful; Therefore my soul keeps them.
2
Ps. 12:6: The words of the LORD are pure words, Like silver tried in a furnace of earth, Purified seven times. **Ps. 119:140:** Your word is very pure; Therefore Your servant loves it.
3
Luke 24:27: And beginning at Moses and all the Prophets, He expounded to them in all the Scriptures the things concerning Himself. **Acts 10:43:** To Him all the prophets witness that, through His name, whoever believes in Him will receive remission of sins. **Acts 26:22:** Therefore, having obtained help from God, to this day I stand, witnessing both to small and great, saying no other things than those which the prophets and Moses said would come.
4
Rom. 3:19, 27: Now we know that whatever the law says, it says to those who are under the law, that every mouth may be stopped, and all the world may become guilty before God.... Where is boasting then? It is excluded. By what law? Of works? No, but by the law of faith. **Rom. 16:25-27:** Now to Him who is able to establish you according to my gospel and the preaching of Jesus Christ, according to the revelation of the mystery kept secret since the world began but now made manifest, and by the prophetic Scriptures made known to all nations, according to the commandment of the everlasting God, for obedience to the faith— to God, alone wise, be glory through Jesus Christ forever. Amen. **See 2 Cor. 3:6-11.**
5
Acts 18:28: ... for he vigorously refuted the Jews publicly, showing from the Scriptures that Jesus is the Christ. **Heb. 4:12:** For the word of God is living and powerful, and sharper than any two-edged sword, piercing even to the division of soul and spirit, and of joints and marrow, and is a discerner of the thoughts and intents of the heart. **James 1:18:** Of His own will He brought us forth by the word of truth, that we might be a kind of firstfruits of His creatures. **Ps. 19:7-9:** The law of the LORD is perfect, converting the soul; The testimony of the LORD is sure, making wise the simple; The statutes of the LORD are right, rejoicing the heart; The commandment of the LORD is pure, enlightening the eyes; The fear of the LORD is clean, enduring forever; The judgments of the LORD are true and righteous altogether. **Rom. 15:4:** For whatever things were written before were written for our learning, that we through the patience and comfort of the Scriptures might have hope. **Acts 20:32:** So now, brethren, I commend you to God and to the word of His grace, which is able to build you up and give you an inheritance among all those who are sanctified.
6
John 16:13-14: However, when He, the Spirit of truth, has come, He will guide you into all truth; for He will not speak on His own authority, but whatever He hears He will speak; and He will tell you things to come. He will glorify Me, for He will take of what is Mine and declare it to you. **See 1 John 2:20, 27. John 20:31:** ... but these are written that you may believe that Jesus is the Christ, the Son of God, and that believing you may have life in His name.

Q. 5. *What do the Scriptures principally teach?*

A. The Scriptures principally teach, what man is to believe concerning God,[1] and what duty God requires of man.[2]

1
Gen. 1:1: In the beginning God created the heavens and the earth. **Ex. 34:5-7:** Now the LORD descended in the cloud and stood with him there, and proclaimed the name of the LORD. And the LORD passed before him and proclaimed, "The LORD, the LORD God, merciful and gracious, longsuffering, and abounding in goodness and truth, keeping mercy for thousands, forgiving iniquity and transgression and sin, by no means clearing the guilty, visiting the iniquity of the fathers upon the children and the children's children to the third and the fourth generation." **Ps. 48:1:** Great is the LORD, and greatly to be praised In the city of our God, In His holy mountain. **John 20:31:** ... but these are written that you may believe that Jesus is the Christ, the Son of God, and that believing you may have life in His name. **See 2 Tim. 3:15.**
2
Deut. 10:12-13: And now, Israel, what does the LORD your God require of you, but to fear the LORD your God, to walk in all His ways and to love Him, to serve the LORD your God with all your heart and with all your soul, *and* to keep the commandments of the LORD and His statutes which I command you today for your good? **2 Tim. 3:15-17:** ... and that from childhood you have known the Holy Scriptures, which are able to make you wise for salvation through faith which is in Christ Jesus. All Scripture *is* given by inspiration of God, and *is* profitable for doctrine, for reproof, for correction, for instruction in righteousness, that the man of God may be complete, thoroughly

equipped for every good work. **Acts 16:30-31:** And he brought them out and said, "Sirs, what must I do to be saved?" So they said, "Believe on the Lord Jesus Christ, and you will be saved, you and your household."

WHAT MAN OUGHT TO BELIEVE CONCERNING GOD

Q. 6. *What do the Scriptures make known of God?*

A. The Scriptures make known what God is,[1] the persons in the Godhead,[2] His decrees,[3] and the execution of His decrees.[4]

1 **John 4:24:** God *is* Spirit, and those who worship Him must worship in spirit and truth. **Ex. 34:6-7:** And the LORD passed before him and proclaimed, "The LORD, the LORD God, merciful and gracious, longsuffering, and abounding in goodness and truth, keeping mercy for thousands, forgiving iniquity and transgression and sin, by no means clearing *the guilty,* visiting the iniquity of the fathers upon the children and the children's children to the third and the fourth generation." **Isa. 40:18, 21-23, 25, 28:** To whom then will you liken God? Or what likeness will you compare to Him? ... Have you not known? Have you not heard? Has it not been told you from the beginning? Have you not understood from the foundations of the earth? It is He who sits above the circle of the earth, And its inhabitants are like grasshoppers, Who stretches out the heavens like a curtain, And spreads them out like a tent to dwell in. He brings the princes to nothing; He makes the judges of the earth useless.... "To whom then will you liken Me, Or to whom shall I be equal?" says the Holy One.... Have you not known? Have you not heard? The everlasting God, the LORD, The Creator of the ends of the earth, Neither faints nor is weary. His understanding is unsearchable. **Heb. 11:6:** But without faith it is impossible to please Him, for he who comes to God must believe that He is, and that He is a rewarder of those who diligently seek Him.

2 **Matt. 3:16-17:** When He had been baptized, Jesus came up immediately from the water; and behold, the heavens were opened to Him, and He saw the Spirit of God descending like a dove and alighting upon Him. And suddenly a voice *came* from heaven, saying, "This is My beloved Son, in whom I am well pleased." **Deut. 6:4-6:** Hear, O Israel: The LORD our God, the LORD is one! You shall love the LORD your God with all your heart, with all your soul, and with all your strength. **Cf. 1 Cor. 8:4, 6:** Therefore concerning the eating of things offered to idols, we know that an idol is nothing in the world, and that there is no other God but one.... yet for us there is one God, the Father, of whom are all things, and we for Him; and one Lord Jesus Christ, through whom are all things, and through whom we live. **See Matt. 28:19-20; 2 Cor. 13:14.**

3 **Acts 15:14-15, 18:** Simon has declared how God at the first visited the Gentiles to take out of them a people for His name. And with this the words of the prophets agree, just as it is written.... Known to God from eternity are all His works. **Isa. 46:9-10:** Remember the former things of old, For I am God, and there is no other; I am God, and there is none like Me, Declaring the end from the beginning, And from ancient times things that are not yet done, Saying, 'My counsel shall stand, And I will do all My pleasure,'

4 **Acts 4:27-28:** For truly against Your holy Servant Jesus, whom You anointed, both Herod and Pontius Pilate, with the Gentiles and the people of Israel, were gathered together to do whatever Your hand and Your purpose determined before to be done.

Q. 7. *What is God?*

A. God is a Spirit,[1] in and of Himself infinite in being,[2] glory,[3] blessedness,[4] and perfection;[5] all-sufficient,[6] eternal,[7] unchangeable,[8] incomprehensible,[9] everywhere present,[10] almighty,[11] knowing all things,[12] most wise,[13] most holy,[14] most just,[15] most merciful and gracious, longsuffering, and abundant in goodness and truth.[16]

1 **John 4:24:** God *is* Spirit, and those who worship Him must worship in spirit and truth.

2
Ex. 3:14: And God said to Moses, "I AM WHO I AM." And He said, "Thus you shall say to the children of Israel, 'I AM has sent me to you.'" **Job 11:7-9:** Can you search out the deep things of God? Can you find out the limits of the Almighty? They are higher than heaven— what can you do? Deeper than Sheol— what can you know? Their measure is longer than the earth And broader than the sea. **Ps. 145:3:** Great *is* the LORD, and greatly to be praised; And His greatness *is* unsearchable. **Ps. 147:5:** Great *is* our Lord, and mighty in power; His understanding *is* infinite.
3
Acts 7:2: And he said, "Brethren and fathers, listen: The God of glory appeared to our father Abraham when he was in Mesopotamia, before he dwelt in Haran.
4
1 Tim. 6:15: ... which He will manifest in His own time, He who is the blessed and only Potentate, the King of kings and Lord of lords.
5
Matt. 5:48: Therefore you shall be perfect, just as your Father in heaven is perfect.
6
Ex. 3:14: And God said to Moses, "I AM WHO I AM." And He said, "Thus you shall say to the children of Israel, 'I AM has sent me to you.'" **Gen. 17:1:** When Abram was ninety-nine years old, the LORD appeared to Abram and said to him, "I *am* Almighty God; walk before Me and be blameless. **Rom. 11:35-36:** "Or who has first given to Him And it shall be repaid to him?" For of Him and through Him and to Him are all things, to whom be glory forever. Amen.
7
Ps. 90:2: Before the mountains were brought forth, Or ever You had formed the earth and the world, Even from everlasting to everlasting, You *are* God. Deut. 33:27: The eternal God is your refuge, And underneath are the everlasting arms; He will thrust out the enemy from before you, And will say, 'Destroy!'
8
Mal. 3:6: For I *am* the LORD, I do not change; Therefore you are not consumed, O sons of Jacob.
9
1 Kings 8:27: But will God indeed dwell on the earth? Behold, heaven and the heaven of heavens cannot contain You. How much less this temple which I have built! **Ps. 145:3:** Great *is* the LORD, and greatly to be praised; And His greatness *is* unsearchable. **See Rom. 11:34.**
10
Ps. 139:1-13: O LORD, You have searched me and known me. You know my sitting down and my rising up; You understand my thought afar off. You comprehend my path and my lying down, And are acquainted with all my ways. For there is not a word on my tongue, But behold, O LORD, You know it altogether. You have hedged me behind and before, And laid Your hand upon me. Such knowledge is too wonderful for me; It is high, I cannot attain it. Where can I go from Your Spirit? Or where can I flee from Your presence? If I ascend into heaven, You are there; If I make my bed in hell, behold, You are there. If I take the wings of the morning, And dwell in the uttermost parts of the sea, Even there Your hand shall lead me, And Your right hand shall hold me. If I say, "Surely the darkness shall fall on me," Even the night shall be light about me; Indeed, the darkness shall not hide from You, But the night shines as the day; The darkness and the light are both alike to You. For You formed my inward parts; You covered me in my mother's womb.
11
Rev. 4:8: The four living creatures, each having six wings, were full of eyes around and within. And they do not rest day or night, saying: "Holy, holy, holy, Lord God Almighty, Who was and is and is to come!" **Gen. 17:1:** When Abram was ninety-nine years old, the LORD appeared to Abram and said to him, "I *am* Almighty God; walk before Me and be blameless. **Matt. 19:26:** But Jesus looked at *them* and said to them, "With men this is impossible, but with God all things are possible."
12
Heb. 4:13: And there is no creature hidden from His sight, but all things *are* naked and open to the eyes of Him to whom we *must give* account. **See Ps. 147:5.**
13
Rom. 11:33-34: For who has known the mind of the LORD? Or who has become His counselor? **Rom. 16:27:** ... to God, alone wise, be glory through Jesus Christ forever. Amen.
14
1 Pet. 1:15-16: but as He who called you *is* holy, you also be holy in all *your* conduct, because it is written, "Be holy, for I am holy." **Rev. 15:4:** Who shall not fear You, O Lord, and glorify Your name? For *You* alone *are* holy. For all nations shall come and worship before You, For Your judgments have been manifested. **Isa. 6:3:** And one cried to another and said: "Holy, holy, holy is the LORD of hosts; The whole earth is full of His glory!"
15
Deut. 32:4: *He is* the Rock, His work *is* perfect; For all His ways *are* justice, A God of truth and without injustice; Righteous and upright *is* He. **Rom. 3:5, 26:** But if our unrighteousness demonstrates the righteousness of God, what shall we say? *Is* God unjust who inflicts wrath? (I speak as a man.) ... to demonstrate at the present time His righteousness, that He might be just and the justifier of the one who has faith in Jesus.
16
Ex. 34:6: And the LORD passed before him and proclaimed, "The LORD, the LORD God, merciful and gracious, longsuffering, and abounding in goodness and truth." **Ps. 117:2:** For His merciful kindness is great toward us, And the truth of the LORD *endures* forever. Praise the LORD! **Deut. 32:4:** *He is* the

Rock, His work *is* perfect; For all His ways *are* justice, A God of truth and without injustice; Righteous and upright *is* He. **Ps. 86:15:** But You, O Lord, *are* a God full of compassion, and gracious, Longsuffering and abundant in mercy and truth.

Q. 8. *Are there more Gods than one?*

A. There is but One only,[1] the living and true God.[2]

[1] **Deut. 6:4:** Hear, O Israel: The LORD our God, the LORD *is* one! **1 Cor. 8:4-6:** Therefore concerning the eating of things offered to idols, we know that an idol *is* nothing in the world, and that *there is* no other God but one.... yet for us *there is* one God, the Father, of whom *are* all things, and we for Him; and one Lord Jesus Christ, through whom *are* all things, and through whom we *live.* **Isa. 45:21-22:** Tell and bring forth *your case;* Yes, let them take counsel together. Who has declared this from ancient time? *Who* has told it from that time? *Have* not I, the LORD? And *there is* no other God besides Me, A just God and a Savior; *There is* none besides Me. Look to Me, and be saved, All you ends of the earth! For I *am* God, and *there is* no other. **Isa. 44:6:** Thus says the LORD, the King of Israel, And his Redeemer, the LORD of hosts: 'I *am* the First and I *am* the Last; Besides Me *there is* no God.'

[2] **Jer. 10:10:** But the LORD *is* the true God; He *is* the living God and the everlasting King. At His wrath the earth will tremble, And the nations will not be able to endure His indignation. **John 17:3:** And this is eternal life, that they may know You, the only true God, and Jesus Christ whom You have sent. **1 Thess. 1:9:** For they themselves declare concerning us what manner of entry we had to you, and how you turned to God from idols to serve the living and true God. **1 John 5:20:** And we know that the Son of God has come and has given us an understanding, that we may know Him who is true; and we are in Him who is true, in His Son Jesus Christ. This is the true God and eternal life.

Q. 9. *How many persons are there in the Godhead?*

A. There be three persons in the Godhead, the Father, the Son, and the Holy Spirit;[1] and these three are one true, eternal God, the same in substance, equal in power and glory; although distinguished by their personal properties.[2]

[1] **Matt. 3:16-17:** When He had been baptized, Jesus came up immediately from the water; and behold, the heavens were opened to Him, and He saw the Spirit of God descending like a dove and alighting upon Him. And suddenly a voice *came* from heaven, saying, "This is My beloved Son, in whom I am well pleased." **Matt. 28:19:** Go therefore and make disciples of all the nations, baptizing them in the name of the Father and of the Son and of the Holy Spirit. **2 Cor. 13:14:** The grace of the Lord Jesus Christ, and the love of God, and the communion of the Holy Spirit *be* with you all. Amen.

[2] **John 1:1:** In the beginning was the Word, and the Word was with God, and the Word was God. **See Gen. 1:1-3:** In the beginning God created the heavens and the earth. The earth was without form, and void; and darkness was on the face of the deep. And the Spirit of God was hovering over the face of the waters. Then God said, "Let there be light"; and there was light. **John 17:5:** And now, O Father, glorify Me together with Yourself, with the glory which I had with You before the world was. **John 10:30:** I and My Father are one. **Ps. 45:6:** Your throne, O God, *is* forever and ever; A scepter of righteousness *is* the scepter of Your kingdom. **See Heb. 1:8-9. Acts 5:3-4:** But Peter said, "Ananias, why has Satan filled your heart to lie to the Holy Spirit and keep back *part* of the price of the land for yourself? While it remained, was it not your own? And after it was sold, was it not in your own control? Why have you conceived this thing in your heart? You have not lied to men but to God." **Rom. 9:5:** ... of whom *are* the fathers and from whom, according to the flesh, Christ *came,* who is over all, *the* eternally blessed God. Amen. **Col. 2:9:** For in Him dwells all the fullness of the Godhead bodily.

Q. 10. *What are the personal properties of the three persons in the Godhead?*

A. It is proper to the Father to beget the Son,[1] and to the Son to be begotten of the Father,[2] and to the Holy Spirit to proceed from the Father and the Son from all eternity.[3]

1
Heb. 1:5-6, 8: For to which of the angels did He ever say: "You are My Son, Today I have begotten You"? And again: "I will be to Him a Father, And He shall be to Me a Son"? But when He again brings the firstborn into the world, He says: "Let all the angels of God worship Him." ... But to the Son He says: "Your throne, O God, is forever and ever; A scepter of righteousness is the scepter of Your kingdom.

2
John 1:14, 18: And the Word became flesh and dwelt among us, and we beheld His glory, the glory as of the only begotten of the Father, full of grace and truth.... No one has seen God at any time. The only begotten Son, who is in the bosom of the Father, He has declared Him.

3
John 15:26: But when the Helper comes, whom I shall send to you from the Father, the Spirit of truth who proceeds from the Father, He will testify of Me. **Gal. 4:6:** And because you are sons, God has sent forth the Spirit of His Son into your hearts, crying out, "Abba, Father!"

Q. 11. *How doth it appear that the Son and the Holy Spirit are God equal with the Father?*

A. The Scriptures manifest that the Son and the Holy Spirit are God equal with the Father, ascribing unto them such names,[1] attributes,[2] works,[3] and worship,[4] as are proper to God only.

1
Isa. 6:3, 5, 8: And one cried to another and said: "Holy, holy, holy is the LORD of hosts; The whole earth is full of His glory!" ... So I said: "Woe is me, for I am undone! Because I am a man of unclean lips, And I dwell in the midst of a people of unclean lips; For my eyes have seen the King, The LORD of hosts." ... Also I heard the voice of the Lord, saying: "Whom shall I send, And who will go for Us?" Then I said, "Here am I! Send me." **John 12:41:** These things Isaiah said when he saw His glory and spoke of Him. **Acts 28:25:** So when they did not agree among themselves, they departed after Paul had said one word: "The Holy Spirit spoke rightly through Isaiah the prophet to our fathers. **1 John 5:20:** And we know that the Son of God has come and has given us an understanding, that we may know Him who is true; and we are in Him who is true, in His Son Jesus Christ. This is the true God and eternal life. **Acts 5:3-4:** But Peter said, "Ananias, why has Satan filled your heart to lie to the Holy Spirit and keep back *part* of the price of the land for yourself? While it remained, was it not your own? And after it was sold, was it not in your own control? Why have you conceived this thing in your heart? You have not lied to men but to God."

2
John 1:1: In the beginning was the Word, and the Word was with God, and the Word was God. **Isa. 9:6:** For unto us a Child is born, Unto us a Son is given; And the government will be upon His shoulder. And His name will be called Wonderful, Counselor, Mighty God, Everlasting Father, Prince of Peace. **John 2:24-25:** But Jesus did not commit Himself to them, because He knew all men, and had no need that anyone should testify of man, for He knew what was in man. **1 Cor. 2:10-11:** But God has revealed them to us through His Spirit. For the Spirit searches all things, yes, the deep things of God. For what man knows the things of a man except the spirit of the man which is in him? Even so no one knows the things of God except the Spirit of God.

3
Col. 1:16: For by Him all things were created that are in heaven and that are on earth, visible and invisible, whether thrones or dominions or principalities or powers. All things were created through Him and for Him. **Gen. 1:2:** The earth was without form, and void; and darkness was on the face of the deep. And the Spirit of God was hovering over the face of the waters.

4
Matt. 28:19: Go therefore and make disciples of all the nations, baptizing them in the name of the Father and of the Son and of the Holy Spirit. **2 Cor. 13:14:** The grace of the Lord Jesus Christ, and the love of God, and the communion of the Holy Spirit *be* with you all. Amen.

Q. 12. *What are the decrees of God?*

A. God's decrees are the wise, free, and holy acts of the counsel of

His will,[1] whereby, from all eternity, He hath, for His own glory, unchangeably foreordained whatsoever comes to pass in time,[2] especially concerning angels and men.

1
Isa. 45:6-7: That they may know from the rising of the sun to its setting That there is none besides Me. I am the LORD, and there is no other; I form the light and create darkness, I make peace and create calamity; I, the LORD, do all these things. **Eph. 1:11:** In Him also we have obtained an inheritance, being predestined according to the purpose of Him who works all things according to the counsel of His will. **Rom. 11:33:** Oh, the depth of the riches both of the wisdom and knowledge of God! How unsearchable are His judgments and His ways past finding out! **Rom. 9:14-15, 18:** What shall we say then? Is there unrighteousness with God? Certainly not! For He says to Moses, "I will have mercy on whomever I will have mercy, and I will have compassion on whomever I will have compassion." ... Therefore He has mercy on whom He wills, and whom He wills He hardens.

2
Ps. 33:11: The counsel of the LORD stands forever, The plans of His heart to all generations. **Isa. 14:24:** The LORD of hosts has sworn, saying, "Surely, as I have thought, so it shall come to pass, And as I have purposed, *so* it shall stand. **Acts 2:23:** Him, being delivered by the determined purpose and foreknowledge of God, you have taken by lawless hands, have crucified, and put to death. **Acts 4:27-28:** For truly against Your holy Servant Jesus, whom You anointed, both Herod and Pontius Pilate, with the Gentiles and the people of Israel, were gathered together to do whatever Your hand and Your purpose determined before to be done. **Rom. 9:22-23:** What if God, wanting to show His wrath and to make His power known, endured with much longsuffering the vessels of wrath prepared for destruction, and that He might make known the riches of His glory on the vessels of mercy, which He had prepared beforehand for glory. **Eph. 1:4, 11:** ... just as He chose us in Him before the foundation of the world, that we should be holy and without blame before Him in love ... In Him also we have obtained an inheritance, being predestined according to the purpose of Him who works all things according to the counsel of His will.

Q. 13. *What hath God especially decreed concerning angels and men?*

A. God, by an eternal and immutable decree, out of His mere love, for the praise of His glorious grace, to be manifested in due time, hath elected some angels to glory;[1] and in Christ hath chosen some men to eternal life, and the means thereof:[2] and also, according to His sovereign power, and the unsearchable counsel of His own will, (whereby He extendeth or withholdeth favor as He pleaseth,) hath passed by and foreordained the rest to dishonour and wrath, to be for their sin inflicted, to the praise of the glory of His justice.[3]

1
1 Tim. 5:21: I charge *you* before God and the Lord Jesus Christ and the elect angels that you observe these things without prejudice, doing nothing with partiality.

2
Eph. 1:4-6: ... just as He chose us in Him before the foundation of the world, that we should be holy and without blame before Him in love, having predestined us to adoption as sons by Jesus Christ to Himself, according to the good pleasure of His will, to the praise of the glory of His grace, by which He made us accepted in the Beloved. **Eph. 2:10:** For we are His workmanship, created in Christ Jesus for good works, which God prepared beforehand that we should walk in them. **2 Thess. 2:13-14:** But we are bound to give thanks to God always for you, brethren beloved by the Lord, because God from the beginning chose you for salvation through sanctification by the Spirit and belief in the truth, to which He called you by our gospel, for the obtaining of the glory of our Lord Jesus Christ. **1 Pet. 1:2:** ... elect according to the foreknowledge of God the Father, in sanctification of the Spirit, for obedience and sprinkling of the blood of Jesus Christ.

3
Rom. 9:17-18, 21-22: For the Scripture says to the Pharaoh, "For this very purpose I have raised you up, that I may show My power in you, and that My name may be declared in all the earth." Therefore He has mercy on whom He wills, and whom He wills He hardens.... Does not the potter

have power over the clay, from the same lump to make one vessel for honor and another for dishonor? *What* if God, wanting to show *His* wrath and to make His power known, endured with much longsuffering the vessels of wrath prepared for destruction. **Matt. 11:25-26:** At that time Jesus answered and said, "I thank You, Father, Lord of heaven and earth, that You have hidden these things from *the* wise and prudent and have revealed them to babes. Even so, Father, for so it seemed good in Your sight. **2 Tim. 2:20:** But in a great house there are not only vessels of gold and silver, but also of wood and clay, some for honor and some for dishonor. **Jude 4:** For certain men have crept in unnoticed, who long ago were marked out for this condemnation, ungodly men, who turn the grace of our God into lewdness and deny the only Lord God and our Lord Jesus Christ. **1 Pet. 2:8:** ... and "A stone of stumbling And a rock of offense." They stumble, being disobedient to the word, to which they also were appointed.

Q. 14. *How doth God execute His decrees?*

A. God executeth His decrees in the works of creation and providence,[1] according to His infallible foreknowledge, and the free and immutable counsel of His own will.[2]

[1] **Rev. 4:11:** You are worthy, O Lord, To receive glory and honor and power; For You created all things, And by Your will they exist and were created. **See Isa. 40:12-31**.

[2] **Eph. 1:11:** In Him also we have obtained an inheritance, being predestined according to the purpose of Him who works all things according to the counsel of His will. **Ps. 148:8:** Fire and hail, snow and clouds; Stormy wind, fulfilling His word. **Dan. 4:35:** All the inhabitants of the earth *are* reputed as nothing; He does according to His will in the army of heaven And *among* the inhabitants of the earth. No one can restrain His hand Or say to Him, "What have You done?" **Acts 4:24-28:** So when they heard that, they raised their voice to God with one accord and said: "Lord, You *are* God, who made heaven and earth and the sea, and all that is in them, who by the mouth of Your servant David have said: 'Why did the nations rage, And the people plot vain things? The kings of the earth took their stand, And the rulers were gathered together Against the LORD and against His Christ.' "For truly against Your holy Servant Jesus, whom You anointed, both Herod and Pontius Pilate, with the Gentiles and the people of Israel, were gathered together to do whatever Your hand and Your purpose determined before to be done."

Q. 15. *What is the work of creation?*

A. The work of creation is that wherein God did in the beginning, by the word of His power, make of nothing the world, and all things therein, for Himself, within the space of six days, and all very good.[1]

[1] **Gen. 1:1:** In the beginning God created the heavens and the earth. **See Gen. 1. Ps. 33:6, 9:** By the word of the LORD the heavens were made, And all the host of them by the breath of His mouth.... For He spoke, and it was *done;* He commanded, and it stood fast. **Heb. 11:3:** By faith we understand that the worlds were framed by the word of God, so that the things which are seen were not made of things which are visible. **Rev. 4:11:** You are worthy, O Lord, To receive glory and honor and power; For You created all things, And by Your will they exist and were created. **See Rom. 11:36.**

Q. 16. *How did God create angels?*

A. God created all the angels[1] spirits,[2] immortal,[3] holy,[4] excelling in knowledge,[5] mighty in power,[6] to execute His commandments, and to praise His name,[7] yet subject to change.[8]

[1] **Col. 1:16:** For by Him all things were created that are in heaven and that are on earth, visible and invisible, whether thrones or dominions or principalities or powers. All things were created through

Him and for Him.

2 **Ps. 104:4:** Who makes His angels spirits, His ministers a flame of fire.

3 **Matt. 22:30:** For in the resurrection they neither marry nor are given in marriage, but are like angels of God in heaven. **Luke 20:36:** ... nor can they die anymore, for they are equal to the angels and are sons of God, being sons of the resurrection.

4 **Matt. 25:31:** When the Son of Man comes in His glory, and all the holy angels with Him, then He will sit on the throne of His glory.

5 **2 Sam. 14:17:** Your maidservant said, 'The word of my lord the king will now be comforting; for as the angel of God, so *is* my lord the king in discerning good and evil. And may the LORD your God be with you.' **Matt. 24:36:** But of that day and hour no one knows, not even the angels of heaven, but My Father only.

6 **2 Thess. 1:7:** ... and to *give* you who are troubled rest with us when the Lord Jesus is revealed from heaven with His mighty angels.

7 **Ps. 91:11-12:** For He shall give His angels charge over you, To keep you in all your ways. In *their* hands they shall bear you up, Lest you dash your foot against a stone. **Ps. 103:20-21:** Bless the LORD, you His angels, Who excel in strength, who do His word, Heeding the voice of His word. Bless the LORD, all *you* His hosts, *You* ministers of His, who do His pleasure.

8 **2 Pet. 2:4:** For if God did not spare the angels who sinned, but cast *them* down to hell and delivered *them* into chains of darkness, to be reserved for judgment.

Q. 17. *How did God create man?*

A. After God had made all other creatures, he created man male and female;[1] formed the body of the man of the dust of the ground,[2] and the woman of the rib of the man,[3] endued them with living, reasonable, and immortal souls;[4] made them after His own image,[5] in knowledge,[6] righteousness, and holiness;[7] having the law of God written in their hearts,[8] and power to fulfill it,[9] and dominion over the creatures;[10] yet subject to fall.[11]

1 **Gen. 1:27:** So God created man in His *own* image; in the image of God He created him; male and female He created them. **Matt. 19:4:** And He answered and said to them, "Have you not read that He who made *them* at the beginning 'made them male and female.'"

2 **Gen. 2:7:** And the LORD God formed man *of* the dust of the ground, and breathed into his nostrils the breath of life; and man became a living being.

3 **Gen. 2:22:** Then the rib which the LORD God had taken from man He made into a woman, and He brought her to the man.

4 **Gen. 2:7:** And the LORD God formed man *of* the dust of the ground, and breathed into his nostrils the breath of life; and man became a living being. **Job 35:11:** Who teaches us more than the beasts of the earth, And makes us wiser than the birds of heaven? **Eccl. 12:7:** Then the dust will return to the earth as it was, And the spirit will return to God who gave it. **Matt. 10:28:** And do not fear those who kill the body but cannot kill the soul. But rather fear Him who is able to destroy both soul and body in hell. **Luke 23:43:** And Jesus said to him, "Assuredly, I say to you, today you will be with Me in Paradise."

5 **Gen. 1:26-27:** Then God said, "Let Us make man in Our image, according to Our likeness; let them have dominion over the fish of the sea, over the birds of the air, and over the cattle, over all the earth and over every creeping thing that creeps on the earth." So God created man in His *own* image; in the image of God He created him; male and female He created them.

6 **Col. 3:10:** ... and have put on the new *man* who is renewed in knowledge according to the image of Him who created him.

7
Eph. 4:24: ... and that you put on the new man which was created according to God, in true righteousness and holiness.
8
Rom. 2:14-15: ... for when Gentiles, who do not have the law, by nature do the things in the law, these, although not having the law, are a law to themselves, who show the work of the law written in their hearts, their conscience also bearing witness, and between themselves *their* thoughts accusing or else excusing *them.*
9
Eccl. 7:29: Truly, this only I have found: That God made man upright, But they have sought out many schemes.
10
Gen. 1:28: Then God blessed them, and God said to them, "Be fruitful and multiply; fill the earth and subdue it; have dominion over the fish of the sea, over the birds of the air, and over every living thing that moves on the earth." **Ps. 8:6-8:** You have made him to have dominion over the works of Your hands; You have put all *things* under his feet, All sheep and oxen— Even the beasts of the field, The birds of the air, And the fish of the sea That pass through the paths of the seas.
11
Gen. 2:16-17: And the LORD God commanded the man, saying, "Of every tree of the garden you may freely eat; but of the tree of the knowledge of good and evil you shall not eat, for in the day that you eat of it you shall surely die." **Gen. 3:6:** So when the woman saw that the tree *was* good for food, that it *was* pleasant to the eyes, and a tree desirable to make *one* wise, she took of its fruit and ate. She also gave to her husband with her, and he ate. **Eccl. 7:29:** Truly, this only I have found: That God made man upright, But they have sought out many schemes.

Q. 18. *What are God's works of providence?*

A. God's works of providence are His most holy,[1] wise,[2] and powerful preserving[3] and governing[4] all His creatures; ordering them, and all their actions,[5] to His own glory.[6]

1
Ps. 145:17: The LORD *is* righteous in all His ways, Gracious in all His works. **Lev. 21:8:** Therefore you shall consecrate him, for he offers the bread of your God. He shall be holy to you, for I the LORD, who sanctify you, *am* holy.
2
Ps. 104:24: O LORD, how manifold are Your works! In wisdom You have made them all. The earth is full of Your possessions. **Isa. 28:29:** This also comes from the LORD of hosts, *Who* is wonderful in counsel *and* excellent in guidance.
3
Heb. 1:3: ... who being the brightness of *His* glory and the express image of His person, and upholding all things by the word of His power, when He had by Himself purged our sins, sat down at the right hand of the Majesty on high. **Ps. 36:6:** Your righteousness *is* like the great mountains; Your judgments *are* a great deep; O LORD, You preserve man and beast. **Neh. 9:6:** You alone *are* the LORD; You have made heaven, The heaven of heavens, with all their host, The earth and everything on it, The seas and all that is in them, And You preserve them all. The host of heaven worships You.
4
Ps. 103:19: The LORD has established His throne in heaven, And His kingdom rules over all. **See Job 38-41; Ps. 145:14-16.**
5
Matt. 10:29-31: Are not two sparrows sold for a copper coin? And not one of them falls to the ground apart from your Father's will. But the very hairs of your head are all numbered. Do not fear therefore; you are of more value than many sparrows. **Gen. 45:7:** And God sent me before you to preserve a posterity for you in the earth, and to save your lives by a great deliverance. **Ps. 135:6:** Whatever the LORD pleases He does, In heaven and in earth, In the seas and in all deep places.
6
Rom. 11:36: For of Him and through Him and to Him *are* all things, to whom *be* glory forever. Amen. **Isa. 63:14:** As a beast goes down into the valley, *And* the Spirit of the LORD causes him to rest, So You lead Your people, To make Yourself a glorious name.

Q. 19. *What is God's providence towards the angels?*

A. God by His providence permitted some of the angels, willfully and irrecoverably, to fall into sin and damnation,[1] limiting and ordering that, and all their sins, to His own glory;[2] and established the rest in holiness and happiness;[3] employing them all,[4] at His pleasure, in the administrations of His power, mercy, and justice.[5]

1 **Jude 6:** And the angels who did not keep their proper domain, but left their own abode, He has reserved in everlasting chains under darkness for the judgment of the great day. **See 2 Pet. 2:4; Heb. 2:16; John 8:44.**

2 **Job 1:12:** And the LORD said to Satan, "Behold, all that he has *is* in your power; only do not lay a hand on his *person.*" So Satan went out from the presence of the LORD. **Matt. 8:31:** So the demons begged Him, saying, "If You cast us out, permit us to go away into the herd of swine." **Luke 10:17:** Then the seventy returned with joy, saying, "Lord, even the demons are subject to us in Your name."

3 **1 Tim. 5:21:** I charge *you* before God and the Lord Jesus Christ and the elect angels that you observe these things without prejudice, doing nothing with partiality. **Mark 8:38:** For whoever is ashamed of Me and My words in this adulterous and sinful generation, of him the Son of Man also will be ashamed when He comes in the glory of His Father with the holy angels. **Heb. 12:22:** But you have come to Mount Zion and to the city of the living God, the heavenly Jerusalem, to an innumerable company of angels.

4 **Ps. 103:20:** Bless the LORD, you His angels, Who excel in strength, who do His word, Heeding the voice of His word. **Ps. 104:4:** Who makes His angels spirits, His ministers a flame of fire.

5 **Heb. 1:14:** Are they not all ministering spirits sent forth to minister for those who will inherit salvation? **See 2 Kings 19:35.**

Q. 20. *What was the providence of God toward man in the estate in which he was created?*

A. The providence of God toward man in the estate in which he was created, was the placing him in paradise, appointing him to dress it, giving him liberty to eat of the fruit of the earth;[1] putting the creatures under his dominion,[2] and ordaining marriage for his help;[3] affording him communion with Himself;[4] instituting the Sabbath;[5] promising continual life to him, upon condition of personal, perfect, and perpetual obedience,[6] of which the tree of life was a token;[7] and forbidding to eat of the tree of the knowledge of good and evil, upon the pain of death.[8]

1 **Gen. 2:8, 15-16:** The LORD God planted a garden eastward in Eden, and there He put the man whom He had formed.... Then the LORD God took the man and put him in the garden of Eden to tend and keep it. And the LORD God commanded the man, saying, "Of every tree of the garden you may freely eat."

2 **Gen. 1:28:** Then God blessed them, and God said to them, "Be fruitful and multiply; fill the earth and subdue it; have dominion over the fish of the sea, over the birds of the air, and over every living thing that moves on the earth."

3 **Gen. 2:18:** And the LORD God said, "*It is* not good that man should be alone; I will make him a helper comparable to him." **See Matt. 19:3-9; Eph. 5:31.**

4 **Gen. 1:26-29:** Then God said, "Let Us make man in Our image, according to Our likeness; let

them have dominion over the fish of the sea, over the birds of the air, and over the cattle, over all the earth and over every creeping thing that creeps on the earth." So God created man in His *own* image; in the image of God He created him; male and female He created them. Then God blessed them, and God said to them, "Be fruitful and multiply; fill the earth and subdue it; have dominion over the fish of the sea, over the birds of the air, and over every living thing that moves on the earth." And God said, "See, I have given you every herb *that* yields seed which *is* on the face of all the earth, and every tree whose fruit yields seed; to you it shall be for food. **Gen. 3:8:** And they heard the sound of the LORD God walking in the garden in the cool of the day, and Adam and his wife hid themselves from the presence of the LORD God among the trees of the garden.

5 **Gen. 2:3:** Then God blessed the seventh day and sanctified it, because in it He rested from all His work which God had created and made. **Cf. Ex. 20:11:** For *in* six days the LORD made the heavens and the earth, the sea, and all that *is* in them, and rested the seventh day. Therefore the LORD blessed the Sabbath day and hallowed it.

6 **Gen. 2:16-17:** And the LORD God commanded the man, saying, "Of every tree of the garden you may freely eat; but of the tree of the knowledge of good and evil you shall not eat, for in the day that you eat of it you shall surely die." **Gal. 3:12:** Yet the law is not of faith, but "the man who does them shall live by them." **Rom. 10:5:** For Moses writes about the righteousness which is of the law, "The man who does those things shall live by them."

7 **Gen. 2:9:** And out of the ground the LORD God made every tree grow that is pleasant to the sight and good for food. The tree of life *was* also in the midst of the garden, and the tree of the knowledge of good and evil. **Gen. 3:22-24:** Then the LORD God said, "Behold, the man has become like one of Us, to know good and evil. And now, lest he put out his hand and take also of the tree of life, and eat, and live forever"— therefore the LORD God sent him out of the garden of Eden to till the ground from which he was taken. So He drove out the man; and He placed cherubim at the east of the garden of Eden, and a flaming sword which turned every way, to guard the way to the tree of life.

8 **Gen. 2:17:** ... but of the tree of the knowledge of good and evil you shall not eat, for in the day that you eat of it you shall surely die. **Cf. James 2:10:** For whoever shall keep the whole law, and yet stumble in one *point,* he is guilty of all.

Q. 21. *Did man continue in that estate wherein God at first created him?*

A. Our first parents being left to the freedom of their own will, through the temptation of Satan, transgressed the commandment of God in eating the forbidden fruit; and thereby fell from the estate of innocency wherein they were created.[1]

1 **Gen. 3:6-8, 13:** So when the woman saw that the tree *was* good for food, that it *was* pleasant to the eyes, and a tree desirable to make *one* wise, she took of its fruit and ate. She also gave to her husband with her, and he ate. Then the eyes of both of them were opened, and they knew that they *were* naked; and they sewed fig leaves together and made themselves coverings. And they heard the sound of the LORD God walking in the garden in the cool of the day, and Adam and his wife hid themselves from the presence of the LORD God among the trees of the garden.... And the LORD God said to the woman, "What *is* this you have done?" The woman said, "The serpent deceived me, and I ate." **Eccl. 7:29:** Truly, this only I have found: That God made man upright, But they have sought out many schemes. **2 Cor. 11:3:** But I fear, lest somehow, as the serpent deceived Eve by his craftiness, so your minds may be corrupted from the simplicity that is in Christ.

Q. 22. *Did all mankind fall in that first transgression?*

A. The divine pledge, communion, and righteous law of God being broken by the sin of Adam as a public person, not for himself only, but for his posterity, all mankind descending from him by ordinary generation,[1] sinned in him, and fell with him in that first transgression.[2]

[1] **Gen. 3:1-7, 22-24:** Now the serpent was more cunning than any beast of the field which the LORD God had made. And he said to the woman, "Has God indeed said, 'You shall not eat of every tree of the garden'?" And the woman said to the serpent, "We may eat the fruit of the trees of the garden; but of the fruit of the tree which *is* in the midst of the garden, God has said, 'You shall not eat it, nor shall you touch it, lest you die.'" Then the serpent said to the woman, "You will not surely die. For God knows that in the day you eat of it your eyes will be opened, and you will be like God, knowing good and evil." So when the woman saw that the tree *was* good for food, that it *was* pleasant to the eyes, and a tree desirable to make *one* wise, she took of its fruit and ate. She also gave to her husband with her, and he ate. Then the eyes of both of them were opened, and they knew that they *were* naked; and they sewed fig leaves together and made themselves coverings.... Then the LORD God said, "Behold, the man has become like one of Us, to know good and evil. And now, lest he put out his hand and take also of the tree of life, and eat, and live forever"— therefore the LORD God sent him out of the garden of Eden to till the ground from which he was taken. So He drove out the man; and He placed cherubim at the east of the garden of Eden, and a flaming sword which turned every way, to guard the way to the tree of life. **Acts 17:26:** And He has made from one blood every nation of men to dwell on all the face of the earth, and has determined their preappointed times and the boundaries of their dwellings. **Rom. 3:23:** ... for all have sinned and fall short of the glory of God.

[2] **Gen. 2:16-17:** And the LORD God commanded the man, saying, "Of every tree of the garden you may freely eat; but of the tree of the knowledge of good and evil you shall not eat, for in the day that you eat of it you shall surely die." **James 2:10:** For whoever shall keep the whole law, and yet stumble in one *point,* he is guilty of all. **Cf. Rom. 5:12-20:** Therefore, just as through one man sin entered the world, and death through sin, and thus death spread to all men, because all sinned— (For until the law sin was in the world, but sin is not imputed when there is no law. Nevertheless death reigned from Adam to Moses, even over those who had not sinned according to the likeness of the transgression of Adam, who is a type of Him who was to come. But the free gift *is* not like the offense. For if by the one man's offense many died, much more the grace of God and the gift by the grace of the one Man, Jesus Christ, abounded to many. And the gift *is* not like *that which came* through the one who sinned. For the judgment *which came* from one *offense resulted* in condemnation, but the free gift *which came* from many offenses *resulted* in justification. For if by the one man's offense death reigned through the one, much more those who receive abundance of grace and of the gift of righteousness will reign in life through the One, Jesus Christ.) Therefore, as through one man's offense *judgment came* to all men, resulting in condemnation, even so through one Man's righteous act *the free gift came* to all men, resulting in justification of life. For as by one man's disobedience many were made sinners, so also by one Man's obedience many will be made righteous. Moreover the law entered that the offense might abound. But where sin abounded, grace abounded much more. **1 Cor. 15:21-22:** For since by man *came* death, by Man also *came* the resurrection of the dead. For as in Adam all die, even so in Christ all shall be made alive.

Q. 23. *Into what estate did the fall bring mankind?*

A. The fall brought mankind into an estate of sin and misery.[1]

[1] **Gen. 3:16-19:** To the woman He said: "I will greatly multiply your sorrow and your conception; In pain you shall bring forth children; Your desire *shall be* for your husband, And he shall rule over you." Then to Adam He said, "Because you have heeded the voice of your wife, and have eaten from the tree of which I commanded you, saying, 'You shall not eat of it': Cursed *is* the ground for your sake; In toil you shall eat *of* it All the days of your life. Both thorns and thistles it shall bring forth for you, And you shall eat the herb of the field. In the sweat of your face you shall eat bread Till you return to the ground, For out of it you were taken; For dust you *are,* And to dust you shall return." **Rom. 5:12:** Therefore, just as through one man sin entered the world, and death through sin, and thus death spread to all men, because all sinned. **Eph. 2:1:** And you *He made alive,* who were dead in trespasses and sins. **Rom. 3:16, 23:** Destruction and misery *are* in their ways ... for all have sinned and fall short of the glory of God.

Q. 24. *What is sin?*

A. Sin is any want of conformity unto, or transgression of, any law of God, given as a rule to the reasonable creature;[1] and is therefore that which doth not give all glory to God.[2]

[1] **Lev. 5:17:** If a person sins, and commits any of these things which are forbidden to be done by the commandments of the LORD, though he does not know *it*, yet he is guilty and shall bear his iniquity. **James 4:17:** Therefore, to him who knows to do good and does not do *it*, to him it is sin. **1 John 3:4:** Whoever commits sin also commits lawlessness, and sin is lawlessness. **See Gal. 3:10, 12.**

[2] **Rom. 3:23:** ... for all have sinned and fall short of the glory of God. **Rom. 11:36:** For of Him and through Him and to Him *are* all things, to whom *be* glory forever. Amen. **1 Cor. 6:20:** For you were bought at a price; therefore glorify God in your body and in your spirit, which are God's. **1 Cor. 10:31:** Therefore, whether you eat or drink, or whatever you do, do all to the glory of God. **1 Pet. 4:11:** If anyone speaks, *let him speak* as the oracles of God. If anyone ministers, *let him do it* as with the ability which God supplies, that in all things God may be glorified through Jesus Christ, to whom belong the glory and the dominion forever and ever. Amen. **Rev. 4:11:** You are worthy, O Lord, To receive glory and honor and power; For You created all things, And by Your will they exist and were created.

Q. 25. *Wherein consisteth the sinfulness of that estate whereinto man fell?*

A. The sinfulness of that estate whereinto man fell, consisteth in the guilt of Adam's first sin,[1] the want of that righteousness wherein he was created, and the corruption of his nature, whereby he is utterly indisposed, disabled, and made opposite unto all that is spiritually good, and wholly inclined to all evil, and that continually;[2] which is commonly called original sin, and from which do proceed all actual transgressions.[3]

[1] **Rom. 5:12, 19:** Therefore, just as through one man sin entered the world, and death through sin, and thus death spread to all men, because all sinned— For as by one man's disobedience many were made sinners, so also by one Man's obedience many will be made righteous. **See 1 Cor. 15:22.**

[2] **Rom. 3:10-12:** As it is written: "There is none righteous, no, not one; There is none who understands; There is none who seeks after God. They have all turned aside; They have together become unprofitable; There is none who does good, no, not one." **See Rom. 3:13-19. Eph. 2:1-3:** And you *He made alive,* who were dead in trespasses and sins, in which you once walked according to the course of this world, according to the prince of the power of the air, the spirit who now works in the sons of disobedience, among whom also we all once conducted ourselves in the lusts of our flesh, fulfilling the desires of the flesh and of the mind, and were by nature children of wrath, just as the others. **Rom. 5:6:** For when we were still without strength, in due time Christ died for the ungodly. **Rom. 8:7-8:** Because the carnal mind *is* enmity against God; for it is not subject to the law of God, nor indeed can be. So then, those who are in the flesh cannot please God. **Gen. 6:5:** Then the LORD saw that the wickedness of man *was* great in the earth, and *that* every intent of the thoughts of his heart *was* only evil continually. **See Col. 3:10; Eph. 4:24.**

[3] **James 1:14-15:** But each one is tempted when he is drawn away by his own desires and enticed. Then, when desire has conceived, it gives birth to sin; and sin, when it is full-grown, brings forth death. **Ps. 53:1-3:** The fool has said in his heart, "*There is* no God." They are corrupt, and have done abominable iniquity; *There is* none who does good. God looks down from heaven upon the children of men, To see if there are *any* who understand, who seek God. Every one of them has turned aside; They have together become corrupt; *There is* none who does good, No, not one. **Matt. 15:19:** For out of the heart proceed evil thoughts, murders, adulteries, fornications, thefts, false witness, blasphemies. **See Rom. 3:10-18, 23; Gal. 5:19-21.**

Q. 26. *How is original sin conveyed from our first parents unto their posterity?*

A. Original sin is conveyed from our first parents unto their posterity by natural generation, so as all that proceed from them in that way are conceived and born in sin.[1]

1 **Ps. 51:5:** Behold, I was brought forth in iniquity, And in sin my mother conceived me. **Job 14:4:** Who can bring a clean *thing* out of an unclean? No one! **John 3:6:** That which is born of the flesh is flesh, and that which is born of the Spirit is spirit.

Q. 27. *What misery did the fall bring upon mankind?*

A. The fall brought upon mankind the loss of communion with God,[1] His displeasure and curse;[2] so as we are by nature children of wrath,[3] bond slaves to Satan,[4] and justly liable to all punishments in this world, and that which is to come.[5]

1 **Gen. 3:8, 10, 24:** And they heard the sound of the LORD God walking in the garden in the cool of the day, and Adam and his wife hid themselves from the presence of the LORD God among the trees of the garden.... So he said, "I heard Your voice in the garden, and I was afraid because I was naked; and I hid myself." ... So He drove out the man; and He placed cherubim at the east of the garden of Eden, and a flaming sword which turned every way, to guard the way to the tree of life. **John 8:34, 42, 44:** Jesus answered them, "Most assuredly, I say to you, whoever commits sin is a slave of sin.... Jesus said to them, "If God were your Father, you would love Me, for I proceeded forth and came from God; nor have I come of Myself, but He sent Me.... You are of *your* father the devil, and the desires of your father you want to do. He was a murderer from the beginning, and does not stand in the truth, because there is no truth in him. When he speaks a lie, he speaks from his own *resources,* for he is a liar and the father of it. **Eph. 2:12:** ... that at that time you were without Christ, being aliens from the commonwealth of Israel and strangers from the covenants of promise, having no hope and without God in the world.

2 **Gen. 3:16-19:** To the woman He said: "I will greatly multiply your sorrow and your conception; In pain you shall bring forth children; Your desire *shall be* for your husband, And he shall rule over you." Then to Adam He said, "Because you have heeded the voice of your wife, and have eaten from the tree of which I commanded you, saying, 'You shall not eat of it': "Cursed *is* the ground for your sake; In toil you shall eat *of* it All the days of your life. Both thorns and thistles it shall bring forth for you, And you shall eat the herb of the field. In the sweat of your face you shall eat bread Till you return to the ground, For out of it you were taken; For dust you *are,* And to dust you shall return." **Job 5:7:** Yet man is born to trouble, As the sparks fly upward. **Eccl. 2:22-23:** For what has man for all his labor, and for the striving of his heart with which he has toiled under the sun? For all his days *are* sorrowful, and his work burdensome; even in the night his heart takes no rest. This also is vanity. **Rom. 8:18-23:** For I consider that the sufferings of this present time are not worthy *to be compared* with the glory which shall be revealed in us. For the earnest expectation of the creation eagerly waits for the revealing of the sons of God. For the creation was subjected to futility, not willingly, but because of Him who subjected *it* in hope; because the creation itself also will be delivered from the bondage of corruption into the glorious liberty of the children of God. For we know that the whole creation groans and labors with birth pangs together until now. Not only *that,* but we also who have the firstfruits of the Spirit, even we ourselves groan within ourselves, eagerly waiting for the adoption, the redemption of our body.

3 **Eph. 2:2-3:** ... in which you once walked according to the course of this world, according to the prince of the power of the air, the spirit who now works in the sons of disobedience, among whom also we all once conducted ourselves in the lusts of our flesh, fulfilling the desires of the flesh and of the mind, and were by nature children of wrath, just as the others. **John 3:36:** He who believes in the Son has everlasting life; and he who does not believe the Son shall not see life, but the wrath of God abides on him. **Rom. 1:18:** For the wrath of God is revealed from heaven against all ungodliness and unrighteousness of men, who suppress the truth in unrighteousness. **Eph. 5:6:** Let no one deceive you with empty words, for because of these things the wrath of God comes upon the sons of disobedience.

4 **2 Tim. 2:26:** ... and *that* they may come to their senses *and escape* the snare of the devil, having been taken captive by him to *do* his will.

5 **Gen. 2:17:** ... but of the tree of the knowledge of good and evil you shall not eat, for in the day that you eat of it you shall surely die. **Lam. 3:39:** Why should a living man complain, A man for the punishment of his sins? **Rom. 6:23:** For the wages of sin *is* death, but the gift of God *is* eternal life in Christ Jesus our Lord. **Matt. 25:41, 46:** Then He will also say to those on the left hand, 'Depart from Me, you cursed, into the everlasting fire prepared for the devil and his angels' ... And these will go away into everlasting punishment, but the righteous into eternal life. **Jude 7:** ... as Sodom and

Gomorrah, and the cities around them in a similar manner to these, having given themselves over to sexual immorality and gone after strange flesh, are set forth as an example, suffering the vengeance of eternal fire.

Q. 28. *What are the punishments of sin in this world?*

A. The punishments of sin in this world are either inward, as blindness of mind,[1] a reprobate sense,[2] strong delusions,[3] hardness of heart,[4] horror of conscience,[5] and vile affections;[6] or outward, as the curse of God upon the creatures for our sakes,[7] and all other evils that befall us in our bodies, names, estates, relations, and employments;[8] together with death itself.[9]

1 **Eph. 4:18:** ... having their understanding darkened, being alienated from the life of God, because of the ignorance that is in them, because of the blindness of their heart.

2 **Rom. 1:28:** And even as they did not like to retain God in *their* knowledge, God gave them over to a debased mind, to do those things which are not fitting.

3 **2 Thess. 2:11:** And for this reason God will send them strong delusion, that they should believe the lie.

4 **Rom. 2:5:** But in accordance with your hardness and your impenitent heart you are treasuring up for yourself wrath in the day of wrath and revelation of the righteous judgment of God.

5 **Isa. 33:14:** The sinners in Zion are afraid; Fearfulness has seized the hypocrites: "Who among us shall dwell with the devouring fire? Who among us shall dwell with everlasting burnings?" **Gen. 4:13:** And Cain said to the Lord, "My punishment *is* greater than I can bear! **Matt. 27:4:** ... saying, "I have sinned by betraying innocent blood." And they said, "What *is that* to us? You see *to it!*"

6 **Rom. 1:26:** For this reason God gave them up to vile passions. For even their women exchanged the natural use for what is against nature.

7 **Gen. 3:17:** Then to Adam He said, "Because you have heeded the voice of your wife, and have eaten from the tree of which I commanded you, saying, 'You shall not eat of it': "Cursed *is* the ground for your sake; In toil you shall eat *of* it All the days of your life.

8 **Deut. 28:15:** But it shall come to pass, if you do not obey the voice of the Lord your God, to observe carefully all His commandments and His statutes which I command you today, that all these curses will come upon you and overtake you. **See Deut. 28:16-68.**

9 **Rom. 6:21, 23:** What fruit did you have then in the things of which you are now ashamed? For the end of those things *is* death.... For the wages of sin *is* death, but the gift of God *is* eternal life in Christ Jesus our Lord.

Q. 29. *What are the punishments of sin in the world to come?*

A. The punishments of sin in the world to come, are everlasting separation from the comfortable presence of God, and most grievous torments in soul and body, without intermission, in hell-fire forever.[1]

1 **2 Thess. 1:9:** These shall be punished with everlasting destruction from the presence of the Lord and from the glory of His power. **Mark 9:43-44:** If your hand causes you to sin, cut it off. It is better for you to enter into life maimed, rather than having two hands, to go to hell, into the fire that shall never be quenched— where 'Their worm does not die And the fire is not quenched.' **Luke 16:24, 26:** Then he cried and said, 'Father Abraham, have mercy on me, and send Lazarus that he may dip the tip of his finger in water and cool my tongue; for I am tormented in this flame.' ... And besides all this, between us and you there is a great gulf fixed, so that those who want to pass from

here to you cannot, nor can those from there pass to us.' **See Matt. 25:41, 46; Rev. 14:11; John 3:36.**

Q. 30. *Doth God leave all mankind to perish in the estate of sin and misery?*

A. God doth not leave all men to perish in the estate of sin and misery,[1] into which they fell under the curse of the law;[2] but of His mere love and mercy delivereth His elect out of it, and bringeth them into an estate of salvation by the promise of Christ, the Seed of the woman, commonly called the covenant of grace.[3]

1 **1 Thess. 5:9:** For God did not appoint us to wrath, but to obtain salvation through our Lord Jesus Christ.

2 **Gen. 3:17:** Then to Adam He said, "Because you have heeded the voice of your wife, and have eaten from the tree of which I commanded you, saying, 'You shall not eat of it': "Cursed *is* the ground for your sake; In toil you shall eat *of* it All the days of your life." **Rom. 5:12, 15:** Therefore, just as through one man sin entered the world, and death through sin, and thus death spread to all men, because all sinned— But the free gift *is* not like the offense. For if by the one man's offense many died, much more the grace of God and the gift by the grace of the one Man, Jesus Christ, abounded to many. **Gal. 3:10, 12:** For as many as are of the works of the law are under the curse; for it is written, "Cursed *is* everyone who does not continue in all things which are written in the book of the law, to do them." ... Yet the law is not of faith, but "the man who does them shall live by them."

3 **Titus 3:4-7:** But when the kindness and the love of God our Savior toward man appeared, not by works of righteousness which we have done, but according to His mercy He saved us, through the washing of regeneration and renewing of the Holy Spirit, whom He poured out on us abundantly through Jesus Christ our Savior, that having been justified by His grace we should become heirs according to the hope of eternal life. **Gal. 3:21:** *Is* the law then against the promises of God? Certainly not! For if there had been a law given which could have given life, truly righteousness would have been by the law. **Rom. 3:20-22:** Therefore by the deeds of the law no flesh will be justified in His sight, for by the law *is* the knowledge of sin. But now the righteousness of God apart from the law is revealed, being witnessed by the Law and the Prophets, even the righteousness of God, through faith in Jesus Christ, to all and on all who believe. For there is no difference. **2 Thess. 2:13-14:** But we are bound to give thanks to God always for you, brethren beloved by the Lord, because God from the beginning chose you for salvation through sanctification by the Spirit and belief in the truth, to which He called you by our gospel, for the obtaining of the glory of our Lord Jesus Christ. **See Acts 13:48; Eph. 1:4-5.**

Q. 31. *What is the covenant of grace?*

A. The covenant of grace is that doctrine of the solemn pledge of God made to Adam wherein He would accomplish redemption by the Seed of the woman,[1] who is Christ, and is therein effectual for the conversion and salvation of the elect.[2]

1 **Gen. 3:15:** And I will put enmity Between you and the woman, And between your seed and her Seed; He shall bruise your head, And you shall bruise His heel. **Gal. 3:16:** Now to Abraham and his Seed were the promises made. He does not say, "And to seeds," as of many, but as of one, "And to your Seed," who is Christ. **Rom. 5:15-21:** But the free gift *is* not like the offense. For if by the one man's offense many died, much more the grace of God and the gift by the grace of the one Man, Jesus Christ, abounded to many. And the gift *is* not like *that which came* through the one who sinned. For the judgment *which came* from one *offense resulted* in condemnation, but the free gift *which came* from many offenses *resulted* in justification. For if by the one man's offense death reigned through the one, much more those who receive abundance of grace and of the gift of

righteousness will reign in life through the One, Jesus Christ.) Therefore, as through one man's offense *judgment came* to all men, resulting in condemnation, even so through one Man's righteous act *the free gift came* to all men, resulting in justification of life. For as by one man's disobedience many were made sinners, so also by one Man's obedience many will be made righteous. Moreover the law entered that the offense might abound. But where sin abounded, grace abounded much more, so that as sin reigned in death, even so grace might reign through righteousness to eternal life through Jesus Christ our Lord. **Isa. 53:10-11:** Yet it pleased the LORD to bruise Him; He has put *Him* to grief. When You make His soul an offering for sin, He shall see *His* seed, He shall prolong *His* days, And the pleasure of the LORD shall prosper in His hand. He shall see the labor of His soul, *and* be satisfied. By His knowledge My righteous Servant shall justify many, For He shall bear their iniquities. **Isa. 59:20-21:** "The Redeemer will come to Zion, And to those who turn from transgression in Jacob," Says the LORD. "As for Me," says the LORD, "this *is* My covenant with them: My Spirit who *is* upon you, and My words which I have put in your mouth, shall not depart from your mouth, nor from the mouth of your descendants, nor from the mouth of your descendants' descendants," says the LORD, "from this time and forevermore."

2 **Eph. 2:4-10:** But God, who is rich in mercy, because of His great love with which He loved us, even when we were dead in trespasses, made us alive together with Christ (by grace you have been saved), and raised *us* up together, and made *us* sit together in the heavenly *places* in Christ Jesus, that in the ages to come He might show the exceeding riches of His grace in *His* kindness toward us in Christ Jesus. For by grace you have been saved through faith, and that not of yourselves; *it is* the gift of God, not of works, lest anyone should boast. For we are His workmanship, created in Christ Jesus for good works, which God prepared beforehand that we should walk in them. **Rom. 5:6-11:** For when we were still without strength, in due time Christ died for the ungodly. For scarcely for a righteous man will one die; yet perhaps for a good man someone would even dare to die. But God demonstrates His own love toward us, in that while we were still sinners, Christ died for us. Much more then, having now been justified by His blood, we shall be saved from wrath through Him. For if when we were enemies we were reconciled to God through the death of His Son, much more, having been reconciled, we shall be saved by His life. And not only *that,* but we also rejoice in God through our Lord Jesus Christ, through whom we have now received the reconciliation.

Q. 32. *How is the covenant of grace revealed?*

A. The covenant of grace is revealed in the gospel; first of all to Adam in the promise of salvation by the Seed of the woman, and afterwards by farther steps,[1] until the full discovery thereof was completed in the New Covenant;[2] in which grace and salvation are held forth in all fullness, evidence, and efficacy,[3] to all nations.[4]

1 **Gen. 3:15:** And I will put enmity Between you and the woman, And between your seed and her Seed; He shall bruise your head, And you shall bruise His heel. **Eph. 2:12:** ... that at that time you were without Christ, being aliens from the commonwealth of Israel and strangers from the covenants of promise, having no hope and without God in the world.

2 **Rom. 1:1-4:** Paul, a bondservant of Jesus Christ, called *to be* an apostle, separated to the gospel of God which He promised before through His prophets in the Holy Scriptures, concerning His Son Jesus Christ our Lord, who was born of the seed of David according to the flesh, *and* declared *to be* the Son of God with power according to the Spirit of holiness, by the resurrection from the dead. **Rom. 16:25-27:** Now to Him who is able to establish you according to my gospel and the preaching of Jesus Christ, according to the revelation of the mystery kept secret since the world began but now made manifest, and by the prophetic Scriptures made known to all nations, according to the commandment of the everlasting God, for obedience to the faith— to God, alone wise, *be* glory through Jesus Christ forever. Amen. **Eph. 3:5:** ... which in other ages was not made known to the sons of men, as it has now been revealed by the Spirit to His holy apostles and prophets.

3 **Heb. 12:22-24:** But you have come to Mount Zion and to the city of the living God, the heavenly Jerusalem, to an innumerable company of angels, to the general assembly and church of the firstborn *who are* registered in heaven, to God the Judge of all, to the spirits of just men made perfect, to Jesus the Mediator of the new covenant, and to the blood of sprinkling that speaks better things than *that of* Abel. **2 Cor. 3:9-11:** For if the ministry of condemnation *had* glory, the ministry of righteousness exceeds much more in glory. For even what was made glorious had no glory in this respect, because of the glory that excels. For if what is passing away *was* glorious, what remains *is* much more glorious. **Jer. 31:33-34:** But this *is* the covenant that I will make with the house of

Israel after those days, says the LORD: I will put My law in their minds, and write it on their hearts; and I will be their God, and they shall be My people. No more shall every man teach his neighbor, and every man his brother, saying, 'Know the LORD,' for they all shall know Me, from the least of them to the greatest of them, says the LORD. For I will forgive their iniquity, and their sin I will remember no more.

4

Luke 2:30-32: For my eyes have seen Your salvation Which You have prepared before the face of all peoples, A light to *bring* revelation to the Gentiles, And the glory of Your people Israel. **Acts 10:34-35:** Then Peter opened *his* mouth and said: "In truth I perceive that God shows no partiality. But in every nation whoever fears Him and works righteousness is accepted by Him." **Eph. 2:14-22:** For He Himself is our peace, who has made both one, and has broken down the middle wall of separation, having abolished in His flesh the enmity, *that is,* the law of commandments *contained* in ordinances, so as to create in Himself one new man *from* the two, *thus* making peace, and that He might reconcile them both to God in one body through the cross, thereby putting to death the enmity. And He came and preached peace to you who were afar off and to those who were near. For through Him we both have access by one Spirit to the Father. Now, therefore, you are no longer strangers and foreigners, but fellow citizens with the saints and members of the household of God, having been built on the foundation of the apostles and prophets, Jesus Christ Himself being the chief corner*stone,* in whom the whole building, being fitted together, grows into a holy temple in the Lord, in whom you also are being built together for a dwelling place of God in the Spirit. **Eph. 3:1-7:** For this reason I, Paul, the prisoner of Christ Jesus for you Gentiles— if indeed you have heard of the dispensation of the grace of God which was given to me for you, how that by revelation He made known to me the mystery (as I have briefly written already, by which, when you read, you may understand my knowledge in the mystery of Christ), which in other ages was not made known to the sons of men, as it has now been revealed by the Spirit to His holy apostles and prophets: that the Gentiles should be fellow heirs, of the same body, and partakers of His promise in Christ through the gospel, of which I became a minister according to the gift of the grace of God given to me by the effective working of His power.

Q. 33. *What are the steps wherein the covenant of grace is revealed?*

A. The steps wherein the covenant of grace is revealed are seven divine covenants of promise[1] which is the fulfillment of that pledge made to Adam in the promise of salvation.[2]

1

Gen. 6:18: But I will establish My covenant with you; and you shall go into the ark—you, your sons, your wife, and your sons' wives with you. **Gen. 9:8-11:** Then God spoke to Noah and to his sons with him, saying: "And as for Me, behold, I establish My covenant with you and with your descendants after you, and with every living creature that *is* with you: the birds, the cattle, and every beast of the earth with you, of all that go out of the ark, every beast of the earth. Thus I establish My covenant with you: Never again shall all flesh be cut off by the waters of the flood; never again shall there be a flood to destroy the earth." **Gen. 17:1-8:** When Abram was ninety-nine years old, the LORD appeared to Abram and said to him, "I *am* Almighty God; walk before Me and be blameless. And I will make My covenant between Me and you, and will multiply you exceedingly." Then Abram fell on his face, and God talked with him, saying: "As for Me, behold, My covenant is with you, and you shall be a father of many nations. No longer shall your name be called Abram, but your name shall be Abraham; for I have made you a father of many nations. I will make you exceedingly fruitful; and I will make nations of you, and kings shall come from you. And I will establish My covenant between Me and you and your descendants after you in their generations, for an everlasting covenant, to be God to you and your descendants after you. Also I give to you and your descendants after you the land in which you are a stranger, all the land of Canaan, as an everlasting possession; and I will be their God." **Ex. 19:1-6:** In the third month after the children of Israel had gone out of the land of Egypt, on the same day, they came *to* the Wilderness of Sinai. For they had departed from Rephidim, had come *to* the Wilderness of Sinai, and camped in the wilderness. So Israel camped there before the mountain. And Moses went up to God, and the LORD called to him from the mountain, saying, "Thus you shall say to the house of Jacob, and tell the children of Israel: 'You have seen what I did to the Egyptians, and *how* I bore you on eagles' wings and brought you to Myself. Now therefore, if you will indeed obey My voice and keep My covenant, then you shall be a special treasure to Me above all people; for all the earth *is* Mine. And you shall be to Me a kingdom of priests and a holy nation.' These *are* the words which you shall speak to the children of Israel." **Ps. 89:3-4, 34-36:** I have made a covenant with My chosen, I have sworn to My servant David: 'Your seed I will establish forever, And build up your throne to all generations.' ... My covenant I will not break, Nor alter the word that has gone out of My lips. Once I have sworn by My holiness; I will not lie to David: His seed shall endure forever, And his throne as the sun before Me. **Ps. 110:1-4:** The LORD said to my Lord, "Sit at My right hand, Till I make Your enemies Your footstool." The LORD shall send the rod of Your strength out of Zion. Rule in the midst of Your enemies! Your people *shall be* volunteers In the day of Your power; In the beauties of holiness, from the womb of the morning, You have the dew of Your youth. The LORD has sworn And will not relent, "You *are* a priest forever According to the order of Melchizedek." **Heb. 7:** For this Melchizedek, king of Salem, priest of the Most High God, who met Abraham returning from the slaughter of the kings and blessed him, to whom also Abraham gave a tenth part of all, first being translated "king of righteousness," and then also king of Salem, meaning "king of peace," without father, without mother, without genealogy, having neither beginning of days nor end of life, but made like the Son of God, remains a priest continually.... Therefore, if perfection were through the Levitical priesthood (for under it the people received the law), what further need *was there* that another priest should rise according to the order of Melchizedek, and not be called according to the order of Aaron? For the priesthood being changed, of necessity there is also a change of the law. For He of whom these things are spoken belongs to another tribe, from which no man has officiated at the altar. For *it is* evident that our Lord arose from Judah, of which tribe Moses spoke nothing concerning priesthood. And it is yet far more evident if, in the likeness of Melchizedek, there arises another priest who has come, not according to the law of a fleshly commandment, but according to the power of an endless life. For He testifies: "You *are* a priest forever According to the order of Melchizedek." ... And inasmuch as *He was* not *made priest* without an oath (for they have become priests without an oath, but He with an oath by Him who said to Him: "The LORD has sworn And will not relent, 'You *are* a priest forever According to the order of Melchizedek'"), by so much more Jesus has become a surety of a better covenant.... For the law appoints as high priests men who have weakness, but the word of the oath, which came after the law, *appoints* the Son who has been perfected forever. **Jer. 31:31-34:** Behold, the days are coming, says the LORD, when I will make a new covenant with the house of Israel and with the house of Judah— not according to the covenant that I made with their fathers in the day *that* I took them by the hand to lead them out of the land of Egypt, My covenant which they broke, though I was a husband to them, says the LORD. But this *is* the covenant that I will make with the house of Israel after those days, says the LORD: I will put My law in their minds, and write it on their hearts; and I will be their God, and they shall be My people. No more shall every man teach his neighbor, and every man his brother, saying, 'Know the LORD,' for they all shall know Me, from the least of them to the greatest of them, says the LORD. For I will forgive their iniquity, and their sin I will remember no more. **Heb. 8:7-13:** For if that first *covenant* had been faultless, then no place would have been sought for a second. Because finding fault with them, He says: "Behold, the days are coming, says the LORD, when I will make a new covenant with the house of Israel and with the house of Judah— not according to the covenant that I made with their fathers in the day when I took them by the hand to lead them out of the land of Egypt; because they did not continue in My covenant, and I disregarded them, says the LORD. For this *is* the covenant that I will make with the house of Israel after those days, says the LORD: I will put My laws in their mind and write them on their hearts; and I will be their God, and they shall be My people. None of them shall teach his neighbor, and none his brother, saying, 'Know the LORD,' for all shall know Me, from the least of them to the greatest of them. For I will be merciful to their unrighteousness, and their sins and their lawless deeds I will remember no more." In that He says, "A new *covenant*," He has made the first obsolete. Now what is becoming obsolete and growing old is ready to vanish away.

2

Eph. 2:11-13: Therefore remember that you, once Gentiles in the flesh—who are called Uncircumcision by what is called the Circumcision made in the flesh by hands—that at that time you were without Christ, being aliens from the commonwealth of Israel and strangers from the covenants of promise, having no hope and without God in the world. But now in Christ Jesus you who once were far off have been brought near by the blood of Christ. **Luke 24:25-27:** Then He said to them, "O foolish ones, and slow of heart to believe in all that the prophets have spoken! Ought not the Christ to have suffered these things and to enter into His glory?" And beginning at Moses and all the Prophets, He expounded to them in all the Scriptures the things concerning Himself. **Gal. 3:13-17:** Christ has redeemed us from the curse of the law, having become a curse for us (for it is written, "Cursed *is* everyone who hangs on a tree"), that the blessing of Abraham might come upon the Gentiles in Christ Jesus, that we might receive the promise of the Spirit through faith. Brethren, I speak in the manner of men: Though *it is* only a man's covenant, yet *if it is* confirmed, no one annuls or adds to it. Now to Abraham and his Seed were the promises made. He does not say, "And to seeds," as of many, but as of one, "And to your Seed," who is Christ. And this I say, *that* the law, which was four hundred and thirty years later, cannot annul the covenant that was confirmed before by God in Christ, that it should make the promise of no effect. **Acts 2:22-36:** "Men of Israel, hear these words: Jesus of Nazareth, a Man attested by God to you by miracles, wonders, and signs which God did through Him in your midst, as you yourselves also know— Him, being delivered by the determined purpose and foreknowledge of God, you have taken by lawless hands, have crucified, and put to death; whom God raised up, having loosed the pains of death, because it was not possible that He should be held by it. For David says concerning Him: 'I foresaw the LORD always before my face, For He is at my right hand, that I may not be shaken. Therefore my heart rejoiced, and my tongue was glad; Moreover my flesh also will rest in hope. For You will not leave my soul in Hades, Nor will You allow Your Holy One to see corruption. You have made known to me the ways of life; You will make me full of joy in Your presence.' "Men *and* brethren, let *me* speak freely to you of the patriarch David, that he is both dead and buried, and his tomb is with us to this day. Therefore, being a prophet, and knowing that God had sworn with an oath to him that of the fruit of his body, according to the flesh, He would raise up the Christ to sit on his throne, he, foreseeing this, spoke concerning the resurrection of the Christ, that His soul was not left in Hades, nor did His flesh see corruption. This Jesus God has raised up, of which we are all witnesses. Therefore being exalted to the right hand of God, and having received from the Father the promise of the Holy Spirit, He poured out this which you now see and hear. "For David did not ascend into the heavens, but he says himself: 'The LORD said to my Lord, "Sit at My right hand, Till I make Your enemies Your footstool."' "Therefore let all the house of Israel know assuredly that God has made this Jesus, whom you crucified, both Lord and Christ."

Q. 34. *What is a divine covenant?*

A. A divine covenant is a promise pledged by God wherein He swears an oath to confirm it;[1] it is an oath-bound promise of His grace, love, and mercy.[2]

[1] **Gen. 9:8-17:** Then God spoke to Noah and to his sons with him, saying: "And as for Me, behold, I establish My covenant with you and with your descendants after you, and with every living creature that *is* with you: the birds, the cattle, and every beast of the earth with you, of all that go out of the ark, every beast of the earth. Thus I establish My covenant with you: Never again shall all flesh be cut off by the waters of the flood; never again shall there be a flood to destroy the earth." And God said: "This *is* the sign of the covenant which I make between Me and you, and every living creature that *is* with you, for perpetual generations: I set My rainbow in the cloud, and it shall be for the sign of the covenant between Me and the earth. It shall be, when I bring a cloud over the earth, that the rainbow shall be seen in the cloud; and I will remember My covenant which *is* between Me and you and every living creature of all flesh; the waters shall never again become a flood to destroy all flesh. The rainbow shall be in the cloud, and I will look on it to remember the everlasting covenant between God and every living creature of all flesh that *is* on the earth." And God said to Noah, "This *is* the sign of the covenant which I have established between Me and all flesh that *is* on the earth." **Isa. 54:9-10:** "For this *is* like the waters of Noah to Me; For as I have sworn That the waters of Noah would no longer cover the earth, So have I sworn That I would not be angry with you, nor rebuke you. For the mountains shall depart And the hills be removed, But My kindness shall not depart from you, Nor shall My covenant of peace be removed," Says the LORD, who has mercy on you. **Ps. 89:3-4, 34-36:** I have made a covenant with My chosen, I have sworn to My servant David: 'Your seed I will establish forever, And build up your throne to all generations.... My covenant I will not break, Nor alter the word that has gone out of My lips. Once I have sworn by My holiness; I will not lie to David: His seed shall endure forever, And his throne as the sun before Me. **Acts 2:29-31:** Men *and* brethren, let *me* speak freely to you of the patriarch David, that he is both dead and buried, and his tomb is with us to this day. Therefore, being a prophet, and knowing that God had sworn with an oath to him that of the fruit of his body, according to the flesh, He would raise up the Christ to sit on his throne, he, foreseeing this, spoke concerning the resurrection of the Christ, that His soul was not left in Hades, nor did His flesh see corruption.

[2] **Gen. 6:8:** But Noah found grace in the eyes of the LORD. **Deut. 7:9:** Therefore know that the LORD your God, He *is* God, the faithful God who keeps covenant and mercy for a thousand generations with those who love Him and keep His commandments. **Luke 1:72:** To perform the mercy *promised* to our fathers And to remember His holy covenant. **1 Kings 8:23:** ... and he said: "LORD God of Israel, *there is* no God in heaven above or on earth below like You, who keep *Your* covenant and mercy with Your servants who walk before You with all their hearts."

Q. 35. *What rules are to be observed for the right understanding of the covenants of promise?*

A. For the right understanding of the covenants of promise, these rules are to be observed:

1. That a divine covenant is neither a pledge nor a promise alone but a solemn promise of God confirmed with an oath wherein is manifested His grace, love, and mercy.[1]

[1] **Ps. 89:3-4, 34-36:** I have made a covenant with My chosen, I have sworn to My servant David: 'Your seed I will establish forever, And build up your throne to all generations.... My covenant I will

not break, Nor alter the word that has gone out of My lips. Once I have sworn by My holiness; I will not lie to David: His seed shall endure forever, And his throne as the sun before Me. **Deut. 4:31:** ... (for the LORD your God *is* a merciful God), He will not forsake you nor destroy you, nor forget the covenant of your fathers which He swore to them. **Ezek. 16:8:** "When I passed by you again and looked upon you, indeed your time *was* the time of love; so I spread My wing over you and covered your nakedness. Yes, I swore an oath to you and entered into a covenant with you, and you became Mine," says the Lord God.

2. That the doctrine of the covenant of grace is the foundation and unity of all the divine covenants.[2]

2 **Eph. 2:11-13:** Therefore remember that you, once Gentiles in the flesh—who are called Uncircumcision by what is called the Circumcision made in the flesh by hands—that at that time you were without Christ, being aliens from the commonwealth of Israel and strangers from the covenants of promise, having no hope and without God in the world. But now in Christ Jesus you who once were far off have been brought near by the blood of Christ. **Gal. 3:15-18:** Brethren, I speak in the manner of men: Though *it is* only a man's covenant, yet *if it is* confirmed, no one annuls or adds to it. Now to Abraham and his Seed were the promises made. He does not say, "And to seeds," as of many, but as of one, "And to your Seed," who is Christ. And this I say, *that* the law, which was four hundred and thirty years later, cannot annul the covenant that was confirmed before by God in Christ, that it should make the promise of no effect. For if the inheritance *is* of the law, *it is* no longer of promise; but God gave *it* to Abraham by promise. **Luke 24:25-27:** Then He said to them, "O foolish ones, and slow of heart to believe in all that the prophets have spoken! Ought not the Christ to have suffered these things and to enter into His glory?" And beginning at Moses and all the Prophets, He expounded to them in all the Scriptures the things concerning Himself.

3. That although the covenants of promise are united through the covenant of grace and are, therefore, the same in substance, yet they differ in their essential properties and are truly distinct.[3]

3 **Gen. 6:18:** But I will establish My covenant with you; and you shall go into the ark—you, your sons, your wife, and your sons' wives with you. **Gen. 9:8-11:** Then God spoke to Noah and to his sons with him, saying: "And as for Me, behold, I establish My covenant with you and with your descendants after you, and with every living creature that *is* with you: the birds, the cattle, and every beast of the earth with you, of all that go out of the ark, every beast of the earth. Thus I establish My covenant with you: Never again shall all flesh be cut off by the waters of the flood; never again shall there be a flood to destroy the earth." **Gen. 17:1-8:** When Abram was ninety-nine years old, the LORD appeared to Abram and said to him, "I *am* Almighty God; walk before Me and be blameless. And I will make My covenant between Me and you, and will multiply you exceedingly." Then Abram fell on his face, and God talked with him, saying: "As for Me, behold, My covenant is with you, and you shall be a father of many nations. No longer shall your name be called Abram, but your name shall be Abraham; for I have made you a father of many nations. I will make you exceedingly fruitful; and I will make nations of you, and kings shall come from you. And I will establish My covenant between Me and you and your descendants after you in their generations, for an everlasting covenant, to be God to you and your descendants after you. Also I give to you and your descendants after you the land in which you are a stranger, all the land of Canaan, as an everlasting possession; and I will be their God." **Ex. 19:1-6:** In the third month after the children of Israel had gone out of the land of Egypt, on the same day, they came *to* the Wilderness of Sinai. For they had departed from Rephidim, had come *to* the Wilderness of Sinai, and camped in the wilderness. So Israel camped there before the mountain. And Moses went up to God, and the LORD called to him from the mountain, saying, "Thus you shall say to the house of Jacob, and tell the children of Israel: 'You have seen what I did to the Egyptians, and *how* I bore you on eagles' wings and brought you to Myself. Now therefore, if you will indeed obey My voice and keep My covenant, then you shall be a special treasure to Me above all people; for all the earth *is* Mine. And you shall be to Me a kingdom of priests and a holy nation.' These *are* the words which you shall speak to the children of Israel." **Ps. 89:3-4, 34-36, See footnote 1 above. Ps. 110:1-4:** The LORD said to my Lord, "Sit at My right hand, Till I make Your enemies Your footstool." The LORD shall send the rod of Your strength out of Zion. Rule in the midst of Your enemies! Your people *shall be* volunteers In the day of Your power; In the beauties of holiness, from the womb of the morning, You have the dew of Your youth. The LORD has sworn And will not relent, "You *are* a priest forever According to the order of Melchizedek." **Heb. 7:** For this Melchizedek, king of Salem, priest of the Most High God, who met Abraham returning from the slaughter of the kings and blessed him, to whom also Abraham gave a tenth part of all, first being translated "king of righteousness," and then also king of Salem, meaning "king of peace," without father, without mother, without genealogy, having neither beginning of days nor end of life, but made like the Son of God, remains a priest continually.... Therefore, if perfection were through the Levitical priesthood (for under it the people received the law), what further need

was there that another priest should rise according to the order of Melchizedek, and not be called according to the order of Aaron? For the priesthood being changed, of necessity there is also a change of the law. For He of whom these things are spoken belongs to another tribe, from which no man has officiated at the altar. For *it is* evident that our Lord arose from Judah, of which tribe Moses spoke nothing concerning priesthood. And it is yet far more evident if, in the likeness of Melchizedek, there arises another priest who has come, not according to the law of a fleshly commandment, but according to the power of an endless life. For He testifies: "You *are* a priest forever According to the order of Melchizedek." ... And inasmuch as *He was* not *made priest* without an oath (for they have become priests without an oath, but He with an oath by Him who said to Him: "The LORD has sworn And will not relent, 'You *are* a priest forever According to the order of Melchizedek'"), by so much more Jesus has become a surety of a better covenant.... For the law appoints as high priests men who have weakness, but the word of the oath, which came after the law, *appoints* the Son who has been perfected forever. **Jer. 31:31-34:** Behold, the days are coming, says the LORD, when I will make a new covenant with the house of Israel and with the house of Judah— not according to the covenant that I made with their fathers in the day *that* I took them by the hand to lead them out of the land of Egypt, My covenant which they broke, though I was a husband to them, says the LORD. But this *is* the covenant that I will make with the house of Israel after those days, says the LORD: I will put My law in their minds, and write it on their hearts; and I will be their God, and they shall be My people. No more shall every man teach his neighbor, and every man his brother, saying, 'Know the LORD,' for they all shall know Me, from the least of them to the greatest of them, says the LORD. For I will forgive their iniquity, and their sin I will remember no more. **Heb. 8:7-13:** For if that first *covenant* had been faultless, then no place would have been sought for a second. Because finding fault with them, He says: "Behold, the days are coming, says the LORD, when I will make a new covenant with the house of Israel and with the house of Judah— not according to the covenant that I made with their fathers in the day when I took them by the hand to lead them out of the land of Egypt; because they did not continue in My covenant, and I disregarded them, says the LORD. For this *is* the covenant that I will make with the house of Israel after those days, says the LORD: I will put My laws in their mind and write them on their hearts; and I will be their God, and they shall be My people. None of them shall teach his neighbor, and none his brother, saying, 'Know the LORD,' for all shall know Me, from the least of them to the greatest of them. For I will be merciful to their unrighteousness, and their sins and their lawless deeds I will remember no more." In that He says, "A new *covenant*," He has made the first obsolete. Now what is becoming obsolete and growing old is ready to vanish away.

4. That the revelation of the covenant of grace is made in divers times and by sundry parts successively through the covenants of promise with the full discovery thereof completed in the New Covenant.[4]

[4] **Rom. 16:25-27:** Now to Him who is able to establish you according to my gospel and the preaching of Jesus Christ, according to the revelation of the mystery kept secret since the world began but now made manifest, and by the prophetic Scriptures made known to all nations, according to the commandment of the everlasting God, for obedience to the faith— to God, alone wise, *be* glory through Jesus Christ forever. Amen. **Eph. 3:1-7:** For this reason I, Paul, the prisoner of Christ Jesus for you Gentiles— if indeed you have heard of the dispensation of the grace of God which was given to me for you, how that by revelation He made known to me the mystery (as I have briefly written already, by which, when you read, you may understand my knowledge in the mystery of Christ), which in other ages was not made known to the sons of men, as it has now been revealed by the Spirit to His holy apostles and prophets: that the Gentiles should be fellow heirs, of the same body, and partakers of His promise in Christ through the gospel, of which I became a minister according to the gift of the grace of God given to me by the effective working of His power. **Heb. 1:1-4:** God, who at various times and in various ways spoke in time past to the fathers by the prophets, has in these last days spoken to us by *His* Son, whom He has appointed heir of all things, through whom also He made the worlds; who being the brightness of *His* glory and the express image of His person, and upholding all things by the word of His power, when He had by Himself purged our sins, sat down at the right hand of the Majesty on high, having become so much better than the angels, as He has by inheritance obtained a more excellent name than they.

Q. 36. *What special things are we to consider in the covenants of promise?*

A. We are to consider, in the covenants of promise, the various dispensations,[1] the substance of the covenants themselves,[2] and several tokens annexed to some, the more to exhibit them.[3]

1 **2 Pet. 3:6-13:** ... by which the world *that* then existed perished, being flooded with water. But the heavens and the earth *which* are now preserved by the same word, are reserved for fire until the day of judgment and perdition of ungodly men. But, beloved, do not forget this one thing, that with the Lord one day *is* as a thousand years, and a thousand years as one day. The Lord is not slack concerning *His* promise, as some count slackness, but is longsuffering toward us, not willing that any should perish but that all should come to repentance. But the day of the Lord will come as a thief in the night, in which the heavens will pass away with a great noise, and the elements will melt with fervent heat; both the earth and the works that are in it will be burned up. Therefore, since all these things will be dissolved, what manner *of persons* ought you to be in holy conduct and godliness, looking for and hastening the coming of the day of God, because of which the heavens will be dissolved, being on fire, and the elements will melt with fervent heat? Nevertheless we, according to His promise, look for new heavens and a new earth in which righteousness dwells. **Gal. 3:19-25:** What purpose then *does* the law *serve?* It was added because of transgressions, till the Seed should come to whom the promise was made; *and it was* appointed through angels by the hand of a mediator. Now a mediator does not *mediate* for one *only,* but God is one. *Is* the law then against the promises of God? Certainly not! For if there had been a law given which could have given life, truly righteousness would have been by the law. But the Scripture has confined all under sin, that the promise by faith in Jesus Christ might be given to those who believe. But before faith came, we were kept under guard by the law, kept for the faith which would afterward be revealed. Therefore the law was our tutor *to bring us* to Christ, that we might be justified by faith. But after faith has come, we are no longer under a tutor. **Eph. 1:9-10:** ... having made known to us the mystery of His will, according to His good pleasure which He purposed in Himself, that in the dispensation of the fullness of the times He might gather together in one all things in Christ, both which are in heaven and which are on earth—in Him.

2 **Rom. 16:25-26:** Now to Him who is able to establish you according to my gospel and the preaching of Jesus Christ, according to the revelation of the mystery kept secret since the world began but now made manifest, and by the prophetic Scriptures made known to all nations, according to the commandment of the everlasting God, for obedience to the faith. **Gal. 4:4-5:** But when the fullness of the time had come, God sent forth His Son, born of a woman, born under the law, to redeem those who were under the law, that we might receive the adoption as sons. **Col. 2:17:** ... which are a shadow of things to come, but the substance is of Christ. **Rev. 12:** Now a great sign appeared in heaven: a woman clothed with the sun, with the moon under her feet, and on her head a garland of twelve stars. Then being with child, she cried out in labor and in pain to give birth. And another sign appeared in heaven: behold, a great, fiery red dragon having seven heads and ten horns, and seven diadems on his heads. His tail drew a third of the stars of heaven and threw them to the earth. And the dragon stood before the woman who was ready to give birth, to devour her Child as soon as it was born. She bore a male Child who was to rule all nations with a rod of iron. And her Child was caught up to God and His throne.... And war broke out in heaven: Michael and his angels fought with the dragon; and the dragon and his angels fought, but they did not prevail, nor was a place found for them in heaven any longer. So the great dragon was cast out, that serpent of old, called the Devil and Satan, who deceives the whole world; he was cast to the earth, and his angels were cast out with him. Then I heard a loud voice saying in heaven, "Now salvation, and strength, and the kingdom of our God, and the power of His Christ have come, for the accuser of our brethren, who accused them before our God day and night, has been cast down.... Now when the dragon saw that he had been cast to the earth, he persecuted the woman who gave birth to the male *Child*.... So the serpent spewed water out of his mouth like a flood after the woman, that he might cause her to be carried away by the flood.... And the dragon was enraged with the woman, and he went to make war with the rest of her offspring, who keep the commandments of God and have the testimony of Jesus Christ.

3 **Gen. 9:13:** I set My rainbow in the cloud, and it shall be for the sign of the covenant between Me and the earth. **Gen. 17:11:** ... and you shall be circumcised in the flesh of your foreskins, and it shall be a sign of the covenant between Me and you. **Ex. 31:16-17:** Therefore the children of Israel shall keep the Sabbath, to observe the Sabbath throughout their generations *as* a perpetual covenant. It *is* a sign between Me and the children of Israel forever; for *in* six days the LORD made the heavens and the earth, and on the seventh day He rested and was refreshed. **Luke 22:19-20:** And He took bread, gave thanks and broke *it,* and gave *it* to them, saying, "This is My body which is given for you; do this in remembrance of Me." Likewise He also *took* the cup after supper, saying, "This cup *is* the new covenant in My blood, which is shed for you.

Q. 37. *What are the various dispensations of the covenants of promise?*

A. The various dispensations of the covenants of promise are the

Noahic,[1] the law,[2] and the gospel[3] dispensations.

[1] **2 Pet. 3:6-13:** ... by which the world *that* then existed perished, being flooded with water. But the heavens and the earth *which* are now preserved by the same word, are reserved for fire until the day of judgment and perdition of ungodly men. But, beloved, do not forget this one thing, that with the Lord one day *is* as a thousand years, and a thousand years as one day. The Lord is not slack concerning *His* promise, as some count slackness, but is longsuffering toward us, not willing that any should perish but that all should come to repentance. But the day of the Lord will come as a thief in the night, in which the heavens will pass away with a great noise, and the elements will melt with fervent heat; both the earth and the works that are in it will be burned up. Therefore, since all these things will be dissolved, what manner *of persons* ought you to be in holy conduct and godliness, looking for and hastening the coming of the day of God, because of which the heavens will be dissolved, being on fire, and the elements will melt with fervent heat? Nevertheless we, according to His promise, look for new heavens and a new earth in which righteousness dwells. **Isa. 54:9:** For this *is* like the waters of Noah to Me; For as I have sworn That the waters of Noah would no longer cover the earth, So have I sworn That I would not be angry with you, nor rebuke you. **Gen. 8:20-22:** Then Noah built an altar to the LORD, and took of every clean animal and of every clean bird, and offered burnt offerings on the altar. And the LORD smelled a soothing aroma. Then the LORD said in His heart, "I will never again curse the ground for man's sake, although the imagination of man's heart *is* evil from his youth; nor will I again destroy every living thing as I have done. "While the earth remains, Seedtime and harvest, Cold and heat, Winter and summer, And day and night Shall not cease." **Gen. 9:1-11:** So God blessed Noah and his sons, and said to them: "Be fruitful and multiply, and fill the earth. And the fear of you and the dread of you shall be on every beast of the earth, on every bird of the air, on all that move *on* the earth, and on all the fish of the sea. They are given into your hand. Every moving thing that lives shall be food for you. I have given you all things, even as the green herbs. But you shall not eat flesh with its life, *that is,* its blood. Surely for your lifeblood I will demand *a reckoning;* from the hand of every beast I will require it, and from the hand of man. From the hand of every man's brother I will require the life of man. "Whoever sheds man's blood, By man his blood shall be shed; For in the image of God He made man. And as for you, be fruitful and multiply; Bring forth abundantly in the earth And multiply in it." Then God spoke to Noah and to his sons with him, saying: "And as for Me, behold, I establish My covenant with you and with your descendants after you, and with every living creature that *is* with you: the birds, the cattle, and every beast of the earth with you, of all that go out of the ark, every beast of the earth. Thus I establish My covenant with you: Never again shall all flesh be cut off by the waters of the flood; never again shall there be a flood to destroy the earth."

[2] **Gal. 3:19-25:** What purpose then *does* the law *serve?* It was added because of transgressions, till the Seed should come to whom the promise was made; *and it was* appointed through angels by the hand of a mediator. Now a mediator does not *mediate* for one *only,* but God is one. *Is* the law then against the promises of God? Certainly not! For if there had been a law given which could have given life, truly righteousness would have been by the law. But the Scripture has confined all under sin, that the promise by faith in Jesus Christ might be given to those who believe. But before faith came, we were kept under guard by the law, kept for the faith which would afterward be revealed. Therefore the law was our tutor *to bring us* to Christ, that we might be justified by faith. But after faith has come, we are no longer under a tutor. **Heb. 7:11-19:** Therefore, if perfection were through the Levitical priesthood (for under it the people received the law), what further need *was there* that another priest should rise according to the order of Melchizedek, and not be called according to the order of Aaron? For the priesthood being changed, of necessity there is also a change of the law. For He of whom these things are spoken belongs to another tribe, from which no man has officiated at the altar. For *it is* evident that our Lord arose from Judah, of which tribe Moses spoke nothing concerning priesthood. And it is yet far more evident if, in the likeness of Melchizedek, there arises another priest who has come, not according to the law of a fleshly commandment, but according to the power of an endless life. For He testifies: "You *are* a priest forever According to the order of Melchizedek." For on the one hand there is an annulling of the former commandment because of its weakness and unprofitableness, for the law made nothing perfect; on the other hand, *there is the* bringing in of a better hope, through which we draw near to God. **Heb. 9:8-10:** ... the Holy Spirit indicating this, that the way into the Holiest of All was not yet made manifest while the first tabernacle was still standing. It *was* symbolic for the present time in which both gifts and sacrifices are offered which cannot make him who performed the service perfect in regard to the conscience— *concerned* only with foods and drinks, various washings, and fleshly ordinances imposed until the time of reformation. **Heb. 10:1:** For the law, having a shadow of the good things to come, *and* not the very image of the things, can never with these same sacrifices, which they offer continually year by year, make those who approach perfect. **2 Cor. 3:7-11:** But if the ministry of death, written *and* engraved on stones, was glorious, so that the children of Israel could not look steadily at the face of Moses because of the glory of his countenance, which *glory* was passing away, how will the ministry of the Spirit not be more glorious? For if the ministry of condemnation *had* glory, the ministry of righteousness exceeds much more in glory. For even what was made glorious had no glory in this respect, because of the glory that excels. For if what is passing away *was* glorious, what remains *is* much more glorious.

[3] **Eph. 1:9-10:** ... having made known to us the mystery of His will, according to His good pleasure

which He purposed in Himself, that in the dispensation of the fullness of the times He might gather together in one all things in Christ, both which are in heaven and which are on earth—in Him. **Eph. 3:1-10:** For this reason I, Paul, the prisoner of Christ Jesus for you Gentiles— if indeed you have heard of the dispensation of the grace of God which was given to me for you, how that by revelation He made known to me the mystery (as I have briefly written already, by which, when you read, you may understand my knowledge in the mystery of Christ), which in other ages was not made known to the sons of men, as it has now been revealed by the Spirit to His holy apostles and prophets: that the Gentiles should be fellow heirs, of the same body, and partakers of His promise in Christ through the gospel, of which I became a minister according to the gift of the grace of God given to me by the effective working of His power. To me, who am less than the least of all the saints, this grace was given, that I should preach among the Gentiles the unsearchable riches of Christ, and to make all see what *is* the fellowship of the mystery, which from the beginning of the ages has been hidden in God who created all things through Jesus Christ; to the intent that now the manifold wisdom of God might be made known by the church to the principalities and powers in the heavenly *places*. **Col. 1:25-27:** ... of which I became a minister according to the stewardship from God which was given to me for you, to fulfill the word of God, the mystery which has been hidden from ages and from generations, but now has been revealed to His saints. To them God willed to make known what are the riches of the glory of this mystery among the Gentiles: which is Christ in you, the hope of glory. **Rom. 3:21-22, 30:** But now the righteousness of God apart from the law is revealed, being witnessed by the Law and the Prophets, even the righteousness of God, through faith in Jesus Christ, to all and on all who believe. For there is no difference ... since *there is* one God who will justify the circumcised by faith and the uncircumcised through faith. **2 Cor. 3:6-11:** ... who also made us sufficient as ministers of the new covenant, not of the letter but of the Spirit; for the letter kills, but the Spirit gives life. But if the ministry of death, written *and* engraved on stones, was glorious, so that the children of Israel could not look steadily at the face of Moses because of the glory of his countenance, which *glory* was passing away, how will the ministry of the Spirit not be more glorious? For if the ministry of condemnation *had* glory, the ministry of righteousness exceeds much more in glory. For even what was made glorious had no glory in this respect, because of the glory that excels. For if what is passing away *was* glorious, what remains *is* much more glorious.

Q. 38. *What is the general scope of a dispensation of the covenants of promise?*

A. The general scope of a dispensation of the covenants of promise is the relation of two divine covenants, the first between God and His servant, and the other with his posterity as a society; the second covenant being made after God had mercifully delivered them in a special manner.[1]

[1] **Gen. 6:18:** But I will establish My covenant with you; and you shall go into the ark—you, your sons, your wife, and your sons' wives with you. **Gen. 8:18-19:** So Noah went out, and his sons and his wife and his sons' wives with him. Every animal, every creeping thing, every bird, *and* whatever creeps on the earth, according to their families, went out of the ark. **Gen. 9:8-11:** Then God spoke to Noah and to his sons with him, saying: "And as for Me, behold, I establish My covenant with you and with your descendants after you, and with every living creature that *is* with you: the birds, the cattle, and every beast of the earth with you, of all that go out of the ark, every beast of the earth. Thus I establish My covenant with you: Never again shall all flesh be cut off by the waters of the flood; never again shall there be a flood to destroy the earth." **Gen. 17:1-8:** When Abram was ninety-nine years old, the LORD appeared to Abram and said to him, "I *am* Almighty God; walk before Me and be blameless. And I will make My covenant between Me and you, and will multiply you exceedingly." Then Abram fell on his face, and God talked with him, saying: "As for Me, behold, My covenant is with you, and you shall be a father of many nations. No longer shall your name be called Abram, but your name shall be Abraham; for I have made you a father of many nations. I will make you exceedingly fruitful; and I will make nations of you, and kings shall come from you. And I will establish My covenant between Me and you and your descendants after you in their generations, for an everlasting covenant, to be God to you and your descendants after you. Also I give to you and your descendants after you the land in which you are a stranger, all the land of Canaan, as an everlasting possession; and I will be their God." **Ex. 19:1-6:** In the third month after the children of Israel had gone out of the land of Egypt, on the same day, they came *to* the Wilderness of Sinai. For they had departed from Rephidim, had come *to* the Wilderness of Sinai, and camped in the wilderness. So Israel camped there before the mountain. And Moses went up to God, and the LORD called to him from the mountain, saying, "Thus you shall say to the house of Jacob, and tell the children of Israel: 'You have seen what I did to the Egyptians, and *how* I bore you on eagles' wings and brought you to Myself. Now therefore, if you will indeed obey My voice and keep My covenant, then you shall be a special treasure to Me above all people; for all the earth *is* Mine. And you shall

be to Me a kingdom of priests and a holy nation.' These *are* the words which you shall speak to the children of Israel." **Heb. 7:** For this Melchizedek, king of Salem, priest of the Most High God, who met Abraham returning from the slaughter of the kings and blessed him, to whom also Abraham gave a tenth part of all, first being translated "king of righteousness," and then also king of Salem, meaning "king of peace," without father, without mother, without genealogy, having neither beginning of days nor end of life, but made like the Son of God, remains a priest continually.... Therefore, if perfection were through the Levitical priesthood (for under it the people received the law), what further need *was there* that another priest should rise according to the order of Melchizedek, and not be called according to the order of Aaron? For the priesthood being changed, of necessity there is also a change of the law. For He of whom these things are spoken belongs to another tribe, from which no man has officiated at the altar. For *it is* evident that our Lord arose from Judah, of which tribe Moses spoke nothing concerning priesthood. And it is yet far more evident if, in the likeness of Melchizedek, there arises another priest who has come, not according to the law of a fleshly commandment, but according to the power of an endless life. For He testifies: "You *are* a priest forever According to the order of Melchizedek." ... And inasmuch as *He was* not *made priest* without an oath (for they have become priests without an oath, but He with an oath by Him who said to Him: "The LORD has sworn And will not relent, 'You *are* a priest forever According to the order of Melchizedek'"), by so much more Jesus has become a surety of a better covenant.... For the law appoints as high priests men who have weakness, but the word of the oath, which came after the law, *appoints* the Son who has been perfected forever. **John 7:28-29:** Then Jesus cried out, as He taught in the temple, saying, "You both know Me, and you know where I am from; and I have not come of Myself, but He who sent Me is true, whom you do not know. But I know Him, for I am from Him, and He sent Me." **Matt. 1:21:** And she will bring forth a Son, and you shall call His name Jesus, for He will save His people from their sins. **Heb. 8:7-13:** For if that first *covenant* had been faultless, then no place would have been sought for a second. Because finding fault with them, He says: "Behold, the days are coming, says the LORD, when I will make a new covenant with the house of Israel and with the house of Judah— not according to the covenant that I made with their fathers in the day when I took them by the hand to lead them out of the land of Egypt; because they did not continue in My covenant, and I disregarded them, says the LORD. For this *is* the covenant that I will make with the house of Israel after those days, says the LORD: I will put My laws in their mind and write them on their hearts; and I will be their God, and they shall be My people. None of them shall teach his neighbor, and none his brother, saying, 'Know the LORD,' for all shall know Me, from the least of them to the greatest of them. For I will be merciful to their unrighteousness, and their sins and their lawless deeds I will remember no more." In that He says, "A new *covenant*," He has made the first obsolete. Now what is becoming obsolete and growing old is ready to vanish away.

Q. 39. *Which is the first covenant?*

A. The first covenant is that oath sworn to Noah, commonly called the antediluvian Noahic Covenant.[1]

1

Gen. 6-8: Then the LORD saw that the wickedness of man *was* great in the earth, and *that* every intent of the thoughts of his heart *was* only evil continually. And the LORD was sorry that He had made man on the earth, and He was grieved in His heart. So the LORD said, "I will destroy man whom I have created from the face of the earth, both man and beast, creeping thing and birds of the air, for I am sorry that I have made them." But Noah found grace in the eyes of the LORD.... And God said to Noah, "The end of all flesh has come before Me, for the earth is filled with violence through them; and behold, I will destroy them with the earth. Make yourself an ark of gopherwood.... And behold, I Myself am bringing floodwaters on the earth, to destroy from under heaven all flesh in which *is* the breath of life; everything that *is* on the earth shall die. But I will establish My covenant with you; and you shall go into the ark—you, your sons, your wife, and your sons' wives with you. And of every living thing of all flesh you shall bring two of every *sort* into the ark, to keep *them* alive with you; they shall be male and female.... And Noah did according to all that the LORD commanded him.... So those that entered, male and female of all flesh, went in as God had commanded him; and the LORD shut him in.... So He destroyed all living things which were on the face of the ground: both man and cattle, creeping thing and bird of the air. They were destroyed from the earth. Only Noah and those who *were* with him in the ark remained *alive*.... Then God remembered Noah, and every living thing, and all the animals that *were* with him in the ark. And God made a wind to pass over the earth, and the waters subsided. The fountains of the deep and the windows of heaven were also stopped, and the rain from heaven was restrained.... Then God spoke to Noah, saying, "Go out of the ark, you and your wife, and your sons and your sons' wives with you. Bring out with you every living thing of all flesh that *is* with you: birds and cattle and every creeping thing that creeps on the earth, so that they may abound on the earth, and be fruitful and multiply on the earth." ... Then Noah built an altar to the LORD, and took of every clean animal and of every clean bird, and offered burnt offerings on the altar. And the LORD smelled a soothing aroma.

Q. 40. *In what way is the covenant of grace revealed in the first covenant?*

A. When God had sworn to Noah,[1] who found grace in the eyes of the LORD,[2] He entered into a covenant with him promising salvation from His wrath, not only for himself, but for his posterity.[3]

1 **Gen. 6:18:** But I will establish My covenant with you; and you shall go into the ark—you, your sons, your wife, and your sons' wives with you.

2 **Gen. 6:8-9:** But Noah found grace in the eyes of the LORD. This is the genealogy of Noah. Noah was a just man, perfect in his generations. Noah walked with God. **Gen. 7:1:** Then the LORD said to Noah, "Come into the ark, you and all your household, because I have seen *that* you *are* righteous before Me in this generation.

3 **Matt. 24:37-39:** But as the days of Noah were, so also will the coming of the Son of Man be. For as in the days before the flood, they were eating and drinking, marrying and giving in marriage, until the day that Noah entered the ark, and did not know until the flood came and took them all away, so also will the coming of the Son of Man be. **Luke 17:26-27, 30:** And as it was in the days of Noah, so it will be also in the days of the Son of Man: They ate, they drank, they married wives, they were given in marriage, until the day that Noah entered the ark, and the flood came and destroyed them all.... Even so will it be in the day when the Son of Man is revealed. **Rom. 5:9:** Much more then, having now been justified by His blood, we shall be saved from wrath through Him. **1 Thess. 1:10:** ... and to wait for His Son from heaven, whom He raised from the dead, *even* Jesus who delivers us from the wrath to come. **Heb. 11:7:** By faith Noah, being divinely warned of things not yet seen, moved with godly fear, prepared an ark for the saving of his household, by which he condemned the world and became heir of the righteousness which is according to faith. **1 Pet. 3:19-22:** ... by whom also He went and preached to the spirits in prison, who formerly were disobedient, when once the Divine longsuffering waited in the days of Noah, while *the* ark was being prepared, in which a few, that is, eight souls, were saved through water. There is also an antitype which now saves us—baptism (not the removal of the filth of the flesh, but the answer of a good conscience toward God), through the resurrection of Jesus Christ, who has gone into heaven and is at the right hand of God, angels and authorities and powers having been made subject to Him. **2 Pet. 2:5:** ... and did not spare the ancient world, but saved Noah, *one of* eight *people*, a preacher of righteousness, bringing in the flood on the world of the ungodly. **Rev. 6:16-17:** ... and said to the mountains and rocks, "Fall on us and hide us from the face of Him who sits on the throne and from the wrath of the Lamb! For the great day of His wrath has come, and who is able to stand?" **Rev. 11:18:** The nations were angry, and Your wrath has come, And the time of the dead, that they should be judged, And that You should reward Your servants the prophets and the saints, And those who fear Your name, small and great, And should destroy those who destroy the earth.

Q. 41. *Which is the second covenant?*

A. The second covenant is that oath sworn to Noah, his posterity and the animals with him, commonly called the postdiluvian Noahic Covenant.[1]

1 **Gen. 9:1-18:** So God blessed Noah and his sons, and said to them: "Be fruitful and multiply, and fill the earth. And the fear of you and the dread of you shall be on every beast of the earth, on every bird of the air, on all that move *on* the earth, and on all the fish of the sea. They are given into your hand. Every moving thing that lives shall be food for you. I have given you all things, even as the green herbs. But you shall not eat flesh with its life, *that is,* its blood. Surely for your lifeblood I will demand *a reckoning;* from the hand of every beast I will require it, and from the hand of man. From the hand of every man's brother I will require the life of man. "Whoever sheds man's blood, By man his blood shall be shed; For in the image of God He made man. And as for you, be fruitful and multiply; Bring forth abundantly in the earth And multiply in it." Then God spoke to Noah and to his sons with him, saying: "And as for Me, behold, I establish My covenant with you and with your descendants after you, and with every living creature that *is* with you: the birds, the cattle, and every beast of the earth with you, of all that go out of the ark, every beast of the earth. Thus I establish My covenant with you: Never again shall all flesh be cut off by the waters of the flood;

never again shall there be a flood to destroy the earth." And God said: "This *is* the sign of the covenant which I make between Me and you, and every living creature that *is* with you, for perpetual generations: I set My rainbow in the cloud, and it shall be for the sign of the covenant between Me and the earth. It shall be, when I bring a cloud over the earth, that the rainbow shall be seen in the cloud; and I will remember My covenant which *is* between Me and you and every living creature of all flesh; the waters shall never again become a flood to destroy all flesh. The rainbow shall be in the cloud, and I will look on it to remember the everlasting covenant between God and every living creature of all flesh that *is* on the earth." And God said to Noah, "This *is* the sign of the covenant which I have established between Me and all flesh that *is* on the earth." **Isa. 54:9:** For this *is* like the waters of Noah to Me; For as I have sworn That the waters of Noah would no longer cover the earth, So have I sworn That I would not be angry with you, nor rebuke you.

Q. 42. *In what way is the covenant of grace revealed in the second covenant?*

A. In fulfillment of the covenant made with Noah,[1] God entered into a covenant with the remnant and their seed after them wherein few, that is, eight souls were saved,[2] promising never again to cut off all flesh by the waters of a flood.[3]

1 **Gen. 8:15-22:** Then God spoke to Noah, saying, "Go out of the ark, you and your wife, and your sons and your sons' wives with you. Bring out with you every living thing of all flesh that *is* with you: birds and cattle and every creeping thing that creeps on the earth, so that they may abound on the earth, and be fruitful and multiply on the earth." So Noah went out, and his sons and his wife and his sons' wives with him. Every animal, every creeping thing, every bird, *and* whatever creeps on the earth, according to their families, went out of the ark. Then Noah built an altar to the LORD, and took of every clean animal and of every clean bird, and offered burnt offerings on the altar. And the LORD smelled a soothing aroma. Then the LORD said in His heart, "I will never again curse the ground for man's sake, although the imagination of man's heart *is* evil from his youth; nor will I again destroy every living thing as I have done. "While the earth remains, Seedtime and harvest, Cold and heat, Winter and summer, And day and night Shall not cease."

2 **Gen. 9:1-11:** So God blessed Noah and his sons, and said to them: "Be fruitful and multiply, and fill the earth. And the fear of you and the dread of you shall be on every beast of the earth, on every bird of the air, on all that move *on* the earth, and on all the fish of the sea. They are given into your hand. Every moving thing that lives shall be food for you. I have given you all things, even as the green herbs. But you shall not eat flesh with its life, *that is,* its blood. Surely for your lifeblood I will demand *a reckoning;* from the hand of every beast I will require it, and from the hand of man. From the hand of every man's brother I will require the life of man. "Whoever sheds man's blood, By man his blood shall be shed; For in the image of God He made man. And as for you, be fruitful and multiply; Bring forth abundantly in the earth And multiply in it." Then God spoke to Noah and to his sons with him, saying: "And as for Me, behold, I establish My covenant with you and with your descendants after you, and with every living creature that *is* with you: the birds, the cattle, and every beast of the earth with you, of all that go out of the ark, every beast of the earth. Thus I establish My covenant with you: Never again shall all flesh be cut off by the waters of the flood; never again shall there be a flood to destroy the earth." **Isa. 10:20-23:** And it shall come to pass in that day *That* the remnant of Israel, And such as have escaped of the house of Jacob, Will never again depend on him who defeated them, But will depend on the LORD, the Holy One of Israel, in truth. The remnant will return, the remnant of Jacob, To the Mighty God. For though your people, O Israel, be as the sand of the sea, A remnant of them will return; The destruction decreed shall overflow with righteousness. For the Lord God of hosts Will make a determined end In the midst of all the land. **Isa. 54:9-10:** "For this *is* like the waters of Noah to Me; For as I have sworn That the waters of Noah would no longer cover the earth, So have I sworn That I would not be angry with you, nor rebuke you. For the mountains shall depart And the hills be removed, But My kindness shall not depart from you, Nor shall My covenant of peace be removed," Says the LORD, who has mercy on you. **Rom. 9:27:** Isaiah also cries out concerning Israel: "Though the number of the children of Israel be as the sand of the sea, The remnant will be saved. **Rom. 11:1-7:** I say then, has God cast away His people? Certainly not! For I also am an Israelite, of the seed of Abraham, *of* the tribe of Benjamin. God has not cast away His people whom He foreknew. Or do you not know what the Scripture says of Elijah, how he pleads with God against Israel, saying, "LORD, they have killed Your prophets and torn down Your altars, and I alone am left, and they seek my life"? But what does the divine response say to him? "I have reserved for Myself seven thousand men who have not bowed the knee to Baal." Even so then, at this present time there is a remnant according to the election of grace. And if by grace, then *it is* no longer of works; otherwise grace is no longer grace. But if *it is* of works, it is no longer grace; otherwise work is no longer work. What then? Israel has not obtained

what it seeks; but the elect have obtained it, and the rest were blinded. **1 Pet. 3:20-22:** ... who formerly were disobedient, when once the Divine longsuffering waited in the days of Noah, while *the* ark was being prepared, in which a few, that is, eight souls, were saved through water. There is also an antitype which now saves us—baptism (not the removal of the filth of the flesh, but the answer of a good conscience toward God), through the resurrection of Jesus Christ, who has gone into heaven and is at the right hand of God, angels and authorities and powers having been made subject to Him.

3 **1 Thess. 1:10:** ... and to wait for His Son from heaven, whom He raised from the dead, *even* Jesus who delivers us from the wrath to come. **1 Thess. 5:9:** For God did not appoint us to wrath, but to obtain salvation through our Lord Jesus Christ. **2 Pet. 3:6-13:** ... by which the world *that* then existed perished, being flooded with water. But the heavens and the earth *which* are now preserved by the same word, are reserved for fire until the day of judgment and perdition of ungodly men. But, beloved, do not forget this one thing, that with the Lord one day *is* as a thousand years, and a thousand years as one day. The Lord is not slack concerning *His* promise, as some count slackness, but is longsuffering toward us, not willing that any should perish but that all should come to repentance. But the day of the Lord will come as a thief in the night, in which the heavens will pass away with a great noise, and the elements will melt with fervent heat; both the earth and the works that are in it will be burned up. Therefore, since all these things will be dissolved, what manner *of persons* ought you to be in holy conduct and godliness, looking for and hastening the coming of the day of God, because of which the heavens will be dissolved, being on fire, and the elements will melt with fervent heat? Nevertheless we, according to His promise, look for new heavens and a new earth in which righteousness dwells.

Q. 43. *What is the token annexed to the second covenant?*

A. The token annexed to the second covenant is the bow set in the cloud.[1]

1 **Gen. 9:12-17:** And God said: "This *is* the sign of the covenant which I make between Me and you, and every living creature that *is* with you, for perpetual generations: I set My rainbow in the cloud, and it shall be for the sign of the covenant between Me and the earth. It shall be, when I bring a cloud over the earth, that the rainbow shall be seen in the cloud; and I will remember My covenant which *is* between Me and you and every living creature of all flesh; the waters shall never again become a flood to destroy all flesh. The rainbow shall be in the cloud, and I will look on it to remember the everlasting covenant between God and every living creature of all flesh that *is* on the earth." And God said to Noah, "This *is* the sign of the covenant which I have established between Me and all flesh that *is* on the earth."

Q. 44. *Which is the third covenant?*

A. The third covenant is that oath sworn to Abraham, commonly called the Abrahamic Covenant.[1]

1 **Gen. 15:** After these things the word of the LORD came to Abram in a vision, saying, "Do not be afraid, Abram. I *am* your shield, your exceedingly great reward." ... Then He brought him outside and said, "Look now toward heaven, and count the stars if you are able to number them." And He said to him, "So shall your descendants be." And he believed in the LORD, and He accounted it to him for righteousness.... Then He said to Abram: "Know certainly that your descendants will be strangers in a land *that is* not theirs, and will serve them, and they will afflict them four hundred years. And also the nation whom they serve I will judge; afterward they shall come out with great possessions.... And it came to pass, when the sun went down and it was dark, that behold, there appeared a smoking oven and a burning torch that passed between those pieces. On the same day the LORD made a covenant with Abram, saying: "To your descendants I have given this land, from the river of Egypt to the great river, the River Euphrates— the Kenites, the Kenezzites, the Kadmonites, the Hittites, the Perizzites, the Rephaim, the Amorites, the Canaanites, the Girgashites, and the Jebusites." **Gen. 17:** When Abram was ninety-nine years old, the LORD appeared to Abram and said to him, "I *am* Almighty God; walk before Me and be blameless. And I will make My covenant between Me and you, and will multiply you exceedingly." Then Abram fell on his face, and God talked with him, saying: "As for Me, behold, My covenant is with you, and you shall be a father of many nations.... And I will establish My covenant between Me and you and your descendants after you in their generations, for an everlasting covenant, to be God to you and your descendants after you. Also I give to you and your descendants after you the land in which you are a stranger, all the land of Canaan, as an everlasting possession; and I will be their God." ... My covenant I will establish

with Isaac, whom Sarah shall bear to you at this set time next year." Then He finished talking with him, and God went up from Abraham.... That very same day Abraham was circumcised, and his son Ishmael; and all the men of his house, born in the house or bought with money from a foreigner, were circumcised with him. **Gen. 22:16-18:** ... and said: "By Myself I have sworn, says the LORD, because you have done this thing, and have not withheld your son, your only *son*— blessing I will bless you, and multiplying I will multiply your descendants as the stars of the heaven and as the sand which *is* on the seashore; and your descendants shall possess the gate of their enemies. In your seed all the nations of the earth shall be blessed, because you have obeyed My voice." **Gen. 26:3:** Dwell in this land, and I will be with you and bless you; for to you and your descendants I give all these lands, and I will perform the oath which I swore to Abraham your father. **Luke 1:72-73:** To perform the mercy *promised* to our fathers And to remember His holy covenant, The oath which He swore to our father Abraham.

Q. 45. *In what way is the covenant of grace revealed in the third covenant?*

A. When God had sworn to Abraham, who believed in the LORD,[1] He entered into a covenant with him[2] promising that Abraham would be a father of many nations;[3] to be a God unto him and to his seed after him;[4] and the land of Canaan, for an everlasting possession.[5]

1 **Gen. 15:6:** And he believed in the LORD, and He accounted it to him for righteousness.

2 **Luke 1:72-73:** To perform the mercy *promised* to our fathers And to remember His holy covenant, The oath which He swore to our father Abraham.

3 **Ps. 22:27-28:** All the ends of the world Shall remember and turn to the LORD, And all the families of the nations Shall worship before You. For the kingdom *is* the LORD's, And He rules over the nations. **Acts 3:25-26:** You are sons of the prophets, and of the covenant which God made with our fathers, saying to Abraham, 'And in your seed all the families of the earth shall be blessed.' To you first, God, having raised up His Servant Jesus, sent Him to bless you, in turning away every one *of you* from your iniquities. **Gal. 3:** ... Abraham "believed God, and it was accounted to him for righteousness." Therefore know that *only* those who are of faith are sons of Abraham. And the Scripture, foreseeing that God would justify the Gentiles by faith, preached the gospel to Abraham beforehand, *saying,* "In you all the nations shall be blessed." So then those who *are* of faith are blessed with believing Abraham.... Brethren, I speak in the manner of men: Though *it is* only a man's covenant, yet *if it is* confirmed, no one annuls or adds to it. Now to Abraham and his Seed were the promises made. He does not say, "And to seeds," as of many, but as of one, "And to your Seed," who is Christ. And this I say, *that* the law, which was four hundred and thirty years later, cannot annul the covenant that was confirmed before by God in Christ, that it should make the promise of no effect. For if the inheritance *is* of the law, *it is* no longer of promise; but God gave *it* to Abraham by promise.... For you are all sons of God through faith in Christ Jesus. For as many of you as were baptized into Christ have put on Christ. There is neither Jew nor Greek, there is neither slave nor free, there is neither male nor female; for you are all one in Christ Jesus. And if you *are* Christ's, then you are Abraham's seed, and heirs according to the promise. **Rom. 4:** ... "Blessed *are those* whose lawless deeds are forgiven, And whose sins are covered; Blessed *is the* man to whom the LORD shall not impute sin." *Does* this blessedness then *come* upon the circumcised *only,* or upon the uncircumcised also? For we say that faith was accounted to Abraham for righteousness. How then was it accounted? While he was circumcised, or uncircumcised? Not while circumcised, but while uncircumcised. And he received the sign of circumcision, a seal of the righteousness of the faith which *he had while still* uncircumcised, that he might be the father of all those who believe, though they are uncircumcised, that righteousness might be imputed to them also, and the father of circumcision to those who not only *are* of the circumcision, but who also walk in the steps of the faith which our father Abraham *had while still* uncircumcised. For the promise that he would be the heir of the world *was* not to Abraham or to his seed through the law, but through the righteousness of faith. For if those who are of the law *are* heirs, faith is made void and the promise made of no effect ... Therefore *it is* of faith that *it might be* according to grace, so that the promise might be sure to all the seed, not only to those who are of the law, but also to those who are of the faith of Abraham, who is the father of us all (as it is written, "I have made you a father of many nations") in the presence of Him whom he believed ... in hope believed, so that he became the father of many nations, according to what was spoken, "So shall your descendants be." **Rev. 21:22-27:** But I saw no temple in it, for the Lord God Almighty and the Lamb are its temple. The city had no need of the sun or of the moon to shine in it, for the glory of God illuminated it. The Lamb *is* its light. And the

nations of those who are saved shall walk in its light, and the kings of the earth bring their glory and honor into it. Its gates shall not be shut at all by day (there shall be no night there). And they shall bring the glory and the honor of the nations into it. But there shall by no means enter it anything that defiles, or causes an abomination or a lie, but only those who are written in the Lamb's Book of Life.

4
2 Cor. 6:16: And what agreement has the temple of God with idols? For you are the temple of the living God. As God has said: "I will dwell in them And walk among them. I will be their God, And they shall be My people." **Heb. 2:13:** And again: "I will put My trust in Him." And again: "Here am I and the children whom God has given Me." **1 Pet. 2:9-10:** But you *are* a chosen generation, a royal priesthood, a holy nation, His own special people, that you may proclaim the praises of Him who called you out of darkness into His marvelous light; who once *were* not a people but *are* now the people of God, who had not obtained mercy but now have obtained mercy. **Rev. 21:7:** He who overcomes shall inherit all things, and I will be his God and he shall be My son.

5
Ps. 105:11: Saying, "To you I will give the land of Canaan As the allotment of your inheritance," **Matt 5:5:** Blessed *are* the meek, For they shall inherit the earth. **Cf. Rom. 4:13:** For the promise that he would be the heir of the world *was* not to Abraham or to his seed through the law, but through the righteousness of faith. **Gal. 3:14:** ... that the blessing of Abraham might come upon the Gentiles in Christ Jesus, that we might receive the promise of the Spirit through faith. **Eph. 1:13-14:** In Him you also *trusted,* after you heard the word of truth, the gospel of your salvation; in whom also, having believed, you were sealed with the Holy Spirit of promise, who is the guarantee of our inheritance until the redemption of the purchased possession, to the praise of His glory. **Heb. 11:8-10:** By faith Abraham obeyed when he was called to go out to the place which he would receive as an inheritance. And he went out, not knowing where he was going. By faith he dwelt in the land of promise as *in* a foreign country, dwelling in tents with Isaac and Jacob, the heirs with him of the same promise; for he waited for the city which has foundations, whose builder and maker *is* God. **2 Pet. 3:13:** Nevertheless we, according to His promise, look for new heavens and a new earth in which righteousness dwells.

Q. 46. *What is the token annexed to the third covenant?*

A. The token annexed to the third covenant is the circumcision of the flesh.[1]

1
Gen. 17:10-11: This *is* My covenant which you shall keep, between Me and you and your descendants after you: Every male child among you shall be circumcised; and you shall be circumcised in the flesh of your foreskins, and it shall be a sign of the covenant between Me and you. **Rom. 4:11:** And he received the sign of circumcision, a seal of the righteousness of the faith which *he had while still* uncircumcised, that he might be the father of all those who believe, though they are uncircumcised, that righteousness might be imputed to them also.

Q. 47. *Which is the fourth covenant?*

A. The fourth covenant is that oath sworn to Israel of old, commonly called the Old Covenant.[1]

1
Ex. 19:1-9: In the third month after the children of Israel had gone out of the land of Egypt, on the same day, they came *to* the Wilderness of Sinai. For they had departed from Rephidim, had come *to* the Wilderness of Sinai, and camped in the wilderness. So Israel camped there before the mountain. And Moses went up to God, and the LORD called to him from the mountain, saying, "Thus you shall say to the house of Jacob, and tell the children of Israel: 'You have seen what I did to the Egyptians, and *how* I bore you on eagles' wings and brought you to Myself. Now therefore, if you will indeed obey My voice and keep My covenant, then you shall be a special treasure to Me above all people; for all the earth *is* Mine. And you shall be to Me a kingdom of priests and a holy nation.' These *are* the words which you shall speak to the children of Israel." So Moses came and called for the elders of the people, and laid before them all these words which the LORD commanded him. Then all the people answered together and said, "All that the LORD has spoken we will do." So Moses brought back the words of the people to the LORD. And the LORD said to Moses, "Behold, I come to you in the thick cloud, that the people may hear when I speak with you, and believe you forever." So Moses told the words of the people to the LORD. **Deut. 29:10-15:** "All of you stand today before the LORD your God: your leaders and your tribes and your elders and your officers, all the men of Israel, your little ones and your wives—also the stranger who *is* in your camp, from the one who cuts your wood to the one who draws your water— that you may enter into covenant with the LORD

your God, and into His oath, which the LORD your God makes with you today, that He may establish you today as a people for Himself, and *that* He may be God to you, just as He has spoken to you, and just as He has sworn to your fathers, to Abraham, Isaac, and Jacob. "I make this covenant and this oath, not with you alone, but with *him* who stands here with us today before the LORD our God, as well as with *him* who *is* not here with us today."

Q. 48. *In what way is the covenant of grace revealed in the fourth covenant?*

A. In fulfillment of the covenant made with Abraham,[1] God entered into a covenant with the Israel of old and their seed;[2] who, as He brought them out of their bondage to Egypt,[3] promised, if they would obey His voice,[4] they would be a peculiar treasure unto Him above all people, a kingdom of priests, and a holy nation.[5]

1 **Ex. 6:2-8:** And God spoke to Moses and said to him: "I *am* the LORD. I appeared to Abraham, to Isaac, and to Jacob, as God Almighty, but *by* My name LORD I was not known to them. I have also established My covenant with them, to give them the land of Canaan, the land of their pilgrimage, in which they were strangers. And I have also heard the groaning of the children of Israel whom the Egyptians keep in bondage, and I have remembered My covenant. Therefore say to the children of Israel: 'I *am* the LORD; I will bring you out from under the burdens of the Egyptians, I will rescue you from their bondage, and I will redeem you with an outstretched arm and with great judgments. I will take you as My people, and I will be your God. Then you shall know that I *am* the LORD your God who brings you out from under the burdens of the Egyptians. And I will bring you into the land which I swore to give to Abraham, Isaac, and Jacob; and I will give it to you *as* a heritage: I *am* the LORD.'"

2 **Ex. 19:1-9, See footnote 1 above.**

3 **Rom. 6:16-22:** Do you not know that to whom you present yourselves slaves to obey, you are that one's slaves whom you obey, whether of sin *leading* to death, or of obedience *leading* to righteousness? But God be thanked that *though* you were slaves of sin, yet you obeyed from the heart that form of doctrine to which you were delivered. And having been set free from sin, you became slaves of righteousness. I speak in human *terms* because of the weakness of your flesh. For just as you presented your members *as* slaves of uncleanness, and of lawlessness *leading* to *more* lawlessness, so now present your members *as* slaves *of* righteousness for holiness. For when you were slaves of sin, you were free in regard to righteousness. What fruit did you have then in the things of which you are now ashamed? For the end of those things *is* death. But now having been set free from sin, and having become slaves of God, you have your fruit to holiness, and the end, everlasting life. **Gal. 4:1-7, 21-31:** Now I say *that* the heir, as long as he is a child, does not differ at all from a slave, though he is master of all, but is under guardians and stewards until the time appointed by the father. Even so we, when we were children, were in bondage under the elements of the world. But when the fullness of the time had come, God sent forth His Son, born of a woman, born under the law, to redeem those who were under the law, that we might receive the adoption as sons. And because you are sons, God has sent forth the Spirit of His Son into your hearts, crying out, "Abba, Father!" Therefore you are no longer a slave but a son, and if a son, then an heir of God through Christ.... Tell me, you who desire to be under the law, do you not hear the law? For it is written that Abraham had two sons: the one by a bondwoman, the other by a freewoman. But he *who was* of the bondwoman was born according to the flesh, and he of the freewoman through promise, which things are symbolic. For these are the two covenants: the one from Mount Sinai which gives birth to bondage, which is Hagar— for this Hagar is Mount Sinai in Arabia, and corresponds to Jerusalem which now is, and is in bondage with her children— but the Jerusalem above is free, which is the mother of us all. For it is written: "Rejoice, O barren, *You* who do not bear! Break forth and shout, You who are not in labor! For the desolate has many more children Than she who has a husband." Now we, brethren, as Isaac *was,* are children of promise. But, as he who was born according to the flesh then persecuted him *who was born* according to the Spirit, even so *it is* now. Nevertheless what does the Scripture say? "Cast out the bondwoman and her son, for the son of the bondwoman shall not be heir with the son of the freewoman." So then, brethren, we are not children of the bondwoman but of the free. **Col. 1:13-14:** He has delivered us from the power of darkness and conveyed *us* into the kingdom of the Son of His love, in whom we have redemption through His blood, the forgiveness of sins. **2 Tim. 2:26:** ... and *that* they may come to their senses *and escape* the snare of the devil, having been taken captive by him to *do* his will. **Heb.**

2:14-15: Inasmuch then as the children have partaken of flesh and blood, He Himself likewise shared in the same, that through death He might destroy him who had the power of death, that is, the devil, and release those who through fear of death were all their lifetime subject to bondage.
4
John 14:15-18: If you love Me, keep My commandments. And I will pray the Father, and He will give you another Helper, that He may abide with you forever— the Spirit of truth, whom the world cannot receive, because it neither sees Him nor knows Him; but you know Him, for He dwells with you and will be in you. I will not leave you orphans; I will come to you. **Acts 8:35-37:** Then Philip opened his mouth, and beginning at this Scripture, preached Jesus to him. Now as they went down the road, they came to some water. And the eunuch said, "See, *here is* water. What hinders me from being baptized?" Then Philip said, "If you believe with all your heart, you may." And he answered and said, "I believe that Jesus Christ is the Son of God." **Rom. 10:8-9:** But what does it say? "The word is near you, in your mouth and in your heart" (that is, the word of faith which we preach): that if you confess with your mouth the Lord Jesus and believe in your heart that God has raised Him from the dead, you will be saved. **1 John 2:3-6:** Now by this we know that we know Him, if we keep His commandments. He who says, "I know Him," and does not keep His commandments, is a liar, and the truth is not in him. But whoever keeps His word, truly the love of God is perfected in him. By this we know that we are in Him. He who says he abides in Him ought himself also to walk just as He walked.
5
1 Pet. 2:5-10: ... you also, as living stones, are being built up a spiritual house, a holy priesthood, to offer up spiritual sacrifices acceptable to God through Jesus Christ. Therefore it is also contained in the Scripture, "Behold, I lay in Zion A chief cornerstone, elect, precious, And he who believes on Him will by no means be put to shame." Therefore, to you who believe, *He is* precious; but to those who are disobedient, "The stone which the builders rejected Has become the chief cornerstone," and "A stone of stumbling And a rock of offense." They stumble, being disobedient to the word, to which they also were appointed. But you *are* a chosen generation, a royal priesthood, a holy nation, His own special people, that you may proclaim the praises of Him who called you out of darkness into His marvelous light; who once *were* not a people but *are* now the people of God, who had not obtained mercy but now have obtained mercy. **Rev. 1:5-6:** ... and from Jesus Christ, the faithful witness, the firstborn from the dead, and the ruler over the kings of the earth. To Him who loved us and washed us from our sins in His own blood, and has made us kings and priests to His God and Father, to Him *be* glory and dominion forever and ever. Amen. **Rev. 5:9-10:** And they sang a new song, saying: "You are worthy to take the scroll, And to open its seals; For You were slain, And have redeemed us to God by Your blood Out of every tribe and tongue and people and nation, And have made us kings and priests to our God; And we shall reign on the earth."

Q. 49. *What is the token annexed to the fourth covenant?*

A. The token annexed to the fourth covenant is the Sabbath wherein God rested and was refreshed.[1]

1
Ex. 31:13, 16-17: Speak also to the children of Israel, saying: 'Surely My Sabbaths you shall keep, for it *is* a sign between Me and you throughout your generations, that *you* may know that I *am* the LORD who sanctifies you.... Therefore the children of Israel shall keep the Sabbath, to observe the Sabbath throughout their generations *as* a perpetual covenant. It *is* a sign between Me and the children of Israel forever; for *in* six days the LORD made the heavens and the earth, and on the seventh day He rested and was refreshed.' **Ezek. 20:12:** Moreover I also gave them My Sabbaths, to be a sign between them and Me, that they might know that I *am* the LORD who sanctifies them.

Q. 50. *Which is the fifth covenant?*

A. The fifth covenant is that oath sworn to David, commonly called the Davidic Covenant.[1]

1
Ps. 89:3-4, 34-36: I have made a covenant with My chosen, I have sworn to My servant David: 'Your seed I will establish forever, And build up your throne to all generations.' ... My covenant I will not break, Nor alter the word that has gone out of My lips. Once I have sworn by My holiness; I will not lie to David: His seed shall endure forever, And his throne as the sun before Me. **Acts 2:30:** Therefore, being a prophet, and knowing that God had sworn with an oath to him that of the fruit of his body, according to the flesh, He would raise up the Christ to sit on his throne.

Q. 51. *In what way is the covenant of grace revealed in the fifth covenant?*

A. When God had sworn to David,[1] a man after His own heart,[2] He entered into a covenant with him promising to raise up his seed after him[3] and to establish his house,[4] and his kingdom,[5] and his throne forevermore.[6]

1 **Acts 2:30:** Therefore, being a prophet, and knowing that God had sworn with an oath to him that of the fruit of his body, according to the flesh, He would raise up the Christ to sit on his throne.

2 **Acts 13:22:** And when He had removed him, He raised up for them David as king, to whom also He gave testimony and said, 'I have found David the *son* of Jesse, a man after My *own* heart, who will do all My will.'

3 **Acts 2:24, 30-35:** ... whom God raised up, having loosed the pains of death, because it was not possible that He should be held by it.... Therefore, being a prophet, and knowing that God had sworn with an oath to him that of the fruit of his body, according to the flesh, He would raise up the Christ to sit on his throne, he, foreseeing this, spoke concerning the resurrection of the Christ, that His soul was not left in Hades, nor did His flesh see corruption. This Jesus God has raised up, of which we are all witnesses. Therefore being exalted to the right hand of God, and having received from the Father the promise of the Holy Spirit, He poured out this which you now see and hear. "For David did not ascend into the heavens, but he says himself: 'The LORD said to my Lord, "Sit at My right hand, Till I make Your enemies Your footstool."' **Acts 3:26:** To you first, God, having raised up His Servant Jesus, sent Him to bless you, in turning away every one *of you* from your iniquities. **Acts 5:30-31:** The God of our fathers raised up Jesus whom you murdered by hanging on a tree. Him God has exalted to His right hand *to be* Prince and Savior, to give repentance to Israel and forgiveness of sins. **Acts 13:30-37:** But God raised Him from the dead. He was seen for many days by those who came up with Him from Galilee to Jerusalem, who are His witnesses to the people. And we declare to you glad tidings—that promise which was made to the fathers. God has fulfilled this for us their children, in that He has raised up Jesus. As it is also written in the second Psalm: 'You are My Son, Today I have begotten You.' And that He raised Him from the dead, no more to return to corruption, He has spoken thus: 'I will give you the sure mercies of David.' Therefore He also says in another *Psalm:* 'You will not allow Your Holy One to see corruption.' "For David, after he had served his own generation by the will of God, fell asleep, was buried with his fathers, and saw corruption; but He whom God raised up saw no corruption. **1 Cor. 6:14:** And God both raised up the Lord and will also raise us up by His power. **1 Cor. 15:15:** Yes, and we are found false witnesses of God, because we have testified of God that He raised up Christ, whom He did not raise up—if in fact the dead do not rise. **2 Cor. 4:14:** ... knowing that He who raised up the Lord Jesus will also raise us up with Jesus, and will present *us* with you. **Gal. 1:1:** Paul, an apostle (not from men nor through man, but through Jesus Christ and God the Father who raised Him from the dead). **Heb. 13:20:** Now may the God of peace who brought up our Lord Jesus from the dead, that great Shepherd of the sheep, through the blood of the everlasting covenant.

4 **Eph. 2:19-22:** Now, therefore, you are no longer strangers and foreigners, but fellow citizens with the saints and members of the household of God, having been built on the foundation of the apostles and prophets, Jesus Christ Himself being the chief corner*stone,* in whom the whole building, being fitted together, grows into a holy temple in the Lord, in whom you also are being built together for a dwelling place of God in the Spirit. **Heb. 3:6:** ... but Christ as a Son over His own house, whose house we are if we hold fast the confidence and the rejoicing of the hope firm to the end. **Heb. 8:8-10:** Because finding fault with them, He says: "Behold, the days are coming, says the LORD, when I will make a new covenant with the house of Israel and with the house of Judah—not according to the covenant that I made with their fathers in the day when I took them by the hand to lead them out of the land of Egypt; because they did not continue in My covenant, and I disregarded them, says the LORD. For this *is* the covenant that I will make with the house of Israel after those days, says the LORD: I will put My laws in their mind and write them on their hearts; and I will be their God, and they shall be My people. **Heb. 10:21:** ... and *having* a High Priest over the house of God. **1 Pet. 2:5:** ... you also, as living stones, are being built up a spiritual house, a holy priesthood, to offer up spiritual sacrifices acceptable to God through Jesus Christ.

5 **Mark 11:9-10:** Then those who went before and those who followed cried out, saying: "Hosanna! 'Blessed *is* He who comes in the name of the LORD!' Blessed *is* the kingdom of our father David That comes in the name of the Lord! Hosanna in the highest!" **Luke 1:30-33:** Then the angel said to her, "Do not be afraid, Mary, for you have found favor with God. And behold, you will conceive in your womb and bring forth a Son, and shall call His name Jesus. He will be great, and will be called the Son of the Highest; and the Lord God will give Him the throne of His father David. And He will reign

over the house of Jacob forever, and of His kingdom there will be no end."

6 **Ps. 89:34-37:** My covenant I will not break, Nor alter the word that has gone out of My lips. Once I have sworn by My holiness; I will not lie to David: His seed shall endure forever, And his throne as the sun before Me; It shall be established forever like the moon, Even *like* the faithful witness in the sky. **Acts 2:29-36:** "Men *and* brethren, let *me* speak freely to you of the patriarch David, that he is both dead and buried, and his tomb is with us to this day. Therefore, being a prophet, and knowing that God had sworn with an oath to him that of the fruit of his body, according to the flesh, He would raise up the Christ to sit on his throne, he, foreseeing this, spoke concerning the resurrection of the Christ, that His soul was not left in Hades, nor did His flesh see corruption. This Jesus God has raised up, of which we are all witnesses. Therefore being exalted to the right hand of God, and having received from the Father the promise of the Holy Spirit, He poured out this which you now see and hear. "For David did not ascend into the heavens, but he says himself: 'The LORD said to my Lord, "Sit at My right hand, Till I make Your enemies Your footstool."' "Therefore let all the house of Israel know assuredly that God has made this Jesus, whom you crucified, both Lord and Christ." **Eph. 1:20:** ... which He worked in Christ when He raised Him from the dead and seated *Him* at His right hand in the heavenly *places*. **Rev. 11:15:** Then the seventh angel sounded: And there were loud voices in heaven, saying, "The kingdoms of this world have become *the kingdoms* of our Lord and of His Christ, and He shall reign forever and ever!"

Q. 52. *Which is the sixth covenant?*

A. The sixth covenant is that oath sworn to the promised Messiah, the Lord Jesus Christ, commonly called the Messianic Covenant.[1]

1 **Ps. 110:1-4:** The LORD said to my Lord, "Sit at My right hand, Till I make Your enemies Your footstool." The LORD shall send the rod of Your strength out of Zion. Rule in the midst of Your enemies! Your people *shall be* volunteers In the day of Your power; In the beauties of holiness, from the womb of the morning, You have the dew of Your youth. The LORD has sworn And will not relent, "You *are* a priest forever According to the order of Melchizedek." **Heb. 7:** For this Melchizedek, king of Salem, priest of the Most High God, who met Abraham returning from the slaughter of the kings and blessed him, to whom also Abraham gave a tenth part of all, first being translated "king of righteousness," and then also king of Salem, meaning "king of peace," without father, without mother, without genealogy, having neither beginning of days nor end of life, but made like the Son of God, remains a priest continually.... Therefore, if perfection were through the Levitical priesthood (for under it the people received the law), what further need *was there* that another priest should rise according to the order of Melchizedek, and not be called according to the order of Aaron? For the priesthood being changed, of necessity there is also a change of the law. For He of whom these things are spoken belongs to another tribe, from which no man has officiated at the altar. For *it is* evident that our Lord arose from Judah, of which tribe Moses spoke nothing concerning priesthood. And it is yet far more evident if, in the likeness of Melchizedek, there arises another priest who has come, not according to the law of a fleshly commandment, but according to the power of an endless life. For He testifies: "You *are* a priest forever According to the order of Melchizedek." ... And inasmuch as *He was* not *made priest* without an oath (for they have become priests without an oath, but He with an oath by Him who said to Him: "The LORD has sworn And will not relent, 'You *are* a priest forever According to the order of Melchizedek'"), by so much more Jesus has become a surety of a better covenant.... For the law appoints as high priests men who have weakness, but the word of the oath, which came after the law, *appoints* the Son who has been perfected forever.

Q. 53. *In what way is the covenant of grace revealed in the sixth covenant?*

A. In fulfillment of the pledge made to Adam in the promise of salvation and the covenants made with Abraham and David,[1] God entered into a covenant with His only Son Jesus Christ, the Seed,[2] promising that He would be a Priest forever after the order of Melchizedek,[3] to sit upon the throne of David and reign over the house of Israel forevermore.[4]

1
Rom. 5:12-21: Therefore, just as through one man sin entered the world, and death through sin, and thus death spread to all men, because all sinned— (For until the law sin was in the world, but sin is not imputed when there is no law. Nevertheless death reigned from Adam to Moses, even over those who had not sinned according to the likeness of the transgression of Adam, who is a type of Him who was to come. But the free gift *is* not like the offense. For if by the one man's offense many died, much more the grace of God and the gift by the grace of the one Man, Jesus Christ, abounded to many. And the gift *is* not like *that which came* through the one who sinned. For the judgment *which came* from one *offense resulted* in condemnation, but the free gift *which came* from many offenses *resulted* in justification. For if by the one man's offense death reigned through the one, much more those who receive abundance of grace and of the gift of righteousness will reign in life through the One, Jesus Christ.) Therefore, as through one man's offense *judgment came* to all men, resulting in condemnation, even so through one Man's righteous act *the free gift came* to all men, resulting in justification of life. For as by one man's disobedience many were made sinners, so also by one Man's obedience many will be made righteous. Moreover the law entered that the offense might abound. But where sin abounded, grace abounded much more, so that as sin reigned in death, even so grace might reign through righteousness to eternal life through Jesus Christ our Lord. **Gal. 4:4:** But when the fullness of the time had come, God sent forth His Son, born of a woman, born under the law. **Eph. 3:8-11:** To me, who am less than the least of all the saints, this grace was given, that I should preach among the Gentiles the unsearchable riches of Christ, and to make all see what *is* the fellowship of the mystery, which from the beginning of the ages has been hidden in God who created all things through Jesus Christ; to the intent that now the manifold wisdom of God might be made known by the church to the principalities and powers in the heavenly *places,* according to the eternal purpose which He accomplished in Christ Jesus our Lord. **Rev. 12:** Now a great sign appeared in heaven: a woman clothed with the sun, with the moon under her feet, and on her head a garland of twelve stars. Then being with child, she cried out in labor and in pain to give birth. And another sign appeared in heaven: behold, a great, fiery red dragon having seven heads and ten horns, and seven diadems on his heads. His tail drew a third of the stars of heaven and threw them to the earth. And the dragon stood before the woman who was ready to give birth, to devour her Child as soon as it was born. She bore a male Child who was to rule all nations with a rod of iron. And her Child was caught up to God and His throne.... And war broke out in heaven: Michael and his angels fought with the dragon; and the dragon and his angels fought, but they did not prevail, nor was a place found for them in heaven any longer. So the great dragon was cast out, that serpent of old, called the Devil and Satan, who deceives the whole world; he was cast to the earth, and his angels were cast out with him. Then I heard a loud voice saying in heaven, "Now salvation, and strength, and the kingdom of our God, and the power of His Christ have come, for the accuser of our brethren, who accused them before our God day and night, has been cast down.... Now when the dragon saw that he had been cast to the earth, he persecuted the woman who gave birth to the male *Child....* So the serpent spewed water out of his mouth like a flood after the woman, that he might cause her to be carried away by the flood.... And the dragon was enraged with the woman, and he went to make war with the rest of her offspring, who keep the commandments of God and have the testimony of Jesus Christ.

2
Matt. 1:1: The book of the genealogy of Jesus Christ, the Son of David, the Son of Abraham. **Acts 3:25:** You are sons of the prophets, and of the covenant which God made with our fathers, saying to Abraham, 'And in your seed all the families of the earth shall be blessed.' **Gal. 3:15:-19:** Brethren, I speak in the manner of men: Though *it is* only a man's covenant, yet *if it is* confirmed, no one annuls or adds to it. Now to Abraham and his Seed were the promises made. He does not say, "And to seeds," as of many, but as of one, "And to your Seed," who is Christ. And this I say, *that* the law, which was four hundred and thirty years later, cannot annul the covenant that was confirmed before by God in Christ, that it should make the promise of no effect. For if the inheritance *is* of the law, *it is* no longer of promise; but God gave *it* to Abraham by promise. What purpose then *does* the law *serve?* It was added because of transgressions, till the Seed should come to whom the promise was made; *and it was* appointed through angels by the hand of a mediator. Now a mediator does not *mediate* for one *only,* but God is one.

3
Gen. 14:18-20: Then Melchizedek king of Salem brought out bread and wine; he *was* the priest of God Most High. And he blessed him and said: "Blessed be Abram of God Most High, Possessor of heaven and earth; And blessed be God Most High, Who has delivered your enemies into your hand." And he gave him a tithe of all. **Ps. 110 and Heb. 7, See Q. 52, footnote 1 above.**

4
Acts 2:25-36: For David says concerning Him: 'I foresaw the LORD always before my face, For He is at my right hand, that I may not be shaken. Therefore my heart rejoiced, and my tongue was glad; Moreover my flesh also will rest in hope. For You will not leave my soul in Hades, Nor will You allow Your Holy One to see corruption. You have made known to me the ways of life; You will make me full of joy in Your presence.' "Men *and* brethren, let *me* speak freely to you of the patriarch David, that he is both dead and buried, and his tomb is with us to this day. Therefore, being a prophet, and knowing that God had sworn with an oath to him that of the fruit of his body, according to the flesh, He would raise up the Christ to sit on his throne, he, foreseeing this, spoke concerning the resurrection of the Christ, that His soul was not left in Hades, nor did His flesh see corruption. This Jesus God has raised up, of which we are all witnesses. Therefore being exalted to the right hand of God, and having received from the Father the promise of the Holy Spirit, He

poured out this which you now see and hear. "For David did not ascend into the heavens, but he says himself: 'The LORD said to my Lord, "Sit at My right hand, Till I make Your enemies Your footstool."' "Therefore let all the house of Israel know assuredly that God has made this Jesus, whom you crucified, both Lord and Christ." **Acts 13:22-23:** And when He had removed him, He raised up for them David as king, to whom also He gave testimony and said, 'I have found David the *son* of Jesse, a man after My *own* heart, who will do all My will.' From this man's seed, according to *the* promise, God raised up for Israel a Savior—Jesus. **Luke 1:30-33:** Then the angel said to her, "Do not be afraid, Mary, for you have found favor with God. And behold, you will conceive in your womb and bring forth a Son, and shall call His name Jesus. He will be great, and will be called the Son of the Highest; and the Lord God will give Him the throne of His father David. And He will reign over the house of Jacob forever, and of His kingdom there will be no end."

Q. 54. *Which is the seventh covenant?*

A. The seventh covenant is that oath sworn to the remnant according to the election of grace,[1] commonly called the New Covenant.[2]

1 **Heb. 8:6:** But now He has obtained a more excellent ministry, inasmuch as He is also Mediator of a better covenant, which was established on better promises. **Rom. 11:1-5, 25-27:** I say then, has God cast away His people? Certainly not! For I also am an Israelite, of the seed of Abraham, *of* the tribe of Benjamin. God has not cast away His people whom He foreknew. Or do you not know what the Scripture says of Elijah, how he pleads with God against Israel, saying, "LORD, they have killed Your prophets and torn down Your altars, and I alone am left, and they seek my life"? But what does the divine response say to him? "I have reserved for Myself seven thousand men who have not bowed the knee to Baal." Even so then, at this present time there is a remnant according to the election of grace.... For I do not desire, brethren, that you should be ignorant of this mystery, lest you should be wise in your own opinion, that blindness in part has happened to Israel until the fullness of the Gentiles has come in. And so all Israel will be saved, as it is written: "The Deliverer will come out of Zion, And He will turn away ungodliness from Jacob; For this *is* My covenant with them, When I take away their sins."

2 **Jer. 31:31-40:** "Behold, the days are coming, says the LORD, when I will make a new covenant with the house of Israel and with the house of Judah— not according to the covenant that I made with their fathers in the day *that* I took them by the hand to lead them out of the land of Egypt, My covenant which they broke, though I was a husband to them, says the LORD. But this *is* the covenant that I will make with the house of Israel after those days, says the LORD: I will put My law in their minds, and write it on their hearts; and I will be their God, and they shall be My people. No more shall every man teach his neighbor, and every man his brother, saying, 'Know the LORD,' for they all shall know Me, from the least of them to the greatest of them, says the LORD. For I will forgive their iniquity, and their sin I will remember no more." Thus says the LORD, Who gives the sun for a light by day, The ordinances of the moon and the stars for a light by night, Who disturbs the sea, And its waves roar (The LORD of hosts *is* His name): "If those ordinances depart From before Me, says the LORD, *Then* the seed of Israel shall also cease From being a nation before Me forever." Thus says the LORD: "If heaven above can be measured, And the foundations of the earth searched out beneath, I will also cast off all the seed of Israel For all that they have done, says the LORD. "Behold, the days are coming, says the LORD, that the city shall be built for the LORD from the Tower of Hananel to the Corner Gate. The surveyor's line shall again extend straight forward over the hill Gareb; then it shall turn toward Goath. And the whole valley of the dead bodies and of the ashes, and all the fields as far as the Brook Kidron, to the corner of the Horse Gate toward the east, *shall be* holy to the LORD. It shall not be plucked up or thrown down anymore forever." **Heb. 8:7-13:** For if that first *covenant* had been faultless, then no place would have been sought for a second. Because finding fault with them, He says: "Behold, the days are coming, says the LORD, when I will make a new covenant with the house of Israel and with the house of Judah— not according to the covenant that I made with their fathers in the day when I took them by the hand to lead them out of the land of Egypt; because they did not continue in My covenant, and I disregarded them, says the LORD. For this *is* the covenant that I will make with the house of Israel after those days, says the LORD: I will put My laws in their mind and write them on their hearts; and I will be their God, and they shall be My people. None of them shall teach his neighbor, and none his brother, saying, 'Know the LORD,' for all shall know Me, from the least of them to the greatest of them. For I will be merciful to their unrighteousness, and their sins and their lawless deeds I will remember no more." In that He says, "A new *covenant*," He has made the first obsolete. Now what is becoming obsolete and growing old is ready to vanish away.

Q. 55. *In what way is the covenant of grace revealed in the seventh covenant?*

A. In fulfillment of the covenants made with Abraham[1] and David,[2] yea, of all the covenants of promise,[3] God entered into a New Covenant with the house of Israel,[4] the seed of Christ;[5] promising to write His law in their hearts, to be their God and they His people; that all shall know the LORD, and He would remember their sins no more.[6]

1 **Luke 1:67-75:** Now his father Zacharias was filled with the Holy Spirit, and prophesied, saying: "Blessed *is* the Lord God of Israel, For He has visited and redeemed His people, And has raised up a horn of salvation for us In the house of His servant David, As He spoke by the mouth of His holy prophets, Who *have been* since the world began, That we should be saved from our enemies And from the hand of all who hate us, To perform the mercy *promised* to our fathers And to remember His holy covenant, The oath which He swore to our father Abraham: To grant us that we, Being delivered from the hand of our enemies, Might serve Him without fear, In holiness and righteousness before Him all the days of our life. **Acts 3:25-26:** You are sons of the prophets, and of the covenant which God made with our fathers, saying to Abraham, 'And in your seed all the families of the earth shall be blessed.' To you first, God, having raised up His Servant Jesus, sent Him to bless you, in turning away every one *of you* from your iniquities. **Gal. 3:7-18, 29:** Therefore know that *only* those who are of faith are sons of Abraham. And the Scripture, foreseeing that God would justify the Gentiles by faith, preached the gospel to Abraham beforehand, *saying,* "In you all the nations shall be blessed." So then those who *are* of faith are blessed with believing Abraham. For as many as are of the works of the law are under the curse; for it is written, "Cursed *is* everyone who does not continue in all things which are written in the book of the law, to do them." But that no one is justified by the law in the sight of God *is* evident, for "the just shall live by faith." Yet the law is not of faith, but "the man who does them shall live by them." Christ has redeemed us from the curse of the law, having become a curse for us (for it is written, "Cursed *is* everyone who hangs on a tree"), that the blessing of Abraham might come upon the Gentiles in Christ Jesus, that we might receive the promise of the Spirit through faith. Brethren, I speak in the manner of men: Though *it is* only a man's covenant, yet *if it is* confirmed, no one annuls or adds to it. Now to Abraham and his Seed were the promises made. He does not say, "And to seeds," as of many, but as of one, "And to your Seed," who is Christ. And this I say, *that* the law, which was four hundred and thirty years later, cannot annul the covenant that was confirmed before by God in Christ, that it should make the promise of no effect. For if the inheritance *is* of the law, *it is* no longer of promise; but God gave *it* to Abraham by promise.... And if you *are* Christ's, then you are Abraham's seed, and heirs according to the promise.

2 **Isa. 55:3:** Incline your ear, and come to Me. Hear, and your soul shall live; And I will make an everlasting covenant with you—The sure mercies of David. **Cf. Acts 13:34:** And that He raised Him from the dead, no more to return to corruption, He has spoken thus: 'I will give you the sure mercies of David.' **Jer. 33:14-26:** 'Behold, the days are coming,' says the LORD, 'that I will perform that good thing which I have promised to the house of Israel and to the house of Judah: 'In those days and at that time I will cause to grow up to David A Branch of righteousness; He shall execute judgment and righteousness in the earth. In those days Judah will be saved, And Jerusalem will dwell safely. And this *is the name* by which she will be called: THE LORD OUR RIGHTEOUSNESS.' "For thus says the LORD: 'David shall never lack a man to sit on the throne of the house of Israel; nor shall the priests, the Levites, lack a man to offer burnt offerings before Me, to kindle grain offerings, and to sacrifice continually.'" And the word of the LORD came to Jeremiah, saying, "Thus says the LORD: 'If you can break My covenant with the day and My covenant with the night, so that there will not be day and night in their season, then My covenant may also be broken with David My servant, so that he shall not have a son to reign on his throne, and with the Levites, the priests, My ministers. As the host of heaven cannot be numbered, nor the sand of the sea measured, so will I multiply the descendants of David My servant and the Levites who minister to Me.'" Moreover the word of the LORD came to Jeremiah, saying, "Have you not considered what these people have spoken, saying, 'The two families which the LORD has chosen, He has also cast them off'? Thus they have despised My people, as if they should no more be a nation before them. "Thus says the LORD: 'If My covenant *is* not with day and night, *and if* I have not appointed the ordinances of heaven and earth, then I will cast away the descendants of Jacob and David My servant, *so* that I will not take *any* of his descendants *to be* rulers over the descendants of Abraham, Isaac, and Jacob. For I will cause their captives to return, and will have mercy on them.'" **Ezek. 34:23-24:** I will establish one shepherd over them, and he shall feed them—My servant David. He shall feed them and be their shepherd. And I, the LORD, will be their God, and My servant David a prince among them; I, the

LORD, have spoken. **Ezek. 37:24-26:** David My servant *shall be* king over them, and they shall all have one shepherd; they shall also walk in My judgments and observe My statutes, and do them. Then they shall dwell in the land that I have given to Jacob My servant, where your fathers dwelt; and they shall dwell there, they, their children, and their children's children, forever; and My servant David *shall be* their prince forever. Moreover I will make a covenant of peace with them, and it shall be an everlasting covenant with them; I will establish them and multiply them, and I will set My sanctuary in their midst forevermore. **Hos. 3:4-5:** For the children of Israel shall abide many days without king or prince, without sacrifice or *sacred* pillar, without ephod or teraphim. Afterward the children of Israel shall return and seek the LORD their God and David their king. They shall fear the LORD and His goodness in the latter days. **Amos 9:11-12:** "On that day I will raise up The tabernacle of David, which has fallen down, And repair its damages; I will raise up its ruins, And rebuild it as in the days of old; That they may possess the remnant of Edom, And all the Gentiles who are called by My name," Says the LORD who does this thing. **Cf. Acts 15:6-21:** Now the apostles and elders came together to consider this matter. And when there had been much dispute, Peter rose up *and* said to them: "Men *and* brethren, you know that a good while ago God chose among us, that by my mouth the Gentiles should hear the word of the gospel and believe. So God, who knows the heart, acknowledged them by giving them the Holy Spirit, just as *He did* to us, and made no distinction between us and them, purifying their hearts by faith. Now therefore, why do you test God by putting a yoke on the neck of the disciples which neither our fathers nor we were able to bear? But we believe that through the grace of the Lord Jesus Christ we shall be saved in the same manner as they." Then all the multitude kept silent and listened to Barnabas and Paul declaring how many miracles and wonders God had worked through them among the Gentiles. And after they had become silent, James answered, saying, "Men *and* brethren, listen to me: Simon has declared how God at the first visited the Gentiles to take out of them a people for His name. And with this the words of the prophets agree, just as it is written: 'After this I will return And will rebuild the tabernacle of David, which has fallen down; I will rebuild its ruins, And I will set it up; So that the rest of mankind may seek the LORD, Even all the Gentiles who are called by My name, Says the LORD who does all these things.' "Known to God from eternity are all His works. Therefore I judge that we should not trouble those from among the Gentiles who are turning to God, but that we write to them to abstain from things polluted by idols, *from* sexual immorality, *from* things strangled, and *from* blood. For Moses has had throughout many generations those who preach him in every city, being read in the synagogues every Sabbath." **Mark 11:9-10:** Then those who went before and those who followed cried out, saying: "Hosanna! 'Blessed *is* He who comes in the name of the LORD!' Blessed *is* the kingdom of our father David That comes in the name of the Lord! Hosanna in the highest!"

3

1 Pet. 3:18-22: For Christ also suffered once for sins, the just for the unjust, that He might bring us to God, being put to death in the flesh but made alive by the Spirit, by whom also He went and preached to the spirits in prison, who formerly were disobedient, when once the Divine longsuffering waited in the days of Noah, while *the* ark was being prepared, in which a few, that is, eight souls, were saved through water. There is also an antitype which now saves us—baptism (not the removal of the filth of the flesh, but the answer of a good conscience toward God), through the resurrection of Jesus Christ, who has gone into heaven and is at the right hand of God, angels and authorities and powers having been made subject to Him. **Isa. 54:9:** For this *is* like the waters of Noah to Me; For as I have sworn That the waters of Noah would no longer cover the earth, So have I sworn That I would not be angry with you, nor rebuke you.

4

Gen. 17:7-8: And I will establish My covenant between Me and you and your descendants after you in their generations, for an everlasting covenant, to be God to you and your descendants after you. Also I give to you and your descendants after you the land in which you are a stranger, all the land of Canaan, as an everlasting possession; and I will be their God. **Jer. 31:32:** ... not according to the covenant that I made with their fathers in the day *that* I took them by the hand to lead them out of the land of Egypt, My covenant which they broke, though I was a husband to them, says the LORD.

5

Isa. 53:10: Yet it pleased the LORD to bruise Him; He has put *Him* to grief. When You make His soul an offering for sin, He shall see *His* seed, He shall prolong *His* days, And the pleasure of the LORD shall prosper in His hand. **Heb. 2:10-17:** For it was fitting for Him, for whom *are* all things and by whom *are* all things, in bringing many sons to glory, to make the captain of their salvation perfect through sufferings. For both He who sanctifies and those who are being sanctified *are* all of one, for which reason He is not ashamed to call them brethren, saying: "I will declare Your name to My brethren; In the midst of the assembly I will sing praise to You." And again: "I will put My trust in Him." And again: "Here am I and the children whom God has given Me." Inasmuch then as the children have partaken of flesh and blood, He Himself likewise shared in the same, that through death He might destroy him who had the power of death, that is, the devil, and release those who through fear of death were all their lifetime subject to bondage. For indeed He does not give aid to angels, but He does give aid to the seed of Abraham. Therefore, in all things He had to be made like *His* brethren, that He might be a merciful and faithful High Priest in things *pertaining* to God, to make propitiation for the sins of the people.

6

Ex. 6:7: I will take you as My people, and I will be your God. Then you shall know that I *am* the LORD your God who brings you out from under the burdens of the Egyptians. **2 Sam. 7:24:** For You have made Your people Israel Your very own people forever; and You, LORD, have become their God. **Jer. 31:33-34:** But this *is* the covenant that I will make with the house of Israel after those days, says the LORD: I will put My law in their minds, and write it on their hearts; and I will be their God, and they shall be My people. No more shall every man teach his neighbor, and every man his brother, saying, 'Know the LORD,' for they all shall know Me, from the least of them to the greatest of them, says the LORD. For I will forgive their iniquity, and their sin I will remember no more.

Q. 56. *What is the token annexed to the seventh covenant?*

A. The token annexed to the seventh covenant is the bread and cup of the Lord,[1] commonly called the Lord's Supper.[2]

1 **Luke 22:19-20:** And He took bread, gave thanks and broke *it,* and gave *it* to them, saying, "This is My body which is given for you; do this in remembrance of Me." Likewise He also *took* the cup after supper, saying, "This cup *is* the new covenant in My blood, which is shed for you." **1 Cor. 11:23-26:** For I received from the Lord that which I also delivered to you: that the Lord Jesus on the *same* night in which He was betrayed took bread; and when He had given thanks, He broke *it* and said, "Take, eat; this is My body which is broken for you; do this in remembrance of Me." In the same manner *He* also *took* the cup after supper, saying, "This cup is the new covenant in My blood. This do, as often as you drink *it,* in remembrance of Me." For as often as you eat this bread and drink this cup, you proclaim the Lord's death till He comes.

2 **1 Cor. 11:20:** Therefore when you come together in one place, it is not to eat the Lord's Supper.

Q. 57. *Who is the Mediator between God and man?*

A. The only Mediator between God and man is the Lord Jesus Christ,[1] who, being the eternal Son of God, of one substance and equal with the Father,[2] in the fullness of time became man,[3] and so was and continues to be God and man, in two entire distinct natures, and one person, forever.[4]

1 **1 Tim. 2:5:** For *there is* one God and one Mediator between God and men, *the* Man Christ Jesus. **John 14:6:** Jesus said to him, "I am the way, the truth, and the life. No one comes to the Father except through Me. **Acts 4:12:** Nor is there salvation in any other, for there is no other name under heaven given among men by which we must be saved.

2 **John 1:1, 14, 18:** In the beginning was the Word, and the Word was with God, and the Word was God.... And the Word became flesh and dwelt among us, and we beheld His glory, the glory as of the only begotten of the Father, full of grace and truth.... No one has seen God at any time. The only begotten Son, who is in the bosom of the Father, He has declared *Him.* **John 10:30:** I and *My* Father are one. **Phil. 2:6:** ... who, being in the form of God, did not consider it robbery to be equal with God. **Ps. 2:7:** I will declare the decree: The LORD has said to Me, 'You *are* My Son, Today I have begotten You. **Matt. 3:17:** And suddenly a voice *came* from heaven, saying, "This is My beloved Son, in whom I am well pleased." **Matt. 17:5:** While he was still speaking, behold, a bright cloud overshadowed them; and suddenly a voice came out of the cloud, saying, "This is My beloved Son, in whom I am well pleased. Hear Him!"

3 **Gal. 4:4:** But when the fullness of the time had come, God sent forth His Son, born of a woman, born under the law. **Matt. 1:23:** "Behold, the virgin shall be with child, and bear a Son, and they shall call His name Immanuel," which is translated, "God with us." **See John 1:14.**

4 **Luke 1:35:** And the angel answered and said to her, "*The* Holy Spirit will come upon you, and the power of the Highest will overshadow you; therefore, also, that Holy One who is to be born will be called the Son of God. **Acts 1:11:** ... who also said, "Men of Galilee, why do you stand gazing up into heaven? This *same* Jesus, who was taken up from you into heaven, will so come in like manner as you saw Him go into heaven." **Rom. 9:5:** ... of whom *are* the fathers and from whom, according to the flesh, Christ *came,* who is over all, *the* eternally blessed God. Amen. **Col. 2:9:** For in Him dwells all the fullness of the Godhead bodily. **Heb. 7:24-25:** But He, because He continues forever, has an unchangeable priesthood. Therefore He is also able to save to the uttermost those who come to God through Him, since He always lives to make intercession for them. **Heb. 13:8:** Jesus Christ *is* the

same yesterday, today, and forever. **See Phil. 2:5-11.**

Q. 58. *How did Christ, being the Son of God, become man?*

A. Christ the Son of God became man, by taking to Himself a true body, and a reasonable soul,[1] being conceived by the power of the Holy Spirit in the womb of the virgin Mary, of her substance, and born of her,[2] yet without sin.[3]

1 **John 1:14:** And the Word became flesh and dwelt among us, and we beheld His glory, the glory as of the only begotten of the Father, full of grace and truth. **Matt. 26:38:** Then He said to them, "My soul is exceedingly sorrowful, even to death. Stay here and watch with Me." **Phil. 2:7:** ... but made Himself of no reputation, taking the form of a bondservant, *and* coming in the likeness of men. **Heb. 2:14-17:** Inasmuch then as the children have partaken of flesh and blood, He Himself likewise shared in the same, that through death He might destroy him who had the power of death, that is, the devil, and release those who through fear of death were all their lifetime subject to bondage. For indeed He does not give aid to angels, but He does give aid to the seed of Abraham. Therefore, in all things He had to be made like *His* brethren, that He might be a merciful and faithful High Priest in things *pertaining* to God, to make propitiation for the sins of the people. **See Luke 2:40, 52; John 11:33.**

2 **Luke 1:27, 31, 35:** ... to a virgin betrothed to a man whose name was Joseph, of the house of David. The virgin's name *was* Mary.... And behold, you will conceive in your womb and bring forth a Son, and shall call His name Jesus.... And the angel answered and said to her, "*The* Holy Spirit will come upon you, and the power of the Highest will overshadow you; therefore, also, that Holy One who is to be born will be called the Son of God. **Gal. 4:4:** But when the fullness of the time had come, God sent forth His Son, born of a woman, born under the law.

3 **Heb. 4:15:** For we do not have a High Priest who cannot sympathize with our weaknesses, but was in all *points* tempted as *we are, yet* without sin. **Heb. 7:26:** For such a High Priest was fitting for us, *who is* holy, harmless, undefiled, separate from sinners, and has become higher than the heavens. **2 Cor. 5:21:** For He made Him who knew no sin *to be* sin for us, that we might become the righteousness of God in Him. **1 John 3:5:** And you know that He was manifested to take away our sins, and in Him there is no sin.

Q. 59. *Why was it requisite that the Mediator should be God?*

A. It was requisite that the Mediator should be God, that He might sustain and keep the human nature from sinking under the infinite wrath of God, and the power of death;[1] give worth and efficacy to His sufferings, obedience, and intercession;[2] and to satisfy God's justice,[3] procure His favor,[4] purchase a peculiar people,[5] give His Spirit to them,[6] conquer all their enemies,[7] and bring them to everlasting salvation.[8]

1 **Acts 2:24-25:** ... whom God raised up, having loosed the pains of death, because it was not possible that He should be held by it. For David says concerning Him: 'I foresaw the LORD always before my face, For He is at my right hand, that I may not be shaken. **Rom. 1:4:** ... *and* declared *to be* the Son of God with power according to the Spirit of holiness, by the resurrection from the dead. **Rom. 4:25:** ... who was delivered up because of our offenses, and was raised because of our justification. **Heb. 9:14:** ... how much more shall the blood of Christ, who through the eternal Spirit offered Himself without spot to God, cleanse your conscience from dead works to serve the living God?

2 **Acts 20:28:** Therefore take heed to yourselves and to all the flock, among which the Holy Spirit has made you overseers, to shepherd the church of God which He purchased with His own blood. **Heb. 9:14:** ... how much more shall the blood of Christ, who through the eternal Spirit offered

Himself without spot to God, cleanse your conscience from dead works to serve the living God? **Heb. 7:25-28:** Therefore He is also able to save to the uttermost those who come to God through Him, since He always lives to make intercession for them. For such a High Priest was fitting for us, *who is* holy, harmless, undefiled, separate from sinners, and has become higher than the heavens; who does not need daily, as those high priests, to offer up sacrifices, first for His own sins and then for the people's, for this He did once for all when He offered up Himself. For the law appoints as high priests men who have weakness, but the word of the oath, which came after the law, *appoints* the Son who has been perfected forever. **See John 17.**

[3] **Rom. 3:24-26:** ... being justified freely by His grace through the redemption that is in Christ Jesus, whom God set forth *as* a propitiation by His blood, through faith, to demonstrate His righteousness, because in His forbearance God had passed over the sins that were previously committed, to demonstrate at the present time His righteousness, that He might be just and the justifier of the one who has faith in Jesus.

[4] **Eph. 1:6:** ... to the praise of the glory of His grace, by which He made us accepted in the Beloved. **Matt. 3:17:** And suddenly a voice *came* from heaven, saying, "This is My beloved Son, in whom I am well pleased."

[5] **Titus 2:13-14:** ... looking for the blessed hope and glorious appearing of our great God and Savior Jesus Christ, who gave Himself for us, that He might redeem us from every lawless deed and purify for Himself *His* own special people, zealous for good works.

[6] **Gal. 4:6:** And because you are sons, God has sent forth the Spirit of His Son into your hearts, crying out, "Abba, Father!" **John 15:26:** But when the Helper comes, whom I shall send to you from the Father, the Spirit of truth who proceeds from the Father, He will testify of Me. **See John 16:7, 14:26.**

[7] **Luke 1:68-69, 71, 74:** Blessed *is* the Lord God of Israel, For He has visited and redeemed His people, And has raised up a horn of salvation for us In the house of His servant David ... That we should be saved from our enemies And from the hand of all who hate us ... To grant us that we, Being delivered from the hand of our enemies, Might serve Him without fear.

[8] **Heb. 5:8-9:** ... though He was a Son, *yet* He learned obedience by the things which He suffered. And having been perfected, He became the author of eternal salvation to all who obey Him. **Heb. 9:11-15:** But Christ came *as* High Priest of the good things to come, with the greater and more perfect tabernacle not made with hands, that is, not of this creation. Not with the blood of goats and calves, but with His own blood He entered the Most Holy Place once for all, having obtained eternal redemption. For if the blood of bulls and goats and the ashes of a heifer, sprinkling the unclean, sanctifies for the purifying of the flesh, how much more shall the blood of Christ, who through the eternal Spirit offered Himself without spot to God, cleanse your conscience from dead works to serve the living God? And for this reason He is the Mediator of the new covenant, by means of death, for the redemption of the transgressions under the first covenant, that those who are called may receive the promise of the eternal inheritance.

Q. 60. *Why was it requisite that the Mediator should be man?*

A. It was requisite that the Mediator should be man, that He might advance our nature,[1] perform obedience to the law,[2] suffer and make intercession for us in our nature,[3] have a fellow-feeling of our infirmities;[4] that we might receive the adoption of sons,[5] and have comfort and access with boldness unto the throne of grace.[6]

[1] **Heb. 2:16:** For indeed He does not give aid to angels, but He does give aid to the seed of Abraham. **2 Pet. 1:4:** ... by which have been given to us exceedingly great and precious promises, that through these you may be partakers of the divine nature, having escaped the corruption *that is* in the world through lust.

[2] **Gal. 4:4:** But when the fullness of the time had come, God sent forth His Son, born of a woman, born under the law. **Matt. 5:17:** Do not think that I came to destroy the Law or the Prophets. I did not come to destroy but to fulfill. **Rom. 5:19:** For as by one man's disobedience many were made sinners, so also by one Man's obedience many will be made righteous. **Phil. 2:8:** And being found in appearance as a man, He humbled Himself and became obedient to *the point of* death, even the

death of the cross.

[3] **Heb. 2:14:** Inasmuch then as the children have partaken of flesh and blood, He Himself likewise shared in the same, that through death He might destroy him who had the power of death, that is, the devil. **Heb. 7:24-25:** But He, because He continues forever, has an unchangeable priesthood. Therefore He is also able to save to the uttermost those who come to God through Him, since He always lives to make intercession for them.

[4] **Heb. 4:15:** For we do not have a High Priest who cannot sympathize with our weaknesses, but was in all *points* tempted as *we are, yet* without sin.

[5] **Gal. 4:5:** ... to redeem those who were under the law, that we might receive the adoption as sons.

[6] **Heb. 4:16:** Let us therefore come boldly to the throne of grace, that we may obtain mercy and find grace to help in time of need.

Q. 61. *Why was it requisite that the Mediator should be God and man in one person?*

A. It was requisite that the Mediator, who was to reconcile God and man, should Himself be both God and man, and this in one person, that the proper works of each nature might be accepted of God for us,[1] and relied on by us, as the works of the whole person.[2]

[1] **Matt. 1:21, 23:** And she will bring forth a Son, and you shall call His name Jesus, for He will save His people from their sins.... "Behold, the virgin shall be with child, and bear a Son, and they shall call His name Immanuel," which is translated, "God with us." **Matt. 3:17:** And suddenly a voice *came* from heaven, saying, "This is My beloved Son, in whom I am well pleased." **Heb. 9:14:** ... how much more shall the blood of Christ, who through the eternal Spirit offered Himself without spot to God, cleanse your conscience from dead works to serve the living God?

[2] **1 Pet. 2:6:** Therefore it is also contained in the Scripture, "Behold, I lay in Zion A chief cornerstone, elect, precious, And he who believes on Him will by no means be put to shame."

Q. 62. *Why was our Mediator called Jesus?*

A. Our Mediator was called Jesus, because He saveth His people from their sins.[1]

[1] **Matt. 1:21:** And she will bring forth a Son, and you shall call His name Jesus, for He will save His people from their sins.

Q. 63. *Why was our Mediator called Christ?*

A. Our Mediator was called Christ, because He was anointed with the Holy Spirit above measure;[1] and so set apart, and fully furnished with all authority and ability,[2] to execute the offices of Prophet,[3] Priest,[4] and King of His church,[5] in the estate both of His humiliation and exaltation.

[1] **Matt. 3:16:** When He had been baptized, Jesus came up immediately from the water; and behold, the heavens were opened to Him, and He saw the Spirit of God descending like a dove and alighting upon Him. **Cf. Acts 10:37-38:** ... that word you know, which was proclaimed throughout all Judea,

and began from Galilee after the baptism which John preached: how God anointed Jesus of Nazareth with the Holy Spirit and with power, who went about doing good and healing all who were oppressed by the devil, for God was with Him. **John 3:34:** For He whom God has sent speaks the words of God, for God does not give the Spirit by measure. **Ps. 45:7:** You love righteousness and hate wickedness; Therefore God, Your God, has anointed You With the oil of gladness more than Your companions.

2

John 6:27: Do not labor for the food which perishes, but for the food which endures to everlasting life, which the Son of Man will give you, because God the Father has set His seal on Him. **Matt. 28:18-20:** And Jesus came and spoke to them, saying, "All authority has been given to Me in heaven and on earth. Go therefore and make disciples of all the nations, baptizing them in the name of the Father and of the Son and of the Holy Spirit, teaching them to observe all things that I have commanded you; and lo, I am with you always, *even* to the end of the age." Amen. **Rom. 1:3-4:** ... concerning His Son Jesus Christ our Lord, who was born of the seed of David according to the flesh, *and* declared *to be* the Son of God with power according to the Spirit of holiness, by the resurrection from the dead.

3

Acts 3:21-22: ... whom heaven must receive until the times of restoration of all things, which God has spoken by the mouth of all His holy prophets since the world began. For Moses truly said to the fathers, 'The LORD your God will raise up for you a Prophet like me from your brethren. Him you shall hear in all things, whatever He says to you. **Luke 4:18, 21:** The Spirit of the LORD *is* upon Me, Because He has anointed Me To preach the gospel to *the* poor; He has sent Me to heal the brokenhearted, To proclaim liberty to *the* captives And recovery of sight to *the* blind, *To* set at liberty those who are oppressed.... And He began to say to them, "Today this Scripture is fulfilled in your hearing." **Heb. 1:1-2:** God, who at various times and in various ways spoke in time past to the fathers by the prophets, has in these last days spoken to us by *His* Son, whom He has appointed heir of all things, through whom also He made the worlds. **Deut. 18:18:** I will raise up for them a Prophet like you from among their brethren, and will put My words in His mouth, and He shall speak to them all that I command Him.

4

Heb. 5:5-7: So also Christ did not glorify Himself to become High Priest, but *it was* He who said to Him: "You are My Son, Today I have begotten You." As *He* also *says* in another *place:* "You *are* a priest forever According to the order of Melchizedek"; who, in the days of His flesh, when He had offered up prayers and supplications, with vehement cries and tears to Him who was able to save Him from death, and was heard because of His godly fear. **Heb. 4:14-15:** Seeing then that we have a great High Priest who has passed through the heavens, Jesus the Son of God, let us hold fast *our* confession. For we do not have a High Priest who cannot sympathize with our weaknesses, but was in all *points* tempted as *we are, yet* without sin.

5

Ps. 2:6: Yet I have set My King On My holy hill of Zion. **Luke 1:32-34:** He will be great, and will be called the Son of the Highest; and the Lord God will give Him the throne of His father David. And He will reign over the house of Jacob forever, and of His kingdom there will be no end." Then Mary said to the angel, "How can this be, since I do not know a man?" **John 18:37:** Pilate therefore said to Him, "Are You a king then?" Jesus answered, "You say *rightly* that I am a king. For this cause I was born, and for this cause I have come into the world, that I should bear witness to the truth. Everyone who is of the truth hears My voice." **Matt. 21:5:** Tell the daughter of Zion, 'Behold, your King is coming to you, Lowly, and sitting on a donkey, A colt, the foal of a donkey.' **Isa. 9:6-7:** For unto us a Child is born, Unto us a Son is given; And the government will be upon His shoulder. And His name will be called Wonderful, Counselor, Mighty God, Everlasting Father, Prince of Peace. Of the increase of *His* government and peace *There will be* no end, Upon the throne of David and over His kingdom, To order it and establish it with judgment and justice From that time forward, even forever. The zeal of the LORD of hosts will perform this. **Phil. 2:8-11:** And being found in appearance as a man, He humbled Himself and became obedient to *the point of* death, even the death of the cross. Therefore God also has highly exalted Him and given Him the name which is above every name, that at the name of Jesus every knee should bow, of those in heaven, and of those on earth, and of those under the earth, and *that* every tongue should confess that Jesus Christ *is* Lord, to the glory of God the Father.

Q. 64. *How doth Christ execute the office of a Prophet?*

A. Christ executeth the office of a Prophet, in His revealing to the church,[1] in all ages, by His Spirit and word,[2] in divers ways of administration,[3] the whole will of God,[4] in all things concerning their edification and salvation.[5]

1

John 1:18: No one has seen God at any time. The only begotten Son, who is in the bosom of the

Father, He has declared *Him.*

2 **1 Pet. 1:10-12:** Of this salvation the prophets have inquired and searched carefully, who prophesied of the grace *that would come* to you, searching what, or what manner of time, the Spirit of Christ who was in them was indicating when He testified beforehand the sufferings of Christ and the glories that would follow. To them it was revealed that, not to themselves, but to us they were ministering the things which now have been reported to you through those who have preached the gospel to you by the Holy Spirit sent from heaven—things which angels desire to look into.

3 **Heb. 1:1-2:** God, who at various times and in various ways spoke in time past to the fathers by the prophets, has in these last days spoken to us by *His* Son, whom He has appointed heir of all things, through whom also He made the worlds.

4 **John 15:15:** No longer do I call you servants, for a servant does not know what his master is doing; but I have called you friends, for all things that I heard from My Father I have made known to you.

5 **Acts 20:32:** So now, brethren, I commend you to God and to the word of His grace, which is able to build you up and give you an inheritance among all those who are sanctified. **Eph. 4:11-13:** And He Himself gave some *to be* apostles, some prophets, some evangelists, and some pastors and teachers, for the equipping of the saints for the work of ministry, for the edifying of the body of Christ, till we all come to the unity of the faith and of the knowledge of the Son of God, to a perfect man, to the measure of the stature of the fullness of Christ. **John 20:31:** ... but these are written that you may believe that Jesus is the Christ, the Son of God, and that believing you may have life in His name.

Q. 65. *How doth Christ execute the office of a Priest?*

A. Christ executeth the office of a Priest, in His once offering Himself a sacrifice without spot to God,[1] to be a reconciliation for the sins of His people;[2] and in making continual intercession for them.[3]

1 **Heb. 9:14, 28:** ... how much more shall the blood of Christ, who through the eternal Spirit offered Himself without spot to God, cleanse your conscience from dead works to serve the living God? ... so Christ was offered once to bear the sins of many. To those who eagerly wait for Him He will appear a second time, apart from sin, for salvation. **Heb. 10:12:** But this Man, after He had offered one sacrifice for sins forever, sat down at the right hand of God. **See Isa. 53.**

2 **Heb. 2:17:** Therefore, in all things He had to be made like *His* brethren, that He might be a merciful and faithful High Priest in things *pertaining* to God, to make propitiation for the sins of the people. **2 Cor. 5:18:** Now all things *are* of God, who has reconciled us to Himself through Jesus Christ, and has given us the ministry of reconciliation. **Col. 1:21-22:** And you, who once were alienated and enemies in your mind by wicked works, yet now He has reconciled in the body of His flesh through death, to present you holy, and blameless, and above reproach in His sight.

3 **Heb. 7:25:** Therefore He is also able to save to the uttermost those who come to God through Him, since He always lives to make intercession for them. **Heb. 9:24:** For Christ has not entered the holy places made with hands, *which are* copies of the true, but into heaven itself, now to appear in the presence of God for us.

Q. 66. *How doth Christ execute the office of a King?*

A. Christ executeth the office of a King, in calling out of the world a people to Himself,[1] and giving them officers,[2] laws,[3] and censures, by which He visibly governs them;[4] in bestowing saving grace upon His elect,[5] rewarding their obedience,[6] and correcting them for their sins,[7] preserving and supporting them under all their temptations and sufferings,[8] restraining and overcoming all their enemies,[9] and powerfully ordering all things for His own glory,[10] and their good;[11] and also in taking vengeance on the rest, who know not God, and obey not the gospel.[12]

1 **Acts 15:14-16:** Simon has declared how God at the first visited the Gentiles to take out of them a people for His name. And with this the words of the prophets agree, just as it is written: 'After this I will return And will rebuild the tabernacle of David, which has fallen down; I will rebuild its ruins, And I will set it up.' **Gen. 49:10:** The scepter shall not depart from Judah, Nor a lawgiver from between his feet, Until Shiloh comes; And to Him *shall be* the obedience of the people. **Ps. 110:3:** Your people *shall be* volunteers In the day of Your power; In the beauties of holiness, from the womb of the morning, You have the dew of Your youth. **John 17:2:** ... as You have given Him authority over all flesh, that He should give eternal life to as many as You have given Him.

2 **Eph. 4:11-12:** And He Himself gave some *to be* apostles, some prophets, some evangelists, and some pastors and teachers, for the equipping of the saints for the work of ministry, for the edifying of the body of Christ. **1 Cor. 12:28:** And God has appointed these in the church: first apostles, second prophets, third teachers, after that miracles, then gifts of healings, helps, administrations, varieties of tongues.

3 **Isa. 33:22:** For the LORD *is* our Judge, The LORD *is* our Lawgiver, The LORD *is* our King; He will save us.

4 **Matt. 18:17-18:** And if he refuses to hear them, tell *it* to the church. But if he refuses even to hear the church, let him be to you like a heathen and a tax collector. "Assuredly, I say to you, whatever you bind on earth will be bound in heaven, and whatever you loose on earth will be loosed in heaven." **1 Cor. 5:4-5:** In the name of our Lord Jesus Christ, when you are gathered together, along with my spirit, with the power of our Lord Jesus Christ, deliver such a one to Satan for the destruction of the flesh, that his spirit may be saved in the day of the Lord Jesus.

5 **Acts 5:31:** Him God has exalted to His right hand *to be* Prince and Savior, to give repentance to Israel and forgiveness of sins.

6 **Rev. 22:12:** And behold, I am coming quickly, and My reward *is* with Me, to give to every one according to his work. **Rev. 2:10:** Do not fear any of those things which you are about to suffer. Indeed, the devil is about to throw *some* of you into prison, that you may be tested, and you will have tribulation ten days. Be faithful until death, and I will give you the crown of life.

7 **Rev. 3:19:** As many as I love, I rebuke and chasten. Therefore be zealous and repent.

8 **Isa. 63:9:** In all their affliction He was afflicted, And the Angel of His Presence saved them; In His love and in His pity He redeemed them; And He bore them and carried them All the days of old.

9 **1 Cor. 15:25:** For He must reign till He has put all enemies under His feet. **Ps. 110:1-2:** The LORD said to my Lord, "Sit at My right hand, Till I make Your enemies Your footstool." The LORD shall send the rod of Your strength out of Zion. Rule in the midst of Your enemies!

10 **Rom. 14:10-11:** But why do you judge your brother? Or why do you show contempt for your brother? For we shall all stand before the judgment seat of Christ. For it is written: "*As* I live, says the LORD, Every knee shall bow to Me, And every tongue shall confess to God."

11 **Rom. 8:28:** And we know that all things work together for good to those who love God, to those who are the called according to *His* purpose.

12 **2 Thess. 1:8-9:** ... in flaming fire taking vengeance on those who do not know God, and on those who do not obey the gospel of our Lord Jesus Christ. These shall be punished with everlasting destruction from the presence of the Lord and from the glory of His power. **Ps. 2:8-9:** Ask of Me, and I will give *You* The nations *for* Your inheritance, And the ends of the earth *for* Your possession. You shall break them with a rod of iron; You shall dash them to pieces like a potter's vessel.

Q. 67. *What was the estate of Christ's humiliation?*

A. The estate of Christ's humiliation was that low condition, wherein He for our sakes, emptying Himself of His glory, took upon Him the form of a servant,[1] in His conception[2] and birth,[3] life,[4] death,[5] and after His death,[6] until His resurrection.[7]

1 **Phil. 2:6-8:** ... who, being in the form of God, did not consider it robbery to be equal with God, but made Himself of no reputation, taking the form of a bondservant, *and* coming in the likeness of men. And being found in appearance as a man, He humbled Himself and became obedient to *the point of* death, even the death of the cross.

2 **Luke 1:31:** And behold, you will conceive in your womb and bring forth a Son, and shall call His name Jesus.

3 **Luke 2:7:** And she brought forth her firstborn Son, and wrapped Him in swaddling cloths, and laid Him in a manger, because there was no room for them in the inn.

4 **Gal. 4:4:** But when the fullness of the time had come, God sent forth His Son, born of a woman, born under the law. **2 Cor. 8:9:** For you know the grace of our Lord Jesus Christ, that though He was rich, yet for your sakes He became poor, that you through His poverty might become rich. **Luke 9:58:** And Jesus said to him, "Foxes have holes and birds of the air *have* nests, but the Son of Man has nowhere to lay *His* head." **Heb. 2:18:** For in that He Himself has suffered, being tempted, He is able to aid those who are tempted. **Isa. 53:3:** He is despised and rejected by men, A Man of sorrows and acquainted with grief. And we hid, as it were, *our* faces from Him; He was despised, and we did not esteem Him.

5 **Ps. 22:1:** My God, My God, why have You forsaken Me? *Why are You so* far from helping Me, *And from* the words of My groaning? **Cf. Matt. 27:46:** And about the ninth hour Jesus cried out with a loud voice, saying, "Eli, Eli, lama sabachthani?" that is, "My God, My God, why have You forsaken Me?" **Isa. 53:10:** Yet it pleased the Lord to bruise Him; He has put *Him* to grief. When You make His soul an offering for sin, He shall see *His* seed, He shall prolong *His* days, And the pleasure of the Lord shall prosper in His hand. **1 John 2:2:** And He Himself is the propitiation for our sins, and not for ours only but also for the whole world. **Phil. 2:8:** And being found in appearance as a man, He humbled Himself and became obedient to *the point of* death, even the death of the cross.

6 **Matt. 12:40:** For as Jonah was three days and three nights in the belly of the great fish, so will the Son of Man be three days and three nights in the heart of the earth. **1 Cor. 15:3-4:** For I delivered to you first of all that which I also received: that Christ died for our sins according to the Scriptures, and that He was buried, and that He rose again the third day according to the Scriptures.

7 **Acts 2:24-27, 31:** ... whom God raised up, having loosed the pains of death, because it was not possible that He should be held by it. For David says concerning Him: 'I foresaw the Lord always before my face, For He is at my right hand, that I may not be shaken. Therefore my heart rejoiced, and my tongue was glad; Moreover my flesh also will rest in hope. For You will not leave my soul in Hades, Nor will You allow Your Holy One to see corruption.... he, foreseeing this, spoke concerning the resurrection of the Christ, that His soul was not left in Hades, nor did His flesh see corruption.

Q. 68. *How did Christ humble Himself in His conception and birth?*

A. Christ humbled Himself in His conception and birth, in that, being from all eternity the Son of God, in the bosom of the Father, He was pleased in the fullness of time to become the son of man, made of a woman of low estate, and to be born of her; with divers circumstances of more than ordinary abasement.[1]

1 **John 1:14, 18:** And the Word became flesh and dwelt among us, and we beheld His glory, the glory as of the only begotten of the Father, full of grace and truth.... No one has seen God at any time. The only begotten Son, who is in the bosom of the Father, He has declared *Him*. **Gal. 4:4:** But when the fullness of the time had come, God sent forth His Son, born of a woman, born under the law. **Luke 2:7:** And she brought forth her firstborn Son, and wrapped Him in swaddling cloths, and laid Him in a manger, because there was no room for them in the inn.

Q. 69. *How did Christ humble Himself in His life?*

A. Christ humbled Himself in His life, by subjecting Himself to the law,[1] which He perfectly fulfilled;[2] and by conflicting with the indignities of the world,[3] temptations of Satan,[4] and infirmities in His flesh, whether common to the nature of man, or particularly accompanying that His low condition.[5]

1 **Gal. 4:4:** But when the fullness of the time had come, God sent forth His Son, born of a woman, born under the law.

2 **Matt. 5:17:** Do not think that I came to destroy the Law or the Prophets. I did not come to destroy but to fulfill. **Rom. 5:19:** For as by one man's disobedience many were made sinners, so also by one Man's obedience many will be made righteous.

3 **Ps. 22:6:** But I *am* a worm, and no man; A reproach of men, and despised by the people. **Isa. 53:2-3:** For He shall grow up before Him as a tender plant, And as a root out of dry ground. He has no form or comeliness; And when we see Him, *There is* no beauty that we should desire Him. He is despised and rejected by men, A Man of sorrows and acquainted with grief. And we hid, as it were, *our* faces from Him; He was despised, and we did not esteem Him. **Heb. 12:2-3:** ... looking unto Jesus, the author and finisher of *our* faith, who for the joy that was set before Him endured the cross, despising the shame, and has sat down at the right hand of the throne of God. For consider Him who endured such hostility from sinners against Himself, lest you become weary and discouraged in your souls.

4 **Matt. 4:1-11:** Then Jesus was led up by the Spirit into the wilderness to be tempted by the devil. And when He had fasted forty days and forty nights, afterward He was hungry. Now when the tempter came to Him, he said, "If You are the Son of God, command that these stones become bread." But He answered and said, "It is written, 'Man shall not live by bread alone, but by every word that proceeds from the mouth of God.'" Then the devil took Him up into the holy city, set Him on the pinnacle of the temple, and said to Him, "If You are the Son of God, throw Yourself down. For it is written: 'He shall give His angels charge over you,' and, 'In *their* hands they shall bear you up, Lest you dash your foot against a stone.'" Jesus said to him, "It is written again, 'You shall not tempt the LORD your God.'" Again, the devil took Him up on an exceedingly high mountain, and showed Him all the kingdoms of the world and their glory. And he said to Him, "All these things I will give You if You will fall down and worship me." Then Jesus said to him, "Away with you, Satan! For it is written, 'You shall worship the LORD your God, and Him only you shall serve.'" Then the devil left Him, and behold, angels came and ministered to Him. **Luke 4:13:** Now when the devil had ended every temptation, he departed from Him until an opportune time.

5 **Heb. 2:17-18:** Therefore, in all things He had to be made like *His* brethren, that He might be a merciful and faithful High Priest in things *pertaining* to God, to make propitiation for the sins of the people. For in that He Himself has suffered, being tempted, He is able to aid those who are tempted. **Heb. 4:15:** For we do not have a High Priest who cannot sympathize with our weaknesses, but was in all *points* tempted as *we are, yet* without sin. **Isa. 52:13-14:** Behold, My Servant shall deal prudently; He shall be exalted and extolled and be very high. Just as many were astonished at you, So His visage was marred more than any man, And His form more than the sons of men.

Q. 70. *How did Christ humble Himself in His death?*

A. Christ humbled Himself in His death, in that having been betrayed by Judas,[1] forsaken by His disciples,[2] scorned and rejected by the world,[3] condemned by Pilate, and tormented by His persecutors;[4] having also conflicted with the terrors of death, and the powers of darkness, felt and borne the weight of God's wrath,[5] He laid down His life an offering for sin,[6] enduring the painful, shameful, and cursed death of the cross.[7]

[1] **Matt. 27:4:** ... saying, "I have sinned by betraying innocent blood." And they said, "What *is that* to us? You see *to it!*"

[2] **Matt. 26:56:** "But all this was done that the Scriptures of the prophets might be fulfilled." Then all the disciples forsook Him and fled.

[3] **Isa. 53:2-3:** For He shall grow up before Him as a tender plant, And as a root out of dry ground. He has no form or comeliness; And when we see Him, *There is* no beauty that we should desire Him. He is despised and rejected by men, A Man of sorrows and acquainted with grief. And we hid, as it were, *our* faces from Him; He was despised, and we did not esteem Him.

[4] **Matt. 27:26-50:** Then he released Barabbas to them; and when he had scourged Jesus, he delivered *Him* to be crucified.... **John 19:34:** But one of the soldiers pierced His side with a spear, and immediately blood and water came out. **See Luke 22:63-64.**

[5] **Luke 22:44:** And being in agony, He prayed more earnestly. Then His sweat became like great drops of blood falling down to the ground. **Matt. 27:46:** And about the ninth hour Jesus cried out with a loud voice, saying, "Eli, Eli, lama sabachthani?" that is, "My God, My God, why have You forsaken Me?"

[6] **Isa. 53:10:** Yet it pleased the Lord to bruise Him; He has put *Him* to grief. When You make His soul an offering for sin, He shall see *His* seed, He shall prolong *His* days, And the pleasure of the Lord shall prosper in His hand. **Matt. 20:28:** ... just as the Son of Man did not come to be served, but to serve, and to give His life a ransom for many. **See Mark 10:45.**

[7] **Phil. 2:8:** And being found in appearance as a man, He humbled Himself and became obedient to *the point of* death, even the death of the cross. **Heb. 12:2:** ... looking unto Jesus, the author and finisher of *our* faith, who for the joy that was set before Him endured the cross, despising the shame, and has sat down at the right hand of the throne of God. **Gal. 3:13:** Christ has redeemed us from the curse of the law, having become a curse for us (for it is written, "Cursed *is* everyone who hangs on a tree").

Q. 71. *Wherein consisted Christ's humiliation after His death?*

A. Christ's humiliation after His death consisted in His being buried,[1] and continuing in the state of the dead, and under the power of death till the third day;[2] which hath been otherwise expressed in these words, He descended into hell.

[1] **1 Cor. 15:3-4:** For I delivered to you first of all that which I also received: that Christ died for our sins according to the Scriptures, and that He was buried, and that He rose again the third day according to the Scriptures.

[2] **Ps. 16:10:** For You will not leave my soul in Sheol, Nor will You allow Your Holy One to see corruption. **Acts 2:24-27, 31:** ... whom God raised up, having loosed the pains of death, because it was not possible that He should be held by it. For David says concerning Him: 'I foresaw the Lord always before my face, For He is at my right hand, that I may not be shaken. Therefore my heart rejoiced, and my tongue was glad; Moreover my flesh also will rest in hope. For You will not leave my soul in Hades, Nor will You allow Your Holy One to see corruption.... he, foreseeing this, spoke concerning the resurrection of the Christ, that His soul was not left in Hades, nor did His flesh see corruption. **Rom. 6:9:** ... knowing that Christ, having been raised from the dead, dies no more. Death no longer has dominion over Him. **Matt. 12:40:** For as Jonah was three days and three nights in the belly of the great fish, so will the Son of Man be three days and three nights in the heart of the earth.

Q. 72. *What was the estate of Christ's exaltation?*

A. The estate of Christ's exaltation comprehendeth His resurrection,[1] ascension,[2] sitting at the right hand of the Father,[3] and His coming again to judge the world.[4]

1 **1 Cor. 15:4:** ... and that He was buried, and that He rose again the third day according to the Scriptures.

2 **Ps. 68:18:** You have ascended on high, You have led captivity captive; You have received gifts among men, Even *from* the rebellious, That the LORD God might dwell *there.* **Acts 1:11:** ... who also said, "Men of Galilee, why do you stand gazing up into heaven? This *same* Jesus, who was taken up from you into heaven, will so come in like manner as you saw Him go into heaven." **Eph. 4:8:** Therefore He says: "When He ascended on high, He led captivity captive, And gave gifts to men."

3 **Eph. 1:20:** ... which He worked in Christ when He raised Him from the dead and seated *Him* at His right hand in the heavenly *places.* **Ps. 110:1:** The LORD said to my Lord, "Sit at My right hand, Till I make Your enemies Your footstool." **Acts 2:33-34:** Therefore being exalted to the right hand of God, and having received from the Father the promise of the Holy Spirit, He poured out this which you now see and hear. "For David did not ascend into the heavens, but he says himself: 'The LORD said to my Lord, "Sit at My right hand." **Heb. 1:3:** ... who being the brightness of *His* glory and the express image of His person, and upholding all things by the word of His power, when He had by Himself purged our sins, sat down at the right hand of the Majesty on high.

4 **Acts 1:11:** ... who also said, "Men of Galilee, why do you stand gazing up into heaven? This *same* Jesus, who was taken up from you into heaven, will so come in like manner as you saw Him go into heaven." **Acts 17:31:** ... because He has appointed a day on which He will judge the world in righteousness by the Man whom He has ordained. He has given assurance of this to all by raising Him from the dead. **See Matt. 16:27.**

Q. 73. *How was Christ exalted in His resurrection?*

A. Christ was exalted in His resurrection, in that, not having seen corruption in death, (of which it was not possible for Him to be held)[1] and having the very same body in which He suffered, with the essential properties thereof,[2] (but without mortality, and other common infirmities belonging to this life,) really united to His soul,[3] He rose again from the dead the third day by His own power;[4] whereby He declared Himself to be the Son of God,[5] to have satisfied divine justice,[6] to have vanquished death, and him that had the power of it,[7] and to be Lord of quick and dead:[8] all which He did as a public person,[9] the Head of His church,[10] for their justification,[11] quickening in grace,[12] support against enemies,[13] and to assure them of their resurrection from the dead at the last day.[14]

1 **Acts 2:24, 27:** ... whom God raised up, having loosed the pains of death, because it was not possible that He should be held by it.... For You will not leave my soul in Hades, Nor will You allow Your Holy One to see corruption.

2 **Luke 24:39:** Behold My hands and My feet, that it is I Myself. Handle Me and see, for a spirit does not have flesh and bones as you see I have.

3 **Rom. 6:9:** ... knowing that Christ, having been raised from the dead, dies no more. Death no longer has dominion over Him. **Rev. 1:18:** I *am* He who lives, and was dead, and behold, I am alive forevermore. Amen. And I have the keys of Hades and of Death.

4 **John 10:18:** No one takes it from Me, but I lay it down of Myself. I have power to lay it down, and I have power to take it again. This command I have received from My Father.

5 **Rom. 1:4:** ... *and* declared *to be* the Son of God with power according to the Spirit of holiness, by the resurrection from the dead.

6
Rom. 8:34: Who *is* he who condemns? *It is* Christ who died, and furthermore is also risen, who is even at the right hand of God, who also makes intercession for us. **Rom. 3:25-26:** ... whom God set forth *as* a propitiation by His blood, through faith, to demonstrate His righteousness, because in His forbearance God had passed over the sins that were previously committed, to demonstrate at the present time His righteousness, that He might be just and the justifier of the one who has faith in Jesus. **Heb. 9:13-14:** For if the blood of bulls and goats and the ashes of a heifer, sprinkling the unclean, sanctifies for the purifying of the flesh, how much more shall the blood of Christ, who through the eternal Spirit offered Himself without spot to God, cleanse your conscience from dead works to serve the living God?

7
Heb. 2:14: Inasmuch then as the children have partaken of flesh and blood, He Himself likewise shared in the same, that through death He might destroy him who had the power of death, that is, the devil.

8
Rom. 14:9: For to this end Christ died and rose and lived again, that He might be Lord of both the dead and the living.

9
1 Cor. 15:21-22: For since by man *came* death, by Man also *came* the resurrection of the dead. For as in Adam all die, even so in Christ all shall be made alive. **Isa. 53:10-11:** Yet it pleased the LORD to bruise Him; He has put *Him* to grief. When You make His soul an offering for sin, He shall see *His* seed, He shall prolong *His* days, And the pleasure of the LORD shall prosper in His hand. He shall see the labor of His soul, *and* be satisfied. By His knowledge My righteous Servant shall justify many, For He shall bear their iniquities.

10
Eph. 1:20-23: ... which He worked in Christ when He raised Him from the dead and seated *Him* at His right hand in the heavenly *places,* far above all principality and power and might and dominion, and every name that is named, not only in this age but also in that which is to come. And He put all *things* under His feet, and gave Him *to be* head over all *things* to the church, which is His body, the fullness of Him who fills all in all. **Col. 1:18:** And He is the head of the body, the church, who is the beginning, the firstborn from the dead, that in all things He may have the preeminence.

11
Rom. 4:25: ... who was delivered up because of our offenses, and was raised because of our justification.

12
Eph. 2:1, 5-6: And you *He made alive,* who were dead in trespasses and sins ... even when we were dead in trespasses, made us alive together with Christ (by grace you have been saved), and raised *us* up together, and made *us* sit together in the heavenly *places* in Christ Jesus. **Col. 2:12:** ... buried with Him in baptism, in which you also were raised with *Him* through faith in the working of God, who raised Him from the dead.

13
1 Cor. 15:25-27: For He must reign till He has put all enemies under His feet. The last enemy *that* will be destroyed *is* death. For "He has put all things under His feet." But when He says "all things are put under *Him,*" *it is* evident that He who put all things under Him is excepted. **Ps. 2:7-9:** I will declare the decree: The LORD has said to Me, 'You *are* My Son, Today I have begotten You. Ask of Me, and I will give *You* The nations *for* Your inheritance, And the ends of the earth *for* Your possession. You shall break them with a rod of iron; You shall dash them to pieces like a potter's vessel.'

14
1 Cor. 15:20: But now Christ is risen from the dead, *and* has become the firstfruits of those who have fallen asleep. **1 Thess. 4:14:** For if we believe that Jesus died and rose again, even so God will bring with Him those who sleep in JESUS.

Q. 74. *How was Christ exalted in His ascension?*

A. Christ was exalted in His ascension, in that having after His resurrection often appeared unto and conversed with His apostles, speaking to them of the things pertaining to the kingdom of God,[1] and giving them commission to preach the gospel to all nations,[2] forty days after His resurrection, He, in our nature, and as our Head,[3] triumphing over enemies,[4] visibly went up into the highest heavens, there to receive gifts for men,[5] to raise up our affections thither,[6] and to prepare a place for us,[7] where Himself is, and shall continue till His second coming at the end of the world.[8]

[1] **Acts 1:2-3:** … until the day in which He was taken up, after He through the Holy Spirit had given commandments to the apostles whom He had chosen, to whom He also presented Himself alive after His suffering by many infallible proofs, being seen by them during forty days and speaking of the things pertaining to the kingdom of God.

[2] **Matt. 28:19-20:** "Go therefore and make disciples of all the nations, baptizing them in the name of the Father and of the Son and of the Holy Spirit, teaching them to observe all things that I have commanded you; and lo, I am with you always, *even* to the end of the age." Amen.

[3] **John 20:17:** Jesus said to her, "Do not cling to Me, for I have not yet ascended to My Father; but go to My brethren and say to them, 'I am ascending to My Father and your Father, and *to* My God and your God.'" **Heb. 6:20:** … where the forerunner has entered for us, *even* Jesus, having become High Priest forever according to the order of Melchizedek.

[4] **Eph. 4:8:** Therefore He says: "When He ascended on high, He led captivity captive, And gave gifts to men."

[5] **Acts 1:9-11:** Now when He had spoken these things, while they watched, He was taken up, and a cloud received Him out of their sight. And while they looked steadfastly toward heaven as He went up, behold, two men stood by them in white apparel, who also said, "Men of Galilee, why do you stand gazing up into heaven? This *same* Jesus, who was taken up from you into heaven, will so come in like manner as you saw Him go into heaven." **Eph. 4:7-8:** But to each one of us grace was given according to the measure of Christ's gift. Therefore He says: "When He ascended on high, He led captivity captive, And gave gifts to men." **Ps. 68:18:** You have ascended on high, You have led captivity captive; You have received gifts among men, Even *from* the rebellious, That the LORD God might dwell *there*. **Eph. 4:10:** He who descended is also the One who ascended far above all the heavens, that He might fill all things. **Acts 2:33:** Therefore being exalted to the right hand of God, and having received from the Father the promise of the Holy Spirit, He poured out this which you now see and hear.

[6] **Col. 3:1-2:** If then you were raised with Christ, seek those things which are above, where Christ is, sitting at the right hand of God. Set your mind on things above, not on things on the earth.

[7] **John 14:3:** And if I go and prepare a place for you, I will come again and receive you to Myself; that where I am, *there* you may be also.

[8] **Acts 3:21:** … whom heaven must receive until the times of restoration of all things, which God has spoken by the mouth of all His holy prophets since the world began.

Q. 75. *How is Christ exalted in His sitting at the right hand of God?*

A. Christ is exalted in His sitting at the right hand of God, in that as God-man He is advanced to the highest favor with God the Father,[1] with all fullness of joy,[2] glory,[3] and power over all things in heaven and earth;[4] and doth gather and defend His church, and subdue their enemies; furnisheth His ministers and people with gifts and graces,[5] and maketh intercession for them.[6]

[1] **Phil. 2:9:** Therefore God also has highly exalted Him and given Him the name which is above every name.

[2] **Acts 2:28:** You have made known to me the ways of life; You will make me full of joy in Your presence. **Ps. 16:11:** You will show me the path of life; In Your presence *is* fullness of joy; At Your right hand *are* pleasures forevermore.

[3] **John 17:5:** And now, O Father, glorify Me together with Yourself, with the glory which I had with

You before the world was.

4 **Dan. 7:13-14:** I was watching in the night visions, And behold, *One* like the Son of Man, Coming with the clouds of heaven! He came to the Ancient of Days, And they brought Him near before Him. Then to Him was given dominion and glory and a kingdom, That all peoples, nations, and languages should serve Him. His dominion *is* an everlasting dominion, Which shall not pass away, And His kingdom *the one* Which shall not be destroyed. **Eph. 1:22:** And He put all *things* under His feet, and gave Him *to be* head over all *things* to the church. **1 Pet. 3:22:** ... who has gone into heaven and is at the right hand of God, angels and authorities and powers having been made subject to Him.

5 **Eph. 4:10-12:** (He who descended is also the One who ascended far above all the heavens, that He might fill all things.) And He Himself gave some *to be* apostles, some prophets, some evangelists, and some pastors and teachers, for the equipping of the saints for the work of ministry, for the edifying of the body of Christ. **Ps. 110:1:** The LORD said to my Lord, "Sit at My right hand, Till I make Your enemies Your footstool." **Heb. 10:12-14:** But this Man, after He had offered one sacrifice for sins forever, sat down at the right hand of God, from that time waiting till His enemies are made His footstool. For by one offering He has perfected forever those who are being sanctified. **Ezek. 37:24:** David My servant *shall be* king over them, and they shall all have one shepherd; they shall also walk in My judgments and observe My statutes, and do them.

6 **Rom. 8:34:** Who *is* he who condemns? *It is* Christ who died, and furthermore is also risen, who is even at the right hand of God, who also makes intercession for us. **1 John 2:1:** My little children, these things I write to you, so that you may not sin. And if anyone sins, we have an Advocate with the Father, Jesus Christ the righteous. **Heb. 7:25:** Therefore He is also able to save to the uttermost those who come to God through Him, since He always lives to make intercession for them.

Q. 76. *How doth Christ make intercession?*

A. Christ maketh intercession, by His appearing in our nature continually before the Father in heaven,[1] in the merit of His obedience and sacrifice on earth,[2] declaring His will to have it applied to all believers;[3] answering all accusations against them,[4] and procuring for them quiet of conscience, notwithstanding daily failings,[5] access with boldness to the throne of grace,[6] and acceptance of their persons[7] and services.[8]

1 **Heb. 9:12, 24:** Not with the blood of goats and calves, but with His own blood He entered the Most Holy Place once for all, having obtained eternal redemption.... For Christ has not entered the holy places made with hands, *which are* copies of the true, but into heaven itself, now to appear in the presence of God for us.

2 **Isa. 53:12:** Therefore I will divide Him a portion with the great, And He shall divide the spoil with the strong, Because He poured out His soul unto death, And He was numbered with the transgressors, And He bore the sin of many, And made intercession for the transgressors. **Heb. 1:3:** ... who being the brightness of *His* glory and the express image of His person, and upholding all things by the word of His power, when He had by Himself purged our sins, sat down at the right hand of the Majesty on high.

3 **John 3:16:** For God so loved the world that He gave His only begotten Son, that whoever believes in Him should not perish but have everlasting life. **John 17:9, 20, 24:** I pray for them. I do not pray for the world but for those whom You have given Me, for they are Yours.... I do not pray for these alone, but also for those who will believe in Me through their word ... Father, I desire that they also whom You gave Me may be with Me where I am, that they may behold My glory which You have given Me; for You loved Me before the foundation of the world.

4 **Rom. 8:33-34:** Who shall bring a charge against God's elect? *It is* God who justifies. Who *is* he who condemns? *It is* Christ who died, and furthermore is also risen, who is even at the right hand of God, who also makes intercession for us.

5 **Rom. 5:1-2:** Therefore, having been justified by faith, we have peace with God through our Lord Jesus Christ, through whom also we have access by faith into this grace in which we stand, and rejoice in hope of the glory of God. **1 John 2:1-2:** My little children, these things I write to you, so

that you may not sin. And if anyone sins, we have an Advocate with the Father, Jesus Christ the righteous. And He Himself is the propitiation for our sins, and not for ours only but also for the whole world.

6 **Heb. 4:16:** Let us therefore come boldly to the throne of grace, that we may obtain mercy and find grace to help in time of need.

7 **Eph. 1:6:** ... to the praise of the glory of His grace, by which He made us accepted in the Beloved.

8 **1 Pet. 2:5:** ... you also, as living stones, are being built up a spiritual house, a holy priesthood, to offer up spiritual sacrifices acceptable to God through Jesus Christ.

Q. 77. *How is Christ to be exalted in His coming again to judge the world?*

A. Christ is to be exalted in His coming again to judge the world, in that He, who was unjustly judged and condemned by wicked men,[1] shall come again at the last day in great power,[2] and in the full manifestation of His own glory, and of His Father's, with all His holy angels,[3] with a shout, with the voice of the archangel, and with the trumpet of God,[4] to judge the world in righteousness.[5]

1 **Acts 3:14-15:** But you denied the Holy One and the Just, and asked for a murderer to be granted to you, and killed the Prince of life, whom God raised from the dead, of which we are witnesses.

2 **Matt. 24:30:** Then the sign of the Son of Man will appear in heaven, and then all the tribes of the earth will mourn, and they will see the Son of Man coming on the clouds of heaven with power and great glory. **2 Thess. 1:9-10:** These shall be punished with everlasting destruction from the presence of the Lord and from the glory of His power, when He comes, in that Day, to be glorified in His saints and to be admired among all those who believe, because our testimony among you was believed.

3 **Luke 9:26:** For whoever is ashamed of Me and My words, of him the Son of Man will be ashamed when He comes in His *own* glory, and *in His* Father's, and of the holy angels. **Matt. 25:31:** When the Son of Man comes in His glory, and all the holy angels with Him, then He will sit on the throne of His glory.

4 **1 Thess. 4:16:** For the Lord Himself will descend from heaven with a shout, with the voice of an archangel, and with the trumpet of God. And the dead in Christ will rise first.

5 **Acts 17:31:** ... because He has appointed a day on which He will judge the world in righteousness by the Man whom He has ordained. He has given assurance of this to all by raising Him from the dead. **2 Thess. 1:6-8:** ... since *it is* a righteous thing with God to repay with tribulation those who trouble you, and to *give* you who are troubled rest with us when the Lord Jesus is revealed from heaven with His mighty angels, in flaming fire taking vengeance on those who do not know God, and on those who do not obey the gospel of our Lord Jesus Christ.

Q. 78. *What benefits hath Christ procured by His mediation?*

A. Christ, by His mediation, hath procured redemption,[1] with all other benefits[2] of His perfect obedience[3] and sacrifice of Himself.[4]

1 **1 Tim. 2:5-6:** For *there is* one God and one Mediator between God and men, *the* Man Christ Jesus, who gave Himself a ransom for all, to be testified in due time. **Heb. 9:12:** Not with the blood of goats and calves, but with His own blood He entered the Most Holy Place once for all, having obtained eternal redemption. **Eph. 1:7:** In Him we have redemption through His blood, the forgiveness of sins, according to the riches of His grace.

[2] **2 Cor. 1:20:** For all the promises of God in Him *are* Yes, and in Him Amen, to the glory of God through us. **Eph. 1:3-6:** Blessed *be* the God and Father of our Lord Jesus Christ, who has blessed us with every spiritual blessing in the heavenly *places* in Christ, just as He chose us in Him before the foundation of the world, that we should be holy and without blame before Him in love, having predestined us to adoption as sons by Jesus Christ to Himself, according to the good pleasure of His will, to the praise of the glory of His grace, by which He made us accepted in the Beloved. **2 Pet. 1:3-4:** ... as His divine power has given to us all things that *pertain* to life and godliness, through the knowledge of Him who called us by glory and virtue, by which have been given to us exceedingly great and precious promises, that through these you may be partakers of the divine nature, having escaped the corruption *that is* in the world through lust.

[3] **Gal. 4:4:** But when the fullness of the time had come, God sent forth His Son, born of a woman, born under the law. **Matt. 5:17:** Do not think that I came to destroy the Law or the Prophets. I did not come to destroy but to fulfill. **Rom. 5:19:** For as by one man's disobedience many were made sinners, so also by one Man's obedience many will be made righteous. **Heb. 5:8:** ... though He was a Son, *yet* He learned obedience by the things which He suffered.

[4] **Heb. 9:14, 28:** ... how much more shall the blood of Christ, who through the eternal Spirit offered Himself without spot to God, cleanse your conscience from dead works to serve the living God? ... so Christ was offered once to bear the sins of many. To those who eagerly wait for Him He will appear a second time, apart from sin, for salvation. **Heb. 10:12:** But this Man, after He had offered one sacrifice for sins forever, sat down at the right hand of God. **See Isa. 53.**

Q. 79. *How do we come to be made partakers of the benefits which Christ hath procured?*

A. We are made partakers of the benefits which Christ hath procured, by the application of them unto us,[1] which is the work especially of God the Holy Spirit.[2]

[1] **John 1:11-12:** He came to His own, and His own did not receive Him. But as many as received Him, to them He gave the right to become children of God, to those who believe in His name.

[2] **Titus 3:4-7:** But when the kindness and the love of God our Savior toward man appeared, not by works of righteousness which we have done, but according to His mercy He saved us, through the washing of regeneration and renewing of the Holy Spirit, whom He poured out on us abundantly through Jesus Christ our Savior, that having been justified by His grace we should become heirs according to the hope of eternal life. **John 16:14-15:** He will glorify Me, for He will take of what is Mine and declare *it* to you. All things that the Father has are Mine. Therefore I said that He will take of Mine and declare *it* to you. **See John 3:3-8.**

Q. 80. *Who are made partakers of redemption through Christ?*

A. Redemption is certainly applied, and effectually communicated, to all those for whom Christ hath purchased it;[1] who are in time by the Holy Spirit enabled to believe in Christ according to the gospel.[2]

[1] **Eph. 1:13-14:** In Him you also *trusted,* after you heard the word of truth, the gospel of your salvation; in whom also, having believed, you were sealed with the Holy Spirit of promise, who is the guarantee of our inheritance until the redemption of the purchased possession, to the praise of His glory. **John 6:37, 39:** All that the Father gives Me will come to Me, and the one who comes to Me I will by no means cast out.... This is the will of the Father who sent Me, that of all He has given Me I should lose nothing, but should raise it up at the last day. **John 10:15-16:** As the Father knows Me, even so I know the Father; and I lay down My life for the sheep. And other sheep I have which are not of this fold; them also I must bring, and they will hear My voice; and there will be one flock *and* one shepherd.

[2] **Rom. 10:17:** So then faith *comes* by hearing, and hearing by the word of God. **1 Cor. 2:12-16:**

Now we have received, not the spirit of the world, but the Spirit who is from God, that we might know the things that have been freely given to us by God. These things we also speak, not in words which man's wisdom teaches but which the Holy Spirit teaches, comparing spiritual things with spiritual. But the natural man does not receive the things of the Spirit of God, for they are foolishness to him; nor can he know *them,* because they are spiritually discerned. But he who is spiritual judges all things, yet he himself is *rightly* judged by no one. For "who has known the mind of the LORD that he may instruct Him?" But we have the mind of Christ. **Eph. 2:8:** For by grace you have been saved through faith, and that not of yourselves; *it is* the gift of God. **Rom. 8:9, 14:** But you are not in the flesh but in the Spirit, if indeed the Spirit of God dwells in you. Now if anyone does not have the Spirit of Christ, he is not His.... For as many as are led by the Spirit of God, these are sons of God.

Q. 81. *Can they who have never heard the gospel, and so know not Jesus Christ, nor believe in Him, be saved by their living according to the light of nature?*

A. They who, having never heard the gospel,[1] know not Jesus Christ,[2] and believe not in Him, cannot be saved,[3] be they never so diligent to frame their lives according to the light of nature,[4] or the laws of that religion which they profess;[5] neither is there salvation in any other, but in Christ alone,[6] who is the Savior only of His body the church.[7]

1 **Rom. 10:14:** How then shall they call on Him in whom they have not believed? And how shall they believe in Him of whom they have not heard? And how shall they hear without a preacher?

2 **2 Thess. 1:8-9:** ... in flaming fire taking vengeance on those who do not know God, and on those who do not obey the gospel of our Lord Jesus Christ. These shall be punished with everlasting destruction from the presence of the Lord and from the glory of His power. **Eph. 2:12:** ... that at that time you were without Christ, being aliens from the commonwealth of Israel and strangers from the covenants of promise, having no hope and without God in the world. **John 1:10-12:** He was in the world, and the world was made through Him, and the world did not know Him. He came to His own, and His own did not receive Him. But as many as received Him, to them He gave the right to become children of God, to those who believe in His name.

3 **John 8:24:** Therefore I said to you that you will die in your sins; for if you do not believe that I am *He,* you will die in your sins. **John 3:18:** He who believes in Him is not condemned; but he who does not believe is condemned already, because he has not believed in the name of the only begotten Son of God.

4 **1 Cor. 1:20-24:** Where *is* the wise? Where *is* the scribe? Where *is* the disputer of this age? Has not God made foolish the wisdom of this world? For since, in the wisdom of God, the world through wisdom did not know God, it pleased God through the foolishness of the message preached to save those who believe. For Jews request a sign, and Greeks seek after wisdom; but we preach Christ crucified, to the Jews a stumbling block and to the Greeks foolishness, but to those who are called, both Jews and Greeks, Christ the power of God and the wisdom of God.

5 **John 4:22:** You worship what you do not know; we know what we worship, for salvation is of the Jews. **Rom. 9:31-32:** ... but Israel, pursuing the law of righteousness, has not attained to the law of righteousness. Why? Because *they did* not *seek it* by faith, but as it were, by the works of the law. For they stumbled at that stumbling stone. **Phil. 3:4-9:** ... though I also might have confidence in the flesh. If anyone else thinks he may have confidence in the flesh, I more so: circumcised the eighth day, of the stock of Israel, *of* the tribe of Benjamin, a Hebrew of the Hebrews; concerning the law, a Pharisee; concerning zeal, persecuting the church; concerning the righteousness which is in the law, blameless. But what things were gain to me, these I have counted loss for Christ. Yet indeed I also count all things loss for the excellence of the knowledge of Christ Jesus my Lord, for whom I have suffered the loss of all things, and count them as rubbish, that I may gain Christ and be found in Him, not having my own righteousness, which *is* from the law, but that which *is* through faith in Christ, the righteousness which is from God by faith.

6 **Acts 4:12:** Nor is there salvation in any other, for there is no other name under heaven given among men by which we must be saved.

[7] **Eph. 5:23:** For the husband is head of the wife, as also Christ is head of the church; and He is the Savior of the body.

Q. 82. *Are all they saved who hear the gospel, and live in the church?*

A. All that hear the gospel, and live in the visible church, are not saved; but they only who are true members of the church invisible.[1]

[1] **John 12:38-40:** ... that the word of Isaiah the prophet might be fulfilled, which he spoke: "Lord, who has believed our report? And to whom has the arm of the LORD been revealed?" Therefore they could not believe, because Isaiah said again: "He has blinded their eyes and hardened their hearts, Lest they should see with *their* eyes, Lest they should understand with *their* hearts and turn, So that I should heal them." **Rom. 9:6:** But it is not that the word of God has taken no effect. For they *are* not all Israel who *are* of Israel. **Matt. 22:14:** For many are called, but few *are* chosen. **Matt. 7:21:** Not everyone who says to Me, 'Lord, Lord,' shall enter the kingdom of heaven, but he who does the will of My Father in heaven. **Rom. 11:7:** What then? Israel has not obtained what it seeks; but the elect have obtained it, and the rest were blinded. **1 Cor. 10:2-5:** ... all were baptized into Moses in the cloud and in the sea, all ate the same spiritual food, and all drank the same spiritual drink. For they drank of that spiritual Rock that followed them, and that Rock was Christ. But with most of them God was not well pleased, for *their bodies* were scattered in the wilderness.

Q. 83. *What is the visible church?*

A. The visible church is the organized society of professing believers, in all ages and places, wherein the gospel is truly preached and the ordinances of baptism and the Lord's Supper rightly administered.[1]

[1] **Acts 2:42:** And they continued steadfastly in the apostles' doctrine and fellowship, in the breaking of bread, and in prayers. **Acts 20:7:** Now on the first *day* of the week, when the disciples came together to break bread, Paul, ready to depart the next day, spoke to them and continued his message until midnight. **Acts 7:38:** This is he who was in the congregation in the wilderness with the Angel who spoke to him on Mount Sinai, and *with* our fathers, the one who received the living oracles to give to us. **1 Cor. 1:2:** To the church of God which is at Corinth, to those who are sanctified in Christ Jesus, called *to be* saints, with all who in every place call on the name of Jesus Christ our Lord, both theirs and ours. **Eph. 4:11-12:** And He Himself gave some *to be* apostles, some prophets, some evangelists, and some pastors and teachers, for the equipping of the saints for the work of ministry, for the edifying of the body of Christ.

Q. 84. *What are the special privileges of the visible church?*

A. The visible church hath the privilege of being under God's special care and government;[1] of being protected and preserved in all ages, notwithstanding the opposition of all enemies;[2] and of enjoying the communion of saints, the ordinary means of salvation,[3] and offers of grace by Christ to all the members of it in the ministry of the gospel, testifying, that whosoever believes in Him shall be saved,[4] and excluding none that will come unto Him.[5]

[1] **1 Tim. 4:10:** For to this *end* we both labor and suffer reproach, because we trust in the living God,

who is *the* Savior of all men, especially of those who believe. **Eph. 4:11-13:** And He Himself gave some *to be* apostles, some prophets, some evangelists, and some pastors and teachers, for the equipping of the saints for the work of ministry, for the edifying of the body of Christ, till we all come to the unity of the faith and of the knowledge of the Son of God, to a perfect man, to the measure of the stature of the fullness of Christ.

2

Matt. 16:18: And I also say to you that you are Peter, and on this rock I will build My church, and the gates of Hades shall not prevail against it. **Rom. 8:31-39:** What then shall we say to these things? If God *is* for us, who *can be* against us? He who did not spare His own Son, but delivered Him up for us all, how shall He not with Him also freely give us all things? Who shall bring a charge against God's elect? *It is* God who justifies. Who *is* he who condemns? *It is* Christ who died, and furthermore is also risen, who is even at the right hand of God, who also makes intercession for us. Who shall separate us from the love of Christ? *Shall* tribulation, or distress, or persecution, or famine, or nakedness, or peril, or sword? As it is written: "For Your sake we are killed all day long; We are accounted as sheep for the slaughter." Yet in all these things we are more than conquerors through Him who loved us. For I am persuaded that neither death nor life, nor angels nor principalities nor powers, nor things present nor things to come, nor height nor depth, nor any other created thing, shall be able to separate us from the love of God which is in Christ Jesus our Lord. **Heb. 12:28-29:** Therefore, since we are receiving a kingdom which cannot be shaken, let us have grace, by which we may serve God acceptably with reverence and godly fear. For our God *is* a consuming fire.

3

Acts 2:39, 42: For the promise is to you and to your children, and to all who are afar off, as many as the Lord our God will call.... And they continued steadfastly in the apostles' doctrine and fellowship, in the breaking of bread, and in prayers. **Matt. 28:19-20:** "Go therefore and make disciples of all the nations, baptizing them in the name of the Father and of the Son and of the Holy Spirit, teaching them to observe all things that I have commanded you; and lo, I am with you always, *even* to the end of the age." Amen. **1 Cor. 12:12-13:** For as the body is one and has many members, but all the members of that one body, being many, are one body, so also *is* Christ. For by one Spirit we were all baptized into one body—whether Jews or Greeks, whether slaves or free—and have all been made to drink into one Spirit.

4

Rom. 9:4: ... who are Israelites, to whom *pertain* the adoption, the glory, the covenants, the giving of the law, the service *of God,* and the promises. **Eph. 4:11-12:** And He Himself gave some *to be* apostles, some prophets, some evangelists, and some pastors and teachers, for the equipping of the saints for the work of ministry, for the edifying of the body of Christ. **Acts 22:16:** And now why are you waiting? Arise and be baptized, and wash away your sins, calling on the name of the Lord. **Acts 2:21:** And it shall come to pass *That* whoever calls on the name of the LORD Shall be saved. **See Joel 2:32. Rom. 10:10-13, 17:** For with the heart one believes unto righteousness, and with the mouth confession is made unto salvation. For the Scripture says, "Whoever believes on Him will not be put to shame." For there is no distinction between Jew and Greek, for the same LORD over all is rich to all who call upon Him. For "whoever calls on the name of the LORD shall be saved." ... So then faith *comes* by hearing, and hearing by the word of God.

5

Matt. 11:28-29: Come to Me, all *you* who labor and are heavy laden, and I will give you rest. Take My yoke upon you and learn from Me, for I am gentle and lowly in heart, and you will find rest for your souls. **John 6:37:** All that the Father gives Me will come to Me, and the one who comes to Me I will by no means cast out.

Q. 85. *What is the invisible church?*

A. The invisible church is the whole number of the elect, that have been, are, or shall be gathered into one under Christ the Head.[1]

1

Eph. 1:10, 22-23: ... that in the dispensation of the fullness of the times He might gather together in one all things in Christ, both which are in heaven and which are on earth—in Him.... And He put all *things* under His feet, and gave Him *to be* head over all *things* to the church, which is His body, the fullness of Him who fills all in all. **John 10:16:** And other sheep I have which are not of this fold; them also I must bring, and they will hear My voice; and there will be one flock *and* one shepherd. **John 11:52: ...** and not for that nation only, but also that He would gather together in one the children of God who were scattered abroad. **Eph. 5:23, 27, 32:** For the husband is head of the wife, as also Christ is head of the church; and He is the Savior of the body.... that He might present her to Himself a glorious church, not having spot or wrinkle or any such thing, but that she should be holy and without blemish.... This is a great mystery, but I speak concerning Christ and the church.

Q. 86. *What special benefits do the members of the invisible church enjoy by Christ?*

A. The members of the invisible church by Christ enjoy union and communion with Him in grace and glory.[1]

[1] **John 17:21:** ... that they all may be one, as You, Father, *are* in Me, and I in You; that they also may be one in Us, that the world may believe that You sent Me. **Eph. 2:5-6:** ... even when we were dead in trespasses, made us alive together with Christ (by grace you have been saved), and raised *us* up together, and made *us* sit together in the heavenly *places* in Christ Jesus. **John 17:24:** Father, I desire that they also whom You gave Me may be with Me where I am, that they may behold My glory which You have given Me; for You loved Me before the foundation of the world. **1 John 1:3:** ... that which we have seen and heard we declare to you, that you also may have fellowship with us; and truly our fellowship *is* with the Father and with His Son Jesus Christ. **John 1:16:** And of His fullness we have all received, and grace for grace. **Eph. 3:16-19:** ... that He would grant you, according to the riches of His glory, to be strengthened with might through His Spirit in the inner man, that Christ may dwell in your hearts through faith; that you, being rooted and grounded in love, may be able to comprehend with all the saints what *is* the width and length and depth and height— to know the love of Christ which passes knowledge; that you may be filled with all the fullness of God. **Phil. 3:10:** ... that I may know Him and the power of His resurrection, and the fellowship of His sufferings, being conformed to His death. **Rom. 6:5-6:** For if we have been united together in the likeness of His death, certainly we also shall be *in the likeness* of *His* resurrection, knowing this, that our old man was crucified with *Him,* that the body of sin might be done away with, that we should no longer be slaves of sin.

Q. 87. *What is that union which the elect have with Christ?*

A. The union which the elect have with Christ is the work of God's grace,[1] whereby they are spiritually and mystically, yet really and inseparably, joined to Christ as their Head and husband;[2] which is done in their effectual calling.[3]

[1] **Eph. 2:6-7:** ... and raised *us* up together, and made *us* sit together in the heavenly *places* in Christ Jesus, that in the ages to come He might show the exceeding riches of His grace in *His* kindness toward us in Christ Jesus.

[2] **Eph. 1:22:** And He put all *things* under His feet, and gave Him *to be* head over all *things* to the church. **1 Cor. 6:17:** But he who is joined to the Lord is one spirit *with Him.* **John 10:28:** And I give them eternal life, and they shall never perish; neither shall anyone snatch them out of My hand. **Eph. 5:23, 30:** For the husband is head of the wife, as also Christ is head of the church; and He is the Savior of the body.... For we are members of His body, of His flesh and of His bones. **John 15:5:** I am the vine, you *are* the branches. He who abides in Me, and I in him, bears much fruit; for without Me you can do nothing. **Eph. 3:17:** ... that Christ may dwell in your hearts through faith; that you, being rooted and grounded in love.

[3] **1 Pet. 5:10:** But may the God of all grace, who called us to His eternal glory by Christ Jesus, after you have suffered a while, perfect, establish, strengthen, and settle *you.* **1 Cor. 1:9:** God *is* faithful, by whom you were called into the fellowship of His Son, Jesus Christ our Lord.

Q. 88. *What is effectual calling?*

A. Effectual calling is the work of God's almighty power and grace,[1] whereby (out of His free and special love to His elect, and from nothing in them moving Him thereunto)[2] He doth, in His accepted time, invite and draw them to Jesus Christ, by His word and Spirit;[3] savingly enlightening their minds,[4] renewing and powerfully determining their wills,[5] so as they (although in themselves dead in sin) are hereby made willing and able freely to answer His call, and to accept and embrace the grace offered and conveyed therein.[6]

1 **Ezek. 37:9, 14:** Also He said to me, "Prophesy to the breath, prophesy, son of man, and say to the breath, 'Thus says the Lord GOD: "Come from the four winds, O breath, and breathe on these slain, that they may live.... I will put My Spirit in you, and you shall live, and I will place you in your own land. Then you shall know that I, the Lord, have spoken *it* and performed *it,*" says the LORD.'" **John 5:25:** Most assuredly, I say to you, the hour is coming, and now is, when the dead will hear the voice of the Son of God; and those who hear will live. **Eph. 1:18-20:** ... the eyes of your understanding being enlightened; that you may know what is the hope of His calling, what are the riches of the glory of His inheritance in the saints, and what *is* the exceeding greatness of His power toward us who believe, according to the working of His mighty power which He worked in Christ when He raised Him from the dead and seated *Him* at His right hand in the heavenly *places.* **2 Tim. 1:8-9:** Therefore do not be ashamed of the testimony of our Lord, nor of me His prisoner, but share with me in the sufferings for the gospel according to the power of God, who has saved us and called *us* with a holy calling, not according to our works, but according to His own purpose and grace which was given to us in Christ Jesus before time began.

2 **Titus 3:4-5:** But when the kindness and the love of God our Savior toward man appeared, not by works of righteousness which we have done, but according to His mercy He saved us, through the washing of regeneration and renewing of the Holy Spirit,. **Eph. 2:4-5, 7-9:** But God, who is rich in mercy, because of His great love with which He loved us, even when we were dead in trespasses, made us alive together with Christ (by grace you have been saved) ... that in the ages to come He might show the exceeding riches of His grace in *His* kindness toward us in Christ Jesus. For by grace you have been saved through faith, and that not of yourselves; *it is* the gift of God, not of works, lest anyone should boast. **Rom. 9:11:** ... for *the children* not yet being born, nor having done any good or evil, that the purpose of God according to election might stand, not of works but of Him who calls. **Deut. 9:5:** *It is* not because of your righteousness or the uprightness of your heart *that* you go in to possess their land, but because of the wickedness of these nations *that* the LORD your God drives them out from before you, and that He may fulfill the word which the LORD swore to your fathers, to Abraham, Isaac, and Jacob.

3 **John 3:5:** Jesus answered, "Most assuredly, I say to you, unless one is born of water and the Spirit, he cannot enter the kingdom of God. **Titus 3:5:** ... not by works of righteousness which we have done, but according to His mercy He saved us, through the washing of regeneration and renewing of the Holy Spirit. **2 Cor. 5:20:** Now then, we are ambassadors for Christ, as though God were pleading through us: we implore *you* on Christ's behalf, be reconciled to God. **2 Cor. 6:1-2:** We then, *as* workers together *with Him* also plead with *you* not to receive the grace of God in vain. For He says: "In an acceptable time I have heard you, And in the day of salvation I have helped you." Behold, now *is* the accepted time; behold, now *is* the day of salvation. **John 6:44-45:** No one can come to Me unless the Father who sent Me draws him; and I will raise him up at the last day. It is written in the prophets, 'And they shall all be taught by God.' Therefore everyone who has heard and learned from the Father comes to Me. **Acts 16:14:** Now a certain woman named Lydia heard *us.* She was a seller of purple from the city of Thyatira, who worshiped God. The Lord opened her heart to heed the things spoken by Paul. **2 Thess. 2:13-14:** But we are bound to give thanks to God always for you, brethren beloved by the Lord, because God from the beginning chose you for salvation through sanctification by the Spirit and belief in the truth, to which He called you by our gospel, for the obtaining of the glory of our Lord Jesus Christ.

4 **Acts 26:18:** ... to open their eyes, *in order* to turn *them* from darkness to light, and *from* the power of Satan to God, that they may receive forgiveness of sins and an inheritance among those who are sanctified by faith in Me. **1 Cor. 2:10, 12:** But God has revealed *them* to us through His Spirit. For the Spirit searches all things, yes, the deep things of God.... Now we have received, not the spirit of the world, but the Spirit who is from God, that we might know the things that have been freely given to us by God. **2 Cor. 4:6:** For it is the God who commanded light to shine out of darkness, who has shone in our hearts to *give* the light of the knowledge of the glory of God in the face of Jesus Christ. **Eph. 1:17-18:** ... that the God of our Lord Jesus Christ, the Father of glory, may give to you the spirit of wisdom and revelation in the knowledge of Him, the eyes of your understanding being enlightened; that you may know what is the hope of His calling, what are the riches of the glory of His inheritance in the saints.

5 **Ezek. 11:19:** Then I will give them one heart, and I will put a new spirit within them, and take the stony heart out of their flesh, and give them a heart of flesh. **Ezek. 36:26-27:** I will give you a new heart and put a new spirit within you; I will take the heart of stone out of your flesh and give you a heart of flesh. I will put My Spirit within you and cause you to walk in My statutes, and you will keep My judgments and do *them.* **John 6:45:** It is written in the prophets, 'And they shall all be taught

by God.' Therefore everyone who has heard and learned from the Father comes to Me.

6 **Eph. 2:5:** ... even when we were dead in trespasses, made us alive together with Christ (by grace you have been saved). **Phil. 2:13:** ... for it is God who works in you both to will and to do for *His* good pleasure. **Deut. 30:6:** And the LORD your God will circumcise your heart and the heart of your descendants, to love the LORD your God with all your heart and with all your soul, that you may live. **Isa. 45:22:** Look to Me, and be saved, All you ends of the earth! For I *am* God, and *there is* no other. **Matt. 11:28-30:** Come to Me, all *you* who labor and are heavy laden, and I will give you rest. Take My yoke upon you and learn from Me, for I am gentle and lowly in heart, and you will find rest for your souls. For My yoke *is* easy and My burden is light. **Rev. 22:17:** And the Spirit and the bride say, "Come!" And let him who hears say, "Come!" And let him who thirsts come. Whoever desires, let him take the water of life freely.

Q. 89. *Are the elect only effectually called?*

A. All the elect, and they only, are effectually called;[1] although others may be, and often are, outwardly called by the ministry of the word,[2] and have some common operations of the Spirit;[3] who, for their willful neglect and contempt of the grace offered to them, being justly left in their unbelief, do never truly come to Jesus Christ.[4]

1 **Acts 13:48:** Now when the Gentiles heard this, they were glad and glorified the word of the Lord. And as many as had been appointed to eternal life believed.

2 **Matt. 22:14:** For many are called, but few *are* chosen. **Acts 8:13, 20-21:** Then Simon himself also believed; and when he was baptized he continued with Philip, and was amazed, seeing the miracles and signs which were done.... But Peter said to him, "Your money perish with you, because you thought that the gift of God could be purchased with money! You have neither part nor portion in this matter, for your heart is not right in the sight of God.

3 **Matt. 7:22:** Many will say to Me in that day, 'Lord, Lord, have we not prophesied in Your name, cast out demons in Your name, and done many wonders in Your name?' **Matt. 13:20-21:** But he who received the seed on stony places, this is he who hears the word and immediately receives it with joy; yet he has no root in himself, but endures only for a while. For when tribulation or persecution arises because of the word, immediately he stumbles. **Heb. 6:4-6:** For *it is* impossible for those who were once enlightened, and have tasted the heavenly gift, and have become partakers of the Holy Spirit, and have tasted the good word of God and the powers of the age to come, if they fall away, to renew them again to repentance, since they crucify again for themselves the Son of God, and put *Him* to an open shame.

4 **John 12:38-40:** ... that the word of Isaiah the prophet might be fulfilled, which he spoke: "Lord, who has believed our report? And to whom has the arm of the LORD been revealed?" Therefore they could not believe, because Isaiah said again: "He has blinded their eyes and hardened their hearts, Lest they should see with *their* eyes, Lest they should understand with *their* hearts and turn, So that I should heal them." **Acts 28:25-27:** So when they did not agree among themselves, they departed after Paul had said one word: "The Holy Spirit spoke rightly through Isaiah the prophet to our fathers, saying, 'Go to this people and say: "Hearing you will hear, and shall not understand; And seeing you will see, and not perceive; For the hearts of this people have grown dull. *Their* ears are hard of hearing, And their eyes they have closed, Lest they should see with *their* eyes and hear with *their* ears, Lest they should understand with *their* hearts and turn, So that I should heal them."' **John 6:64-65:** "But there are some of you who do not believe." For Jesus knew from the beginning who they were who did not believe, and who would betray Him. And He said, "Therefore I have said to you that no one can come to Me unless it has been granted to him by My Father." **Ps. 81:11-12:** But My people would not heed My voice, And Israel would *have* none of Me. So I gave them over to their own stubborn heart, To walk in their own counsels. **Heb. 10:29:** Of how much worse punishment, do you suppose, will he be thought worthy who has trampled the Son of God underfoot, counted the blood of the covenant by which he was sanctified a common thing, and insulted the Spirit of grace? **1 John 2:19:** They went out from us, but they were not of us; for if they had been of us, they would have continued with us; but *they went out* that they might be made manifest, that none of them were of us.

Q. 90. *What is the communion in grace which the members of the invisible church have with Christ?*

A. The communion in grace which the members of the invisible church have with Christ, is their partaking of the virtue of His mediation, in their justification,[1] adoption,[2] sanctification, and whatever else, in this life, manifests their union with Him.[3]

[1] **Rom. 8:30:** Moreover whom He predestined, these He also called; whom He called, these He also justified; and whom He justified, these He also glorified.

[2] **Eph. 1:5:** ... having predestined us to adoption as sons by Jesus Christ to Himself, according to the good pleasure of His will.

[3] **1 Cor. 1:30:** But of Him you are in Christ Jesus, who became for us wisdom from God—and righteousness and sanctification and redemption. **1 Cor. 6:11:** And such were some of you. But you were washed, but you were sanctified, but you were justified in the name of the Lord Jesus and by the Spirit of our God.

Q. 91. *What is justification?*

A. Justification is an act of God's free grace unto sinners,[1] in which He pardoneth all their sins, accepteth and accounteth their persons righteous in His sight;[2] not for anything wrought in them, or done by them,[3] but only for the perfect obedience and full satisfaction of Christ, by God imputed to them,[4] and received by faith alone.[5]

[1] **Rom. 3:22, 24-25:** ... even the righteousness of God, through faith in Jesus Christ, to all and on all who believe. For there is no difference ... being justified freely by His grace through the redemption that is in Christ Jesus, whom God set forth *as* a propitiation by His blood, through faith, to demonstrate His righteousness, because in His forbearance God had passed over the sins that were previously committed. **Rom. 4:5:** But to him who does not work but believes on Him who justifies the ungodly, his faith is accounted for righteousness.

[2] **Jer. 23:6:** In His days Judah will be saved, And Israel will dwell safely; Now this *is* His name by which He will be called: THE LORD OUR RIGHTEOUSNESS. **Rom. 4:6-8:** ... just as David also describes the blessedness of the man to whom God imputes righteousness apart from works: "Blessed *are those* whose lawless deeds are forgiven, And whose sins are covered; Blessed *is the* man to whom the LORD shall not impute sin." **2 Cor. 5:19, 21:** ... that is, that God was in Christ reconciling the world to Himself, not imputing their trespasses to them, and has committed to us the word of reconciliation.... For He made Him who knew no sin *to be* sin for us, that we might become the righteousness of God in Him. **Rom. 3:22, 24-25, 27-28:** ... even the righteousness of God, through faith in Jesus Christ, to all and on all who believe. For there is no difference ... being justified freely by His grace through the redemption that is in Christ Jesus, whom God set forth *as* a propitiation by His blood, through faith, to demonstrate His righteousness, because in His forbearance God had passed over the sins that were previously committed ... Where *is* boasting then? It is excluded. By what law? Of works? No, but by the law of faith. Therefore we conclude that a man is justified by faith apart from the deeds of the law.

[3] **Titus 3:5, 7:** ... not by works of righteousness which we have done, but according to His mercy He saved us, through the washing of regeneration and renewing of the Holy Spirit.... that having been justified by His grace we should become heirs according to the hope of eternal life. **Eph. 1:7:** In Him we have redemption through His blood, the forgiveness of sins, according to the riches of His grace.

[4] **Rom. 4:6-8, 11:** ... just as David also describes the blessedness of the man to whom God imputes righteousness apart from works: "Blessed *are those* whose lawless deeds are forgiven, And whose sins are covered; Blessed *is the* man to whom the LORD shall not impute sin." ... And he received the

sign of circumcision, a seal of the righteousness of the faith which *he had while still* uncircumcised, that he might be the father of all those who believe, though they are uncircumcised, that righteousness might be imputed to them also. **Rom. 5:17-19:** For if by the one man's offense death reigned through the one, much more those who receive abundance of grace and of the gift of righteousness will reign in life through the One, Jesus Christ.) Therefore, as through one man's offense *judgment came* to all men, resulting in condemnation, even so through one Man's righteous act *the free gift came* to all men, resulting in justification of life. For as by one man's disobedience many were made sinners, so also by one Man's obedience many will be made righteous.

5

Acts 10:43: To Him all the prophets witness that, through His name, whoever believes in Him will receive remission of sins. **Gal. 2:16:** ... knowing that a man is not justified by the works of the law but by faith in Jesus Christ, even we have believed in Christ Jesus, that we might be justified by faith in Christ and not by the works of the law; for by the works of the law no flesh shall be justified. **Phil. 3:9:** ... and be found in Him, not having my own righteousness, which *is* from the law, but that which *is* through faith in Christ, the righteousness which is from God by faith.

Q. 92. *How is justification an act of God's free grace?*

A. Although Christ, by His obedience and death, did make a proper, real, and full satisfaction to God's justice in the behalf of them that are justified;[1] yet inasmuch as God accepteth the satisfaction from a surety, which He might have demanded of them, and did provide this surety, His own only Son,[2] imputing His righteousness to them,[3] and requiring nothing of them for their justification but faith,[4] which also is His gift,[5] their justification is to them of free grace.[6]

1

Rom. 5:8-10, 19: But God demonstrates His own love toward us, in that while we were still sinners, Christ died for us. Much more then, having now been justified by His blood, we shall be saved from wrath through Him. For if when we were enemies we were reconciled to God through the death of His Son, much more, having been reconciled, we shall be saved by His life.... For as by one man's disobedience many were made sinners, so also by one Man's obedience many will be made righteous.

2

1 Tim. 2:5-6: For *there is* one God and one Mediator between God and men, *the* Man Christ Jesus, who gave Himself a ransom for all, to be testified in due time. **Heb. 10:10:** By that will we have been sanctified through the offering of the body of Jesus Christ once *for all.* **Matt. 20:28:** ... just as the Son of Man did not come to be served, but to serve, and to give His life a ransom for many. **Dan. 9:24, 26:** Seventy weeks are determined For your people and for your holy city, To finish the transgression, To make an end of sins, To make reconciliation for iniquity, To bring in everlasting righteousness, To seal up vision and prophecy, And to anoint the Most Holy.... And after the sixty-two weeks Messiah shall be cut off, but not for Himself; And the people of the prince who is to come Shall destroy the city and the sanctuary. The end of it *shall be* with a flood, And till the end of the war desolations are determined. **Isa. 53:4-6, 10-12:** Surely He has borne our griefs And carried our sorrows; Yet we esteemed Him stricken, Smitten by God, and afflicted. But He *was* wounded for our transgressions, *He was* bruised for our iniquities; The chastisement for our peace *was* upon Him, And by His stripes we are healed. All we like sheep have gone astray; We have turned, every one, to his own way; And the LORD has laid on Him the iniquity of us all.... Yet it pleased the LORD to bruise Him; He has put *Him* to grief. When You make His soul an offering for sin, He shall see *His* seed, He shall prolong *His* days, And the pleasure of the LORD shall prosper in His hand. He shall see the labor of His soul, *and* be satisfied. By His knowledge My righteous Servant shall justify many, For He shall bear their iniquities. Therefore I will divide Him a portion with the great, And He shall divide the spoil with the strong, Because He poured out His soul unto death, And He was numbered with the transgressors, And He bore the sin of many, And made intercession for the transgressors. **Heb. 7:22:** ... by so much more Jesus has become a surety of a better covenant. **Rom. 8:32:** He who did not spare His own Son, but delivered Him up for us all, how shall He not with Him also freely give us all things? **1 Pet. 1:18-19:** ... knowing that you were not redeemed with corruptible things, *like* silver or gold, from your aimless conduct *received* by tradition from your fathers, but with the precious blood of Christ, as of a lamb without blemish and without spot.

3

2 Cor. 5:21: For He made Him who knew no sin *to be* sin for us, that we might become the righteousness of God in Him. **Rom. 4:6, 11:** ... just as David also describes the blessedness of the man to whom God imputes righteousness apart from works ... And he received the sign of circumcision, a seal of the righteousness of the faith which *he had while still* uncircumcised, that he might be the father of all those who believe, though they are uncircumcised, that righteousness might be imputed to them also.

4
Rom. 3:24-25: ... being justified freely by His grace through the redemption that is in Christ Jesus, whom God set forth *as* a propitiation by His blood, through faith, to demonstrate His righteousness, because in His forbearance God had passed over the sins that were previously committed.

5
Eph. 2:8: For by grace you have been saved through faith, and that not of yourselves; *it is* the gift of God.

6
Eph. 1:7: In Him we have redemption through His blood, the forgiveness of sins, according to the riches of His grace. **Rom. 3:24-25:** ... being justified freely by His grace through the redemption that is in Christ Jesus, whom God set forth *as* a propitiation by His blood, through faith, to demonstrate His righteousness, because in His forbearance God had passed over the sins that were previously committed.

Q. 93. *What is justifying faith?*

A. Justifying faith is a saving grace,[1] wrought in the heart of a sinner by the Spirit[2] and word of God,[3] whereby he, being convinced of his sin and misery, and of the disability in himself and all other creatures to recover him out of his lost condition,[4] not only assenteth to the truth of the promise of the gospel,[5] but receiveth and resteth upon Christ and His righteousness, therein held forth, for pardon of sin,[6] and for the accepting and accounting of his person righteous in the sight of God for salvation.[7]

1
Heb. 10:39: But we are not of those who draw back to perdition, but of those who believe to the saving of the soul.

2
2 Cor. 4:13: And since we have the same spirit of faith, according to what is written, "I believed and therefore I spoke," we also believe and therefore speak. **Eph. 1:17-19:** ... that the God of our Lord Jesus Christ, the Father of glory, may give to you the spirit of wisdom and revelation in the knowledge of Him, the eyes of your understanding being enlightened; that you may know what is the hope of His calling, what are the riches of the glory of His inheritance in the saints, and what *is* the exceeding greatness of His power toward us who believe, according to the working of His mighty power. **1 Cor. 12:3:** Therefore I make known to you that no one speaking by the Spirit of God calls Jesus accursed, and no one can say that Jesus is Lord except by the Holy Spirit. **1 Pet. 1:2:** ... elect according to the foreknowledge of God the Father, in sanctification of the Spirit, for obedience and sprinkling of the blood of Jesus Christ: Grace to you and peace be multiplied.

3
Rom. 10:14-17: How then shall they call on Him in whom they have not believed? And how shall they believe in Him of whom they have not heard? And how shall they hear without a preacher? And how shall they preach unless they are sent? As it is written: "How beautiful are the feet of those who preach the gospel of peace, Who bring glad tidings of good things!" But they have not all obeyed the gospel. For Isaiah says, LORD, who has believed our report?" So then faith *comes* by hearing, and hearing by the word of God. **1 Cor. 1:21:** For since, in the wisdom of God, the world through wisdom did not know God, it pleased God through the foolishness of the message preached to save those who believe.

4
Acts 2:37: Now when they heard *this,* they were cut to the heart, and said to Peter and the rest of the apostles, "Men *and* brethren, what shall we do?" **Acts 16:30:** And he brought them out and said, "Sirs, what must I do to be saved?" **John 16:8-9:** And when He has come, He will convict the world of sin, and of righteousness, and of judgment: of sin, because they do not believe in Me. **Rom. 6:6:** ... knowing this, that our old man was crucified with *Him,* that the body of sin might be done away with, that we should no longer be slaves of sin. **Eph. 2:1:** And you *He made alive,* who were dead in trespasses and sins. **Acts 4:12:** Nor is there salvation in any other, for there is no other name under heaven given among men by which we must be saved.

5
Eph. 1:13: In Him you also *trusted,* after you heard the word of truth, the gospel of your salvation; in whom also, having believed, you were sealed with the Holy Spirit of promise. **Heb. 11:13:** These all died in faith, not having received the promises, but having seen them afar off were assured of them, embraced *them* and confessed that they were strangers and pilgrims on the earth.
6
John 1:12: But as many as received Him, to them He gave the right to become children of God, to those who believe in His name. **Acts 16:31:** So they said, "Believe on the Lord Jesus Christ, and you will be saved, you and your household." **Acts 10:43:** To Him all the prophets witness that, through His name, whoever believes in Him will receive remission of sins. **Zech. 3:8-9:** 'Hear, O Joshua, the high priest, You and your companions who sit before you, For they are a wondrous sign; For behold, I am bringing forth My Servant the BRANCH. For behold, the stone That I have laid before Joshua: Upon the stone *are* seven eyes. Behold, I will engrave its inscription,' Says the LORD of hosts, 'And I will remove the iniquity of that land in one day.'
7
Phil. 3:9: ... and be found in Him, not having my own righteousness, which *is* from the law, but that which *is* through faith in Christ, the righteousness which is from God by faith. **Acts 15:11:** But we believe that through the grace of the Lord Jesus Christ we shall be saved in the same manner as they.

Q. 94. *How doth faith justify a sinner in the sight of God?*

A. Faith justifies a sinner in the sight of God, not because of those other graces which do always accompany it, or of good works that are the fruits of it,[1] nor as if the grace of faith, or any act thereof, were imputed to him for his justification;[2] but only as it is an instrument by which he receiveth and applieth Christ and His righteousness.[3]

1
Gal. 3:11: But that no one is justified by the law in the sight of God *is* evident, for "the just shall live by faith." **Rom. 3:28:** Therefore we conclude that a man is justified by faith apart from the deeds of the law.
2
Rom. 4:5: But to him who does not work but believes on Him who justifies the ungodly, his faith is accounted for righteousness. **Rom. 10:10:** For with the heart one believes unto righteousness, and with the mouth confession is made unto salvation.
3
John 1:12: But as many as received Him, to them He gave the right to become children of God, to those who believe in His name. **Phil. 3:9:** ... and be found in Him, not having my own righteousness, which *is* from the law, but that which *is* through faith in Christ, the righteousness which is from God by faith. **Gal. 2:16:** ... knowing that a man is not justified by the works of the law but by faith in Jesus Christ, even we have believed in Christ Jesus, that we might be justified by faith in Christ and not by the works of the law; for by the works of the law no flesh shall be justified.

Q. 95. *What is adoption?*

A. Adoption is an act of the free grace of God,[1] in and for His only Son Jesus Christ,[2] whereby all those that are justified are received into the number of His children,[3] have His name put upon them,[4] the Spirit of His Son given to them,[5] are under His fatherly care and dispensations,[6] admitted to all the liberties and privileges of the sons of God, made heirs of all the promises, and fellow-heirs with Christ in glory.[7]

1
1 John 3:1: Behold what manner of love the Father has bestowed on us, that we should be called

children of God! Therefore the world does not know us, because it did not know Him.

2 **Eph. 1:5:** ... having predestined us to adoption as sons by Jesus Christ to Himself, according to the good pleasure of His will. **Gal. 4:4-5:** But when the fullness of the time had come, God sent forth His Son, born of a woman, born under the law, to redeem those who were under the law, that we might receive the adoption as sons.

3 **John 1:12:** But as many as received Him, to them He gave the right to become children of God, to those who believe in His name. **Rom. 8:15-16:** For you did not receive the spirit of bondage again to fear, but you received the Spirit of adoption by whom we cry out, "Abba, Father." The Spirit Himself bears witness with our spirit that we are children of God.

4 **Num. 6:24-27:** The LORD bless you and keep you; The LORD make His face shine upon you, And be gracious to you; The LORD lift up His countenance upon you, And give you peace. **Amos 9:12:** "That they may possess the remnant of Edom, And all the Gentiles who are called by My name," Says the LORD who does this thing. **2 Cor. 6:18:** I will be a Father to you, And you shall be My sons and daughters, Says the LORD Almighty. **Rev. 3:12:** He who overcomes, I will make him a pillar in the temple of My God, and he shall go out no more. I will write on him the name of My God and the name of the city of My God, the New Jerusalem, which comes down out of heaven from My God. And *I will write on him* My new name.

5 **Gal. 4:6:** And because you are sons, God has sent forth the Spirit of His Son into your hearts, crying out, "Abba, Father!"

6 **Ps. 103:13:** As a father pities *his* children, *So* the LORD pities those who fear Him. **Prov. 14:26:** In the fear of the LORD *there is* strong confidence, And His children will have a place of refuge. **Matt. 6:32:** For after all these things the Gentiles seek. For your heavenly Father knows that you need all these things. **Heb. 12:5-7, 11:** And you have forgotten the exhortation which speaks to you as to sons: "My son, do not despise the chastening of the LORD, Nor be discouraged when you are rebuked by Him; For whom the LORD loves He chastens, And scourges every son whom He receives." If you endure chastening, God deals with you as with sons; for what son is there whom a father does not chasten? ... Now no chastening seems to be joyful for the present, but painful; nevertheless, afterward it yields the peaceable fruit of righteousness to those who have been trained by it.

7 **Heb. 6:12:** ... that you do not become sluggish, but imitate those who through faith and patience inherit the promises. **Rom. 8:17:** ... and if children, then heirs—heirs of God and joint heirs with Christ, if indeed we suffer with *Him,* that we may also be glorified together. **1 Pet. 1:3-4:** Blessed *be* the God and Father of our Lord Jesus Christ, who according to His abundant mercy has begotten us again to a living hope through the resurrection of Jesus Christ from the dead, to an inheritance incorruptible and undefiled and that does not fade away, reserved in heaven for you.

Q. 96. *What is sanctification?*

A. Sanctification is a work of God's grace, whereby they whom God hath, before the foundation of the world, chosen to be holy, are in time, through the powerful operation of His Spirit[1] applying the death and resurrection of Christ unto them,[2] renewed in their whole man after the image of God;[3] having the seeds of repentance unto life, and all other saving graces, put into their hearts,[4] and those graces so stirred up, increased, and strengthened,[5] as that they more and more die unto sin, and rise unto newness of life.[6]

1 **Ezek. 36:27:** I will put My Spirit within you and cause you to walk in My statutes, and you will keep My judgments and do *them.* **Phil. 2:13:** ... for it is God who works in you both to will and to do for *His* good pleasure. **2 Thess. 2:13:** But we are bound to give thanks to God always for you, brethren beloved by the Lord, because God from the beginning chose you for salvation through sanctification by the Spirit and belief in the truth. **Eph. 1:4:** ... just as He chose us in Him before the foundation of the world, that we should be holy and without blame before Him in love. **1 Cor. 6:11:** And such were some of you. But you were washed, but you were sanctified, but you were justified in the name of the Lord Jesus and by the Spirit of our God.

2
Rom. 6:4-6: Therefore we were buried with Him through baptism into death, that just as Christ was raised from the dead by the glory of the Father, even so we also should walk in newness of life. For if we have been united together in the likeness of His death, certainly we also shall be *in the likeness* of *His* resurrection, knowing this, that our old man was crucified with *Him,* that the body of sin might be done away with, that we should no longer be slaves of sin. **Col. 3:1-3:** ... If then you were raised with Christ, seek those things which are above, where Christ is, sitting at the right hand of God. Set your mind on things above, not on things on the earth. For you died, and your life is hidden with Christ in God. **Phil. 3:10:** ... that I may know Him and the power of His resurrection, and the fellowship of His sufferings, being conformed to His death.
3
2 Cor. 5:17: Therefore, if anyone *is* in Christ, *he is* a new creation; old things have passed away; behold, all things have become new. **Eph. 4:23-24:** ... and be renewed in the spirit of your mind, and that you put on the new man which was created according to God, in true righteousness and holiness. **1 Thess. 5:23:** Now may the God of peace Himself sanctify you completely; and may your whole spirit, soul, and body be preserved blameless at the coming of our Lord Jesus Christ.
4
Acts 11:18: When they heard these things they became silent; and they glorified God, saying, "Then God has also granted to the Gentiles repentance to life." **1 John 3:9:** Whoever has been born of God does not sin, for His seed remains in him; and he cannot sin, because he has been born of God.
5
Jude 20: But you, beloved, building yourselves up on your most holy faith, praying in the Holy Spirit. **Heb. 6:11-12:** And we desire that each one of you show the same diligence to the full assurance of hope until the end, that you do not become sluggish, but imitate those who through faith and patience inherit the promises. **Eph. 3:16-19:** ... that He would grant you, according to the riches of His glory, to be strengthened with might through His Spirit in the inner man, that Christ may dwell in your hearts through faith; that you, being rooted and grounded in love, may be able to comprehend with all the saints what *is* the width and length and depth and height— to know the love of Christ which passes knowledge; that you may be filled with all the fullness of God. **Col. 1:10-11:** ... that you may walk worthy of the Lord, fully pleasing *Him,* being fruitful in every good work and increasing in the knowledge of God; strengthened with all might, according to His glorious power, for all patience and longsuffering with joy.
6
Ezek. 36:25-27: Then I will sprinkle clean water on you, and you shall be clean; I will cleanse you from all your filthiness and from all your idols. I will give you a new heart and put a new spirit within you; I will take the heart of stone out of your flesh and give you a heart of flesh. I will put My Spirit within you and cause you to walk in My statutes, and you will keep My judgments and do *them.* **Rom. 6:4, 6, 12-14:** Therefore we were buried with Him through baptism into death, that just as Christ was raised from the dead by the glory of the Father, even so we also should walk in newness of life.... knowing this, that our old man was crucified with *Him,* that the body of sin might be done away with, that we should no longer be slaves of sin.... Therefore do not let sin reign in your mortal body, that you should obey it in its lusts. And do not present your members *as* instruments of unrighteousness to sin, but present yourselves to God as being alive from the dead, and your members *as* instruments of righteousness to God. For sin shall not have dominion over you, for you are not under law but under grace. **2 Cor. 7:1:** Therefore, having these promises, beloved, let us cleanse ourselves from all filthiness of the flesh and spirit, perfecting holiness in the fear of God. **1 Pet. 2:24:** ... who Himself bore our sins in His own body on the tree, that we, having died to sins, might live for righteousness—by whose stripes you were healed. **Gal. 5:24:** And those *who are* Christ's have crucified the flesh with its passions and desires.

Q. 97. *What is repentance unto life?*

A. Repentance unto life is a saving grace,[1] wrought in the heart of a sinner by the Spirit[2] and word of God,[3] whereby, out of the sight and sense, not only of the danger,[4] but also of the filthiness and odiousness of his sins,[5] and upon the apprehension of God's mercy in Christ to such as are penitent,[6] he so grieves for[7] and hates his sins,[8] as that he turns from them all to God,[9] purposing and endeavoring constantly to walk with Him in all the ways of new obedience.[10]

1
2 Tim. 2:25: ... in humility correcting those who are in opposition, if God perhaps will grant them repentance, so that they may know the truth. **Acts 11:18:** When they heard these things they became silent; and they glorified God, saying, "Then God has also granted to the Gentiles repentance to life."
2
Zech. 12:10: And I will pour on the house of David and on the inhabitants of Jerusalem the Spirit of grace and supplication; then they will look on Me whom they pierced. Yes, they will mourn for Him as one mourns for *his* only *son,* and grieve for Him as one grieves for a firstborn.
3
Acts 11:18, 20-21: When they heard these things they became silent; and they glorified God, saying, "Then God has also granted to the Gentiles repentance to life." ... But some of them were men from Cyprus and Cyrene, who, when they had come to Antioch, spoke to the Hellenists, preaching the Lord Jesus. And the hand of the Lord was with them, and a great number believed and turned to the Lord.
4
Ezek. 18:28, 30, 32: Because he considers and turns away from all the transgressions which he committed, he shall surely live; he shall not die.... "Therefore I will judge you, O house of Israel, every one according to his ways," says the Lord God. "Repent, and turn from all your transgressions, so that iniquity will not be your ruin.... For I have no pleasure in the death of one who dies," says the Lord God. "Therefore turn and live!" **Luke 15:17-18:** But when he came to himself, he said, 'How many of my father's hired servants have bread enough and to spare, and I perish with hunger! I will arise and go to my father, and will say to him, "Father, I have sinned against heaven and before you." **Hos. 2:6-7:** Therefore, behold, I will hedge up your way with thorns, And wall her in, So that she cannot find her paths. She will chase her lovers, But not overtake them; Yes, she will seek them, but not find *them.* Then she will say, 'I will go and return to my first husband, For then *it was* better for me than now.'
5
Ezek. 36:31: Then you will remember your evil ways and your deeds that *were* not good; and you will loathe yourselves in your own sight, for your iniquities and your abominations. **Isa. 30:22:** You will also defile the covering of your images of silver, And the ornament of your molded images of gold. You will throw them away as an unclean thing; You will say to them, "Get away!" **Phil. 3:7-8:** But what things were gain to me, these I have counted loss for Christ. Yet indeed I also count all things loss for the excellence of the knowledge of Christ Jesus my Lord, for whom I have suffered the loss of all things, and count them as rubbish, that I may gain Christ.
6
Joel 2:12-13: "Now, therefore," says the LORD, "Turn to Me with all your heart, With fasting, with weeping, and with mourning." So rend your heart, and not your garments; Return to the LORD your God, For He *is* gracious and merciful, Slow to anger, and of great kindness; And He relents from doing harm. **Ps. 51:1-4:** Have mercy upon me, O God, According to Your lovingkindness; According to the multitude of Your tender mercies, Blot out my transgressions. Wash me thoroughly from my iniquity, And cleanse me from my sin. For I acknowledge my transgressions, And my sin *is* always before me. Against You, You only, have I sinned, And done *this* evil in Your sight—That You may be found just when You speak, *And* blameless when You judge. **Luke 15:7, 10:** I say to you that likewise there will be more joy in heaven over one sinner who repents than over ninety-nine just persons who need no repentance.... Likewise, I say to you, there is joy in the presence of the angels of God over one sinner who repents. **Acts 2:37:** Now when they heard *this,* they were cut to the heart, and said to Peter and the rest of the apostles, "Men *and* brethren, what shall we do?"
7
Jer. 31:18-19: I have surely heard Ephraim bemoaning himself: 'You have chastised me, and I was chastised, Like an untrained bull; Restore me, and I will return, For You *are* the LORD my God. Surely, after my turning, I repented; And after I was instructed, I struck myself on the thigh; I was ashamed, yes, even humiliated, Because I bore the reproach of my youth.' **Ps. 32:5:** I acknowledged my sin to You, And my iniquity I have not hidden. I said, "I will confess my transgressions to the LORD," And You forgave the iniquity of my sin. *Selah.*
8
2 Cor. 7:11: For observe this very thing, that you sorrowed in a godly manner: What diligence it produced in you, *what clearing of yourselves, what* indignation, *what* fear, *what* vehement desire, *what* zeal, *what* vindication! In all *things* you proved yourselves to be clear in this matter.
9
Luke 1:16-17: And he will turn many of the children of Israel to the Lord their God. He will also go before Him in the spirit and power of Elijah, 'to turn the hearts of the fathers to the children,' and the disobedient to the wisdom of the just, to make ready a people prepared for the Lord. **1 Thess. 1:9:** For they themselves declare concerning us what manner of entry we had to you, and how you turned to God from idols to serve the living and true God. **Acts 26:18:** ... to open their eyes, *in order* to turn *them* from darkness to light, and *from* the power of Satan to God, that they may receive forgiveness of sins and an inheritance among those who are sanctified by faith in Me. **Ezek. 14:6:** Therefore say to the house of Israel, 'Thus says the Lord GOD: "Repent, turn away from your idols, and turn your faces away from all your abominations." **1 Kings 8:47-48:** ... *yet* when they come to themselves in the land where they were carried captive, and repent, and make supplication to You in the land of those who took them captive, saying, 'We have sinned and done wrong, we have committed wickedness'; and *when* they return to You with all their heart and with all their soul

in the land of their enemies who led them away captive, and pray to You toward their land which You gave to their fathers, the city which You have chosen and the temple which I have built for Your name.

10 **2 Chron. 7:14:** … if My people who are called by My name will humble themselves, and pray and seek My face, and turn from their wicked ways, then I will hear from heaven, and will forgive their sin and heal their land. **Ps. 119:57-64:** *You are* my portion, O LORD; I have said that I would keep Your words. I entreated Your favor with *my* whole heart; Be merciful to me according to Your word. I thought about my ways, And turned my feet to Your testimonies. I made haste, and did not delay To keep Your commandments. The cords of the wicked have bound me, *But* I have not forgotten Your law. At midnight I will rise to give thanks to You, Because of Your righteous judgments. I *am* a companion of all who fear You, And of those who keep Your precepts. The earth, O LORD, is full of Your mercy; Teach me Your statutes. **Matt. 3:8:** Therefore bear fruits worthy of repentance. **2 Cor. 7:10:** For godly sorrow produces repentance *leading* to salvation, not to be regretted; but the sorrow of the world produces death. **Luke 1:6:** And they were both righteous before God, walking in all the commandments and ordinances of the Lord blameless.

Q. 98. *Wherein do justification and sanctification differ?*

A. Although sanctification be inseparably joined with justification,[1] yet they differ, in that God in justification imputeth the righteousness of Christ;[2] in sanctification His Spirit infuseth grace, and enableth to the exercise thereof;[3] in the former, sin is pardoned;[4] in the other, it is subdued:[5] the one doth equally free all believers from the revenging wrath of God, and that perfectly in this life, that they never fall into condemnation;[6] the other is neither equal in all,[7] nor in this life perfect in any,[8] but growing up to perfection.[9]

1 **1 Cor. 6:11:** And such were some of you. But you were washed, but you were sanctified, but you were justified in the name of the Lord Jesus and by the Spirit of our God. **1 Cor. 1:30:** But of Him you are in Christ Jesus, who became for us wisdom from God—and righteousness and sanctification and redemption.

2 **Rom. 4:6, 8:** … just as David also describes the blessedness of the man to whom God imputes righteousness apart from works.… Blessed *is the* man to whom the LORD shall not impute sin.

3 **Ezek. 36:27:** I will put My Spirit within you and cause you to walk in My statutes, and you will keep My judgments and do *them.* **Heb. 9:13-14:** For if the blood of bulls and goats and the ashes of a heifer, sprinkling the unclean, sanctifies for the purifying of the flesh, how much more shall the blood of Christ, who through the eternal Spirit offered Himself without spot to God, cleanse your conscience from dead works to serve the living God?

4 **Rom. 3:24-25:** … being justified freely by His grace through the redemption that is in Christ Jesus, whom God set forth *as* a propitiation by His blood, through faith, to demonstrate His righteousness, because in His forbearance God had passed over the sins that were previously committed.

5 **Rom. 6:6, 14:** … knowing this, that our old man was crucified with *Him,* that the body of sin might be done away with, that we should no longer be slaves of sin.… For sin shall not have dominion over you, for you are not under law but under grace.

6 **Rom. 8:33-34:** Who shall bring a charge against God's elect? *It is* God who justifies. Who *is* he who condemns? *It is* Christ who died, and furthermore is also risen, who is even at the right hand of God, who also makes intercession for us.

7 **1 John 2:12-14:** I write to you, little children, Because your sins are forgiven you for His name's sake. I write to you, fathers, Because you have known Him *who is* from the beginning. I write to you, young men, Because you have overcome the wicked one. I write to you, little children, Because you have known the Father. I have written to you, fathers, Because you have known Him *who is* from the beginning. I have written to you, young men, Because you are strong, and the word of God abides in you, And you have overcome the wicked one. **Heb. 5:12-14:** For though by this time you

ought to be teachers, you need *someone* to teach you again the first principles of the oracles of God; and you have come to need milk and not solid food. For everyone who partakes *only* of milk *is* unskilled in the word of righteousness, for he is a babe. But solid food belongs to those who are of full age, *that is,* those who by reason of use have their senses exercised to discern both good and evil.

8 **1 John 1:8, 10:** If we say that we have no sin, we deceive ourselves, and the truth is not in us.... If we say that we have not sinned, we make Him a liar, and His word is not in us.

9 **2 Cor. 7:1:** Therefore, having these promises, beloved, let us cleanse ourselves from all filthiness of the flesh and spirit, perfecting holiness in the fear of God.... **Phil. 3:12-14:** Not that I have already attained, or am already perfected; but I press on, that I may lay hold of that for which Christ Jesus has also laid hold of me. Brethren, I do not count myself to have apprehended; but one thing *I do,* forgetting those things which are behind and reaching forward to those things which are ahead, I press toward the goal for the prize of the upward call of God in Christ Jesus.

Q. 99. *Whence ariseth the imperfection of sanctification in believers?*

A. The imperfection of sanctification in believers ariseth from the remnants of sin abiding in every part of them, and the perpetual lustings of the flesh against the Spirit; whereby they are often foiled with temptations, and fall into many sins,[1] are hindered in all their spiritual services,[2] and their best works are imperfect and defiled in the sight of God.[3]

1 **Rom. 7:18, 23:** For I know that in me (that is, in my flesh) nothing good dwells; for to will is present with me, but *how* to perform what is good I do not find.... But I see another law in my members, warring against the law of my mind, and bringing me into captivity to the law of sin which is in my members. **See Mark 14:66-72. Gal. 2:11-12:** Now when Peter had come to Antioch, I withstood him to his face, because he was to be blamed; for before certain men came from James, he would eat with the Gentiles; but when they came, he withdrew and separated himself, fearing those who were of the circumcision.

2 **Heb. 12:1:** Therefore we also, since we are surrounded by so great a cloud of witnesses, let us lay aside every weight, and the sin which so easily ensnares *us,* and let us run with endurance the race that is set before us.

3 **Isa. 64:6:** But we are all like an unclean *thing,* And all our righteousnesses *are* like filthy rags; We all fade as a leaf, And our iniquities, like the wind, Have taken us away. **Ex. 28:38:** So it shall be on Aaron's forehead, that Aaron may bear the iniquity of the holy things which the children of Israel hallow in all their holy gifts; and it shall always be on his forehead, that they may be accepted before the LORD. **Gal. 5:16-18:** I say then: Walk in the Spirit, and you shall not fulfill the lust of the flesh. For the flesh lusts against the Spirit, and the Spirit against the flesh; and these are contrary to one another, so that you do not do the things that you wish. But if you are led by the Spirit, you are not under the law.

Q. 100. *May not true believers, by reason of their imperfections, and the many temptations and sins they are overtaken with, fall away from the state of grace?*

A. True believers, by reason of the unchangeable love of God,[1] and His decree and covenant to give them perseverance,[2] their inseparable union with Christ,[3] His continual intercession for them,[4] and the Spirit and seed of God abiding in them,[5] can neither totally nor finally fall away from the state of grace,[6] but are kept by the power of God through faith unto salvation.[7]

[1] **Jer. 31:3:** The LORD has appeared of old to me, *saying:* "Yes, I have loved you with an everlasting love; Therefore with lovingkindness I have drawn you."

[2] **2 Tim. 2:19:** Nevertheless the solid foundation of God stands, having this seal: "The Lord knows those who are His," and, "Let everyone who names the name of Christ depart from iniquity." **Heb. 13:20-21:** Now may the God of peace who brought up our Lord Jesus from the dead, that great Shepherd of the sheep, through the blood of the everlasting covenant, make you complete in every good work to do His will, working in you what is well pleasing in His sight, through Jesus Christ, to whom *be* glory forever and ever. Amen. **2 Sam. 23:5:** "Although my house *is* not so with God, Yet He has made with me an everlasting covenant, Ordered in all *things* and secure. For *this is* all my salvation and all *my* desire; Will He not make *it* increase?"

[3] **1 Cor. 1:8-9:** ... who will also confirm you to the end, *that you may be* blameless in the day of our Lord Jesus Christ. God *is* faithful, by whom you were called into the fellowship of His Son, Jesus Christ our Lord.

[4] **Heb. 7:25:** Therefore He is also able to save to the uttermost those who come to God through Him, since He always lives to make intercession for them. **Luke 22:32:** But I have prayed for you, that your faith should not fail; and when you have returned to *Me,* strengthen your brethren.

[5] **1 John 3:9:** Whoever has been born of God does not sin, for His seed remains in him; and he cannot sin, because he has been born of God. **1 John 2:27:** But the anointing which you have received from Him abides in you, and you do not need that anyone teach you; but as the same anointing teaches you concerning all things, and is true, and is not a lie, and just as it has taught you, you will abide in Him.

[6] **Jer. 32:40:** And I will make an everlasting covenant with them, that I will not turn away from doing them good; but I will put My fear in their hearts so that they will not depart from Me. **John 10:28:** And I give them eternal life, and they shall never perish; neither shall anyone snatch them out of My hand.

[7] **1 Pet. 1:5:** ... who are kept by the power of God through faith for salvation ready to be revealed in the last time.

Q. 101. *Can true believers be infallibly assured that they are in the estate of grace, and that they shall persevere therein unto salvation?*

A. Such as truly believe in Christ, and endeavor to walk in all good conscience before Him,[1] may, without extraordinary revelation, by faith grounded upon the truth of God's promises, and by the Spirit enabling them to discern in themselves those graces to which the promises of life are made,[2] and bearing witness with their spirits that they are the children of God,[3] be infallibly assured that they are in the estate of grace, and shall persevere therein unto salvation.[4]

[1] **1 John 2:3:** Now by this we know that we know Him, if we keep His commandments. **Heb. 10:19-23:** Therefore, brethren, having boldness to enter the Holiest by the blood of Jesus, by a new and living way which He consecrated for us, through the veil, that is, His flesh, and *having* a High Priest over the house of God, let us draw near with a true heart in full assurance of faith, having our hearts sprinkled from an evil conscience and our bodies washed with pure water. Let us hold fast the confession of *our* hope without wavering, for He who promised *is* faithful.

[2] **1 Cor. 2:12:** Now we have received, not the spirit of the world, but the Spirit who is from God, that we might know the things that have been freely given to us by God. **1 John 3:14, 18-19, 21,**

24: We know that we have passed from death to life, because we love the brethren. He who does not love *his* brother abides in death.... My little children, let us not love in word or in tongue, but in deed and in truth. And by this we know that we are of the truth, and shall assure our hearts before Him.... Beloved, if our heart does not condemn us, we have confidence toward God.... Now he who keeps His commandments abides in Him, and He in him. And by this we know that He abides in us, by the Spirit whom He has given us. **1 John. 4:13, 16:** By this we know that we abide in Him, and He in us, because He has given us of His Spirit.... And we have known and believed the love that God has for us. God is love, and he who abides in love abides in God, and God in him. **Heb. 6:11-12:** And we desire that each one of you show the same diligence to the full assurance of hope until the end, that you do not become sluggish, but imitate those who through faith and patience inherit the promises.

3

Rom. 8:15-16: For you did not receive the spirit of bondage again to fear, but you received the Spirit of adoption by whom we cry out, "Abba, Father." The Spirit Himself bears witness with our spirit that we are children of God.

4

1 John 5:13: These things I have written to you who believe in the name of the Son of God, that you may know that you have eternal life, and that you may *continue to* believe in the name of the Son of God. **Heb. 6:19-20:** This *hope* we have as an anchor of the soul, both sure and steadfast, and which enters the *Presence* behind the veil, where the forerunner has entered for us, *even* Jesus, having become High Priest forever according to the order of Melchizedek. **2 Pet. 1:5-11:** But also for this very reason, giving all diligence, add to your faith virtue, to virtue knowledge, to knowledge self-control, to self-control perseverance, to perseverance godliness, to godliness brotherly kindness, and to brotherly kindness love. For if these things are yours and abound, *you* will be neither barren nor unfruitful in the knowledge of our Lord Jesus Christ. For he who lacks these things is shortsighted, even to blindness, and has forgotten that he was cleansed from his old sins. Therefore, brethren, be even more diligent to make your call and election sure, for if you do these things you will never stumble; for so an entrance will be supplied to you abundantly into the everlasting kingdom of our Lord and Savior Jesus Christ.

Q. 102. *Are all true believers at all times assured of their present being in the estate of grace, and that they shall be saved?*

A. Assurance of grace and salvation not being of the essence of faith,[1] true believers may wait long before they obtain it;[2] and, after the enjoyment thereof, may have it weakened and intermitted, through manifold distempers, sins, temptations, and desertions;[3] yet are they never left without such a presence and support of the Spirit of God as keeps them from sinking into utter despair.[4]

1

Eph. 1:13: In Him you also *trusted,* after you heard the word of truth, the gospel of your salvation; in whom also, having believed, you were sealed with the Holy Spirit of promise.

2

Isa. 50:10: Who among you fears the LORD? Who obeys the voice of His Servant? Who walks in darkness And has no light? Let him trust in the name of the LORD And rely upon his God. **Ps. 88:1-3, 6-7, 9-10, 13-15:** O LORD, God of my salvation, I have cried out day and night before You. Let my prayer come before You; Incline Your ear to my cry. For my soul is full of troubles, And my life draws near to the grave.... You have laid me in the lowest pit, In darkness, in the depths. Your wrath lies heavy upon me, And You have afflicted *me* with all Your waves.... My eye wastes away because of affliction. LORD, I have called daily upon You; I have stretched out my hands to You. Will You work wonders for the dead? Shall the dead arise *and* praise You? ... But to You I have cried out, O LORD, And in the morning my prayer comes before You. LORD, why do You cast off my soul? *Why* do You hide Your face from me? I *have been* afflicted and ready to die from *my* youth; I suffer Your terrors; I am distraught.

3

Ps. 77:1-12: I cried out to God with my voice—To God with my voice; And He gave ear to me. In the day of my trouble I sought the Lord.... Will the Lord cast off forever? And will He be favorable no more? Has His mercy ceased forever? Has *His* promise failed forevermore? Has God forgotten to be gracious? Has He in anger shut up His tender mercies? *Selah*. And I said, "This *is* my anguish; *But I will remember* the years of the right hand of the Most High." I will remember the works of the LORD;

Surely I will remember Your wonders of old. I will also meditate on all Your work, And talk of Your deeds. **Ps. 51:8, 12:** Make me hear joy and gladness, *That* the bones You have broken may rejoice.... Restore to me the joy of Your salvation, And uphold me *by Your* generous Spirit. **Ps. 31:22:** For I said in my haste, "I am cut off from before Your eyes"; Nevertheless You heard the voice of my supplications When I cried out to You. **Ps. 22:1:** My God, My God, why have You forsaken Me? *Why are You so* far from helping Me, *And from* the words of My groaning? **Eph. 4:30:** And do not grieve the Holy Spirit of God, by whom you were sealed for the day of redemption. **Luke 22:31-34:** And the Lord said, "Simon, Simon! Indeed, Satan has asked for you, that he may sift *you* as wheat. But I have prayed for you, that your faith should not fail; and when you have returned to *Me,* strengthen your brethren." But he said to Him, "Lord, I am ready to go with You, both to prison and to death." Then He said, "I tell you, Peter, the rooster shall not crow this day before you will deny three times that you know Me."

[4] **1 John 3:9:** Whoever has been born of God does not sin, for His seed remains in him; and he cannot sin, because he has been born of God. **Ps. 73:15, 23:** If I had said, "I will speak thus," Behold, I would have been untrue to the generation of Your children.... Nevertheless I *am* continually with You; You hold *me* by my right hand. **Isa. 54:7-10:** "For a mere moment I have forsaken you, But with great mercies I will gather you. With a little wrath I hid My face from you for a moment; But with everlasting kindness I will have mercy on you," Says the LORD, your Redeemer. "For this *is* like the waters of Noah to Me; For as I have sworn That the waters of Noah would no longer cover the earth, So have I sworn That I would not be angry with you, nor rebuke you. For the mountains shall depart And the hills be removed, But My kindness shall not depart from you, Nor shall My covenant of peace be removed," Says the LORD, who has mercy on you. **1 Pet. 4:12-14:** Beloved, do not think it strange concerning the fiery trial which is to try you, as though some strange thing happened to you; but rejoice to the extent that you partake of Christ's sufferings, that when His glory is revealed, you may also be glad with exceeding joy. If you are reproached for the name of Christ, blessed *are you,* for the Spirit of glory and of God rests upon you. On their part He is blasphemed, but on your part He is glorified.

Q. 103. *What is the communion in glory which the members of the invisible church have with Christ?*

A. The communion in glory which the members of the invisible church have with Christ, is in this life,[1] immediately after death,[2] and at last perfected at the resurrection and day of judgment.[3]

[1] **2 Cor. 3:18:** But we all, with unveiled face, beholding as in a mirror the glory of the Lord, are being transformed into the same image from glory to glory, just as by the Spirit of the Lord.

[2] **Luke 23:43:** And Jesus said to him, "Assuredly, I say to you, today you will be with Me in Paradise."

[3] **1 Thess. 4:17:** Then we who are alive and remain shall be caught up together with them in the clouds to meet the Lord in the air. And thus we shall always be with the Lord.

Q. 104. *What is the communion in glory with Christ which the members of the invisible church enjoy in this life?*

A. The members of the invisible church have communicated to them in this life the firstfruits of glory with Christ, as they are members of Him their Head, and so in Him are interested in that glory which He is fully possessed of;[1] and, as an earnest thereof, enjoy the sense of God's love,[2] peace of conscience, joy in the Holy Spirit, and hope of glory;[3] as, on the contrary, sense of God's revenging wrath, horror of conscience, and a fearful expectation of judgment, are to the wicked the beginning of their torments which they shall endure after death.[4]

1 **Eph. 2:5-6:** ... even when we were dead in trespasses, made us alive together with Christ (by grace you have been saved), and raised *us* up together, and made *us* sit together in the heavenly *places* in Christ Jesus.

2 **Rom. 5:5:** Now hope does not disappoint, because the love of God has been poured out in our hearts by the Holy Spirit who was given to us. **2 Cor. 1:22:** ... who also has sealed us and given us the Spirit in our hearts as a guarantee.

3 **Rom. 5:1-2:** Therefore, having been justified by faith, we have peace with God through our Lord Jesus Christ, through whom also we have access by faith into this grace in which we stand, and rejoice in hope of the glory of God. **Rom. 14:17:** ... for the kingdom of God is not eating and drinking, but righteousness and peace and joy in the Holy Spirit. **2 Pet. 3:18:** ... but grow in the grace and knowledge of our Lord and Savior Jesus Christ. To Him *be* the glory both now and forever. Amen.

4 **Gen. 4:13:** And Cain said to the LORD, "My punishment *is* greater than I can bear! **Matt. 27:4:** ... saying, "I have sinned by betraying innocent blood." And they said, "What *is that* to us? You see *to it!*" **Heb. 10:27:** ... but a certain fearful expectation of judgment, and fiery indignation which will devour the adversaries. **Rom. 2:9:** ... tribulation and anguish, on every soul of man who does evil, of the Jew first and also of the Greek. **Mark 9:44:** ... where 'Their worm does not die And the fire is not quenched.'

Q. 105. *Shall all men die?*

A. Death being threatened as the wages of sin,[1] it is appointed unto all men once to die;[2] for that all have sinned.[3]

1 **Rom. 6:23:** For the wages of sin *is* death, but the gift of God *is* eternal life in Christ Jesus our Lord.

2 **Heb. 9:27:** And as it is appointed for men to die once, but after this the judgment.

3 **Rom. 5:12:** Therefore, just as through one man sin entered the world, and death through sin, and thus death spread to all men, because all sinned.

Q. 106. *Death, being the wages of sin, why are not the righteous delivered from death, seeing all their sins are forgiven in Christ?*

A. The righteous shall be delivered from death itself at the last day, and even in death are delivered from the sting and curse of it;[1] so that, although they die, yet it is out of God's love,[2] to free them perfectly from sin and misery,[3] and to make them capable of further communion with Christ in glory, which they then enter upon.[4]

1 **1 Cor. 15:26, 55-57:** The last enemy *that* will be destroyed *is* death.... "O Death, where *is* your sting? O Hades, where *is* your victory?" The sting of death *is* sin, and the strength of sin *is* the law. But thanks *be* to God, who gives us the victory through our Lord Jesus Christ. **Heb. 2:15:** ... and release those who through fear of death were all their lifetime subject to bondage. **John 11:25-26:** Jesus said to her, "I am the resurrection and the life. He who believes in Me, though he may die, he shall live. And whoever lives and believes in Me shall never die. Do you believe this?"

2 **Isa. 57:1-2:** The righteous perishes, And no man takes *it* to heart; Merciful men *are* taken away, While no one considers That the righteous is taken away from evil. He shall enter into peace; They shall rest in their beds, *Each one* walking *in* his uprightness. **2 Kings 22:20:** "Surely, therefore, I

will gather you to your fathers, and you shall be gathered to your grave in peace; and your eyes shall not see all the calamity which I will bring on this place." So they brought back word to the king.

3

Rev. 14:13: Then I heard a voice from heaven saying to me, "Write: 'Blessed *are* the dead who die in the Lord from now on.'" "Yes," says the Spirit, "that they may rest from their labors, and their works follow them." **Eph. 5:27:** ... that He might present her to Himself a glorious church, not having spot or wrinkle or any such thing, but that she should be holy and without blemish.

4

Luke 23:43: And Jesus said to him, "Assuredly, I say to you, today you will be with Me in Paradise." **Phil. 1:23:** For I am hard-pressed between the two, having a desire to depart and be with Christ, *which is* far better.

Q. 107. *What is the communion in glory with Christ, which the members of the invisible church enjoy immediately after death?*

A. The communion in glory with Christ, which the members of the invisible church enjoy immediately after death, is, in that their souls are then made perfect in holiness,[1] and received into the highest heavens,[2] where they behold the face of God in light and glory,[3] waiting for the full redemption of their bodies,[4] which even in death continue united to Christ,[5] and rest in their graves as in their beds,[6] till at the last day they be again united to their souls.[7] Whereas the souls of the wicked are at their death cast into hell, where they remain in torments and utter darkness, and their bodies kept in their graves, as in their prisons, till the resurrection and judgment of the great day.[8]

1

Heb. 12:23: ... to the general assembly and church of the firstborn *who are* registered in heaven, to God the Judge of all, to the spirits of just men made perfect. **Acts 7:55, 59:** But he, being full of the Holy Spirit, gazed into heaven and saw the glory of God, and Jesus standing at the right hand of God.... And they stoned Stephen as he was calling on *God* and saying, "Lord Jesus, receive my spirit."

2

2 Cor. 5:1, 6, 8: For we know that if our earthly house, *this* tent, is destroyed, we have a building from God, a house not made with hands, eternal in the heavens.... So *we are* always confident, knowing that while we are at home in the body we are absent from the Lord.... We are confident, yes, well pleased rather to be absent from the body and to be present with the Lord. **Phil. 1:23:** For I am hard-pressed between the two, having a desire to depart and be with Christ, *which is* far better. **Acts 3:21:** ... whom heaven must receive until the times of restoration of all things, which God has spoken by the mouth of all His holy prophets since the world began. **Eph. 4:10:** He who descended is also the One who ascended far above all the heavens, that He might fill all things. **Luke 23:43:** And Jesus said to him, "Assuredly, I say to you, today you will be with Me in Paradise."

3

1 John 3:2: Beloved, now we are children of God; and it has not yet been revealed what we shall be, but we know that when He is revealed, we shall be like Him, for we shall see Him as He is. **1 Cor. 13:12:** For now we see in a mirror, dimly, but then face to face. Now I know in part, but then I shall know just as I also am known.

4

Rom. 8:23: Not only *that,* but we also who have the firstfruits of the Spirit, even we ourselves groan within ourselves, eagerly waiting for the adoption, the redemption of our body. **Ps. 16:9:** Therefore my heart is glad, and my glory rejoices; My flesh also will rest in hope.

5

1 Thess. 4:14, 16: For if we believe that Jesus died and rose again, even so God will bring with Him those who sleep in Jesus.... For the Lord Himself will descend from heaven with a shout, with the voice of an archangel, and with the trumpet of God. And the dead in Christ will rise first.

6
Isa. 57:2: He shall enter into peace; They shall rest in their beds, *Each one* walking *in* his uprightness.
7
Job 19:26-27: And after my skin is destroyed, this *I know,* That in my flesh I shall see God, Whom I shall see for myself, And my eyes shall behold, and not another. *How* my heart yearns within me!
8
Luke 16:23-24: And being in torments in Hades, he lifted up his eyes and saw Abraham afar off, and Lazarus in his bosom. "Then he cried and said, 'Father Abraham, have mercy on me, and send Lazarus that he may dip the tip of his finger in water and cool my tongue; for I am tormented in this flame.'" **Acts 1:25:** ... to take part in this ministry and apostleship from which Judas by transgression fell, that he might go to his own place. **Jude 6-7:** And the angels who did not keep their proper domain, but left their own abode, He has reserved in everlasting chains under darkness for the judgment of the great day; as Sodom and Gomorrah, and the cities around them in a similar manner to these, having given themselves over to sexual immorality and gone after strange flesh, are set forth as an example, suffering the vengeance of eternal fire.

Q. 108. *What are we to believe concerning the resurrection?*

A. We are to believe, that at the last day there shall be a general resurrection of the dead, both of the just and unjust:[1] when they that are then found alive shall in a moment be changed; and the selfsame bodies of the dead which were laid in the grave, being then again united to their souls forever, shall be raised up by the power of Christ.[2] The bodies of the just, by the Spirit of Christ, and by virtue of His resurrection as their Head, shall be raised in power, spiritual, incorruptible, and made like to His glorious body;[3] and the bodies of the wicked shall be raised up in dishonour by Him, as an offended judge.[4]

1
Dan. 12:2: And many of those who sleep in the dust of the earth shall awake, Some to everlasting life, Some to shame *and* everlasting contempt. **Acts 24:15:** I have hope in God, which they themselves also accept, that there will be a resurrection of *the* dead, both of *the* just and *the* unjust.
2
Job 19:26: And after my skin is destroyed, this *I know,* That in my flesh I shall see God. **1 Cor. 15:51-53:** Behold, I tell you a mystery: We shall not all sleep, but we shall all be changed— in a moment, in the twinkling of an eye, at the last trumpet. For the trumpet will sound, and the dead will be raised incorruptible, and we shall be changed. For this corruptible must put on incorruption, and this mortal *must* put on immortality. **1 Thess. 4:15-17:** For this we say to you by the word of the Lord, that we who are alive *and* remain until the coming of the Lord will by no means precede those who are asleep. For the Lord Himself will descend from heaven with a shout, with the voice of an archangel, and with the trumpet of God. And the dead in Christ will rise first. Then we who are alive *and* remain shall be caught up together with them in the clouds to meet the Lord in the air. And thus we shall always be with the Lord. **John 5:28-29:** Do not marvel at this; for the hour is coming in which all who are in the graves will hear His voice and come forth—those who have done good, to the resurrection of life, and those who have done evil, to the resurrection of condemnation. **Rom. 8:11:** But if the Spirit of Him who raised Jesus from the dead dwells in you, He who raised Christ from the dead will also give life to your mortal bodies through His Spirit who dwells in you.
3
1 Cor. 15:21-23, 42-44: For since by man *came* death, by Man also *came* the resurrection of the dead. For as in Adam all die, even so in Christ all shall be made alive. But each one in his own order: Christ the firstfruits, afterward those *who are* Christ's at His coming.... So also *is* the resurrection of the dead. *The body* is sown in corruption, it is raised in incorruption. It is sown in dishonor, it is raised in glory. It is sown in weakness, it is raised in power. It is sown a natural body, it is raised a spiritual body. There is a natural body, and there is a spiritual body. **Phil. 3:21:** ... who will transform our lowly body that it may be conformed to His glorious body, according to the working by which He is able even to subdue all things to Himself.
4
John 5:27-29: ... and has given Him authority to execute judgment also, because He is the Son of Man. Do not marvel at this; for the hour is coming in which all who are in the graves will hear His

voice and come forth—those who have done good, to the resurrection of life, and those who have done evil, to the resurrection of condemnation. **Matt. 25:33:** And He will set the sheep on His right hand, but the goats on the left.

Q. 109. *What shall immediately follow after the resurrection?*

A. Immediately after the resurrection shall follow the general and final judgment of angels and men;[1] the day and hour whereof no man knoweth, that all may watch and pray, and be ever ready for the coming of the Lord.[2]

1 **Eccl. 12:14:** For God will bring every work into judgment, Including every secret thing, Whether good or evil. **2 Pet. 2:4, 6-7, 14-15:** For if God did not spare the angels who sinned, but cast *them* down to hell and delivered *them* into chains of darkness, to be reserved for judgment.... and turning the cities of Sodom and Gomorrah into ashes, condemned *them* to destruction, making *them* an example to those who afterward would live ungodly; and delivered righteous Lot, *who was* oppressed by the filthy conduct of the wicked ... having eyes full of adultery and that cannot cease from sin, enticing unstable souls. They have a heart trained in covetous practices, *and are* accursed children. They have forsaken the right way and gone astray, following the way of Balaam the *son* of Beor, who loved the wages of unrighteousness. **Matt. 25:46:** And these will go away into everlasting punishment, but the righteous into eternal life. **2 Cor. 5:10:** For we must all appear before the judgment seat of Christ, that each one may receive the things *done* in the body, according to what he has done, whether good or bad. **Rom. 14:10, 12:** But why do you judge your brother? Or why do you show contempt for your brother? For we shall all stand before the judgment seat of Christ.... So then each of us shall give account of himself to God.

2 **Matt. 24:36, 42, 44:** But of that day and hour no one knows, not even the angels of heaven, but My Father only.... Watch therefore, for you do not know what hour your Lord is coming.... Therefore you also be ready, for the Son of Man is coming at an hour you do not expect. **Mark 13:35-37:** Watch therefore, for you do not know when the master of the house is coming—in the evening, at midnight, at the crowing of the rooster, or in the morning— lest, coming suddenly, he find you sleeping. And what I say to you, I say to all: Watch!

Q. 110. *What shall be done to the wicked at the day of judgment?*

A. At the day of judgment, the wicked shall be set on Christ's left hand,[1] and, upon clear evidence, and full conviction of their own consciences,[2] shall have the fearful but just sentence of condemnation pronounced against them;[3] and thereupon shall be cast out from the favorable presence of God, and the glorious fellowship with Christ, His saints, and all His holy angels, into hell, to be punished with unspeakable torments, both of body and soul, with the devil and his angels forever.[4]

1 **Matt. 25:33:** And He will set the sheep on His right hand, but the goats on the left.

2 **Rom. 2:15-16:** ... who show the work of the law written in their hearts, their conscience also bearing witness, and between themselves *their* thoughts accusing or else excusing *them*) in the day when God will judge the secrets of men by Jesus Christ, according to my gospel.

3 **Matt. 25:41-43:** Then He will also say to those on the left hand, 'Depart from Me, you cursed, into the everlasting fire prepared for the devil and his angels: for I was hungry and you gave Me no food; I was thirsty and you gave Me no drink; I was a stranger and you did not take Me in, naked and you did not clothe Me, sick and in prison and you did not visit Me.'

4 **Luke 16:26:** And besides all this, between us and you there is a great gulf fixed, so that those who want to pass from here to you cannot, nor can those from there pass to us. **2 Thess. 1:8-9:** ... in flaming fire taking vengeance on those who do not know God, and on those who do not obey the gospel of our Lord Jesus Christ. These shall be punished with everlasting destruction from the presence of the Lord and from the glory of His power.

Q. 111. *What shall be done to the righteous at the day of judgment?*

A. At the day of judgment, the righteous, being caught up to Christ in the clouds,[1] shall be set on His right hand, and there openly acknowledged and acquitted,[2] shall join with Him in the judging of reprobate angels and men,[3] and shall be received into heaven,[4] where they shall be fully and forever freed from all sin and misery;[5] filled with inconceivable joys,[6] made perfectly holy and happy both in body and soul, in the company of innumerable saints and holy angels,[7] but especially in the immediate vision and fruition of God the Father, of our Lord Jesus Christ, and of the Holy Spirit, to all eternity.[8] And this is the perfect and full communion, which the members of the invisible church shall enjoy with Christ in glory, at the resurrection and day of judgment.

1 **1 Thess. 4:17:** Then we who are alive *and* remain shall be caught up together with them in the clouds to meet the Lord in the air. And thus we shall always be with the Lord. **1 Cor. 15:42-43:** So also *is* the resurrection of the dead. *The body* is sown in corruption, it is raised in incorruption. It is sown in dishonor, it is raised in glory. It is sown in weakness, it is raised in power.

2 **Matt. 25:33:** And He will set the sheep on His right hand, but the goats on the left. **Matt. 10:32:** Therefore whoever confesses Me before men, him I will also confess before My Father who is in heaven.

3 **1 Cor. 6:2-3:** Do you not know that the saints will judge the world? And if the world will be judged by you, are you unworthy to judge the smallest matters? Do you not know that we shall judge angels? How much more, things that pertain to this life?

4 **Matt. 25:34, 46:** Then the King will say to those on His right hand, 'Come, you blessed of My Father, inherit the kingdom prepared for you from the foundation of the world.

5 **Eph. 5:27:** ... that He might present her to Himself a glorious church, not having spot or wrinkle or any such thing, but that she should be holy and without blemish. **Rev. 14:13:** Then I heard a voice from heaven saying to me, "Write: 'Blessed *are* the dead who die in the Lord from now on.'" "Yes," says the Spirit, "that they may rest from their labors, and their works follow them."

6 **Ps. 16:11:** You will show me the path of life; In Your presence *is* fullness of joy; At Your right hand *are* pleasures forevermore.

7 **Heb. 12:22-23:** But you have come to Mount Zion and to the city of the living God, the heavenly Jerusalem, to an innumerable company of angels, to the general assembly and church of the firstborn *who are* registered in heaven, to God the Judge of all, to the spirits of just men made perfect.

8 **1 John 3:2:** Beloved, now we are children of God; and it has not yet been revealed what we shall be, but we know that when He is revealed, we shall be like Him, for we shall see Him as He is. **Rom. 8:29:** For whom He foreknew, He also predestined *to be* conformed to the image of His Son, that He might be the firstborn among many brethren. **1 Cor. 13:12:** For now we see in a mirror, dimly, but

then face to face. Now I know in part, but then I shall know just as I also am known. **1 Thess. 4:17-18:** Then we who are alive *and* remain shall be caught up together with them in the clouds to meet the Lord in the air. And thus we shall always be with the Lord. Therefore comfort one another with these words.

HAVING SEEN WHAT THE SCRIPTURES PRINCIPALLY TEACH US TO BELIEVE CONCERNING GOD, IT FOLLOWS TO CONSIDER WHAT THEY REQUIRE AS THE DUTY OF MAN

Q. 112. *What is the duty which God requireth of man?*

A. The duty which God requireth of man, is obedience to His revealed will.[1]

[1] **Deut. 29:29:** The secret *things belong* to the LORD our God, but those *things which are* revealed *belong* to us and to our children forever, that *we* may do all the words of this law. **Mic. 6:8:** He has shown you, O man, what *is* good; And what does the LORD require of you But to do justly, To love mercy, And to walk humbly with your God? **1 John 5:2-3:** By this we know that we love the children of God, when we love God and keep His commandments. For this is the love of God, that we keep His commandments. And His commandments are not burdensome. **Rom. 12:1-2:** I beseech you therefore, brethren, by the mercies of God, that you present your bodies a living sacrifice, holy, acceptable to God, *which is* your reasonable service. And do not be conformed to this world, but be transformed by the renewing of your mind, that you may prove what *is* that good and acceptable and perfect will of God. **1 Sam. 15:22:** So Samuel said: "Has the LORD *as great* delight in burnt offerings and sacrifices, As in obeying the voice of the LORD? Behold, to obey is better than sacrifice, *And* to heed than the fat of rams.

Q. 113. *What did God at first reveal unto man as the rule of his obedience?*

A. The rule of obedience revealed to Adam in the estate of innocence, and to all mankind in him, besides a special command not to eat of the fruit of the tree of the knowledge of good and evil, was the moral law.[1]

[1] **Gen. 1:26-27:** Then God said, "Let Us make man in Our image, according to Our likeness; let them have dominion over the fish of the sea, over the birds of the air, and over the cattle, over all the earth and over every creeping thing that creeps on the earth." So God created man in His *own* image; in the image of God He created him; male and female He created them. **Rom. 2:14-15:** ... for when Gentiles, who do not have the law, by nature do the things in the law, these, although not having the law, are a law to themselves, who show the work of the law written in their hearts, their conscience also bearing witness, and between themselves *their* thoughts accusing or else excusing *them*. **Rom. 10:5:** For Moses writes about the righteousness which is of the law, "The man who does those things shall live by them." **Gen. 2:17:** ... but of the tree of the knowledge of good and evil you shall not eat, for in the day that you eat of it you shall surely die.

Q. 114 *What is the moral law?*

A. The moral law is the declaration of the will of God to mankind, directing and binding every one to personal, perfect, and perpetual conformity and obedience thereunto, in the frame and disposition of the whole man, soul and body,[1] and in performance of all those duties of holiness and righteousness which he oweth to God and man:[2] promising life upon the fulfilling, and threatening death upon the breach of it.[3]

1 **Deut. 5:1-3, 31, 33:** And Moses called all Israel, and said to them: "Hear, O Israel, the statutes and judgments which I speak in your hearing today, that you may learn them and be careful to observe them. The LORD our God made a covenant with us in Horeb. The LORD did not make this covenant with our fathers, but with us, those who *are* here today, all of us who *are* alive.... But as for you, stand here by Me, and I will speak to you all the commandments, the statutes, and the judgments which you shall teach them, that they may observe *them* in the land which I am giving them to possess.... You shall walk in all the ways which the LORD your God has commanded you, that you may live and *that it may be* well with you, and *that* you may prolong *your* days in the land which you shall possess. **Luke 10:26-27:** He said to him, "What is written in the law? What is your reading *of it?*" So he answered and said, "'You shall love the LORD your God with all your heart, with all your soul, with all your strength, and with all your mind,' and 'your neighbor as yourself.'" **1 Thess. 5:23:** Now may the God of peace Himself sanctify you completely; and may your whole spirit, soul, and body be preserved blameless at the coming of our Lord Jesus Christ. **Eph. 4:24:** ... and that you put on the new man which was created according to God, in true righteousness and holiness.

2 **Luke 1:75:** In holiness and righteousness before Him all the days of our life. **Acts 24:16:** This *being* so, I myself always strive to have a conscience without offense toward God and men. **1 Pet. 1:15-16:** ... but as He who called you *is* holy, you also be holy in all *your* conduct, because it is written, "Be holy, for I am holy."

3 **Rom. 10:5:** For Moses writes about the righteousness which is of the law, "The man who does those things shall live by them." **Gal. 3:10, 12:** For as many as are of the works of the law are under the curse; for it is written, "Cursed *is* everyone who does not continue in all things which are written in the book of the law, to do them." ... Yet the law is not of faith, but "the man who does them shall live by them." **Rom. 5:12:** Therefore, just as through one man sin entered the world, and death through sin, and thus death spread to all men, because all sinned.

Q. 115. *Is there any use of the moral law to man since the fall?*

A. Although no man, since the fall, can attain to righteousness and life by the moral law;[1] yet there is great use thereof, as well common to all men, as peculiar either to the unregenerate, or the regenerate.[2]

1 **Rom. 8:3:** For what the law could not do in that it was weak through the flesh, God *did* by sending His own Son in the likeness of sinful flesh, on account of sin: He condemned sin in the flesh. **Gal. 2:16:** ... knowing that a man is not justified by the works of the law but by faith in Jesus Christ, even we have believed in Christ Jesus, that we might be justified by faith in Christ and not by the works of the law; for by the works of the law no flesh shall be justified.

2 **1 Tim. 1:8:** But we know that the law *is* good if one uses it lawfully.

Q. 116. *Of what use is the moral law to all men?*

A. The moral law is of use to all men, to inform them of the holy nature and will of God,[1] and of their duty, binding them to walk accordingly;[2] to convince them of their disability to keep it, and of the sinful pollution of their nature, hearts, and lives:[3] to humble them in the sense of their sin and misery,[4] and thereby help them to a clearer sight of the need they have of Christ,[5] and of the perfection of His obedience.[6]

1
Rom. 1:20: For since the creation of the world His invisible *attributes* are clearly seen, being understood by the things that are made, *even* His eternal power and Godhead, so that they are without excuse. **Lev. 11:44-45:** For I *am* the LORD your God. You shall therefore consecrate yourselves, and you shall be holy; for I *am* holy. Neither shall you defile yourselves with any creeping thing that creeps on the earth. For I *am* the LORD who brings you up out of the land of Egypt, to be your God. You shall therefore be holy, for I *am* holy. **Lev. 20:7-8:** Consecrate yourselves therefore, and be holy, for I *am* the LORD your God. And you shall keep My statutes, and perform them: I *am* the LORD who sanctifies you. **Rom. 7:12:** Therefore the law *is* holy, and the commandment holy and just and good.
2
Mic. 6:8: He has shown you, O man, what *is* good; And what does the LORD require of you But to do justly, To love mercy, And to walk humbly with your God? **James 2:10-11:** For whoever shall keep the whole law, and yet stumble in one *point,* he is guilty of all. For He who said, "Do not commit adultery," also said, "Do not murder." Now if you do not commit adultery, but you do murder, you have become a transgressor of the law. **Rom. 1:32:** ... who, knowing the righteous judgment of God, that those who practice such things are deserving of death, not only do the same but also approve of those who practice them.
3
Ps. 19:11-12: Moreover by them Your servant is warned, *And* in keeping them *there is* great reward. Who can understand *his* errors? Cleanse me from secret *faults.* **Rom. 3:20:** Therefore by the deeds of the law no flesh will be justified in His sight, for by the law *is* the knowledge of sin. **Rom. 7:7:** What shall we say then? *Is* the law sin? Certainly not! On the contrary, I would not have known sin except through the law. For I would not have known covetousness unless the law had said, "You shall not covet."
4
Rom. 3:9, 23: What then? Are we better *than they?* Not at all. For we have previously charged both Jews and Greeks that they are all under sin.... for all have sinned and fall short of the glory of God.
5
Gal. 3:21-22, 24: *Is* the law then against the promises of God? Certainly not! For if there had been a law given which could have given life, truly righteousness would have been by the law. But the Scripture has confined all under sin, that the promise by faith in Jesus Christ might be given to those who believe.... Therefore the law was our tutor *to bring us* to Christ, that we might be justified by faith.
6
Rom. 10:4: For Christ *is* the end of the law for righteousness to everyone who believes.

Q. 117. *What particular use is there of the moral law to unregenerate men?*

A. The moral law is of use to unregenerate men, to awaken their consciences to flee from the wrath to come,[1] and to drive them to Christ;[2] or, upon their continuance in the estate and way of sin, to leave them inexcusable,[3] and under the curse thereof.[4]

1
Ps. 51:13: *Then* I will teach transgressors Your ways, And sinners shall be converted to You. **1 Tim. 1:9-11:** ... knowing this: that the law is not made for a righteous person, but for *the* lawless and insubordinate, for *the* ungodly and for sinners, for *the* unholy and profane, for murderers of fathers and murderers of mothers, for manslayers, for fornicators, for sodomites, for kidnappers, for liars, for perjurers, and if there is any other thing that is contrary to sound doctrine, according to the glorious gospel of the blessed God which was committed to my trust.
2
Gal. 3:24: Therefore the law was our tutor *to bring us* to Christ, that we might be justified by faith.
3
Rom. 1:20: For since the creation of the world His invisible *attributes* are clearly seen, being understood by the things that are made, *even* His eternal power and Godhead, so that they are without excuse. **Rom. 2:15:** ... who show the work of the law written in their hearts, their conscience also bearing witness, and between themselves *their* thoughts accusing or else excusing *them.*
4
Gal. 3:10: For as many as are of the works of the law are under the curse; for it is written, "Cursed *is* everyone who does not continue in all things which are written in the book of the law, to do them."

Q. 118. *What special use is there of the moral law to the regenerate?*

A. Although they that are regenerate, and believe in Christ, be delivered from the moral law as a covenant of works,[1] so as thereby they are neither justified[2] nor condemned;[3] yet besides the general uses thereof common to them with all men, it is of special use, to show them how much they are bound to Christ for His fulfilling it, and enduring the curse thereof in their stead, and for their good;[4] and thereby to provoke them to more thankfulness,[5] and to express the same in their greater care to conform themselves thereunto as the rule of their obedience.[6]

1

Rom. 6:14: For sin shall not have dominion over you, for you are not under law but under grace. **Rom. 7:4, 6:** Therefore, my brethren, you also have become dead to the law through the body of Christ, that you may be married to another—to Him who was raised from the dead, that we should bear fruit to God.... But now we have been delivered from the law, having died to what we were held by, so that we should serve in the newness of the Spirit and not *in* the oldness of the letter. **Gal. 4:4-5:** But when the fullness of the time had come, God sent forth His Son, born of a woman, born under the law, to redeem those who were under the law, that we might receive the adoption as sons. **Col. 2:13-14:** And you, being dead in your trespasses and the uncircumcision of your flesh, He has made alive together with Him, having forgiven you all trespasses, having wiped out the handwriting of requirements that was against us, which was contrary to us. And He has taken it out of the way, having nailed it to the cross.

2

Rom. 3:20: Therefore by the deeds of the law no flesh will be justified in His sight, for by the law *is* the knowledge of sin.

3

Gal. 5:23: ... gentleness, self-control. Against such there is no law. **Rom. 8:1:** *There is* therefore now no condemnation to those who are in Christ Jesus, who do not walk according to the flesh, but according to the Spirit.

4

Rom. 7:24-25: O wretched man that I am! Who will deliver me from this body of death? I thank God—through Jesus Christ our Lord! So then, with the mind I myself serve the law of God, but with the flesh the law of sin. **Gal. 3:13-14:** Christ has redeemed us from the curse of the law, having become a curse for us (for it is written, "Cursed *is* everyone who hangs on a tree"), that the blessing of Abraham might come upon the Gentiles in Christ Jesus, that we might receive the promise of the Spirit through faith. **Rom. 8:3-4:** For what the law could not do in that it was weak through the flesh, God *did* by sending His own Son in the likeness of sinful flesh, on account of sin: He condemned sin in the flesh, that the righteous requirement of the law might be fulfilled in us who do not walk according to the flesh but according to the Spirit. **Acts 13:38-39:** Therefore let it be known to you, brethren, that through this Man is preached to you the forgiveness of sins; and by Him everyone who believes is justified from all things from which you could not be justified by the law of Moses.

5

Luke 1:68-69, 74-75: Blessed *is* the Lord God of Israel, For He has visited and redeemed His people, And has raised up a horn of salvation for us In the house of His servant David.... To grant us that we, Being delivered from the hand of our enemies, Might serve Him without fear, In holiness and righteousness before Him all the days of our life. **Col. 1:12-14:** ... giving thanks to the Father who has qualified us to be partakers of the inheritance of the saints in the light. He has delivered us from the power of darkness and conveyed *us* into the kingdom of the Son of His love, in whom we have redemption through His blood, the forgiveness of sins. **Rom. 6:14:** For sin shall not have dominion over you, for you are not under law but under grace.

6

Deut. 30:19-20: I call heaven and earth as witnesses today against you, *that* I have set before you life and death, blessing and cursing; therefore choose life, that both you and your descendants may live; that you may love the LORD your God, that you may obey His voice, and that you may cling to Him, for He *is* your life and the length of your days; and that you may dwell in the land which the LORD swore to your fathers, to Abraham, Isaac, and Jacob, to give them. **Rom. 7:22:** For I delight in the law of God according to the inward man. **Rom. 12:2:** And do not be conformed to this world, but be transformed by the renewing of your mind, that you may prove what *is* that good and acceptable and perfect will of God. **Titus 2:11-14:** For the grace of God that brings salvation has appeared to all men, teaching us that, denying ungodliness and worldly lusts, we should live soberly, righteously, and godly in the present age, looking for the blessed hope and glorious appearing of our great God and Savior Jesus Christ, who gave Himself for us, that He might redeem us from every lawless deed and purify for Himself *His* own special people, zealous for good works. **James 1:25:** But he who looks into the perfect law of liberty and continues *in it,* and is not a forgetful hearer but a doer of the work, this one will be blessed in what he does.

Q. 119. *Where is the moral law summarily comprehended?*

A. The moral law is summarily comprehended in the ten commandments, which were delivered by the voice of God upon mount Sinai, and written by Him in two tables of stone;[1] and are recorded in the twentieth chapter of Exodus: The four first commandments containing our duty to God, and the other six our duty to man.[2]

1 **Deut. 4:13:** So He declared to you His covenant which He commanded you to perform, the Ten Commandments; and He wrote them on two tablets of stone. **Deut. 10:4:** And He wrote on the tablets according to the first writing, the Ten Commandments, which the LORD had spoken to you in the mountain from the midst of the fire in the day of the assembly; and the LORD gave them to me. **Ex. 34:1-4:** And the LORD said to Moses, "Cut two tablets of stone like the first *ones,* and I will write on *these* tablets the words that were on the first tablets which you broke. So be ready in the morning, and come up in the morning to Mount Sinai, and present yourself to Me there on the top of the mountain. And no man shall come up with you, and let no man be seen throughout all the mountain; let neither flocks nor herds feed before that mountain." So he cut two tablets of stone like the first *ones.* Then Moses rose early in the morning and went up Mount Sinai, as the LORD had commanded him; and he took in his hand the two tablets of stone. **Rom. 13:8-10:** Owe no one anything except to love one another, for he who loves another has fulfilled the law. For the commandments, "You shall not commit adultery," "You shall not murder," "You shall not steal," "You shall not bear false witness," "You shall not covet," and if *there is* any other commandment, are *all* summed up in this saying, namely, "You shall love your neighbor as yourself." Love does no harm to a neighbor; therefore love *is* the fulfillment of the law. **James 2:8, 10-12:** If you really fulfill *the* royal law according to the Scripture, "You shall love your neighbor as yourself," you do well ... For whoever shall keep the whole law, and yet stumble in one *point,* he is guilty of all. For He who said, "Do not commit adultery," also said, "Do not murder." Now if you do not commit adultery, but you do murder, you have become a transgressor of the law. So speak and so do as those who will be judged by the law of liberty.

2 **Matt. 22:37-40:** Jesus said to him, "'You shall love the LORD your God with all your heart, with all your soul, and with all your mind.' This is *the* first and great commandment. And *the* second *is* like it: 'You shall love your neighbor as yourself.' On these two commandments hang all the Law and the Prophets." **Matt. 19:17-19:** So He said to him, "Why do you call Me good? No one *is* good but One, *that is,* God. But if you want to enter into life, keep the commandments." He said to Him, "Which ones?" Jesus said, "'You shall not murder,' 'You shall not commit adultery,' 'You shall not steal,' 'You shall not bear false witness,' 'Honor your father and *your* mother,' and, 'You shall love your neighbor as yourself.'"

Q. 120. *What rules are to be observed for the right understanding of the ten commandments?*

A. For the right understanding of the ten commandments, these rules are to be observed:

1. That the law is perfect, and bindeth every one to full conformity in the whole man unto the righteousness thereof, and unto entire obedience forever; so as to require the utmost perfection of every duty, and to forbid the least degree of every

sin.[1]

[1] **Ps. 19:7:** The law of the LORD *is* perfect, converting the soul; The testimony of the LORD *is* sure, making wise the simple. **James 2:10:** For whoever shall keep the whole law, and yet stumble in one *point,* he is guilty of all. **Matt. 5:21-22:** You have heard that it was said to those of old, 'You shall not murder, and whoever murders will be in danger of the judgment.' But I say to you that whoever is angry with his brother without a cause shall be in danger of the judgment. And whoever says to his brother, 'Raca!' shall be in danger of the council. But whoever says, 'You fool!' shall be in danger of hell fire.

2. That it is spiritual, and so reacheth the understanding, will, affections, and all other powers of the soul; as well as words, works, and gestures.[2]

[2] **Rom. 7:14:** For we know that the law is spiritual, but I am carnal, sold under sin. **Deut. 6:5:** You shall love the LORD your God with all your heart, with all your soul, and with all your strength. **Matt. 22:37-39:** Jesus said to him, "'You shall love the LORD your God with all your heart, with all your soul, and with all your mind.' This is *the* first and great commandment. And *the* second *is* like it: 'You shall love your neighbor as yourself.' **Matt. 5:21-22, 27-28, 33-34, 37-39, 43-44:** You have heard that it was said to those of old, 'You shall not murder, and whoever murders will be in danger of the judgment.' But I say to you that whoever is angry with his brother without a cause shall be in danger of the judgment. And whoever says to his brother, 'Raca!' shall be in danger of the council. But whoever says, 'You fool!' shall be in danger of hell fire.... You have heard that it was said to those of old, 'You shall not commit adultery.' But I say to you that whoever looks at a woman to lust for her has already committed adultery with her in his heart.... Again you have heard that it was said to those of old, 'You shall not swear falsely, but shall perform your oaths to the Lord.' But I say to you, do not swear at all: neither by heaven, for it is God's throne.... But let your 'Yes' be 'Yes,' and your 'No,' 'No.' For whatever is more than these is from the evil one. You have heard that it was said, 'An eye for an eye and a tooth for a tooth.' But I tell you not to resist an evil person. But whoever slaps you on your right cheek, turn the other to him also.... You have heard that it was said, 'You shall love your neighbor and hate your enemy.' But I say to you, love your enemies, bless those who curse you, do good to those who hate you, and pray for those who spitefully use you and persecute you.

3. That one and the same thing, in divers respects, is required or forbidden in several commandments.[3]

[3] **Col. 3:5:** Therefore put to death your members which are on the earth: fornication, uncleanness, passion, evil desire, and covetousness, which is idolatry. **Amos 8:5:** Saying: "When will the New Moon be past, That we may sell grain? And the Sabbath, That we may trade wheat? Making the ephah small and the shekel large, Falsifying the scales by deceit. **Prov. 1:19:** So *are* the ways of everyone who is greedy for gain; It takes away the life of its owners. **1 Tim. 6:10:** For the love of money is a root of all *kinds of* evil, for which some have strayed from the faith in their greediness, and pierced themselves through with many sorrows.

4. That as, where a duty is commanded, the contrary sin is forbidden;[4] and, where a sin is forbidden, the contrary duty is commanded:[5] so, where a promise is annexed, the contrary threatening is included;[6] and, where a threatening is annexed, the contrary promise is included.[7]

[4] **Isa. 58:13:** If you turn away your foot from the Sabbath, *From* doing your pleasure on My holy day, And call the Sabbath a delight, The holy *day* of the LORD honorable, And shall honor Him, not doing your own ways, Nor finding your own pleasure, Nor speaking *your own* words. **Deut. 6:13:** You shall fear the LORD your God and serve Him, and shall take oaths in His name. **Matt. 4:9-10:** And he said to Him, "All these things I will give You if You will fall down and worship me." Then Jesus said to him, "Away with you, Satan! For it is written, 'You shall worship the LORD your God, and Him only you shall serve.'" **Matt. 15:4-6:** For God commanded, saying, 'Honor your father and your mother'; and, 'He who curses father or mother, let him be put to death.' But you say, 'Whoever says to his father or mother, "Whatever profit you might have received from me *is* a gift *to God*"—

then he need not honor his father or mother.' Thus you have made the commandment of God of no effect by your tradition.

5 **Matt. 5:21-25:** You have heard that it was said to those of old, 'You shall not murder, and whoever murders will be in danger of the judgment.' But I say to you that whoever is angry with his brother without a cause shall be in danger of the judgment. And whoever says to his brother, 'Raca!' shall be in danger of the council. But whoever says, 'You fool!' shall be in danger of hell fire. Therefore if you bring your gift to the altar, and there remember that your brother has something against you, leave your gift there before the altar, and go your way. First be reconciled to your brother, and then come and offer your gift. Agree with your adversary quickly, while you are on the way with him, lest your adversary deliver you to the judge, the judge hand you over to the officer, and you be thrown into prison. **Eph. 4:28:** Let him who stole steal no longer, but rather let him labor, working with *his* hands what is good, that he may have something to give him who has need.

6 **Ex. 20:12:** Honor your father and your mother, that your days may be long upon the land which the LORD your God is giving you. **Prov. 30:17:** The eye *that* mocks *his* father, And scorns obedience to *his* mother, The ravens of the valley will pick it out, And the young eagles will eat it.

7 **Jer. 18:7-8:** The instant I speak concerning a nation and concerning a kingdom, to pluck up, to pull down, and to destroy *it,* if that nation against whom I have spoken turns from its evil, I will relent of the disaster that I thought to bring upon it. **Ex. 20:7:** You shall not take the name of the LORD your God in vain, for the LORD will not hold *him* guiltless who takes His name in vain. **Ps. 15:1, 4-5:** LORD, who may abide in Your tabernacle? Who may dwell in Your holy hill? ... In whose eyes a vile person is despised, But he honors those who fear the LORD; He *who* swears to his own hurt and does not change; He *who* does not put out his money at usury, Nor does he take a bribe against the innocent. He who does these *things* shall never be moved. **Ps. 24:4-5:** He who has clean hands and a pure heart, Who has not lifted up his soul to an idol, Nor sworn deceitfully. He shall receive blessing from the LORD, And righteousness from the God of his salvation.

5. That what God forbids, is at no time to be done;[8] what He commands, is always our duty;[9] and yet every particular duty is not to be done at all times.[10]

8 **Job 13:7-8:** Will you speak wickedly for God, And talk deceitfully for Him? Will you show partiality for Him? Will you contend for God? **Rom. 3:8:** And *why* not *say,* "Let us do evil that good may come"?—as we are slanderously reported and as some affirm that we say. Their condemnation is just. **Job 36:21:** Take heed, do not turn to iniquity, For you have chosen this rather than affliction. **Heb. 11:25:** ... choosing rather to suffer affliction with the people of God than to enjoy the passing pleasures of sin.

9 **Deut. 4:8-9:** And what great nation *is there* that has *such* statutes and righteous judgments as are in all this law which I set before you this day? Only take heed to yourself, and diligently keep yourself, lest you forget the things your eyes have seen, and lest they depart from your heart all the days of your life. And teach them to your children and your grandchildren. **Luke 17:10:** So likewise you, when you have done all those things which you are commanded, say, 'We are unprofitable servants. We have done what was our duty to do.'

10 **Matt. 12:7:** But if you had known what *this* means, 'I desire mercy and not sacrifice,' you would not have condemned the guiltless.

6. That under one sin or duty, all of the same kind are forbidden or commanded; together with all the causes, means, occasions, and appearances thereof, and provocations thereunto.[11]

11 **Matt. 5:21-22, 27-28:** You have heard that it was said to those of old, 'You shall not murder, and whoever murders will be in danger of the judgment.' But I say to you that whoever is angry with his brother without a cause shall be in danger of the judgment. And whoever says to his brother, 'Raca!' shall be in danger of the council. But whoever says, 'You fool!' shall be in danger of hell fire ... You have heard that it was said to those of old, 'You shall not commit adultery.' But I say to you that whoever looks at a woman to lust for her has already committed adultery with her in his heart. **Matt. 15:4-6:** For God commanded, saying, 'Honor your father and your mother'; and, 'He who curses father or mother, let him be put to death.' But you say, 'Whoever says to his father or mother, "Whatever profit you might have received from me *is* a gift *to God*"— then he need not honor his father or mother.' Thus you have made the commandment of God of no effect by your tradition. **1 Thess. 5:22:** Abstain from every form of evil. **Jude 23:** ... but others save with fear,

pulling them out of the fire, hating even the garment defiled by the flesh. **Gal. 5:26:** Let us not become conceited, provoking one another, envying one another. **Col. 3:21:** Fathers, do not provoke your children, lest they become discouraged.

7. That what is forbidden or commanded to ourselves, we are bound, according to our places, to endeavor that it may be avoided or performed by others, according to the duty of their places.[12]

12 **Ex. 20:10:** ... but the seventh day *is* the Sabbath of the LORD your God. *In it* you shall do no work: you, nor your son, nor your daughter, nor your male servant, nor your female servant, nor your cattle, nor your stranger who *is* within your gates. **Lev. 19:17:** You shall not hate your brother in your heart. You shall surely rebuke your neighbor, and not bear sin because of him. **Gen. 18:19:** For I have known him, in order that he may command his children and his household after him, that they keep the way of the LORD, to do righteousness and justice, that the LORD may bring to Abraham what He has spoken to him. **Josh. 24:15:** And if it seems evil to you to serve the LORD, choose for yourselves this day whom you will serve, whether the gods which your fathers served that *were* on the other side of the River, or the gods of the Amorites, in whose land you dwell. But as for me and my house, we will serve the LORD. **Deut. 6:6-7:** And these words which I command you today shall be in your heart. You shall teach them diligently to your children, and shall talk of them when you sit in your house, when you walk by the way, when you lie down, and when you rise up. **Heb. 10:24-25:** And let us consider one another in order to stir up love and good works, not forsaking the assembling of ourselves together, as *is* the manner of some, but exhorting *one another,* and so much the more as you see the Day approaching.

8. That in what is commanded to others, we are bound, according to our places and callings, to be helpful to them;[13] and to take heed of partaking with others in what is forbidden them.[14]

13 **2 Cor. 1:24:** Not that we have dominion over your faith, but are fellow workers for your joy; for by faith you stand.

14 **1 Tim. 5:22:** Do not lay hands on anyone hastily, nor share in other people's sins; keep yourself pure. **Eph. 5:11:** And have no fellowship with the unfruitful works of darkness, but rather expose *them.*

Q. 121. *What special things are we to consider in the ten commandments?*

A. We are to consider, in the ten commandments, the preface, the substance of the commandments themselves, and several reasons annexed to some of them, the more to enforce them.[1]

1 **Eph. 6:1-3:** Children, obey your parents in the Lord, for this is right. "Honor your father and mother," which is the first commandment with promise: "that it may be well with you and you may live long on the earth."

Q. 122. *What is the preface to the ten commandments?*

A. The preface to the ten commandments is contained in these words, *I am the LORD thy God, which have brought thee out of the land of Egypt, out of the house of bondage.*[1] Wherein God manifesteth His sovereignty, as being JEHOVAH, the eternal, immutable, and almighty God;[2] having His being in and of Himself,[3] and giving being to all His words[4] and works:[5] and that He is a God in covenant, as with Israel of old, so with all His people;[6] who, as He brought them out of their bondage in Egypt, so He delivereth us from our spiritual thraldom;[7] and that therefore we are bound to take Him for our God alone, and to keep all His commandments.[8]

1 **Ex. 20:2:** I *am* the LORD your God, who brought you out of the land of Egypt, out of the house of bondage. **Cf. Deut. 5:6.**

2 **Isa. 44:6:** Thus says the LORD, the King of Israel, And his Redeemer, the LORD of hosts: 'I *am* the First and I *am* the Last; Besides Me *there is* no God.'

3 **Ex. 3:14:** And God said to Moses, "I AM WHO I AM." And He said, "Thus you shall say to the children of Israel, 'I AM has sent me to you.'"

4 **Ex. 6:3:** I appeared to Abraham, to Isaac, and to Jacob, as God Almighty, but *by* My name LORD I was not known to them.

5 **Acts 17:24, 28:** God, who made the world and everything in it, since He is Lord of heaven and earth, does not dwell in temples made with hands.... for in Him we live and move and have our being, as also some of your own poets have said, 'For we are also His offspring.'

6 **Gen. 17:7:** And I will establish My covenant between Me and you and your descendants after you in their generations, for an everlasting covenant, to be God to you and your descendants after you. **Rom. 3:29:** Or *is He* the God of the Jews only? *Is He* not also the God of the Gentiles? Yes, of the Gentiles also.

7 **Luke 1:74-75:** To grant us that we, Being delivered from the hand of our enemies, Might serve Him without fear, In holiness and righteousness before Him all the days of our life. **Gal. 5:1:** Stand fast therefore in the liberty by which Christ has made us free, and do not be entangled again with a yoke of bondage.

8 **1 Pet. 1:15-19:** ... but as He who called you *is* holy, you also be holy in all *your* conduct, because it is written, "Be holy, for I am holy." And if you call on the Father, who without partiality judges according to each one's work, conduct yourselves throughout the time of your stay *here* in fear; knowing that you were not redeemed with corruptible things, *like* silver or gold, from your aimless conduct *received* by tradition from your fathers, but with the precious blood of Christ, as of a lamb without blemish and without spot. **Lev. 18:30:** 'Therefore you shall keep My ordinance, so that *you* do not commit *any* of these abominable customs which were committed before you, and that you do not defile yourselves by them: I *am* the LORD your God.' **Lev. 19:37:** 'Therefore you shall observe all My statutes and all My judgments, and perform them: I *am* the LORD.'

Q. 123. *What is the sum of the four commandments which contain our duty to God?*

A. The sum of the four commandments containing our duty to God, is, to love the LORD our God with all our heart, and with all our soul, and with all our strength, and with all our mind.[1]

1 **Luke 10:27:** So he answered and said, "'You shall love the LORD your God with all your heart, with all your soul, with all your strength, and with all your mind,' and 'your neighbor as yourself.'" **Matt. 22:37-40:** Jesus said to him, "'You shall love the LORD your God with all your heart, with all your soul, and with all your mind.' This is *the* first and great commandment. And *the* second *is* like it: 'You shall love your neighbor as yourself.' On these two commandments hang all the Law and the Prophets."

Q. 124. *Which is the first commandment?*

A. The first commandment is, *Thou shalt have no other gods before me.*[1]

1 **Ex. 20:3:** You shall have no other gods before Me. **Cf. Deut. 5:7.**

Q. 125. *What are the duties required in the first commandment?*

A. The duties required in the first commandment are, the knowing and acknowledging of God to be the only true God, and our God;[1] and to worship and glorify Him accordingly,[2] by thinking,[3] meditating,[4] remembering,[5] highly esteeming,[6] honouring,[7] adoring,[8] choosing,[9] loving,[10] desiring,[11] fearing of Him;[12] believing Him;[13] trusting,[14] hoping,[15] delighting,[16] rejoicing in Him;[17] being zealous for Him;[18] calling upon Him, giving all praise and thanks,[19] and yielding all obedience and submission to Him with the whole man;[20] being careful in all things to please Him,[21] and sorrowful when in anything He is offended;[22] and walking humbly with Him.[23]

1 **1 Chron. 28:9:** As for you, my son Solomon, know the God of your father, and serve Him with a loyal heart and with a willing mind; for the LORD searches all hearts and understands all the intent of the thoughts. If you seek Him, He will be found by you; but if you forsake Him, He will cast you off forever. **Deut. 26:7:** Then we cried out to the LORD God of our fathers, and the LORD heard our voice and looked on our affliction and our labor and our oppression. **Isa. 43:10:** "You *are* My witnesses," says the LORD, "And My servant whom I have chosen, That you may know and believe Me, And understand that I *am* He. Before Me there was no God formed, Nor shall there be after Me. **See Jer. 14:22.**

2 **Ps. 95:6-7:** Oh come, let us worship and bow down; Let us kneel before the LORD our Maker. For He *is* our God, And we *are* the people of His pasture, And the sheep of His hand. Today, if you will hear His voice. **Matt. 4:10:** Then Jesus said to him, "Away with you, Satan! For it is written, 'You shall worship the LORD your God, and Him only you shall serve.'" **Ps. 29:2:** Give unto the LORD the glory due to His name; Worship the LORD in the beauty of holiness.

3 **Mal. 3:16:** Then those who feared the LORD spoke to one another, And the LORD listened and heard them; So a book of remembrance was written before Him For those who fear the LORD And who meditate on His name.

4 **Ps. 63:6:** When I remember You on my bed, I meditate on You in the *night* watches.

5 **Eccl. 12:1:** Remember now your Creator in the days of your youth, Before the difficult days come, And the years draw near when you say, "I have no pleasure in them."

6 **Ps. 71:19:** Also Your righteousness, O God, *is* very high, You who have done great things; O God, who *is* like You?

7 **Mal. 1:6:** A son honors *his* father, And a servant *his* master. If then I am the Father, Where *is* My honor? And if I *am* a Master, Where *is* My reverence? Says the LORD of hosts To you priests who despise My name. Yet you say, 'In what way have we despised Your name?'

8 **Isa. 45:23:** I have sworn by Myself; The word has gone out of My mouth *in* righteousness, And shall not return, That to Me every knee shall bow, Every tongue shall take an oath. **See Ps. 96.**

9
Josh. 24:15, 22: And if it seems evil to you to serve the LORD, choose for yourselves this day whom you will serve, whether the gods which your fathers served that *were* on the other side of the River, or the gods of the Amorites, in whose land you dwell. But as for me and my house, we will serve the LORD." ... So Joshua said to the people, "You *are* witnesses against yourselves that you have chosen the LORD for yourselves, to serve Him." And they said, "*We are* witnesses!"

10
Deut. 6:5: You shall love the LORD your God with all your heart, with all your soul, and with all your strength.

11
Ps. 73:25: Whom have I in heaven *but You?* And *there is* none upon earth *that* I desire besides You.

12
Isa. 8:13: The LORD of hosts, Him you shall hallow; *Let* Him *be* your fear, And *let* Him *be* your dread.

13
Ex. 14:31: Thus Israel saw the great work which the LORD had done in Egypt; so the people feared the LORD, and believed the LORD and His servant Moses.

14
Isa. 26:4: Trust in the LORD forever, For in YAH, the LORD, *is* everlasting strength.

15
Ps. 130:7: O Israel, hope in the LORD; For with the LORD *there is* mercy, And with Him *is* abundant redemption.

16
Ps. 37:4: Delight yourself also in the LORD, And He shall give you the desires of your heart.

17
Ps. 32:11: Be glad in the LORD and rejoice, you righteous; And shout for joy, all *you* upright in heart!

18
Rom. 12:11: ... not lagging in diligence, fervent in spirit, serving the Lord. **See Num. 25:11.**

19
Phil. 4:6: Be anxious for nothing, but in everything by prayer and supplication, with thanksgiving, let your requests be made known to God.

20
Jer. 7:23: But this is what I commanded them, saying, 'Obey My voice, and I will be your God, and you shall be My people. And walk in all the ways that I have commanded you, that it may be well with you.' **James 4:7:** Therefore submit to God. Resist the devil and he will flee from you.

21
1 John 3:22: And whatever we ask we receive from Him, because we keep His commandments and do those things that are pleasing in His sight.

22
Ps. 119:136: Rivers of water run down from my eyes, Because *men* do not keep Your law. **Jer. 31:18:** I have surely heard Ephraim bemoaning himself: 'You have chastised me, and I was chastised, Like an untrained bull; Restore me, and I will return, For You *are* the LORD my God."

23
Mic. 6:8: He has shown you, O man, what *is* good; And what does the LORD require of you But to do justly, To love mercy, And to walk humbly with your God?

Q. 126. *What are the sins forbidden in the first commandment?*

A. The sins forbidden in the first commandment, are, atheism, in denying or not having a God;[1] idolatry, in having or worshiping more gods than one, or any with or instead of the true God;[2] the not having and avouching Him for God, and our God;[3] the omission or neglect of anything due to Him, required in this commandment;[4] ignorance,[5] forgetfulness,[6] misapprehensions,[7] false opinions,[8] unworthy and wicked thoughts of Him;[9] bold and curious searching into His secrets;[10] all profaneness,[11] hatred of God;[12] self-love,[13] self-seeking,[14] and all other inordinate and immoderate setting of our mind, will, or affections upon other things, and taking them off from Him in whole or in part;[15] vain credulity,[16] unbelief,[17] heresy,[18] misbelief,[19] distrust,[20] despair,[21] incorrigibleness,[22] and insensibleness under judgments,[23] hardness of heart,[24] pride,[25] presumption,[26] carnal security,[27] tempting of God;[28] using unlawful means,[29] and trusting in lawful means;[30] carnal delights and joys;[31] corrupt, blind, and indiscreet zeal;[32] lukewarmness,[33] and deadness in the things of God;[34] estranging ourselves, and apostatizing from God;[35] praying, or giving any religious worship, to saints, angels, or any other creatures;[36] all compacts and consulting with the devil,[37] and hearkening to his suggestions;[38] making men the lords of our faith and conscience;[39] slighting and despising God and His commands;[40] resisting and grieving of His Spirit,[41] discontent and impatience at His dispensations, charging Him foolishly for the evils He inflicts on us;[42] and ascribing the praise of any good we either are, have, or can do, to fortune,[43] idols,[44] ourselves,[45] or any other creature.[46]

1 **Ps. 14:1:** The fool has said in his heart, "*There is* no God." They are corrupt, They have done abominable works, There is none who does good. **Eph. 2:12:** ... that at that time you were without Christ, being aliens from the commonwealth of Israel and strangers from the covenants of promise, having no hope and without God in the world.

2 **Jer. 2:27-28:** Saying to a tree, 'You *are* my father,' And to a stone, 'You gave birth to me.' For they have turned *their* back to Me, and not *their* face. But in the time of their trouble They will say, 'Arise and save us.' But where *are* your gods that you have made for yourselves? Let them arise, If they can save you in the time of your trouble; For *according to* the number of your cities Are your gods, O Judah. **1 Thess. 1:9:** For they themselves declare concerning us what manner of entry we had to you, and how you turned to God from idols to serve the living and true God.

3 **Ps. 81:10-11:** I *am* the LORD your God, Who brought you out of the land of Egypt; Open your mouth wide, and I will fill it. "But My people would not heed My voice, And Israel would *have* none of Me. **See Rom. 1:21.**

4 **Isa. 43:22-24:** But you have not called upon Me, O Jacob; And you have been weary of Me, O Israel. You have not brought Me the sheep for your burnt offerings, Nor have you honored Me with your sacrifices. I have not caused you to serve with grain offerings, Nor wearied you with incense. You have bought Me no sweet cane with money, Nor have you satisfied Me with the fat of your sacrifices; But you have burdened Me with your sins, You have wearied Me with your iniquities.

5 **Jer. 4:22:** For My people *are* foolish, They have not known Me. They *are* silly children, And they have no understanding. They *are* wise to do evil, But to do good they have no knowledge. **Hos. 4:1, 6:** Hear the word of the LORD, You children of Israel, For the LORD *brings* a charge against the inhabitants of the land: "There is no truth or mercy Or knowledge of God in the land.... My people are destroyed for lack of knowledge. Because you have rejected knowledge, I also will reject you from being priest for Me; Because you have forgotten the law of your God, I also will forget your children.

6 **Jer. 2:32:** Can a virgin forget her ornaments, *Or* a bride her attire? Yet My people have forgotten Me days without number.

7 **Acts 17:23, 29:** ... for as I was passing through and considering the objects of your worship, I even found an altar with this inscription: TO THE UNKNOWN GOD. Therefore, the One whom you

worship without knowing, Him I proclaim to you.... Therefore, since we are the offspring of God, we ought not to think that the Divine Nature is like gold or silver or stone, something shaped by art and man's devising.

8

Isa. 40:18: To whom then will you liken God? Or what likeness will you compare to Him?

9

Ps. 50:21: These *things* you have done, and I kept silent; You thought that I was altogether like you; *But* I will rebuke you, And set *them* in order before your eyes.

10

Deut. 29:29: The secret *things belong* to the LORD our God, but those *things which are* revealed *belong* to us and to our children forever, that *we* may do all the words of this law.

11

Titus 1:16: They profess to know God, but in works they deny *Him,* being abominable, disobedient, and disqualified for every good work. **Heb. 12:16:** ... lest there *be* any fornicator or profane person like Esau, who for one morsel of food sold his birthright.

12

Rom. 1:30: ... backbiters, haters of God, violent, proud, boasters, inventors of evil things, disobedient to parents.

13

2 Tim. 3:2: For men will be lovers of themselves, lovers of money, boasters, proud, blasphemers, disobedient to parents, unthankful, unholy.

14

Phil. 2:21: For all seek their own, not the things which are of Christ Jesus.

15

1 John 2:15-16: Do not love the world or the things in the world. If anyone loves the world, the love of the Father is not in him. For all that *is* in the world—the lust of the flesh, the lust of the eyes, and the pride of life—is not of the Father but is of the world. **Col. 3:2, 5:** Set your mind on things above, not on things on the earth.... Therefore put to death your members which are on the earth: fornication, uncleanness, passion, evil desire, and covetousness, which is idolatry. **See 1 Sam. 2:29.**

16

1 John 4:1: Beloved, do not believe every spirit, but test the spirits, whether they are of God; because many false prophets have gone out into the world.

17

Heb. 3:12: Beware, brethren, lest there be in any of you an evil heart of unbelief in departing from the living God.

18

Gal. 5:20: ... idolatry, sorcery, hatred, contentions, jealousies, outbursts of wrath, selfish ambitions, dissensions, heresies. **Titus 3:10:** Reject a divisive man after the first and second admonition.

19

Acts 26:9: Indeed, I myself thought I must do many things contrary to the name of Jesus of Nazareth.

20

Ps. 78:22: Because they did not believe in God, And did not trust in His salvation.

21

Gen. 4:13: And Cain said to the LORD, "My punishment *is* greater than I can bear!"

22

Jer. 5:3: O LORD, *are* not Your eyes on the truth? You have stricken them, But they have not grieved; You have consumed them, But they have refused to receive correction. They have made their faces harder than rock; They have refused to return.

23

Isa. 42:25: Therefore He has poured on him the fury of His anger And the strength of battle; It has set him on fire all around, Yet he did not know; And it burned him, Yet he did not take *it* to heart.

24

Rom. 2:5: But in accordance with your hardness and your impenitent heart you are treasuring up for yourself wrath in the day of wrath and revelation of the righteous judgment of God.

25

Jer. 13:15: Hear and give ear: Do not be proud, For the LORD has spoken.

26

Ps. 19:13: Keep back Your servant also from presumptuous *sins;* Let them not have dominion over me. Then I shall be blameless, And I shall be innocent of great transgression.

27

Zeph. 1:12: And it shall come to pass at that time *That* I will search Jerusalem with lamps, And punish the men Who are settled in complacency, Who say in their heart, 'The LORD will not do good, Nor will He do evil.'

28

Matt. 4:7: Jesus said to him, "It is written again, 'You shall not tempt the LORD your God.'"

29

Rom. 3:8: And *why* not *say,* "Let us do evil that good may come"?—as we are slanderously reported and as some affirm that we say. Their condemnation is just.

30
Jer. 17:5: Thus says the LORD: "Cursed *is* the man who trusts in man And makes flesh his strength, Whose heart departs from the LORD.
31
2 Tim. 3:4: ... traitors, headstrong, haughty, lovers of pleasure rather than lovers of God.
32
Gal. 4:17: They zealously court you, *but* for no good; yes, they want to exclude you, that you may be zealous for them. **Rom. 10:2:** For I bear them witness that they have a zeal for God, but not according to knowledge. **See John 16:2; Luke 9:54-55.**
33
Rev. 3:16: So then, because you are lukewarm, and neither cold nor hot, I will vomit you out of My mouth.
34
Rev. 3:1: And to the angel of the church in Sardis write, 'These things says He who has the seven Spirits of God and the seven stars: "I know your works, that you have a name that you are alive, but you are dead."'
35
Ezek. 14:5: ... that I may seize the house of Israel by their heart, because they are all estranged from Me by their idols. **Isa. 1:4-5:** Alas, sinful nation, A people laden with iniquity, A brood of evildoers, Children who are corrupters! They have forsaken the LORD, They have provoked to anger The Holy One of Israel, They have turned away backward. Why should you be stricken again? You will revolt more and more. The whole head is sick, And the whole heart faints.
36
Hos. 4:12: My people ask counsel from their wooden *idols,* And their staff informs them. For the spirit of harlotry has caused *them* to stray, And they have played the harlot against their God. **Acts 10:25-26:** As Peter was coming in, Cornelius met him and fell down at his feet and worshiped *him.* But Peter lifted him up, saying, "Stand up; I myself am also a man." **Rev. 19:10:** And I fell at his feet to worship him. But he said to me, "See *that you do* not *do that!* I am your fellow servant, and of your brethren who have the testimony of Jesus. Worship God! For the testimony of Jesus is the spirit of prophecy." **Matt. 4:10:** Then Jesus said to him, "Away with you, Satan! For it is written, 'You shall worship the LORD your God, and Him only you shall serve.'" **Col. 2:18:** Let no one cheat you of your reward, taking delight in *false* humility and worship of angels, intruding into those things which he has not seen, vainly puffed up by his fleshly mind. **Rom. 1:25:** ... who exchanged the truth of God for the lie, and worshiped and served the creature rather than the Creator, who is blessed forever. Amen.
37
Lev. 20:6: And the person who turns to mediums and familiar spirits, to prostitute himself with them, I will set My face against that person and cut him off from his people. **See 1 Sam. 28:7, 11; 1 Chron. 10:13-14.**
38
Acts 5:3: But Peter said, "Ananias, why has Satan filled your heart to lie to the Holy Spirit and keep back *part* of the price of the land for yourself?"
39
2 Cor. 1:24: Not that we have dominion over your faith, but are fellow workers for your joy; for by faith you stand. **See Matt. 23:9.**
40
Deut. 32:15: But Jeshurun grew fat and kicked; You grew fat, you grew thick, You are obese! Then he forsook God *who* made him, And scornfully esteemed the Rock of his salvation. **Prov. 13:13:** He who despises the word will be destroyed, But he who fears the commandment will be rewarded. **See 2 Sam. 12:9.**
41
Acts 7:51: *You* stiff-necked and uncircumcised in heart and ears! You always resist the Holy Spirit; as your fathers *did,* so *do* you. **Eph. 4:30:** And do not grieve the Holy Spirit of God, by whom you were sealed for the day of redemption.
42
Job 1:22: In all this Job did not sin nor charge God with wrong. **Ps. 73:2-3:** But as for me, my feet had almost stumbled; My steps had nearly slipped. For I *was* envious of the boastful, When I saw the prosperity of the wicked. **See Ps. 73:13-15, 22.**
43
1 Sam. 6:7-9: Now therefore, make a new cart, take two milk cows which have never been yoked, and hitch the cows to the cart; and take their calves home, away from them. Then take the ark of the LORD and set it on the cart; and put the articles of gold which you are returning to Him *as* a trespass offering in a chest by its side. Then send it away, and let it go. And watch: if it goes up the road to its own territory, to Beth Shemesh, *then* He has done us this great evil. But if not, then we shall know that *it is* not His hand *that* struck us—it happened to us by chance. **Luke 12:19:** And I will say to my soul, "Soul, you have many goods laid up for many years; take your ease; eat, drink, *and* be merry."'
44
Dan. 5:23: And you have lifted yourself up against the Lord of heaven. They have brought the vessels of His house before you, and you and your lords, your wives and your concubines, have drunk wine from them. And you have praised the gods of silver and gold, bronze and iron, wood and stone, which do not see or hear or know; and the God who *holds* your breath in His hand and owns

all your ways, you have not glorified.

45 **Deut. 8:17:** ... then you say in your heart, 'My power and the might of my hand have gained me this wealth.' **See Dan. 4:30.**

46 **Hab. 1:16:** Therefore they sacrifice to their net, And burn incense to their dragnet; Because by them their share *is* sumptuous And their food plentiful.

Q. 127. *What are we specially taught by these words,* before me, *in the first commandment?*

A. These words, *before me*, or before My face, in the first commandment, teach us, that God, who seeth all things, taketh special notice of, and is much displeased with, the sin of having any other God: that so it may be an argument to dissuade from it, and to aggravate it as a most impudent provocation:[1] as also to persuade us to do as in His sight, whatever we do in His service.[2]

1 **Ps. 44:20-21:** If we had forgotten the name of our God, Or stretched out our hands to a foreign god, Would not God search this out? For He knows the secrets of the heart. **See Deut. 30:17-18; Ezek. 8:5-6, 12.**

2 **1 Chron. 28:9:** As for you, my son Solomon, know the God of your father, and serve Him with a loyal heart and with a willing mind; for the LORD searches all hearts and understands all the intent of the thoughts. If you seek Him, He will be found by you; but if you forsake Him, He will cast you off forever.

Q. 128. *Which is the second commandment?*

A. The second commandment is, *Thou shalt not make unto thee any graven image, or any likeness of any thing that is in heaven above, or that is in the earth beneath, or that is in the water under the earth: thou shalt not bow down thyself to them, nor serve them: for I the LORD thy God am a jealous God, visiting the iniquity of the fathers upon the children unto the third and fourth generation of them that hate me; and shewing mercy unto thousands of them that love me, and keep my commandments.*[1]

1 **Ex. 20:4-6:** You shall not make for yourself a carved image—any likeness *of anything* that *is* in heaven above, or that *is* in the earth beneath, or that *is* in the water under the earth; you shall not bow down to them nor serve them. For I, the LORD your God, *am* a jealous God, visiting the iniquity of the fathers upon the children to the third and fourth *generations* of those who hate Me, but showing mercy to thousands, to those who love Me and keep My commandments. **Cf. Deut. 5:8-10.**

Q. 129. *What are the duties required in the second commandment?*

A. The duties required in the second commandment are, the receiving, observing, and keeping pure and entire, all such religious worship and ordinances as God hath instituted in His word;[1] particularly prayer and thanksgiving in the name of Christ;[2] the reading, preaching, and hearing of the word;[3] the administration and receiving of the ordinances;[4] church government and discipline;[5] the ministry and maintenance thereof;[6] religious fasting;[7] swearing by the name of God,[8] and vowing unto Him:[9] as also the disapproving, detesting, opposing, all false worship;[10] and, according to each one's place and calling, removing it, and all monuments of idolatry.[11]

1 **Deut. 12:32:** Whatever I command you, be careful to observe it; you shall not add to it nor take away from it. **Deut. 32:46-47:** ... and he said to them: "Set your hearts on all the words which I testify among you today, which you shall command your children to be careful to observe—all the words of this law. For it *is* not a futile thing for you, because it *is* your life, and by this word you shall prolong *your* days in the land which you cross over the Jordan to possess." **Matt. 28:20:** "... teaching them to observe all things that I have commanded you; and lo, I am with you always, *even* to the end of the age." Amen. **1 Tim. 6:13-14:** ... I urge you in the sight of God who gives life to all things, and *before* Christ Jesus who witnessed the good confession before Pontius Pilate, that you keep *this* commandment without spot, blameless until our Lord Jesus Christ's appearing. **See Acts 2:42.**

2 **Phil. 4:6:** Be anxious for nothing, but in everything by prayer and supplication, with thanksgiving, let your requests be made known to God. **Eph. 5:20:** ... giving thanks always for all things to God the Father in the name of our Lord Jesus Christ.

3 **Deut. 17:18-19:** Also it shall be, when he sits on the throne of his kingdom, that he shall write for himself a copy of this law in a book, from *the one* before the priests, the Levites. And it shall be with him, and he shall read it all the days of his life, that he may learn to fear the LORD his God and be careful to observe all the words of this law and these statutes. **Acts 15:21:** For Moses has had throughout many generations those who preach him in every city, being read in the synagogues every Sabbath. **2 Tim. 4:2:** Preach the word! Be ready in season *and* out of season. Convince, rebuke, exhort, with all longsuffering and teaching. **James 1:21-22:** Therefore lay aside all filthiness and overflow of wickedness, and receive with meekness the implanted word, which is able to save your souls. But be doers of the word, and not hearers only, deceiving yourselves. **Acts 10:33:** So I sent to you immediately, and you have done well to come. Now therefore, we are all present before God, to hear all the things commanded you by God.

4 **Matt. 28:19:** Go therefore and make disciples of all the nations, baptizing them in the name of the Father and of the Son and of the Holy Spirit. **See 1 Cor. 11:23-30.**

5 **Matt. 18:15-17:** Moreover if your brother sins against you, go and tell him his fault between you and him alone. If he hears you, you have gained your brother. But if he will not hear, take with you one or two more, that 'by the mouth of two or three witnesses every word may be established.' And if he refuses to hear them, tell *it* to the church. But if he refuses even to hear the church, let him be to you like a heathen and a tax collector. **Matt. 16:19:** And I will give you the keys of the kingdom of heaven, and whatever you bind on earth will be bound in heaven, and whatever you loose on earth will be loosed in heaven. **1 Cor. 12:28:** And God has appointed these in the church: first apostles, second prophets, third teachers, after that miracles, then gifts of healings, helps, administrations, varieties of tongues. **See 1 Cor. 5.**

6 **Eph. 4:11-12:** And He Himself gave some *to be* apostles, some prophets, some evangelists, and some pastors and teachers, for the equipping of the saints for the work of ministry, for the edifying of the body of Christ. **1 Tim. 5:17-18:** Let the elders who rule well be counted worthy of double honor, especially those who labor in the word and doctrine. For the Scripture says, "You shall not muzzle an ox while it treads out the grain," and, "The laborer *is* worthy of his wages." **See 1 Cor. 9:7-15.**

7 **Joel 2:12-13:** "Now, therefore," says the LORD, "Turn to Me with all your heart, With fasting, with weeping, and with mourning." So rend your heart, and not your garments; Return to the LORD your God, For He *is* gracious and merciful, Slow to anger, and of great kindness; And He relents from doing harm. **1 Cor. 7:5:** Do not deprive one another except with consent for a time, that you may give yourselves to fasting and prayer; and come together again so that Satan does not tempt you because of your lack of self-control.

8 **Deut. 6:13:** You shall fear the LORD your God and serve Him, and shall take oaths in His name.

9
Ps. 76:11: Make vows to the LORD your God, and pay *them;* Let all who are around Him bring presents to Him who ought to be feared. **Isa. 19:21:** Then the LORD will be known to Egypt, and the Egyptians will know the LORD in that day, and will make sacrifice and offering; yes, they will make a vow to the LORD and perform *it.* **See Ps. 116:14, 18.**
10
Acts 17:16-17: Now while Paul waited for them at Athens, his spirit was provoked within him when he saw that the city was given over to idols. Therefore he reasoned in the synagogue with the Jews and with the *Gentile* worshipers, and in the marketplace daily with those who happened to be there. **Ps. 16:4:** Their sorrows shall be multiplied who hasten *after* another *god;* Their drink offerings of blood I will not offer, Nor take up their names on my lips.
11
Deut. 7:5: But thus you shall deal with them: you shall destroy their altars, and break down their *sacred* pillars, and cut down their wooden images, and burn their carved images with fire. **Isa. 30:22:** You will also defile the covering of your images of silver, And the ornament of your molded images of gold. You will throw them away as an unclean thing; You will say to them, "Get away!"

Q. 130. *What are the sins forbidden in the second commandment?*

A. The sins forbidden in the second commandment are, all devising,[1] counseling,[2] commanding,[3] using,[4] and anywise approving, any religious worship not instituted by God Himself;[5] tolerating a false religion;[6] the making any representation of God, of all or of any of the three persons, either inwardly in our mind, or outwardly in any kind of image or likeness of any creature whatsoever;[7] all worshiping of it,[8] or God in it or by it;[9] the making of any representation of feigned deities,[10] and all worship of them, or service belonging to them;[11] all superstitious devices,[12] corrupting the worship of God,[13] adding to it, or taking from it,[14] whether invented and taken up of ourselves,[15] or received by tradition from others,[16] though under the title of antiquity,[17] custom,[18] devotion,[19] good intent, or any other pretense whatsoever;[20] simony;[21] sacrilege;[22] all neglect,[23] contempt,[24] hindering,[25] and opposing the worship and ordinances which God hath appointed.[26]

1
Num. 15:39: And you shall have the tassel, that you may look upon it and remember all the commandments of the LORD and do them, and that you *may* not follow the harlotry to which your own heart and your own eyes are inclined.
2
Deut. 13:6-8: If your brother, the son of your mother, your son or your daughter, the wife of your bosom, or your friend who is as your own soul, secretly entices you, saying, 'Let us go and serve other gods,' which you have not known, neither you nor your fathers, of the gods of the people which *are* all around you, near to you or far off from you, from *one* end of the earth to the *other* end of the earth, you shall not consent to him or listen to him, nor shall your eye pity him, nor shall you spare him or conceal him.
3
Hos. 5:11: Ephraim is oppressed *and* broken in judgment, Because he willingly walked by *human* precept. **Mic. 6:16:** For the statutes of Omri are kept; All the works of Ahab's house *are done;* And you walk in their counsels, That I may make you a desolation, And your inhabitants a hissing. Therefore you shall bear the reproach of My people.
4
1 Kings 11:33: ... because they have forsaken Me, and worshiped Ashtoreth the goddess of the

Sidonians, Chemosh the god of the Moabites, and Milcom the god of the people of Ammon, and have not walked in My ways to do *what is* right in My eyes and *keep* My statutes and My judgments, as *did* his father David. **1 Kings 12:33:** So he made offerings on the altar which he had made at Bethel on the fifteenth day of the eighth month, in the month which he had devised in his own heart. And he ordained a feast for the children of Israel, and offered sacrifices on the altar and burned incense.

5

Deut. 12:30-32: ... take heed to yourself that you are not ensnared to follow them, after they are destroyed from before you, and that you do not inquire after their gods, saying, 'How did these nations serve their gods? I also will do likewise.' You shall not worship the LORD your God in that way; for every abomination to the LORD which He hates they have done to their gods; for they burn even their sons and daughters in the fire to their gods. "Whatever I command you, be careful to observe it; you shall not add to it nor take away from it. **Lev. 10:1-2:** Then Nadab and Abihu, the sons of Aaron, each took his censer and put fire in it, put incense on it, and offered profane fire before the LORD, which He had not commanded them. So fire went out from the LORD and devoured them, and they died before the LORD. **Jer. 19:5:** ... they have also built the high places of Baal, to burn their sons with fire *for* burnt offerings to Baal, which I did not command or speak, nor did it come into My mind.

6

Deut. 13:6-12: If your brother, the son of your mother, your son or your daughter, the wife of your bosom, or your friend who is as your own soul, secretly entices you, saying, 'Let us go and serve other gods,' which you have not known, neither you nor your fathers, of the gods of the people which *are* all around you, near to you or far off from you, from *one* end of the earth to the *other* end of the earth, you shall not consent to him or listen to him, nor shall your eye pity him, nor shall you spare him or conceal him; but you shall surely kill him; your hand shall be first against him to put him to death, and afterward the hand of all the people. And you shall stone him with stones until he dies, because he sought to entice you away from the LORD your God, who brought you out of the land of Egypt, from the house of bondage. So all Israel shall hear and fear, and not again do such wickedness as this among you. If you hear someone in one of your cities, which the LORD your God gives you to dwell in, saying. **Zech. 13:2-3:** It shall be in that day," says the LORD of hosts, "*that* I will cut off the names of the idols from the land, and they shall no longer be remembered. I will also cause the prophets and the unclean spirit to depart from the land. It shall come to pass *that* if anyone still prophesies, then his father and mother who begot him will say to him, 'You shall not live, because you have spoken lies in the name of the LORD.' And his father and mother who begot him shall thrust him through when he prophesies. **Rev. 2:2, 14-15, 20:** I know your works, your labor, your patience, and that you cannot bear those who are evil. And you have tested those who say they are apostles and are not, and have found them liars.... But I have a few things against you, because you have there those who hold the doctrine of Balaam, who taught Balak to put a stumbling block before the children of Israel, to eat things sacrificed to idols, and to commit sexual immorality. Thus you also have those who hold the doctrine of the Nicolaitans, which thing I hate.... Nevertheless I have a few things against you, because you allow that woman Jezebel, who calls herself a prophetess, to teach and seduce My servants to commit sexual immorality and eat things sacrificed to idols. **Rev. 17:12, 16-17:** The ten horns which you saw are ten kings who have received no kingdom as yet, but they receive authority for one hour as kings with the beast.... And the ten horns which you saw on the beast, these will hate the harlot, make her desolate and naked, eat her flesh and burn her with fire. For God has put it into their hearts to fulfill His purpose, to be of one mind, and to give their kingdom to the beast, until the words of God are fulfilled.

7

Deut. 4:15-16: Take careful heed to yourselves, for you saw no form when the LORD spoke to you at Horeb out of the midst of the fire, lest you act corruptly and make for yourselves a carved image in the form of any figure: the likeness of male or female. **See Deut. 4:17-19. Acts 17:29:** Therefore, since we are the offspring of God, we ought not to think that the Divine Nature is like gold or silver or stone, something shaped by art and man's devising. **Rom. 1:21-23, 25:** ... because, although they knew God, they did not glorify *Him* as God, nor were thankful, but became futile in their thoughts, and their foolish hearts were darkened. Professing to be wise, they became fools, and changed the glory of the incorruptible God into an image made like corruptible man—and birds and four-footed animals and creeping things.... who exchanged the truth of God for the lie, and worshiped and served the creature rather than the Creator, who is blessed forever. Amen.

8

Gal. 4:8: But then, indeed, when you did not know God, you served those which by nature are not gods. **See Dan. 3:18.**

9

Ex. 32:5: So when Aaron saw *it,* he built an altar before it. And Aaron made a proclamation and said, "Tomorrow *is* a feast to the LORD."

10

Ex. 32:8: They have turned aside quickly out of the way which I commanded them. They have made themselves a molded calf, and worshiped it and sacrificed to it, and said, 'This *is* your god, O Israel, that brought you out of the land of Egypt!'

11

1 Kings 18:26, 28: So they took the bull which was given them, and they prepared *it,* and called on the name of Baal from morning even till noon, saying, "O Baal, hear us!" But *there was* no voice; no one answered. Then they leaped about the altar which they had made.... So they cried aloud, and cut themselves, as was their custom, with knives and lances, until the blood gushed out on them. **See Isa. 65:11.**

12

Acts 17:22: Then Paul stood in the midst of the Areopagus and said, "Men of Athens, I perceive that in all things you are very religious." **Col. 2:21-23:** "Do not touch, do not taste, do not handle," which all concern things which perish with the using—according to the commandments and doctrines of men? These things indeed have an appearance of wisdom in self-imposed religion, *false* humility, and neglect of the body, *but are* of no value against the indulgence of the flesh.

13

Mal. 1:7-8, 14: "You offer defiled food on My altar, But say, 'In what way have we defiled You?' By saying, 'The table of the LORD is contemptible.' And when you offer the blind as a sacrifice, *Is it* not evil? And when you offer the lame and sick, *Is it* not evil? Offer it then to your governor! Would he be pleased with you? Would he accept you favorably?" Says the LORD of hosts.... "But cursed *be* the deceiver Who has in his flock a male, And takes a vow, But sacrifices to the Lord what is blemished— For I *am* a great King," Says the LORD of hosts, "And My name *is to be* feared among the nations."

14

Deut. 4:2: You shall not add to the word which I command you, nor take from it, that you may keep the commandments of the LORD your God which I command you.

15

Ps. 106:39: Thus they were defiled by their own works, And played the harlot by their own deeds.

16

Matt. 15:9: And in vain they worship Me, Teaching *as* doctrines the commandments of men.

17

1 Pet. 1:18: ... knowing that you were not redeemed with corruptible things, *like* silver or gold, from your aimless conduct *received* by tradition from your fathers.

18

Jer. 44:17: But we will certainly do whatever has gone out of our own mouth, to burn incense to the queen of heaven and pour out drink offerings to her, as we have done, we and our fathers, our kings and our princes, in the cities of Judah and in the streets of Jerusalem. For *then* we had plenty of food, were well-off, and saw no trouble.

19

Isa. 65:3-5: A people who provoke Me to anger continually to My face; Who sacrifice in gardens, And burn incense on altars of brick; Who sit among the graves, And spend the night in the tombs; Who eat swine's flesh, And the broth of abominable things is *in* their vessels; Who say, 'Keep to yourself, Do not come near me, For I am holier than you!' These *are* smoke in My nostrils, A fire that burns all the day. **Gal. 1:13-14:** For you have heard of my former conduct in Judaism, how I persecuted the church of God beyond measure and *tried to* destroy it. And I advanced in Judaism beyond many of my contemporaries in my own nation, being more exceedingly zealous for the traditions of my fathers.

20

1 Sam. 13:11-12: And Samuel said, "What have you done?" Saul said, "When I saw that the people were scattered from me, and *that* you did not come within the days appointed, and *that* the Philistines gathered together at Michmash, then I said, 'The Philistines will now come down on me at Gilgal, and I have not made supplication to the LORD.' Therefore I felt compelled, and offered a burnt offering." **1 Sam. 15:21:** But the people took of the plunder, sheep and oxen, the best of the things which should have been utterly destroyed, to sacrifice to the LORD your God in Gilgal.

21

Acts 8:18-19: And when Simon saw that through the laying on of the apostles' hands the Holy Spirit was given, he offered them money, saying, "Give me this power also, that anyone on whom I lay hands may receive the Holy Spirit."

22

Rom. 2:22: You who say, "Do not commit adultery," do you commit adultery? You who abhor idols, do you rob temples? **Mal. 3:8:** Will a man rob God? Yet you have robbed Me! But you say, 'In what way have we robbed You?' In tithes and offerings.

23

Ex. 4:24-26: And it came to pass on the way, at the encampment, that the LORD met him and sought to kill him. Then Zipporah took a sharp stone and cut off the foreskin of her son and cast *it* at *Moses'* feet, and said, "Surely you *are* a husband of blood to me!" So He let him go. Then she said, "*You are* a husband of blood!"—because of the circumcision.

24

Matt. 22:5: But they made light of it and went their ways, one to his own farm, another to his business. **Mal. 1:7, 13:** "You offer defiled food on My altar, But say, 'In what way have we defiled You?' By saying, 'The table of the LORD is contemptible.' ... You also say, 'Oh, what a weariness!' And you sneer at it," Says the LORD of hosts. "And you bring the stolen, the lame, and the sick; Thus you bring an offering! Should I accept this from your hand?" Says the LORD.

25

Matt. 23:13: But woe to you, scribes and Pharisees, hypocrites! For you shut up the kingdom of heaven against men; for you neither go in *yourselves,* nor do you allow those who are entering to go in.

26
Acts 13:44-45: On the next Sabbath almost the whole city came together to hear the word of God. But when the Jews saw the multitudes, they were filled with envy; and contradicting and blaspheming, they opposed the things spoken by Paul. **See 1 Thess. 2:15-16.**

Q. 131. *What are the reasons annexed to the second commandment, the more to enforce it?*

A. The reasons annexed to the second commandment, the more to enforce it, contained in these words, *for I the LORD thy God am a jealous God, visiting the iniquity of the fathers upon the children unto the third and fourth generation of them that hate me; and shewing mercy unto thousands of them that love me, and keep my commandments;*[1] are, besides God's sovereignty over us, and propriety in us,[2] His fervent zeal for His own worship,[3] and His revengeful indignation against all false worship, as being a spiritual whoredom;[4] accounting the breakers of this commandment such as hate Him, and threatening to punish them unto divers generations;[5] and esteeming the observers of it such as love Him and keep His commandments, and promising mercy to them unto many generations.[6]

1
Ex. 20:5-6: ... you shall not bow down to them nor serve them. For I, the LORD your God, *am* a jealous God, visiting the iniquity of the fathers upon the children to the third and fourth *generations* of those who hate Me, but showing mercy to thousands, to those who love Me and keep My commandments.

2
Ps. 45:11: So the King will greatly desire your beauty; Because He *is* your Lord, worship Him. **Rev. 15:3-4:** They sing the song of Moses, the servant of God, and the song of the Lamb, saying: "Great and marvelous *are* Your works, Lord God Almighty! Just and true *are* Your ways, O King of the saints! Who shall not fear You, O Lord, and glorify Your name? For *You* alone *are* holy. For all nations shall come and worship before You, For Your judgments have been manifested." **See Ps. 95:2-3, 6-7; Ex. 19:5; Isa. 54:5.**

3
Ex. 34:13-14: But you shall destroy their altars, break their *sacred* pillars, and cut down their wooden images (for you shall worship no other god, for the LORD, whose name *is* Jealous, *is* a jealous God).

4
1 Cor. 10:20-22: Rather, that the things which the Gentiles sacrifice they sacrifice to demons and not to God, and I do not want you to have fellowship with demons. You cannot drink the cup of the Lord and the cup of demons; you cannot partake of the Lord's table and of the table of demons. Or do we provoke the Lord to jealousy? Are we stronger than He? **Ezek. 16:26-27:** You also committed harlotry with the Egyptians, your very fleshly neighbors, and increased your acts of harlotry to provoke Me to anger. "Behold, therefore, I stretched out My hand against you, diminished your allotment, and gave you up to the will of those who hate you, the daughters of the Philistines, who were ashamed of your lewd behavior. **See Jer. 7:18-20; Deut. 32:16-20.**

5
Hos. 2:2-4: Bring charges against your mother, bring charges; For she *is* not My wife, nor *am* I her Husband! Let her put away her harlotries from her sight, And her adulteries from between her breasts; Lest I strip her naked And expose her, as in the day she was born, And make her like a wilderness, And set her like a dry land, And slay her with thirst. I will not have mercy on her children, For they *are* the children of harlotry.

6
Deut. 5:29: Oh, that they had such a heart in them that they would fear Me and always keep all My commandments, that it might be well with them and with their children forever!

Q. 132. *Which is the third commandment?*

A. The third commandment is, *Thou shalt not take the name of the LORD thy God in vain; for the LORD will not hold him guiltless that taketh his name in vain.*[1]

[1] **Ex. 20:7:** You shall not take the name of the LORD your God in vain, for the LORD will not hold *him* guiltless who takes His name in vain. **Cf. Deut. 5:11.**

Q. 133. *What is required in the third commandment?*

A. The third commandment requires, that the name of God, His titles, attributes,[1] ordinances,[2] the word,[3] prayer,[4] oaths,[5] vows,[6] lots,[7] His works,[8] and whatsoever else there is whereby He makes Himself known, be holily and reverently used in thought,[9] meditation,[10] word,[11] and writing;[12] by an holy profession,[13] and answerable conversation,[14] to the glory of God,[15] and the good of ourselves,[16] and others.[17]

[1] **Matt. 6:9:** In this manner, therefore, pray: Our Father in heaven, Hallowed be Your name. **Deut. 28:58:** If you do not carefully observe all the words of this law that are written in this book, that you may fear this glorious and awesome name, THE LORD YOUR GOD. **Ps. 68:4:** Sing to God, sing praises to His name; Extol Him who rides on the clouds, By His name YAH, And rejoice before Him. **See Ps. 29:2; 1 Chron. 29:10-13; Rev. 15:3-4.**

[2] **Eccl. 5:1:** Walk prudently when you go to the house of God; and draw near to hear rather than to give the sacrifice of fools, for they do not know that they do evil. **Luke 1:6:** And they were both righteous before God, walking in all the commandments and ordinances of the Lord blameless. **1 Cor. 11:24-25, 28-29:** ... and when He had given thanks, He broke *it* and said, "Take, eat; this is My body which is broken for you; do this in remembrance of Me." In the same manner *He* also *took* the cup after supper, saying, "This cup is the new covenant in My blood. This do, as often as you drink *it,* in remembrance of Me." ... But let a man examine himself, and so let him eat of the bread and drink of the cup. For he who eats and drinks in an unworthy manner eats and drinks judgment to himself, not discerning the Lord's body.

[3] **Ps. 138:2:** I will worship toward Your holy temple, And praise Your name For Your lovingkindness and Your truth; For You have magnified Your word above all Your name.

[4] **1 Tim. 2:8:** I desire therefore that the men pray everywhere, lifting up holy hands, without wrath and doubting.

[5] **Jer. 4:2:** And you shall swear, 'The LORD lives,' In truth, in judgment, and in righteousness; The nations shall bless themselves in Him, And in Him they shall glory.

[6] **Eccl. 5:2, 4-6:** Do not be rash with your mouth, And let not your heart utter anything hastily before God. For God *is* in heaven, and you on earth; Therefore let your words be few.... When you make a vow to God, do not delay to pay it; For *He has* no pleasure in fools. Pay what you have vowed— Better not to vow than to vow and not pay. Do not let your mouth cause your flesh to sin, nor say before the messenger *of God* that it *was* an error. Why should God be angry at your excuse and destroy the work of your hands?

[7] **Acts 1:24, 26:** And they prayed and said, "You, O Lord, who know the hearts of all, show which of these two You have chosen." ... And they cast their lots, and the lot fell on Matthias. And he was numbered with the eleven apostles.

[8] **Job 36:24:** Remember to magnify His work, Of which men have sung.

[9] **Mal. 3:16:** Then those who feared the LORD spoke to one another, And the LORD listened and heard them; So a book of remembrance was written before Him For those who fear the LORD And who

meditate on His name.

10
Ps. 8:1, 3-4: O LORD, our Lord, How excellent *is* Your name in all the earth, Who have set Your glory above the heavens! ... When I consider Your heavens, the work of Your fingers, The moon and the stars, which You have ordained, What is man that You are mindful of him, And the son of man that You visit him?

11
Ps. 105:2, 5: Sing to Him, sing psalms to Him; Talk of all His wondrous works! ... Remember His marvelous works which He has done, His wonders, and the judgments of His mouth. **See Col. 3:17.**

12
Ps. 102:18: This will be written for the generation to come, That a people yet to be created may praise the LORD.

13
1 Pet. 3:15: But sanctify the Lord God in your hearts, and always *be* ready to *give* a defense to everyone who asks you a reason for the hope that is in you, with meekness and fear. **Mic. 4:5:** For all people walk each in the name of his god, But we will walk in the name of the LORD our God Forever and ever.

14
Phil. 1:27: Only let your conduct be worthy of the gospel of Christ, so that whether I come and see you or am absent, I may hear of your affairs, that you stand fast in one spirit, with one mind striving together for the faith of the gospel.

15
1 Cor. 10:31: Therefore, whether you eat or drink, or whatever you do, do all to the glory of God.

16
Jer. 32:39: ... then I will give them one heart and one way, that they may fear Me forever, for the good of them and their children after them.

17
1 Pet. 2:12: ... having your conduct honorable among the Gentiles, that when they speak against you as evildoers, they may, by *your* good works which they observe, glorify God in the day of visitation.

Q. 134. *What are the sins forbidden in the third commandment?*

A. The sins forbidden in the third commandment are, the not using of God's name as is required;[1] and the abuse of it in an ignorant,[2] vain,[3] irreverent, profane,[4] superstitious,[5] or wicked mentioning or otherwise using His titles, attributes,[6] ordinances,[7] or works,[8] by blasphemy,[9] perjury;[10] all sinful cursings,[11] oaths,[12] vows,[13] and lots;[14] violating of our oaths and vows, if lawful;[15] and fulfilling them, if of things unlawful;[16] murmuring and quarreling at,[17] curious prying into,[18] and misapplying of God's decrees[19] and providences;[20] misinterpreting,[21] misapplying,[22] or any way perverting the word, or any part of it,[23] to profane jests,[24] curious or unprofitable questions, vain janglings, or the maintaining of false doctrines;[25] abusing it, the creatures, or anything contained under the name of God, to charms,[26] or sinful lusts and practices;[27] the maligning,[28] scorning,[29] reviling,[30] or any wise opposing of God's truth, grace, and ways;[31] making profession of religion in hypocrisy, or for sinister ends;[32] being ashamed of it,[33] or a shame to it, by unconformable,[34] unwise,[35] unfruitful,[36] and offensive walking,[37] or backsliding from it.[38]

1
Mal. 2:2: "If you will not hear, And if you will not take *it* to heart, To give glory to My name," Says the LORD of hosts, "I will send a curse upon you, And I will curse your blessings. Yes, I have cursed them already, Because you do not take *it* to heart."

2
Acts 17:23: ... for as I was passing through and considering the objects of your worship, I even found an altar with this inscription: TO THE UNKNOWN GOD. Therefore, the One whom you worship without knowing, Him I proclaim to you.

3
Prov. 30:9: Lest I be full and deny *You,* And say, "Who *is* the LORD?" Or lest I be poor and steal, And profane the name of my God.

4
Mal. 1:6-7, 12: A son honors *his* father, And a servant *his* master. If then I am the Father, Where *is* My honor? And if I *am* a Master, Where *is* My reverence? Says the LORD of hosts To you priests who despise My name. Yet you say, 'In what way have we despised Your name?' You offer defiled food on My altar, But say, 'In what way have we defiled You?' By saying, 'The table of the LORD is contemptible.' ... But you profane it, In that you say, 'The table of the LORD is defiled; And its fruit, its food, *is* contemptible.' **Mal. 3:14:** You have said, 'It is useless to serve God; What profit *is it* that we have kept His ordinance, And that we have walked as mourners Before the LORD of hosts?'

5
1 Sam. 4:3-5: And when the people had come into the camp, the elders of Israel said, "Why has the LORD defeated us today before the Philistines? Let us bring the ark of the covenant of the LORD from Shiloh to us, that when it comes among us it may save us from the hand of our enemies." So the people sent to Shiloh, that they might bring from there the ark of the covenant of the LORD of hosts, who dwells *between* the cherubim. And the two sons of Eli, Hophni and Phinehas, *were* there with the ark of the covenant of God. And when the ark of the covenant of the LORD came into the camp, all Israel shouted so loudly that the earth shook. **Jer. 7:4, 9-10, 14, 31:** Do not trust in these lying words, saying, 'The temple of the LORD, the temple of the LORD, the temple of the LORD *are* these.' ... Will you steal, murder, commit adultery, swear falsely, burn incense to Baal, and walk after other gods whom you do not know, and *then* come and stand before Me in this house which is called by My name, and say, 'We are delivered to do all these abominations'? ... therefore I will do to the house which is called by My name, in which you trust, and to this place which I gave to you and your fathers, as I have done to Shiloh.... And they have built the high places of Tophet, which *is* in the Valley of the Son of Hinnom, to burn their sons and their daughters in the fire, which I did not command, nor did it come into My heart. **Col. 2:20-22:** Therefore, if you died with Christ from the basic principles of the world, why, as *though* living in the world, do you subject yourselves to regulations— "Do not touch, do not taste, do not handle," which all concern things which perish with the using—according to the commandments and doctrines of men?

6
2 Kings 18:30, 35: ... nor let Hezekiah make you trust in the LORD, saying, "The LORD will surely deliver us; this city shall not be given into the hand of the king of Assyria."' ... Who among all the gods of the lands have delivered their countries from my hand, that the LORD should deliver Jerusalem from my hand?'" **Ex. 5:2:** And Pharaoh said, "Who *is* the LORD, that I should obey His voice to let Israel go? I do not know the LORD, nor will I let Israel go." **Ps. 139:20:** For they speak against You wickedly; Your enemies take *Your name* in vain.

7
Ps. 50:16-17: But to the wicked God says: "What *right* have you to declare My statutes, Or take My covenant in your mouth, Seeing you hate instruction And cast My words behind you?"

8
Isa. 5:12: The harp and the strings, The tambourine and flute, And wine are in their feasts; But they do not regard the work of the LORD, Nor consider the operation of His hands.

9
2 Kings 19:22: Whom have you reproached and blasphemed? Against whom have you raised *your* voice, And lifted up your eyes on high? Against the Holy *One* of Israel. **Lev. 24:11:** And the Israelite woman's son blasphemed the name of *the LORD* and cursed; and so they brought him to Moses. (His mother's name *was* Shelomith the daughter of Dibri, of the tribe of Dan.)

10
Zech. 5:4: "I will send out *the curse,"* says the LORD of hosts; "It shall enter the house of the thief And the house of the one who swears falsely by My name. It shall remain in the midst of his house And consume it, with its timber and stones." **Zech. 8:17:** 'Let none of you think evil in your heart against your neighbor; And do not love a false oath. For all these *are things* that I hate,' Says the LORD.

11
1 Sam. 17:43: So the Philistine said to David, *"Am* I a dog, that you come to me with sticks?" And the Philistine cursed David by his gods. **2 Sam. 16:5:** Now when King David came to Bahurim, there was a man from the family of the house of Saul, whose name *was* Shimei the son of Gera, coming from there. He came out, cursing continuously as he came.

12
Jer. 5:7: How shall I pardon you for this? Your children have forsaken Me And sworn by *those that are* not gods. When I had fed them to the full, Then they committed adultery And assembled

themselves by troops in the harlots' houses. **Jer. 23:10:** For the land is full of adulterers; For because of a curse the land mourns. The pleasant places of the wilderness are dried up. Their course of life is evil, And their might *is* not right.

13

Deut. 23:18: You shall not bring the wages of a harlot or the price of a dog to the house of the LORD your God for any vowed offering, for both of these *are* an abomination to the LORD your God. **Acts 23:12, 14:** And when it was day, some of the Jews banded together and bound themselves under an oath, saying that they would neither eat nor drink till they had killed Paul.... They came to the chief priests and elders, and said, "We have bound ourselves under a great oath that we will eat nothing until we have killed Paul."

14

Est. 3:7: In the first month, which is the month of Nisan, in the twelfth year of King Ahasuerus, they cast Pur (that *is,* the lot), before Haman to determine the day and the month, until *it fell on the* twelfth *month,* which *is* the month of Adar. **Est. 9:24:** ... because Haman, the son of Hammedatha the Agagite, the enemy of all the Jews, had plotted against the Jews to annihilate them, and had cast Pur (that *is,* the lot), to consume them and destroy them. **Ps. 22:18:** They divide My garments among them, And for My clothing they cast lots.

15

Ps. 24:4: He who has clean hands and a pure heart, Who has not lifted up his soul to an idol, Nor sworn deceitfully. **Ezek. 17:16, 18-19:** '*As* I live,' says the Lord GOD, 'surely in the place *where* the king *dwells* who made him king, whose oath he despised and whose covenant he broke—with him in the midst of Babylon he shall die.... Since he despised the oath by breaking the covenant, and in fact gave his hand and still did all these *things,* he shall not escape.'" Therefore thus says the Lord GOD: "*As* I live, surely My oath which he despised, and My covenant which he broke, I will recompense on his own head."

16

Mark 6:26: And the king was exceedingly sorry; *yet,* because of the oaths and because of those who sat with him, he did not want to refuse her. **1 Sam. 25:22, 32-34:** May God do so, and more also, to the enemies of David, if I leave one male of all who *belong* to him by morning light.... Then David said to Abigail: "Blessed *is* the LORD God of Israel, who sent you this day to meet me! And blessed *is* your advice and blessed *are* you, because you have kept me this day from coming to bloodshed and from avenging myself with my own hand. For indeed, *as* the LORD God of Israel lives, who has kept me back from hurting you, unless you had hurried and come to meet me, surely by morning light no males would have been left to Nabal!"

17

Rom. 9:14, 19-20: What shall we say then? *Is there* unrighteousness with God? Certainly not! ... You will say to me then, "Why does He still find fault? For who has resisted His will?" But indeed, O man, who are you to reply against God? Will the thing formed say to him who formed *it,* "Why have you made me like this?"

18

Deut. 29:29: The secret *things belong* to the LORD our God, but those *things which are* revealed *belong* to us and to our children forever, that *we* may do all the words of this law.

19

Rom. 3:5, 7: But if our unrighteousness demonstrates the righteousness of God, what shall we say? *Is* God unjust who inflicts wrath? (I speak as a man.) ... For if the truth of God has increased through my lie to His glory, why am I also still judged as a sinner? **Rom. 6:1-2:** What shall we say then? Shall we continue in sin that grace may abound? Certainly not! How shall we who died to sin live any longer in it?

20

Eccl. 8:11: Because the sentence against an evil work is not executed speedily, therefore the heart of the sons of men is fully set in them to do evil. **Eccl. 9:3:** This *is* an evil in all that is done under the sun: that one thing *happens* to all. Truly the hearts of the sons of men are full of evil; madness *is* in their hearts while they live, and after that *they go* to the dead. **See Ps. 39.**

21

Matt. 5:21-22, 27-28, 31-35, 38-39, 43-44: You have heard that it was said to those of old, 'You shall not murder, and whoever murders will be in danger of the judgment.' But I say to you that whoever is angry with his brother without a cause shall be in danger of the judgment. And whoever says to his brother, 'Raca!' shall be in danger of the council. But whoever says, 'You fool!' shall be in danger of hell fire.... You have heard that it was said to those of old, 'You shall not commit adultery.' But I say to you that whoever looks at a woman to lust for her has already committed adultery with her in his heart.... Furthermore it has been said, 'Whoever divorces his wife, let him give her a certificate of divorce.' But I say to you that whoever divorces his wife for any reason except sexual immorality causes her to commit adultery; and whoever marries a woman who is divorced commits adultery. Again you have heard that it was said to those of old, 'You shall not swear falsely, but shall perform your oaths to the Lord.' But I say to you, do not swear at all: neither by heaven, for it is God's throne; nor by the earth, for it is His footstool; nor by Jerusalem, for it is the city of the great King.... You have heard that it was said, 'An eye for an eye and a tooth for a tooth.' But I tell you not to resist an evil person. But whoever slaps you on your right cheek, turn the other to him also.... You have heard that it was said, 'You shall love your neighbor and hate your enemy.' But I say to you, love your enemies, bless those who curse you, do good to those who hate you, and pray for those who spitefully use you and persecute you.

22
Ezek. 13:22: Because with lies you have made the heart of the righteous sad, whom I have not made sad; and you have strengthened the hands of the wicked, so that he does not turn from his wicked way to save his life.
23
2 Pet. 3:16: ... as also in all his epistles, speaking in them of these things, in which are some things hard to understand, which untaught and unstable *people* twist to their own destruction, as *they do* also the rest of the Scriptures. **See Matt. 22:24-31.**
24
Isa. 22:13: But instead, joy and gladness, Slaying oxen and killing sheep, Eating meat and drinking wine: "Let us eat and drink, for tomorrow we die!" **Jer. 23:34, 36, 38:** And *as for* the prophet and the priest and the people who say, 'The oracle of the LORD!' I will even punish that man and his house.... And the oracle of the LORD you shall mention no more. For every man's word will be his oracle, for you have perverted the words of the living God, the LORD of hosts, our God.... But since you say, 'The oracle of the LORD!' therefore thus says the LORD: 'Because you say this word, "The oracle of the LORD!" and I have sent to you, saying, "Do not say, 'The oracle of the LORD!'"
25
1 Tim. 1:4, 6-7: ... nor give heed to fables and endless genealogies, which cause disputes rather than godly edification which is in faith.... from which some, having strayed, have turned aside to idle talk, desiring to be teachers of the law, understanding neither what they say nor the things which they affirm. **1 Tim. 6:4-5, 20:** ... he is proud, knowing nothing, but is obsessed with disputes and arguments over words, from which come envy, strife, reviling, evil suspicions, useless wranglings of men of corrupt minds and destitute of the truth, who suppose that godliness is a *means of* gain. From such withdraw yourself.... O Timothy! Guard what was committed to your trust, avoiding the profane *and* idle babblings and contradictions of what is falsely called knowledge. **2 Tim. 2:14:** Remind *them* of these things, charging *them* before the Lord not to strive about words to no profit, to the ruin of the hearers. **Titus 3:9:** But avoid foolish disputes, genealogies, contentions, and strivings about the law; for they are unprofitable and useless.
26
Deut. 18:10-14: There shall not be found among you *anyone* who makes his son or his daughter pass through the fire, *or one* who practices witchcraft, *or* a soothsayer, or one who interprets omens, or a sorcerer, or one who conjures spells, or a medium, or a spiritist, or one who calls up the dead. For all who do these things *are* an abomination to the LORD, and because of these abominations the LORD your God drives them out from before you. You shall be blameless before the LORD your God. For these nations which you will dispossess listened to soothsayers and diviners; but as for you, the LORD your God has not appointed such for you. **Acts 19:13:** Then some of the itinerant Jewish exorcists took it upon themselves to call the name of the Lord Jesus over those who had evil spirits, saying, "We exorcise you by the Jesus whom Paul preaches."
27
2 Tim. 4:3-4: For the time will come when they will not endure sound doctrine, but according to their own desires, *because* they have itching ears, they will heap up for themselves teachers; and they will turn *their* ears away from the truth, and be turned aside to fables. **1 Kings 21:9-10:** She wrote in the letters, saying, Proclaim a fast, and seat Naboth with high honor among the people; and seat two men, scoundrels, before him to bear witness against him, saying, "You have blasphemed God and the king." *Then* take him out, and stone him, that he may die. **See Rom. 13:13-14.**
28
Acts 13:45: But when the Jews saw the multitudes, they were filled with envy; and contradicting and blaspheming, they opposed the things spoken by Paul. **1 John 3:12:** ... not as Cain *who* was of the wicked one and murdered his brother. And why did he murder him? Because his works were evil and his brother's righteous.
29
Ps. 1:1: Blessed *is* the man Who walks not in the counsel of the ungodly, Nor stands in the path of sinners, Nor sits in the seat of the scornful. **2 Pet. 3:3:** ... knowing this first: that scoffers will come in the last days, walking according to their own lusts.
30
1 Pet. 4:4: In regard to these, they think it strange that you do not run with *them* in the same flood of dissipation, speaking evil of *you.*
31
Acts 13:45-46, 50: But when the Jews saw the multitudes, they were filled with envy; and contradicting and blaspheming, they opposed the things spoken by Paul. Then Paul and Barnabas grew bold and said, "It was necessary that the word of God should be spoken to you first; but since you reject it, and judge yourselves unworthy of everlasting life, behold, we turn to the Gentiles." ... But the Jews stirred up the devout and prominent women and the chief men of the city, raised up persecution against Paul and Barnabas, and expelled them from their region. **Acts 4:18:** So they called them and commanded them not to speak at all nor teach in the name of Jesus. **1 Thess. 2:16:** ... forbidding us to speak to the Gentiles that they may be saved, so as always to fill up *the measure of* their sins; but wrath has come upon them to the uttermost. **Heb. 10:29:** Of how much worse punishment, do you suppose, will he be thought worthy who has trampled the Son of God underfoot, counted the blood of the covenant by which he was sanctified a common thing, and insulted the Spirit of grace? **See Acts 19:9.**

32
2 Tim. 3:5: ... having a form of godliness but denying its power. And from such people turn away! **Matt. 23:14:** Woe to you, scribes and Pharisees, hypocrites! For you devour widows' houses, and for a pretense make long prayers. Therefore you will receive greater condemnation. **See Matt. 6:1-2, 5, 16.**
33
Mark 8:38: For whoever is ashamed of Me and My words in this adulterous and sinful generation, of him the Son of Man also will be ashamed when He comes in the glory of His Father with the holy angels.
34
Ps. 73:14-15: For all day long I have been plagued, And chastened every morning. If I had said, "I will speak thus," Behold, I would have been untrue to the generation of Your children.
35
Eph. 5:15-17: See then that you walk circumspectly, not as fools but as wise, redeeming the time, because the days are evil. Therefore do not be unwise, but understand what the will of the Lord *is.* **See 1 Cor. 6:5-6.**
36
Isa. 5:4: What more could have been done to My vineyard That I have not done in it? Why then, when I expected *it* to bring forth *good* grapes, Did it bring forth wild grapes? **See 2 Pet. 1:8-9.**
37
Rom. 2:23-24: You who make your boast in the law, do you dishonor God through breaking the law? For "the name of God is blasphemed among the Gentiles because of you," as it is written.
38
Gal. 3:1, 3: O foolish Galatians! Who has bewitched you that you should not obey the truth, before whose eyes Jesus Christ was clearly portrayed among you as crucified? ... Are you so foolish? Having begun in the Spirit, are you now being made perfect by the flesh? **See Heb. 6:6.**

Q. 135. *What reasons are annexed to the third commandment?*

A. The reasons annexed to the third commandment, in these words, *The LORD thy God*, and, *for the LORD will not hold him guiltless that taketh his name in vain,*[1] are, because He is the LORD and our God, therefore His name is not to be profaned, or any way abused by us;[2] especially because He will be so far from acquitting and sparing the transgressors of this commandment, as that He will not suffer them to escape His righteous judgment,[3] albeit many such escape the censures and punishments of men.[4]

1
Ex. 20:7: You shall not take the name of the LORD your God in vain, for the LORD will not hold *him* guiltless who takes His name in vain.
2
Lev. 19:12: And you shall not swear by My name falsely, nor shall you profane the name of your God: I *am* the LORD.
3
Deut. 28:58-59: If you do not carefully observe all the words of this law that are written in this book, that you may fear this glorious and awesome name, THE LORD YOUR GOD, then the LORD will bring upon you and your descendants extraordinary plagues—great and prolonged plagues—and serious and prolonged sicknesses. **See Ezek. 36:21-23.**
4
1 Sam. 2:29: Why do you kick at My sacrifice and My offering which I have commanded *in My* dwelling place, and honor your sons more than Me, to make yourselves fat with the best of all the offerings of Israel My people? **1 Sam. 3:13:** For I have told him that I will judge his house forever for the iniquity which he knows, because his sons made themselves vile, and he did not restrain them. **See 1 Sam. 2:12-17; 22-25.**

Q. 136. *Which is the fourth commandment?*

A. The fourth commandment is, *Remember the sabbath day, to keep it holy. Six days shalt thou labour, and do all thy work: but the seventh day is the sabbath of the LORD thy God: in it thou shalt not do any work, thou, nor thy son, nor thy daughter, thy manservant, nor thy maidservant, nor thy cattle, nor thy stranger that is within thy gates: for in six days the LORD made heaven and earth, the sea, and all that in them is, and rested the seventh day: wherefore the LORD blessed the sabbath day, and hallowed it.*[1]

[1] **Ex. 20:8-11:** Remember the Sabbath day, to keep it holy. Six days you shall labor and do all your work, but the seventh day *is* the Sabbath of the LORD your God. *In it* you shall do no work: you, nor your son, nor your daughter, nor your male servant, nor your female servant, nor your cattle, nor your stranger who *is* within your gates. For *in* six days the LORD made the heavens and the earth, the sea, and all that *is* in them, and rested the seventh day. Therefore the LORD blessed the Sabbath day and hallowed it. **Cf. Deut. 5:12-15.**

Q. 137. *What is required in the fourth commandment?*

A. The fourth commandment requireth of all men the sanctifying or keeping holy to God such set times as He hath appointed in His word, expressly one whole day in seven; which was the seventh from the beginning of the world to the resurrection of Christ, and the first day of the week ever since, and so to continue to the end of the world; which is the Christian Sabbath,[1] and in the New Covenant called *The Lord's Day.*[2]

[1] **Deut. 5:12-14:** Observe the Sabbath day, to keep it holy, as the LORD your God commanded you. Six days you shall labor and do all your work, but the seventh day *is* the Sabbath of the LORD your God. *In it* you shall do no work: you, nor your son, nor your daughter, nor your male servant, nor your female servant, nor your ox, nor your donkey, nor any of your cattle, nor your stranger who *is* within your gates, that your male servant and your female servant may rest as well as you. **Gen. 2:2-3:** And on the seventh day God ended His work which He had done, and He rested on the seventh day from all His work which He had done. Then God blessed the seventh day and sanctified it, because in it He rested from all His work which God had created and made. **1 Cor. 16:1-2:** Now concerning the collection for the saints, as I have given orders to the churches of Galatia, so you must do also: On the first *day* of the week let each one of you lay something aside, storing up as he may prosper, that there be no collections when I come. **Acts 20:7:** Now on the first *day* of the week, when the disciples came together to break bread, Paul, ready to depart the next day, spoke to them and continued his message until midnight. **John 20:19, 26:** Then, the same day at evening, being the first *day* of the week, when the doors were shut where the disciples were assembled, for fear of the Jews, Jesus came and stood in the midst, and said to them, "Peace *be* with you." ... And after eight days His disciples were again inside, and Thomas with them. Jesus came, the doors being shut, and stood in the midst, and said, "Peace to you!" **See Matt. 5:17-18; Isa. 56:2, 4, 6-7.**

[2] **Rev. 1:10:** I was in the Spirit on the Lord's Day, and I heard behind me a loud voice, as of a trumpet.

Q. 138. *How is the Sabbath or the Lord's Day to be sanctified?*

A. The Sabbath or Lord's Day is to be sanctified by an holy resting all the day,[1] not only from such works as are at all times sinful, but even from such worldly employments and recreations as are on other days lawful;[2] and making it our delight to spend the whole time (except so much of it as is to be taken up in works of necessity and mercy)[3] in the public and private exercises of God's worship:[4] and, to that end, we are to prepare our hearts, and with such foresight, diligence, and moderation, to dispose and seasonably dispatch our worldly business, that we may be the more free and fit for the duties of that day.[5]

1 **Ex. 20:8, 10:** Remember the Sabbath day, to keep it holy.... but the seventh day *is* the Sabbath of the LORD your God. *In it* you shall do no work: you, nor your son, nor your daughter, nor your male servant, nor your female servant, nor your cattle, nor your stranger who *is* within your gates.

2 **Ex. 16:25-28:** Then Moses said, "Eat that today, for today *is* a Sabbath to the LORD; today you will not find it in the field. Six days you shall gather it, but on the seventh day, the Sabbath, there will be none." Now it happened *that some* of the people went out on the seventh day to gather, but they found none. And the LORD said to Moses, "How long do you refuse to keep My commandments and My laws? **Jer. 17:21-22:** Thus says the LORD: "Take heed to yourselves, and bear no burden on the Sabbath day, nor bring *it* in by the gates of Jerusalem; nor carry a burden out of your houses on the Sabbath day, nor do any work, but hallow the Sabbath day, as I commanded your fathers. **See Neh. 13:15-22.**

3 **Matt. 12:1-5:** At that time Jesus went through the grainfields on the Sabbath. And His disciples were hungry, and began to pluck heads of grain and to eat. And when the Pharisees saw *it,* they said to Him, "Look, Your disciples are doing what is not lawful to do on the Sabbath!" But He said to them, "Have you not read what David did when he was hungry, he and those who were with him: how he entered the house of God and ate the showbread which was not lawful for him to eat, nor for those who were with him, but only for the priests? Or have you not read in the law that on the Sabbath the priests in the temple profane the Sabbath, and are blameless? **See Matt. 12:6-13.**

4 **Isa. 58:13-14:** If you turn away your foot from the Sabbath, *From* doing your pleasure on My holy day, And call the Sabbath a delight, The holy *day* of the LORD honorable, And shall honor Him, not doing your own ways, Nor finding your own pleasure, Nor speaking *your own* words, Then you shall delight yourself in the LORD; And I will cause you to ride on the high hills of the earth, And feed you with the heritage of Jacob your father. The mouth of the LORD has spoken. **Luke 4:16:** So He came to Nazareth, where He had been brought up. And as His custom was, He went into the synagogue on the Sabbath day, and stood up to read. **Acts 20:7:** Now on the first *day* of the week, when the disciples came together to break bread, Paul, ready to depart the next day, spoke to them and continued his message until midnight. **1 Cor. 16:1-2:** Now concerning the collection for the saints, as I have given orders to the churches of Galatia, so you must do also: On the first *day* of the week let each one of you lay something aside, storing up as he may prosper, that there be no collections when I come. **Lev. 23:3:** Six days shall work be done, but the seventh day *is* a Sabbath of solemn rest, a holy convocation. You shall do no work *on it;* it *is* the Sabbath of the LORD in all your dwellings. **See Ps. 92; Isa. 66:23.**

5 **Ex. 20:8:** Remember the Sabbath day, to keep it holy. **Luke 23:54, 56:** That day was the Preparation, and the Sabbath drew near.... Then they returned and prepared spices and fragrant oils. And they rested on the Sabbath according to the commandment. **Ex. 16:22, 25-26, 29:** And so it was, on the sixth day, *that* they gathered twice as much bread, two omers for each one. And all the rulers of the congregation came and told Moses.... Then Moses said, "Eat that today, for today *is* a Sabbath to the LORD; today you will not find it in the field. Six days you shall gather it, but on the seventh day, the Sabbath, there will be none." ... See! For the LORD has given you the Sabbath; therefore He gives you on the sixth day bread for two days. Let every man remain in his place; let no man go out of his place on the seventh day." **Neh. 13:19:** So it was, at the gates of Jerusalem, as it began to be dark before the Sabbath, that I commanded the gates to be shut, and charged that they must not be opened till after the Sabbath. Then I posted *some* of my servants at the gates, *so that* no burdens would be brought in on the Sabbath day.

Q. 139. *Why is the charge of keeping the Sabbath more specially directed to governors of families, and other superiors?*

A. The charge of keeping the Sabbath is more specially directed to governors of families, and other superiors, because they are bound not only to keep it themselves, but to see that it be observed by all those that are under their charge; and because they are prone ofttimes to hinder them by employments of their own.[1]

[1] **Ex. 20:10:** ... but the seventh day *is* the Sabbath of the LORD your God. *In it* you shall do no work: you, nor your son, nor your daughter, nor your male servant, nor your female servant, nor your cattle, nor your stranger who *is* within your gates. **Ex. 23:12:** Six days you shall do your work, and on the seventh day you shall rest, that your ox and your donkey may rest, and the son of your female servant and the stranger may be refreshed. **See Josh. 24:15; Neh. 13:15-17; Jer. 17:20-22.**

Q. 140. *What are the sins forbidden in the fourth commandment?*

A. The sins forbidden in the fourth commandment are, all omissions of the duties required,[1] all careless, negligent, and unprofitable performing of them, and being weary of them;[2] all profaning the day by idleness, and doing that which is in itself sinful;[3] and by all needless works, words, and thoughts, about our worldly employments and recreations.[4]

[1] **Ezek. 22:26:** Her priests have violated My law and profaned My holy things; they have not distinguished between the holy and unholy, nor have they made known *the difference* between the unclean and the clean; and they have hidden their eyes from My Sabbaths, so that I am profaned among them.

[2] **Amos 8:5:** Saying: "When will the New Moon be past, That we may sell grain? And the Sabbath, That we may trade wheat? Making the ephah small and the shekel large, Falsifying the scales by deceit." **See Acts 20:7, 9; Ezek. 33:30-32; Mal. 1:13.**

[3] **Ezek. 23:38:** Moreover they have done this to Me: They have defiled My sanctuary on the same day and profaned My Sabbaths.

[4] **Jer. 17:24, 27:** "And it shall be, if you heed Me carefully," says the LORD, "to bring no burden through the gates of this city on the Sabbath day, but hallow the Sabbath day, to do no work in it ... But if you will not heed Me to hallow the Sabbath day, such as not carrying a burden when entering the gates of Jerusalem on the Sabbath day, then I will kindle a fire in its gates, and it shall devour the palaces of Jerusalem, and it shall not be quenched." **See Isa. 58:13-14.**

Q. 141. *What are the reasons annexed to the fourth commandment, the more to enforce it?*

A. The reasons annexed to the fourth commandment, the more to enforce it, are taken from the equity of it, God allowing us six days of seven for our own affairs, and reserving but one for Himself, in these words, *Six days shalt thou labour, and do all thy work:*[1] from God's challenging a special propriety in that day, *The seventh day is the sabbath of the LORD thy God:*[2] from the example of God, who *in six days ... made heaven and earth, the sea, and all that in them is, and rested the seventh day:* and from that blessing which God put upon that day, not only in sanctifying it to be a day for His service, but in ordaining it to be a means of blessing to us in our sanctifying it; *Wherefore the LORD blessed the sabbath day, and hallowed it.*[3]

1 **Ex. 20:9:** Six days you shall labor and do all your work.

2 **Ex. 20:10:** ... but the seventh day *is* the Sabbath of the LORD your God. *In it* you shall do no work: you, nor your son, nor your daughter, nor your male servant, nor your female servant, nor your cattle, nor your stranger who *is* within your gates.

3 **Ex. 20:11:** For *in* six days the LORD made the heavens and the earth, the sea, and all that *is* in them, and rested the seventh day. Therefore the LORD blessed the Sabbath day and hallowed it.

Q. 142. *Why is the word* Remember *set in the beginning of the fourth commandment?*

A. The word *Remember* is set in the beginning of the fourth commandment,[1] partly, because of the great benefit of remembering it, we being thereby helped in our preparation to keep it,[2] and, in keeping it, better to keep all the rest of the commandments,[3] and to continue a thankful remembrance of the two great benefits of creation and redemption, which contain a short abridgment of religion;[4] and partly, because we are very ready to forget it,[5] for that there is less light of nature for it,[6] and yet it restraineth our natural liberty in things at other times lawful;[7] that it cometh but once in seven days, and many worldly businesses come between, and too often take off our minds from thinking of it, either to prepare for it, or to sanctify it;[8] and that Satan with his instruments much labour to blot out the glory, and even the memory of it, to bring in all irreligion and impiety.[9]

1 **Ex. 20:8:** Remember the Sabbath day, to keep it holy.

2 **Ex. 16:23:** Then he said to them, "This *is what* the LORD has said: 'Tomorrow *is* a Sabbath rest, a holy Sabbath to the LORD. Bake what you will bake *today,* and boil what you will boil; and lay up for yourselves all that remains, to be kept until morning.'" **Luke 23:54, 56:** That day was the Preparation, and the Sabbath drew near.... Then they returned and prepared spices and fragrant oils. And they rested on the Sabbath according to the commandment. **See Mark 15:42; Neh. 13:19.**

3 **Ezek. 20:12, 19-20:** Moreover I also gave them My Sabbaths, to be a sign between them and Me, that they might know that I *am* the LORD who sanctifies them.... I *am* the LORD your God: Walk in My statutes, keep My judgments, and do them; hallow My Sabbaths, and they will be a sign between Me and you, that you may know that I *am* the LORD your God. **Ps. 92:13-14:** Those who are planted in the house of the LORD Shall flourish in the courts of our God. They shall still bear fruit in old age; They shall be fresh and flourishing.

4 **Gen. 2:2-3:** And on the seventh day God ended His work which He had done, and He rested on the seventh day from all His work which He had done. Then God blessed the seventh day and sanctified it, because in it He rested from all His work which God had created and made. **Ps. 118:22, 24:** The stone *which* the builders rejected Has become the chief cornerstone.... This *is* the day the LORD has

made; We will rejoice and be glad in it. **Rev. 1:10:** I was in the Spirit on the Lord's Day, and I heard behind me a loud voice, as of a trumpet.

5 **Ezek. 22:26:** Her priests have violated My law and profaned My holy things; they have not distinguished between the holy and unholy, nor have they made known *the difference* between the unclean and the clean; and they have hidden their eyes from My Sabbaths, so that I am profaned among them.

6 **Neh. 9:14:** You made known to them Your holy Sabbath, And commanded them precepts, statutes and laws, By the hand of Moses Your servant.

7 **Ex. 34:21:** Six days you shall work, but on the seventh day you shall rest; in plowing time and in harvest you shall rest.

8 **Deut. 5:14-15:** ... but the seventh day *is* the Sabbath of the LORD your God. *In it* you shall do no work: you, nor your son, nor your daughter, nor your male servant, nor your female servant, nor your ox, nor your donkey, nor any of your cattle, nor your stranger who *is* within your gates, that your male servant and your female servant may rest as well as you. And remember that you were a slave in the land of Egypt, and the LORD your God brought you out from there by a mighty hand and by an outstretched arm; therefore the LORD your God commanded you to keep the Sabbath day. **Amos 8:5:** When will the New Moon be past, That we may sell grain? And the Sabbath, That we may trade wheat? Making the ephah small and the shekel large, Falsifying the scales by deceit.

9 **Lam. 1:7:** In the days of her affliction and roaming, Jerusalem remembers all her pleasant things That she had in the days of old. When her people fell into the hand of the enemy, With no one to help her, The adversaries saw her *And* mocked at her downfall. **Jer. 17:21-23:** Thus says the LORD: "Take heed to yourselves, and bear no burden on the Sabbath day, nor bring *it* in by the gates of Jerusalem; nor carry a burden out of your houses on the Sabbath day, nor do any work, but hallow the Sabbath day, as I commanded your fathers. But they did not obey nor incline their ear, but made their neck stiff, that they might not hear nor receive instruction. **See Neh. 13:15-22.**

Q. 143. *What is the sum of the six commandments which contain our duty to man?*

A. The sum of the six commandments which contain our duty to man, is, to love our neighbour as ourselves,[1] and to do to others what we would have them to do to us.[2]

1 **Matt. 22:39:** And *the* second *is* like it: 'You shall love your neighbor as yourself.'

2 **Matt. 7:12:** Therefore, whatever you want men to do to you, do also to them, for this is the Law and the Prophets.

Q. 144. *Which is the fifth commandment?*

A. The fifth commandment is, *Honour thy father and thy mother: that thy days may be long upon the land which the LORD thy God giveth thee.*[1]

1 **Ex. 20:12:** Honor your father and your mother, that your days may be long upon the land which the LORD your God is giving you. **Cf. Deut. 5:16.**

Q. 145. *Who are meant by* father *and* mother *in the fifth commandment?*

A. By *father* and *mother*, in the fifth commandment, are meant, not only natural parents,[1] but all superiors in age[2] and gifts;[3] and especially such as, by God's ordinance, are over us in place of authority, whether in family,[4] church,[5] or commonwealth.[6]

[1] **Prov. 23:22, 25:** Listen to your father who begot you, And do not despise your mother when she is old.... Let your father and your mother be glad, And let her who bore you rejoice. **See Eph. 6:1-2.**

[2] **1 Tim. 5:1-2:** Do not rebuke an older man, but exhort *him* as a father, younger men as brothers, older women as mothers, younger women as sisters, with all purity.

[3] **Gen. 4:20-21:** And Adah bore Jabal. He was the father of those who dwell in tents and have livestock. His brother's name *was* Jubal. He was the father of all those who play the harp and flute. **Gen. 45:8:** So now *it was* not you *who* sent me here, but God; and He has made me a father to Pharaoh, and lord of all his house, and a ruler throughout all the land of Egypt.

[4] **2 Kings 5:13:** And his servants came near and spoke to him, and said, "My father, *if* the prophet had told you *to do* something great, would you not have done *it?* How much more then, when he says to you, 'Wash, and be clean'?"

[5] **2 Kings 2:12:** And Elisha saw *it,* and he cried out, "My father, my father, the chariot of Israel and its horsemen!" So he saw him no more. And he took hold of his own clothes and tore them into two pieces. **Gal. 4:19:** My little children, for whom I labor in birth again until Christ is formed in you. **See 2 Kings 13:14.**

[6] **Isa. 49:23:** Kings shall be your foster fathers, And their queens your nursing mothers; They shall bow down to you with *their* faces to the earth, And lick up the dust of your feet. Then you will know that I *am* the LORD, For they shall not be ashamed who wait for Me.

Q. 146. *Why are superiors styled* Father *and* Mother?

A. Superiors are styled *Father* and *Mother*, both to teach them in all duties toward their inferiors, like natural parents, to express love and tenderness to them, according to their several relations;[1] and to work inferiors to a greater willingness and cheerfulness in performing their duties to their superiors, as to their parents.[2]

[1] **Eph. 6:4:** And you, fathers, do not provoke your children to wrath, but bring them up in the training and admonition of the Lord. **2 Cor. 12:14:** Now *for* the third time I am ready to come to you. And I will not be burdensome to you; for I do not seek yours, but you. For the children ought not to lay up for the parents, but the parents for the children. **1 Thess. 2:7-8, 11:** But we were gentle among you, just as a nursing *mother* cherishes her own children. So, affectionately longing for you, we were well pleased to impart to you not only the gospel of God, but also our own lives, because you had become dear to us.... as you know how we exhorted, and comforted, and charged every one of you, as a father *does* his own children. **See Num. 11:11-12.**

[2] **1 Cor. 4:14-16:** I do not write these things to shame you, but as my beloved children I warn *you.* For though you might have ten thousand instructors in Christ, yet *you do* not *have* many fathers; for in Christ Jesus I have begotten you through the gospel. Therefore I urge you, imitate me. **See 2 Kings 5:13.**

Q. 147. *What is the general scope of the fifth commandment?*

A. The general scope of the fifth commandment is, the performance of those duties which we mutually owe in our several relations, as inferiors, superiors, or equals.[1]

[1] **Eph. 5:21:** ... submitting to one another in the fear of God. **1 Pet. 2:17:** Honor all *people.* Love the brotherhood. Fear God. Honor the king. **Rom. 12:10:** *Be* kindly affectionate to one another with brotherly love, in honor giving preference to one another. **See Rom. 13:1, 7; Eph. 5:22, 24; 6:1, 4-5, 9.**

Q. 148. *What is the honour that inferiors owe to their superiors?*

A. The honour which inferiors owe to their superiors is, all due reverence in heart,[1] word,[2] and behaviour;[3] prayer and thanksgiving for them;[4] imitation of their virtues and graces;[5] willing obedience to their lawful commands and counsels;[6] due submission to their corrections;[7] fidelity to,[8] defense,[9] and maintenance of their persons and authority, according to their several ranks, and the nature of their places;[10] bearing with their infirmities, and covering them in love,[11] that so they may be an honour to them and to their government.[12]

1
Mal. 1:6: A son honors *his* father, And a servant *his* master. If then I am the Father, Where *is* My honor? And if I *am* a Master, Where *is* My reverence? Says the LORD of hosts To you priests who despise My name. Yet you say, 'In what way have we despised Your name?' **Lev. 19:3:** Every one of you shall revere his mother and his father, and keep My Sabbaths: I *am* the LORD your God.

2
Prov. 31:28: Her children rise up and call her blessed; Her husband *also,* and he praises her. **1 Pet. 3:6:** ... as Sarah obeyed Abraham, calling him lord, whose daughters you are if you do good and are not afraid with any terror.

3
Lev. 19:32: You shall rise before the gray headed and honor the presence of an old man, and fear your God: I am the LORD. **1 Kings 2:19:** Bathsheba therefore went to King Solomon, to speak to him for Adonijah. And the king rose up to meet her and bowed down to her, and sat down on his throne and had a throne set for the king's mother; so she sat at his right hand.

4
1 Tim. 2:1-2: Therefore I exhort first of all that supplications, prayers, intercessions, *and* giving of thanks be made for all men, for kings and all who are in authority, that we may lead a quiet and peaceable life in all godliness and reverence.

5
Heb. 13:7: Remember those who rule over you, who have spoken the word of God to you, whose faith follow, considering the outcome of *their* conduct. **Phil. 3:17:** Brethren, join in following my example, and note those who so walk, as you have us for a pattern.

6
Eph. 6:1-2, 5-7: Children, obey your parents in the Lord, for this is right. "Honor your father and mother," which is the first commandment with promise... Bondservants, be obedient to those who are your masters according to the flesh, with fear and trembling, in sincerity of heart, as to Christ; not with eyeservice, as men-pleasers, but as bondservants of Christ, doing the will of God from the heart, with goodwill doing service, as to the Lord, and not to men. **1 Pet. 2:13-14:** Therefore submit yourselves to every ordinance of man for the Lord's sake, whether to the king as supreme, or to governors, as to those who are sent by him for the punishment of evildoers and *for the* praise of those who do good. **Heb. 13:17:** Obey those who rule over you, and be submissive, for they watch out for your souls, as those who must give account. Let them do so with joy and not with grief, for that would be unprofitable for you. **See Rom. 13:1-5; Prov. 4:3-4, 23:22; Ex. 18:19, 24.**

7
Heb. 12:9: Furthermore, we have had human fathers who corrected *us,* and we paid *them* respect. Shall we not much more readily be in subjection to the Father of spirits and live? **1 Pet. 2:18-20:** Servants, *be* submissive to *your* masters with all fear, not only to the good and gentle, but also to the harsh. For this *is* commendable, if because of conscience toward God one endures grief, suffering wrongfully. For what credit *is it* if, when you are beaten for your faults, you take it patiently? But when you do good and suffer, if you take it patiently, this *is* commendable before God.

8
Titus 2:9-10: *Exhort* bondservants to be obedient to their own masters, to be well pleasing in all *things,* not answering back, not pilfering, but showing all good fidelity, that they may adorn the doctrine of God our Savior in all things.

9
1 Sam. 26:15-16: So David said to Abner, "*Are* you not a man? And who *is* like you in Israel? Why then have you not guarded your lord the king? For one of the people came in to destroy your lord

the king. This thing that you have done *is* not good. *As* the LORD lives, you deserve to die, because you have not guarded your master, the LORD's anointed. And now see where the king's spear *is,* and the jug of water that *was* by his head." **See 2 Sam. 18:3; Est. 6:2.**

10

Matt. 22:21: They said to Him, "Caesar's." And He said to them, "Render therefore to Caesar the things that are Caesar's, and to God the things that are God's." **Rom. 13:6-7:** For because of this you also pay taxes, for they are God's ministers attending continually to this very thing. Render therefore to all their due: taxes to whom taxes *are due,* customs to whom customs, fear to whom fear, honor to whom honor. **1 Tim. 5:17-18:** Let the elders who rule well be counted worthy of double honor, especially those who labor in the word and doctrine. For the Scripture says, "You shall not muzzle an ox while it treads out the grain," and, "The laborer *is* worthy of his wages." **See Gal. 6:6; Gen. 45:11, 47:12.**

11

Gen. 9:23: But Shem and Japheth took a garment, laid *it* on both their shoulders, and went backward and covered the nakedness of their father. Their faces *were* turned away, and they did not see their father's nakedness. **See 1 Pet. 2:18; Prov. 23:22.**

12

Ps. 127:3-5: Behold, children *are* a heritage from the LORD, The fruit of the womb *is* a reward. Like arrows in the hand of a warrior, So *are* the children of one's youth. Happy *is* the man who has his quiver full of them; They shall not be ashamed, But shall speak with their enemies in the gate. **Prov. 31:23:** Her husband is known in the gates, When he sits among the elders of the land.

Q. 149. *What are the sins of inferiors against their superiors?*

A. The sins of inferiors against their superiors are, all neglect of the duties required toward them;[1] envying at,[2] contempt of,[3] and rebellion[4] against their persons[5] and places,[6] in their lawful counsels,[7] commands, and corrections;[8] cursing, mocking,[9] and all such refractory and scandalous carriage, as proves a shame and dishonour to them and their government.[10]

1

Matt. 15:4-6: For God commanded, saying, 'Honor your father and your mother'; and, 'He who curses father or mother, let him be put to death.' But you say, 'Whoever says to his father or mother, "Whatever profit you might have received from me *is* a gift *to God*"— then he need not honor his father or mother.' Thus you have made the commandment of God of no effect by your tradition. **Rom. 13:8:** Owe no one anything except to love one another, for he who loves another has fulfilled the law.

2

Num. 11:28-29: So Joshua the son of Nun, Moses' assistant, *one* of his choice men, answered and said, "Moses my lord, forbid them!" Then Moses said to him, "Are you zealous for my sake? Oh, that all the LORD's people were prophets *and* that the LORD would put His Spirit upon them!"

3

1 Sam. 8:7: And the LORD said to Samuel, "Heed the voice of the people in all that they say to you; for they have not rejected you, but they have rejected Me, that I should not reign over them. **Isa. 3:5:** The people will be oppressed, Every one by another and every one by his neighbor; The child will be insolent toward the elder, And the base toward the honorable."

4

2 Sam. 15:10: Then Absalom sent spies throughout all the tribes of Israel, saying, "As soon as you hear the sound of the trumpet, then you shall say, 'Absalom reigns in Hebron!'" **See 2 Sam. 15:1-12.**

5

Ex. 21:15: And he who strikes his father or his mother shall surely be put to death.

6

1 Sam. 10:27: But some rebels said, "How can this man save us?" So they despised him, and brought him no presents. But he held his peace.

7

1 Sam. 2:25: If one man sins against another, God will judge him. But if a man sins against the LORD, who will intercede for him?" Nevertheless they did not heed the voice of their father, because the LORD desired to kill them.

8

Deut. 21:18-21: If a man has a stubborn and rebellious son who will not obey the voice of his father or the voice of his mother, and *who,* when they have chastened him, will not heed them, then his father and his mother shall take hold of him and bring him out to the elders of his city, to the gate of his city. And they shall say to the elders of his city, 'This son of ours is stubborn and rebellious; he will not obey our voice; he is a glutton and a drunkard.' Then all the men of his city shall stone him to death with stones; so you shall put away the evil from among you, and all Israel shall hear and fear.

9 **Prov. 30:11, 17:** *There is* a generation *that* curses its father, And does not bless its mother.... The eye *that* mocks *his* father, And scorns obedience to *his* mother, The ravens of the valley will pick it out, And the young eagles will eat it.

10 **Prov. 19:26:** He who mistreats *his* father *and* chases away *his* mother *Is* a son who causes shame and brings reproach.

Q. 150. *What is required of superiors towards their inferiors?*

A. It is required of superiors, according to that power they receive from God, and that relation wherein they stand, to love,[1] pray for,[2] and bless their inferiors;[3] to instruct,[4] counsel, and admonish them;[5] countenancing,[6] commending,[7] and rewarding such as do well;[8] and discountenancing,[9] reproving, and chastising such as do ill;[10] protecting,[11] and providing for them all things necessary for soul[12] and body:[13] and by grave, wise, holy, and exemplary carriage, to procure glory to God,[14] honour to themselves,[15] and so to preserve that authority which God hath put upon them.[16]

1 **Col. 3:19:** Husbands, love your wives and do not be bitter toward them. **Titus 2:4:** ... that they admonish the young women to love their husbands, to love their children.

2 **1 Sam. 12:23:** Moreover, as for me, far be it from me that I should sin against the LORD in ceasing to pray for you; but I will teach you the good and the right way. **Job 1:5:** So it was, when the days of feasting had run their course, that Job would send and sanctify them, and he would rise early in the morning and offer burnt offerings *according to* the number of them all. For Job said, "It may be that my sons have sinned and cursed God in their hearts." Thus Job did regularly.

3 **1 Kings 8:55-56:** Then he stood and blessed all the assembly of Israel with a loud voice, saying: "Blessed *be* the LORD, who has given rest to His people Israel, according to all that He promised. There has not failed one word of all His good promise, which He promised through His servant Moses. **Heb. 7:7:** Now beyond all contradiction the lesser is blessed by the better. **See Gen. 49:28.**

4 **Deut. 6:6-7:** And these words which I command you today shall be in your heart. You shall teach them diligently to your children, and shall talk of them when you sit in your house, when you walk by the way, when you lie down, and when you rise up.

5 **Eph. 6:4:** And you, fathers, do not provoke your children to wrath, but bring them up in the training and admonition of the Lord.

6 **1 Pet. 3:7:** Husbands, likewise, dwell with *them* with understanding, giving honor to the wife, as to the weaker vessel, and as *being* heirs together of the grace of life, that your prayers may not be hindered.

7 **1 Pet. 2:14:** ... or to governors, as to those who are sent by him for the punishment of evildoers and *for the* praise of those who do good. **Rom. 13:3:** For rulers are not a terror to good works, but to evil. Do you want to be unafraid of the authority? Do what is good, and you will have praise from the same.

8 **Est. 6:3:** Then the king said, "What honor or dignity has been bestowed on Mordecai for this?" And the king's servants who attended him said, "Nothing has been done for him."

9 **Rom. 13:3-4:** For rulers are not a terror to good works, but to evil. Do you want to be unafraid of the authority? Do what is good, and you will have praise from the same. For he is God's minister to you for good. But if you do evil, be afraid; for he does not bear the sword in vain; for he is God's

minister, an avenger to *execute* wrath on him who practices evil.

10

Prov. 29:15: The rod and rebuke give wisdom, But a child left *to himself* brings shame to his mother. **1 Pet. 2:14:** or to governors, as to those who are sent by him for the punishment of evildoers and *for the* praise of those who do good.

11

Isa. 1:10, 17: Hear the word of the LORD, You rulers of Sodom; Give ear to the law of our God, You people of Gomorrah.... Learn to do good; Seek justice, Rebuke the oppressor; Defend the fatherless, Plead for the widow. **See Job 29:12-17.**

12

Eph. 6:4: And you, fathers, do not provoke your children to wrath, but bring them up in the training and admonition of the Lord.

13

1 Tim. 5:8: But if anyone does not provide for his own, and especially for those of his household, he has denied the faith and is worse than an unbeliever.

14

1 Tim. 4:12: Let no one despise your youth, but be an example to the believers in word, in conduct, in love, in spirit, in faith, in purity. **See Titus 2:3-5.**

15

1 Kings 3:28: And all Israel heard of the judgment which the king had rendered; and they feared the king, for they saw that the wisdom of God *was* in him to administer justice.

16

Titus 2:15: Speak these things, exhort, and rebuke with all authority. Let no one despise you.

Q. 151. *What are the sins of superiors?*

A. The sins of superiors are, besides the neglect of the duties required of them,[1] an inordinate seeking of themselves,[2] their own glory,[3] ease, profit, or pleasure;[4] commanding things unlawful,[5] or not in the power of inferiors to perform;[6] counseling,[7] encouraging,[8] or favoring them in that which is evil;[9] dissuading, discouraging, or discountenancing them in that which is good;[10] correcting them unduly;[11] careless exposing, or leaving them to wrong, temptation, and danger;[12] provoking them to wrath;[13] or any way dishonouring themselves, or lessening their authority, by an unjust, indiscreet, rigorous, or remiss behaviour.[14]

1

Ezek. 34:2-4: Son of man, prophesy against the shepherds of Israel, prophesy and say to them, 'Thus says the Lord God to the shepherds: "Woe to the shepherds of Israel who feed themselves! Should not the shepherds feed the flocks? You eat the fat and clothe yourselves with the wool; you slaughter the fatlings, *but* you do not feed the flock. The weak you have not strengthened, nor have you healed those who were sick, nor bound up the broken, nor brought back what was driven away, nor sought what was lost; but with force and cruelty you have ruled them."'

2

Phil. 2:21: For all seek their own, not the things which are of Christ Jesus.

3

John 5:44: How can you believe, who receive honor from one another, and do not seek the honor that *comes* from the only God? **See John 7:18.**

4

Isa. 56:10-11: His watchmen *are* blind, They are all ignorant; They *are* all dumb dogs, They cannot bark; Sleeping, lying down, loving to slumber. Yes, *they are* greedy dogs *Which* never have enough. And they *are* shepherds Who cannot understand; They all look to their own way, Every one for his own gain, From his *own* territory. **See Deut. 17:17.**

5

Acts 4:17-18: "But so that it spreads no further among the people, let us severely threaten them, that from now on they speak to no man in this name." So they called them and commanded them not to speak at all nor teach in the name of Jesus. **See Dan. 3:4-6.**

6
Ex. 5:18: Therefore go now *and* work; for no straw shall be given you, yet you shall deliver the quota of bricks. **See Ex. 5:10-19; Matt. 23:2, 4:** ... saying: "The scribes and the Pharisees sit in Moses' seat.... For they bind heavy burdens, hard to bear, and lay *them* on men's shoulders; but they *themselves* will not move them with one of their fingers.
7
Matt. 14:8: So she, having been prompted by her mother, said, "Give me John the Baptist's head here on a platter." **See Mark 6:24.**
8
2 Sam. 13:28: Now Absalom had commanded his servants, saying, "Watch now, when Amnon's heart is merry with wine, and when I say to you, 'Strike Amnon!' then kill him. Do not be afraid. Have I not commanded you? Be courageous and valiant."
9
Jer. 6:13-14: Because from the least of them even to the greatest of them, Everyone *is* given to covetousness; And from the prophet even to the priest, Everyone deals falsely. They have also healed the hurt of My people slightly, Saying, 'Peace, peace!' When *there is* no peace. **Judg. 20:13-14:** Now therefore, deliver up the men, the perverted men who *are* in Gibeah, that we may put them to death and remove the evil from Israel!" But the children of Benjamin would not listen to the voice of their brethren, the children of Israel. Instead, the children of Benjamin gathered together from their cities to Gibeah, to go to battle against the children of Israel. **See Judg. 20.**
10
John 7:46-49: The officers answered, "No man ever spoke like this Man!" Then the Pharisees answered them, "Are you also deceived? Have any of the rulers or the Pharisees believed in Him? But this crowd that does not know the law is accursed." **See Col. 3:21; Ex. 5:17; John 9:28.**
11
1 Pet. 2:18-20: Servants, *be* submissive to *your* masters with all fear, not only to the good and gentle, but also to the harsh. For this *is* commendable, if because of conscience toward God one endures grief, suffering wrongfully. For what credit *is it* if, when you are beaten for your faults, you take it patiently? But when you do good and suffer, if you take it patiently, this *is* commendable before God. **Deut. 25:3:** Forty blows he may give him *and* no more, lest he should exceed this and beat him with many blows above these, and your brother be humiliated in your sight.
12
Gen. 38:11, 26: Then Judah said to Tamar his daughter-in-law, "Remain a widow in your father's house till my son Shelah is grown." For he said, "Lest he also die like his brothers." And Tamar went and dwelt in her father's house.... So Judah acknowledged *them* and said, "She has been more righteous than I, because I did not give her to Shelah my son." And he never knew her again. **Acts 18:17:** Then all the Greeks took Sosthenes, the ruler of the synagogue, and beat *him* before the judgment seat. But Gallio took no notice of these things. **See 1 Sam. 23:15-17; Lev. 19:29; Isa. 58:7.**
13
Eph. 6:4: And you, fathers, do not provoke your children to wrath, but bring them up in the training and admonition of the Lord.
14
Gen. 9:21: Then he drank of the wine and was drunk, and became uncovered in his tent. **1 Kings 12:13-16:** Then the king answered the people roughly, and rejected the advice which the elders had given him; and he spoke to them according to the advice of the young men, saying, "My father made your yoke heavy, but I will add to your yoke; my father chastised you with whips, but I will chastise you with scourges!" So the king did not listen to the people; for the turn *of events* was from the LORD, that He might fulfill His word, which the LORD had spoken by Ahijah the Shilonite to Jeroboam the son of Nebat. Now when all Israel saw that the king did not listen to them, the people answered the king, saying: "What share have we in David? *We have* no inheritance in the son of Jesse. To your tents, O Israel! Now, see to your own house, O David!" So Israel departed to their tents. **1 Kings 1:6:** And his father had not rebuked him at any time by saying, "Why have you done so?" He *was* also very good-looking. *His mother* had borne him after Absalom. **See 1 Sam. 2:29-31; 3:13.**

Q. 152. *What are the duties of equals?*

A. The duties of equals are, to regard the dignity and worth of each other,[1] in giving honour to go one before another;[2] and to rejoice in each others' gifts and advancement, as their own.[3]

1
1 Pet. 2:17: Honor all *people.* Love the brotherhood. Fear God. Honor the king.
2
Rom. 12:10: *Be* kindly affectionate to one another with brotherly love, in honor giving preference to one another. **Phil. 2:3:** *Let* nothing *be done* through selfish ambition or conceit, but in lowliness of mind let each esteem others better than himself.

[3] **Rom. 12:15-16:** Rejoice with those who rejoice, and weep with those who weep. Be of the same mind toward one another. Do not set your mind on high things, but associate with the humble. Do not be wise in your own opinion. **Phil. 2:3:** *Let* nothing *be done* through selfish ambition or conceit, but in lowliness of mind let each esteem others better than himself.

Q. 153. *What are the sins of equals?*

A. The sins of equals are, besides the neglect of the duties required,[1] the undervaluing of the worth,[2] envying the gifts,[3] grieving at the advancement or prosperity one of another;[4] and usurping preeminence one over another.[5]

[1] **Rom. 13:8:** Owe no one anything except to love one another, for he who loves another has fulfilled the law.

[2] **2 Tim. 3:3:** ... unloving, unforgiving, slanderers, without self-control, brutal, despisers of good. **See Prov. 14:21; Isa. 65:5.**

[3] **Acts 7:9:** And the patriarchs, becoming envious, sold Joseph into Egypt. But God was with him. **Gal. 5:26:** Let us not become conceited, provoking one another, envying one another.

[4] **Num. 12:2:** So they said, "Has the LORD indeed spoken only through Moses? Has He not spoken through us also?" And the LORD heard *it.*

[5] **3 John 9:** I wrote to the church, but Diotrephes, who loves to have the preeminence among them, does not receive us. **Luke 22:24:** Now there was also a dispute among them, as to which of them should be considered the greatest.

Q. 154. *What is the reason annexed to the fifth commandment, the more to enforce it?*

A. The reason annexed to the fifth commandment, in these words, *That thy days may be long upon the land which the LORD thy God giveth thee,*[1] is an express promise of long life and prosperity, as far as it shall serve for God's glory and their own good, to all such as keep this commandment.[2]

[1] **Ex. 20:12:** Honor your father and your mother, that your days may be long upon the land which the LORD your God is giving you.

[2] **Eph. 6:2-3:** "Honor your father and mother," which is the first commandment with promise: "that it may be well with you and you may live long on the earth." **See Deut. 5:16; 1 Kings 8:25.**

Q. 155. *Which is the sixth commandment?*

A. The sixth commandment is, *Thou shalt not kill.*[1]

[1] **Ex. 20:13:** You shall not murder. **Cf. Deut. 5:17.**

Q. 156. *What are the duties required in the sixth commandment?*

A. The duties required in the sixth commandment are, all careful studies, and lawful endeavors, to preserve the life of ourselves[1] and others[2] by resisting all thoughts and purposes,[3] subduing all passions,[4] and avoiding all occasions,[5] temptations,[6] and practices, which tend to the unjust taking away the life of any;[7] by just defense thereof against violence,[8] patient bearing of the hand of God,[9] quietness of mind,[10] cheerfulness of spirit;[11] a sober use of meat,[12] drink,[13] physic,[14] sleep,[15] labour,[16] and recreations;[17] by charitable thoughts,[18] love,[19] compassion,[20] meekness, gentleness, kindness;[21] peaceable,[22] mild and courteous speeches and behaviour;[23] forbearance, readiness to be reconciled, patient bearing and forgiving of injuries, and requiting good for evil;[24] comforting and succoring the distressed, and protecting and defending the innocent.[25]

1
Eph. 5:28-29: So husbands ought to love their own wives as their own bodies; he who loves his wife loves himself. For no one ever hated his own flesh, but nourishes and cherishes it, just as the Lord *does* the church.

2
1 Kings 18:4: For so it was, while Jezebel massacred the prophets of the LORD, that Obadiah had taken one hundred prophets and hidden them, fifty to a cave, and had fed them with bread and water.

3
Jer. 26:15-16: But know for certain that if you put me to death, you will surely bring innocent blood on yourselves, on this city, and on its inhabitants; for truly the LORD has sent me to you to speak all these words in your hearing." So the princes and all the people said to the priests and the prophets, "This man does not deserve to die. For he has spoken to us in the name of the LORD our God." **See Acts 23:12, 16-17, 21, 27.**

4
Eph. 4:26-27: "Be angry, and do not sin": do not let the sun go down on your wrath, nor give place to the devil.

5
2 Sam. 2:22-23: So Abner said again to Asahel, "Turn aside from following me. Why should I strike you to the ground? How then could I face your brother Joab?" However, he refused to turn aside. Therefore Abner struck him in the stomach with the blunt end of the spear, so that the spear came out of his back; and he fell down there and died on the spot. So it was *that* as many as came to the place where Asahel fell down and died, stood still. **Deut. 22:8:** When you build a new house, then you shall make a parapet for your roof, that you may not bring guilt of bloodshed on your household if anyone falls from it.

6
Matt. 4:6-7: ... and said to Him, "If You are the Son of God, throw Yourself down. For it is written: 'He shall give His angels charge over you,' and, 'In *their* hands they shall bear you up, Lest you dash your foot against a stone.'" Jesus said to him, "It is written again, 'You shall not tempt the LORD your God.'" **Prov. 1:10-11, 15-16:** My son, if sinners entice you, Do not consent. If they say, "Come with us, Let us lie in wait to *shed* blood; Let us lurk secretly for the innocent without cause." ... My son, do not walk in the way with them, Keep your foot from their path; For their feet run to evil, And they make haste to shed blood.

7
Gen. 37:21-22: But Reuben heard *it,* and he delivered him out of their hands, and said, "Let us not kill him." And Reuben said to them, "Shed no blood, *but* cast him into this pit which *is* in the wilderness, and do not lay a hand on him"—that he might deliver him out of their hands, and bring him back to his father. **See 1 Sam. 24:12, 26:9-11.**

8
Ps. 82:4: Deliver the poor and needy; Free *them* from the hand of the wicked. **Prov. 24:11-12:** Deliver *those who* are drawn toward death, And hold back *those* stumbling to the slaughter. If you say, "Surely we did not know this," Does not He who weighs the hearts consider *it?* He who keeps your soul, does He *not* know *it?* And will He *not* render to *each* man according to his deeds? **See 1 Sam. 14:45; Jer. 38:7-13.**

9
James 5:10-11: My brethren, take the prophets, who spoke in the name of the Lord, as an example of suffering and patience. Indeed we count them blessed who endure. You have heard of the perseverance of Job and seen the end *intended by* the Lord—that the Lord is very compassionate and merciful. **Heb. 12:9:** Furthermore, we have had human fathers who corrected *us,* and we paid *them* respect. Shall we not much more readily be in subjection to the Father of spirits and live? **See 2 Sam. 16:10-12.**

10
1 Thess. 4:11: ... that you also aspire to lead a quiet life, to mind your own business, and to work with your own hands, as we commanded you. **1 Pet. 3:3-4:** Do not let your adornment be *merely* outward—arranging the hair, wearing gold, or putting on *fine* apparel— rather *let it be* the hidden person of the heart, with the incorruptible *beauty* of a gentle and quiet spirit, which is very precious in the sight of God. **Ps. 37:8, 11:** Cease from anger, and forsake wrath; Do not fret—*it* only *causes* harm.... But the meek shall inherit the earth, And shall delight themselves in the abundance of peace.

11
Prov. 17:22: A merry heart does good, *like* medicine, But a broken spirit dries the bones.

12
Prov. 23:20: Do not mix with winebibbers, *Or* with gluttonous eaters of meat. **Prov. 25:16, 27:** Have you found honey? Eat only as much as you need, Lest you be filled with it and vomit.... *It is* not good to eat much honey; So to seek one's own glory *is not* glory.

13
1 Tim. 5:23: No longer drink only water, but use a little wine for your stomach's sake and your frequent infirmities.

14
Isa. 38:21: Now Isaiah had said, "Let them take a lump of figs, and apply *it* as a poultice on the boil, and he shall recover."

15
Ps. 127:2: *It is* vain for you to rise up early, To sit up late, To eat the bread of sorrows; *For* so He gives His beloved sleep.

16
2 Thess. 3:12: Now those who are such we command and exhort through our Lord Jesus Christ that they work in quietness and eat their own bread. **See Eccl. 5:12.**

17
Eccl. 3:4, 11: A time to weep, And a time to laugh; A time to mourn, And a time to dance.... He has made everything beautiful in its time. Also He has put eternity in their hearts, except that no one can find out the work that God does from beginning to end. **Mark 6:31:** And He said to them, "Come aside by yourselves to a deserted place and rest a while." For there were many coming and going, and they did not even have time to eat.

18
1 Sam. 19:4-5: Thus Jonathan spoke well of David to Saul his father, and said to him, "Let not the king sin against his servant, against David, because he has not sinned against you, and because his works *have been* very good toward you. For he took his life in his hands and killed the Philistine, and the LORD brought about a great deliverance for all Israel. You saw *it* and rejoiced. Why then will you sin against innocent blood, to kill David without a cause?" **See 1 Sam. 22:13-14.**

19
Rom. 13:10: Love does no harm to a neighbor; therefore love *is* the fulfillment of the law.

20
Luke 10:33-34: But a certain Samaritan, as he journeyed, came where he was. And when he saw him, he had compassion. So he went to *him* and bandaged his wounds, pouring on oil and wine; and he set him on his own animal, brought him to an inn, and took care of him.

21
Col. 3:12-13: Therefore, as *the* elect of God, holy and beloved, put on tender mercies, kindness, humility, meekness, longsuffering; bearing with one another, and forgiving one another, if anyone has a complaint against another; even as Christ forgave you, so you also *must do.*

22
James 3:17: But the wisdom that is from above is first pure, then peaceable, gentle, willing to yield, full of mercy and good fruits, without partiality and without hypocrisy.

23
1 Pet. 3:8-11: Finally, all *of you be* of one mind, having compassion for one another; love as brothers, *be* tenderhearted, *be* courteous; not returning evil for evil or reviling for reviling, but on the contrary blessing, knowing that you were called to this, that you may inherit a blessing. For "He who would love life And see good days, Let him refrain his tongue from evil, And his lips from speaking deceit. Let him turn away from evil and do good; Let him seek peace and pursue it." **1 Cor. 4:12-13:** And we labor, working with our own hands. Being reviled, we bless; being persecuted, we endure; being defamed, we entreat. We have been made as the filth of the world, the offscouring of all things until now. **See Prov. 15:1; Judg. 8:1-3.**

24
Matt. 5:24: ... leave your gift there before the altar, and go your way. First be reconciled to your brother, and then come and offer your gift. **Eph. 4:2, 32:** ... with all lowliness and gentleness, with longsuffering, bearing with one another in love ... And be kind to one another, tenderhearted, forgiving one another, even as God in Christ forgave you. **Rom. 12:17, 20-21:** Repay no one evil

for evil. Have regard for good things in the sight of all men.... Therefore "If your enemy is hungry, feed him; If he is thirsty, give him a drink; For in so doing you will heap coals of fire on his head." Do not be overcome by evil, but overcome evil with good.

25

1 Thess. 5:14: Now we exhort you, brethren, warn those who are unruly, comfort the fainthearted, uphold the weak, be patient with all. **Matt. 25:35-36:** ... for I was hungry and you gave Me food; I was thirsty and you gave Me drink; I was a stranger and you took Me in; I *was* naked and you clothed Me; I was sick and you visited Me; I was in prison and you came to Me. **Prov. 31:8-9:** Open your mouth for the speechless, In the cause of all *who are* appointed to die. Open your mouth, judge righteously, And plead the cause of the poor and needy. **See Job 31:19-20; Isa. 58:7.**

Q. 157. *What are the sins forbidden in the sixth commandment?*

A. The sins forbidden in the sixth commandment are, all taking away the life of ourselves,[1] or of others,[2] except in case of public justice,[3] lawful war,[4] or necessary defense;[5] the neglecting or withdrawing the lawful and necessary means of preservation of life;[6] sinful anger,[7] hatred,[8] envy,[9] desire of revenge;[10] all excessive passions,[11] distracting cares;[12] immoderate use of meat, drink,[13] labour,[14] and recreations;[15] provoking words,[16] oppression,[17] quarreling,[18] striking, wounding,[19] and whatsoever else tends to the destruction of the life of any.[20]

1

Acts 16:28: But Paul called with a loud voice, saying, "Do yourself no harm, for we are all here."

2

Gen. 9:6: Whoever sheds man's blood, By man his blood shall be shed; For in the image of God He made man.

3

Num. 35:31, 33: Moreover you shall take no ransom for the life of a murderer who *is* guilty of death, but he shall surely be put to death.... So you shall not pollute the land where you *are;* for blood defiles the land, and no atonement can be made for the land, for the blood that is shed on it, except by the blood of him who shed it. **Rom. 13:4:** For he is God's minister to you for good. But if you do evil, be afraid; for he does not bear the sword in vain; for he is God's minister, an avenger to *execute* wrath on him who practices evil.

4

Heb. 11:32-34: And what more shall I say? For the time would fail me to tell of Gideon and Barak and Samson and Jephthah, also *of* David and Samuel and the prophets: who through faith subdued kingdoms, worked righteousness, obtained promises, stopped the mouths of lions, quenched the violence of fire, escaped the edge of the sword, out of weakness were made strong, became valiant in battle, turned to flight the armies of the aliens. **Cf. Deut. 20.**

5

Ex. 22:2: If the thief is found breaking in, and he is struck so that he dies, *there shall be* no guilt for his bloodshed.

6

Matt. 25:42-43: ... for I was hungry and you gave Me no food; I was thirsty and you gave Me no drink; I was a stranger and you did not take Me in, naked and you did not clothe Me, sick and in prison and you did not visit Me. **James 2:15-16:** If a brother or sister is naked and destitute of daily food, and one of you says to them, "Depart in peace, be warmed and filled," but you do not give them the things which are needed for the body, what *does it* profit?

7

Matt. 5:22: But I say to you that whoever is angry with his brother without a cause shall be in danger of the judgment. And whoever says to his brother, 'Raca!' shall be in danger of the council. But whoever says, 'You fool!' shall be in danger of hell fire.

8

1 John 3:15: Whoever hates his brother is a murderer, and you know that no murderer has eternal life abiding in him. **Lev. 19:17:** You shall not hate your brother in your heart. You shall surely rebuke your neighbor, and not bear sin because of him.

9
Prov. 14:30: A sound heart *is* life to the body, But envy *is* rottenness to the bones.
10
Rom. 12:19: Beloved, do not avenge yourselves, but *rather* give place to wrath; for it is written, "Vengeance *is* Mine, I will repay," says the Lord.
11
Eph. 4:31: Let all bitterness, wrath, anger, clamor, and evil speaking be put away from you, with all malice.
12
Matt. 6:31, 34: Therefore do not worry, saying, 'What shall we eat?' or 'What shall we drink?' or 'What shall we wear?' ... Therefore do not worry about tomorrow, for tomorrow will worry about its own things. Sufficient for the day *is* its own trouble.
13
Luke 21:34: But take heed to yourselves, lest your hearts be weighed down with carousing, drunkenness, and cares of this life, and that Day come on you unexpectedly. **Rom. 13:13:** Let us walk properly, as in the day, not in revelry and drunkenness, not in lewdness and lust, not in strife and envy.
14
Eccl. 12:12: And further, my son, be admonished by these. Of making many books *there is* no end, and much study *is* wearisome to the flesh. **Eccl. 2:22-23:** For what has man for all his labor, and for the striving of his heart with which he has toiled under the sun? For all his days *are* sorrowful, and his work burdensome; even in the night his heart takes no rest. This also is vanity.
15
Isa. 5:12: The harp and the strings, The tambourine and flute, And wine are in their feasts; But they do not regard the work of the LORD, Nor consider the operation of His hands.
16
Prov. 15:1: A soft answer turns away wrath, But a harsh word stirs up anger. **Prov. 12:18:** There is one who speaks like the piercings of a sword, But the tongue of the wise *promotes* health.
17
Ex. 1:14: And they made their lives bitter with hard bondage—in mortar, in brick, and in all manner of service in the field. All their service in which they made them serve *was* with rigor. **See Isa. 3:15.**
18
Gal. 5:15: But if you bite and devour one another, beware lest you be consumed by one another! **Prov. 23:29:** Who has woe? Who has sorrow? Who has contentions? Who has complaints? Who has wounds without cause? Who has redness of eyes?
19
Num. 35:16-17: But if he strikes him with an iron implement, so that he dies, he *is* a murderer; the murderer shall surely be put to death. And if he strikes him with a stone in the hand, by which one could die, and he does die, he *is* a murderer; the murderer shall surely be put to death. **See Num. 35:18-21.**
20
Ex. 21:29: But if the ox tended to thrust with its horn in times past, and it has been made known to his owner, and he has not kept it confined, so that it has killed a man or a woman, the ox shall be stoned and its owner also shall be put to death. **See Ex. 21:18-36.**

Q. 158. *Which is the seventh commandment?*

A. The seventh commandment is, *Thou shalt not commit adultery.*[1]

1
Ex. 20:14: You shall not commit adultery. **Cf. Deut. 5:18.**

Q. 159. *What are the duties required in the seventh commandment?*

A. The duties required in the seventh commandment are, chastity in body, mind, affections,[1] words,[2] and behaviour;[3] and the preservation of it in ourselves and others;[4] watchfulness over the eyes and all the senses;[5] temperance,[6] keeping of chaste company,[7] modesty in apparel;[8] marriage by those that have not the gift of continency,[9] conjugal love,[10] and cohabitation;[11] diligent labour in our callings;[12] shunning all occasions of uncleanness, and resisting temptations thereunto.[13]

1
1 Thess. 4:4-5: ... that each of you should know how to possess his own vessel in sanctification and honor, not in passion of lust, like the Gentiles who do not know God. **Job 31:1:** I have made a covenant with my eyes; Why then should I look upon a young woman? **1 Cor. 7:34:** There is a difference between a wife and a virgin. The unmarried woman cares about the things of the Lord, that she may be holy both in body and in spirit. But she who is married cares about the things of the world—how she may please *her* husband.

2
Eph. 4:29: Let no corrupt word proceed out of your mouth, but what is good for necessary edification, that it may impart grace to the hearers. **Col. 4:6:** *Let* your speech always *be* with grace, seasoned with salt, that you may know how you ought to answer each one.

3
1 Pet. 3:2: ... when they observe your chaste conduct *accompanied* by fear.

4
1 Cor. 7:2-5, 34-36: Nevertheless, because of sexual immorality, let each man have his own wife, and let each woman have her own husband. Let the husband render to his wife the affection due her, and likewise also the wife to her husband. The wife does not have authority over her own body, but the husband *does.* And likewise the husband does not have authority over his own body, but the wife *does.* Do not deprive one another except with consent for a time, that you may give yourselves to fasting and prayer; and come together again so that Satan does not tempt you because of your lack of self-control.... There is a difference between a wife and a virgin. The unmarried woman cares about the things of the Lord, that she may be holy both in body and in spirit. But she who is married cares about the things of the world—how she may please *her* husband. And this I say for your own profit, not that I may put a leash on you, but for what is proper, and that you may serve the Lord without distraction. But if any man thinks he is behaving improperly toward his virgin, if she is past the flower of youth, and thus it must be, let him do what he wishes. He does not sin; let them marry.

5
Matt. 5:28: But I say to you that whoever looks at a woman to lust for her has already committed adultery with her in his heart. **Job 31:1:** I have made a covenant with my eyes; Why then should I look upon a young woman?

6
Acts 24:24-25: And after some days, when Felix came with his wife Drusilla, who was Jewish, he sent for Paul and heard him concerning the faith in Christ. Now as he reasoned about righteousness, self-control, and the judgment to come, Felix was afraid and answered, "Go away for now; when I have a convenient time I will call for you."

7
Prov. 2:16-20: To deliver you from the immoral woman, From the seductress *who* flatters with her words, Who forsakes the companion of her youth, And forgets the covenant of her God. For her house leads down to death, And her paths to the dead; None who go to her return, Nor do they regain the paths of life— So you may walk in the way of goodness, And keep *to* the paths of righteousness.

8
1 Tim. 2:9: ... in like manner also, that the women adorn themselves in modest apparel, with propriety and moderation, not with braided hair or gold or pearls or costly clothing.

9
1 Cor. 7:2, 9: Nevertheless, because of sexual immorality, let each man have his own wife, and let each woman have her own husband.... but if they cannot exercise self-control, let them marry. For it is better to marry than to burn *with passion.*

10
Prov. 5:19-20: *As a* loving deer and a graceful doe, Let her breasts satisfy you at all times; And always be enraptured with her love. For why should you, my son, be enraptured by an immoral woman, And be embraced in the arms of a seductress?

11
1 Pet. 3:7: Husbands, likewise, dwell with *them* with understanding, giving honor to the wife, as to the weaker vessel, and as *being* heirs together of the grace of life, that your prayers may not be hindered. **1 Cor. 7:5:** Do not deprive one another except with consent for a time, that you may give yourselves to fasting and prayer; and come together again so that Satan does not tempt you because of your lack of self-control.

12
Prov. 31:11, 27-28: The heart of her husband safely trusts her; So he will have no lack of gain.... She watches over the ways of her household, And does not eat the bread of idleness. Her children rise up and call her blessed; Her husband *also,* and he praises her.

13
Prov. 5:8: Remove your way far from her, And do not go near the door of her house. **See Gen. 39:8-10.**

Q. 160. *What are the sins forbidden in the seventh commandment?*

A. The sins forbidden in the seventh commandment, besides the neglect of the duties required,[1] are, adultery, fornication,[2] rape, incest,[3] sodomy, and all unnatural lusts;[4] all unclean imaginations, thoughts, purposes, and affections;[5] all corrupt or filthy communications, or listening thereunto;[6] wanton looks,[7] impudent or light behaviour, immodest apparel;[8] prohibiting of lawful,[9] and dispensing with unlawful marriages;[10] allowing, tolerating, keeping of stews, and resorting to them;[11] entangling vows of single life,[12] undue delay of marriage;[13] having more wives or husbands than one at the same time;[14] unjust divorce,[15] or desertion;[16] idleness, gluttony, drunkenness,[17] unchaste company;[18] lascivious songs, books, pictures, dancings, stage plays;[19] and all other provocations to, or acts of uncleanness, either in ourselves or others.[20]

[1] **Prov. 5:7:** Therefore hear me now, *my* children, And do not depart from the words of my mouth. **See Prov. 4:23, 27.**

[2] **Heb. 13:4:** Marriage *is* honorable among all, and the bed undefiled; but fornicators and adulterers God will judge. **Eph. 5:5:** For this you know, that no fornicator, unclean person, nor covetous man, who is an idolater, has any inheritance in the kingdom of Christ and God. **See Gal. 5:19.**

[3] **2 Sam. 13:14:** However, he would not heed her voice; and being stronger than she, he forced her and lay with her. **1 Cor. 5:1:** It is actually reported *that there is* sexual immorality among you, and such sexual immorality as is not even named among the Gentiles—that a man has his father's wife! **Mark 6:18:** Because John had said to Herod, "It is not lawful for you to have your brother's wife."

[4] **Rom. 1:24, 26-27:** Therefore God also gave them up to uncleanness, in the lusts of their hearts, to dishonor their bodies among themselves ... For this reason God gave them up to vile passions. For even their women exchanged the natural use for what is against nature. Likewise also the men, leaving the natural use of the woman, burned in their lust for one another, men with men committing what is shameful, and receiving in themselves the penalty of their error which was due. **Lev. 20:15-16:** If a man mates with an animal, he shall surely be put to death, and you shall kill the animal. If a woman approaches any animal and mates with it, you shall kill the woman and the animal. They shall surely be put to death. Their blood *is* upon them.

[5] **Matt. 5:28:** But I say to you that whoever looks at a woman to lust for her has already committed adultery with her in his heart. **Matt. 15:19:** For out of the heart proceed evil thoughts, murders, adulteries, fornications, thefts, false witness, blasphemies. **Col. 3:5:** Therefore put to death your members which are on the earth: fornication, uncleanness, passion, evil desire, and covetousness, which is idolatry.

[6] **Eph. 5:3-4:** But fornication and all uncleanness or covetousness, let it not even be named among you, as is fitting for saints; neither filthiness, nor foolish talking, nor coarse jesting, which are not fitting, but rather giving of thanks. **See Prov. 7:5, 21-22.**

[7] **Isa. 3:16:** Moreover the LORD says: "Because the daughters of Zion are haughty, And walk with outstretched necks And wanton eyes, Walking and mincing *as* they go, Making a jingling with their feet." **2 Pet. 2:14:** ... having eyes full of adultery and that cannot cease from sin, enticing unstable souls. They have a heart trained in covetous practices, *and are* accursed children.

[8] **Prov. 7:10, 13:** And there a woman met him, *With* the attire of a harlot, and a crafty heart.... So she caught him and kissed him; With an impudent face she said to him.

9
1 Tim. 4:3: ... forbidding to marry, *and commanding* to abstain from foods which God created to be received with thanksgiving by those who believe and know the truth.
10
Mark 6:18: Because John had said to Herod, "It is not lawful for you to have your brother's wife." **Mal. 2:11-12:** Judah has dealt treacherously, And an abomination has been committed in Israel and in Jerusalem, For Judah has profaned The LORD's holy *institution* which He loves: He has married the daughter of a foreign god. May the LORD cut off from the tents of Jacob The man who does this, being awake and aware, Yet who brings an offering to the LORD of hosts! **See Lev. 18:1-21.**
11
1 Kings 15:12: And he banished the perverted persons from the land, and removed all the idols that his fathers had made. **2 Kings 23:7:** Then he tore down the *ritual* booths of the perverted persons that *were* in the house of the LORD, where the women wove hangings for the wooden image. **Lev. 19:29:** Do not prostitute your daughter, to cause her to be a harlot, lest the land fall into harlotry, and the land become full of wickedness. **Jer. 5:7:** How shall I pardon you for this? Your children have forsaken Me And sworn by *those that are* not gods. When I had fed them to the full, Then they committed adultery And assembled themselves by troops in the harlots' houses. **See Deut. 23:17-18; Prov. 7:24-27.**
12
Matt. 19:10-11: His disciples said to Him, "If such is the case of the man with *his* wife, it is better not to marry." But He said to them, "All cannot accept this saying, but only *those* to whom it has been given."
13
1 Cor. 7:7-9: For I wish that all men were even as I myself. But each one has his own gift from God, one in this manner and another in that. But I say to the unmarried and to the widows: It is good for them if they remain even as I am; but if they cannot exercise self-control, let them marry. For it is better to marry than to burn *with passion.* **Gen. 38:26:** So Judah acknowledged *them* and said, "She has been more righteous than I, because I did not give her to Shelah my son." And he never knew her again.
14
Mal. 2:14-15: Yet you say, "For what reason?" Because the LORD has been witness Between you and the wife of your youth, With whom you have dealt treacherously; Yet she is your companion And your wife by covenant. But did He not make *them* one, Having a remnant of the Spirit? And why one? He seeks godly offspring. Therefore take heed to your spirit, And let none deal treacherously with the wife of his youth. **Matt. 19:5:** ... and said, 'For this reason a man shall leave his father and mother and be joined to his wife, and the two shall become one flesh'?
15
Mal. 2:16: "For the LORD God of Israel says That He hates divorce, For it covers one's garment with violence," Says the LORD of hosts. "Therefore take heed to your spirit, That you do not deal treacherously." **Matt. 5:32:** But I say to you that whoever divorces his wife for any reason except sexual immorality causes her to commit adultery; and whoever marries a woman who is divorced commits adultery. **Matt. 19:8-9:** He said to them, "Moses, because of the hardness of your hearts, permitted you to divorce your wives, but from the beginning it was not so. And I say to you, whoever divorces his wife, except for sexual immorality, and marries another, commits adultery; and whoever marries her who is divorced commits adultery."
16
1 Cor. 7:12-13: But to the rest I, not the Lord, say: If any brother has a wife who does not believe, and she is willing to live with him, let him not divorce her. And a woman who has a husband who does not believe, if he is willing to live with her, let her not divorce him.
17
Ezek. 16:49: Look, this was the iniquity of your sister Sodom: She and her daughter had pride, fullness of food, and abundance of idleness; neither did she strengthen the hand of the poor and needy. **See Prov. 23:30-33.**
18
Gen. 39:19: So it was, when his master heard the words which his wife spoke to him, saying, "Your servant did to me after this manner," that his anger was aroused. **See Prov. 5:8.**
19
Eph. 5:4: ... neither filthiness, nor foolish talking, nor coarse jesting, which are not fitting, but rather giving of thanks. **Rom. 13:13:** Let us walk properly, as in the day, not in revelry and drunkenness, not in lewdness and lust, not in strife and envy. **1 Pet. 4:3:** For we *have spent* enough of our past lifetime in doing the will of the Gentiles—when we walked in lewdness, lusts, drunkenness, revelries, drinking parties, and abominable idolatries. **See Ezek. 23:14-16; Isa. 3:16, 23:15-17; Mark 6:22.**
20
2 Kings 9:30: Now when Jehu had come to Jezreel, Jezebel heard *of it;* and she put paint on her eyes and adorned her head, and looked through a window. **Jer. 4:30:** And *when* you *are* plundered, What will you do? Though you clothe yourself with crimson, Though you adorn *yourself* with ornaments of gold, Though you enlarge your eyes with paint, In vain you will make yourself fair; *Your* lovers will despise you; They will seek your life. **Ezek. 23:40:** Furthermore you sent for men to come from afar, to whom a messenger *was* sent; and there they came. And you washed yourself for them, painted your eyes, and adorned yourself with ornaments.

Q. 161. *Which is the eighth commandment?*

A. The eighth commandment is, *Thou shalt not steal.*[1]

[1] **Ex. 20:15:** You shall not steal. **Cf. Deut. 5:19.**

Q. 162. *What are the duties required in the eighth commandment?*

A. The duties required in the eighth commandment are, truth, faithfulness, and justice in contracts and commerce between man and man;[1] rendering to every one his due;[2] restitution of goods unlawfully detained from the right owners thereof;[3] giving and lending freely, according to our abilities, and the necessities of others;[4] moderation of our judgments, wills, and affections concerning worldly goods;[5] a provident care and study to get,[6] keep, use, and dispose these things which are necessary and convenient for the sustentation of our nature, and suitable to our condition;[7] a lawful calling,[8] and diligence in it;[9] frugality;[10] avoiding unnecessary lawsuits,[11] and suretyship, or other like engagements;[12] and an endeavor, by all just and lawful means, to procure, preserve, and further the wealth and outward estate of others, as well as our own.[13]

[1] **Ps. 15:2, 4:** He who walks uprightly, And works righteousness, And speaks the truth in his heart ... In whose eyes a vile person is despised, But he honors those who fear the LORD; He *who* swears to his own hurt and does not change. **Mic. 6:8:** He has shown you, O man, what *is* good; And what does the LORD require of you But to do justly, To love mercy, And to walk humbly with your God? **Zech. 8:16-17:** These *are* the things you shall do: Speak each man the truth to his neighbor; Give judgment in your gates for truth, justice, and peace; Let none of you think evil in your heart against your neighbor; And do not love a false oath. For all these *are things* that I hate,' Says the LORD." **See Zech. 7:4, 10.**

[2] **Rom. 13:7:** Render therefore to all their due: taxes to whom taxes *are due,* customs to whom customs, fear to whom fear, honor to whom honor.

[3] **Lev. 6:2-5:** If a person sins and commits a trespass against the LORD by lying to his neighbor about what was delivered to him for safekeeping, or about a pledge, or about a robbery, or if he has extorted from his neighbor, or if he has found what was lost and lies concerning it, and swears falsely—in any one of these things that a man may do in which he sins: then it shall be, because he has sinned and is guilty, that he shall restore what he has stolen, or the thing which he has extorted, or what was delivered to him for safekeeping, or the lost thing which he found, or all that about which he has sworn falsely. He shall restore its full value, add one-fifth more to it, *and* give it to whomever it belongs, on the day of his trespass offering. **See Luke 19:8.**

[4] **Luke 6:30, 38:** Give to everyone who asks of you. And from him who takes away your goods do not ask *them* back.... Give, and it will be given to you: good measure, pressed down, shaken together, and running over will be put into your bosom. For with the same measure that you use, it will be measured back to you. **1 John 3:17:** But whoever has this world's goods, and sees his brother in need, and shuts up his heart from him, how does the love of God abide in him? **Eph. 4:28:** Let him who stole steal no longer, but rather let him labor, working with *his* hands what is good, that he may have something to give him who has need. **Gal. 6:10:** Therefore, as we have opportunity, let us do good to all, especially to those who are of the household of faith.

5
1 Tim. 6:6-9: Now godliness with contentment is great gain. For we brought nothing into *this* world, *and it is* certain we can carry nothing out. And having food and clothing, with these we shall be content. But those who desire to be rich fall into temptation and a snare, and *into* many foolish and harmful lusts which drown men in destruction and perdition. **See Gal. 6:14.**
6
1 Tim. 5:8: But if anyone does not provide for his own, and especially for those of his household, he has denied the faith and is worse than an unbeliever.
7
Prov. 27:23: Be diligent to know the state of your flocks, *And* attend to your herds. **See Prov. 27:24-27. Eccl. 2:24:** Nothing *is* better for a man *than* that he should eat and drink, and *that* his soul should enjoy good in his labor. This also, I saw, was from the hand of God. **Eccl. 3:12-13:** I know that nothing *is* better for them than to rejoice, and to do good in their lives, and also that every man should eat and drink and enjoy the good of all his labor—it *is* the gift of God. **1 Tim. 6:17-18:** Command those who are rich in this present age not to be haughty, nor to trust in uncertain riches but in the living God, who gives us richly all things to enjoy. *Let them* do good, that they be rich in good works, ready to give, willing to share. **See Isa. 38:1; Matt. 11:8.**
8
1 Cor. 7:20: Let each one remain in the same calling in which he was called. **See Gen. 2:15, 3:19.**
9
Eph. 4:28: Let him who stole steal no longer, but rather let him labor, working with *his* hands what is good, that he may have something to give him who has need. **Prov. 10:4:** He who has a slack hand becomes poor, But the hand of the diligent makes rich. **Rom. 12:11:** ... not lagging in diligence, fervent in spirit, serving the Lord.
10
John 6:12: So when they were filled, He said to His disciples, "Gather up the fragments that remain, so that nothing is lost." **Prov. 21:20:** *There is* desirable treasure, And oil in the dwelling of the wise, But a foolish man squanders it.
11
1 Cor. 6:1: Dare any of you, having a matter against another, go to law before the unrighteous, and not before the saints? **See 1 Cor. 6:2-9.**
12
Prov. 11:15: He who is surety for a stranger will suffer, But one who hates being surety is secure. **See Prov. 6:1-6.**
13
Lev. 25:35: If one of your brethren becomes poor, and falls into poverty among you, then you shall help him, like a stranger or a sojourner, that he may live with you. **Phil. 2:4:** Let each of you look out not only for his own interests, but also for the interests of others. **See Deut. 22:1-4; Ex. 23:4-5; Gen. 47:14, 20; Matt. 22:39.**

Q. 163. *What are the sins forbidden in the eighth commandment?*

A. The sins forbidden in the eighth commandment, besides the neglect of the duties required,[1] are, theft,[2] robbery,[3] man-stealing,[4] and receiving anything that is stolen;[5] fraudulent dealing,[6] false weights and measures,[7] removing landmarks,[8] injustice and unfaithfulness in contracts between man and man,[9] or in matters of trust;[10] oppression,[11] extortion,[12] usury,[13] bribery,[14] vexatious lawsuits,[15] unjust enclosures and depopulations;[16] engrossing commodities to enhance the price;[17] unlawful callings,[18] and all other unjust or sinful ways of taking or withholding from our neighbour what belongs to him, or of enriching ourselves;[19] covetousness;[20] inordinate prizing and affecting worldly goods;[21] distrustful and distracting cares and studies in getting, keeping, and using them;[22] envying at the prosperity of others;[23] as likewise idleness,[24] prodigality, wasteful gaming; and all other ways whereby we do unduly prejudice our own outward estate,[25] and defrauding ourselves of the due use and comfort of that estate which God hath given us.[26]

1 **James 2:15-16:** If a brother or sister is naked and destitute of daily food, and one of you says to them, "Depart in peace, be warmed and filled," but you do not give them the things which are needed for the body, what *does it* profit? **1 John 3:17:** But whoever has this world's goods, and sees his brother in need, and shuts up his heart from him, how does the love of God abide in him?

2 **Eph. 4:28:** Let him who stole steal no longer, but rather let him labor, working with *his* hands what is good, that he may have something to give him who has need.

3 **Ps. 62:10:** Do not trust in oppression, Nor vainly hope in robbery; If riches increase, Do not set *your* heart *on them.*

4 **1 Tim. 1:10:** ... for fornicators, for sodomites, for kidnappers, for liars, for perjurers, and if there is any other thing that is contrary to sound doctrine.

5 **Prov. 29:24:** Whoever is a partner with a thief hates his own life; He swears to tell the truth, but reveals nothing. **Ps. 50:18:** When you saw a thief, you consented with him, And have been a partaker with adulterers.

6 **1 Thess. 4:6:** ... that no one should take advantage of and defraud his brother in this matter, because the Lord *is* the avenger of all such, as we also forewarned you and testified. **Lev. 19:13:** You shall not cheat your neighbor, nor rob *him*. The wages of him who is hired shall not remain with you all night until morning.

7 **Prov. 11:1:** Dishonest scales *are* an abomination to the LORD, But a just weight *is* His delight. **Prov. 20:10:** Diverse weights *and* diverse measures, They *are* both alike, an abomination to the LORD.

8 **Deut. 19:14:** You shall not remove your neighbor's landmark, which the men of old have set, in your inheritance which you will inherit in the land that the LORD your God is giving you to possess. **See Prov. 23:10.**

9 **Amos 8:5:** Saying: "When will the New Moon be past, That we may sell grain? And the Sabbath, That we may trade wheat? Making the ephah small and the shekel large, Falsifying the scales by deceit. **Ps. 37:21:** The wicked borrows and does not repay, But the righteous shows mercy and gives.

10 **Luke 16:10-12:** He who *is* faithful in *what is* least is faithful also in much; and he who is unjust in *what is* least is unjust also in much. Therefore if you have not been faithful in the unrighteous mammon, who will commit to your trust the true *riches?* And if you have not been faithful in what is another man's, who will give you what is your own?

11 **Ezek. 22:29:** The people of the land have used oppressions, committed robbery, and mistreated the poor and needy; and they wrongfully oppress the stranger. **Lev. 25:17:** Therefore you shall not oppress one another, but you shall fear your God; for I *am* the LORD your God.

12 **Matt. 23:25:** Woe to you, scribes and Pharisees, hypocrites! For you cleanse the outside of the cup and dish, but inside they are full of extortion and self-indulgence. **Ezek. 22:12:** "In you they take bribes to shed blood; you take usury and increase; you have made profit from your neighbors by extortion, and have forgotten Me," says the Lord God.

13 **Ps. 15:5:** He *who* does not put out his money at usury, Nor does he take a bribe against the innocent. He who does these *things* shall never be moved.

14 **Job 15:34:** For the company of hypocrites *will be* barren, And fire will consume the tents of bribery.

15 **1 Cor. 6:6-8:** But brother goes to law against brother, and that before unbelievers! Now therefore, it is already an utter failure for you that you go to law against one another. Why do you not rather accept wrong? Why do you not rather *let yourselves* be cheated? No, you yourselves do wrong and cheat, and *you do* these things *to your* brethren! **Prov. 3:29-30:** Do not devise evil against your neighbor, For he dwells by you for safety's sake. Do not strive with a man without cause, If he has done you no harm.

16
Isa. 5:8: Woe to those who join house to house; They add field to field, Till *there is* no place Where they may dwell alone in the midst of the land! **Mic. 2:2:** They covet fields and take *them* by violence, Also houses, and seize *them.* So they oppress a man and his house, A man and his inheritance.
17
Prov. 11:26: The people will curse him who withholds grain, But blessing *will be* on the head of him who sells *it.*
18
Acts 19:19: Also, many of those who had practiced magic brought their books together and burned *them* in the sight of all. And they counted up the value of them, and *it* totaled fifty thousand *pieces* of silver. **See Acts 19:24-25.**
19
James 5:4: Indeed the wages of the laborers who mowed your fields, which you kept back by fraud, cry out; and the cries of the reapers have reached the ears of the Lord of Sabaoth. **Prov. 21:6:** Getting treasures by a lying tongue *Is* the fleeting fantasy of those who seek death. **See Job 20:19.**
20
Luke 12:15: And He said to them, "Take heed and beware of covetousness, for one's life does not consist in the abundance of the things he possesses."
21
1 Tim. 6:5: ... useless wranglings of men of corrupt minds and destitute of the truth, who suppose that godliness is a *means of* gain. From such withdraw yourself. **Col. 3:2:** Set your mind on things above, not on things on the earth. **1 John 2:15-16:** Do not love the world or the things in the world. If anyone loves the world, the love of the Father is not in him. For all that *is* in the world—the lust of the flesh, the lust of the eyes, and the pride of life—is not of the Father but is of the world. **See Prov. 23:5; Ps. 62:10.**
22
Matt. 6:25, 31, 34: Therefore I say to you, do not worry about your life, what you will eat or what you will drink; nor about your body, what you will put on. Is not life more than food and the body more than clothing? ... Therefore do not worry, saying, 'What shall we eat?' or 'What shall we drink?' or 'What shall we wear?'... Therefore do not worry about tomorrow, for tomorrow will worry about its own things. Sufficient for the day *is* its own trouble. **Eccl. 5:12:** The sleep of a laboring man *is* sweet, Whether he eats little or much; But the abundance of the rich will not permit him to sleep.
23
Ps. 73:3: For I *was* envious of the boastful, When I saw the prosperity of the wicked. **See Ps. 37:1, 7.**
24
2 Thess. 3:10-11: For even when we were with you, we commanded you this: If anyone will not work, neither shall he eat. For we hear that there are some who walk among you in a disorderly manner, not working at all, but are busybodies. **See Prov. 18:9.**
25
Prov. 21:17: He who loves pleasure *will be* a poor man; He who loves wine and oil will not be rich. **Prov. 23:20-21:** Do not mix with winebibbers, *Or* with gluttonous eaters of meat; For the drunkard and the glutton will come to poverty, And drowsiness will clothe *a man* with rags. **See Prov. 28:19.**
26
Eccl. 4:8: There is one alone, without companion: He has neither son nor brother. Yet *there is* no end to all his labors, Nor is his eye satisfied with riches. *But he never asks,* "For whom do I toil and deprive myself of good?" This also *is* vanity and a grave misfortune. **Eccl. 6:2:** A man to whom God has given riches and wealth and honor, so that he lacks nothing for himself of all he desires; yet God does not give him power to eat of it, but a foreigner consumes it. This *is* vanity, and it *is* an evil affliction. **1 Tim. 4:3-5:** ... forbidding to marry, *and commanding* to abstain from foods which God created to be received with thanksgiving by those who believe and know the truth. For every creature of God *is* good, and nothing is to be refused if it is received with thanksgiving; for it is sanctified by the word of God and prayer. **1 Tim. 5:8:** But if anyone does not provide for his own, and especially for those of his household, he has denied the faith and is worse than an unbeliever.

Q. 164. *Which is the ninth commandment?*

A. The ninth commandment is, *Thou shalt not bear false witness against thy neighbour.*[1]

1
Ex. 20:16: You shall not bear false witness against your neighbor. **Cf. Deut. 5:20.**

Q. 165. *What are the duties required in the ninth commandment?*

A. The duties required in the ninth commandment are, the preserving and promoting of truth between man and man,[1] and the good name of our neighbour, as well as our own;[2] appearing and standing for the truth;[3] and from the heart,[4] sincerely,[5] freely,[6] clearly,[7] and fully,[8] speaking the truth, and only the truth, in matters of judgment and justice,[9] and in all other things whatsoever;[10] a charitable esteem of our neighbours;[11] loving, desiring, and rejoicing in their good name;[12] sorrowing for,[13] and covering of their infirmities;[14] freely acknowledging of their gifts and graces,[15] defending their innocency;[16] a ready receiving of a good report,[17] and unwillingness to admit of an evil report,[18] concerning them; discouraging talebearers,[19] flatterers,[20] and slanderers;[21] love and care of our own good name, and defending it when need requireth;[22] keeping of lawful promises;[23] studying and practicing of whatsoever things are true, honest, lovely, and of good report.[24]

1 **Zech. 8:16:** These *are* the things you shall do: Speak each man the truth to his neighbor; Give judgment in your gates for truth, justice, and peace. **Eph. 4:25:** Therefore, putting away lying, "*Let* each one *of you* speak truth with his neighbor," for we are members of one another.

2 **3 John 12:** Demetrius has a *good* testimony from all, and from the truth itself. And we also bear witness, and you know that our testimony is true.

3 **Prov. 31:8-9:** Open your mouth for the speechless, In the cause of all *who are* appointed to die. Open your mouth, judge righteously, And plead the cause of the poor and needy.

4 **Ps. 15:2:** He who walks uprightly, And works righteousness, And speaks the truth in his heart.

5 **2 Chron. 19:9:** And he commanded them, saying, "Thus you shall act in the fear of the LORD, faithfully and with a loyal heart."

6 **1 Sam. 19:4-5:** Thus Jonathan spoke well of David to Saul his father, and said to him, "Let not the king sin against his servant, against David, because he has not sinned against you, and because his works *have been* very good toward you. For he took his life in his hands and killed the Philistine, and the LORD brought about a great deliverance for all Israel. You saw *it* and rejoiced. Why then will you sin against innocent blood, to kill David without a cause?"

7 **Josh. 7:19:** Now Joshua said to Achan, "My son, I beg you, give glory to the LORD God of Israel, and make confession to Him, and tell me now what you have done; do not hide *it* from me." **See Josh. 7:15-20.**

8 **2 Sam. 14:18:** Then the king answered and said to the woman, "Please do not hide from me anything that I ask you." And the woman said, "Please, let my lord the king speak." **See 2 Sam. 14:19-20; Acts 20:27:** For I have not shunned to declare to you the whole counsel of God.

9 **Lev. 19:15:** You shall do no injustice in judgment. You shall not be partial to the poor, nor honor the person of the mighty. In righteousness you shall judge your neighbor. **Prov. 14:5, 25:** A faithful witness does not lie, But a false witness will utter lies.... A true witness delivers souls, But a deceitful *witness* speaks lies.

10
2 Cor. 1:17-18: Therefore, when I was planning this, did I do it lightly? Or the things I plan, do I plan according to the flesh, that with me there should be Yes, Yes, and No, No? But *as* God *is* faithful, our word to you was not Yes and No. **Eph. 4:25:** Therefore, putting away lying, "*Let* each one *of you* speak truth with his neighbor," for we are members of one another. **See Col. 3:9.**
11
Heb. 6:9: But, beloved, we are confident of better things concerning you, yes, things that accompany salvation, though we speak in this manner. **1 Cor. 13:7:** ... bears all things, believes all things, hopes all things, endures all things.
12
Rom. 1:8: First, I thank my God through Jesus Christ for you all, that your faith is spoken of throughout the whole world. **2 John 4:** I rejoiced greatly that I have found *some* of your children walking in truth, as we received commandment from the Father. **3 John 3-4:** For I rejoiced greatly when brethren came and testified of the truth *that is* in you, just as you walk in the truth. I have no greater joy than to hear that my children walk in truth.
13
2 Cor. 2:4: For out of much affliction and anguish of heart I wrote to you, with many tears, not that you should be grieved, but that you might know the love which I have so abundantly for you. **2 Cor. 12:21:** ... lest, when I come again, my God will humble me among you, and I shall mourn for many who have sinned before and have not repented of the uncleanness, fornication, and lewdness which they have practiced. **See Ps. 119:158.**
14
Prov. 17:9: He who covers a transgression seeks love, But he who repeats a matter separates friends. **1 Pet. 4:8:** And above all things have fervent love for one another, for "love will cover a multitude of sins."
15
1 Cor. 1:4-5, 7: I thank my God always concerning you for the grace of God which was given to you by Christ Jesus, that you were enriched in everything by Him in all utterance and all knowledge ... so that you come short in no gift, eagerly waiting for the revelation of our Lord Jesus Christ. **See 2 Tim. 1:4-5.**
16
1 Sam. 22:14: So Ahimelech answered the king and said, "And who among all your servants *is as* faithful as David, who is the king's son-in-law, who goes at your bidding, and is honorable in your house?"
17
1 Cor. 13:6-7: ... does not rejoice in iniquity, but rejoices in the truth; bears all things, believes all things, hopes all things, endures all things.
18
Ps. 15:3: He *who* does not backbite with his tongue, Nor does evil to his neighbor, Nor does he take up a reproach against his friend.
19
Prov. 25:23: The north wind brings forth rain, And a backbiting tongue an angry countenance.
20
Prov. 26:24-25: He who hates, disguises *it* with his lips, And lays up deceit within himself; When he speaks kindly, do not believe him, For *there are* seven abominations in his heart.
21
Ps. 101:5: Whoever secretly slanders his neighbor, Him I will destroy; The one who has a haughty look and a proud heart, Him I will not endure.
22
Prov. 22:1: A *good* name is to be chosen rather than great riches, Loving favor rather than silver and gold. **John 8:49:** Jesus answered, "I do not have a demon; but I honor My Father, and you dishonor Me." **See 2 Cor. 11:1-12:13.**
23
Ps. 15:4: In whose eyes a vile person is despised, But he honors those who fear the LORD; He *who* swears to his own hurt and does not change.
24
Phil. 4:8: Finally, brethren, whatever things are true, whatever things *are* noble, whatever things *are* just, whatever things *are* pure, whatever things *are* lovely, whatever things *are* of good report, if *there is* any virtue and if *there is* anything praiseworthy—meditate on these things.

Q. 166. *What are the sins forbidden in the ninth commandment?*

A. The sins forbidden in the ninth commandment are, all prejudicing the truth, and the good name of our neighbours, as well as our own,[1] especially in public judicature;[2] giving false evidence,[3] suborning false witnesses,[4] wittingly appearing and pleading for an evil cause, outfacing and overbearing the truth;[5] passing unjust sentence,[6] calling evil good, and good evil; rewarding the wicked according to the work of the righteous, and the righteous according to the work of the wicked;[7] forgery,[8] concealing the truth, undue silence in a just cause,[9] and holding our peace when iniquity calleth for either a reproof from ourselves,[10] or complaint to others;[11] speaking the truth unseasonably,[12] or maliciously to a wrong end,[13] or perverting it to a wrong meaning,[14] or in doubtful or equivocal expressions, to the prejudice of truth or justice;[15] speaking untruth,[16] lying,[17] slandering,[18] backbiting,[19] detracting,[20] talebearing,[21] whispering,[22] scoffing,[23] reviling,[24] rash,[25] harsh,[26] and partial censuring;[27] misconstructing intentions, words, and actions;[28] flattering,[29] vainglorious boasting,[30] thinking or speaking too highly or too meanly of ourselves or others;[31] denying the gifts and graces of God;[32] aggravating smaller faults;[33] hiding, excusing, or extenuating of sins, when called to a free confession;[34] unnecessary discovering of infirmities;[35] raising false rumours,[36] receiving and countenancing evil reports,[37] and stopping our ears against just defense;[38] evil suspicion;[39] envying or grieving at the deserved credit of any,[40] endeavoring or desiring to impair it,[41] rejoicing in their disgrace and infamy;[42] scornful contempt,[43] fond admiration;[44] breach of lawful promises;[45] neglecting such things as are of good report,[46] and practicing, or not avoiding ourselves, or not hindering what we can in others, such things as procure an ill name.[47]

[1] **Luke 3:14:** Likewise the soldiers asked him, saying, "And what shall we do?" So he said to them, "Do not intimidate anyone or accuse falsely, and be content with your wages." **See 1 Sam. 17:28; 2 Sam. 16:3, 1:9-10, 15-16.**

[2] **Lev. 19:15:** You shall do no injustice in judgment. You shall not be partial to the poor, nor honor the person of the mighty. In righteousness you shall judge your neighbor. **See Hab. 1:4.**

[3] **Prov. 19:5:** A false witness will not go unpunished, And *he who* speaks lies will not escape. **See Prov. 6:16, 19.**

[4] **Acts 6:13:** They also set up false witnesses who said, "This man does not cease to speak blasphemous words against this holy place and the law"

[5] **Jer. 9:3, 5:** "And *like* their bow they have bent their tongues *for* lies. They are not valiant for the truth on the earth. For they proceed from evil to evil, And they do not know Me," says the LORD.... Everyone will deceive his neighbor, And will not speak the truth; They have taught their tongue to speak lies; They weary themselves to commit iniquity. **Ps. 12:3-4:** May the LORD cut off all flattering

lips, *And* the tongue that speaks proud things, Who have said, "With our tongue we will prevail; Our lips *are* our own; Who *is* lord over us?" **See Acts 24:2, 5; Ps. 52:1-4.**

6

Prov. 17:15: He who justifies the wicked, and he who condemns the just, Both of them alike *are* an abomination to the LORD. **See 1 Kings 21:9-14.**

7

Isa. 5:23: Who justify the wicked for a bribe, And take away justice from the righteous man!

8

1 Kings 21:8: And she wrote letters in Ahab's name, sealed *them* with his seal, and sent the letters to the elders and the nobles who *were* dwelling in the city with Naboth.

9

Lev. 5:1: If a person sins in hearing the utterance of an oath, and *is* a witness, whether he has seen or known *of the matter*—if he does not tell *it*, he bears guilt. **Acts 5:3:** But Peter said, "Ananias, why has Satan filled your heart to lie to the Holy Spirit and keep back *part* of the price of the land for yourself? **See Acts 5:8-9; Deut. 13:8; 2 Tim. 4:16.**

10

1 Kings 1:6: And his father had not rebuked him at any time by saying, "Why have you done so?" He *was* also very good-looking. *His mother* had borne him after Absalom. **Lev. 19:17:** You shall not hate your brother in your heart. You shall surely rebuke your neighbor, and not bear sin because of him.

11

Isa. 59:4: No one calls for justice, Nor does *any* plead for truth. They trust in empty words and speak lies; They conceive evil and bring forth iniquity.

12

Prov. 29:11: A fool vents all his feelings, But a wise *man* holds them back.

13

1 Sam. 22:9-10: Then answered Doeg the Edomite, who was set over the servants of Saul, and said, "I saw the son of Jesse going to Nob, to Ahimelech the son of Ahitub. And he inquired of the LORD for him, gave him provisions, and gave him the sword of Goliath the Philistine." **Ps. 52:1-5:** Why do you boast in evil, O mighty man? The goodness of God *endures* continually. Your tongue devises destruction, Like a sharp razor, working deceitfully. You love evil more than good, Lying rather than speaking righteousness. *Selah*. You love all devouring words, *You* deceitful tongue. God shall likewise destroy you forever; He shall take you away, and pluck you out of *your* dwelling place, And uproot you from the land of the living. *Selah*.

14

Ps. 56:5: All day they twist my words; All their thoughts *are* against me for evil. **Matt. 26:60-61:** ... but found none. Even though many false witnesses came forward, they found none. But at last two false witnesses came forward and said, "This *fellow* said, 'I am able to destroy the temple of God and to build it in three days.'" **See John 2:19.**

15

Gen. 3:5: "For God knows that in the day you eat of it your eyes will be opened, and you will be like God, knowing good and evil." **See Gen. 26:7, 9.**

16

Isa. 59:13: In transgressing and lying against the LORD, And departing from our God, Speaking oppression and revolt, Conceiving and uttering from the heart words of falsehood.

17

Col. 3:9: Do not lie to one another, since you have put off the old man with his deeds. **See Lev. 19:11.**

18

Ps. 50:20: You sit *and* speak against your brother; You slander your own mother's son.

19

Ps. 15:3: He *who* does not backbite with his tongue, Nor does evil to his neighbor, Nor does he take up a reproach against his friend.

20

James 4:11: Do not speak evil of one another, brethren. He who speaks evil of a brother and judges his brother, speaks evil of the law and judges the law. But if you judge the law, you are not a doer of the law but a judge. **See Jer. 38:4.**

21

Lev. 19:16: You shall not go about *as* a talebearer among your people; nor shall you take a stand against the life of your neighbor: I *am* the LORD.

22

Rom. 1:29-30: ... being filled with all unrighteousness, sexual immorality, wickedness, covetousness, maliciousness; full of envy, murder, strife, deceit, evil-mindedness; *they are* whisperers, backbiters, haters of God, violent, proud, boasters, inventors of evil things, disobedient to parents.

23

Gen. 21:9: And Sarah saw the son of Hagar the Egyptian, whom she had borne to Abraham, scoffing. **Gal. 4:29:** But, as he who was born according to the flesh then persecuted him *who was born* according to the Spirit, even so *it is* now.

24

1 Cor. 6:10: ... nor thieves, nor covetous, nor drunkards, nor revilers, nor extortioners will inherit the kingdom of God.

25
Matt. 7:1: Judge not, that you be not judged.
26
Acts 28:4: So when the natives saw the creature hanging from his hand, they said to one another, "No doubt this man is a murderer, whom, though he has escaped the sea, yet justice does not allow to live." **See James 2:13.**
27
Gen. 38:24: And it came to pass, about three months after, that Judah was told, saying, "Tamar your daughter-in-law has played the harlot; furthermore she *is* with child by harlotry." So Judah said, "Bring her out and let her be burned!" **Rom. 2:1:** Therefore you are inexcusable, O man, whoever you are who judge, for in whatever you judge another you condemn yourself; for you who judge practice the same things.
28
Rom. 3:8: And *why* not *say,* "Let us do evil that good may come"?—as we are slanderously reported and as some affirm that we say. Their condemnation is just. **Ps. :10:** When I wept *and chastened* my soul with fasting, That became my reproach. **See Neh. 6:6-8; 1 Sam. 1:13-15; 2 Sam. 10:3.**
29
Ps. 12:2-3: They speak idly everyone with his neighbor; *With* flattering lips *and* a double heart they speak. May the LORD cut off all flattering lips, *And* the tongue that speaks proud things.
30
2 Tim. 3:2: For men will be lovers of themselves, lovers of money, boasters, proud, blasphemers, disobedient to parents, unthankful, unholy.
31
Luke 18:9, 11: Also He spoke this parable to some who trusted in themselves that they were righteous, and despised others.... The Pharisee stood and prayed thus with himself, 'God, I thank You that I am not like other men—extortioners, unjust, adulterers, or even as this tax collector.' **Acts 12:22:** And the people kept shouting, "The voice of a god and not of a man!" **Ex. 4:10-14:** Then Moses said to the LORD, "O my Lord, I *am* not eloquent, neither before nor since You have spoken to Your servant; but I *am* slow of speech and slow of tongue." So the LORD said to him, "Who has made man's mouth? Or who makes the mute, the deaf, the seeing, or the blind? *Have* not I, the LORD? Now therefore, go, and I will be with your mouth and teach you what you shall say." But he said, "O my Lord, please send by the hand of whomever *else* You may send." So the anger of the LORD was kindled against Moses, and He said: "Is not Aaron the Levite your brother? I know that he can speak well. And look, he is also coming out to meet you. When he sees you, he will be glad in his heart. **See Rom. 12:16; Gal. 5:26; 1 Cor. 4:6.**
32
Luke 9:49-50: Now John answered and said, "Master, we saw someone casting out demons in Your name, and we forbade him because he does not follow with us." But Jesus said to him, "Do not forbid *him,* for he who is not against us is on our side." **2 Cor. 10:10:** "For *his* letters," they say, "*are* weighty and powerful, but *his* bodily presence *is* weak, and *his* speech contemptible." **Acts 2:13:** Others mocking said, "They are full of new wine." **See Job 27:5-6; 4:6.**
33
Matt. 7:3-5: And why do you look at the speck in your brother's eye, but do not consider the plank in your own eye? Or how can you say to your brother, 'Let me remove the speck from your eye'; and look, a plank *is* in your own eye? Hypocrite! First remove the plank from your own eye, and then you will see clearly to remove the speck from your brother's eye.
34
Prov. 28:13: He who covers his sins will not prosper, But whoever confesses and forsakes *them* will have mercy. **Gen. 3:12-13:** Then the man said, "The woman whom You gave *to be* with me, she gave me of the tree, and I ate." And the LORD God said to the woman, "What *is* this you have done?" The woman said, "The serpent deceived me, and I ate." **See Prov. 30:20; Jer. 2:35; 2 Kings 5:25; Gen. 4:9.**
35
Prov. 25:9-10: Debate your case with your neighbor, And do not disclose the secret to another; Lest he who hears *it* expose your shame, And your reputation be ruined. **See Gen. 9:22.**
36
Ex. 23:1: You shall not circulate a false report. Do not put your hand with the wicked to be an unrighteous witness.
37
Prov. 29:12: If a ruler pays attention to lies, All his servants *become* wicked. **See Ps. 41:7-8.**
38
Acts 7:56-57: ... and said, "Look! I see the heavens opened and the Son of Man standing at the right hand of God!" Then they cried out with a loud voice, stopped their ears, and ran at him with one accord. **Job 31:13-14:** If I have despised the cause of my male or female servant When they complained against me, What then shall I do when God rises up? When He punishes, how shall I answer Him?
39
1 Cor. 13:5: ... does not behave rudely, does not seek its own, is not provoked, thinks no evil. **See 1 Tim. 6:4.**
40
Matt. 21:15: But when the chief priests and scribes saw the wonderful things that He did, and the

children crying out in the temple and saying, "Hosanna to the Son of David!" they were indignant. **See Num. 11:29.**

41 **Ezra. 4:12-13:** Let it be known to the king that the Jews who came up from you have come to us at Jerusalem, and are building the rebellious and evil city, and are finishing *its* walls and repairing the foundations. Let it now be known to the king that, if this city is built and the walls completed, they will not pay tax, tribute, or custom, and the king's treasury will be diminished. **See Dan. 6:3-4.**

42 **Jer. 48:27:** For was not Israel a derision to you? Was he found among thieves? For whenever you speak of him, You shake *your head in scorn.*

43 **Matt. 27:28-29:** And they stripped Him and put a scarlet robe on Him. When they had twisted a crown of thorns, they put *it* on His head, and a reed in His right hand. And they bowed the knee before Him and mocked Him, saying, "Hail, King of the Jews!" **See Ps. 35:15-16, 21.**

44 **Jude 16:** These are grumblers, complainers, walking according to their own lusts; and they mouth great swelling words, flattering people to gain advantage. **Acts 12:22:** And the people kept shouting, "The voice of a god and not of a man!"

45 **Rom. 1:31:** ... undiscerning, untrustworthy, unloving, unforgiving, unmerciful. **2 Tim. 3:3:** ... unloving, unforgiving, slanderers, without self-control, brutal, despisers of good.

46 **1 Sam. 2:24:** No, my sons! For *it is* not a good report that I hear. You make the LORD's people transgress.

47 **2 Sam. 13:12-13:** But she answered him, "No, my brother, do not force me, for no such thing should be done in Israel. Do not do this disgraceful thing! And I, where could I take my shame? And as for you, you would be like one of the fools in Israel. Now therefore, please speak to the king; for he will not withhold me from you." **Prov. 5:8-9:** Remove your way far from her, And do not go near the door of her house, Lest you give your honor to others, And your years to the cruel *one.* **Prov. 6:33:** Wounds and dishonor he will get, And his reproach will not be wiped away.

Q. 167. *Which is the tenth commandment?*

A. The tenth commandment is, *Thou shalt not covet thy neighbour's house, thou shalt not covet thy neighbour's wife, nor his manservant, nor his maidservant, nor his ox, nor his ass, nor any thing that is thy neighbour's.*[1]

1 **Ex. 20:17:** You shall not covet your neighbor's house; you shall not covet your neighbor's wife, nor his male servant, nor his female servant, nor his ox, nor his donkey, nor anything that *is* your neighbor's. **Cf. Deut. 5:21.**

Q. 168. *What are the duties required in the tenth commandment?*

A. The duties required in the tenth commandment are, such a full contentment with our own condition,[1] and such a charitable frame of the whole soul toward our neighbour, as that all our inward motions and affections touching him, tend unto, and further all that good which is his.[2]

1 **Heb. 13:5:** *Let your* conduct *be* without covetousness; *be* content with such things as you have. For He Himself has said, "I will never leave you nor forsake you." **1 Tim. 6:6:** Now godliness with contentment is great gain. **See Phil. 4:11.**

2 **Job 31:29:** If I have rejoiced at the destruction of him who hated me, Or lifted myself up when evil found him. **Rom. 12:15:** Rejoice with those who rejoice, and weep with those who weep. **See**

Ps. 122:7-9; 1 Tim. 1:5; Est. 10:3; 1 Cor. 13:4-7.

Q. 169. *What are the sins forbidden in the tenth commandment?*

A. The sins forbidden in the tenth commandment are, discontentment with our own estate;[1] envying[2] and grieving at the good of our neighbour,[3] together with all inordinate motions and affections to anything that is his.[4]

1 **1 Cor. 10:10:** ... nor complain, as some of them also complained, and were destroyed by the destroyer. **See 1 Kings 21:4; Est. 5:13.**

2 **Gal. 5:26:** Let us not become conceited, provoking one another, envying one another. **James 3:14, 16:** But if you have bitter envy and self-seeking in your hearts, do not boast and lie against the truth.... For where envy and self-seeking *exist,* confusion and every evil thing *are* there.

3 **Ps. 112:9-10:** He has dispersed abroad, He has given to the poor; His righteousness endures forever; His horn will be exalted with honor. The wicked will see *it* and be grieved; He will gnash his teeth and melt away; The desire of the wicked shall perish. **See Neh. 2:10.**

4 **Rom. 7:7-8:** What shall we say then? *Is* the law sin? Certainly not! On the contrary, I would not have known sin except through the law. For I would not have known covetousness unless the law had said, "You shall not covet." But sin, taking opportunity by the commandment, produced in me all *manner of evil* desire. For apart from the law sin *was* dead. **Rom. 13:9:** For the commandments, "You shall not commit adultery," "You shall not murder," "You shall not steal," "You shall not bear false witness," "You shall not covet," and if *there is* any other commandment, are *all* summed up in this saying, namely, "You shall love your neighbor as yourself." **Col. 3:5:** Therefore put to death your members which are on the earth: fornication, uncleanness, passion, evil desire, and covetousness, which is idolatry. **Deut. 5:21:** You shall not covet your neighbor's wife; and you shall not desire your neighbor's house, his field, his male servant, his female servant, his ox, his donkey, or anything that *is* your neighbor's.

Q. 170. *Is any man able perfectly to keep the commandments of God?*

A. No man is able, either of himself,[1] or by any grace received in this life, perfectly to keep the commandments of God;[2] but doth daily break them in thought,[3] word, and deed.[4]

1 **James 3:2:** For we all stumble in many things. If anyone does not stumble in word, he *is* a perfect man, able also to bridle the whole body. **John 15:5:** I am the vine, you *are* the branches. He who abides in Me, and I in him, bears much fruit; for without Me you can do nothing. **Rom. 8:3:** For what the law could not do in that it was weak through the flesh, God *did* by sending His own Son in the likeness of sinful flesh, on account of sin: He condemned sin in the flesh.

2 **Eccl. 7:20:** For *there is* not a just man on earth who does good And does not sin. **1 John 1:8, 10:** If we say that we have no sin, we deceive ourselves, and the truth is not in us.... If we say that we have not sinned, we make Him a liar, and His word is not in us. **Gal. 5:17:** For the flesh lusts against the Spirit, and the Spirit against the flesh; and these are contrary to one another, so that you do not do the things that you wish. **Rom. 7:18-19:** For I know that in me (that is, in my flesh) nothing good dwells; for to will is present with me, but *how* to perform what is good I do not find. For the good that I will *to do,* I do not do; but the evil I will not *to do,* that I practice.

3 **Gen. 6:5:** Then the LORD saw that the wickedness of man *was* great in the earth, and *that* every intent of the thoughts of his heart *was* only evil continually. **Gen. 8:21:** And the LORD smelled a soothing aroma. Then the LORD said in His heart, "I will never again curse the ground for man's sake, although the imagination of man's heart *is* evil from his youth; nor will I again destroy every living thing as I have done. **James 1:14:** But each one is tempted when he is drawn away by his

own desires and enticed.

[4] **Rom. 3:9:** What then? Are we better *than they?* Not at all. For we have previously charged both Jews and Greeks that they are all under sin. **See Rom. 3:10-19; James 3:2-13.**

Q. 171. *Are all transgressions of the law of God equally heinous in themselves, and in the sight of God?*

A. All transgressions of the law of God are not equally heinous; but some sins in themselves, and by reason of several aggravations, are more heinous in the sight of God than others.[1]

[1] **John 19:11:** Jesus answered, "You could have no power at all against Me unless it had been given you from above. Therefore the one who delivered Me to you has the greater sin." **1 John 5:16:** If anyone sees his brother sinning a sin *which does* not *lead* to death, he will ask, and He will give him life for those who commit sin not *leading* to death. There is sin *leading* to death. I do not say that he should pray about that. **Heb. 2:2-3:** For if the word spoken through angels proved steadfast, and every transgression and disobedience received a just reward, how shall we escape if we neglect so great a salvation, which at the first began to be spoken by the Lord, and was confirmed to us by those who heard *Him.* **See Ps. 78:17, 32, 56; Ezek. 8:6, 13, 15.**

Q. 172 *What are those aggravations that make some sins more heinous than others?*

A. Sins receive their aggravations:

1. From the persons offending;[1] if they be of riper age,[2] greater experience or grace,[3] eminent for profession,[4] gifts,[5] place,[6] office,[7] guides to others,[8] and whose example is likely to be followed by others.[9]

[1] **Jer. 2:8:** The priests did not say, 'Where *is* the LORD?' And those who handle the law did not know Me; The rulers also transgressed against Me; The prophets prophesied by Baal, And walked after *things that* do not profit.

[2] **Job 32:7, 9:** I said, 'Age should speak, And multitude of years should teach wisdom.' ... Great men are not *always* wise, Nor do the aged *always* understand justice. **Eccl. 4:13:** Better a poor and wise youth Than an old and foolish king who will be admonished no more.

[3] **1 Kings 11:4, 9:** For it was so, when Solomon was old, that his wives turned his heart after other gods; and his heart was not loyal to the LORD his God, as *was* the heart of his father David.... So the LORD became angry with Solomon, because his heart had turned from the LORD God of Israel, who had appeared to him twice.

[4] **2 Sam. 12:14:** However, because by this deed you have given great occasion to the enemies of the LORD to blaspheme, the child also *who is* born to you shall surely die. **1 Cor. 5:1:** It is actually reported *that there is* sexual immorality among you, and such sexual immorality as is not even named among the Gentiles—that a man has his father's wife!

[5] **James 4:17:** Therefore, to him who knows to do good and does not do *it,* to him it is sin. **Luke 12:47-48**: And that servant who knew his master's will, and did not prepare *himself* or do according to his will, shall be beaten with many *stripes.* But he who did not know, yet committed things deserving of stripes, shall be beaten with few. For everyone to whom much is given, from him much will be required; and to whom much has been committed, of him they will ask the more.

[6] **Jer. 5:4-5:** Therefore I said, "Surely these *are* poor. They are foolish; For they do not know the way of the LORD, The judgment of their God. I will go to the great men and speak to them, For they have known the way of the LORD, The judgment of their God." But these have altogether broken the

yoke *And* burst the bonds.
7
2 Sam. 12:7-9: Then Nathan said to David, "You *are* the man! Thus says the LORD God of Israel: 'I anointed you king over Israel, and I delivered you from the hand of Saul. I gave you your master's house and your master's wives into your keeping, and gave you the house of Israel and Judah. And if *that had been* too little, I also would have given you much more! Why have you despised the commandment of the LORD, to do evil in His sight? You have killed Uriah the Hittite with the sword; you have taken his wife *to be* your wife, and have killed him with the sword of the people of Ammon. **Ezek. 8:11-12:** And there stood before them seventy men of the elders of the house of Israel, and in their midst stood Jaazaniah the son of Shaphan. Each man had a censer in his hand, and a thick cloud of incense went up. Then He said to me, "Son of man, have you seen what the elders of the house of Israel do in the dark, every man in the room of his idols? For they say, 'The LORD does not see us, the LORD has forsaken the land.'"
8
Rom. 2:17-24: Indeed you are called a Jew, and rest on the law, and make your boast in God, and know *His* will, and approve the things that are excellent, being instructed out of the law, and are confident that you yourself are a guide to the blind, a light to those who are in darkness, an instructor of the foolish, a teacher of babes, having the form of knowledge and truth in the law. You, therefore, who teach another, do you not teach yourself? You who preach that a man should not steal, do you steal? You who say, "Do not commit adultery," do you commit adultery? You who abhor idols, do you rob temples? You who make your boast in the law, do you dishonor God through breaking the law? For "the name of God is blasphemed among the Gentiles because of you," as it is written.
9
Gal. 2:11-14: Now when Peter had come to Antioch, I withstood him to his face, because he was to be blamed; for before certain men came from James, he would eat with the Gentiles; but when they came, he withdrew and separated himself, fearing those who were of the circumcision. And the rest of the Jews also played the hypocrite with him, so that even Barnabas was carried away with their hypocrisy. But when I saw that they were not straightforward about the truth of the gospel, I said to Peter before *them* all, "If you, being a Jew, live in the manner of Gentiles and not as the Jews, why do you compel Gentiles to live as Jews?

2. From the parties offended:[10] if immediately against God,[11] His attributes,[12] and worship;[13] against Christ, and His grace;[14] the Holy Spirit,[15] His witness,[16] and workings;[17] against superiors, men of eminency,[18] and such as we stand especially related and engaged unto;[19] against any of the saints,[20] particularly weak brethren,[21] the souls of them, or any other,[22] and the common good of all or many.[23]

10
Ps. 2:12: Kiss the Son, lest He be angry, And you perish *in* the way, When His wrath is kindled but a little. Blessed *are* all those who put their trust in Him. **Matt. 21:38-39:** But when the vinedressers saw the son, they said among themselves, 'This is the heir. Come, let us kill him and seize his inheritance.' So they took him and cast *him* out of the vineyard and killed *him*.
11
1 Sam. 2:25: If one man sins against another, God will judge him. But if a man sins against the LORD, who will intercede for him?" Nevertheless they did not heed the voice of their father, because the LORD desired to kill them. **Acts 5:4:** While it remained, was it not your own? And after it was sold, was it not in your own control? Why have you conceived this thing in your heart? You have not lied to men but to God. **Ps. 5:4:** For You *are* not a God who takes pleasure in wickedness, Nor shall evil dwell with You.
12
Rom. 2:4: Or do you despise the riches of His goodness, forbearance, and longsuffering, not knowing that the goodness of God leads you to repentance?
13
Mal. 1:8, 14: And when you offer the blind as a sacrifice, *Is it* not evil? And when you offer the lame and sick, *Is it* not evil? Offer it then to your governor! Would he be pleased with you? Would he accept you favorably?" Says the LORD of hosts.... "But cursed *be* the deceiver Who has in his flock a male, And takes a vow, But sacrifices to the Lord what is blemished— For I *am* a great King," Says the LORD of hosts, "And My name *is to be* feared among the nations."
14
Heb. 2:2-3: For if the word spoken through angels proved steadfast, and every transgression and disobedience received a just reward, how shall we escape if we neglect so great a salvation, which at the first began to be spoken by the Lord, and was confirmed to us by those who heard *Him*. **Heb.**

12:25: See that you do not refuse Him who speaks. For if they did not escape who refused Him who spoke on earth, much more *shall we not escape* if we turn away from Him who *speaks* from heaven.
15

Heb. 10:28-29: Anyone who has rejected Moses' law dies without mercy on *the testimony of* two or three witnesses. Of how much worse punishment, do you suppose, will he be thought worthy who has trampled the Son of God underfoot, counted the blood of the covenant by which he was sanctified a common thing, and insulted the Spirit of grace? **Matt. 12:31-32:** Therefore I say to you, every sin and blasphemy will be forgiven men, but the blasphemy *against* the Spirit will not be forgiven men. Anyone who speaks a word against the Son of Man, it will be forgiven him; but whoever speaks against the Holy Spirit, it will not be forgiven him, either in this age or in the *age* to come.
16

Eph. 4:30: And do not grieve the Holy Spirit of God, by whom you were sealed for the day of redemption.
17

Heb. 6:4-6: For *it is* impossible for those who were once enlightened, and have tasted the heavenly gift, and have become partakers of the Holy Spirit, and have tasted the good word of God and the powers of the age to come, if they fall away, to renew them again to repentance, since they crucify again for themselves the Son of God, and put *Him* to an open shame.
18

Jude 8: Likewise also these dreamers defile the flesh, reject authority, and speak evil of dignitaries. **Num. 12:8-9:** I speak with him face to face, Even plainly, and not in dark sayings; And he sees the form of the LORD. Why then were you not afraid To speak against My servant Moses? **Isa. 3:5:** The people will be oppressed, Every one by another and every one by his neighbor; The child will be insolent toward the elder, And the base toward the honorable.
19

Prov. 30:17: The eye *that* mocks *his* father, And scorns obedience to *his* mother, The ravens of the valley will pick it out, And the young eagles will eat it. **2 Cor. 12:15:** And I will very gladly spend and be spent for your souls; though the more abundantly I love you, the less I am loved. **Ps. 55:12-15:** For *it is* not an enemy *who* reproaches me; Then I could bear *it.* Nor *is it* one *who* hates me who has exalted *himself* against me; Then I could hide from him. But *it was* you, a man my equal, My companion and my acquaintance. We took sweet counsel together, *And* walked to the house of God in the throng. Let death seize them; Let them go down alive into hell, For wickedness *is* in their dwellings *and* among them.
20

Zeph. 2:8, 10-11: I have heard the reproach of Moab, And the insults of the people of Ammon, With which they have reproached My people, And made arrogant threats against their borders.... This they shall have for their pride, Because they have reproached and made arrogant threats Against the people of the LORD of hosts. The LORD *will be* awesome to them, For He will reduce to nothing all the gods of the earth; *People* shall worship Him, Each one from his place, Indeed all the shores of the nations. **Matt. 18:6:** Whoever causes one of these little ones who believe in Me to sin, it would be better for him if a millstone were hung around his neck, and he were drowned in the depth of the sea. **1 Cor. 6:8:** No, you yourselves do wrong and cheat, and *you do* these things *to your* brethren! **Rev. 17:6:** I saw the woman, drunk with the blood of the saints and with the blood of the martyrs of Jesus. And when I saw her, I marveled with great amazement.
21

1 Cor. 8:11-12: And because of your knowledge shall the weak brother perish, for whom Christ died? But when you thus sin against the brethren, and wound their weak conscience, you sin against Christ. **Rom. 14:13, 15, 21:** Therefore let us not judge one another anymore, but rather resolve this, not to put a stumbling block or a cause to fall in *our* brother's way.... Yet if your brother is grieved because of *your* food, you are no longer walking in love. Do not destroy with your food the one for whom Christ died.... *It is* good neither to eat meat nor drink wine nor *do anything* by which your brother stumbles or is offended or is made weak.
22

Ezek. 13:19: And will you profane Me among My people for handfuls of barley and for pieces of bread, killing people who should not die, and keeping people alive who should not live, by your lying to My people who listen to lies? **1 Cor. 8:12:** But when you thus sin against the brethren, and wound their weak conscience, you sin against Christ. **Rev. 18:12-13:** ... merchandise of gold and silver, precious stones and pearls, fine linen and purple, silk and scarlet, every kind of citron wood, every kind of object of ivory, every kind of object of most precious wood, bronze, iron, and marble; and cinnamon and incense, fragrant oil and frankincense, wine and oil, fine flour and wheat, cattle and sheep, horses and chariots, and bodies and souls of men. **Matt. 23:15:** Woe to you, scribes and Pharisees, hypocrites! For you travel land and sea to win one proselyte, and when he is won, you make him twice as much a son of hell as yourselves.
23

1 Thess. 2:15-16: ... who killed both the Lord Jesus and their own prophets, and have persecuted us; and they do not please God and are contrary to all men, forbidding us to speak to the Gentiles that they may be saved, so as always to fill up *the measure of* their sins; but wrath has come upon them to the uttermost. **Josh. 22:20:** Did not Achan the son of Zerah commit a trespass in the accursed thing, and wrath fell on all the congregation of Israel? And that man did not perish alone in his iniquity.

3. From the nature and quality of the offence:[24] if it be against the express letter of the law,[25] break many commandments, contain in it many sins:[26] if not only conceived in the heart, but breaks forth in words and actions,[27] scandalize others,[28] and admit of no reparation:[29] if against means,[30] mercies,[31] judgments,[32] light of nature,[33] conviction of conscience,[34] public or private admonition,[35] censures of the church,[36] civil punishments;[37] and our prayers, purposes, promises,[38] vows,[39] covenants,[40] and engagements to God or men:[41] if done deliberately,[42] willfully,[43] presumptuously,[44] impudently,[45] boastingly,[46] maliciously,[47] frequently,[48] obstinately,[49] with delight,[50] continuance,[51] or relapsing after repentance.[52]

24

Prov. 6:30-33: *People* do not despise a thief If he steals to satisfy himself when he is starving. Yet *when* he is found, he must restore sevenfold; He may have to give up all the substance of his house. Whoever commits adultery with a woman lacks understanding; He *who* does so destroys his own soul. Wounds and dishonor he will get, And his reproach will not be wiped away.

25

Ezra 9:10-12: And now, O our God, what shall we say after this? For we have forsaken Your commandments, which You commanded by Your servants the prophets, saying, 'The land which you are entering to possess is an unclean land, with the uncleanness of the peoples of the lands, with their abominations which have filled it from one end to another with their impurity. Now therefore, do not give your daughters as wives for their sons, nor take their daughters to your sons; and never seek their peace or prosperity, that you may be strong and eat the good of the land, and leave *it* as an inheritance to your children forever.' **1 Kings 11:9-10:** So the LORD became angry with Solomon, because his heart had turned from the LORD God of Israel, who had appeared to him twice, and had commanded him concerning this thing, that he should not go after other gods; but he did not keep what the LORD had commanded.

26

Col. 3:5: Therefore put to death your members which are on the earth: fornication, uncleanness, passion, evil desire, and covetousness, which is idolatry. **1 Tim. 6:10:** For the love of money is a root of all *kinds of* evil, for which some have strayed from the faith in their greediness, and pierced themselves through with many sorrows. **Prov. 5:8-12:** Remove your way far from her, And do not go near the door of her house, Lest you give your honor to others, And your years to the cruel *one;* Lest aliens be filled with your wealth, And your labors *go* to the house of a foreigner; And you mourn at last, When your flesh and your body are consumed, And say: "How I have hated instruction, And my heart despised correction!" **Prov. 6:32-33:** Whoever commits adultery with a woman lacks understanding; He *who* does so destroys his own soul. Wounds and dishonor he will get, And his reproach will not be wiped away. **Josh. 7:21:** When I saw among the spoils a beautiful Babylonian garment, two hundred shekels of silver, and a wedge of gold weighing fifty shekels, I coveted them and took them. And there they are, hidden in the earth in the midst of my tent, with the silver under it.

27

James 1:14-15: But each one is tempted when he is drawn away by his own desires and enticed. Then, when desire has conceived, it gives birth to sin; and sin, when it is full-grown, brings forth death. **Matt. 5:22:** But I say to you that whoever is angry with his brother without a cause shall be in danger of the judgment. And whoever says to his brother, 'Raca!' shall be in danger of the council. But whoever says, 'You fool!' shall be in danger of hell fire. **Mic. 2:1:** Woe to those who devise iniquity, And work out evil on their beds! At morning light they practice it, Because it is in the power of their hand.

28

Matt. 18:7: Woe to the world because of offenses! For offenses must come, but woe to that man by whom the offense comes! **Rom. 2:23-24:** You who make your boast in the law, do you dishonor God through breaking the law? For "the name of God is blasphemed among the Gentiles because of you," as it is written.

29

Deut. 22:22, 28-29: If a man is found lying with a woman married to a husband, then both of them shall die—the man that lay with the woman, and the woman; so you shall put away the evil from Israel.... If a man finds a young woman *who is* a virgin, who is not betrothed, and he seizes her and lies with her, and they are found out, then the man who lay with her shall give to the young woman's father fifty *shekels* of silver, and she shall be his wife because he has humbled her; he shall not be permitted to divorce her all his days. **Prov. 6:32-35:** Whoever commits adultery with a woman lacks understanding; He *who* does so destroys his own soul. Wounds and dishonor he will get, And his reproach will not be wiped away. For jealousy *is* a husband's fury; Therefore he will not spare in the day of vengeance. He will accept no recompense, Nor will he be appeased though you give many gifts.

30

Matt. 11:21-24: Woe to you, Chorazin! Woe to you, Bethsaida! For if the mighty works which were done in you had been done in Tyre and Sidon, they would have repented long ago in sackcloth and ashes. But I say to you, it will be more tolerable for Tyre and Sidon in the day of judgment than for you. And you, Capernaum, who are exalted to heaven, will be brought down to Hades; for if the mighty works which were done in you had been done in Sodom, it would have remained until this day. But I say to you that it shall be more tolerable for the land of Sodom in the day of judgment than for you. **John 15:22:** If I had not come and spoken to them, they would have no sin, but now they have no excuse for their sin.

31

Isa. 1:3: The ox knows its owner And the donkey its master's crib; *But* Israel does not know, My people do not consider. **Deut. 32:6:** Do you thus deal with the LORD, O foolish and unwise people? *Is* He not your Father, *who* bought you? Has He not made you and established you?

32

Amos 4:8-11: So two *or* three cities wandered to another city to drink water, But they were not satisfied; Yet you have not returned to Me," Says the LORD. "I blasted you with blight and mildew. When your gardens increased, Your vineyards, Your fig trees, And your olive trees, The locust devoured *them;* Yet you have not returned to Me," Says the LORD. "I sent among you a plague after the manner of Egypt; Your young men I killed with a sword, Along with your captive horses; I made the stench of your camps come up into your nostrils; Yet you have not returned to Me," Says the LORD. "I overthrew *some* of you, As God overthrew Sodom and Gomorrah, And you were like a firebrand plucked from the burning; Yet you have not returned to Me," Says the LORD. **Jer. 5:3:** O LORD, *are* not Your eyes on the truth? You have stricken them, But they have not grieved; You have consumed them, But they have refused to receive correction. They have made their faces harder than rock; They have refused to return.

33

Rom. 1:26-27: For this reason God gave them up to vile passions. For even their women exchanged the natural use for what is against nature. Likewise also the men, leaving the natural use of the woman, burned in their lust for one another, men with men committing what is shameful, and receiving in themselves the penalty of their error which was due.

34

Rom. 1:32: ... who, knowing the righteous judgment of God, that those who practice such things are deserving of death, not only do the same but also approve of those who practice them. **Dan. 5:22:** But you his son, Belshazzar, have not humbled your heart, although you knew all this. **Titus 3:10-11:** Reject a divisive man after the first and second admonition, knowing that such a person is warped and sinning, being self-condemned.

35

Prov. 29:1: He who is often rebuked, *and* hardens *his* neck, Will suddenly be destroyed, and that without remedy.

36

Titus 3:10: Reject a divisive man after the first and second admonition. **Matt. 18:17:** And if he refuses to hear them, tell *it* to the church. But if he refuses even to hear the church, let him be to you like a heathen and a tax collector.

37

Prov. 27:22: Though you grind a fool in a mortar with a pestle along with crushed grain, *Yet* his foolishness will not depart from him. **Prov. 23:35:** They have struck me, *but* I was not hurt; They have beaten me, but I did not feel *it.* When shall I awake, that I may seek another *drink?*

38

Ps. 78:34-37: When He slew them, then they sought Him; And they returned and sought earnestly for God. Then they remembered that God *was* their rock, And the Most High God their Redeemer. Nevertheless they flattered Him with their mouth, And they lied to Him with their tongue; For their heart was not steadfast with Him, Nor were they faithful in His covenant. **Jer. 2:20:** For of old I have broken your yoke *and* burst your bonds; And you said, 'I will not transgress,' When on every high hill and under every green tree You lay down, playing the harlot. **Jer. 13:5-6, 20-21:** So I went and hid it by the Euphrates, as the LORD commanded me. Now it came to pass after many days that the LORD said to me, "Arise, go to the Euphrates, and take from there the sash which I commanded you to hide there." ... Lift up your eyes and see Those who come from the north. Where *is* the flock *that* was given to you, Your beautiful sheep? What will you say when He punishes you? For you have taught them *To be* chieftains, to be head over you. Will not pangs seize you, Like a woman in labor?

39

Eccl. 5:4-6: When you make a vow to God, do not delay to pay it; For *He has* no pleasure in fools. Pay what you have vowed— Better not to vow than to vow and not pay. Do not let your mouth cause your flesh to sin, nor say before the messenger *of God* that it *was* an error. Why should God be angry at your excuse and destroy the work of your hands? **Prov. 20:25:** *It is* a snare for a man to devote rashly *something as* holy, And afterward to reconsider *his* vows.

40

Lev. 26:25: And I will bring a sword against you that will execute the vengeance of the covenant;

when you are gathered together within your cities I will send pestilence among you; and you shall be delivered into the hand of the enemy.

41

Prov. 2:17: Who forsakes the companion of her youth, And forgets the covenant of her God. **Ezek. 7:18-19:** They will also be girded with sackcloth; Horror will cover them; Shame *will be* on every face, Baldness on all their heads. 'They will throw their silver into the streets, And their gold will be like refuse; Their silver and their gold will not be able to deliver them In the day of the wrath of the LORD; They will not satisfy their souls, Nor fill their stomachs, Because it became their stumbling block of iniquity.

42

Ps. 36:4: He devises wickedness on his bed; He sets himself in a way *that is* not good; He does not abhor evil.

43

Jer. 6:16: Thus says the LORD: "Stand in the ways and see, And ask for the old paths, where the good way *is,* And walk in it; Then you will find rest for your souls. But they said, 'We will not walk *in it.'*

44

Num. 15:30: But the person who does *anything* presumptuously, *whether he is* native-born or a stranger, that one brings reproach on the LORD, and he shall be cut off from among his people. **Ex. 21:14:** But if a man acts with premeditation against his neighbor, to kill him by treachery, you shall take him from My altar, that he may die.

45

Jer. 3:3: Therefore the showers have been withheld, And there has been no latter rain. You have had a harlot's forehead; You refuse to be ashamed. **Prov. 7:13:** So she caught him and kissed him; With an impudent face she said to him....

46

Ps. 52:1: Why do you boast in evil, O mighty man? The goodness of God *endures* continually.

47

3 John 10: Therefore, if I come, I will call to mind his deeds which he does, prating against us with malicious words. And not content with that, he himself does not receive the brethren, and forbids those who wish to, putting *them* out of the church.

48

Num. 14:22: ... because all these men who have seen My glory and the signs which I did in Egypt and in the wilderness, and have put Me to the test now these ten times, and have not heeded My voice.

49

Zech. 7:11-12: But they refused to heed, shrugged their shoulders, and stopped their ears so that they could not hear. Yes, they made their hearts like flint, refusing to hear the law and the words which the LORD of hosts had sent by His Spirit through the former prophets. Thus great wrath came from the LORD of hosts.

50

Prov. 2:14: Who rejoice in doing evil, *And* delight in the perversity of the wicked.

51

Isa. 57:17: For the iniquity of his covetousness I was angry and struck him; I hid and was angry, And he went on backsliding in the way of his heart.

52

Jer. 34:8-11: *This is* the word that came to Jeremiah from the LORD, after King Zedekiah had made a covenant with all the people who *were* at Jerusalem to proclaim liberty to them: that every man should set free his male and female slave—a Hebrew man or woman—that no one should keep a Jewish brother in bondage. Now when all the princes and all the people, who had entered into the covenant, heard that everyone should set free his male and female slaves, that no one should keep them in bondage anymore, they obeyed and let *them* go. But afterward they changed their minds and made the male and female slaves return, whom they had set free, and brought them into subjection as male and female slaves. **2 Pet. 2:20-22:** For if, after they have escaped the pollutions of the world through the knowledge of the Lord and Savior Jesus Christ, they are again entangled in them and overcome, the latter end is worse for them than the beginning. For it would have been better for them not to have known the way of righteousness, than having known *it,* to turn from the holy commandment delivered to them. But it has happened to them according to the true proverb: "A dog returns to his own vomit," and, "a sow, having washed, to her wallowing in the mire."

4. From circumstances of time[53] and place:[54] if on the Lord's Day,[55] or other times of divine worship;[56] or immediately before[57] or after these,[58] or other helps to prevent or remedy such miscarriages:[59] if in public, or in the presence of others, who are thereby likely to be provoked or defiled.[60]

53
2 Kings 5:26: Then he said to him, "Did not my heart go *with you* when the man turned back from his chariot to meet you? *Is it* time to receive money and to receive clothing, olive groves and vineyards, sheep and oxen, male and female servants?"
54
Jer. 7:10: ... and *then* come and stand before Me in this house which is called by My name, and say, 'We are delivered to do all these abominations'? **Isa. 26:10:** Let grace be shown to the wicked, *Yet* he will not learn righteousness; In the land of uprightness he will deal unjustly, And will not behold the majesty of the LORD.
55
Ezek. 23:37-39: For they have committed adultery, and blood *is* on their hands. They have committed adultery with their idols, and even *sacrificed* their sons whom they bore to Me, passing them through *the fire,* to devour *them.* Moreover they have done this to Me: They have defiled My sanctuary on the same day and profaned My Sabbaths. For after they had slain their children for their idols, on the same day they came into My sanctuary to profane it; and indeed thus they have done in the midst of My house.
56
Isa. 58:3-5: 'Why have we fasted,' *they say,* 'and You have not seen? *Why* have we afflicted our souls, and You take no notice?' "In fact, in the day of your fast you find pleasure, And exploit all your laborers. Indeed you fast for strife and debate, And to strike with the fist of wickedness. You will not fast as *you do* this day, To make your voice heard on high. Is it a fast that I have chosen, A day for a man to afflict his soul? *Is it* to bow down his head like a bulrush, And to spread out sackcloth and ashes? Would you call this a fast, And an acceptable day to the LORD?" **Num. 25:6-7:** And indeed, one of the children of Israel came and presented to his brethren a Midianite woman in the sight of Moses and in the sight of all the congregation of the children of Israel, who *were* weeping at the door of the tabernacle of meeting. Now when Phinehas the son of Eleazar, the son of Aaron the priest, saw *it,* he rose from among the congregation and took a javelin in his hand.
57
1 Cor. 11:20-21: Therefore when you come together in one place, it is not to eat the Lord's Supper. For in eating, each one takes his own supper ahead of *others;* and one is hungry and another is drunk. **Jer. 7:8-10:** Behold, you trust in lying words that cannot profit. Will you steal, murder, commit adultery, swear falsely, burn incense to Baal, and walk after other gods whom you do not know, and *then* come and stand before Me in this house which is called by My name, and say, 'We are delivered to do all these abominations'?
58
Prov. 7:14-15: *I have* peace offerings with me; Today I have paid my vows. So I came out to meet you, Diligently to seek your face, And I have found you. **John 13:27, 30:** Now after the piece of bread, Satan entered him. Then Jesus said to him, "What you do, do quickly." ... Having received the piece of bread, he then went out immediately. And it was night.
59
Ezra 9:13-14: And after all that has come upon us for our evil deeds and for our great guilt, since You our God have punished us less than our iniquities *deserve,* and have given us *such* deliverance as this, should we again break Your commandments, and join in marriage with the people *committing* these abominations? Would You not be angry with us until You had consumed *us,* so that *there would be* no remnant or survivor?
60
2 Sam. 16:22: So they pitched a tent for Absalom on the top of the house, and Absalom went in to his father's concubines in the sight of all Israel. **1 Sam. 2:22-24:** Now Eli was very old; and he heard everything his sons did to all Israel, and how they lay with the women who assembled at the door of the tabernacle of meeting. So he said to them, "Why do you do such things? For I hear of your evil dealings from all the people. No, my sons! For *it is* not a good report that I hear. You make the LORD's people transgress."

Q. 173. *What doth every sin deserve at the hands of God?*

A. Every sin, even the least, being against the sovereignty,[1] goodness,[2] and holiness of God,[3] and against His righteous law,[4] deserveth His wrath and curse,[5] both in this life,[6] and that which is to come;[7] and cannot be expiated but by the blood of Christ.[8]

1
James 2:10-11: For whoever shall keep the whole law, and yet stumble in one *point,* he is guilty of all. For He who said, "Do not commit adultery," also said, "Do not murder." Now if you do not commit adultery, but you do murder, you have become a transgressor of the law.
2
Ex. 20:1-2: I *am* the LORD your God, who brought you out of the land of Egypt, out of the house of

bondage.

3 **Hab. 1:13:** *You are* of purer eyes than to behold evil, And cannot look on wickedness. Why do You look on those who deal treacherously, *And* hold Your tongue when the wicked devours A *person* more righteous than he? **Lev. 10:3:** And Moses said to Aaron, "This is what the LORD spoke, saying: 'By those who come near Me I must be regarded as holy; And before all the people I must be glorified.'" So Aaron held his peace. **Lev. 11:44-45:** For I *am* the LORD your God. You shall therefore consecrate yourselves, and you shall be holy; for I *am* holy. Neither shall you defile yourselves with any creeping thing that creeps on the earth. For I *am* the LORD who brings you up out of the land of Egypt, to be your God. You shall therefore be holy, for I *am* holy.

4 **1 John 3:4:** Whoever commits sin also commits lawlessness, and sin is lawlessness. **Rom. 7:12:** Therefore the law *is* holy, and the commandment holy and just and good.

5 **Eph. 5:6:** Let no one deceive you with empty words, for because of these things the wrath of God comes upon the sons of disobedience. **Gal. 3:10:** For as many as are of the works of the law are under the curse; for it is written, "Cursed *is* everyone who does not continue in all things which are written in the book of the law, to do them."

6 **Lam. 3:39:** Why should a living man complain, A man for the punishment of his sins? **Deut. 28:15-68:** But it shall come to pass, if you do not obey the voice of the LORD your God, to observe carefully all His commandments and His statutes which I command you today, that all these curses will come upon you and overtake you: Cursed *shall* you *be* in the city, and cursed *shall* you *be* in the country. Cursed *shall be* your basket and your kneading bowl....

7 **Matt. 25:41:** Then He will also say to those on the left hand, 'Depart from Me, you cursed, into the everlasting fire prepared for the devil and his angels.'

8 **Heb. 9:22:** And according to the law almost all things are purified with blood, and without shedding of blood there is no remission. **1 Pet. 1:18-19:** ... knowing that you were not redeemed with corruptible things, *like* silver or gold, from your aimless conduct *received* by tradition from your fathers, but with the precious blood of Christ, as of a lamb without blemish and without spot.

Q. 174. *What doth God require of us, that we may escape His wrath and curse due to us by reason of the transgression of the law?*

A. That we may escape the wrath and curse of God due to us by reason of the transgression of the law, He requireth of us repentance toward God, and faith toward our Lord Jesus Christ,[1] and the diligent use of the outward means whereby Christ communicates to us the benefits of His mediation.[2]

1 **Acts 20:21:** ... testifying to Jews, and also to Greeks, repentance toward God and faith toward our Lord Jesus Christ. **Matt. 3:7-8:** But when he saw many of the Pharisees and Sadducees coming to his baptism, he said to them, "Brood of vipers! Who warned you to flee from the wrath to come? Therefore bear fruits worthy of repentance. **Luke 13:3, 5:** I tell you, no; but unless you repent you will all likewise perish.... I tell you, no; but unless you repent you will all likewise perish. **Acts 16:30-31:** And he brought them out and said, "Sirs, what must I do to be saved?" So they said, "Believe on the Lord Jesus Christ, and you will be saved, you and your household." **John 3:16, 18:** For God so loved the world that He gave His only begotten Son, that whoever believes in Him should not perish but have everlasting life.... He who believes in Him is not condemned; but he who does not believe is condemned already, because he has not believed in the name of the only begotten Son of God.

2 **Prov. 2:1-5:** My son, if you receive my words, And treasure my commands within you, So that you incline your ear to wisdom, *And* apply your heart to understanding; Yes, if you cry out for discernment, *And* lift up your voice for understanding, If you seek her as silver, And search for her as *for* hidden treasures; Then you will understand the fear of the LORD, And find the knowledge of God. **Prov. 8:33-36:** Hear instruction and be wise, And do not disdain *it*. Blessed is the man who listens to me, Watching daily at my gates, Waiting at the posts of my doors. For whoever finds me finds life, And obtains favor from the LORD; But he who sins against me wrongs his own soul; All those who hate me love death.

Q. 175. *What are the outward means whereby Christ communicates to us the benefits of His mediation?*

A. The outward and ordinary means whereby Christ communicates to His church the benefits of His mediation, are all His ordinances; especially the word, baptism and the Lord's Supper, and prayer; all which are made effectual to the elect for their salvation.[1]

1

Matt. 28:19-20: Go therefore and make disciples of all the nations, baptizing them in the name of the Father and of the Son and of the Holy Spirit, teaching them to observe all things that I have commanded you; and lo, I am with you always, *even* to the end of the age." Amen. **Acts 2:42, 46-47:** And they continued steadfastly in the apostles' doctrine and fellowship, in the breaking of bread, and in prayers.... So continuing daily with one accord in the temple, and breaking bread from house to house, they ate their food with gladness and simplicity of heart, praising God and having favor with all the people. And the Lord added to the church daily those who were being saved.

Q. 176. *How is the word made effectual to salvation?*

A. The Spirit of God maketh the reading, but especially the preaching of the word, an effectual means of enlightening,[1] convincing, and humbling sinners;[2] of driving them out of themselves, and drawing them unto Christ;[3] of conforming them to his image,[4] and subduing them to his will;[5] of strengthening them against temptations and corruptions;[6] of building them up in grace,[7] and establishing their hearts in holiness and comfort through faith unto salvation.[8]

1

Neh. 8:8: So they read distinctly from the book, in the Law of God; and they gave the sense, and helped *them* to understand the reading. **Acts 26:18:** ... to open their eyes, *in order* to turn *them* from darkness to light, and *from* the power of Satan to God, that they may receive forgiveness of sins and an inheritance among those who are sanctified by faith in Me. **Ps. 19:8:** The statutes of the Lord *are* right, rejoicing the heart; The commandment of the Lord *is* pure, enlightening the eyes.

2

1 Cor. 14:24-25: But if all prophesy, and an unbeliever or an uninformed person comes in, he is convinced by all, he is convicted by all. And thus the secrets of his heart are revealed; and so, falling down on *his* face, he will worship God and report that God is truly among you. **See 2 Chron. 34:18-19, 26-28.**

3

Acts 2:37, 41: Now when they heard *this,* they were cut to the heart, and said to Peter and the rest of the apostles, "Men *and* brethren, what shall we do?" ... Then those who gladly received his word were baptized; and that day about three thousand souls were added *to them.* **See Acts 8:27-38.**

4

2 Cor. 3:18: But we all, with unveiled face, beholding as in a mirror the glory of the Lord, are being transformed into the same image from glory to glory, just as by the Spirit of the Lord. **See Col. 1:27.**

5

2 Cor. 10:4-6: For the weapons of our warfare *are* not carnal but mighty in God for pulling down strongholds, casting down arguments and every high thing that exalts itself against the knowledge of God, bringing every thought into captivity to the obedience of Christ, and being ready to punish all disobedience when your obedience is fulfilled. **See Rom. 6:17-18.**

6

Eph. 6:16-17: ... above all, taking the shield of faith with which you will be able to quench all the fiery darts of the wicked one. And take the helmet of salvation, and the sword of the Spirit, which is the word of God. **Col. 1:28:** Him we preach, warning every man and teaching every man in all wisdom, that we may present every man perfect in Christ Jesus. **Ps. 19:11:** Moreover by them Your servant is warned, *And* in keeping them *there is* great reward. **See Matt. 4:4, 7, 10; 1 Cor. 10:11.**

7 **Eph. 4:11-12:** And He Himself gave some *to be* apostles, some prophets, some evangelists, and some pastors and teachers, for the equipping of the saints for the work of ministry, for the edifying of the body of Christ. **Acts 20:32:** So now, brethren, I commend you to God and to the word of His grace, which is able to build you up and give you an inheritance among all those who are sanctified. **See 2 Tim. 3:15-17.**

8 **Rom. 16:25:** Now to Him who is able to establish you according to my gospel and the preaching of Jesus Christ, according to the revelation of the mystery kept secret since the world began. **1 Thess. 3:2, 10-11, 13:** and sent Timothy, our brother and minister of God, and our fellow laborer in the gospel of Christ, to establish you and encourage you concerning your faith ... night and day praying exceedingly that we may see your face and perfect what is lacking in your faith? Now may our God and Father Himself, and our Lord Jesus Christ, direct our way to you.... so that He may establish your hearts blameless in holiness before our God and Father at the coming of our Lord Jesus Christ with all His saints. **Acts 9:31:** Then the churches throughout all Judea, Galilee, and Samaria had peace and were edified. And walking in the fear of the Lord and in the comfort of the Holy Spirit, they were multiplied. **See Rom. 15:4, 10:13-17, Rom. 1:16.**

Q. 177. *Is the word of God to be read by all?*

A. Although all are not to be permitted to read the word publicly to the congregation,[1] yet all sorts of people are bound to read it apart by themselves,[2] and with their families:[3] to which end, the Holy Scriptures are to be translated out of the original into vulgar languages.[4]

1 **Deut. 31:9, 11-13:** So Moses wrote this law and delivered it to the priests, the sons of Levi, who bore the ark of the covenant of the LORD, and to all the elders of Israel.... when all Israel comes to appear before the LORD your God in the place which He chooses, you shall read this law before all Israel in their hearing. Gather the people together, men and women and little ones, and the stranger who *is* within your gates, that they may hear and that they may learn to fear the LORD your God and carefully observe all the words of this law, and *that* their children, who have not known it, may hear and learn to fear the LORD your God as long as you live in the land which you cross the Jordan to possess. **See Neh. 8:2-3; Neh. 9:3-5.**

2 **Deut. 17:19:** And it shall be with him, and he shall read it all the days of his life, that he may learn to fear the LORD his God and be careful to observe all the words of this law and these statutes. **Rev. 1:3:** Blessed *is* he who reads and those who hear the words of this prophecy, and keep those things which are written in it; for the time *is* near. **John 5:39:** You search the Scriptures, for in them you think you have eternal life; and these are they which testify of Me. **Isa. 34:16:** Search from the book of the LORD, and read: Not one of these shall fail; Not one shall lack her mate. For My mouth has commanded it, and His Spirit has gathered them.

3 **Deut. 6:6-9:** And these words which I command you today shall be in your heart. You shall teach them diligently to your children, and shall talk of them when you sit in your house, when you walk by the way, when you lie down, and when you rise up. You shall bind them as a sign on your hand, and they shall be as frontlets between your eyes. You shall write them on the doorposts of your house and on your gates. **Gen. 18:17, 19:** And the LORD said, "Shall I hide from Abraham what I am doing ... For I have known him, in order that he may command his children and his household after him, that they keep the way of the LORD, to do righteousness and justice, that the LORD may bring to Abraham what He has spoken to him. **Ps. 78:5-7:** For He established a testimony in Jacob, And appointed a law in Israel, Which He commanded our fathers, That they should make them known to their children; That the generation to come might know *them,* The children *who* would be born, *That* they may arise and declare *them* to their children, That they may set their hope in God, And not forget the works of God, But keep His commandments.

4 **1 Cor. 14:6, 9, 11-12, 15-16, 24, 27-28:** But now, brethren, if I come to you speaking with tongues, what shall I profit you unless I speak to you either by revelation, by knowledge, by prophesying, or by teaching? ... So likewise you, unless you utter by the tongue words easy to understand, how will it be known what is spoken? For you will be speaking into the air.... Therefore, if I do not know the meaning of the language, I shall be a foreigner to him who speaks, and he who speaks *will be* a foreigner to me. Even so you, since you are zealous for spiritual *gifts, let it be* for the edification of the church *that* you seek to excel.... What is *the conclusion* then? I will pray with

the spirit, and I will also pray with the understanding. I will sing with the spirit, and I will also sing with the understanding. Otherwise, if you bless with the spirit, how will he who occupies the place of the uninformed say "Amen" at your giving of thanks, since he does not understand what you say? ... But if all prophesy, and an unbeliever or an uninformed person comes in, he is convinced by all, he is convicted by all.... If anyone speaks in a tongue, *let there be* two or at the most three, *each* in turn, and let one interpret. But if there is no interpreter, let him keep silent in church, and let him speak to himself and to God. **Neh. 8:8:** So they read distinctly from the book, in the Law of God; and they gave the sense, and helped *them* to understand the reading.

Q. 178. *How is the word of God to be read?*

A. The Holy Scriptures are to be read with an high and reverent esteem of them;[1] with a firm persuasion that they are the very word of God,[2] and that He only can enable us to understand them;[3] with desire to know, believe, and obey the will of God revealed in them;[4] with diligence,[5] and attention to the matter and scope of them;[6] with meditation,[7] application,[8] self-denial,[9] and prayer.[10]

1 **Ps. 119:97:** Oh, how I love Your law! It *is* my meditation all the day. **Ps. 19:10:** More to be desired *are they* than gold, Yea, than much fine gold; Sweeter also than honey and the honeycomb. **Ex. 24:7:** Then he took the Book of the Covenant and read in the hearing of the people. And they said, "All that the LORD has said we will do, and be obedient." **2 Chron. 34:27:** ... because your heart was tender, and you humbled yourself before God when you heard His words against this place and against its inhabitants, and you humbled yourself before Me, and you tore your clothes and wept before Me, I also have heard *you,*" says the LORD. **Isa. 66:2:** For all those *things* My hand has made, And all those *things* exist," Says the LORD. "But on this *one* will I look: On *him who is* poor and of a contrite spirit, And who trembles at My word. **See Neh. 8:3-10.**

2 **2 Pet. 1:19-21:** And so we have the prophetic word confirmed, which you do well to heed as a light that shines in a dark place, until the day dawns and the morning star rises in your hearts; knowing this first, that no prophecy of Scripture is of any private interpretation, for prophecy never came by the will of man, but holy men of God spoke *as they were* moved by the Holy Spirit. **Matt. 4:4:** But He answered and said, "It is written, 'Man shall not live by bread alone, but by every word that proceeds from the mouth of God.'" **1 Thess. 2:13:** For this reason we also thank God without ceasing, because when you received the word of God which you heard from us, you welcomed *it* not *as* the word of men, but as it is in truth, the word of God, which also effectively works in you who believe. **See Mark 7:13.**

3 **Luke 24:45:** And He opened their understanding, that they might comprehend the Scriptures. **2 Cor. 3:13-16:** ... unlike Moses, *who* put a veil over his face so that the children of Israel could not look steadily at the end of what was passing away. But their minds were blinded. For until this day the same veil remains unlifted in the reading of the Old Testament, because the *veil* is taken away in Christ. But even to this day, when Moses is read, a veil lies on their heart. Nevertheless when one turns to the Lord, the veil is taken away.

4 **Deut. 17:10, 20:** You shall do according to the sentence which they pronounce upon you in that place which the LORD chooses. And you shall be careful to do according to all that they order you.... that his heart may not be lifted above his brethren, that he may not turn aside from the commandment *to* the right hand or *to* the left, and that he may prolong *his* days in his kingdom, he and his children in the midst of Israel.

5 **Acts 17:11:** These were more fair-minded than those in Thessalonica, in that they received the word with all readiness, and searched the Scriptures daily *to find out* whether these things were so.

6 **Acts 8:30, 34:** So Philip ran to him, and heard him reading the prophet Isaiah, and said, "Do you understand what you are reading?" ... So the eunuch answered Philip and said, "I ask you, of whom does the prophet say this, of himself or of some other man?" **Luke 10:26-28:** He said to him, "What is written in the law? What is your reading *of it?*" So he answered and said, "'You shall love the LORD your God with all your heart, with all your soul, with all your strength, and with all your mind,' and 'your neighbor as yourself.'" And He said to him, "You have answered rightly; do this and you will live."

7
Ps. 1:2: But his delight *is* in the law of the LORD, And in His law he meditates day and night. **Ps. 119:97:** Oh, how I love Your law! It *is* my meditation all the day.
8
2 Chron. 34:21: "Go, inquire of the LORD for me, and for those who are left in Israel and Judah, concerning the words of the book that is found; for great *is* the wrath of the LORD that is poured out on us, because our fathers have not kept the word of the LORD, to do according to all that is written in this book."
9
Prov. 3:5: Trust in the LORD with all your heart, And lean not on your own understanding. **Deut. 33:3:** Yes, He loves the people; All His saints *are* in Your hand; They sit down at Your feet; *Everyone* receives Your words. **Matt. 16:24:** Then Jesus said to His disciples, "If anyone desires to come after Me, let him deny himself, and take up his cross, and follow Me." **See Luke 9:23; Gal. 1:15-16.**
10
Prov. 2:1-6: My son, if you receive my words, And treasure my commands within you, So that you incline your ear to wisdom, *And* apply your heart to understanding; Yes, if you cry out for discernment, *And* lift up your voice for understanding, If you seek her as silver, And search for her as *for* hidden treasures; Then you will understand the fear of the LORD, And find the knowledge of God. For the LORD gives wisdom; From His mouth *come* knowledge and understanding. **Ps. 119:18:** Open my eyes, that I may see Wondrous things from Your law. **Neh. 8:6, 8:** And Ezra blessed the LORD, the great God. Then all the people answered, "Amen, Amen!" while lifting up their hands. And they bowed their heads and worshiped the LORD with *their* faces to the ground.... So they read distinctly from the book, in the Law of God; and they gave the sense, and helped *them* to understand the reading.

Q. 179. *By whom is the word of God to be preached?*

A. The word of God is to be preached only by such as are sufficiently gifted,[1] and also duly approved and called to that office.[2]

1
1 Tim. 3:2, 6: A bishop then must be blameless, the husband of one wife, temperate, sober-minded, of good behavior, hospitable, able to teach ... not a novice, lest being puffed up with pride he fall into the *same* condemnation as the devil. **Eph. 4:8-11:** Therefore He says: "When He ascended on high, He led captivity captive, And gave gifts to men." (Now this, "He ascended"—what does it mean but that He also first descended into the lower parts of the earth? He who descended is also the One who ascended far above all the heavens, that He might fill all things.) And He Himself gave some *to be* apostles, some prophets, some evangelists, and some pastors and teachers. **Mal. 2:7:** For the lips of a priest should keep knowledge, And *people* should seek the law from his mouth; For he is the messenger of the LORD of hosts. **2 Cor. 3:6:** ... who also made us sufficient as ministers of the new covenant, not of the letter but of the Spirit; for the letter kills, but the Spirit gives life. **2 Tim. 2:2:** And the things that you have heard from me among many witnesses, commit these to faithful men who will be able to teach others also.
2
Jer. 14:15: Therefore thus says the LORD concerning the prophets who prophesy in My name, whom I did not send, and who say, 'Sword and famine shall not be in this land'—'By sword and famine those prophets shall be consumed! **Rom. 10:15:** And how shall they preach unless they are sent? As it is written: "How beautiful are the feet of those who preach the gospel of peace, Who bring glad tidings of good things!" **Heb. 5:4:** And no man takes this honor to himself, but he who is called by God, just as Aaron *was.* **1 Cor. 12:28-29:** And God has appointed these in the church: first apostles, second prophets, third teachers, after that miracles, then gifts of healings, helps, administrations, varieties of tongues. *Are* all apostles? *Are* all prophets? *Are* all teachers? *Are* all workers of miracles? **1 Tim. 3:10:** But let these also first be tested; then let them serve as deacons, being *found* blameless. **1 Tim. 4:14:** Do not neglect the gift that is in you, which was given to you by prophecy with the laying on of the hands of the eldership. **1 Tim. 5:22:** Do not lay hands on anyone hastily, nor share in other people's sins; keep yourself pure.

Q. 180. *How is the word of God to be preached by those that are called thereunto?*

A. They that are called to labour in the ministry of the word, are to preach sound doctrine,[1] diligently,[2] in season and out of season;[3] plainly,[4] not in the enticing words of man's wisdom, but in demonstration of the Spirit, and of power;[5] faithfully,[6] making known the whole counsel of God;[7] wisely,[8] applying themselves to the necessities and capacities of the hearers;[9] zealously,[10] with fervent love to God[11] and the souls of His people;[12] sincerely,[13] aiming at His glory,[14] and their conversion,[15] edification,[16] and salvation.[17]

1 **Titus 2:1, 8:** But as for you, speak the things which are proper for sound doctrine.... sound speech that cannot be condemned, that one who is an opponent may be ashamed, having nothing evil to say of you.

2 **Acts 18:25:** This man had been instructed in the way of the Lord; and being fervent in spirit, he spoke and taught accurately the things of the Lord, though he knew only the baptism of John.

3 **2 Tim. 4:2:** Preach the word! Be ready in season *and* out of season. Convince, rebuke, exhort, with all longsuffering and teaching.

4 **1 Cor. 14:9:** So likewise you, unless you utter by the tongue words easy to understand, how will it be known what is spoken? For you will be speaking into the air. **See 1 Cor. 14:10-19.**

5 **1 Cor. 2:4:** And my speech and my preaching *were* not with persuasive words of human wisdom, but in demonstration of the Spirit and of power.

6 **Jer. 23:28:** "The prophet who has a dream, let him tell a dream; And he who has My word, let him speak My word faithfully. What *is* the chaff to the wheat?" says the Lord. **1 Cor. 4:1-2:** Let a man so consider us, as servants of Christ and stewards of the mysteries of God. Moreover it is required in stewards that one be found faithful.

7 **Acts 20:27:** For I have not shunned to declare to you the whole counsel of God.

8 **Col. 1:28:** Him we preach, warning every man and teaching every man in all wisdom, that we may present every man perfect in Christ Jesus. **2 Tim. 2:15:** Be diligent to present yourself approved to God, a worker who does not need to be ashamed, rightly dividing the word of truth.

9 **1 Cor. 3:2:** I fed you with milk and not with solid food; for until now you were not able *to receive it,* and even now you are still not able. **Heb. 5:12-14:** For though by this time you ought to be teachers, you need *someone* to teach you again the first principles of the oracles of God; and you have come to need milk and not solid food. For everyone who partakes *only* of milk *is* unskilled in the word of righteousness, for he is a babe. But solid food belongs to those who are of full age, *that is,* those who by reason of use have their senses exercised to discern both good and evil. **Luke 12:42:** And the Lord said, "Who then is that faithful and wise steward, whom *his* master will make ruler over his household, to give *them their* portion of food in due season?"

10 **Acts 18:25:** This man had been instructed in the way of the Lord; and being fervent in spirit, he spoke and taught accurately the things of the Lord, though he knew only the baptism of John. **Ps. 119:139:** My zeal has consumed me, Because my enemies have forgotten Your words. **2 Tim. 4:5:** But you be watchful in all things, endure afflictions, do the work of an evangelist, fulfill your ministry.

11 **2 Cor. 5:13-14:** For if we are beside ourselves, *it is* for God; or if we are of sound mind, *it is* for you. For the love of Christ compels us, because we judge thus: that if One died for all, then all died. **Phil. 1:15-17:** Some indeed preach Christ even from envy and strife, and some also from goodwill: The former preach Christ from selfish ambition, not sincerely, supposing to add affliction to my chains; but the latter out of love, knowing that I am appointed for the defense of the gospel.

12 **Col. 4:12:** Epaphras, who is *one* of you, a bondservant of Christ, greets you, always laboring fervently for you in prayers, that you may stand perfect and complete in all the will of God. **2 Cor. 12:15:** And I will very gladly spend and be spent for your souls; though the more abundantly I love you, the less I am loved.

13 **2 Cor. 2:17:** For we are not, as so many, peddling the word of God; but as of sincerity, but as from God, we speak in the sight of God in Christ. **2 Cor. 4:2:** But we have renounced the hidden

things of shame, not walking in craftiness nor handling the word of God deceitfully, but by manifestation of the truth commending ourselves to every man's conscience in the sight of God.

14 **1 Thess. 2:4-6:** But as we have been approved by God to be entrusted with the gospel, even so we speak, not as pleasing men, but God who tests our hearts. For neither at any time did we use flattering words, as you know, nor a cloak for covetousness—God *is* witness. Nor did we seek glory from men, either from you or from others, when we might have made demands as apostles of Christ. **John 7:18:** He who speaks from himself seeks his own glory; but He who seeks the glory of the One who sent Him is true, and no unrighteousness is in Him.

15 **1 Cor. 9:19-22:** For though I am free from all *men,* I have made myself a servant to all, that I might win the more; and to the Jews I became as a Jew, that I might win Jews; to those *who are* under the law, as under the law, that I might win those *who are* under the law; to those *who are* without law, as without law (not being without law toward God, but under law toward Christ), that I might win those *who are* without law; to the weak I became as weak, that I might win the weak. I have become all things to all *men,* that I might by all means save some.

16 **2 Cor. 12:19:** Again, do you think that we excuse ourselves to you? We speak before God in Christ. But *we do* all things, beloved, for your edification. **Eph. 4:12:** ... for the equipping of the saints for the work of ministry, for the edifying of the body of Christ.

17 **1 Tim. 4:16:** Take heed to yourself and to the doctrine. Continue in them, for in doing this you will save both yourself and those who hear you.... **Acts 26:16-18:** But rise and stand on your feet; for I have appeared to you for this purpose, to make you a minister and a witness both of the things which you have seen and of the things which I will yet reveal to you. I will deliver you from the *Jewish* people, as well as *from* the Gentiles, to whom I now send you, to open their eyes, *in order* to turn *them* from darkness to light, and *from* the power of Satan to God, that they may receive forgiveness of sins and an inheritance among those who are sanctified by faith in Me.

Q. 181. *What is required of those that hear the word preached?*

A. It is required of those that hear the word preached, that they attend upon it with diligence,[1] preparation,[2] and prayer;[3] examine what they hear by the Scriptures;[4] receive the truth with faith,[5] love,[6] meekness,[7] and readiness of mind,[8] as the word of God;[9] meditate,[10] and confer of it;[11] hide it in their hearts,[12] and bring forth the fruit of it in their lives.[13]

1 **Prov. 8:34:** Blessed is the man who listens to me, Watching daily at my gates, Waiting at the posts of my doors.

2 **1 Pet. 2:1-2:** Therefore, laying aside all malice, all deceit, hypocrisy, envy, and all evil speaking, as newborn babes, desire the pure milk of the word, that you may grow thereby. **Luke 8:18:** Therefore take heed how you hear. For whoever has, to him *more* will be given; and whoever does not have, even what he seems to have will be taken from him.

3 **Ps. 119:18:** Open my eyes, that I may see Wondrous things from Your law. **Eph. 6:18-19:** ... praying always with all prayer and supplication in the Spirit, being watchful to this end with all perseverance and supplication for all the saints— and for me, that utterance may be given to me, that I may open my mouth boldly to make known the mystery of the gospel.

4 **Acts 17:11:** These were more fair-minded than those in Thessalonica, in that they received the word with all readiness, and searched the Scriptures daily *to find out* whether these things were so.

5 **Heb. 4:2:** For indeed the gospel was preached to us as well as to them; but the word which they heard did not profit them, not being mixed with faith in those who heard *it.*

6 **2 Thess. 2:10:** ... and with all unrighteous deception among those who perish, because they did not receive the love of the truth, that they might be saved.

7 **James 1:21:** Therefore lay aside all filthiness and overflow of wickedness, and receive with meekness the implanted word, which is able to save your souls.

8
Acts 17:11: These were more fair-minded than those in Thessalonica, in that they received the word with all readiness, and searched the Scriptures daily *to find out* whether these things were so.
9
1 Thess. 2:13: For this reason we also thank God without ceasing, because when you received the word of God which you heard from us, you welcomed *it* not *as* the word of men, but as it is in truth, the word of God, which also effectively works in you who believe.
10
Luke 9:44: Let these words sink down into your ears, for the Son of Man is about to be betrayed into the hands of men. **Heb. 2:1:** Therefore we must give the more earnest heed to the things we have heard, lest we drift away.
11
Luke 24:14: And they talked together of all these things which had happened. **Deut. 6:6-7:** And these words which I command you today shall be in your heart. You shall teach them diligently to your children, and shall talk of them when you sit in your house, when you walk by the way, when you lie down, and when you rise up.
12
Prov. 2:1: My son, if you receive my words, And treasure my commands within you. **Ps. 119:11:** Your word I have hidden in my heart, That I might not sin against You.
13
Luke 8:15: But the ones *that* fell on the good ground are those who, having heard the word with a noble and good heart, keep *it* and bear fruit with patience. **James 1:25:** But he who looks into the perfect law of liberty and continues *in it,* and is not a forgetful hearer but a doer of the work, this one will be blessed in what he does.

Q. 182. *How does baptism and the Lord's Supper become effectual means of salvation?*

A. Baptism and the Lord's Supper become effectual means of salvation, not by any power in themselves, or any virtue derived from the piety or intention of him by whom they are administered, but only by the working of the Holy Spirit, and the blessing of Christ, by whom they are instituted.[1]

1
1 Pet. 3:21: There is also an antitype which now saves us—baptism (not the removal of the filth of the flesh, but the answer of a good conscience toward God), through the resurrection of Jesus Christ. **Acts 8:13, 23:** Then Simon himself also believed; and when he was baptized he continued with Philip, and was amazed, seeing the miracles and signs which were done.... For I see that you are poisoned by bitterness and bound by iniquity. **1 Cor. 3:5-7:** Who then is Paul, and who *is* Apollos, but ministers through whom you believed, as the Lord gave to each one? I planted, Apollos watered, but God gave the increase. So then neither he who plants is anything, nor he who waters, but God who gives the increase. **Cf. 1 Cor. 1:12-17:** Now I say this, that each of you says, "I am of Paul," or "I am of Apollos," or "I am of Cephas," or "I am of Christ." Is Christ divided? Was Paul crucified for you? Or were you baptized in the name of Paul? I thank God that I baptized none of you except Crispus and Gaius, lest anyone should say that I had baptized in my own name. Yes, I also baptized the household of Stephanas. Besides, I do not know whether I baptized any other. For Christ did not send me to baptize, but to preach the gospel, not with wisdom of words, lest the cross of Christ should be made of no effect. **1 Cor. 12:13:** For by one Spirit we were all baptized into one body—whether Jews or Greeks, whether slaves or free—and have all been made to drink into one Spirit. **1 Cor. 6:11:** And such were some of you. But you were washed, but you were sanctified, but you were justified in the name of the Lord Jesus and by the Spirit of our God.

Q. 183. *Wherein do the ordinances of baptism and the Lord's Supper differ from the other ordinances of God?*

A. Baptism and the Lord's Supper differ from the other ordinances of God in that they were specially instituted by Christ[1] to represent and apply to believers the benefits of the New Covenant by visible and outward signs.[2]

[1] **Matt. 28:19-20:** Go therefore and make disciples of all the nations, baptizing them in the name of the Father and of the Son and of the Holy Spirit, teaching them to observe all things that I have commanded you; and lo, I am with you always, *even* to the end of the age." Amen. **1 Cor. 11:23-26:** For I received from the Lord that which I also delivered to you: that the Lord Jesus on the *same* night in which He was betrayed took bread; and when He had given thanks, He broke *it* and said, "Take, eat; this is My body which is broken for you; do this in remembrance of Me." In the same manner *He* also *took* the cup after supper, saying, "This cup is the new covenant in My blood. This do, as often as you drink *it,* in remembrance of Me." For as often as you eat this bread and drink this cup, you proclaim the Lord's death till He comes.

[2] **Acts 22:16:** And now why are you waiting? Arise and be baptized, and wash away your sins, calling on the name of the Lord. **Matt. 26:26-28:** And as they were eating, Jesus took bread, blessed and broke *it,* and gave *it* to the disciples and said, "Take, eat; this is My body." Then He took the cup, and gave thanks, and gave *it* to them, saying, "Drink from it, all of you. For this is My blood of the new covenant, which is shed for many for the remission of sins. **Rom. 6:4:** Therefore we were buried with Him through baptism into death, that just as Christ was raised from the dead by the glory of the Father, even so we also should walk in newness of life.

Q. 184. *What is baptism?*

A. Baptism is a holy ordinance of the New Covenant, wherein Christ hath ordained the washing with water in the name of the Father, and of the Son, and of the Holy Spirit,[1] to be a covenant transaction and sign of ingrafting into Himself,[2] of remission of sins by His blood,[3] of fellowship with Him, in His death and resurrection unto everlasting life;[4] which is not the putting away of the filth of the flesh, but the answer of a good conscience toward God.[5]

[1] **Matt. 28:19:** Go therefore and make disciples of all the nations, baptizing them in the name of the Father and of the Son and of the Holy Spirit.

[2] **Gal. 3:27:** For as many of you as were baptized into Christ have put on Christ. **Rom. 6:3-5:** Or do you not know that as many of us as were baptized into Christ Jesus were baptized into His death? Therefore we were buried with Him through baptism into death, that just as Christ was raised from the dead by the glory of the Father, even so we also should walk in newness of life. For if we have been united together in the likeness of His death, certainly we also shall be *in the likeness* of *His* resurrection.

[3] **Mark 1:4:** John came baptizing in the wilderness and preaching a baptism of repentance for the remission of sins. **Acts 2:38:** Then Peter said to them, "Repent, and let every one of you be baptized in the name of Jesus Christ for the remission of sins; and you shall receive the gift of the Holy Spirit. **Acts 22:16:** And now why are you waiting? Arise and be baptized, and wash away your sins, calling on the name of the Lord.

[4] **Col. 2:12-13:** ... buried with Him in baptism, in which you also were raised with *Him* through faith in the working of God, who raised Him from the dead. And you, being dead in your trespasses and the uncircumcision of your flesh, He has made alive together with Him, having forgiven you all trespasses. **Rom. 6:5:** For if we have been united together in the likeness of His death, certainly we also shall be *in the likeness* of *His* resurrection.

[5] **1 Pet. 3:21:** There is also an antitype which now saves us—baptism (not the removal of the filth of the flesh, but the answer of a good conscience toward God), through the resurrection of Jesus Christ. **Acts 2:38:** Then Peter said to them, "Repent, and let every one of you be baptized in the name of Jesus Christ for the remission of sins; and you shall receive the gift of the Holy Spirit.

Q. 185. *Unto whom is baptism to be administered?*

A. Baptism is to be administered to all those who actually profess repentance towards God, faith in, and obedience to our Lord Jesus Christ;[1] the infants descending from parents, either both, or but one of them, professing faith in Christ are not to be baptized.

1 **Acts 2:38:** Then Peter said to them, "Repent, and let every one of you be baptized in the name of Jesus Christ for the remission of sins; and you shall receive the gift of the Holy Spirit. **Matt. 3:6:** ... and were baptized by him in the Jordan, confessing their sins. **Mark 16:16:** He who believes and is baptized will be saved; but he who does not believe will be condemned. **Acts 8:12, 36:** But when they believed Philip as he preached the things concerning the kingdom of God and the name of Jesus Christ, both men and women were baptized.... Now as they went down the road, they came to some water. And the eunuch said, "See, *here is* water. What hinders me from being baptized?" **Acts 10:47-48:** "Can anyone forbid water, that these should not be baptized who have received the Holy Spirit just as we *have?"* And he commanded them to be baptized in the name of the Lord. Then they asked him to stay a few days.

Q. 186. *How is our baptism to be improved by us?*

A. The needful but much neglected duty of improving our baptism, is to be performed by us all our life long, especially in the time of temptation, and when we are present at the administration of it to others;[1] by serious and thankful consideration of the nature of it, and of the ends for which Christ instituted it, the privileges and benefits conferred thereby, and our solemn vow made therein;[2] by being humbled for our sinful defilement, our falling short of, and walking contrary to, the grace of baptism, and our engagements;[3] by growing up to assurance of pardon of sin, and of all other blessings for us in that holy ordinance;[4] by drawing strength from the death and resurrection of Christ, into whom we are baptized, for the mortifying of sin, and quickening of grace;[5] and by endeavoring to live by faith,[6] to have our conversation in holiness and righteousness,[7] as those that have therein given up their names to Christ;[8] and to walk in brotherly love, as being baptized by the same Spirit into one body.[9]

1 **Col. 2:11-12:** In Him you were also circumcised with the circumcision made without hands, by putting off the body of the sins of the flesh, by the circumcision of Christ, buried with Him in baptism, in which you also were raised with *Him* through faith in the working of God, who raised Him from the dead. **Rom. 6:4, 6, 11:** Therefore we were buried with Him through baptism into death, that just as Christ was raised from the dead by the glory of the Father, even so we also should walk in newness of life.... knowing this, that our old man was crucified with *Him,* that the body of sin might be done away with, that we should no longer be slaves of sin.... Likewise you also, reckon yourselves to be dead indeed to sin, but alive to God in Christ Jesus our Lord.

2 **Rom. 6:3-5:** Or do you not know that as many of us as were baptized into Christ Jesus were baptized into His death? Therefore we were buried with Him through baptism into death, that just as Christ was raised from the dead by the glory of the Father, even so we also should walk in newness of life. For if we have been united together in the likeness of His death, certainly we also shall be *in the likeness* of *His* resurrection. **1 Pet. 3:21:** There is also an antitype which now saves us—baptism (not the removal of the filth of the flesh, but the answer of a good conscience toward God), through the resurrection of Jesus Christ.

3
1 Cor. 1:11-13: For it has been declared to me concerning you, my brethren, by those of Chloe's *household,* that there are contentions among you. Now I say this, that each of you says, "I am of Paul," or "I am of Apollos," or "I am of Cephas," or "I am of Christ." Is Christ divided? Was Paul crucified for you? Or were you baptized in the name of Paul? **Rom. 6:2-3:** Certainly not! How shall we who died to sin live any longer in it? Or do you not know that as many of us as were baptized into Christ Jesus were baptized into His death?
4
Rom. 6:4-7, 22: Therefore we were buried with Him through baptism into death, that just as Christ was raised from the dead by the glory of the Father, even so we also should walk in newness of life. For if we have been united together in the likeness of His death, certainly we also shall be *in the likeness* of *His* resurrection, knowing this, that our old man was crucified with *Him,* that the body of sin might be done away with, that we should no longer be slaves of sin. For he who has died has been freed from sin.... But now having been set free from sin, and having become slaves of God, you have your fruit to holiness, and the end, everlasting life. **1 Pet. 3:21:** There is also an antitype which now saves us—baptism (not the removal of the filth of the flesh, but the answer of a good conscience toward God), through the resurrection of Jesus Christ. **Rom. 5:1-2:** Therefore, having been justified by faith, we have peace with God through our Lord Jesus Christ, through whom also we have access by faith into this grace in which we stand, and rejoice in hope of the glory of God. **Jer. 33:8:** I will cleanse them from all their iniquity by which they have sinned against Me, and I will pardon all their iniquities by which they have sinned and by which they have transgressed against Me.
5
Rom. 6:3-5: Or do you not know that as many of us as were baptized into Christ Jesus were baptized into His death? Therefore we were buried with Him through baptism into death, that just as Christ was raised from the dead by the glory of the Father, even so we also should walk in newness of life. For if we have been united together in the likeness of His death, certainly we also shall be *in the likeness* of *His* resurrection.
6
Gal. 3:26-27: For you are all sons of God through faith in Christ Jesus. For as many of you as were baptized into Christ have put on Christ.
7
Rom. 6:22: But now having been set free from sin, and having become slaves of God, you have your fruit to holiness, and the end, everlasting life.
8
Acts 2:38: Then Peter said to them, "Repent, and let every one of you be baptized in the name of Jesus Christ for the remission of sins; and you shall receive the gift of the Holy Spirit. **Cf. Gal. 2:20:** I have been crucified with Christ; it is no longer I who live, but Christ lives in me; and the *life* which I now live in the flesh I live by faith in the Son of God, who loved me and gave Himself for me. **See Rev. 2:17.**
9
1 Cor. 12:13, 25: For by one Spirit we were all baptized into one body—whether Jews or Greeks, whether slaves or free—and have all been made to drink into one Spirit.... that there should be no schism in the body, but *that* the members should have the same care for one another.

Q. 187. *What is the Lord's Supper?*

A. The Lord's Supper is a holy ordinance of the New Covenant,[1] wherein, by giving and receiving bread and wine according to the appointment of Jesus Christ, His death is showed forth; and they that worthily communicate feed upon His body and blood, to their spiritual nourishment and growth in grace;[2] have their union and communion with Him confirmed;[3] testify and renew their thankfulness,[4] and engagement to God,[5] and their mutual love and fellowship with each other, as members of the same body.[6]

1
Luke 22:20: Likewise He also *took* the cup after supper, saying, "This cup *is* the new covenant in My blood, which is shed for you.
2
Matt. 26:26-28: And as they were eating, Jesus took bread, blessed and broke *it,* and gave *it* to the disciples and said, "Take, eat; this is My body." Then He took the cup, and gave thanks, and

gave *it* to them, saying, "Drink from it, all of you. For this is My blood of the new covenant, which is shed for many for the remission of sins. **1 Cor. 11:23-26:** For I received from the Lord that which I also delivered to you: that the Lord Jesus on the *same* night in which He was betrayed took bread; and when He had given thanks, He broke *it* and said, "Take, eat; this is My body which is broken for you; do this in remembrance of Me." In the same manner *He* also *took* the cup after supper, saying, "This cup is the new covenant in My blood. This do, as often as you drink *it,* in remembrance of Me." For as often as you eat this bread and drink this cup, you proclaim the Lord's death till He comes.

[3] **1 Cor. 10:16:** The cup of blessing which we bless, is it not the communion of the blood of Christ? The bread which we break, is it not the communion of the body of Christ?

[4] **1 Cor. 11:24:** ... and when He had given thanks, He broke *it* and said, "Take, eat; this is My body which is broken for you; do this in remembrance of Me."

[5] **1 Cor. 10:14-16, 21:** Therefore, my beloved, flee from idolatry. I speak as to wise men; judge for yourselves what I say. The cup of blessing which we bless, is it not the communion of the blood of Christ? The bread which we break, is it not the communion of the body of Christ? ... You cannot drink the cup of the Lord and the cup of demons; you cannot partake of the Lord's table and of the table of demons. **Cf. Rom. 7:4:** Therefore, my brethren, you also have become dead to the law through the body of Christ, that you may be married to another—to Him who was raised from the dead, that we should bear fruit to God.

[6] **1 Cor. 10:17:** For we, *though* many, are one bread *and* one body; for we all partake of that one bread.

Q. 188. *How hath Christ appointed bread and wine to be given and received in the ordinance of the Lord's Supper?*

A. Christ hath appointed the ministers of His word, in the administration of this ordinance of the Lord's Supper, to set apart the bread and wine from common use, by the word of institution, thanksgiving, and prayer; to take and break the bread, and to give both the bread and the wine to the communicants: who are, by the same appointment, to take and eat the bread, and to drink the wine, in thankful remembrance that the body of Christ was broken and given, and His blood shed, for them.[1]

[1] **1 Cor. 11:23-24:** For I received from the Lord that which I also delivered to you: that the Lord Jesus on the *same* night in which He was betrayed took bread; and when He had given thanks, He broke *it* and said, "Take, eat; this is My body which is broken for you; do this in remembrance of Me." **See Matt. 26:26-28; Mark 14:22-24; Luke 22:19-20.**

Q. 189. *How do they that worthily communicate in the Lord's Supper feed upon the body and blood of Christ therein?*

A. As the body and blood of Christ are not corporally or carnally present in, with, or under the bread and wine in the Lord's Supper,[1] and yet are spiritually present to the faith of the receiver, no less truly and really than the elements themselves are to their outward senses;[2] so they that worthily communicate in the ordinance of the Lord's Supper, do therein feed upon the body and blood of Christ, not after a corporal and carnal, but in a spiritual manner; yet truly and really,[3] while by faith they receive and apply unto themselves Christ crucified, and all the benefits of His death.[4]

1 **Acts 3:21:** ... whom heaven must receive until the times of restoration of all things, which God has spoken by the mouth of all His holy prophets since the world began.

2 **Matt. 26:26, 28:** And as they were eating, Jesus took bread, blessed and broke *it,* and gave *it* to the disciples and said, "Take, eat; this is My body." ... For this is My blood of the new covenant, which is shed for many for the remission of sins.

3 **1 Cor. 11:24-29:** ... and when He had given thanks, He broke *it* and said, "Take, eat; this is My body which is broken for you; do this in remembrance of Me." In the same manner *He* also *took* the cup after supper, saying, "This cup is the new covenant in My blood. This do, as often as you drink *it,* in remembrance of Me." For as often as you eat this bread and drink this cup, you proclaim the Lord's death till He comes. Therefore whoever eats this bread or drinks *this* cup of the Lord in an unworthy manner will be guilty of the body and blood of the Lord. But let a man examine himself, and so let him eat of the bread and drink of the cup. For he who eats and drinks in an unworthy manner eats and drinks judgment to himself, not discerning the Lord's body. **Cf. John 6:51, 53.**

4 **1 Cor. 10:16:** The cup of blessing which we bless, is it not the communion of the blood of Christ? The bread which we break, is it not the communion of the body of Christ?

Q. 190. *How are they that receive the ordinance of the Lord's Supper to prepare themselves before they come unto it?*

A. They that receive the ordinance of the Lord's Supper are, before they come, to prepare themselves thereunto, by examining themselves[1] of their being in Christ,[2] of their sins and wants;[3] of the truth and measure of their knowledge,[4] faith,[5] repentance;[6] love to God and the brethren,[7] charity to all men,[8] forgiving those that have done them wrong;[9] of their desires after Christ,[10] and of their new obedience;[11] and by renewing the exercise of these graces,[12] by serious meditation,[13] and fervent prayer.[14]

1 **1 Cor. 11:28:** But let a man examine himself, and so let him eat of the bread and drink of the cup.

2 **2 Cor. 13:5:** Examine yourselves *as to* whether you are in the faith. Test yourselves. Do you not know yourselves, that Jesus Christ is in you?—unless indeed you are disqualified.

3 **1 Cor. 5:7:** Therefore purge out the old leaven, that you may be a new lump, since you truly are unleavened. For indeed Christ, our Passover, was sacrificed for us. **Ex. 12:15:** Seven days you shall eat unleavened bread. On the first day you shall remove leaven from your houses. For whoever eats leavened bread from the first day until the seventh day, that person shall be cut off from Israel.

4 **1 Cor. 11:29:** For he who eats and drinks in an unworthy manner eats and drinks judgment to himself, not discerning the Lord's body.

5 **2 Cor. 13:5:** Examine yourselves *as to* whether you are in the faith. Test yourselves. Do you not know yourselves, that Jesus Christ is in you?—unless indeed you are disqualified. **Matt. 26:28:** For this is My blood of the new covenant, which is shed for many for the remission of sins.

6 **Zech. 12:10:** And I will pour on the house of David and on the inhabitants of Jerusalem the Spirit of grace and supplication; then they will look on Me whom they pierced. Yes, they will mourn for Him as one mourns for *his* only *son,* and grieve for Him as one grieves for a firstborn. **1 Cor. 11:31:** For if we would judge ourselves, we would not be judged.

7

1 Cor. 10:16-17: The cup of blessing which we bless, is it not the communion of the blood of Christ? The bread which we break, is it not the communion of the body of Christ? For we, *though* many, are one bread *and* one body; for we all partake of that one bread. **Acts 2:46-47:** So continuing daily with one accord in the temple, and breaking bread from house to house, they ate their food with gladness and simplicity of heart, praising God and having favor with all the people. And the Lord added to the church daily those who were being saved.

8

1 Cor. 5:8: Therefore let us keep the feast, not with old leaven, nor with the leaven of malice and wickedness, but with the unleavened *bread* of sincerity and truth. **1 Cor. 11:18, 20:** For first of all, when you come together as a church, I hear that there are divisions among you, and in part I believe it.... Therefore when you come together in one place, it is not to eat the Lord's Supper.

9

Matt. 5:23-24: Therefore if you bring your gift to the altar, and there remember that your brother has something against you, leave your gift there before the altar, and go your way. First be reconciled to your brother, and then come and offer your gift.

10

Isa. 55:1: Ho! Everyone who thirsts, Come to the waters; And you who have no money, Come, buy and eat. Yes, come, buy wine and milk Without money and without price. **John 7:37:** On the last day, that great *day* of the feast, Jesus stood and cried out, saying, "If anyone thirsts, let him come to Me and drink."

11

1 Cor. 5:7-8: Therefore purge out the old leaven, that you may be a new lump, since you truly are unleavened. For indeed Christ, our Passover, was sacrificed for us. Therefore let us keep the feast, not with old leaven, nor with the leaven of malice and wickedness, but with the unleavened *bread* of sincerity and truth.

12

1 Cor. 11:25-26, 28: In the same manner *He* also *took* the cup after supper, saying, "This cup is the new covenant in My blood. This do, as often as you drink *it,* in remembrance of Me." For as often as you eat this bread and drink this cup, you proclaim the Lord's death till He comes.... But let a man examine himself, and so let him eat of the bread and drink of the cup. **Heb. 10:21-22, 24:** ... and *having* a High Priest over the house of God, let us draw near with a true heart in full assurance of faith, having our hearts sprinkled from an evil conscience and our bodies washed with pure water. And let us consider one another in order to stir up love and good works. **Ps. 26:6:** I will wash my hands in innocence; So I will go about Your altar, O LORD.

13

1 Cor. 11:24-25: ... and when He had given thanks, He broke *it* and said, "Take, eat; this is My body which is broken for you; do this in remembrance of Me." In the same manner *He* also *took* the cup after supper, saying, "This cup is the new covenant in My blood. This do, as often as you drink *it,* in remembrance of Me."

14

2 Chron. 30:18-19: For a multitude of the people, many from Ephraim, Manasseh, Issachar, and Zebulun, had not cleansed themselves, yet they ate the Passover contrary to what was written. But Hezekiah prayed for them, saying, "May the good LORD provide atonement for everyone *who* prepares his heart to seek God, the LORD God of his fathers, though *he is* not *cleansed* according to the purification of the sanctuary." **Matt. 26:26:** And as they were eating, Jesus took bread, blessed and broke *it,* and gave *it* to the disciples and said, "Take, eat; this is My body."

Q. 191. *May one who doubteth of his being in Christ, or of his due preparation, come to the Lord's Supper?*

A. One who doubteth of his being in Christ, or of his due preparation to the ordinance of the Lord's Supper, may have true interest in Christ, though he be not yet assured thereof;[1] and in God's account hath it, if he be duly affected with the apprehension of the want of it,[2] and unfeignedly desires to be found in Christ,[3] and to depart from iniquity:[4] in which case (because promises are made, and this ordinance is appointed, for the relief even of weak and doubting Christians)[5] he is to bewail his unbelief,[6] and labour to have his doubts resolved;[7] and, so doing, he may and ought to come to the Lord's Supper, that he may be further strengthened.[8]

1
Isa. 50:10: Who among you fears the LORD? Who obeys the voice of His Servant? Who walks in darkness And has no light? Let him trust in the name of the LORD And rely upon his God. **1 John 5:13:** These things I have written to you who believe in the name of the Son of God, that you may know that you have eternal life, and that you may *continue to* believe in the name of the Son of God. **Ps. 88:** O LORD, God of my salvation, I have cried out day and night before You. Let my prayer come before You; Incline Your ear to my cry. For my soul is full of troubles, And my life draws near to the grave ... Your wrath lies heavy upon me, And You have afflicted *me* with all Your waves.... My eye wastes away because of affliction. LORD, I have called daily upon You; I have stretched out my hands to You. Will You work wonders for the dead? Shall the dead arise *and* praise You? ... LORD, why do You cast off my soul? *Why* do You hide Your face from me? ... Your fierce wrath has gone over me; Your terrors have cut me off.... Loved one and friend You have put far from me, *And* my acquaintances into darkness. **Ps. 77:1-4, 7-10:** I cried out to God with my voice— To God with my voice; And He gave ear to me. In the day of my trouble I sought the Lord; My hand was stretched out in the night without ceasing; My soul refused to be comforted. I remembered God, and was troubled; I complained, and my spirit was overwhelmed. *Selah*. You hold my eyelids *open;* I am so troubled that I cannot speak.... Will the Lord cast off forever? And will He be favorable no more? Has His mercy ceased forever? Has *His* promise failed forevermore? Has God forgotten to be gracious? Has He in anger shut up His tender mercies? *Selah*. And I said, "This *is* my anguish; *But I will remember* the years of the right hand of the Most High." **Jonah 2:4:** Then I said, 'I have been cast out of Your sight; Yet I will look again toward Your holy temple.'

2
Isa. 54:7-10: "For a mere moment I have forsaken you, But with great mercies I will gather you. With a little wrath I hid My face from you for a moment; But with everlasting kindness I will have mercy on you," Says the LORD, your Redeemer. "For this *is* like the waters of Noah to Me; For as I have sworn That the waters of Noah would no longer cover the earth, So have I sworn That I would not be angry with you, nor rebuke you. For the mountains shall depart And the hills be removed, But My kindness shall not depart from you, Nor shall My covenant of peace be removed," Says the LORD, who has mercy on you. **Matt. 5:3-4:** Blessed *are* the poor in spirit, For theirs is the kingdom of heaven. Blessed *are* those who mourn, For they shall be comforted. **Ps. 31:22:** For I said in my haste, "I am cut off from before Your eyes"; Nevertheless You heard the voice of my supplications When I cried out to You. **Ps. 73:13, 22-23:** Surely I have cleansed my heart *in* vain, And washed my hands in innocence.... I *was* so foolish and ignorant; I was *like* a beast before You. Nevertheless I *am* continually with You; You hold *me* by my right hand.

3
Phil. 3:8-9: Yet indeed I also count all things loss for the excellence of the knowledge of Christ Jesus my Lord, for whom I have suffered the loss of all things, and count them as rubbish, that I may gain Christ and be found in Him, not having my own righteousness, which *is* from the law, but that which *is* through faith in Christ, the righteousness which is from God by faith. **Ps. 10:17:** LORD, You have heard the desire of the humble; You will prepare their heart; You will cause Your ear to hear. **Ps. 42:1-2, 5, 11:** As the deer pants for the water brooks, So pants my soul for You, O God. My soul thirsts for God, for the living God. When shall I come and appear before God? ... Why are you cast down, O my soul? And *why* are you disquieted within me? Hope in God, for I shall yet praise Him *For* the help of His countenance.... Why are you cast down, O my soul? And why are you disquieted within me? Hope in God; For I shall yet praise Him, The help of my countenance and my God.

4
2 Tim. 2:19: Nevertheless the solid foundation of God stands, having this seal: "The Lord knows those who are His," and, "Let everyone who names the name of Christ depart from iniquity." **Isa. 50:10:** Who among you fears the LORD? Who obeys the voice of His Servant? Who walks in darkness And has no light? Let him trust in the name of the LORD And rely upon his God. **Ps. 66:18-20:** If I regard iniquity in my heart, The Lord will not hear. *But* certainly God has heard *me;* He has attended to the voice of my prayer. Blessed *be* God, Who has not turned away my prayer, Nor His mercy from me!

5
Isa. 40:11, 29, 31: He will feed His flock like a shepherd; He will gather the lambs with His arm, And carry *them* in His bosom, *And* gently lead those who are with young.... He gives power to the weak, And to *those who have* no might He increases strength.... But those who wait on the LORD Shall renew *their* strength; They shall mount up with wings like eagles, They shall run and not be weary, They shall walk and not faint. **Matt. 11:28:** Come to Me, all *you* who labor and are heavy laden, and I will give you rest. **Matt. 12:20:** A bruised reed He will not break, And smoking flax He will not quench, Till He sends forth justice to victory. **Matt. 26:28:** For this is My blood of the new covenant, which is shed for many for the remission of sins.

6
Mark 9:24: Immediately the father of the child cried out and said with tears, "Lord, I believe; help my unbelief!"

7
Acts 2:37: Now when they heard *this,* they were cut to the heart, and said to Peter and the rest of

the apostles, "Men *and* brethren, what shall we do?" **Acts 16:30:** And he brought them out and said, "Sirs, what must I do to be saved?"

[8] **Rom. 4:11:** And he received the sign of circumcision, a seal of the righteousness of the faith which *he had while still* uncircumcised, that he might be the father of all those who believe, though they are uncircumcised, that righteousness might be imputed to them also. **1 Cor. 11:28:** But let a man examine himself, and so let him eat of the bread and drink of the cup.

Q. 192. *May any who profess the faith, and desire to come to the Lord's Supper, be kept from it?*

A. Such as are found to be ignorant or scandalous, notwithstanding their profession of the faith, and desire to come to the Lord's Supper, may and ought to be kept from that holy ordinance, by the power which Christ hath left in His church,[1] until they receive instruction, and manifest their reformation.[2]

[1] **1 Cor. 11:27-34:** Therefore whoever eats this bread or drinks *this* cup of the Lord in an unworthy manner will be guilty of the body and blood of the Lord. But let a man examine himself, and so let him eat of the bread and drink of the cup. For he who eats and drinks in an unworthy manner eats and drinks judgment to himself, not discerning the Lord's body. For this reason many *are* weak and sick among you, and many sleep. For if we would judge ourselves, we would not be judged. But when we are judged, we are chastened by the Lord, that we may not be condemned with the world. Therefore, my brethren, when you come together to eat, wait for one another. But if anyone is hungry, let him eat at home, lest you come together for judgment. And the rest I will set in order when I come. **Matt. 7:6:** Do not give what is holy to the dogs; nor cast your pearls before swine, lest they trample them under their feet, and turn and tear you in pieces. **1 Cor. 5:** It is actually reported *that there is* sexual immorality among you, and such sexual immorality as is not even named among the Gentiles—that a man has his father's wife! ... For I indeed, as absent in body but present in spirit, have already judged (as though I were present) him who has so done this deed. In the name of our Lord Jesus Christ, when you are gathered together, along with my spirit, with the power of our Lord Jesus Christ, deliver such a one to Satan for the destruction of the flesh, that his spirit may be saved in the day of the Lord Jesus.... For indeed Christ, our Passover, was sacrificed for us. Therefore let us keep the feast, not with old leaven, nor with the leaven of malice and wickedness, but with the unleavened *bread* of sincerity and truth.... But now I have written to you not to keep company with anyone named a brother, who is sexually immoral, or covetous, or an idolater, or a reviler, or a drunkard, or an extortioner—not even to eat with such a person.... Therefore "put away from yourselves the evil person." **Jude 23:** ... but others save with fear, pulling them out of the fire, hating even the garment defiled by the flesh. **1 Tim. 5:22:** Do not lay hands on anyone hastily, nor share in other people's sins; keep yourself pure.

[2] **2 Cor. 2:7:** ... so that, on the contrary, you *ought* rather to forgive and comfort *him*, lest perhaps such a one be swallowed up with too much sorrow.

Q. 193. *What is required of them that receive the ordinance of the Lord's Supper in the time of the administration of it?*

A. It is required of them that receive the ordinance of the Lord's Supper, that, during the time of the administration of it, with all holy reverence and attention they wait upon God in that ordinance,[1] diligently observe the elements and actions,[2] heedfully discern the Lord's body,[3] and affectionately meditate on His death and sufferings,[4] and thereby stir up themselves to a vigorous exercise of their graces;[5] in judging themselves,[6] and sorrowing for sin;[7] in earnest hungering and thirsting after

Christ,[8] feeding on Him by faith,[9] receiving of His fullness,[10] trusting in His merits,[11] rejoicing in His love,[12] giving thanks for His grace;[13] in renewing of their covenant with God,[14] and love to all the saints.[15]

1 **Lev. 10:3:** And Moses said to Aaron, "This is what the LORD spoke, saying: 'By those who come near Me I must be regarded as holy; And before all the people I must be glorified.'" So Aaron held his peace. **Heb. 12:28:** Therefore, since we are receiving a kingdom which cannot be shaken, let us have grace, by which we may serve God acceptably with reverence and godly fear. **Ps. 5:7:** But as for me, I will come into Your house in the multitude of Your mercy; In fear of You I will worship toward Your holy temple. **1 Cor. 11:17, 26-27:** Now in giving these instructions I do not praise *you,* since you come together not for the better but for the worse.... For as often as you eat this bread and drink this cup, you proclaim the Lord's death till He comes. Therefore whoever eats this bread or drinks *this* cup of the Lord in an unworthy manner will be guilty of the body and blood of the Lord.

2 **Ex. 24:8:** And Moses took the blood, sprinkled *it* on the people, and said, "This is the blood of the covenant which the LORD has made with you according to all these words." **Matt. 26:28:** For this is My blood of the new covenant, which is shed for many for the remission of sins.

3 **1 Cor. 11:29:** For he who eats and drinks in an unworthy manner eats and drinks judgment to himself, not discerning the Lord's body.

4 **Luke 22:19:** And He took bread, gave thanks and broke *it,* and gave *it* to them, saying, "This is My body which is given for you; do this in remembrance of Me."

5 **1 Cor. 11:26:** For as often as you eat this bread and drink this cup, you proclaim the Lord's death till He comes. **1 Cor. 10:3-5, 11, 14:** ... all ate the same spiritual food, and all drank the same spiritual drink. For they drank of that spiritual Rock that followed them, and that Rock was Christ. But with most of them God was not well pleased, for *their bodies* were scattered in the wilderness.... Now all these things happened to them as examples, and they were written for our admonition, upon whom the ends of the ages have come.... Therefore, my beloved, flee from idolatry.

6 **1 Cor. 11:31:** For if we would judge ourselves, we would not be judged.

7 **Zech. 12:10:** And I will pour on the house of David and on the inhabitants of Jerusalem the Spirit of grace and supplication; then they will look on Me whom they pierced. Yes, they will mourn for Him as one mourns for *his* only *son,* and grieve for Him as one grieves for a firstborn.

8 **Rev. 22:17:** And the Spirit and the bride say, "Come!" And let him who hears say, "Come!" And let him who thirsts come. Whoever desires, let him take the water of life freely. **See Matt. 5:6.**

9 **John 6:35:** And Jesus said to them, "I am the bread of life. He who comes to Me shall never hunger, and he who believes in Me shall never thirst." **See John 6:47-58.**

10 **John 1:16:** And of His fullness we have all received, and grace for grace.

11 **Phil. 3:9:** ... and be found in Him, not having my own righteousness, which *is* from the law, but that which *is* through faith in Christ, the righteousness which is from God by faith.

12 **Ps. 63:4-5:** Thus I will bless You while I live; I will lift up my hands in Your name. My soul shall be satisfied as with marrow and fatness, And my mouth shall praise *You* with joyful lips. **2 Chron. 30:21:** So the children of Israel who were present at Jerusalem kept the Feast of Unleavened Bread seven days with great gladness; and the Levites and the priests praised the LORD day by day, *singing* to the LORD, accompanied by loud instruments.

13 **Ps. 22:26:** The poor shall eat and be satisfied; Those who seek Him will praise the LORD. Let your heart live forever! **See 1 Cor. 10:16.**

14 **Jer. 50:5:** They shall ask the way to Zion, With their faces toward it, *saying,* 'Come and let us join ourselves to the LORD *In* a perpetual covenant *That* will not be forgotten.' **Ps. 50:5:** Gather My saints together to Me, Those who have made a covenant with Me by sacrifice.

15 **Acts 2:42:** And they continued steadfastly in the apostles' doctrine and fellowship, in the breaking of bread, and in prayers.

Q. 194. *What is the duty of Christians, after they have received the ordinance of the Lord's Supper?*

A. The duty of Christians, after they have received the ordinance of the Lord's Supper, is seriously to consider how they have behaved themselves therein, and with what success;[1] if they find quickening and comfort, to bless God for it,[2] beg the continuance of it,[3] watch against relapses,[4] fulfill their vows,[5] and encourage themselves to a frequent attendance on that ordinance:[6] but if they find no present benefit, more exactly to review their preparation to, and carriage at, the ordinance;[7] in both which, if they can approve themselves to God and their own consciences, they are to wait for the fruit of it in due time:[8] but, if they see they have failed in either, they are to be humbled,[9] and to attend upon it afterwards with more care and diligence.[10]

1 **Ps. 28:7:** The LORD *is* my strength and my shield; My heart trusted in Him, and I am helped; Therefore my heart greatly rejoices, And with my song I will praise Him. **Ps. 85:8:** I will hear what God the LORD will speak, For He will speak peace To His people and to His saints; But let them not turn back to folly. **1 Cor. 11:17, 30-31:** Now in giving these instructions I do not praise *you,* since you come together not for the better but for the worse.... For this reason many *are* weak and sick among you, and many sleep. For if we would judge ourselves, we would not be judged.

2 **2 Chron. 30:21-23, 25-26:** So the children of Israel who were present at Jerusalem kept the Feast of Unleavened Bread seven days with great gladness; and the Levites and the priests praised the LORD day by day, *singing* to the LORD, accompanied by loud instruments. And Hezekiah gave encouragement to all the Levites who taught the good knowledge of the LORD; and they ate throughout the feast seven days, offering peace offerings and making confession to the LORD God of their fathers. Then the whole assembly agreed to keep *the feast* another seven days, and they kept it *another* seven days with gladness.... The whole assembly of Judah rejoiced, also the priests and Levites, all the assembly that came from Israel, the sojourners who came from the land of Israel, and those who dwelt in Judah. So there was great joy in Jerusalem, for since the time of Solomon the son of David, king of Israel, *there had* been nothing like this in Jerusalem. **Acts 2:42, 46-47:** And they continued steadfastly in the apostles' doctrine and fellowship, in the breaking of bread, and in prayers.... So continuing daily with one accord in the temple, and breaking bread from house to house, they ate their food with gladness and simplicity of heart, praising God and having favor with all the people. And the Lord added to the church daily those who were being saved.

3 **Ps. 36:10:** Oh, continue Your lovingkindness to those who know You, And Your righteousness to the upright in heart. **Song 3:4:** Scarcely had I passed by them, When I found the one I love. I held him and would not let him go, Until I had brought him to the house of my mother, And into the chamber of her who conceived me. **1 Chron. 29:18:** O LORD God of Abraham, Isaac, and Israel, our fathers, keep this forever in the intent of the thoughts of the heart of Your people, and fix their heart toward You.

4 **1 Cor. 10:3-5, 12:** ... all ate the same spiritual food, and all drank the same spiritual drink. For they drank of that spiritual Rock that followed them, and that Rock was Christ. But with most of them God was not well pleased, for *their bodies* were scattered in the wilderness.... Therefore let him who thinks he stands take heed lest he fall.

5 **Ps. 50:14:** Offer to God thanksgiving, And pay your vows to the Most High.

6 **1 Cor. 11:25-26:** In the same manner *He* also *took* the cup after supper, saying, "This cup is the new covenant in My blood. This do, as often as you drink *it,* in remembrance of Me." For as often as you eat this bread and drink this cup, you proclaim the Lord's death till He comes. **Acts 2:42, 46:** And they continued steadfastly in the apostles' doctrine and fellowship, in the breaking of bread, and in prayers.... So continuing daily with one accord in the temple, and breaking bread from house to house, they ate their food with gladness and simplicity of heart.

7

Eccl. 5:1-6: Walk prudently when you go to the house of God; and draw near to hear rather than to give the sacrifice of fools, for they do not know that they do evil. Do not be rash with your mouth, And let not your heart utter anything hastily before God. For God *is* in heaven, and you on earth; Therefore let your words be few. For a dream comes through much activity, And a fool's voice *is known* by *his* many words. When you make a vow to God, do not delay to pay it; For *He has* no pleasure in fools. Pay what you have vowed— Better not to vow than to vow and not pay. Do not let your mouth cause your flesh to sin, nor say before the messenger *of God* that it *was* an error. Why should God be angry at your excuse and destroy the work of your hands? **Ps. 139:23-24:** Search me, O God, and know my heart; Try me, and know my anxieties; And see if *there is any* wicked way in me, And lead me in the way everlasting.

8

Ps. 123:1-2: Unto You I lift up my eyes, O You who dwell in the heavens. Behold, as the eyes of servants *look* to the hand of their masters, As the eyes of a maid to the hand of her mistress, So our eyes *look* to the LORD our God, Until He has mercy on us. **Ps. 42:5, 8:** Why are you cast down, O my soul? And *why* are you disquieted within me? Hope in God, for I shall yet praise Him *For* the help of His countenance.... The LORD will command His lovingkindness in the daytime, And in the night His song *shall be* with me— A prayer to the God of my life. **Ps. 43:3-5:** Oh, send out Your light and Your truth! Let them lead me; Let them bring me to Your holy hill And to Your tabernacle. Then I will go to the altar of God, To God my exceeding joy; And on the harp I will praise You, O God, my God. Why are you cast down, O my soul? And why are you disquieted within me? Hope in God; For I shall yet praise Him, The help of my countenance and my God.

9

2 Chron. 30:18-19: For a multitude of the people, many from Ephraim, Manasseh, Issachar, and Zebulun, had not cleansed themselves, yet they ate the Passover contrary to what was written. But Hezekiah prayed for them, saying, "May the good LORD provide atonement for everyone *who* prepares his heart to seek God, the LORD God of his fathers, though *he is* not *cleansed* according to the purification of the sanctuary."

10

2 Cor. 7:11: For observe this very thing, that you sorrowed in a godly manner: What diligence it produced in you, *what clearing of yourselves, what* indignation, *what* fear, *what* vehement desire, *what* zeal, *what* vindication! In all *things* you proved yourselves to be clear in this matter. **1 Chron. 15:12-14:** He said to them, "You *are* the heads of the fathers' *houses* of the Levites; sanctify yourselves, you and your brethren, that you may bring up the ark of the LORD God of Israel to *the place* I have prepared for it. For because you *did* not *do it* the first *time,* the LORD our God broke out against us, because we did not consult Him about the proper order." So the priests and the Levites sanctified themselves to bring up the ark of the LORD God of Israel.

Q. 195. *Wherein do the ordinances of baptism and the Lord's Supper agree?*

A. The ordinances of baptism and the Lord's Supper agree, in that they are to be administered only unto those who do actually profess repentance and faith,[1] that the author of both is God;[2] the spiritual part of both is Christ and His benefits;[3] both are visible and outward signs of the same covenant,[4] are to be dispensed by ministers of the gospel, and by none other;[5] and to be continued in the church of Christ until His second coming.[6]

1

Acts 2:38: Then Peter said to them, "Repent, and let every one of you be baptized in the name of Jesus Christ for the remission of sins; and you shall receive the gift of the Holy Spirit." **Matt. 3:6:** ... and were baptized by him in the Jordan, confessing their sins. **1 Cor. 11:27-28:** Therefore whoever eats this bread or drinks *this* cup of the Lord in an unworthy manner will be guilty of the body and blood of the Lord. But let a man examine himself, and so let him eat of the bread and drink of the cup.

2

Matt. 28:19: Go therefore and make disciples of all the nations, baptizing them in the name of the Father and of the Son and of the Holy Spirit. **1 Cor. 11:23:** For I received from the Lord that which I also delivered to you: that the Lord Jesus on the *same* night in which He was betrayed took bread.

3

Rom. 6:3-4: Or do you not know that as many of us as were baptized into Christ Jesus were baptized into His death? Therefore we were buried with Him through baptism into death, that just as

Christ was raised from the dead by the glory of the Father, even so we also should walk in newness of life. **1 Cor. 10:16:** The cup of blessing which we bless, is it not the communion of the blood of Christ? The bread which we break, is it not the communion of the body of Christ?

4 **Col. 2:12:** ... buried with Him in baptism, in which you also were raised with *Him* through faith in the working of God, who raised Him from the dead. **Matt. 26:27-28:** Then He took the cup, and gave thanks, and gave *it* to them, saying, "Drink from it, all of you. For this is My blood of the new covenant, which is shed for many for the remission of sins."

5 **John 1:33:** I did not know Him, but He who sent me to baptize with water said to me, 'Upon whom you see the Spirit descending, and remaining on Him, this is He who baptizes with the Holy Spirit.' **Matt. 28:19:** Go therefore and make disciples of all the nations, baptizing them in the name of the Father and of the Son and of the Holy Spirit. **1 Cor.11:23:** For I received from the Lord that which I also delivered to you: that the Lord Jesus on the *same* night in which He was betrayed took bread. **1 Cor. 4:1:** Let a man so consider us, as servants of Christ and stewards of the mysteries of God. **Heb. 5:4:** And no man takes this honor to himself, but he who is called by God, just as Aaron *was.*

6 **Matt. 28:19-20:** "Go therefore and make disciples of all the nations, baptizing them in the name of the Father and of the Son and of the Holy Spirit, teaching them to observe all things that I have commanded you; and lo, I am with you always, *even* to the end of the age." Amen. **1 Cor. 11:20, 23:** Therefore when you come together in one place, it is not to eat the Lord's Supper.... For I received from the Lord that which I also delivered to you: that the Lord Jesus on the *same* night in which He was betrayed took bread. **1 Cor. 4:1:** Let a man so consider us, as servants of Christ and stewards of the mysteries of God. **Eph. 4:11-12:** And He Himself gave some *to be* apostles, some prophets, some evangelists, and some pastors and teachers, for the equipping of the saints for the work of ministry, for the edifying of the body of Christ.

Q. 196. *Wherein do the ordinances of baptism and the Lord's Supper differ?*

A. The ordinances of baptism and the Lord's Supper differ, in that baptism is to be administered but once, with water, to be a covenant transaction with God and a sign of our ingrafting into Christ;[1] whereas the Lord's Supper is to be administered often, in the elements of bread and wine, to represent and exhibit Christ as spiritual nourishment to the soul,[2] and to confirm our union and communion with Him;[3] although both are visible and outward signs of the New Covenant,[4] yet the Lord's Supper is the only express token thereof.[5]

1 **Matt. 3:11:** I indeed baptize you with water unto repentance, but He who is coming after me is mightier than I, whose sandals I am not worthy to carry. He will baptize you with the Holy Spirit and fire. **Rom. 6:3-5:** Or do you not know that as many of us as were baptized into Christ Jesus were baptized into His death? Therefore we were buried with Him through baptism into death, that just as Christ was raised from the dead by the glory of the Father, even so we also should walk in newness of life. For if we have been united together in the likeness of His death, certainly we also shall be *in the likeness* of *His* resurrection. **Gal. 3:27:** For as many of you as were baptized into Christ have put on Christ.

2 **1 Cor. 11:23-26:** For I received from the Lord that which I also delivered to you: that the Lord Jesus on the *same* night in which He was betrayed took bread; and when He had given thanks, He broke *it* and said, "Take, eat; this is My body which is broken for you; do this in remembrance of Me." In the same manner *He* also *took* the cup after supper, saying, "This cup is the new covenant in My blood. This do, as often as you drink *it,* in remembrance of Me." For as often as you eat this bread and drink this cup, you proclaim the Lord's death till He comes.

3 **1 Cor. 10:16-17:** The cup of blessing which we bless, is it not the communion of the blood of Christ? The bread which we break, is it not the communion of the body of Christ? For we, *though* many, are one bread *and* one body; for we all partake of that one bread.

4 **Acts 2:38:** Then Peter said to them, "Repent, and let every one of you be baptized in the name of

Jesus Christ for the remission of sins; and you shall receive the gift of the Holy Spirit." **Acts 10:47:** "Can anyone forbid water, that these should not be baptized who have received the Holy Spirit just as we have?" **1 Cor. 11:23-26:** For I received from the Lord that which I also delivered to you: that the Lord Jesus on the same night in which He was betrayed took bread; and when He had given thanks, He broke it and said, "Take, eat; this is My body which is broken for you; do this in remembrance of Me." In the same manner He also took the cup after supper, saying, "This cup is the new covenant in My blood. This do, as often as you drink it, in remembrance of Me." For as often as you eat this bread and drink this cup, you proclaim the Lord's death till He comes.

5 **Luke 22:20:** Likewise He also *took* the cup after supper, saying, "This cup *is* the new covenant in My blood, which is shed for you.

Q. 197. *What is prayer?*

A. Prayer is an offering up of our desires unto God,[1] in the name of Christ,[2] by the help of His Spirit;[3] with confession of our sins,[4] and thankful acknowledgement of His mercies.[5]

1 **Ps. 10:17:** LORD, You have heard the desire of the humble; You will prepare their heart; You will cause Your ear to hear. **Ps. 62:8:** Trust in Him at all times, you people; Pour out your heart before Him; God *is* a refuge for us. **Matt. 7:7-8:** Ask, and it will be given to you; seek, and you will find; knock, and it will be opened to you. For everyone who asks receives, and he who seeks finds, and to him who knocks it will be opened.

2 **John 16:23:** And in that day you will ask Me nothing. Most assuredly, I say to you, whatever you ask the Father in My name He will give you.

3 **Rom. 8:26:** Likewise the Spirit also helps in our weaknesses. For we do not know what we should pray for as we ought, but the Spirit Himself makes intercession for us with groanings which cannot be uttered.

4 **Ps. 32:5-6:** I acknowledged my sin to You, And my iniquity I have not hidden. I said, "I will confess my transgressions to the LORD," And You forgave the iniquity of my sin. *Selah.* For this cause everyone who is godly shall pray to You In a time when You may be found; Surely in a flood of great waters They shall not come near him. **1 John 1:9:** If we confess our sins, He is faithful and just to forgive us *our* sins and to cleanse us from all unrighteousness. **See Dan. 9:4-19.**

5 **Phil. 4:6:** Be anxious for nothing, but in everything by prayer and supplication, with thanksgiving, let your requests be made known to God. **Ps. 103:1-5:** Bless the LORD, O my soul; And all that is within me, *bless* His holy name! Bless the LORD, O my soul, And forget not all His benefits: Who forgives all your iniquities, Who heals all your diseases, Who redeems your life from destruction, Who crowns you with lovingkindness and tender mercies, Who satisfies your mouth with good *things, So that* your youth is renewed like the eagle's. **See Ps. 136.**

Q. 198. *Are we to pray unto God only?*

A. God only being able to search the hearts,[1] hear the requests,[2] pardon the sins,[3] and fulfill the desires of all;[4] and only to be believed in,[5] and worshiped with religious worship;[6] prayer, which is a special part thereof,[7] is to be made by all to Him alone,[8] and to none other.[9]

1 **1 Kings 8:39:** ... then hear in heaven Your dwelling place, and forgive, and act, and give to everyone according to all his ways, whose heart You know (for You alone know the hearts of all the sons of men). **Acts 1:24:** And they prayed and said, "You, O Lord, who know the hearts of all, show which of these two You have chosen." **Rom. 8:27:** Now He who searches the hearts knows what the mind of the Spirit *is,* because He makes intercession for the saints according to *the will of* God.

2 **Ps. 65:2:** O You who hear prayer, To You all flesh will come.

3
Mic. 7:18: Who *is* a God like You, Pardoning iniquity And passing over the transgression of the remnant of His heritage? He does not retain His anger forever, Because He delights *in* mercy.
4
Ps. 145:18: The LORD *is* near to all who call upon Him, To all who call upon Him in truth.
5
Rom. 10:14: How then shall they call on Him in whom they have not believed? And how shall they believe in Him of whom they have not heard? And how shall they hear without a preacher?
6
Matt. 4:10: Then Jesus said to him, "Away with you, Satan! For it is written, 'You shall worship the LORD your God, and Him only you shall serve.'"
7
1 Cor. 1:2: To the church of God which is at Corinth, to those who are sanctified in Christ Jesus, called *to be* saints, with all who in every place call on the name of Jesus Christ our Lord, both theirs and ours.
8
Isa. 45:22: Look to Me, and be saved, All you ends of the earth! For I *am* God, and *there is* no other. **Matt. 6:9:** In this manner, therefore, pray: Our Father in heaven, Hallowed be Your name. **Ps. 50:15:** Call upon Me in the day of trouble; I will deliver you, and you shall glorify Me.
9
Isa. 43:11: I, *even* I, *am* the LORD, And besides Me *there is* no savior. **Isa. 46:9:** Remember the former things of old, For I *am* God, and *there is* no other; *I am* God, and *there is* none like Me. **See Isa. 46.**

Q. 199. *What is it to pray in the name of Christ?*

A. To pray in the name of Christ is, in obedience to His command, and in confidence on His promises, to ask mercy for His sake;[1] not by bare mentioning of His name,[2] but by drawing our encouragement to pray, and our boldness, strength, and hope of acceptance in prayer, from Christ and His mediation.[3]

1
John 14:13-14: And whatever you ask in My name, that I will do, that the Father may be glorified in the Son. If you ask anything in My name, I will do *it.* **John 16:24:** Until now you have asked nothing in My name. Ask, and you will receive, that your joy may be full. **Dan. 9:17:** Now therefore, our God, hear the prayer of Your servant, and his supplications, and for the Lord's sake cause Your face to shine on Your sanctuary, which is desolate.
2
Matt. 7:21: Not everyone who says to Me, 'Lord, Lord,' shall enter the kingdom of heaven, but he who does the will of My Father in heaven.
3
Heb. 4:14-16: Seeing then that we have a great High Priest who has passed through the heavens, Jesus the Son of God, let us hold fast *our* confession. For we do not have a High Priest who cannot sympathize with our weaknesses, but was in all *points* tempted as *we are, yet* without sin. Let us therefore come boldly to the throne of grace, that we may obtain mercy and find grace to help in time of need. **1 John 5:13-15:** These things I have written to you who believe in the name of the Son of God, that you may know that you have eternal life, and that you may *continue to* believe in the name of the Son of God. Now this is the confidence that we have in Him, that if we ask anything according to His will, He hears us. And if we know that He hears us, whatever we ask, we know that we have the petitions that we have asked of Him.

Q. 200. *Why are we to pray in the name of Christ?*

A. The sinfulness of man, and his distance from God by reason thereof, being so great, as that we can have no access into His presence without a Mediator;[1] and there being none in heaven or earth appointed to, or fit for, that glorious work but Christ alone,[2] we are to pray in no other name but His only.[3]

1
John 14:6: Jesus said to him, "I am the way, the truth, and the life. No one comes to the Father except through Me." **Isa. 59:2:** But your iniquities have separated you from your God; And your sins have hidden *His* face from you, So that He will not hear. **Eph. 3:12:** ... in whom we have boldness and access with confidence through faith in Him.
2
John 6:27: Do not labor for the food which perishes, but for the food which endures to everlasting life, which the Son of Man will give you, because God the Father has set His seal on Him. **Heb. 7:25-27:** Therefore He is also able to save to the uttermost those who come to God through Him, since He always lives to make intercession for them. For such a High Priest was fitting for us, *who is* holy, harmless, undefiled, separate from sinners, and has become higher than the heavens; who does not need daily, as those high priests, to offer up sacrifices, first for His own sins and then for the people's, for this He did once for all when He offered up Himself. **1 Tim. 2:5:** For *there is* one God and one Mediator between God and men, *the* Man Christ Jesus.
3
Col. 3:17: And whatever you do in word or deed, *do* all in the name of the Lord Jesus, giving thanks to God the Father through Him. **Heb. 13:15:** Therefore by Him let us continually offer the sacrifice of praise to God, that is, the fruit of *our* lips, giving thanks to His name.

Q. 201. *How doth the Spirit help us to pray?*

A. We not knowing what to pray for as we ought, the Spirit helpeth our infirmities, by enabling us to understand both for whom, and what, and how prayer is to be made; and by working and quickening in our hearts (although not in all persons, nor at all times, in the same measure) those apprehensions, affections, and graces which are requisite for the right performance of that duty.[1]

1
Rom. 8:26-27: Likewise the Spirit also helps in our weaknesses. For we do not know what we should pray for as we ought, but the Spirit Himself makes intercession for us with groanings which cannot be uttered. Now He who searches the hearts knows what the mind of the Spirit *is,* because He makes intercession for the saints according to *the will of* God. **Ps. 10:17:** LORD, You have heard the desire of the humble; You will prepare their heart; You will cause Your ear to hear. **Zech. 12:10:** And I will pour on the house of David and on the inhabitants of Jerusalem the Spirit of grace and supplication; then they will look on Me whom they pierced. Yes, they will mourn for Him as one mourns for *his* only *son,* and grieve for Him as one grieves for a firstborn.

Q. 202. *For whom are we to pray?*

A. We are to pray for the whole church of Christ upon earth;[1] for magistrates,[2] and ministers;[3] for ourselves,[4] our brethren,[5] yea, our enemies;[6] and for all sorts of men living,[7] or that shall live hereafter;[8] but not for the dead,[9] nor for those that are known to have sinned the sin unto death.[10]

1
Eph. 6:18: ... praying always with all prayer and supplication in the Spirit, being watchful to this end with all perseverance and supplication for all the saints. **Ps. 28:9:** Save Your people, And bless Your inheritance; Shepherd them also, And bear them up forever.
2
1 Tim. 2:1-2: Therefore I exhort first of all that supplications, prayers, intercessions, *and* giving of thanks be made for all men, for kings and all who are in authority, that we may lead a quiet and peaceable life in all godliness and reverence.
3
Col. 4:3: ... meanwhile praying also for us, that God would open to us a door for the word, to speak the mystery of Christ, for which I am also in chains.

4
Gen. 32:11: Deliver me, I pray, from the hand of my brother, from the hand of Esau; for I fear him, lest he come and attack me *and* the mother with the children.
5
James 5:16: Confess *your* trespasses to one another, and pray for one another, that you may be healed. The effective, fervent prayer of a righteous man avails much.
6
Matt. 5:44: But I say to you, love your enemies, bless those who curse you, do good to those who hate you, and pray for those who spitefully use you and persecute you.
7
1 Tim. 2:1-2: Therefore I exhort first of all that supplications, prayers, intercessions, *and* giving of thanks be made for all men, for kings and all who are in authority, that we may lead a quiet and peaceable life in all godliness and reverence.
8
John 17:20: I do not pray for these alone, but also for those who will believe in Me through their word. **2 Sam. 7:29:** Now therefore, let it please You to bless the house of Your servant, that it may continue before You forever; for You, O Lord GOD, have spoken *it,* and with Your blessing let the house of Your servant be blessed forever.
9
2 Sam. 12:21-23: Then his servants said to him, "What *is* this that you have done? You fasted and wept for the child *while he was* alive, but when the child died, you arose and ate food." And he said, "While the child was alive, I fasted and wept; for I said, 'Who can tell *whether* the LORD will be gracious to me, that the child may live?' But now he is dead; why should I fast? Can I bring him back again? I shall go to him, but he shall not return to me."
10
1 John 5:16: If anyone sees his brother sinning a sin *which does* not *lead* to death, he will ask, and He will give him life for those who commit sin not *leading* to death. There is sin *leading* to death. I do not say that he should pray about that.

Q. 203. *For what things are we to pray?*

A. We are to pray for all things tending to the glory of God,[1] the welfare of the church,[2] our own[3] or others' good;[4] but not for anything that is unlawful.[5]

1
Matt. 6:9: Our Father in heaven, Hallowed be Your name.
2
Ps. 51:18: Do good in Your good pleasure to Zion; Build the walls of Jerusalem. **PS. 122:6:** Pray for the peace of Jerusalem: "May they prosper who love you."
3
Matt. 7:11: If you then, being evil, know how to give good gifts to your children, how much more will your Father who is in heaven give good things to those who ask Him!
4
Ps. 125:4: Do good, O LORD, to *those who are* good, And to *those who are* upright in their hearts.
5
1 John 5:14: Now this is the confidence that we have in Him, that if we ask anything according to His will, He hears us.

Q. 204. *How are we to pray?*

A. We are to pray with an awful apprehension of the majesty of God,[1] and deep sense of our own unworthiness,[2] necessities,[3] and sins;[4] with penitent,[5] thankful,[6] and enlarged hearts;[7] with understanding,[8] faith,[9] sincerity,[10] fervency,[11] love,[12] and perseverance,[13] waiting upon Him,[14] with humble submission to His will.[15]

1
Ps. 33:8: Let all the earth fear the LORD; Let all the inhabitants of the world stand in awe of Him. **Ps. 95:6:** Oh come, let us worship and bow down; Let us kneel before the LORD our Maker. **Ps.**

145:5: I will meditate on the glorious splendor of Your majesty, And on Your wondrous works.

2 **Gen. 18:27:** Then Abraham answered and said, "Indeed now, I who *am but* dust and ashes have taken it upon myself to speak to the Lord. **Gen. 32:10:** I am not worthy of the least of all the mercies and of all the truth which You have shown Your servant; for I crossed over this Jordan with my staff, and now I have become two companies.

3 **Luke 15:17-19:** But when he came to himself, he said, 'How many of my father's hired servants have bread enough and to spare, and I perish with hunger! I will arise and go to my father, and will say to him, "Father, I have sinned against heaven and before you, and I am no longer worthy to be called your son. Make me like one of your hired servants."'

4 **Luke 18:13-14:** And the tax collector, standing afar off, would not so much as raise *his* eyes to heaven, but beat his breast, saying, 'God, be merciful to me a sinner!' I tell you, this man went down to his house justified *rather* than the other; for everyone who exalts himself will be humbled, and he who humbles himself will be exalted.

5 **Ps. 51:17:** The sacrifices of God *are* a broken spirit, A broken and a contrite heart— These, O God, You will not despise.

6 **Phil. 4:6:** Be anxious for nothing, but in everything by prayer and supplication, with thanksgiving, let your requests be made known to God.

7 **1 Sam. 1:15:** But Hannah answered and said, "No, my lord, I *am* a woman of sorrowful spirit. I have drunk neither wine nor intoxicating drink, but have poured out my soul before the LORD. **1 Sam. 2:1:** And Hannah prayed and said: "My heart rejoices in the LORD; My horn is exalted in the LORD. I smile at my enemies, Because I rejoice in Your salvation.

8 **1 Cor. 14:15:** What is *the conclusion* then? I will pray with the spirit, and I will also pray with the understanding. I will sing with the spirit, and I will also sing with the understanding.

9 **Mark 11:24:** Therefore I say to you, whatever things you ask when you pray, believe that you receive *them,* and you will have *them.* **James 1:6:** But let him ask in faith, with no doubting, for he who doubts is like a wave of the sea driven and tossed by the wind.

10 **Ps. 145:18:** The LORD *is* near to all who call upon Him, To all who call upon Him in truth. **Ps. 17:1:** Hear a just cause, O LORD, Attend to my cry; Give ear to my prayer *which is* not from deceitful lips.

11 **James 5:16:** Confess *your* trespasses to one another, and pray for one another, that you may be healed. The effective, fervent prayer of a righteous man avails much.

12 **Ps. 116:1-2:** I love the LORD, because He has heard My voice *and* my supplications. Because He has inclined His ear to me, Therefore I will call *upon Him* as long as I live. **Rom. 15:30:** Now I beg you, brethren, through the Lord Jesus Christ, and through the love of the Spirit, that you strive together with me in prayers to God for me.

13 **Eph. 6:18:** ... praying always with all prayer and supplication in the Spirit, being watchful to this end with all perseverance and supplication for all the saints.

14 **Mic. 7:7:** Therefore I will look to the LORD; I will wait for the God of my salvation; My God will hear me.

15 **Matt. 26:39:** He went a little farther and fell on His face, and prayed, saying, "O My Father, if it is possible, let this cup pass from Me; nevertheless, not as I will, but as You *will.*"

Q. 205. *What rule hath God given for our direction in the duty of prayer?*

A. The whole word of God is of use to direct us in the duty of prayer;[1] but the special rule of direction is that form of prayer which our Savior Christ taught His disciples, commonly called *The Lord's Prayer.*[2]

1 **1 John 5:14:** Now this is the confidence that we have in Him, that if we ask anything according to

His will, He hears us.

[2] **Matt. 6:9-13:** In this manner, therefore, pray: Our Father in heaven, Hallowed be Your name. Your kingdom come. Your will be done On earth as *it is* in heaven. Give us this day our daily bread. And forgive us our debts, As we forgive our debtors. And do not lead us into temptation, But deliver us from the evil one. For Yours is the kingdom and the power and the glory forever. Amen. **Luke 11:2-4:** So He said to them, "When you pray, say: Our Father in heaven, Hallowed be Your name. Your kingdom come. Your will be done On earth as *it is* in heaven. Give us day by day our daily bread. And forgive us our sins, For we also forgive everyone who is indebted to us. And do not lead us into temptation, But deliver us from the evil one."

Q. 206. *How is the Lord's Prayer to be used?*

A. The Lord's Prayer is not only for direction, as a pattern, according to which we are to make other prayers; but may also be used as a prayer, so that it be done with understanding, faith, reverence, and other graces necessary to the right performance of the duty of prayer.[1]

[1] **Matt. 6:9:** In this manner, therefore, pray: Our Father in heaven, Hallowed be Your name. **Luke 11:2:** So He said to them, "When you pray, say: Our Father in heaven, Hallowed be Your name. Your kingdom come. Your will be done On earth as *it is* in heaven."

Q. 207. *Of how many parts doth the Lord's Prayer consist?*

A. The Lord's Prayer consists of three parts; a preface, petitions, and a conclusion.[1]

[1] **Matt. 6:9-13:** In this manner, therefore, pray: Our Father in heaven, Hallowed be Your name. Your kingdom come. Your will be done On earth as *it is* in heaven. Give us this day our daily bread. And forgive us our debts, As we forgive our debtors. And do not lead us into temptation, But deliver us from the evil one. For Yours is the kingdom and the power and the glory forever. Amen.

Q. 208. *What doth the preface of the Lord's Prayer teach us?*

A. The preface of the Lord's Prayer (contained in these words, *Our Father which art in heaven*)[1] teacheth us, when we pray, to draw near to God with confidence of His fatherly goodness, and our interest therein;[2] with reverence, and all other childlike dispositions,[3] heavenly affections,[4] and due apprehensions of His sovereign power, majesty, and gracious condescension:[5] as also, to pray with and for others.[6]

[1] **Matt. 6:9:** In this manner, therefore, pray: Our Father in heaven, Hallowed be Your name. **Cf. Luke 11:2.**

[2] **Ps. 103:13:** As a father pities *his* children, *So* the LORD pities those who fear Him. **Luke 11:13:** If you then, being evil, know how to give good gifts to your children, how much more will *your* heavenly Father give the Holy Spirit to those who ask Him! **Rom. 8:15:** For you did not receive the spirit of bondage again to fear, but you received the Spirit of adoption by whom we cry out, "Abba, Father."

[3] **Isa. 64:9:** Do not be furious, O LORD, Nor remember iniquity forever; Indeed, please look—we all

are Your people!

[4] **Col. 3:1-2:** If then you were raised with Christ, seek those things which are above, where Christ is, sitting at the right hand of God. Set your mind on things above, not on things on the earth. **Ps. 123:1:** Unto You I lift up my eyes, O You who dwell in the heavens. **Lam. 3:41:** Let us lift our hearts and hands To God in heaven.

[5] **Isa. 63:15-16:** Look down from heaven, And see from Your habitation, holy and glorious. Where *are* Your zeal and Your strength, The yearning of Your heart and Your mercies toward me? Are they restrained? Doubtless You *are* our Father, Though Abraham was ignorant of us, And Israel does not acknowledge us. You, O LORD, *are* our Father; Our Redeemer from Everlasting *is* Your name. **Neh. 1:4-6:** So it was, when I heard these words, that I sat down and wept, and mourned *for many* days; I was fasting and praying before the God of heaven. And I said: "I pray, LORD God of heaven, O great and awesome God, *You* who keep *Your* covenant and mercy with those who love You and observe Your commandments, please let Your ear be attentive and Your eyes open, that You may hear the prayer of Your servant which I pray before You now, day and night, for the children of Israel Your servants, and confess the sins of the children of Israel which we have sinned against You. Both my father's house and I have sinned. **See Ps. 113:4-6.**

[6] **Acts 12:5:** Peter was therefore kept in prison, but constant prayer was offered to God for him by the church. **1 Tim. 2:1-2:** Therefore I exhort first of all that supplications, prayers, intercessions, *and* giving of thanks be made for all men, for kings and all who are in authority, that we may lead a quiet and peaceable life in all godliness and reverence. **Eph. 6:18:** ... praying always with all prayer and supplication in the Spirit, being watchful to this end with all perseverance and supplication for all the saints.

Q. 209. *What do we pray for in the first petition?*

A. In the first petition (which is, *Hallowed be thy name*),[1] acknowledging the utter inability and indisposition that is in ourselves and all men to honour God aright,[2] we pray, that God would by His grace enable and incline us and others to know, to acknowledge, and highly to esteem Him,[3] His titles,[4] attributes,[5] ordinances, word,[6] works, and whatsoever He is pleased to make Himself known by[7]; and to glorify Him in thought, word,[8] and deed:[9] that He would prevent and remove atheism,[10] ignorance,[11] idolatry,[12] profaneness,[13] and whatsoever is dishonourable to Him;[14] and, by His overruling providence, direct and dispose of all things to His own glory.[15]

[1] **Matt. 6:9:** In this manner, therefore, pray: Our Father in heaven, Hallowed be Your name. **Cf. Luke 11:2.**

[2] **2 Cor. 3:5:** Not that we are sufficient of ourselves to think of anything as *being* from ourselves, but our sufficiency *is* from God. **Ps. 51:15:** O Lord, open my lips, And my mouth shall show forth Your praise.

[3] **Ps. 67:2-3:** That Your way may be known on earth, Your salvation among all nations. Let the peoples praise You, O God; Let all the peoples praise You. **Ps. 99:1-3:** The LORD reigns; Let the peoples tremble! He dwells *between* the cherubim; Let the earth be moved! The LORD *is* great in Zion, And He *is* high above all the peoples. Let them praise Your great and awesome name— He *is* holy.

[4] **Ps. 83:18:** That they may know that You, whose name alone *is* the LORD, *Are* the Most High over all the earth.

[5] **Ps. 86:10-13, 15:** For You *are* great, and do wondrous things; You alone *are* God. Teach me Your way, O LORD; I will walk in Your truth; Unite my heart to fear Your name. I will praise You, O Lord my God, with all my heart, And I will glorify Your name forevermore. For great *is* Your mercy toward

me, And You have delivered my soul from the depths of Sheol.... But You, O Lord, *are* a God full of compassion, and gracious, Longsuffering and abundant in mercy and truth.

6

2 Thess. 3:1: Finally, brethren, pray for us, that the word of the Lord may run *swiftly* and be glorified, just as *it is* with you. **Ps. 147:19-20:** He declares His word to Jacob, His statutes and His judgments to Israel. He has not dealt thus with any nation; And *as for His* judgments, they have not known them. Praise the LORD! **Ps. 138:1-3:** I will praise You with my whole heart; Before the gods I will sing praises to You. I will worship toward Your holy temple, And praise Your name For Your lovingkindness and Your truth; For You have magnified Your word above all Your name. In the day when I cried out, You answered me, *And* made me bold *with* strength in my soul. **2 Cor. 2:14-15:** Now thanks *be* to God who always leads us in triumph in Christ, and through us diffuses the fragrance of His knowledge in every place. For we are to God the fragrance of Christ among those who are being saved and among those who are perishing.

7

Ps. 145: I will extol You, my God, O King; And I will bless Your name forever and ever. Every day I will bless You, And I will praise Your name forever and ever.... **Ps. 8:** O LORD, our Lord, How excellent *is* Your name in all the earth, Who have set Your glory above the heavens....

8

Ps. 103:1: Bless the LORD, O my soul; And all that is within me, *bless* His holy name! **Ps. 19:14:** Let the words of my mouth and the meditation of my heart Be acceptable in Your sight, O LORD, my strength and my Redeemer.

9

Phil. 1:9, 11: And this I pray, that your love may abound still more and more in knowledge and all discernment ... being filled with the fruits of righteousness which *are* by Jesus Christ, to the glory and praise of God. **Ps. 100:3-4:** Know that the LORD, He *is* God; *It is* He *who* has made us, and not we ourselves; *We are* His people and the sheep of His pasture. Enter into His gates with thanksgiving, *And* into His courts with praise. Be thankful to Him, *and* bless His name.

10

Ps. 67:1-4: God be merciful to us and bless us, *And* cause His face to shine upon us, *Selah*. That Your way may be known on earth, Your salvation among all nations. Let the peoples praise You, O God; Let all the peoples praise You. Oh, let the nations be glad and sing for joy! For You shall judge the people righteously, And govern the nations on earth. *Selah*.

11

Eph. 1:17-18: ... that the God of our Lord Jesus Christ, the Father of glory, may give to you the spirit of wisdom and revelation in the knowledge of Him, the eyes of your understanding being enlightened; that you may know what is the hope of His calling, what are the riches of the glory of His inheritance in the saints.

12

Ps. 97:7: Let all be put to shame who serve carved images, Who boast of idols. Worship Him, all *you* gods.

13

Ps. 74:18, 22-23: Remember this, *that* the enemy has reproached, O LORD, And *that* a foolish people has blasphemed Your name.... Arise, O God, plead Your own cause; Remember how the foolish man reproaches You daily. Do not forget the voice of Your enemies; The tumult of those who rise up against You increases continually.

14

2 Kings 19:15-16: Then Hezekiah prayed before the LORD, and said: "O LORD God of Israel, *the One* who dwells *between* the cherubim, You are God, You alone, of all the kingdoms of the earth. You have made heaven and earth. Incline Your ear, O LORD, and hear; open Your eyes, O LORD, and see; and hear the words of Sennacherib, which he has sent to reproach the living God.

15

2 Chron. 20:6: ... and said: "O LORD God of our fathers, *are* You not God in heaven, and do You *not* rule over all the kingdoms of the nations, and in Your hand *is there not* power and might, so that no one is able to withstand You? **See 2 Chron. 20:10-12. Rom. 11:33-36:** Oh, the depth of the riches both of the wisdom and knowledge of God! How unsearchable *are* His judgments and His ways past finding out! "For who has known the mind of the Lord? Or who has become His counselor?" "Or who has first given to Him And it shall be repaid to him?" For of Him and through Him and to Him *are* all things, to whom *be* glory forever. Amen. **Rev. 4:11:** You are worthy, O Lord, To receive glory and honor and power; For You created all things, And by Your will they exist and were created. **See Ps. 83, 140:4, 8.**

Q. 210. *What do we pray for in the second petition?*

A. In the second petition (which is, *Thy kingdom come*),[1] acknowledging ourselves and all mankind to be by nature under the dominion of sin and Satan,[2] we pray, that the kingdom of sin and Satan may be destroyed,[3] the gospel propagated throughout the world,[4] the Jews called,[5] the fullness of the Gentiles brought in;[6] the church furnished with all gospel officers and ordinances,[7] purged from corruption,[8] countenanced and maintained by the common suffrage of the church:[9] that the ordinances of Christ may be purely dispensed, and made effectual to the converting of those that are yet in their sins, and the confirming, comforting, and building up of those that are already converted:[10] that Christ would rule in our hearts here,[11] and hasten the time of His second coming, and our reigning with Him forever:[12] and that He would be pleased so to exercise the kingdom of His power in all the world, as may best conduce to these ends.[13]

1 **Matt. 6:10:** Your kingdom come. Your will be done On earth as *it is* in heaven. **Cf. Luke 11:2.**

2 **Eph. 2:2-3:** ... in which you once walked according to the course of this world, according to the prince of the power of the air, the spirit who now works in the sons of disobedience, among whom also we all once conducted ourselves in the lusts of our flesh, fulfilling the desires of the flesh and of the mind, and were by nature children of wrath, just as the others.

3 **Ps. 68:1, 18:** Let God arise, Let His enemies be scattered; Let those also who hate Him flee before Him.... You have ascended on high, You have led captivity captive; You have received gifts among men, Even *from* the rebellious, That the LORD God might dwell *there.* **Rev. 12:10-11:** Then I heard a loud voice saying in heaven, "Now salvation, and strength, and the kingdom of our God, and the power of His Christ have come, for the accuser of our brethren, who accused them before our God day and night, has been cast down. And they overcame him by the blood of the Lamb and by the word of their testimony, and they did not love their lives to the death."

4 **Ps. 67:1-2:** God be merciful to us and bless us, *And* cause His face to shine upon us, *Selah*. That Your way may be known on earth, Your salvation among all nations. **2 Thess. 3:1:** Finally, brethren, pray for us, that the word of the Lord may run *swiftly* and be glorified, just as *it is* with you.

5 **Rom. 10:1:** Brethren, my heart's desire and prayer to God for Israel is that they may be saved.

6 **John 17:9, 20:** I pray for them. I do not pray for the world but for those whom You have given Me, for they are Yours.... I do not pray for these alone, but also for those who will believe in Me through their word. **Rom. 11:25-26:** For I do not desire, brethren, that you should be ignorant of this mystery, lest you should be wise in your own opinion, that blindness in part has happened to Israel until the fullness of the Gentiles has come in. And so all Israel will be saved, as it is written: "The Deliverer will come out of Zion, And He will turn away ungodliness from Jacob." **See Ps. 67.**

7 **Matt. 9:38:** Therefore pray the Lord of the harvest to send out laborers into His harvest. **2 Thess. 3:1:** Finally, brethren, pray for us, that the word of the Lord may run *swiftly* and be glorified, just as *it is* with you.

8 **Mal. 1:11:** For from the rising of the sun, even to its going down, My name *shall be* great among the Gentiles; In every place incense *shall be* offered to My name, And a pure offering; For My name shall be great among the nations," Says the LORD of hosts. **Zeph. 3:9:** For then I will restore to the peoples a pure language, That they all may call on the name of the LORD, To serve Him with one accord.

9 **Acts 6:1-7:** Now in those days, when *the number of* the disciples was multiplying, there arose a complaint against the Hebrews by the Hellenists, because their widows were neglected in the daily distribution. Then the twelve summoned the multitude of the disciples and said, "It is not desirable that we should leave the word of God and serve tables. Therefore, brethren, seek out from among you seven men of *good* reputation, full of the Holy Spirit and wisdom, whom we may appoint over this business; but we will give ourselves continually to prayer and to the ministry of the word." And the saying pleased the whole multitude. And they chose Stephen, a man full of faith and the Holy Spirit, and Philip, Prochorus, Nicanor, Timon, Parmenas, and Nicolas, a proselyte from Antioch,

whom they set before the apostles; and when they had prayed, they laid hands on them. Then the word of God spread, and the number of the disciples multiplied greatly in Jerusalem, and a great many of the priests were obedient to the faith. **Acts 14:23:** So when they had appointed elders in every church, and prayed with fasting, they commended them to the Lord in whom they had believed.

10

Acts 4:29-30: Now, Lord, look on their threats, and grant to Your servants that with all boldness they may speak Your word, by stretching out Your hand to heal, and that signs and wonders may be done through the name of Your holy Servant Jesus. **Eph. 6:18-20:** ... praying always with all prayer and supplication in the Spirit, being watchful to this end with all perseverance and supplication for all the saints— and for me, that utterance may be given to me, that I may open my mouth boldly to make known the mystery of the gospel, for which I am an ambassador in chains; that in it I may speak boldly, as I ought to speak. **Rom. 15:29-30, 32:** But I know that when I come to you, I shall come in the fullness of the blessing of the gospel of Christ. Now I beg you, brethren, through the Lord Jesus Christ, and through the love of the Spirit, that you strive together with me in prayers to God for me.... that I may come to you with joy by the will of God, and may be refreshed together with you. **2 Thess. 1:11:** Therefore we also pray always for you that our God would count you worthy of *this* calling, and fulfill all the good pleasure of *His* goodness and the work of faith with power. **2 Thess. 2:16-17:** Now may our Lord Jesus Christ Himself, and our God and Father, who has loved us and given *us* everlasting consolation and good hope by grace, comfort your hearts and establish you in every good word and work.

11

Eph. 3:14-20: For this reason I bow my knees to the Father of our Lord Jesus Christ, from whom the whole family in heaven and earth is named, that He would grant you, according to the riches of His glory, to be strengthened with might through His Spirit in the inner man, that Christ may dwell in your hearts through faith; that you, being rooted and grounded in love, may be able to comprehend with all the saints what *is* the width and length and depth and height— to know the love of Christ which passes knowledge; that you may be filled with all the fullness of God. Now to Him who is able to do exceedingly abundantly above all that we ask or think, according to the power that works in us. **Col. 3:15:** And let the peace of God rule in your hearts, to which also you were called in one body; and be thankful.

12

Rev. 22:20: He who testifies to these things says, "Surely I am coming quickly." Amen. Even so, come, Lord Jesus! **2 Tim. 2:12:** If we endure, We shall also reign with *Him.* If we deny *Him,* He also will deny us. **2 Pet. 3:12:** ... looking for and hastening the coming of the day of God, because of which the heavens will be dissolved, being on fire, and the elements will melt with fervent heat?

13

Isa. 64:1-2: Oh, that You would rend the heavens! That You would come down! That the mountains might shake at Your presence— As fire burns brushwood, As fire causes water to boil— To make Your name known to Your adversaries, *That* the nations may tremble at Your presence! **Rev. 4:8-11:** *The* four living creatures, each having six wings, were full of eyes around and within. And they do not rest day or night, saying: "Holy, holy, holy, Lord God Almighty, Who was and is and is to come!" Whenever the living creatures give glory and honor and thanks to Him who sits on the throne, who lives forever and ever, the twenty-four elders fall down before Him who sits on the throne and worship Him who lives forever and ever, and cast their crowns before the throne, saying: "You are worthy, O Lord, To receive glory and honor and power; For You created all things, And by Your will they exist and were created."

Q. 211. *What do we pray for in the third petition?*

A. In the third petition (which is, *Thy will be done in earth, as it is in heaven*),[1] acknowledging, that by nature we and all men are not only utterly unable and unwilling to know and do the will of God,[2] but prone to rebel against His word,[3] to repine and murmur against His providence,[4] and wholly inclined to do the will of the flesh, and of the devil:[5] we pray, that God would by His Spirit take away from ourselves and others all blindness,[6] weakness,[7] indisposition,[8] and perverseness of heart;[9] and by His grace make us able and willing to know, do, and submit to His will in all things,[10] with the like humility,[11] cheerfulness,[12] faithfulness,[13] diligence,[14] zeal,[15] sincerity,[16] and constancy,[17] as the angels do in heaven.[18]

1
Matt. 6:10: Your kingdom come. Your will be done On earth as *it is* in heaven. **Cf. Luke 11:2.**

2
Rom. 7:18: For I know that in me (that is, in my flesh) nothing good dwells; for to will is present with me, but *how* to perform what is good I do not find. **Job 21:14:** Yet they say to God, 'Depart from us, For we do not desire the knowledge of Your ways. **1 Cor. 2:14:** But the natural man does not receive the things of the Spirit of God, for they are foolishness to him; nor can he know *them,* because they are spiritually discerned.

3
Rom. 8:7: Because the carnal mind *is* enmity against God; for it is not subject to the law of God, nor indeed can be.

4
Ex. 17:7: So he called the name of the place Massah and Meribah, because of the contention of the children of Israel, and because they tempted the LORD, saying, "Is the LORD among us or not?" **Num. 14:2:** And all the children of Israel complained against Moses and Aaron, and the whole congregation said to them, "If only we had died in the land of Egypt! Or if only we had died in this wilderness!"

5
Eph. 2:2: ... in which you once walked according to the course of this world, according to the prince of the power of the air, the spirit who now works in the sons of disobedience.

6
Eph. 1:17-18: ... that the God of our Lord Jesus Christ, the Father of glory, may give to you the spirit of wisdom and revelation in the knowledge of Him, the eyes of your understanding being enlightened; that you may know what is the hope of His calling, what are the riches of the glory of His inheritance in the saints.

7
Eph. 3:16: ... that He would grant you, according to the riches of His glory, to be strengthened with might through His Spirit in the inner man.

8
Matt. 26:40-41: Then He came to the disciples and found them sleeping, and said to Peter, "What! Could you not watch with Me one hour? Watch and pray, lest you enter into temptation. The spirit indeed *is* willing, but the flesh *is* weak."

9
Jer. 31:18-19: I have surely heard Ephraim bemoaning himself: 'You have chastised me, and I was chastised, Like an untrained bull; Restore me, and I will return, For You *are* the LORD my God. Surely, after my turning, I repented; And after I was instructed, I struck myself on the thigh; I was ashamed, yes, even humiliated, Because I bore the reproach of my youth.'

10
Ps. 19:14: Let the words of my mouth and the meditation of my heart Be acceptable in Your sight, O LORD, my strength and my Redeemer. **Acts 21:14:** So when he would not be persuaded, we ceased, saying, "The will of the Lord be done." **See Ps. 119; 1 Thess. 5:23; Heb. 13:20-21.**

11
Mic. 6:8: He has shown you, O man, what *is* good; And what does the LORD require of you But to do justly, To love mercy, And to walk humbly with your God?

12
Ps. 100:2: Serve the LORD with gladness; Come before His presence with singing. **Job 1:21:** And he said: "Naked I came from my mother's womb, And naked shall I return there. The LORD gave, and the LORD has taken away; Blessed be the name of the LORD." **2 Sam. 15:25-26:** Then the king said to Zadok, "Carry the ark of God back into the city. If I find favor in the eyes of the LORD, He will bring me back and show me *both* it and His dwelling place. But if He says thus: 'I have no delight in you,' here I am, let Him do to me as seems good to Him."

13
Isa. 38:3: ... and said, "Remember now, O LORD, I pray, how I have walked before You in truth and with a loyal heart, and have done *what is* good in Your sight." And Hezekiah wept bitterly.

14
Ps. 119:4-5: You have commanded *us* To keep Your precepts diligently. Oh, that my ways were directed To keep Your statutes!

15
Ps. 69:9: Because zeal for Your house has eaten me up, And the reproaches of those who reproach You have fallen on me. **John 2:17:** Then His disciples remembered that it was written, "Zeal for Your house has eaten Me up." **Rom. 12:11:** ... not lagging in diligence, fervent in spirit, serving the Lord.

16
Josh. 24:14: Now therefore, fear the LORD, serve Him in sincerity and in truth, and put away the gods which your fathers served on the other side of the River and in Egypt. Serve the LORD! **Ps. 119:80:** Let my heart be blameless regarding Your statutes, That I may not be ashamed. **1 Cor. 5:8:** Therefore let us keep the feast, not with old leaven, nor with the leaven of malice and wickedness, but with the unleavened *bread* of sincerity and truth. **See 2 Cor. 1:12.**

17 **Ps. 119:112:** I have inclined my heart to perform Your statutes Forever, to the very end.

18 **Isa. 6:2-3:** Above it stood seraphim; each one had six wings: with two he covered his face, with two he covered his feet, and with two he flew. And one cried to another and said: "Holy, holy, holy *is* the LORD of hosts; The whole earth *is* full of His glory!" **Ps. 103:20-21:** Bless the LORD, you His angels, Who excel in strength, who do His word, Heeding the voice of His word. Bless the LORD, all *you* His hosts, *You* ministers of His, who do His pleasure. **Matt. 18:10:** Take heed that you do not despise one of these little ones, for I say to you that in heaven their angels always see the face of My Father who is in heaven.

Q. 212. *What do we pray for in the fourth petition?*

A. In the fourth petition (which is, *Give us this day our daily bread*),[1] acknowledging, that in Adam, and by our own sin, we have forfeited our right to all the outward blessings of this life, and deserve to be wholly deprived of them by God, and to have them cursed to us in the use of them;[2] and that neither they of themselves are able to sustain us,[3] nor we to merit,[4] or by our own industry to procure them;[5] but prone to desire,[6] get,[7] and use them unlawfully:[8] we pray for ourselves and others, that both they and we, waiting upon the providence of God from day to day in the use of lawful means, may, of His free gift, and as to His fatherly wisdom shall seem best, enjoy a competent portion of them;[9] and have the same continued and blessed unto us in our holy and comfortable use of them,[10] and contentment in them;[11] and be kept from all things that are contrary to our temporal support and comfort.[12]

1 **Matt. 6:11:** Give us this day our daily bread. **Cf. Luke 11:3.**

2 **Gen. 2:17:** ... but of the tree of the knowledge of good and evil you shall not eat, for in the day that you eat of it you shall surely die. **Gen. 3:17:** Then to Adam He said, "Because you have heeded the voice of your wife, and have eaten from the tree of which I commanded you, saying, 'You shall not eat of it': "Cursed *is* the ground for your sake; In toil you shall eat *of* it All the days of your life." **Rom. 8:20-22:** For the creation was subjected to futility, not willingly, but because of Him who subjected *it* in hope; because the creation itself also will be delivered from the bondage of corruption into the glorious liberty of the children of God. For we know that the whole creation groans and labors with birth pangs together until now. **Jer. 5:25:** Your iniquities have turned these *things* away, And your sins have withheld good from you. **Deut. 28:15-68:** But it shall come to pass, if you do not obey the voice of the LORD your God, to observe carefully all His commandments and His statutes which I command you today, that all these curses will come upon you and overtake you: "Cursed *shall* you *be* in the city, and cursed *shall* you *be* in the country. "Cursed *shall be* your basket and your kneading bowl....

3 **Deut. 8:3:** So He humbled you, allowed you to hunger, and fed you with manna which you did not know nor did your fathers know, that He might make you know that man shall not live by bread alone; but man lives by every *word* that proceeds from the mouth of the LORD.

4 **Gen. 32:10:** I am not worthy of the least of all the mercies and of all the truth which You have shown Your servant; for I crossed over this Jordan with my staff, and now I have become two companies.

5 **Deut. 8:17-18:** ... then you say in your heart, 'My power and the might of my hand have gained me this wealth.' "And you shall remember the LORD your God, for *it is* He who gives you power to get wealth, that He may establish His covenant which He swore to your fathers, as *it is* this day."

6
Jer. 6:13: Because from the least of them even to the greatest of them, Everyone *is* given to covetousness; And from the prophet even to the priest, Everyone deals falsely. **Mark 7:21-22:** For from within, out of the heart of men, proceed evil thoughts, adulteries, fornications, murders, thefts, covetousness, wickedness, deceit, lewdness, an evil eye, blasphemy, pride, foolishness.

7
Hos. 12:7: A cunning Canaanite! Deceitful scales *are* in his hand; He loves to oppress.

8
James 4:3: You ask and do not receive, because you ask amiss, that you may spend *it* on your pleasures.

9
Gen. 43:12-14: Take double money in your hand, and take back in your hand the money that was returned in the mouth of your sacks; perhaps it was an oversight. Take your brother also, and arise, go back to the man. And may God Almighty give you mercy before the man, that he may release your other brother and Benjamin. If I am bereaved, I am bereaved! **Gen. 28:20:** Then Jacob made a vow, saying, "If God will be with me, and keep me in this way that I am going, and give me bread to eat and clothing to put on." **Eph. 4:28:** Let him who stole steal no longer, but rather let him labor, working with *his* hands what is good, that he may have something to give him who has need. **2 Thess. 3:11-12:** For we hear that there are some who walk among you in a disorderly manner, not working at all, but are busybodies. Now those who are such we command and exhort through our Lord Jesus Christ that they work in quietness and eat their own bread. **Phil. 4:6:** Be anxious for nothing, but in everything by prayer and supplication, with thanksgiving, let your requests be made known to God.

10
1 Tim. 4:3-5: ... forbidding to marry, *and commanding* to abstain from foods which God created to be received with thanksgiving by those who believe and know the truth. For every creature of God *is* good, and nothing is to be refused if it is received with thanksgiving; for it is sanctified by the word of God and prayer.

11
1 Tim. 6:6-8: Now godliness with contentment is great gain. For we brought nothing into *this* world, *and it is* certain we can carry nothing out. And having food and clothing, with these we shall be content.

12
Prov. 30:8-9: Remove falsehood and lies far from me; Give me neither poverty nor riches— Feed me with the food allotted to me; Lest I be full and deny *You,* And say, "Who *is* the LORD?" Or lest I be poor and steal, And profane the name of my God.

Q. 213. *What do we pray for in the fifth petition?*

A. In the fifth petition (which is, *Forgive us our debts, as we forgive our debtors*),[1] acknowledging, that we and all others are guilty both of original and actual sin, and thereby become debtors to the justice of God; and that neither we, nor any other creature, can make the least satisfaction for that debt:[2] we pray for ourselves and others, that God of His free grace would, through the obedience and satisfaction of Christ, apprehended and applied by faith, acquit us both from the guilt and punishment of sin,[3] accept us in His Beloved;[4] continue His favor and grace to us,[5] pardon our daily failings,[6] and fill us with peace and joy, in giving us daily more and more assurance of forgiveness;[7] which we are the rather emboldened to ask, and encouraged to expect, when we have this testimony in ourselves, that we from the heart forgive others their offenses.[8]

1
Matt. 6:12: And forgive us our debts, As we forgive our debtors. **Cf. Luke 11:4.**

2
Rom. 3:9-22: What then? Are we better *than they?* Not at all. For we have previously charged both Jews and Greeks that they are all under sin. As it is written: "There is none righteous, no, not

one; There is none who understands; There is none who seeks after God. They have all turned aside; They have together become unprofitable; There is none who does good, no, not one." "Their throat *is* an open tomb; With their tongues they have practiced deceit"; "The poison of asps *is* under their lips"; "Whose mouth *is* full of cursing and bitterness." "Their feet *are* swift to shed blood; Destruction and misery *are* in their ways; And the way of peace they have not known." "There is no fear of God before their eyes." Now we know that whatever the law says, it says to those who are under the law, that every mouth may be stopped, and all the world may become guilty before God. Therefore by the deeds of the law no flesh will be justified in His sight, for by the law *is* the knowledge of sin. But now the righteousness of God apart from the law is revealed, being witnessed by the Law and the Prophets, even the righteousness of God, through faith in Jesus Christ, to all and on all who believe. For there is no difference; **Matt. 18:24-25:** And when he had begun to settle accounts, one was brought to him who owed him ten thousand talents. But as he was not able to pay, his master commanded that he be sold, with his wife and children and all that he had, and that payment be made. **Ps. 130:3-4:** If You, LORD, should mark iniquities, O Lord, who could stand? But *there is* forgiveness with You, That You may be feared.

3 **Rom. 3:24-26:** ... being justified freely by His grace through the redemption that is in Christ Jesus, whom God set forth *as* a propitiation by His blood, through faith, to demonstrate His righteousness, because in His forbearance God had passed over the sins that were previously committed, to demonstrate at the present time His righteousness, that He might be just and the justifier of the one who has faith in Jesus. **Heb. 9:22:** And according to the law almost all things are purified with blood, and without shedding of blood there is no remission.

4 **Eph. 1:6-7:** ... to the praise of the glory of His grace, by which He made us accepted in the Beloved. In Him we have redemption through His blood, the forgiveness of sins, according to the riches of His grace.

5 **2 Pet. 1:2:** Grace and peace be multiplied to you in the knowledge of God and of Jesus our Lord.

6 **Hos. 14:2:** Take words with you, And return to the LORD. Say to Him, "Take away all iniquity; Receive *us* graciously, For we will offer the sacrifices of our lips. **Jer. 14:7:** O LORD, though our iniquities testify against us, Do it for Your name's sake; For our backslidings are many, We have sinned against You. **1 John 1:9:** If we confess our sins, He is faithful and just to forgive us *our* sins and to cleanse us from all unrighteousness. **See Dan. 9:17-19.**

7 **Rom. 15:13:** Now may the God of hope fill you with all joy and peace in believing, that you may abound in hope by the power of the Holy Spirit. **Ps. 51:7-10, 12:** Purge me with hyssop, and I shall be clean; Wash me, and I shall be whiter than snow. Make me hear joy and gladness, *That* the bones You have broken may rejoice. Hide Your face from my sins, And blot out all my iniquities. Create in me a clean heart, O God, And renew a steadfast spirit within me.... Restore to me the joy of Your salvation, And uphold me *by Your* generous Spirit.

8 **Luke 11:4:** And forgive us our sins, For we also forgive everyone who is indebted to us. And do not lead us into temptation, But deliver us from the evil one. **Matt. 6:14-15:** For if you forgive men their trespasses, your heavenly Father will also forgive you. But if you do not forgive men their trespasses, neither will your Father forgive your trespasses. **Eph. 4:32:** And be kind to one another, tenderhearted, forgiving one another, even as God in Christ forgave you. **Col. 3:13:** ... bearing with one another, and forgiving one another, if anyone has a complaint against another; even as Christ forgave you, so you also *must do.* **See Matt. 18:21-35.**

Q. 214. *What do we pray for in the sixth petition?*

A. In the sixth petition (which is, *And lead us not into temptation, but deliver us from evil*),[1] acknowledging, that the most wise, righteous, and gracious God, for divers holy and just ends, may so order things, that we may be assaulted, foiled, and for a time led captive by temptations;[2] that Satan,[3] the world,[4] and the flesh, are ready powerfully to draw us aside, and ensnare us;[5] and that we, even after the pardon of our sins, by reason of our corruption,[6] weakness, and want of watchfulness,[7] are not only subject to be tempted, and forward to expose ourselves unto temptations,[8] but also of ourselves unable and unwilling to resist them, to recover out of them, and to improve them;[9] and worthy to be left under the power of them:[10] we pray, that God would so overrule the world and all in it,[11] subdue the flesh,[12] and restrain Satan,[13] order all things,[14] bestow and bless all means of grace,[15] and quicken us to watchfulness in the use of them, that we and all His people may by His providence be kept from being tempted to sin;[16] or, if tempted, that by His Spirit we may be powerfully supported and enabled to stand in the hour of temptation;[17] or when fallen, raised again and recovered out of it,[18] and have a sanctified use and improvement thereof:[19] that our sanctification and salvation may be perfected,[20] Satan trodden under our feet,[21] and we fully freed from sin, temptation, and all evil, forever.[22]

[1] **Matt. 6:13:** And do not lead us into temptation, But deliver us from the evil one. For Yours is the kingdom and the power and the glory forever. Amen. **Cf. Luke 11:4.**

[2] **2 Chron. 32:31:** However, *regarding* the ambassadors of the princes of Babylon, whom they sent to him to inquire about the wonder that was *done* in the land, God withdrew from him, in order to test him, that He might know all *that was* in his heart.

[3] **1 Chron. 21:1:** Now Satan stood up against Israel, and moved David to number Israel.

[4] **Luke 21:34:** But take heed to yourselves, lest your hearts be weighed down with carousing, drunkenness, and cares of this life, and that Day come on you unexpectedly. **Mark 4:19:** ... and the cares of this world, the deceitfulness of riches, and the desires for other things entering in choke the word, and it becomes unfruitful.

[5] **James 1:14:** But each one is tempted when he is drawn away by his own desires and enticed.

[6] **Gal. 5:17:** For the flesh lusts against the Spirit, and the Spirit against the flesh; and these are contrary to one another, so that you do not do the things that you wish.

[7] **Matt. 26:41:** Watch and pray, lest you enter into temptation. The spirit indeed *is* willing, but the flesh *is* weak.

[8] **Matt. 26:69-72:** Now Peter sat outside in the courtyard. And a servant girl came to him, saying, "You also were with Jesus of Galilee." But he denied it before *them* all, saying, "I do not know what you are saying." And when he had gone out to the gateway, another *girl* saw him and said to those *who were* there, "This *fellow* also was with Jesus of Nazareth." But again he denied with an oath, "I do not know the Man!" **Gal. 2:11-14:** Now when Peter had come to Antioch, I withstood him to his face, because he was to be blamed; for before certain men came from James, he would eat with the Gentiles; but when they came, he withdrew and separated himself, fearing those who were of the circumcision. And the rest of the Jews also played the hypocrite with him, so that even Barnabas was carried away with their hypocrisy. But when I saw that they were not straightforward about the truth of the gospel, I said to Peter before *them* all, "If you, being a Jew, live in the manner of Gentiles and not as the Jews, why do you compel Gentiles to live as Jews? **2 Chron. 18:3:** So Ahab king of Israel said to Jehoshaphat king of Judah, "Will you go with me *against* Ramoth Gilead?" And he answered him, "I *am* as you *are,* and my people as your people; *we will be* with you in the war." **2 Chron. 19:2:** And Jehu the son of Hanani the seer went out to meet him, and said to King Jehoshaphat, "Should you help the wicked and love those who hate the LORD? Therefore the wrath of the LORD *is* upon you."

[9] **Rom. 7:23-24:** But I see another law in my members, warring against the law of my mind, and bringing me into captivity to the law of sin which is in my members. O wretched man that I am! Who will deliver me from this body of death? **1 Chron. 21:1-4:** Now Satan stood up against Israel, and moved David to number Israel. So David said to Joab and to the leaders of the people, "Go, number Israel from Beersheba to Dan, and bring the number of them to me that I may know *it.*" And Joab answered, "May the LORD make His people a hundred times more than they are. But, my

lord the king, *are* they not all my lord's servants? Why then does my lord require this thing? Why should he be a cause of guilt in Israel?" Nevertheless the king's word prevailed against Joab. Therefore Joab departed and went throughout all Israel and came to Jerusalem. **2 Chron. 16:7-10:** And at that time Hanani the seer came to Asa king of Judah, and said to him: "Because you have relied on the king of Syria, and have not relied on the LORD your God, therefore the army of the king of Syria has escaped from your hand. Were the Ethiopians and the Lubim not a huge army with very many chariots and horsemen? Yet, because you relied on the LORD, He delivered them into your hand. For the eyes of the LORD run to and fro throughout the whole earth, to show Himself strong on behalf of *those* whose heart *is* loyal to Him. In this you have done foolishly; therefore from now on you shall have wars." Then Asa was angry with the seer, and put him in prison, for *he was* enraged at him because of this. And Asa oppressed *some* of the people at that time.

10

Ps. 81:11-12: But My people would not heed My voice, And Israel would *have* none of Me. So I gave them over to their own stubborn heart, To walk in their own counsels.

11

John 17:15: I do not pray that You should take them out of the world, but that You should keep them from the evil one.

12

Ps. 51:10: Create in me a clean heart, O God, And renew a steadfast spirit within me. **Ps. 119:133:** Direct my steps by Your word, And let no iniquity have dominion over me.

13

2 Cor. 12:7-8: And lest I should be exalted above measure by the abundance of the revelations, a thorn in the flesh was given to me, a messenger of Satan to buffet me, lest I be exalted above measure. Concerning this thing I pleaded with the Lord three times that it might depart from me.

14

1 Cor. 10:12-13: Therefore let him who thinks he stands take heed lest he fall. No temptation has overtaken you except such as is common to man; but God *is* faithful, who will not allow you to be tempted beyond what you are able, but with the temptation will also make the way of escape, that you may be able to bear *it.*

15

Heb. 13:20-21: Now may the God of peace who brought up our Lord Jesus from the dead, that great Shepherd of the sheep, through the blood of the everlasting covenant, make you complete in every good work to do His will, working in you what is well pleasing in His sight, through Jesus Christ, to whom *be* glory forever and ever. Amen.

16

Matt. 26:41: Watch and pray, lest you enter into temptation. The spirit indeed *is* willing, but the flesh *is* weak. **Ps. 19:13:** Keep back Your servant also from presumptuous *sins;* Let them not have dominion over me. Then I shall be blameless, And I shall be innocent of great transgression.

17

Eph. 3:14-17: For this reason I bow my knees to the Father of our Lord Jesus Christ, from whom the whole family in heaven and earth is named, that He would grant you, according to the riches of His glory, to be strengthened with might through His Spirit in the inner man, that Christ may dwell in your hearts through faith; that you, being rooted and grounded in love. **1 Thess. 3:13:** ... so that He may establish your hearts blameless in holiness before our God and Father at the coming of our Lord Jesus Christ with all His saints. **Jude 24:** Now to Him who is able to keep you from stumbling, And to present you faultless Before the presence of His glory with exceeding joy.

18

Ps. 51:12: Restore to me the joy of Your salvation, And uphold me *by Your* generous Spirit.

19

1 Pet. 5:8-10: Be sober, be vigilant; because your adversary the devil walks about like a roaring lion, seeking whom he may devour. Resist him, steadfast in the faith, knowing that the same sufferings are experienced by your brotherhood in the world. But may the God of all grace, who called us to His eternal glory by Christ Jesus, after you have suffered a while, perfect, establish, strengthen, and settle *you.*

20

2 Cor. 13:7, 9: Now I pray to God that you do no evil, not that we should appear approved, but that you should do what is honorable, though we may seem disqualified.... For we are glad when we are weak and you are strong. And this also we pray, that you may be made complete.

21

Rom. 16:20: And the God of peace will crush Satan under your feet shortly. The grace of our Lord Jesus Christ *be* with you. Amen. **Luke 22:31-32:** And the Lord said, "Simon, Simon! Indeed, Satan has asked for you, that he may sift *you* as wheat. But I have prayed for you, that your faith should not fail; and when you have returned to *Me,* strengthen your brethren."

22

John 17:15: I do not pray that You should take them out of the world, but that You should keep them from the evil one. **1 Thess. 5:23:** Now may the God of peace Himself sanctify you completely; and may your whole spirit, soul, and body be preserved blameless at the coming of our Lord Jesus Christ.

Q. 215. *What doth the conclusion of the Lord's Prayer teach us?*

A. The conclusion of the Lord's Prayer (which is, *For thine is the kingdom, and the power, and the glory, for ever. Amen.*),[1] teacheth us to enforce our petitions with arguments,[2] which are to be taken, not from any worthiness in ourselves, or in any other creature, but from God;[3] and with our prayers to join praises,[4] ascribing to God alone eternal sovereignty, omnipotency, and glorious excellency;[5] in regard whereof, as He is able and willing to help us,[6] so we by faith are emboldened to plead with Him that He would,[7] and quietly to rely upon Him, that He will fulfill our requests.[8] And, to testify this our desire and assurance, we say, *Amen.*[9]

1 **Matt. 6:13:** And do not lead us into temptation, But deliver us from the evil one. For Yours is the kingdom and the power and the glory forever. Amen.

2 **Rom. 15:30:** Now I beg you, brethren, through the Lord Jesus Christ, and through the love of the Spirit, that you strive together with me in prayers to God for me.

3 **Dan. 9:4, 7-9, 16-19:** And I prayed to the LORD my God, and made confession, and said, "O Lord, great and awesome God, who keeps His covenant and mercy with those who love Him, and with those who keep His commandments ... O Lord, righteousness *belongs* to You, but to us shame of face, as *it is* this day—to the men of Judah, to the inhabitants of Jerusalem and all Israel, those near and those far off in all the countries to which You have driven them, because of the unfaithfulness which they have committed against You. O Lord, to us *belongs* shame of face, to our kings, our princes, and our fathers, because we have sinned against You. To the Lord our God *belong* mercy and forgiveness, though we have rebelled against Him.... O Lord, according to all Your righteousness, I pray, let Your anger and Your fury be turned away from Your city Jerusalem, Your holy mountain; because for our sins, and for the iniquities of our fathers, Jerusalem and Your people *are* a reproach to all *those* around us. Now therefore, our God, hear the prayer of Your servant, and his supplications, and for the Lord's sake cause Your face to shine on Your sanctuary, which is desolate. O my God, incline Your ear and hear; open Your eyes and see our desolations, and the city which is called by Your name; for we do not present our supplications before You because of our righteous deeds, but because of Your great mercies. O Lord, hear! O Lord, forgive! O Lord, listen and act! Do not delay for Your own sake, my God, for Your city and Your people are called by Your name.

4 **Phil. 4:6:** Be anxious for nothing, but in everything by prayer and supplication, with thanksgiving, let your requests be made known to God.

5 **1 Chron. 29:10-13:** Therefore David blessed the LORD before all the assembly; and David said: "Blessed are You, LORD God of Israel, our Father, forever and ever. Yours, O LORD, *is* the greatness, The power and the glory, The victory and the majesty; For all *that is* in heaven and in earth *is Yours;* Yours *is* the kingdom, O LORD, And You are exalted as head over all. Both riches and honor *come* from You, And You reign over all. In Your hand *is* power and might; In Your hand *it is* to make great And to give strength to all. Now therefore, our God, We thank You And praise Your glorious name." **1 Tim. 1:17:** Now to the King eternal, immortal, invisible, to God who alone is wise, *be* honor and glory forever and ever. Amen. **Rev. 5:11-13:** Then I looked, and I heard the voice of many angels around the throne, the living creatures, and the elders; and the number of them was ten thousand times ten thousand, and thousands of thousands, saying with a loud voice: "Worthy is the Lamb who was slain To receive power and riches and wisdom, And strength and honor and glory and blessing!" And every creature which is in heaven and on the earth and under the earth and such as are in the sea, and all that are in them, I heard saying: "Blessing and honor and glory and power *Be* to Him who sits on the throne, And to the Lamb, forever and ever!"

6 **Eph. 3:20-21:** Now to Him who is able to do exceedingly abundantly above all that we ask or think, according to the power that works in us, to Him *be* glory in the church by Christ Jesus to all generations, forever and ever. Amen. **Luke 11:13:** If you then, being evil, know how to give good gifts to your children, how much more will *your* heavenly Father give the Holy Spirit to those who

ask Him!

7

2 Chron. 20:6, 11: ... and said: "O LORD God of our fathers, *are* You not God in heaven, and do You *not* rule over all the kingdoms of the nations, and in Your hand *is there not* power and might, so that no one is able to withstand You?"

8

2 Chron. 14:11: And Asa cried out to the LORD his God, and said, "LORD, *it is* nothing for You to help, whether with many or with those who have no power; help us, O LORD our God, for we rest on You, and in Your name we go against this multitude. O LORD, You *are* our God; do not let man prevail against You!"

9

1 Cor. 14:16: Otherwise, if you bless with the spirit, how will he who occupies the place of the uninformed say "Amen" at your giving of thanks, since he does not understand what you say? **Rev. 22:20-21:** He who testifies to these things says, "Surely I am coming quickly." Amen. Even so, come, Lord Jesus! The grace of our Lord Jesus Christ *be* with you all. Amen.

THE

SHORTER CATECHISM

TO BE A DIRECTORY FOR CATECHISING SUCH AS ARE CHILDREN, NEW CONVERTS, AND AS MANY AS ARE OF WEAKER CAPACITY,

WITH

THE PROOFS FROM THE SCRIPTURE

THE

SHORTER CATECHISM

Q. 1. *What is the chief end of man?*

A. Man's chief end is to glorify God,[1] and to enjoy Him forever.[2]

[1] **Ps. 86:9:** All nations whom You have made Shall come and worship before You, O Lord, And shall glorify Your name. **Isa. 60:21:** Also your people *shall* all *be* righteous; They shall inherit the land forever, The branch of My planting, The work of My hands, That I may be glorified. **Rom. 11:36:** For of Him and through Him and to Him *are* all things, to whom *be* glory forever. Amen. **1 Cor. 6:20:** For you were bought at a price; therefore glorify God in your body and in your spirit, which are God's. **1 Cor. 10:31:** Therefore, whether you eat or drink, or whatever you do, do all to the glory of God. **Rev. 4:11:** "You are worthy, O Lord, To receive glory and honor and power; For You created all things, And by Your will they exist and were created."

[2] **Ps. 16:5-11:** O LORD, *You are* the portion of my inheritance and my cup; You maintain my lot. The lines have fallen to me in pleasant *places;* Yes, I have a good inheritance. I will bless the LORD who has given me counsel; My heart also instructs me in the night seasons. I have set the LORD always before me; Because *He is* at my right hand I shall not be moved. Therefore my heart is glad, and my glory rejoices; My flesh also will rest in hope. For You will not leave my soul in Sheol, Nor will You allow Your Holy One to see corruption. You will show me the path of life; In Your presence *is* fullness of joy; At Your right hand *are* pleasures forevermore. **Ps. 144:15:** Happy *are* the people who are in such a state; Happy *are* the people whose God *is* the LORD! **Isa. 12:2:** Behold, God *is* my salvation, I will trust and not be afraid; 'For YAH, the LORD, *is* my strength and song; He also has become my salvation.'" **Luke 2:10:** Then the angel said to them, "Do not be afraid, for behold, I bring you good tidings of great joy which will be to all people. **Phil. 4:4:** Rejoice in the Lord always. Again I will say, rejoice! **Rev. 21:3-4:** And I heard a loud voice from heaven saying, "Behold, the tabernacle of God *is* with men, and He will dwell with them, and they shall be His people. God Himself will be with them *and be* their God. And God will wipe away every tear from their eyes; there shall be no more death, nor sorrow, nor crying. There shall be no more pain, for the former things have passed away."

Q. 2. *What rule hath God given to direct us how we may glorify and enjoy Him?*

A. The word of God, which is contained in the Scriptures of the Old and New Testaments,[1] is the only rule to direct us how we may glorify and enjoy Him.[2]

[1] **Matt. 19:4-5:** And He answered and said to them, "Have you not read that He who made *them* at the beginning 'made them male and female,' and said, 'For this reason a man shall leave his father and mother and be joined to his wife, and the two shall become one flesh'? **Cf. Gen. 2:24:** Therefore a man shall leave his father and mother and be joined to his wife, and they shall become one flesh. **Luke 24:27, 44:** And beginning at Moses and all the Prophets, He expounded to them in all the Scriptures the things concerning Himself.... Then He said to them, "These *are* the words which I spoke to you while I was still with you, that all things must be fulfilled which were written in the Law of Moses and *the* Prophets and *the* Psalms concerning Me." **1 Cor. 2:13:** These things we also speak, not in words which man's wisdom teaches but which the Holy Spirit teaches, comparing spiritual things with spiritual. **1 Cor. 14:37:** If anyone thinks himself to be a prophet or spiritual, let him acknowledge that the things which I write to you are the commandments of the Lord. **2 Pet. 1:20-21:** ... knowing this first, that no prophecy of Scripture is of any private interpretation, for prophecy never came by the will of man, but holy men of God spoke *as they were* moved by the Holy Spirit. **2 Pet. 3:2, 15-16:** ... that you may be mindful of the words which were spoken before by the holy prophets, and of the commandment of us, the apostles of the Lord and Savior ... and consider *that* the longsuffering of our Lord *is* salvation—as also our beloved brother Paul, according to the wisdom given to him, has written to you, as also in all his epistles, speaking in them of these things, in which are some things hard to understand, which untaught and unstable *people* twist to their own destruction, as *they do* also the rest of the Scriptures.

[2] **Deut. 4:2:** You shall not add to the word which I command you, nor take from it, that you may keep the commandments of the LORD your God which I command you. **Ps. 19:7-11:** The law of the LORD *is* perfect, converting the soul; The testimony of the LORD *is* sure, making wise the simple; The statutes of the LORD *are* right, rejoicing the heart; The commandment of the LORD *is* pure, enlightening the eyes; The fear of the LORD *is* clean, enduring forever; The judgments of the LORD *are* true *and* righteous altogether. More to be desired *are they* than gold, Yea, than much fine gold; Sweeter also than honey and the honeycomb. Moreover by them Your servant is warned, *And* in keeping them *there is* great reward. **Isa. 8:20:** To the law and to the testimony! If they do not speak according to this word, *it is* because *there is* no light in them. **John 15:11:** These things I have spoken to you, that My joy may remain in you, and *that* your joy may be full. **John 20:30-31:** And truly Jesus did many other signs in the presence of His disciples, which are not written in this book; but these are written that you may believe that Jesus is the Christ, the Son of God, and that believing you may have life in His name. **Acts 17:11:** These were more fair-minded than those in Thessalonica, in that they received the word with all readiness, and searched the Scriptures daily *to find out* whether these things were so. **2 Tim. 3:15-17:** ... and that from childhood you have known the Holy Scriptures, which are able to make you wise for salvation through faith which is in Christ Jesus. All Scripture *is* given by inspiration of God, and *is* profitable for doctrine, for reproof, for correction, for instruction in righteousness, that the man of God may be complete, thoroughly equipped for every good work. **1 John 1:4:** And these things we write to you that your joy may be full.

Q. 3. *What do the Scriptures principally teach?*

A. The Scriptures principally teach what man is to believe concerning God,[1] and what duty God requires of man.[2]

[1] **Gen. 1:1:** In the beginning God created the heavens and the earth. **John 5:39:** You search the Scriptures, for in them you think you have eternal life; and these are they which testify of Me. **John 20:31:** ... but these are written that you may believe that Jesus is the Christ, the Son of God, and that believing you may have life in His name. **Rom. 10:17:** So then faith *comes* by hearing, and hearing by the word of God. **2 Tim. 3:15:** ... and that from childhood you have known the Holy Scriptures, which are able to make you wise for salvation through faith which is in Christ Jesus.

[2] **Deut. 10:12-13:** And now, Israel, what does the LORD your God require of you, but to fear the LORD your God, to walk in all His ways and to love Him, to serve the LORD your God with all your heart and with all your soul, *and* to keep the commandments of the LORD and His statutes which I command you today for your good? **Josh. 1:8:** This Book of the Law shall not depart from your mouth, but you shall meditate in it day and night, that you may observe to do according to all that is written in it. For then you will make your way prosperous, and then you will have good success. **Ps. 119:105:** Your word *is* a lamp to my feet And a light to my path. **Mic. 6:8:** He has shown you, O man, what *is* good; And what does the LORD require of you But to do justly, To love mercy, And to walk humbly with your God? **2 Tim. 3:16-17:** All Scripture *is* given by inspiration of God, and *is* profitable for doctrine, for reproof, for correction, for instruction in righteousness, that the man of God may be complete, thoroughly equipped for every good work.

Q. 4. *What is God?*

A. God is a Spirit,[1] infinite,[2] eternal,[3] and unchangeable,[4] in His being,[5] wisdom,[6] power,[7] holiness,[8] justice,[9] goodness[10] and truth.[11]

[1] **Deut. 4:15-19:** Take careful heed to yourselves, for you saw no form when the LORD spoke to you at Horeb out of the midst of the fire, lest you act corruptly and make for yourselves a carved image in the form of any figure: the likeness of male or female, the likeness of any animal that *is* on the earth or the likeness of any winged bird that flies in the air, the likeness of anything that creeps on the ground or the likeness of any fish that *is* in the water beneath the earth. And *take heed,* lest you lift your eyes to heaven, and *when* you see the sun, the moon, and the stars, all the host of heaven, you feel driven to worship them and serve them, which the LORD your God has given to all the peoples under the whole heaven as a heritage. **Luke 24:39:** Behold My hands and My feet, that it is I Myself. Handle Me and see, for a spirit does not have flesh and bones as you see I have. **John 1:18:** No one has seen God at any time. The only begotten Son, who is in the bosom of the Father, He has declared *Him.* **John 4:24:** God *is* Spirit, and those who worship Him must worship in spirit and truth. **Acts 17:29:** Therefore, since we are the offspring of God, we ought not to think that the Divine Nature is like gold or silver or stone, something shaped by art and man's devising.

2
1 Kings 8:27: But will God indeed dwell on the earth? Behold, heaven and the heaven of heavens cannot contain You. How much less this temple which I have built! **Ps. 139:7-10:** Where can I go from Your Spirit? Or where can I flee from Your presence? If I ascend into heaven, You *are* there; If I make my bed in hell, behold, You *are there. If* I take the wings of the morning, *And* dwell in the uttermost parts of the sea, Even there Your hand shall lead me, And Your right hand shall hold me. **Ps. 145:3:** Great *is* the LORD, and greatly to be praised; And His greatness *is* unsearchable. **Ps. 147:5:** Great *is* our Lord, and mighty in power; His understanding *is* infinite. **Jer. 23:24:** Can anyone hide himself in secret places, So I shall not see him?" says the LORD; "Do I not fill heaven and earth?" says the LORD. **Rom. 11:33-36:** Oh, the depth of the riches both of the wisdom and knowledge of God! How unsearchable *are* His judgments and His ways past finding out! "For who has known the mind of the LORD? Or who has become His counselor?" "Or who has first given to Him And it shall be repaid to him?" For of Him and through Him and to Him *are* all things, to whom *be* glory forever. Amen.
3
Deut. 33:27: The eternal God *is your* refuge, And underneath *are* the everlasting arms; He will thrust out the enemy from before you, And will say, 'Destroy!' **Ps. 90:2:** Before the mountains were brought forth, Or ever You had formed the earth and the world, Even from everlasting to everlasting, You *are* God. **Ps. 102:12, 24-27:** But You, O LORD, shall endure forever, And the remembrance of Your name to all generations.... I said, "O my God, Do not take me away in the midst of my days; Your years *are* throughout all generations. Of old You laid the foundation of the earth, And the heavens *are* the work of Your hands. They will perish, but You will endure; Yes, they will all grow old like a garment; Like a cloak You will change them, And they will be changed. But You *are* the same, And Your years will have no end." **Rev. 1:4, 8:** John, to the seven churches which are in Asia: Grace to you and peace from Him who is and who was and who is to come, and from the seven Spirits who are before His throne ... "I am the Alpha and the Omega, *the* Beginning and *the* End," says the Lord, "who is and who was and who is to come, the Almighty."
4
Ps. 33:11: The counsel of the LORD stands forever, The plans of His heart to all generations. **Mal. 3:6:** For I *am* the LORD, I do not change; Therefore you are not consumed, O sons of Jacob. **Heb. 1:12:** Like a cloak You will fold them up, And they will be changed. But You are the same, And Your years will not fail. **Heb. 6:17-18:** Thus God, determining to show more abundantly to the heirs of promise the immutability of His counsel, confirmed *it* by an oath, that by two immutable things, in which it *is* impossible for God to lie, we might have strong consolation, who have fled for refuge to lay hold of the hope set before *us.* **Heb. 13:8:** Jesus Christ *is* the same yesterday, today, and forever. **James 1:17:** Every good gift and every perfect gift is from above, and comes down from the Father of lights, with whom there is no variation or shadow of turning.
5
Ex. 3:14: And God said to Moses, "I AM WHO I AM." And He said, "Thus you shall say to the children of Israel, 'I AM has sent me to you.'" **Ps. 115:2-3:** Why should the Gentiles say, "So where *is* their God?" But our God *is* in heaven; He does whatever He pleases. **1 Tim. 1:17:** Now to the King eternal, immortal, invisible, to God who alone is wise, *be* honor and glory forever and ever. Amen. **1 Tim. 6:15-16:** ... which He will manifest in His own time, *He who is* the blessed and only Potentate, the King of kings and Lord of lords, who alone has immortality, dwelling in unapproachable light, whom no man has seen or can see, to whom *be* honor and everlasting power. Amen.
6
Ps. 104:24: O LORD, how manifold are Your works! In wisdom You have made them all. The earth is full of Your possessions. **Rom. 11:33-34:** For who has known the mind of the LORD? Or who has become His counselor? **Heb. 4:13:** And there is no creature hidden from His sight, but all things *are* naked and open to the eyes of Him to whom we *must give* account. **1 John 3:20:** For if our heart condemns us, God is greater than our heart, and knows all things.
7
Gen. 17:1: When Abram was ninety-nine years old, the LORD appeared to Abram and said to him, "I *am* Almighty God; walk before Me and be blameless. **Ps. 62:11:** God has spoken once, Twice I have heard this: That power *belongs* to God. **Jer. 32:17:** Ah, LORD God! Behold, You have made the heavens and the earth by Your great power and outstretched arm. There is nothing too hard for You. **Matt. 19:26:** But Jesus looked at *them* and said to them, "With men this is impossible, but with God all things are possible." **Rev. 1:8:** I am the Alpha and the Omega, *the* Beginning and *the* End," says the LORD, "who is and who was and who is to come, the Almighty.
8
Hab. 1:13: *You are* of purer eyes than to behold evil, And cannot look on wickedness. Why do You look on those who deal treacherously, *And* hold Your tongue when the wicked devours A *person* more righteous than he? **1 Pet. 1:15-16:** but as He who called you *is* holy, you also be holy in all *your* conduct, because it is written, "Be holy, for I am holy." **1 John 3:3, 5:** And everyone who has this hope in Him purifies himself, just as He is pure.... And you know that He was manifested to take away our sins, and in Him there is no sin. **Rev. 15:4:** Who shall not fear You, O Lord, and glorify Your name? For *You* alone *are* holy. For all nations shall come and worship before You, For Your judgments have been manifested.
9
Gen. 18:25: Far be it from You to do such a thing as this, to slay the righteous with the wicked, so that the righteous should be as the wicked; far be it from You! Shall not the Judge of all the earth do

right? **Ex. 34:6-7:** And the LORD passed before him and proclaimed, "The LORD, the LORD God, merciful and gracious, longsuffering, and abounding in goodness and truth, keeping mercy for thousands, forgiving iniquity and transgression and sin, by no means clearing *the guilty,* visiting the iniquity of the fathers upon the children and the children's children to the third and the fourth generation." **Deut. 32:4:** *He is* the Rock, His work *is* perfect; For all His ways *are* justice, A God of truth and without injustice; Righteous and upright *is* He. **Ps. 96:13:** For He is coming, for He is coming to judge the earth. He shall judge the world with righteousness, And the peoples with His truth. **Rom. 3:5, 26:** But if our unrighteousness demonstrates the righteousness of God, what shall we say? *Is* God unjust who inflicts wrath? (I speak as a man.) ... to demonstrate at the present time His righteousness, that He might be just and the justifier of the one who has faith in Jesus.

10

Ps. 103:5: Who satisfies your mouth with good *things, So that* your youth is renewed like the eagle's. **Ps. 107:8:** Oh, that *men* would give thanks to the LORD *for* His goodness, And *for* His wonderful works to the children of men! **Matt. 19:17:** So He said to him, "Why do you call Me good? No one *is* good but One, *that is,* God. But if you want to enter into life, keep the commandments." **Rom. 2:4:** Or do you despise the riches of His goodness, forbearance, and longsuffering, not knowing that the goodness of God leads you to repentance?

11

Ex. 34:6: And the LORD passed before him and proclaimed, "The LORD, the LORD God, merciful and gracious, longsuffering, and abounding in goodness and truth." **Deut. 32:4:** *He is* the Rock, His work *is* perfect; For all His ways *are* justice, A God of truth and without injustice; Righteous and upright *is* He. **Ps. 86:15:** But You, O Lord, *are* a God full of compassion, and gracious, Longsuffering and abundant in mercy and truth. **Ps. 117:2:** For His merciful kindness is great toward us, And the truth of the LORD *endures* forever. Praise the LORD! **Heb. 6:18:** ... that by two immutable things, in which it *is* impossible for God to lie, we might have strong consolation, who have fled for refuge to lay hold of the hope set before *us.*

Q. 5. *Are there more Gods than one?*

A. There is but One only,[1] the living and true God.[2]

1

Deut. 6:4: Hear, O Israel: The LORD our God, the LORD *is* one! **Isa. 44:6:** Thus says the LORD, the King of Israel, And his Redeemer, the LORD of hosts: 'I *am* the First and I *am* the Last; Besides Me *there is* no God.' **Isa. 45:21-22:** Tell and bring forth *your case;* Yes, let them take counsel together. Who has declared this from ancient time? *Who* has told it from that time? *Have* not I, the LORD? And *there is* no other God besides Me, A just God and a Savior; *There is* none besides Me. Look to Me, and be saved, All you ends of the earth! For I *am* God, and *there is* no other. **1 Cor. 8:4-6:** Therefore concerning the eating of things offered to idols, we know that an idol *is* nothing in the world, and that *there is* no other God but one. For even if there are so-called gods, whether in heaven or on earth (as there are many gods and many lords), yet for us *there is* one God, the Father, of whom *are* all things, and we for Him; and one Lord Jesus Christ, through whom *are* all things, and through whom we *live.*

2

Jer. 10:10: But the LORD *is* the true God; He *is* the living God and the everlasting King. At His wrath the earth will tremble, And the nations will not be able to endure His indignation. **John 17:3:** And this is eternal life, that they may know You, the only true God, and Jesus Christ whom You have sent. **1 Thess. 1:9:** For they themselves declare concerning us what manner of entry we had to you, and how you turned to God from idols to serve the living and true God. **1 John 5:20:** And we know that the Son of God has come and has given us an understanding, that we may know Him who is true; and we are in Him who is true, in His Son Jesus Christ. This is the true God and eternal life.

Q. 6. *How many persons are there in the Godhead?*

A. There are three persons in the Godhead; the Father, the Son, and the Holy Spirit;[1] and these three are one God, the same in substance, equal in power and glory.[2]

1

Matt. 3:16-17: When He had been baptized, Jesus came up immediately from the water; and behold, the heavens were opened to Him, and He saw the Spirit of God descending like a dove and alighting upon Him. And suddenly a voice *came* from heaven, saying, "This is My beloved Son, in whom I am well pleased." **Matt. 28:19:** Go therefore and make disciples of all the nations, baptizing them in the name of the Father and of the Son and of the Holy Spirit. **2 Cor. 13:14:** The grace of the Lord Jesus Christ, and the love of God, and the communion of the Holy Spirit *be* with you all. Amen. **1 Pet. 1:2:** ... elect according to the foreknowledge of God the Father, in sanctification of the

Spirit, for obedience and sprinkling of the blood of Jesus Christ: Grace to you and peace be multiplied.

2 **Ps. 45:6:** Your throne, O God, *is* forever and ever; A scepter of righteousness *is* the scepter of Your kingdom. **John 1:1:** In the beginning was the Word, and the Word was with God, and the Word was God. **John 17:5:** And now, O Father, glorify Me together with Yourself, with the glory which I had with You before the world was. **Acts 5:3-4:** But Peter said, "Ananias, why has Satan filled your heart to lie to the Holy Spirit and keep back *part* of the price of the land for yourself? While it remained, was it not your own? And after it was sold, was it not in your own control? Why have you conceived this thing in your heart? You have not lied to men but to God." **Rom. 9:5:** ... of whom *are* the fathers and from whom, according to the flesh, Christ *came,* who is over all, *the* eternally blessed God. Amen. **Col. 2:9:** For in Him dwells all the fullness of the Godhead bodily. **Jude 24-25:** Now to Him who is able to keep you from stumbling, And to present you faultless Before the presence of His glory with exceeding joy, To God our Savior, Who alone is wise, Be glory and majesty, Dominion and power, Both now and forever. Amen.

Q. 7. *What are the decrees of God?*

A. The decrees of God are His eternal purpose, according to the counsel of His will, whereby, for His own glory, He hath foreordained whatsoever comes to pass.[1]

1 **Ps. 33:11:** The counsel of the LORD stands forever, The plans of His heart to all generations. **Isa. 14:24:** The LORD of hosts has sworn, saying, "Surely, as I have thought, so it shall come to pass, And as I have purposed, *so* it shall stand. **Acts 2:23:** Him, being delivered by the determined purpose and foreknowledge of God, you have taken by lawless hands, have crucified, and put to death. **Eph. 1:11-12:** In Him also we have obtained an inheritance, being predestined according to the purpose of Him who works all things according to the counsel of His will, that we who first trusted in Christ should be to the praise of His glory.

Q. 8. *How doth God execute His decrees?*

A. God executeth His decrees in the works of creation and providence.[1]

1 **Ps. 148:8:** Fire and hail, snow and clouds; Stormy wind, fulfilling His word. **Isa. 40:26:** Lift up your eyes on high, And see who has created these *things,* Who brings out their host by number; He calls them all by name, By the greatness of His might And the strength of *His* power; Not one is missing. **Dan. 4:35:** All the inhabitants of the earth *are* reputed as nothing; He does according to His will in the army of heaven And *among* the inhabitants of the earth. No one can restrain His hand Or say to Him, "What have You done?" **Acts 4:24-28:** So when they heard that, they raised their voice to God with one accord and said: "Lord, You *are* God, who made heaven and earth and the sea, and all that is in them, who by the mouth of Your servant David have said: 'Why did the nations rage, And the people plot vain things? The kings of the earth took their stand, And the rulers were gathered together Against the LORD and against His Christ.' "For truly against Your holy Servant Jesus, whom You anointed, both Herod and Pontius Pilate, with the Gentiles and the people of Israel, were gathered together to do whatever Your hand and Your purpose determined before to be done. **Rev. 4:11:** You are worthy, O Lord, To receive glory and honor and power; For You created all things, And by Your will they exist and were created.

Q. 9. *What is the work of creation?*

A. The work of creation is God's making all things of nothing, by the word of His power,[1] in the space of six days, and all very good.[2]

1 **Gen. 1:1:** In the beginning God created the heavens and the earth. **Ps. 33:6, 9:** By the word of the LORD the heavens were made, And all the host of them by the breath of His mouth.... For He

spoke, and it was *done;* He commanded, and it stood fast. **Heb. 11:3:** By faith we understand that the worlds were framed by the word of God, so that the things which are seen were not made of things which are visible.

[2] **Gen. 1:31:** Then God saw everything that He had made, and indeed *it was* very good. So the evening and the morning were the sixth day.

Q. 10. *How did God create man?*

A. God created man male and female, after His own image,[1] in knowledge,[2] righteousness and holiness,[3] with dominion over the creatures.[4]

[1] **Gen. 1:27:** So God created man in His *own* image; in the image of God He created him; male and female He created them.

[2] **Col. 3:10:** ... and have put on the new *man* who is renewed in knowledge according to the image of Him who created him.

[3] **Eph. 4:24:** ... and that you put on the new man which was created according to God, in true righteousness and holiness.

[4] **Gen. 1:28:** Then God blessed them, and God said to them, "Be fruitful and multiply; fill the earth and subdue it; have dominion over the fish of the sea, over the birds of the air, and over every living thing that moves on the earth." **See Ps. 8.**

Q. 11. *What are God's works of providence?*

A. God's works of providence are His most holy,[1] wise[2] and powerful[3] preserving[4] and governing[5] all His creatures, and all their actions.[6]

[1] **Ps. 145:17:** The LORD *is* righteous in all His ways, Gracious in all His works.

[2] **Ps. 104:24:** O LORD, how manifold are Your works! In wisdom You have made them all. The earth is full of Your possessions.

[3] **Heb. 1:3:** ... who being the brightness of *His* glory and the express image of His person, and upholding all things by the word of His power, when He had by Himself purged our sins, sat down at the right hand of the Majesty on high.

[4] **Neh. 9:6:** You alone *are* the LORD; You have made heaven, The heaven of heavens, with all their host, The earth and everything on it, The seas and all that is in them, And You preserve them all. The host of heaven worships You.

[5] **Eph. 1:19-22:** ... and what *is* the exceeding greatness of His power toward us who believe, according to the working of His mighty power which He worked in Christ when He raised Him from the dead and seated *Him* at His right hand in the heavenly *places,* far above all principality and power and might and dominion, and every name that is named, not only in this age but also in that which is to come. And He put all *things* under His feet, and gave Him *to be* head over all *things* to the church.

[6] **Ps. 36:6:** Your righteousness *is* like the great mountains; Your judgments *are* a great deep; O LORD, You preserve man and beast. **Prov. 16:33:** The lot is cast into the lap, But its every decision *is* from the LORD. **Matt. 10:30:** But the very hairs of your head are all numbered.

Q. 12. *What special act of providence did God exercise toward man in the estate wherein he was created?*

A. When God had created man, He promised continual life to him, upon condition of perfect obedience; forbidding him to eat of the tree of the knowledge of good and evil, upon the pain of death.[1]

[1] **Gen. 2:16-17:** And the LORD God commanded the man, saying, "Of every tree of the garden you may freely eat; but of the tree of the knowledge of good and evil you shall not eat, for in the day that you eat of it you shall surely die." **James 2:10:** For whoever shall keep the whole law, and yet stumble in one *point,* he is guilty of all.

Q. 13. *Did our first parents continue in the estate wherein they were created?*

A. Our first parents, being left to the freedom of their own will, fell from the estate wherein they were created, by sinning against God.[1]

[1] **Gen. 3:6-8, 13:** So when the woman saw that the tree *was* good for food, that it *was* pleasant to the eyes, and a tree desirable to make *one* wise, she took of its fruit and ate. She also gave to her husband with her, and he ate. Then the eyes of both of them were opened, and they knew that they *were* naked; and they sewed fig leaves together and made themselves coverings. And they heard the sound of the LORD God walking in the garden in the cool of the day, and Adam and his wife hid themselves from the presence of the LORD God among the trees of the garden.... And the LORD God said to the woman, "What *is* this you have done?" The woman said, "The serpent deceived me, and I ate." **2 Cor. 11:3:** But I fear, lest somehow, as the serpent deceived Eve by his craftiness, so your minds may be corrupted from the simplicity that is in Christ.

Q. 14. *What is sin?*

A. Sin is any want of conformity unto, or transgression of, the law of God;[1] and is therefore that which doth not give all glory to God.[2]

[1] **Lev. 5:17:** If a person sins, and commits any of these things which are forbidden to be done by the commandments of the LORD, though he does not know *it,* yet he is guilty and shall bear his iniquity. **James 4:17:** Therefore, to him who knows to do good and does not do *it,* to him it is sin. **1 John 3:4:** Whoever commits sin also commits lawlessness, and sin is lawlessness.

[2] **Rom. 3:23:** ... for all have sinned and fall short of the glory of God. **Rom. 11:36:** For of Him and through Him and to Him *are* all things, to whom *be* glory forever. Amen. **1 Cor. 6:20:** For you were bought at a price; therefore glorify God in your body and in your spirit, which are God's. **1 Cor. 10:31:** Therefore, whether you eat or drink, or whatever you do, do all to the glory of God. **1 Pet. 4:11:** If anyone speaks, *let him speak* as the oracles of God. If anyone ministers, *let him do it* as with the ability which God supplies, that in all things God may be glorified through Jesus Christ, to whom belong the glory and the dominion forever and ever. Amen.

Q. 15. *What was the sin whereby our first parents fell from the estate wherein they were created?*

A. The sin whereby our first parents fell from the estate wherein they were created was their eating the forbidden fruit.[1]

[1] **Gen. 3:6:** So when the woman saw that the tree *was* good for food, that it *was* pleasant to the eyes, and a tree desirable to make *one* wise, she took of its fruit and ate. She also gave to her husband with her, and he ate.

Q. 16. *Did all mankind fall in Adam's first transgression?*

A. The divine pledge, communion, and righteous law of God being broken by the sin of Adam,[1] not only for himself, but for his posterity; all mankind, descending from him by ordinary generation, sinned in him, and fell with him, in his first transgression.[2]

[1] **Gen. 2:16-17:** And the LORD God commanded the man, saying, "Of every tree of the garden you may freely eat; but of the tree of the knowledge of good and evil you shall not eat, for in the day that you eat of it you shall surely die." **James 2:10:** For whoever shall keep the whole law, and yet stumble in one *point,* he is guilty of all. **Gen. 3:1-7, 22-24:** Now the serpent was more cunning than any beast of the field which the LORD God had made. And he said to the woman, "Has God indeed said, 'You shall not eat of every tree of the garden'?" And the woman said to the serpent, "We may eat the fruit of the trees of the garden; but of the fruit of the tree which *is* in the midst of the garden, God has said, 'You shall not eat it, nor shall you touch it, lest you die.'" Then the serpent said to the woman, "You will not surely die. For God knows that in the day you eat of it your eyes will be opened, and you will be like God, knowing good and evil." So when the woman saw that the tree *was* good for food, that it *was* pleasant to the eyes, and a tree desirable to make *one* wise, she took of its fruit and ate. She also gave to her husband with her, and he ate. Then the eyes of both of them were opened, and they knew that they *were* naked; and they sewed fig leaves together and made themselves coverings.... Then the LORD God said, "Behold, the man has become like one of Us, to know good and evil. And now, lest he put out his hand and take also of the tree of life, and eat, and live forever"— therefore the LORD God sent him out of the garden of Eden to till the ground from which he was taken. So He drove out the man; and He placed cherubim at the east of the garden of Eden, and a flaming sword which turned every way, to guard the way to the tree of life.

[2] **Rom. 5:12-21:** Therefore, just as through one man sin entered the world, and death through sin, and thus death spread to all men, because all sinned— (For until the law sin was in the world, but sin is not imputed when there is no law. Nevertheless death reigned from Adam to Moses, even over those who had not sinned according to the likeness of the transgression of Adam, who is a type of Him who was to come. But the free gift *is* not like the offense. For if by the one man's offense many died, much more the grace of God and the gift by the grace of the one Man, Jesus Christ, abounded to many. And the gift *is* not like *that which came* through the one who sinned. For the judgment *which came* from one *offense resulted* in condemnation, but the free gift *which came* from many offenses *resulted* in justification. For if by the one man's offense death reigned through the one, much more those who receive abundance of grace and of the gift of righteousness will reign in life through the One, Jesus Christ.) Therefore, as through one man's offense *judgment came* to all men, resulting in condemnation, even so through one Man's righteous act *the free gift came* to all men, resulting in justification of life. For as by one man's disobedience many were made sinners, so also by one Man's obedience many will be made righteous. Moreover the law entered that the offense might abound. But where sin abounded, grace abounded much more, so that as sin reigned in death, even so grace might reign through righteousness to eternal life through Jesus Christ our Lord. **1 Cor. 15:22:** For as in Adam all die, even so in Christ all shall be made alive.

Q. 17. *Into what estate did the fall bring mankind?*

A. The fall brought mankind into an estate of sin and misery.[1]

[1] **Gen. 3:16-19, 23:** To the woman He said: "I will greatly multiply your sorrow and your conception; In pain you shall bring forth children; Your desire *shall be* for your husband, And he shall rule over you." Then to Adam He said, "Because you have heeded the voice of your wife, and have eaten from the tree of which I commanded you, saying, 'You shall not eat of it': "Cursed *is* the ground for your sake; In toil you shall eat *of* it All the days of your life. Both thorns and thistles it shall bring forth for you, And you shall eat the herb of the field. In the sweat of your face you shall eat bread Till you return to the ground, For out of it you were taken; For dust you *are,* And to dust you shall return." ... therefore the LORD God sent him out of the garden of Eden to till the ground

from which he was taken. **Rom. 3:16:** Destruction and misery *are* in their ways. **Rom. 5:12:** Therefore, just as through one man sin entered the world, and death through sin, and thus death spread to all men, because all sinned. **Eph. 2:1:** And you *He made alive,* who were dead in trespasses and sins.

Q. 18. *Wherein consists the sinfulness of that estate whereinto man fell?*

A. The sinfulness of that estate whereinto man fell consists in the guilt of Adam's first sin,[1] the want of original righteousness,[2] and the corruption of his whole nature,[3] which is commonly called original sin; together with all actual transgressions which proceed from it.[4]

1 **Rom. 5:12, 19:** Therefore, just as through one man sin entered the world, and death through sin, and thus death spread to all men, because all sinned ... For as by one man's disobedience many were made sinners, so also by one Man's obedience many will be made righteous.

2 **Rom. 3:10:** As it is written: "There is none righteous, no, not one." **Col. 3:10:** ... and have put on the new *man* who is renewed in knowledge according to the image of Him who created him. **Eph. 4:24:** ... and that you put on the new man which was created according to God, in true righteousness and holiness.

3 **Ps. 51:5:** Behold, I was brought forth in iniquity, And in sin my mother conceived me. **John 3:6:** That which is born of the flesh is flesh, and that which is born of the Spirit is spirit. **Rom. 3:18:** There is no fear of God before their eyes. **Rom. 8:7-8:** Because the carnal mind *is* enmity against God; for it is not subject to the law of God, nor indeed can be. So then, those who are in the flesh cannot please God. **Eph. 2:3:** ... among whom also we all once conducted ourselves in the lusts of our flesh, fulfilling the desires of the flesh and of the mind, and were by nature children of wrath, just as the others.

4 **Gen. 6:5**: Then the LORD saw that the wickedness of man *was* great in the earth, and *that* every intent of the thoughts of his heart *was* only evil continually. **Ps. 53:1-3:** The fool has said in his heart, "*There is* no God." They are corrupt, and have done abominable iniquity; *There is* none who does good. God looks down from heaven upon the children of men, To see if there are *any* who understand, who seek God. Every one of them has turned aside; They have together become corrupt; *There is* none who does good, No, not one. **Matt. 15:19:** For out of the heart proceed evil thoughts, murders, adulteries, fornications, thefts, false witness, blasphemies. **Rom. 3:10-18, 23:** As it is written: "There is none righteous, no, not one; There is none who understands; There is none who seeks after God. They have all turned aside; They have together become unprofitable; There is none who does good, no, not one." "Their throat *is* an open tomb; With their tongues they have practiced deceit"; "The poison of asps *is* under their lips"; "Whose mouth *is* full of cursing and bitterness." "Their feet *are* swift to shed blood; Destruction and misery *are* in their ways; And the way of peace they have not known." "There is no fear of God before their eyes." ... for all have sinned and fall short of the glory of God. **Gal. 5:19-21:** Now the works of the flesh are evident, which are: adultery, fornication, uncleanness, lewdness, idolatry, sorcery, hatred, contentions, jealousies, outbursts of wrath, selfish ambitions, dissensions, heresies, envy, murders, drunkenness, revelries, and the like; of which I tell you beforehand, just as I also told *you* in time past, that those who practice such things will not inherit the kingdom of God. **James 1:14-15:** But each one is tempted when he is drawn away by his own desires and enticed. Then, when desire has conceived, it gives birth to sin; and sin, when it is full-grown, brings forth death.

Q. 19. *What is the misery of that estate whereinto man fell?*

A. All mankind by their fall lost communion with God,[1] are under His wrath[2] and curse,[3] and so made liable to all miseries in this life,[4] to death[5] itself, and to the pains of hell forever.[6]

1 **Gen. 3:8, 24:** And they heard the sound of the LORD God walking in the garden in the cool of the

day, and Adam and his wife hid themselves from the presence of the LORD God among the trees of the garden.... So He drove out the man; and He placed cherubim at the east of the garden of Eden, and a flaming sword which turned every way, to guard the way to the tree of life. **John 8:34, 42, 44:** Jesus answered them, "Most assuredly, I say to you, whoever commits sin is a slave of sin.... Jesus said to them, "If God were your Father, you would love Me, for I proceeded forth and came from God; nor have I come of Myself, but He sent Me.... You are of *your* father the devil, and the desires of your father you want to do. He was a murderer from the beginning, and does not stand in the truth, because there is no truth in him. When he speaks a lie, he speaks from his own *resources,* for he is a liar and the father of it.... **Eph. 2:12:** ... that at that time you were without Christ, being aliens from the commonwealth of Israel and strangers from the covenants of promise, having no hope and without God in the world. **Eph. 4:18:** ... having their understanding darkened, being alienated from the life of God, because of the ignorance that is in them, because of the blindness of their heart.

2

John 3:36: He who believes in the Son has everlasting life; and he who does not believe the Son shall not see life, but the wrath of God abides on him. **Rom. 1:18:** For the wrath of God is revealed from heaven against all ungodliness and unrighteousness of men, who suppress the truth in unrighteousness. **Eph. 2:3:** ... among whom also we all once conducted ourselves in the lusts of our flesh, fulfilling the desires of the flesh and of the mind, and were by nature children of wrath, just as the others. **Eph. 5:6:** Let no one deceive you with empty words, for because of these things the wrath of God comes upon the sons of disobedience.

3

Gal. 3:10: For as many as are of the works of the law are under the curse; for it is written, "Cursed *is* everyone who does not continue in all things which are written in the book of the law, to do them." **Rev. 22:3:** And there shall be no more curse, but the throne of God and of the Lamb shall be in it, and His servants shall serve Him.

4

Gen. 3:16-19: To the woman He said:"I will greatly multiply your sorrow and your conception; In pain you shall bring forth children; Your desire *shall be* for your husband, And he shall rule over you." Then to Adam He said, "Because you have heeded the voice of your wife, and have eaten from the tree of which I commanded you, saying, 'You shall not eat of it': "Cursed *is* the ground for your sake; In toil you shall eat *of* it All the days of your life. Both thorns and thistles it shall bring forth for you, And you shall eat the herb of the field. In the sweat of your face you shall eat bread Till you return to the ground, For out of it you were taken; For dust you *are,* And to dust you shall return." **Job 5:7:** Yet man is born to trouble, As the sparks fly upward. **Eccl. 2:22-23:** For what has man for all his labor, and for the striving of his heart with which he has toiled under the sun? For all his days *are* sorrowful, and his work burdensome; even in the night his heart takes no rest. This also is vanity. **Rom. 8:18-23:** For I consider that the sufferings of this present time are not worthy *to be compared* with the glory which shall be revealed in us. For the earnest expectation of the creation eagerly waits for the revealing of the sons of God. For the creation was subjected to futility, not willingly, but because of Him who subjected *it* in hope; because the creation itself also will be delivered from the bondage of corruption into the glorious liberty of the children of God. For we know that the whole creation groans and labors with birth pangs together until now. Not only *that,* but we also who have the firstfruits of the Spirit, even we ourselves groan within ourselves, eagerly waiting for the adoption, the redemption of our body.

5

Ezek. 18:4: Behold, all souls are Mine; The soul of the father As well as the soul of the son is Mine; The soul who sins shall die. **Rom. 5:12:** Therefore, just as through one man sin entered the world, and death through sin, and thus death spread to all men, because all sinned. **Rom. 6:23:** For the wages of sin *is* death, but the gift of God *is* eternal life in Christ Jesus our Lord.

6

Matt. 25:41, 46: Then He will also say to those on the left hand, 'Depart from Me, you cursed, into the everlasting fire prepared for the devil and his angels....' And these will go away into everlasting punishment, but the righteous into eternal life." **2 Thess. 1:9:** These shall be punished with everlasting destruction from the presence of the Lord and from the glory of His power. **Rev. 14:9-11:** Then a third angel followed them, saying with a loud voice, "If anyone worships the beast and his image, and receives *his* mark on his forehead or on his hand, he himself shall also drink of the wine of the wrath of God, which is poured out full strength into the cup of His indignation. He shall be tormented with fire and brimstone in the presence of the holy angels and in the presence of the Lamb. And the smoke of their torment ascends forever and ever; and they have no rest day or night, who worship the beast and his image, and whoever receives the mark of his name."

Q. 20. *Did God leave all mankind to perish in the estate of sin and misery?*

A. God having, out of His mere good pleasure, from all eternity, elected some to everlasting life,[1] did pledge to deliver them out of the estate of sin and misery, and to bring them into an estate of salvation by a Redeemer, commonly called the covenant of grace.[2]

1
Acts 13:48: Now when the Gentiles heard this, they were glad and glorified the word of the Lord. And as many as had been appointed to eternal life believed. **Eph. 1:4-5:** ... just as He chose us in Him before the foundation of the world, that we should be holy and without blame before Him in love, having predestined us to adoption as sons by Jesus Christ to Himself, according to the good pleasure of His will. **2 Thess. 2:13-14:** But we are bound to give thanks to God always for you, brethren beloved by the Lord, because God from the beginning chose you for salvation through sanctification by the Spirit and belief in the truth, to which He called you by our gospel, for the obtaining of the glory of our Lord Jesus Christ.

2
Gen. 3:15: And I will put enmity Between you and the woman, And between your seed and her Seed; He shall bruise your head, And you shall bruise His heel. **Gen. 17:7:** And I will establish My covenant between Me and you and your descendants after you in their generations, for an everlasting covenant, to be God to you and your descendants after you. **Ex. 19:5-6:** 'Now therefore, if you will indeed obey My voice and keep My covenant, then you shall be a special treasure to Me above all people; for all the earth *is* Mine. And you shall be to Me a kingdom of priests and a holy nation.' These *are* the words which you shall speak to the children of Israel. **Jer. 31:31-34:** Behold, the days are coming, says the LORD, when I will make a new covenant with the house of Israel and with the house of Judah— not according to the covenant that I made with their fathers in the day *that* I took them by the hand to lead them out of the land of Egypt, My covenant which they broke, though I was a husband to them, says the LORD. But this *is* the covenant that I will make with the house of Israel after those days, says the LORD: I will put My law in their minds, and write it on their hearts; and I will be their God, and they shall be My people. No more shall every man teach his neighbor, and every man his brother, saying, 'Know the LORD,' for they all shall know Me, from the least of them to the greatest of them, says the LORD. For I will forgive their iniquity, and their sin I will remember no more. **Matt. 20:28:** ... just as the Son of Man did not come to be served, but to serve, and to give His life a ransom for many. **1 Cor. 11:25:** In the same manner *He* also *took* the cup after supper, saying, "This cup is the new covenant in My blood. This do, as often as you drink *it,* in remembrance of Me." **Heb. 9:15:** And for this reason He is the Mediator of the new covenant, by means of death, for the redemption of the transgressions under the first covenant, that those who are called may receive the promise of the eternal inheritance.

Q. 21. *How is the covenant of grace revealed?*

A. The covenant of grace is revealed first of all to Adam in the promise of salvation,[1] and afterwards successively through the seven divine covenants of promise.[2]

1
Gen. 3:15: And I will put enmity Between you and the woman, And between your seed and her Seed; He shall bruise your head, And you shall bruise His heel.

2
Eph. 2:12: ... that at that time you were without Christ, being aliens from the commonwealth of Israel and strangers from the covenants of promise, having no hope and without God in the world. Gen. 6:18: But I will establish My covenant with you; and you shall go into the ark—you, your sons, your wife, and your sons' wives with you. **Gen. 9:8-11:** Then God spoke to Noah and to his sons with him, saying: "And as for Me, behold, I establish My covenant with you and with your descendants after you, and with every living creature that *is* with you: the birds, the cattle, and every beast of the earth with you, of all that go out of the ark, every beast of the earth. Thus I establish My covenant with you: Never again shall all flesh be cut off by the waters of the flood; never again shall there be a flood to destroy the earth." **Gen. 17:1-8:** When Abram was ninety-nine years old, the LORD appeared to Abram and said to him, "I *am* Almighty God; walk before Me and be blameless. And I will make My covenant between Me and you, and will multiply you exceedingly." Then Abram fell on his face, and God talked with him, saying: "As for Me, behold, My covenant is with you, and you shall be a father of many nations. No longer shall your name be called Abram, but your name shall be Abraham; for I have made you a father of many nations. I will make you exceedingly fruitful; and I will make nations of you, and kings shall come from you. And I will establish My covenant between Me and you and your descendants after you in their generations, for an everlasting covenant, to be God to you and your descendants after you. Also I give to you and your descendants after you the land in which you are a stranger, all the land of Canaan, as an everlasting possession; and I will be their God." **Ex. 19:1-6:** In the third month after the children of Israel had gone out of the land of Egypt, on the same day, they came *to* the Wilderness of Sinai. For they had departed from Rephidim, had come *to* the Wilderness of Sinai, and camped in the wilderness. So Israel camped there before the mountain. And Moses went up to God, and the LORD

called to him from the mountain, saying, "Thus you shall say to the house of Jacob, and tell the children of Israel: 'You have seen what I did to the Egyptians, and *how* I bore you on eagles' wings and brought you to Myself. Now therefore, if you will indeed obey My voice and keep My covenant, then you shall be a special treasure to Me above all people; for all the earth *is* Mine. And you shall be to Me a kingdom of priests and a holy nation.' These *are* the words which you shall speak to the children of Israel." **Ps. 89:3-4, 34-36:** I have made a covenant with My chosen, I have sworn to My servant David: 'Your seed I will establish forever, And build up your throne to all generations.' ... My covenant I will not break, Nor alter the word that has gone out of My lips. Once I have sworn by My holiness; I will not lie to David: His seed shall endure forever, And his throne as the sun before Me. **Ps. 110:1-4:** The LORD said to my Lord, "Sit at My right hand, Till I make Your enemies Your footstool." The LORD shall send the rod of Your strength out of Zion. Rule in the midst of Your enemies! Your people *shall be* volunteers In the day of Your power; In the beauties of holiness, from the womb of the morning, You have the dew of Your youth. The LORD has sworn And will not relent, "You *are* a priest forever According to the order of Melchizedek." **Heb. 7:** For this Melchizedek, king of Salem, priest of the Most High God, who met Abraham returning from the slaughter of the kings and blessed him, to whom also Abraham gave a tenth part of all, first being translated "king of righteousness," and then also king of Salem, meaning "king of peace," without father, without mother, without genealogy, having neither beginning of days nor end of life, but made like the Son of God, remains a priest continually.... Therefore, if perfection were through the Levitical priesthood (for under it the people received the law), what further need *was there* that another priest should rise according to the order of Melchizedek, and not be called according to the order of Aaron? For the priesthood being changed, of necessity there is also a change of the law. For He of whom these things are spoken belongs to another tribe, from which no man has officiated at the altar. For *it is* evident that our Lord arose from Judah, of which tribe Moses spoke nothing concerning priesthood. And it is yet far more evident if, in the likeness of Melchizedek, there arises another priest who has come, not according to the law of a fleshly commandment, but according to the power of an endless life. For He testifies: "You *are* a priest forever According to the order of Melchizedek." ... And inasmuch as *He was* not *made priest* without an oath (for they have become priests without an oath, but He with an oath by Him who said to Him: "The LORD has sworn And will not relent, 'You *are* a priest forever According to the order of Melchizedek'"), by so much more Jesus has become a surety of a better covenant.... For the law appoints as high priests men who have weakness, but the word of the oath, which came after the law, *appoints* the Son who has been perfected forever. **Jer. 31:31-34:** Behold, the days are coming, says the LORD, when I will make a new covenant with the house of Israel and with the house of Judah— not according to the covenant that I made with their fathers in the day *that* I took them by the hand to lead them out of the land of Egypt, My covenant which they broke, though I was a husband to them, says the LORD. But this *is* the covenant that I will make with the house of Israel after those days, says the LORD: I will put My law in their minds, and write it on their hearts; and I will be their God, and they shall be My people. No more shall every man teach his neighbor, and every man his brother, saying, 'Know the LORD,' for they all shall know Me, from the least of them to the greatest of them, says the LORD. For I will forgive their iniquity, and their sin I will remember no more. **Heb. 8:7-13:** For if that first *covenant* had been faultless, then no place would have been sought for a second. Because finding fault with them, He says: "Behold, the days are coming, says the LORD, when I will make a new covenant with the house of Israel and with the house of Judah— not according to the covenant that I made with their fathers in the day when I took them by the hand to lead them out of the land of Egypt; because they did not continue in My covenant, and I disregarded them, says the LORD. For this *is* the covenant that I will make with the house of Israel after those days, says the LORD: I will put My laws in their mind and write them on their hearts; and I will be their God, and they shall be My people. None of them shall teach his neighbor, and none his brother, saying, 'Know the LORD,' for all shall know Me, from the least of them to the greatest of them. For I will be merciful to their unrighteousness, and their sins and their lawless deeds I will remember no more." In that He says, "A new *covenant*," He has made the first obsolete. Now what is becoming obsolete and growing old is ready to vanish away.

Q. 22. *What is a divine covenant?*

A. A divine covenant is a promise pledged by God wherein He swears an oath to confirm it;[1] it is an oath-bound promise of His grace, love, and mercy.[2]

1 **Gen. 9:8-17:** Then God spoke to Noah and to his sons with him, saying: "And as for Me, behold, I establish My covenant with you and with your descendants after you, and with every living creature that *is* with you: the birds, the cattle, and every beast of the earth with you, of all that go out of the ark, every beast of the earth. Thus I establish My covenant with you: Never again shall all flesh be cut off by the waters of the flood; never again shall there be a flood to destroy the earth." And God said: "This *is* the sign of the covenant which I make between Me and you, and every living creature that *is* with you, for perpetual generations: I set My rainbow in the cloud, and it shall be for the sign of the covenant between Me and the earth. It shall be, when I bring a cloud over the earth, that the

rainbow shall be seen in the cloud; and I will remember My covenant which *is* between Me and you and every living creature of all flesh; the waters shall never again become a flood to destroy all flesh. The rainbow shall be in the cloud, and I will look on it to remember the everlasting covenant between God and every living creature of all flesh that *is* on the earth." And God said to Noah, "This *is* the sign of the covenant which I have established between Me and all flesh that *is* on the earth." **Isa. 54:9-10:** "For this *is* like the waters of Noah to Me; For as I have sworn That the waters of Noah would no longer cover the earth, So have I sworn That I would not be angry with you, nor rebuke you. For the mountains shall depart And the hills be removed, But My kindness shall not depart from you, Nor shall My covenant of peace be removed," Says the LORD, who has mercy on you. **Ps. 89:3-4, 34-36:** I have made a covenant with My chosen, I have sworn to My servant David: 'Your seed I will establish forever, And build up your throne to all generations.... My covenant I will not break, Nor alter the word that has gone out of My lips. Once I have sworn by My holiness; I will not lie to David: His seed shall endure forever, And his throne as the sun before Me. **Acts 2:29-31:** Men *and* brethren, let *me* speak freely to you of the patriarch David, that he is both dead and buried, and his tomb is with us to this day. Therefore, being a prophet, and knowing that God had sworn with an oath to him that of the fruit of his body, according to the flesh, He would raise up the Christ to sit on his throne, he, foreseeing this, spoke concerning the resurrection of the Christ, that His soul was not left in Hades, nor did His flesh see corruption.

[2] **Gen. 6:8:** But Noah found grace in the eyes of the LORD. **Deut. 7:9:** Therefore know that the LORD your God, He *is* God, the faithful God who keeps covenant and mercy for a thousand generations with those who love Him and keep His commandments. **Luke 1:72:** To perform the mercy *promised* to our fathers And to remember His holy covenant. **1 Kings 8:23:** ... and he said: "LORD God of Israel, *there is* no God in heaven above or on earth below like You, who keep *Your* covenant and mercy with Your servants who walk before You with all their hearts."

Q. 23. *Which is the first covenant?*

A. The first covenant is that oath sworn to Noah,[1] commonly called the antediluvian Noahic Covenant.

[1] **Gen. 6-8:** Then the LORD saw that the wickedness of man *was* great in the earth, and *that* every intent of the thoughts of his heart *was* only evil continually. And the LORD was sorry that He had made man on the earth, and He was grieved in His heart. So the LORD said, "I will destroy man whom I have created from the face of the earth, both man and beast, creeping thing and birds of the air, for I am sorry that I have made them." But Noah found grace in the eyes of the LORD.... And God said to Noah, "The end of all flesh has come before Me, for the earth is filled with violence through them; and behold, I will destroy them with the earth. Make yourself an ark of gopherwood.... And behold, I Myself am bringing floodwaters on the earth, to destroy from under heaven all flesh in which *is* the breath of life; everything that *is* on the earth shall die. But I will establish My covenant with you; and you shall go into the ark—you, your sons, your wife, and your sons' wives with you. And of every living thing of all flesh you shall bring two of every *sort* into the ark, to keep *them* alive with you; they shall be male and female.... And Noah did according to all that the LORD commanded him.... So those that entered, male and female of all flesh, went in as God had commanded him; and the LORD shut him in.... So He destroyed all living things which were on the face of the ground: both man and cattle, creeping thing and bird of the air. They were destroyed from the earth. Only Noah and those who *were* with him in the ark remained *alive*.... Then God remembered Noah, and every living thing, and all the animals that *were* with him in the ark. And God made a wind to pass over the earth, and the waters subsided. The fountains of the deep and the windows of heaven were also stopped, and the rain from heaven was restrained.... Then God spoke to Noah, saying, "Go out of the ark, you and your wife, and your sons and your sons' wives with you. Bring out with you every living thing of all flesh that *is* with you: birds and cattle and every creeping thing that creeps on the earth, so that they may abound on the earth, and be fruitful and multiply on the earth." ... Then Noah built an altar to the LORD, and took of every clean animal and of every clean bird, and offered burnt offerings on the altar. And the LORD smelled a soothing aroma.

Q. 24. *Which is the second covenant?*

A. The second covenant is that oath sworn to Noah, his posterity, and the animals with him,[1] commonly called the postdiluvian Noahic Covenant.

[1] **Gen. 9:1-18:** So God blessed Noah and his sons, and said to them: "Be fruitful and multiply, and fill the earth. And the fear of you and the dread of you shall be on every beast of the earth, on every bird of the air, on all that move *on* the earth, and on all the fish of the sea. They are given into your hand. Every moving thing that lives shall be food for you. I have given you all things, even as the green herbs. But you shall not eat flesh with its life, *that is,* its blood. Surely for your lifeblood I will demand *a reckoning;* from the hand of every beast I will require it, and from the hand of man. From the hand of every man's brother I will require the life of man. "Whoever sheds man's blood, By man his blood shall be shed; For in the image of God He made man. And as for you, be fruitful and multiply; Bring forth abundantly in the earth And multiply in it." Then God spoke to Noah and to his sons with him, saying: "And as for Me, behold, I establish My covenant with you and with your descendants after you, and with every living creature that *is* with you: the birds, the cattle, and every beast of the earth with you, of all that go out of the ark, every beast of the earth. Thus I establish My covenant with you: Never again shall all flesh be cut off by the waters of the flood; never again shall there be a flood to destroy the earth." And God said: "This *is* the sign of the covenant which I make between Me and you, and every living creature that *is* with you, for perpetual generations: I set My rainbow in the cloud, and it shall be for the sign of the covenant between Me and the earth. It shall be, when I bring a cloud over the earth, that the rainbow shall be seen in the cloud; and I will remember My covenant which *is* between Me and you and every living creature of all flesh; the waters shall never again become a flood to destroy all flesh. The rainbow shall be in the cloud, and I will look on it to remember the everlasting covenant between God and every living creature of all flesh that *is* on the earth." And God said to Noah, "This *is* the sign of the covenant which I have established between Me and all flesh that *is* on the earth." Now the sons of Noah who went out of the ark were Shem, Ham, and Japheth. And Ham *was* the father of Canaan. **Isa. 54:9:** For this *is* like the waters of Noah to Me; For as I have sworn That the waters of Noah would no longer cover the earth, So have I sworn That I would not be angry with you, nor rebuke you.

Q. 25. *What is the token annexed to the second covenant?*

A. The token annexed to the second covenant is the bow set in the cloud.[1]

[1] **Gen. 9:12-17:** And God said: "This *is* the sign of the covenant which I make between Me and you, and every living creature that *is* with you, for perpetual generations: I set My rainbow in the cloud, and it shall be for the sign of the covenant between Me and the earth. It shall be, when I bring a cloud over the earth, that the rainbow shall be seen in the cloud; and I will remember My covenant which *is* between Me and you and every living creature of all flesh; the waters shall never again become a flood to destroy all flesh. The rainbow shall be in the cloud, and I will look on it to remember the everlasting covenant between God and every living creature of all flesh that *is* on the earth." And God said to Noah, "This *is* the sign of the covenant which I have established between Me and all flesh that *is* on the earth."

Q. 26. *Which is the third covenant?*

A. The third covenant is that oath sworn to Abraham,[1] commonly called the Abrahamic Covenant.

[1] **Gen. 15:** And behold, the word of the Lord *came* to him, saying, "This one shall not be your heir, but one who will come from your own body shall be your heir." Then He brought him outside and said, "Look now toward heaven, and count the stars if you are able to number them." And He said to him, "So shall your descendants be." And he believed in the Lord, and He accounted it to him for righteousness.... So He said to him, "Bring Me a three-year-old heifer, a three-year-old female goat, a three-year-old ram, a turtledove, and a young pigeon." Then he brought all these to Him and cut them in two, down the middle, and placed each piece opposite the other ... And it came to pass, when the sun went down and it was dark, that behold, there appeared a smoking oven and a burning torch that passed between those pieces. On the same day the Lord made a covenant with Abram, saying: "To your descendants I have given this land, from the river of Egypt to the great river, the River Euphrates—the Kenites, the Kenezzites, the Kadmonites, the Hittites, the Perizzites, the Rephaim, the Amorites, the Canaanites, the Girgashites, and the Jebusites." **Gen. 17:** When Abram was ninety-nine years old, the Lord appeared to Abram and said to him, "I *am* Almighty God; walk before Me and be blameless. And I will make My covenant between Me and you, and will multiply you exceedingly." Then Abram fell on his face, and God talked with him, saying: "As for Me, behold, My covenant is with you, and you shall be a father of many nations. No longer shall your

name be called Abram, but your name shall be Abraham; for I have made you a father of many nations. I will make you exceedingly fruitful; and I will make nations of you, and kings shall come from you. And I will establish My covenant between Me and you and your descendants after you in their generations, for an everlasting covenant, to be God to you and your descendants after you. Also I give to you and your descendants after you the land in which you are a stranger, all the land of Canaan, as an everlasting possession; and I will be their God." ... "As for you, you shall keep My covenant, you and your descendants after you throughout their generations. This *is* My covenant which you shall keep, between Me and you and your descendants after you: Every male child among you shall be circumcised; and you shall be circumcised in the flesh of your foreskins, and it shall be a sign of the covenant between Me and you.... and My covenant shall be in your flesh for an everlasting covenant. And the uncircumcised male child, who is not circumcised in the flesh of his foreskin, that person shall be cut off from his people; he has broken My covenant." ... Sarah your wife shall bear you a son, and you shall call his name Isaac; I will establish My covenant with him for an everlasting covenant, *and* with his descendants after him.... **Gen. 22:16-18:** ... and said: "By Myself I have sworn, says the LORD, because you have done this thing, and have not withheld your son, your only *son*— blessing I will bless you, and multiplying I will multiply your descendants as the stars of the heaven and as the sand which *is* on the seashore; and your descendants shall possess the gate of their enemies. In your seed all the nations of the earth shall be blessed, because you have obeyed My voice." **Gen. 26:3:** Dwell in this land, and I will be with you and bless you; for to you and your descendants I give all these lands, and I will perform the oath which I swore to Abraham your father. **Luke 1:72-73:** To perform the mercy *promised* to our fathers And to remember His holy covenant, The oath which He swore to our father Abraham.

Q. 27. *What is the token annexed to the third covenant?*

A. The token annexed to the third covenant is the circumcision of the flesh.[1]

[1] **Gen. 17:10-11:** This *is* My covenant which you shall keep, between Me and you and your descendants after you: Every male child among you shall be circumcised; and you shall be circumcised in the flesh of your foreskins, and it shall be a sign of the covenant between Me and you. **Rom. 4:11:** And he received the sign of circumcision, a seal of the righteousness of the faith which *he had while still* uncircumcised, that he might be the father of all those who believe, though they are uncircumcised, that righteousness might be imputed to them also.

Q. 28. *Which is the fourth covenant?*

A. The fourth covenant is that oath sworn to Israel of old,[1] commonly called the Old Covenant.

[1] **Ex. 19:1-9:** In the third month after the children of Israel had gone out of the land of Egypt, on the same day, they came *to* the Wilderness of Sinai. For they had departed from Rephidim, had come *to* the Wilderness of Sinai, and camped in the wilderness. So Israel camped there before the mountain. And Moses went up to God, and the LORD called to him from the mountain, saying, "Thus you shall say to the house of Jacob, and tell the children of Israel: 'You have seen what I did to the Egyptians, and *how* I bore you on eagles' wings and brought you to Myself. Now therefore, if you will indeed obey My voice and keep My covenant, then you shall be a special treasure to Me above all people; for all the earth *is* Mine. And you shall be to Me a kingdom of priests and a holy nation.' These *are* the words which you shall speak to the children of Israel." So Moses came and called for the elders of the people, and laid before them all these words which the LORD commanded him. Then all the people answered together and said, "All that the LORD has spoken we will do." So Moses brought back the words of the people to the LORD. And the LORD said to Moses, "Behold, I come to you in the thick cloud, that the people may hear when I speak with you, and believe you forever." So Moses told the words of the people to the LORD. **Deut. 29:10-15:** "All of you stand today before the LORD your God: your leaders and your tribes and your elders and your officers, all the men of Israel, your little ones and your wives—also the stranger who *is* in your camp, from the one who cuts your wood to the one who draws your water— that you may enter into covenant with the LORD your God, and into His oath, which the LORD your God makes with you today, that He may establish you today as a people for Himself, and *that* He may be God to you, just as He has spoken to you, and just as He has sworn to your fathers, to Abraham, Isaac, and Jacob. "I make this covenant and this oath, not with you alone, but with *him* who stands here with us today before the LORD our God, as well as with *him* who *is* not here with us today."

Q. 29. *What is the token annexed to the fourth covenant?*

A. The token annexed to the fourth covenant is the Sabbath wherein God rested and was refreshed.[1]

[1] **Ex. 31:13, 16-17:** "Speak also to the children of Israel, saying: 'Surely My Sabbaths you shall keep, for it *is* a sign between Me and you throughout your generations, that *you* may know that I *am* the LORD who sanctifies you.... Therefore the children of Israel shall keep the Sabbath, to observe the Sabbath throughout their generations *as* a perpetual covenant. It *is* a sign between Me and the children of Israel forever; for *in* six days the LORD made the heavens and the earth, and on the seventh day He rested and was refreshed.'" **Ezek. 20:12:** Moreover I also gave them My Sabbaths, to be a sign between them and Me, that they might know that I *am* the LORD who sanctifies them.

Q. 30. *Which is the fifth covenant?*

A. The fifth covenant is that oath sworn to David,[1] commonly called the Davidic Covenant.

[1] **Ps. 89:3-4, 34-36:** I have made a covenant with My chosen, I have sworn to My servant David: 'Your seed I will establish forever, And build up your throne to all generations.... My covenant I will not break, Nor alter the word that has gone out of My lips. Once I have sworn by My holiness; I will not lie to David: His seed shall endure forever, And his throne as the sun before Me. **Acts 2:30:** Therefore, being a prophet, and knowing that God had sworn with an oath to him that of the fruit of his body, according to the flesh, He would raise up the Christ to sit on his throne.

Q. 31. *Which is the sixth covenant?*

A. The sixth covenant is that oath sworn to the promised Messiah, the Lord Jesus Christ,[1] commonly called the Messianic Covenant.

[1] **Ps. 110:1-4:** The LORD said to my Lord, "Sit at My right hand, Till I make Your enemies Your footstool." The LORD shall send the rod of Your strength out of Zion. Rule in the midst of Your enemies! Your people *shall be* volunteers In the day of Your power; In the beauties of holiness, from the womb of the morning, You have the dew of Your youth. The LORD has sworn And will not relent, "You *are* a priest forever According to the order of Melchizedek." **Heb. 7:** For this Melchizedek, king of Salem, priest of the Most High God, who met Abraham returning from the slaughter of the kings and blessed him, to whom also Abraham gave a tenth part of all, first being translated "king of righteousness," and then also king of Salem, meaning "king of peace," without father, without mother, without genealogy, having neither beginning of days nor end of life, but made like the Son of God, remains a priest continually.... Therefore, if perfection were through the Levitical priesthood (for under it the people received the law), what further need *was there* that another priest should rise according to the order of Melchizedek, and not be called according to the order of Aaron? For the priesthood being changed, of necessity there is also a change of the law. For He of whom these things are spoken belongs to another tribe, from which no man has officiated at the altar. For *it is* evident that our Lord arose from Judah, of which tribe Moses spoke nothing concerning priesthood. And it is yet far more evident if, in the likeness of Melchizedek, there arises another priest who has come, not according to the law of a fleshly commandment, but according to the power of an endless life. For He testifies: "You *are* a priest forever According to the order of Melchizedek." ... And inasmuch as *He was* not *made priest* without an oath (for they have become priests without an oath, but He with an oath by Him who said to Him: "The LORD has sworn And will not relent, 'You *are* a priest forever According to the order of Melchizedek'"), by so much more Jesus has become a surety of a better covenant.... For the law appoints as high priests men who have weakness, but the word of the oath, which came after the law, *appoints* the Son who has been perfected forever.

Q. 32. *Which is the seventh covenant?*

A. The seventh covenant is that oath sworn to the remnant according to the election of grace,[1] commonly called the New Covenant.[2]

1

Heb. 8:6: But now He has obtained a more excellent ministry, inasmuch as He is also Mediator of a better covenant, which was established on better promises. **Rom. 11:1-5, 25-27:** I say then, has God cast away His people? Certainly not! For I also am an Israelite, of the seed of Abraham, *of* the tribe of Benjamin. God has not cast away His people whom He foreknew. Or do you not know what the Scripture says of Elijah, how he pleads with God against Israel, saying, "LORD, they have killed Your prophets and torn down Your altars, and I alone am left, and they seek my life"? But what does the divine response say to him? "I have reserved for Myself seven thousand men who have not bowed the knee to Baal." Even so then, at this present time there is a remnant according to the election of grace.... For I do not desire, brethren, that you should be ignorant of this mystery, lest you should be wise in your own opinion, that blindness in part has happened to Israel until the fullness of the Gentiles has come in. And so all Israel will be saved, as it is written: "The Deliverer will come out of Zion, And He will turn away ungodliness from Jacob; For this *is* My covenant with them, When I take away their sins."

2

Jer. 31:31-40: "Behold, the days are coming, says the LORD, when I will make a new covenant with the house of Israel and with the house of Judah— not according to the covenant that I made with their fathers in the day *that* I took them by the hand to lead them out of the land of Egypt, My covenant which they broke, though I was a husband to them, says the LORD. But this *is* the covenant that I will make with the house of Israel after those days, says the LORD: I will put My law in their minds, and write it on their hearts; and I will be their God, and they shall be My people. No more shall every man teach his neighbor, and every man his brother, saying, 'Know the LORD,' for they all shall know Me, from the least of them to the greatest of them, says the LORD. For I will forgive their iniquity, and their sin I will remember no more." Thus says the LORD, Who gives the sun for a light by day, The ordinances of the moon and the stars for a light by night, Who disturbs the sea, And its waves roar (The LORD of hosts *is* His name): "If those ordinances depart From before Me, says the LORD, *Then* the seed of Israel shall also cease From being a nation before Me forever." Thus says the LORD: "If heaven above can be measured, And the foundations of the earth searched out beneath, I will also cast off all the seed of Israel For all that they have done, says the LORD. "Behold, the days are coming, says the LORD, that the city shall be built for the LORD from the Tower of Hananel to the Corner Gate. The surveyor's line shall again extend straight forward over the hill Gareb; then it shall turn toward Goath. And the whole valley of the dead bodies and of the ashes, and all the fields as far as the Brook Kidron, to the corner of the Horse Gate toward the east, *shall be* holy to the LORD. It shall not be plucked up or thrown down anymore forever." **Heb. 8:7-13:** For if that first *covenant* had been faultless, then no place would have been sought for a second. Because finding fault with them, He says: "Behold, the days are coming, says the LORD, when I will make a new covenant with the house of Israel and with the house of Judah— not according to the covenant that I made with their fathers in the day when I took them by the hand to lead them out of the land of Egypt; because they did not continue in My covenant, and I disregarded them, says the LORD. For this *is* the covenant that I will make with the house of Israel after those days, says the LORD: I will put My laws in their mind and write them on their hearts; and I will be their God, and they shall be My people. None of them shall teach his neighbor, and none his brother, saying, 'Know the LORD,' for all shall know Me, from the least of them to the greatest of them. For I will be merciful to their unrighteousness, and their sins and their lawless deeds I will remember no more." In that He says, "A new *covenant*," He has made the first obsolete. Now what is becoming obsolete and growing old is ready to vanish away.

Q. 33. *What is the token annexed to the seventh covenant?*

A. The token annexed to the seventh covenant is the bread and cup of the Lord,[1] commonly called the Lord's Supper.[2]

1

Luke 22:19-20: And He took bread, gave thanks and broke *it,* and gave *it* to them, saying, "This is My body which is given for you; do this in remembrance of Me." Likewise He also *took* the cup after supper, saying, "This cup *is* the new covenant in My blood, which is shed for you. **1 Cor. 11:23-26:** For I received from the Lord that which I also delivered to you: that the Lord Jesus on the *same* night in which He was betrayed took bread; and when He had given thanks, He broke *it* and said, "Take, eat; this is My body which is broken for you; do this in remembrance of Me." In the same manner *He* also *took* the cup after supper, saying, "This cup is the new covenant in My blood. This do, as often as you drink *it,* in remembrance of Me." For as often as you eat this bread and drink this cup, you proclaim the Lord's death till He comes.

[2] **1 Cor. 11:20:** Therefore when you come together in one place, it is not to eat the Lord's Supper.

Q. 34. *Who is the Redeemer of God's elect?*

A. The only Redeemer of God's elect is the Lord Jesus Christ,[1] who, being the eternal Son of God,[2] became man,[3] and so was, and continueth to be, God and man in two distinct natures, and one person, forever.[4]

[1] **John 14:6:** Jesus said to him, "I am the way, the truth, and the life. No one comes to the Father except through Me. **Acts 4:12:** Nor is there salvation in any other, for there is no other name under heaven given among men by which we must be saved. **1 Tim. 2:5-6:** For *there is* one God and one Mediator between God and men, *the* Man Christ Jesus, who gave Himself a ransom for all, to be testified in due time.

[2] **Ps. 2:7:** I will declare the decree: The LORD has said to Me, 'You *are* My Son, Today I have begotten You. **Matt. 3:17:** And suddenly a voice *came* from heaven, saying, "This is My beloved Son, in whom I am well pleased." **Matt. 17:5:** While he was still speaking, behold, a bright cloud overshadowed them; and suddenly a voice came out of the cloud, saying, "This is My beloved Son, in whom I am well pleased. Hear Him!" **John 1:18:** No one has seen God at any time. The only begotten Son, who is in the bosom of the Father, He has declared *Him.*

[3] **Isa. 9:6:** For unto us a Child is born, Unto us a Son is given; And the government will be upon His shoulder. And His name will be called Wonderful, Counselor, Mighty God, Everlasting Father, Prince of Peace. **Matt. 1:23:** "Behold, the virgin shall be with child, and bear a Son, and they shall call His name Immanuel," which is translated, "God with us." **John 1:14:** And the Word became flesh and dwelt among us, and we beheld His glory, the glory as of the only begotten of the Father, full of grace and truth. **Gal. 4:4:** But when the fullness of the time had come, God sent forth His Son, born of a woman, born under the law.

[4] **Acts 1:11:** who also said, "Men of Galilee, why do you stand gazing up into heaven? This *same* Jesus, who was taken up from you into heaven, will so come in like manner as you saw Him go into heaven." **Heb. 7:24-25:** But He, because He continues forever, has an unchangeable priesthood. Therefore He is also able to save to the uttermost those who come to God through Him, since He always lives to make intercession for them.

Q. 35. *How did Christ, being the Son of God, become man?*

A. Christ, the Son of God, became man, by taking to Himself a true body and a reasonable soul,[1] being conceived by the power of the Holy Spirit in the womb of the virgin Mary, and born of her,[2] yet without sin.[3]

[1] **Phil. 2:7:** ... but made Himself of no reputation, taking the form of a bondservant, *and* coming in the likeness of men. **Heb. 2:14, 17:** Inasmuch then as the children have partaken of flesh and blood, He Himself likewise shared in the same, that through death He might destroy him who had the power of death, that is, the devil.... Therefore, in all things He had to be made like *His* brethren, that He might be a merciful and faithful High Priest in things *pertaining* to God, to make propitiation for the sins of the people.

[2] **Luke 1:27, 31, 35:** ... to a virgin betrothed to a man whose name was Joseph, of the house of David. The virgin's name *was* Mary.... And behold, you will conceive in your womb and bring forth a Son, and shall call His name Jesus.... And the angel answered and said to her, "*The* Holy Spirit will come upon you, and the power of the Highest will overshadow you; therefore, also, that Holy One who is to be born will be called the Son of God.

[3] **2 Cor. 5:21:** For He made Him who knew no sin *to be* sin for us, that we might become the righteousness of God in Him. **Heb. 4:15:** For we do not have a High Priest who cannot sympathize with our weaknesses, but was in all *points* tempted as *we are, yet* without sin. **Heb. 7:26:** For such

a High Priest was fitting for us, *who is* holy, harmless, undefiled, separate from sinners, and has become higher than the heavens. **1 John 3:5:** And you know that He was manifested to take away our sins, and in Him there is no sin.

Q. 36. *What offices doth Christ execute as our Redeemer?*

A. Christ, as our Redeemer, executeth the offices of a Prophet,[1] of a Priest,[2] and of a King,[3] both in His estate of humiliation and exaltation.

1 **Deut. 18:18:** I will raise up for them a Prophet like you from among their brethren, and will put My words in His mouth, and He shall speak to them all that I command Him. **Acts 2:33:** Therefore being exalted to the right hand of God, and having received from the Father the promise of the Holy Spirit, He poured out this which you now see and hear. **Acts 3:22-23:** For Moses truly said to the fathers, 'The LORD your God will raise up for you a Prophet like me from your brethren. Him you shall hear in all things, whatever He says to you. And it shall be *that* every soul who will not hear that Prophet shall be utterly destroyed from among the people.' **Heb. 1:1-2:** God, who at various times and in various ways spoke in time past to the fathers by the prophets, has in these last days spoken to us by *His* Son, whom He has appointed heir of all things, through whom also He made the worlds.

2 **Heb. 4:14-15:** Seeing then that we have a great High Priest who has passed through the heavens, Jesus the Son of God, let us hold fast *our* confession. For we do not have a High Priest who cannot sympathize with our weaknesses, but was in all *points* tempted as *we are, yet* without sin. **Heb. 5:5-6:** So also Christ did not glorify Himself to become High Priest, but *it was* He who said to Him: "You are My Son, Today I have begotten You." As *He* also *says* in another *place:* "You *are* a priest forever According to the order of Melchizedek".

3 **Isa. 9:6-7:** For unto us a Child is born, Unto us a Son is given; And the government will be upon His shoulder. And His name will be called Wonderful, Counselor, Mighty God, Everlasting Father, Prince of Peace. Of the increase of *His* government and peace *There will be* no end, Upon the throne of David and over His kingdom, To order it and establish it with judgment and justice From that time forward, even forever. The zeal of the LORD of hosts will perform this. **Luke 1:32-33:** He will be great, and will be called the Son of the Highest; and the Lord God will give Him the throne of His father David. And He will reign over the house of Jacob forever, and of His kingdom there will be no end. **John 18:37:** Pilate therefore said to Him, "Are You a king then?" Jesus answered, "You say *rightly* that I am a king. For this cause I was born, and for this cause I have come into the world, that I should bear witness to the truth. Everyone who is of the truth hears My voice." **1 Cor. 15:25:** For He must reign till He has put all enemies under His feet.

Q. 37. *How doth Christ execute the office of a Prophet?*

A. Christ executeth the office of a Prophet, in revealing to us, by His word[1] and Spirit,[2] the will of God for our salvation.[3]

1 **Luke 4:18-19, 21:** "The Spirit of the LORD *is* upon Me, Because He has anointed Me To preach the gospel to *the* poor; He has sent Me to heal the brokenhearted, To proclaim liberty to *the* captives And recovery of sight to *the* blind, *To* set at liberty those who are oppressed; To proclaim the acceptable year of the LORD." ... And He began to say to them, "Today this Scripture is fulfilled in your hearing." **Acts 1:1-2:** The former account I made, O Theophilus, of all that Jesus began both to do and teach, until the day in which He was taken up, after He through the Holy Spirit had given commandments to the apostles whom He had chosen. **Heb. 2:3:** ... how shall we escape if we neglect so great a salvation, which at the first began to be spoken by the Lord, and was confirmed to us by those who heard *Him.*

2 **John 15:26-27:** But when the Helper comes, whom I shall send to you from the Father, the Spirit of truth who proceeds from the Father, He will testify of Me. And you also will bear witness, because you have been with Me from the beginning. **Acts 1:8:** But you shall receive power when the Holy Spirit has come upon you; and you shall be witnesses to Me in Jerusalem, and in all Judea and Samaria, and to the end of the earth. **1 Pet. 1:11:** ... searching what, or what manner of time, the Spirit of Christ who was in them was indicating when He testified beforehand the sufferings of Christ and the glories that would follow.

3 **John 4:41-42:** Then they said to the woman, "Now we believe, not because of what you said, for

we ourselves have heard *Him* and we know that this is indeed the Christ, the Savior of the world." **John 20:30-31:** And truly Jesus did many other signs in the presence of His disciples, which are not written in this book; but these are written that you may believe that Jesus is the Christ, the Son of God, and that believing you may have life in His name.

Q. 38. *How doth Christ execute the office of a Priest?*

A. Christ executeth the office of a Priest, in His once offering up of Himself a sacrifice to satisfy divine justice,[1] and reconcile us to God;[2] and in making continual intercession for us.[3]

1 **Isa. 53:** ... All we like sheep have gone astray; We have turned, every one, to his own way; And the LORD has laid on Him the iniquity of us all. He was oppressed and He was afflicted, Yet He opened not His mouth; He was led as a lamb to the slaughter, And as a sheep before its shearers is silent, So He opened not His mouth. He was taken from prison and from judgment, And who will declare His generation? For He was cut off from the land of the living; For the transgressions of My people He was stricken.... Yet it pleased the LORD to bruise Him; He has put *Him* to grief. When You make His soul an offering for sin, He shall see *His* seed, He shall prolong *His* days, And the pleasure of the LORD shall prosper in His hand. He shall see the labor of His soul, *and* be satisfied. By His knowledge My righteous Servant shall justify many, For He shall bear their iniquities. **Acts 8:32-35:** The place in the Scripture which he read was this: "He was led as a sheep to the slaughter; And as a lamb before its shearer *is* silent, So He opened not His mouth. In His humiliation His justice was taken away, And who will declare His generation? For His life is taken from the earth." So the eunuch answered Philip and said, "I ask you, of whom does the prophet say this, of himself or of some other man?" Then Philip opened his mouth, and beginning at this Scripture, preached Jesus to him. **Heb. 9:26-28:** He then would have had to suffer often since the foundation of the world; but now, once at the end of the ages, He has appeared to put away sin by the sacrifice of Himself. And as it is appointed for men to die once, but after this the judgment, so Christ was offered once to bear the sins of many. To those who eagerly wait for Him He will appear a second time, apart from sin, for salvation. **Heb. 10:12:** But this Man, after He had offered one sacrifice for sins forever, sat down at the right hand of God.

2 **Rom. 5:10-11:** For if when we were enemies we were reconciled to God through the death of His Son, much more, having been reconciled, we shall be saved by His life. And not only *that,* but we also rejoice in God through our Lord Jesus Christ, through whom we have now received the reconciliation. **2 Cor. 5:18:** Now all things *are* of God, who has reconciled us to Himself through Jesus Christ, and has given us the ministry of reconciliation. **Col. 1:21-22:** And you, who once were alienated and enemies in your mind by wicked works, yet now He has reconciled in the body of His flesh through death, to present you holy, and blameless, and above reproach in His sight.

3 **Rom. 8:34:** Who *is* he who condemns? *It is* Christ who died, and furthermore is also risen, who is even at the right hand of God, who also makes intercession for us. **Heb. 7:25:** Therefore He is also able to save to the uttermost those who come to God through Him, since He always lives to make intercession for them. **Heb. 9:24:** For Christ has not entered the holy places made with hands, *which are* copies of the true, but into heaven itself, now to appear in the presence of God for us.

Q. 39. *How doth Christ execute the office of a King?*

A. Christ executeth the office of a King, in subduing us to Himself, in ruling and defending us,[1] and in restraining and conquering all His and our enemies.[2]

1 **Ps. 110:3:** Your people *shall be* volunteers In the day of Your power; In the beauties of holiness, from the womb of the morning, You have the dew of Your youth. **Matt. 28:18-20:** And Jesus came and spoke to them, saying, "All authority has been given to Me in heaven and on earth. Go therefore and make disciples of all the nations, baptizing them in the name of the Father and of the Son and of the Holy Spirit, teaching them to observe all things that I have commanded you; and lo, I am with you always, *even* to the end of the age." Amen. **John 17:2:** ... as You have given Him authority over all flesh, that He should give eternal life to as many as You have given Him. **Col. 1:13:** He has delivered us from the power of darkness and conveyed *us* into the kingdom of the Son of His love.

2 **Ps. 2:6-9:** "Yet I have set My King On My holy hill of Zion." "I will declare the decree: The LORD has

said to Me, 'You *are* My Son, Today I have begotten You. Ask of Me, and I will give *You* The nations *for* Your inheritance, And the ends of the earth *for* Your possession. You shall break them with a rod of iron; You shall dash them to pieces like a potter's vessel.'" **Ps. 110:1-2:** The LORD said to my Lord, "Sit at My right hand, Till I make Your enemies Your footstool." The LORD shall send the rod of Your strength out of Zion. Rule in the midst of Your enemies! **Matt. 12:28:** But if I cast out demons by the Spirit of God, surely the kingdom of God has come upon you. **1 Cor. 15:24-26:** Then *comes* the end, when He delivers the kingdom to God the Father, when He puts an end to all rule and all authority and power. For He must reign till He has put all enemies under His feet. The last enemy *that* will be destroyed *is* death. **Col. 2:15:** Having disarmed principalities and powers, He made a public spectacle of them, triumphing over them in it.

Q. 40. *Wherein did Christ's humiliation consist?*

A. Christ's humiliation consisted in His being born, and that in a low condition,[1] made under the law[2] undergoing the miseries of this life,[3] the wrath of God,[4] and the cursed death of the cross;[5] in being buried, and continuing under the power of death for a time.[6]

1 **Luke 2:7:** And she brought forth her firstborn Son, and wrapped Him in swaddling cloths, and laid Him in a manger, because there was no room for them in the inn. **2 Cor. 8:9:** For you know the grace of our Lord Jesus Christ, that though He was rich, yet for your sakes He became poor, that you through His poverty might become rich. **Gal. 4:4:** But when the fullness of the time had come, God sent forth His Son, born of a woman, born under the law.

2 **Gal. 4:4:** But when the fullness of the time had come, God sent forth His Son, born of a woman, born under the law.

3 **Isa. 53:3:** He is despised and rejected by men, A Man of sorrows and acquainted with grief. And we hid, as it were, *our* faces from Him; He was despised, and we did not esteem Him. **Luke 9:58:** And Jesus said to him, "Foxes have holes and birds of the air *have* nests, but the Son of Man has nowhere to lay *His* head." **John 4:6:** Now Jacob's well was there. Jesus therefore, being wearied from *His* journey, sat thus by the well. It was about the sixth hour. **John 11:35:** Jesus wept. **Heb. 2:18:** For in that He Himself has suffered, being tempted, He is able to aid those who are tempted.

4 **Ps. 22:1:** My God, My God, why have You forsaken Me? *Why are You so* far from helping Me, *And from* the words of My groaning? **Matt. 27:46:** And about the ninth hour Jesus cried out with a loud voice, saying, "Eli, Eli, lama sabachthani?" that is, "My God, My God, why have You forsaken Me?" **Isa. 53:10:** Yet it pleased the LORD to bruise Him; He has put *Him* to grief. When You make His soul an offering for sin, He shall see *His* seed, He shall prolong *His* days, And the pleasure of the LORD shall prosper in His hand. **1 John 2:2:** And He Himself is the propitiation for our sins, and not for ours only but also for the whole world.

5 **Gal. 3:13:** Christ has redeemed us from the curse of the law, having become a curse for us (for it is written, "Cursed *is* everyone who hangs on a tree"). **Phil. 2:8:** And being found in appearance as a man, He humbled Himself and became obedient to *the point of* death, even the death of the cross.

6 **Matt. 12:40:** For as Jonah was three days and three nights in the belly of the great fish, so will the Son of Man be three days and three nights in the heart of the earth. **1 Cor. 15:3-4:** For I delivered to you first of all that which I also received: that Christ died for our sins according to the Scriptures, and that He was buried, and that He rose again the third day according to the Scriptures.

Q. 41. *Wherein consisteth Christ's exaltation?*

A. Christ's exaltation consisteth in His rising again from the dead on the third day,[1] in ascending up into heaven,[2] in sitting at the right hand of God the Father,[3] and in coming to judge the world at the last day.[4]

1
1 Cor. 15:4: ... and that He was buried, and that He rose again the third day according to the Scriptures.
2
Ps. 68:18: You have ascended on high, You have led captivity captive; You have received gifts among men, Even *from* the rebellious, That the LORD God might dwell *there.* **Acts 1:11:** ... who also said, "Men of Galilee, why do you stand gazing up into heaven? This *same* Jesus, who was taken up from you into heaven, will so come in like manner as you saw Him go into heaven." **Eph. 4:8:** Therefore He says: "When He ascended on high, He led captivity captive, And gave gifts to men."
3
Ps. 110:1: The LORD said to my Lord, "Sit at My right hand, Till I make Your enemies Your footstool." **Acts 2:33-34:** Therefore being exalted to the right hand of God, and having received from the Father the promise of the Holy Spirit, He poured out this which you now see and hear. "For David did not ascend into the heavens, but he says himself: 'The LORD said to my Lord, "Sit at My right hand." **Heb. 1:3:** ... who being the brightness of *His* glory and the express image of His person, and upholding all things by the word of His power, when He had by Himself purged our sins, sat down at the right hand of the Majesty on high.
4
Matt. 16:27: For the Son of Man will come in the glory of His Father with His angels, and then He will reward each according to his works. **Acts 17:31:** ... because He has appointed a day on which He will judge the world in righteousness by the Man whom He has ordained. He has given assurance of this to all by raising Him from the dead."

Q. 42. *How are we made partakers of the redemption purchased by Christ?*

A. We are made partakers of the redemption purchased by Christ, by the effectual application of it to us by His Holy Spirit.[1]

1
Titus 3:4-7: But when the kindness and the love of God our Savior toward man appeared, not by works of righteousness which we have done, but according to His mercy He saved us, through the washing of regeneration and renewing of the Holy Spirit, whom He poured out on us abundantly through Jesus Christ our Savior, that having been justified by His grace we should become heirs according to the hope of eternal life.

Q. 43. *How doth the Spirit apply to us the redemption purchased by Christ?*

A. The Spirit applieth to us the redemption purchased by Christ, by working faith in us,[1] and thereby uniting us to Christ in our effectual calling.[2]

1
Rom. 10:17: So then faith *comes* by hearing, and hearing by the word of God. **1 Cor. 2:12-16:** Now we have received, not the spirit of the world, but the Spirit who is from God, that we might know the things that have been freely given to us by God. These things we also speak, not in words which man's wisdom teaches but which the Holy Spirit teaches, comparing spiritual things with spiritual. But the natural man does not receive the things of the Spirit of God, for they are foolishness to him; nor can he know *them,* because they are spiritually discerned. But he who is spiritual judges all things, yet he himself is *rightly* judged by no one. For "who has known the mind of the LORD that he may instruct Him?" But we have the mind of Christ. **Eph. 2:8:** For by grace you have been saved through faith, and that not of yourselves; *it is* the gift of God. **Phil. 1:29:** For to you it has been granted on behalf of Christ, not only to believe in Him, but also to suffer for His sake.
2
John 15:5: I am the vine, you *are* the branches. He who abides in Me, and I in him, bears much fruit; for without Me you can do nothing. **1 Cor. 1:9:** God *is* faithful, by whom you were called into the fellowship of His Son, Jesus Christ our Lord. **Eph. 3:17:** ... that Christ may dwell in your hearts through faith; that you, being rooted and grounded in love.

Q. 44. *What is effectual calling?*

A. Effectual calling is the work of God's Spirit, whereby, convincing us of our sin and misery, enlightening our minds in the knowledge of Christ,[1] and renewing our wills,[2] He doth persuade and enable us to embrace Jesus Christ,[3] freely offered to us in the gospel.[4]

1 **Acts 26:18:** ... to open their eyes, *in order* to turn *them* from darkness to light, and *from* the power of Satan to God, that they may receive forgiveness of sins and an inheritance among those who are sanctified by faith in Me. **1 Cor. 2:10, 12:** But God has revealed *them* to us through His Spirit. For the Spirit searches all things, yes, the deep things of God.... Now we have received, not the spirit of the world, but the Spirit who is from God, that we might know the things that have been freely given to us by God. **2 Cor. 4:6:** For it is the God who commanded light to shine out of darkness, who has shone in our hearts to *give* the light of the knowledge of the glory of God in the face of Jesus Christ. **Eph. 1:17-18:** ... that the God of our Lord Jesus Christ, the Father of glory, may give to you the spirit of wisdom and revelation in the knowledge of Him, the eyes of your understanding being enlightened; that you may know what is the hope of His calling, what are the riches of the glory of His inheritance in the saints.

2 **Deut. 30:6:** And the LORD your God will circumcise your heart and the heart of your descendants, to love the LORD your God with all your heart and with all your soul, that you may live. **Ezek. 36:26-27:** I will give you a new heart and put a new spirit within you; I will take the heart of stone out of your flesh and give you a heart of flesh. I will put My Spirit within you and cause you to walk in My statutes, and you will keep My judgments and do *them.* **John 3:5**: Jesus answered, "Most assuredly, I say to you, unless one is born of water and the Spirit, he cannot enter the kingdom of God. **Titus 3:5:** ... not by works of righteousness which we have done, but according to His mercy He saved us, through the washing of regeneration and renewing of the Holy Spirit.

3 **John 6:44-45:** No one can come to Me unless the Father who sent Me draws him; and I will raise him up at the last day. It is written in the prophets, 'And they shall all be taught by God.' Therefore everyone who has heard and learned from the Father comes to Me. **Acts 16:14:** Now a certain woman named Lydia heard *us.* She was a seller of purple from the city of Thyatira, who worshiped God. The Lord opened her heart to heed the things spoken by Paul.

4 **Isa. 45:22:** Look to Me, and be saved, All you ends of the earth! For I *am* God, and *there is* no other. **Matt. 11:28-30:** Come to Me, all *you* who labor and are heavy laden, and I will give you rest. Take My yoke upon you and learn from Me, for I am gentle and lowly in heart, and you will find rest for your souls. For My yoke *is* easy and My burden is light. **Rev. 22:17:** And the Spirit and the bride say, "Come!" And let him who hears say, "Come!" And let him who thirsts come. Whoever desires, let him take the water of life freely.

Q. 45. *What benefits do they that are effectually called partake of in this life?*

A. They that are effectually called do in this life partake of justification, adoption and sanctification, and the several benefits which in this life do either accompany or flow from them.[1]

1 **Rom. 8:30:** Moreover whom He predestined, these He also called; whom He called, these He also justified; and whom He justified, these He also glorified. **1 Cor. 1:30:** But of Him you are in Christ Jesus, who became for us wisdom from God—and righteousness and sanctification and redemption. **1 Cor. 6:11:** And such were some of you. But you were washed, but you were sanctified, but you were justified in the name of the Lord Jesus and by the Spirit of our God. **Eph. 1:5:** ... having predestined us to adoption as sons by Jesus Christ to Himself, according to the good pleasure of His will.

Q. 46. *What is justification?*

A. Justification is an act of God's free grace,[1] wherein He pardoneth all our sins,[2] and accepteth us as righteous in His sight,[3] only for the righteousness of Christ imputed to us,[4] and received by faith alone.[5]

1 **Rom. 3:24:** ... being justified freely by His grace through the redemption that is in Christ Jesus.

2 **Rom. 4:6-8:** ... just as David also describes the blessedness of the man to whom God imputes righteousness apart from works: "Blessed *are those* whose lawless deeds are forgiven, And whose sins are covered; Blessed *is the* man to whom the LORD shall not impute sin." **2 Cor. 5:19:** ... that is, that God was in Christ reconciling the world to Himself, not imputing their trespasses to them, and has committed to us the word of reconciliation.

3 **2 Cor. 5:21:** For He made Him who knew no sin *to be* sin for us, that we might become the righteousness of God in Him.

4 **Rom. 4:6, 11:** ... just as David also describes the blessedness of the man to whom God imputes righteousness apart from works.... And he received the sign of circumcision, a seal of the righteousness of the faith which *he had while still* uncircumcised, that he might be the father of all those who believe, though they are uncircumcised, that righteousness might be imputed to them also. **Rom. 5:19:** For as by one man's disobedience many were made sinners, so also by one Man's obedience many will be made righteous.

5 **Gal. 2:16:** ... knowing that a man is not justified by the works of the law but by faith in Jesus Christ, even we have believed in Christ Jesus, that we might be justified by faith in Christ and not by the works of the law; for by the works of the law no flesh shall be justified. **Phil. 3:9:** ... and be found in Him, not having my own righteousness, which *is* from the law, but that which *is* through faith in Christ, the righteousness which is from God by faith.

Q. 47. *What is adoption?*

A. Adoption is an act of God's free grace,[1] whereby we are received into the number, and have a right to all the privileges, of the sons of God.[2]

1 **1 John 3:1:** Behold what manner of love the Father has bestowed on us, that we should be called children of God! Therefore the world does not know us, because it did not know Him.

2 **John 1:12:** But as many as received Him, to them He gave the right to become children of God, to those who believe in His name. **Rom. 8:17:** ... and if children, then heirs—heirs of God and joint heirs with Christ, if indeed we suffer with *Him,* that we may also be glorified together.

Q. 48. *What is sanctification?*

A. Sanctification is the work of God's free grace,[1] whereby we are renewed in the whole man after the image of God,[2] and are enabled more and more to die unto sin, and live unto righteousness.[3]

1 **Ezek. 36:27:** I will put My Spirit within you and cause you to walk in My statutes, and you will keep My judgments and do *them.* **Phil. 2:13:** ... for it is God who works in you both to will and to do for *His* good pleasure. **2 Thess. 2:13:** But we are bound to give thanks to God always for you, brethren beloved by the Lord, because God from the beginning chose you for salvation through

sanctification by the Spirit and belief in the truth.

2 **2 Cor. 5:17:** Therefore, if anyone *is* in Christ, *he is* a new creation; old things have passed away; behold, all things have become new. **Eph. 4:23-24:** ... and be renewed in the spirit of your mind, and that you put on the new man which was created according to God, in true righteousness and holiness. **1 Thess. 5:23:** Now may the God of peace Himself sanctify you completely; and may your whole spirit, soul, and body be preserved blameless at the coming of our Lord Jesus Christ.

3 **Ezek. 36:25-27:** Then I will sprinkle clean water on you, and you shall be clean; I will cleanse you from all your filthiness and from all your idols. I will give you a new heart and put a new spirit within you; I will take the heart of stone out of your flesh and give you a heart of flesh. I will put My Spirit within you and cause you to walk in My statutes, and you will keep My judgments and do *them.* **Rom. 6:4, 6, 12-14:** Therefore we were buried with Him through baptism into death, that just as Christ was raised from the dead by the glory of the Father, even so we also should walk in newness of life.... knowing this, that our old man was crucified with *Him,* that the body of sin might be done away with, that we should no longer be slaves of sin.... Therefore do not let sin reign in your mortal body, that you should obey it in its lusts. And do not present your members *as* instruments of unrighteousness to sin, but present yourselves to God as being alive from the dead, and your members *as* instruments of righteousness to God. For sin shall not have dominion over you, for you are not under law but under grace. **2 Cor. 7:1:** Therefore, having these promises, beloved, let us cleanse ourselves from all filthiness of the flesh and spirit, perfecting holiness in the fear of God. **1 Pet. 2:24:** ... who Himself bore our sins in His own body on the tree, that we, having died to sins, might live for righteousness—by whose stripes you were healed.

Q. 49. *What are the benefits which in this life do accompany or flow from justification, adoption and sanctification?*

A. The benefits which in this life do accompany or flow from justification, adoption and sanctification, are, assurance of God's love,[1] peace of conscience,[2] joy in the Holy Spirit,[3] increase of grace,[4] and perseverance therein to the end.[5]

1 **Rom. 5:5:** Now hope does not disappoint, because the love of God has been poured out in our hearts by the Holy Spirit who was given to us.

2 **Rom. 5:1:** Therefore, having been justified by faith, we have peace with God through our Lord Jesus Christ.

3 **Rom. 14:17:** ... for the kingdom of God is not eating and drinking, but righteousness and peace and joy in the Holy Spirit.

4 **2 Pet. 3:18:** ... but grow in the grace and knowledge of our Lord and Savior Jesus Christ. To Him *be* the glory both now and forever. Amen.

5 **Phil. 1:6:** ... being confident of this very thing, that He who has begun a good work in you will complete *it* until the day of Jesus Christ. **1 Pet. 1:5:** ... who are kept by the power of God through faith for salvation ready to be revealed in the last time.

Q. 50. *What benefits do believers receive from Christ at death?*

A. The souls of believers are at their death made perfect in holiness,[1] and do immediately pass into glory;[2] and their bodies, being still united to Christ,[3] do rest in their graves till the resurrection.[4]

1 **Heb. 12:23:** ... to the general assembly and church of the firstborn *who are* registered in heaven, to God the Judge of all, to the spirits of just men made perfect

2 **Luke 23:43:** And Jesus said to him, "Assuredly, I say to you, today you will be with Me in

Paradise." **2 Cor. 5:6, 8:** So *we are* always confident, knowing that while we are at home in the body we are absent from the Lord.... We are confident, yes, well pleased rather to be absent from the body and to be present with the Lord. **Phil. 1:23:** For I am hard-pressed between the two, having a desire to depart and be with Christ, *which is* far better.

[3] **1 Thess. 4:14:** For if we believe that Jesus died and rose again, even so God will bring with Him those who sleep in Jesus.

[4] **Dan. 12:2:** And many of those who sleep in the dust of the earth shall awake, Some to everlasting life, Some to shame *and* everlasting contempt. **John 5:28-29:** Do not marvel at this; for the hour is coming in which all who are in the graves will hear His voice and come forth—those who have done good, to the resurrection of life, and those who have done evil, to the resurrection of condemnation. **Acts 24:15:** I have hope in God, which they themselves also accept, that there will be a resurrection of *the* dead, both of *the* just and *the* unjust.

Q. 51. *What benefits do believers receive from Christ at the resurrection?*

A. At the resurrection, believers being raised up in glory,[1] shall be openly acknowledged and acquitted in the day of judgment,[2] and made perfectly blessed in the full enjoying of God[3] to all eternity.[4]

[1] **1 Cor. 15:42-43:** So also *is* the resurrection of the dead. *The body* is sown in corruption, it is raised in incorruption. It is sown in dishonor, it is raised in glory. It is sown in weakness, it is raised in power.

[2] **Matt. 25:33-34, 46:** And He will set the sheep on His right hand, but the goats on the left. Then the King will say to those on His right hand, 'Come, you blessed of My Father, inherit the kingdom prepared for you from the foundation of the world.' ... And these will go away into everlasting punishment, but the righteous into eternal life."

[3] **Rom. 8:29:** And suddenly they cried out, saying, "What have we to do with You, Jesus, You Son of God? Have You come here to torment us before the time?" **1 John 3:2:** Beloved, now we are children of God; and it has not yet been revealed what we shall be, but we know that when He is revealed, we shall be like Him, for we shall see Him as He is.

[4] **Ps. 16:11:** You will show me the path of life; In Your presence *is* fullness of joy; At Your right hand *are* pleasures forevermore. **1 Thess. 4:17:** Then we who are alive *and* remain shall be caught up together with them in the clouds to meet the Lord in the air. And thus we shall always be with the Lord.

Q. 52. *What is the duty which God requireth of man?*

A. The duty which God requireth of man is obedience to His revealed will.[1]

[1] **Deut. 29:29:** The secret *things belong* to the LORD our God, but those *things which are* revealed *belong* to us and to our children forever, that *we* may do all the words of this law. **Mic. 6:8:** He has shown you, O man, what *is* good; And what does the LORD require of you But to do justly, To love mercy, And to walk humbly with your God? **1 John 5:2-3:** By this we know that we love the children of God, when we love God and keep His commandments. For this is the love of God, that we keep His commandments. And His commandments are not burdensome.

Q. 53. *What did God at first reveal to man for the rule of his obedience?*

A. The rule which God at first revealed to man for his obedience was the moral law.[1]

[1] **Rom. 2:14-15:** for when Gentiles, who do not have the law, by nature do the things in the law, these, although not having the law, are a law to themselves, who show the work of the law written in their hearts, their conscience also bearing witness, and between themselves *their* thoughts accusing or else excusing *them*. **Rom. 10:5:** For Moses writes about the righteousness which is of the law, "The man who does those things shall live by them."

Q. 54. *Where is the moral law summarily comprehended?*

A. The moral law is summarily comprehended in the ten commandments.[1]

[1] **Deut. 4:13:** So He declared to you His covenant which He commanded you to perform, the Ten Commandments; and He wrote them on two tablets of stone. **Matt. 19:17-19:** So He said to him, "Why do you call Me good? No one *is* good but One, *that is,* God. But if you want to enter into life, keep the commandments." He said to Him, "Which ones?" Jesus said, "'You shall not murder,' 'You shall not commit adultery,' 'You shall not steal,' 'You shall not bear false witness,' 'Honor your father and *your* mother,' and, 'You shall love your neighbor as yourself.'"

Q. 55. *What is the sum of the ten commandments?*

A. The sum of the ten commandments is to love the LORD our God with all our heart, with all our soul, with all our strength, and with all our mind; and our neighbour as ourselves.[1]

[1] **Matt. 22:37-40:** Jesus said to him, "'You shall love the LORD your God with all your heart, with all your soul, and with all your mind.' This is *the* first and great commandment. And *the* second *is* like it: 'You shall love your neighbor as yourself.' On these two commandments hang all the Law and the Prophets."

Q. 56. *What is the preface to the ten commandments?*

A. The preface to the ten commandments is in these words, *I am the LORD thy God, which have brought thee out of the land of Egypt, out of the house of bondage.*[1]

[1] **Ex. 20:2:** I *am* the LORD your God, who brought you out of the land of Egypt, out of the house of bondage. **Deut. 5:6:** I *am* the LORD your God who brought you out of the land of Egypt, out of the house of bondage.

Q. 57. *What doth the preface to the ten commandments teach us?*

A. The preface to the ten commandments teacheth us that because God is the LORD, and our God, and Redeemer, therefore we are bound to keep all His commandments.[1]

[1] **Luke 1:74-75:** To grant us that we, Being delivered from the hand of our enemies, Might serve Him without fear, In holiness and righteousness before Him all the days of our life. **1 Pet. 1:14-19:** ... as obedient children, not conforming yourselves to the former lusts, *as* in your ignorance; but as He who called you *is* holy, you also be holy in all *your* conduct, because it is

written, "Be holy, for I am holy." And if you call on the Father, who without partiality judges according to each one's work, conduct yourselves throughout the time of your stay *here* in fear; knowing that you were not redeemed with corruptible things, *like* silver or gold, from your aimless conduct *received* by tradition from your fathers, but with the precious blood of Christ, as of a lamb without blemish and without spot.

Q. 58. *Which is the first commandment?*

A. The first commandment is, *Thou shalt have no other gods before me.*[1]

[1] **Ex. 20:3:** You shall have no other gods before Me. **Cf. Deut. 5:7.**

Q. 59. *What is required in the first commandment?*

A. The first commandment requireth us to know and acknowledge God to be the only true God, and our God; and to worship and glorify Him accordingly.[1]

[1] **1 Chron. 28:9:** As for you, my son Solomon, know the God of your father, and serve Him with a loyal heart and with a willing mind; for the LORD searches all hearts and understands all the intent of the thoughts. If you seek Him, He will be found by you; but if you forsake Him, He will cast you off forever. **Isa. 45:20-25:** "Assemble yourselves and come; Draw near together, You *who have* escaped from the nations. They have no knowledge, Who carry the wood of their carved image, And pray to a god *that* cannot save. Tell and bring forth *your case;* Yes, let them take counsel together. Who has declared this from ancient time? *Who* has told it from that time? *Have* not I, the LORD? And *there is* no other God besides Me, A just God and a Savior; *There is* none besides Me. "Look to Me, and be saved, All you ends of the earth! For I *am* God, and *there is* no other. I have sworn by Myself; The word has gone out of My mouth *in* righteousness, And shall not return, That to Me every knee shall bow, Every tongue shall take an oath. He shall say, 'Surely in the LORD I have righteousness and strength. To Him *men* shall come, And all shall be ashamed Who are incensed against Him. In the LORD all the descendants of Israel Shall be justified, and shall glory.'" **Matt. 4:10:** Then Jesus said to him, "Away with you, Satan! For it is written, 'You shall worship the LORD your God, and Him only you shall serve.'"

Q. 60. *What is forbidden in the first commandment?*

A. The first commandment forbiddeth the denying,[1] or not worshiping and glorifying the true God as God,[2] and our God;[3] and the giving of that worship and glory to any other, which is due to Him alone.[4]

[1] **Ps. 14:1:** The fool has said in his heart, "*There is* no God." They are corrupt, They have done abominable works, There is none who does good.

[2] **Rom. 1:20-21:** For since the creation of the world His invisible *attributes* are clearly seen, being understood by the things that are made, *even* His eternal power and Godhead, so that they are without excuse, because, although they knew God, they did not glorify *Him* as God, nor were thankful, but became futile in their thoughts, and their foolish hearts were darkened.

[3] **Ps. 81:10-11:** I *am* the LORD your God, Who brought you out of the land of Egypt; Open your mouth wide, and I will fill it. "But My people would not heed My voice, And Israel would *have* none of Me.

[4] **Ezek. 8:16-18:** So He brought me into the inner court of the LORD's house; and there, at the door of the temple of the LORD, between the porch and the altar, *were* about twenty-five men with their backs toward the temple of the LORD and their faces toward the east, and they were worshiping the

sun toward the east. And He said to me, "Have you seen *this,* O son of man? Is it a trivial thing to the house of Judah to commit the abominations which they commit here? For they have filled the land with violence; then they have returned to provoke Me to anger. Indeed they put the branch to their nose. Therefore I also will act in fury. My eye will not spare nor will I have pity; and though they cry in My ears with a loud voice, I will not hear them." **Rom. 1:25:** ... who exchanged the truth of God for the lie, and worshiped and served the creature rather than the Creator, who is blessed forever. Amen.

Q. 61. *What are we specially taught by these words,* before me, *in the first commandment?*

A. These words, *before me,* in the first commandment teach us that God, who seeth all things, taketh notice of, and is much displeased with, the sin of having any other god.[1]

[1] **Deut. 30:17-18:** But if your heart turns away so that you do not hear, and are drawn away, and worship other gods and serve them, I announce to you today that you shall surely perish; you shall not prolong *your* days in the land which you cross over the Jordan to go in and possess. **Ps. 44:20-21:** ... If we had forgotten the name of our God, Or stretched out our hands to a foreign god, Would not God search this out? For He knows the secrets of the heart. **Ezek. 8:12:** Then He said to me, "Son of man, have you seen what the elders of the house of Israel do in the dark, every man in the room of his idols? For they say, 'The LORD does not see us, the LORD has forsaken the land.'"

Q. 62. *Which is the second commandment?*

A. The second commandment is, *Thou shalt not make unto thee any graven image, or any likeness of any thing that is in heaven above, or that is in the earth beneath, or that is in the water under the earth. Thou shalt not bow down thyself to them, nor serve them: for I the LORD thy God am a jealous God, visiting the iniquity of the fathers upon the children unto the third and fourth generation of them that hate me; and shewing mercy unto thousands of them that love me, and keep my commandments.*[1]

[1] **Ex. 20:4-6:** You shall not make for yourself a carved image—any likeness *of anything* that *is* in heaven above, or that *is* in the earth beneath, or that *is* in the water under the earth; you shall not bow down to them nor serve them. For I, the LORD your God, *am* a jealous God, visiting the iniquity of the fathers upon the children to the third and fourth *generations* of those who hate Me, but showing mercy to thousands, to those who love Me and keep My commandments. **Cf. Deut. 5:8-10.**

Q. 63. *What is required in the second commandment?*

A. The second commandment requireth the receiving, observing, and keeping pure and entire, all such religious worship and ordinances as God hath appointed in His word.[1]

[1] **Deut. 12:32:** Whatever I command you, be careful to observe it; you shall not add to it nor take away from it. **Matt. 28:20:** "...teaching them to observe all things that I have commanded you; and lo, I am with you always, *even* to the end of the age." Amen.

Q. 64. *What is forbidden in the second commandment?*

A. The second commandment forbiddeth the worshiping of God by images,[1] or any other way not appointed in His word.[2]

[1] **Deut. 4:15-19:** Take careful heed to yourselves, for you saw no form when the LORD spoke to you at Horeb out of the midst of the fire, lest you act corruptly and make for yourselves a carved image in the form of any figure: the likeness of male or female, the likeness of any animal that *is* on the earth or the likeness of any winged bird that flies in the air, the likeness of anything that creeps on the ground or the likeness of any fish that *is* in the water beneath the earth. And *take heed,* lest you lift your eyes to heaven, and *when* you see the sun, the moon, and the stars, all the host of heaven, you feel driven to worship them and serve them, which the LORD your God has given to all the peoples under the whole heaven as a heritage. **Rom. 1:22-23:** Professing to be wise, they became fools, and changed the glory of the incorruptible God into an image made like corruptible man—and birds and four-footed animals and creeping things.

[2] **Lev. 10:1-2:** Then Nadab and Abihu, the sons of Aaron, each took his censer and put fire in it, put incense on it, and offered profane fire before the LORD, which He had not commanded them. So fire went out from the LORD and devoured them, and they died before the LORD. **Jer. 19:4-5:** Because they have forsaken Me and made this an alien place, because they have burned incense in it to other gods whom neither they, their fathers, nor the kings of Judah have known, and have filled this place with the blood of the innocents (they have also built the high places of Baal, to burn their sons with fire *for* burnt offerings to Baal, which I did not command or speak, nor did it come into My mind). **Col. 2:18-23:** Let no one cheat you of your reward, taking delight in *false* humility and worship of angels, intruding into those things which he has not seen, vainly puffed up by his fleshly mind, and not holding fast to the Head, from whom all the body, nourished and knit together by joints and ligaments, grows with the increase *that is* from God. Therefore, if you died with Christ from the basic principles of the world, why, as *though* living in the world, do you subject yourselves to regulations— "Do not touch, do not taste, do not handle," which all concern things which perish with the using—according to the commandments and doctrines of men? These things indeed have an appearance of wisdom in self-imposed religion, *false* humility, and neglect of the body, *but are* of no value against the indulgence of the flesh.

Q. 65. *What are the reasons annexed to the second commandment?*

A. The reasons annexed to the second commandment are, God's sovereignty over us,[1] His propriety in us,[2] and the zeal He hath to His own worship.[3]

[1] **Ps. 95:2-3, 6-7:** Let us come before His presence with thanksgiving; Let us shout joyfully to Him with psalms. For the LORD *is* the great God, And the great King above all gods.... Oh come, let us worship and bow down; Let us kneel before the LORD our Maker. For He *is* our God, And we *are* the people of His pasture, And the sheep of His hand. Today, if you will hear His voice. **Ps. 96:9-10:** Oh, worship the LORD in the beauty of holiness! Tremble before Him, all the earth. Say among the nations, "The LORD reigns; The world also is firmly established, It shall not be moved; He shall judge the peoples righteously."

[2] **Ex. 19:5:** Now therefore, if you will indeed obey My voice and keep My covenant, then you shall be a special treasure to Me above all people; for all the earth *is* Mine. **Ps. 45:11:** So the King will greatly desire your beauty; Because He *is* your Lord, worship Him. **Isa. 54:5:** For your Maker *is* your husband, The LORD of hosts *is* His name; And your Redeemer *is* the Holy One of Israel; He is called the God of the whole earth.

[3] **Ex. 34:14:** ... for you shall worship no other god, for the LORD, whose name *is* Jealous, *is* a jealous God. **1 Cor. 10:22:** Or do we provoke the Lord to jealousy? Are we stronger than He?

Q. 66. *Which is the third commandment?*

A. The third commandment is, *Thou shalt not take the name of the*

LORD thy God in vain: for the LORD will not hold him guiltless that taketh his name in vain.[1]

1 **Ex. 20:7:** You shall not take the name of the LORD your God in vain, for the LORD will not hold *him* guiltless who takes His name in vain. **Cf. Deut. 5:11.**

Q. 67. *What is required in the third commandment?*

A. The third commandment requireth the holy and reverent use of God's names, titles,[1] attributes[2] ordinances,[3] word[4] and works.[5]

1 **Deut. 10:20:** You shall fear the LORD your God; you shall serve Him, and to Him you shall hold fast, and take oaths in His name. **Ps. 29:2:** Give unto the LORD the glory due to His name; Worship the LORD in the beauty of holiness. **Matt. 6:9:** In this manner, therefore, pray: Our Father in heaven, Hallowed be Your name.

2 **1 Chron. 29:10-13:** Therefore David blessed the LORD before all the assembly; and David said: "Blessed are You, LORD God of Israel, our Father, forever and ever. Yours, O LORD, *is* the greatness, The power and the glory, The victory and the majesty; For all *that is* in heaven and in earth *is Yours;* Yours *is* the kingdom, O LORD, And You are exalted as head over all. Both riches and honor *come* from You, And You reign over all. In Your hand *is* power and might; In Your hand *it is* to make great And to give strength to all. "Now therefore, our God, We thank You And praise Your glorious name. **Rev. 15:3-4:** They sing the song of Moses, the servant of God, and the song of the Lamb, saying: "Great and marvelous *are* Your works, Lord God Almighty! Just and true *are* Your ways, O King of the saints! Who shall not fear You, O Lord, and glorify Your name? For *You* alone *are* holy. For all nations shall come and worship before You, For Your judgments have been manifested."

3 **Acts 2:42:** And they continued steadfastly in the apostles' doctrine and fellowship, in the breaking of bread, and in prayers. **1 Cor. 11:27-28:** Therefore whoever eats this bread or drinks *this* cup of the Lord in an unworthy manner will be guilty of the body and blood of the Lord. But let a man examine himself, and so let him eat of the bread and drink of the cup.

4 **Ps. 138:2:** I will worship toward Your holy temple, And praise Your name For Your lovingkindness and Your truth; For You have magnified Your word above all Your name. **Rev. 22:18-19:** For I testify to everyone who hears the words of the prophecy of this book: If anyone adds to these things, God will add to him the plagues that are written in this book; and if anyone takes away from the words of the book of this prophecy, God shall take away his part from the Book of Life, from the holy city, and *from* the things which are written in this book.

5 **Ps. 107:21-22:** Oh, that *men* would give thanks to the LORD *for* His goodness, And *for* His wonderful works to the children of men! Let them sacrifice the sacrifices of thanksgiving, And declare His works with rejoicing. **Rev. 4:11:** "You are worthy, O Lord, To receive glory and honor and power; For You created all things, And by Your will they exist and were created."

Q. 68. *What is forbidden in the third commandment?*

A. The third commandment forbiddeth all profaning or abusing of anything whereby God maketh Himself known.[1]

1 **Lev. 19:12:** And you shall not swear by My name falsely, nor shall you profane the name of your God: I *am* the LORD. **Matt. 5:33-37:** "Again you have heard that it was said to those of old, 'You shall not swear falsely, but shall perform your oaths to the Lord.' But I say to you, do not swear at all: neither by heaven, for it is God's throne; nor by the earth, for it is His footstool; nor by Jerusalem, for it is the city of the great King. Nor shall you swear by your head, because you cannot make one hair white or black. But let your 'Yes' be 'Yes,' and your 'No,' 'No.' For whatever is more than these is from the evil one." **James 5:12:** But above all, my brethren, do not swear, either by heaven or by earth or with any other oath. But let your "Yes" be "Yes," and *your* "No," "No," lest you fall into judgment.

Q. 69. *What is the reason annexed to the third commandment?*

A. The reason annexed to the third commandment is that however the breakers of this commandment may escape punishment from men, yet the LORD our God will not suffer them to escape His righteous judgment.[1]

[1] **Deut. 28:58-59:** If you do not carefully observe all the words of this law that are written in this book, that you may fear this glorious and awesome name, THE LORD YOUR GOD, then the LORD will bring upon you and your descendants extraordinary plagues—great and prolonged plagues—and serious and prolonged sicknesses. **1 Sam. 3:13:** For I have told him that I will judge his house forever for the iniquity which he knows, because his sons made themselves vile, and he did not restrain them. **1 Sam. 4:11:** Also the ark of God was captured; and the two sons of Eli, Hophni and Phinehas, died.

Q. 70. *Which is the fourth commandment?*

A. The fourth commandment is, *Remember the sabbath day, to keep it holy. Six days shalt thou labour, and do all thy work; but the seventh day is the sabbath of the LORD thy God: in it thou shalt not do any work, thou, nor thy son, nor thy daughter, thy manservant, nor thy maidservant, nor thy cattle, nor thy stranger that is within thy gates. For in six days the LORD made heaven and earth, the sea, and all that in them is, and rested the seventh day: wherefore the LORD blessed the sabbath day, and hallowed it.*[1]

[1] **Ex. 20:8-11:** Remember the Sabbath day, to keep it holy. Six days you shall labor and do all your work, but the seventh day *is* the Sabbath of the LORD your God. *In it* you shall do no work: you, nor your son, nor your daughter, nor your male servant, nor your female servant, nor your cattle, nor your stranger who *is* within your gates. For *in* six days the LORD made the heavens and the earth, the sea, and all that *is* in them, and rested the seventh day. Therefore the LORD blessed the Sabbath day and hallowed it. **Cf. Deut. 5:12-15.**

Q. 71. *What is required in the fourth commandment?*

A. The fourth commandment requireth the keeping holy to God such set times as He hath appointed in His word; expressly one whole day in seven, to be a holy Sabbath to Himself.[1]

[1] **Ex. 31:13, 16-17:** "Speak also to the children of Israel, saying: 'Surely My Sabbaths you shall keep, for it *is* a sign between Me and you throughout your generations, that *you* may know that I *am* the LORD who sanctifies you.' ... Therefore the children of Israel shall keep the Sabbath, to observe the Sabbath throughout their generations *as* a perpetual covenant. It *is* a sign between Me and the children of Israel forever; for *in* six days the LORD made the heavens and the earth, and on the seventh day He rested and was refreshed.'"

Q. 72. *Which day of the seven hath God appointed to be the weekly Sabbath?*

A. From the beginning of the world to the resurrection of Christ, God appointed the seventh day of the week to be the weekly Sabbath;[1] and the first day of the week ever since, to continue to the end of the world, which is the Christian Sabbath.[2]

[1] **Gen. 2:2-3:** And on the seventh day God ended His work which He had done, and He rested on the seventh day from all His work which He had done. Then God blessed the seventh day and sanctified it, because in it He rested from all His work which God had created and made. **Ex. 20:11:** For *in* six days the LORD made the heavens and the earth, the sea, and all that *is* in them, and rested the seventh day. Therefore the LORD blessed the Sabbath day and hallowed it.

[2] **Mark 2:27-28:** And He said to them, "The Sabbath was made for man, and not man for the Sabbath. Therefore the Son of Man is also Lord of the Sabbath." **Acts 20:7:** Now on the first *day* of the week, when the disciples came together to break bread, Paul, ready to depart the next day, spoke to them and continued his message until midnight. **1 Cor. 16:2:** On the first *day* of the week let each one of you lay something aside, storing up as he may prosper, that there be no collections when I come. **Rev. 1:10:** I was in the Spirit on the Lord's Day, and I heard behind me a loud voice, as of a trumpet.

Q. 73. *How is the Sabbath to be sanctified?*

A. The Sabbath is to be sanctified by a holy resting all that day, even from such worldly employments and recreations as are lawful on other days;[1] and spending the whole time in the public and private exercises of God's worship,[2] except so much as is to be taken up in the works of necessity and mercy.[3]

[1] **Ex. 20:10:** ... but the seventh day *is* the Sabbath of the LORD your God. *In it* you shall do no work: you, nor your son, nor your daughter, nor your male servant, nor your female servant, nor your cattle, nor your stranger who *is* within your gates. **Neh. 13:15-22:** In those days I saw *people* in Judah treading wine presses on the Sabbath, and bringing in sheaves, and loading donkeys with wine, grapes, figs, and all *kinds of* burdens, which they brought into Jerusalem on the Sabbath day. And I warned *them* about the day on which they were selling provisions. Men of Tyre dwelt there also, who brought in fish and all kinds of goods, and sold *them* on the Sabbath to the children of Judah, and in Jerusalem. Then I contended with the nobles of Judah, and said to them, "What evil thing *is* this that you do, by which you profane the Sabbath day? Did not your fathers do thus, and did not our God bring all this disaster on us and on this city? Yet you bring added wrath on Israel by profaning the Sabbath." So it was, at the gates of Jerusalem, as it began to be dark before the Sabbath, that I commanded the gates to be shut, and charged that they must not be opened till after the Sabbath. Then I posted *some* of my servants at the gates, *so that* no burdens would be brought in on the Sabbath day. Now the merchants and sellers of all kinds of wares lodged outside Jerusalem once or twice. Then I warned them, and said to them, "Why do you spend the night around the wall? If you do *so* again, I will lay hands on you!" From that time on they came no *more* on the Sabbath. And I commanded the Levites that they should cleanse themselves, and that they should go and guard the gates, to sanctify the Sabbath day. Remember me, O my God, *concerning* this also, and spare me according to the greatness of Your mercy! **Isa. 58:13-14:** If you turn away your foot from the Sabbath, *From* doing your pleasure on My holy day, And call the Sabbath a delight, The holy *day* of the LORD honorable, And shall honor Him, not doing your own ways, Nor finding your own pleasure, Nor speaking *your own* words, Then you shall delight yourself in the LORD; And I will cause you to ride on the high hills of the earth, And feed you with the heritage of Jacob your father. The mouth of the LORD has spoken.

[2] **Ex. 20:8:** Remember the Sabbath day, to keep it holy. **Lev. 23:3:** Six days shall work be done, but the seventh day *is* a Sabbath of solemn rest, a holy convocation. You shall do no work *on it;* it *is* the Sabbath of the LORD in all your dwellings. **Luke 4:16:** So He came to Nazareth, where He had been brought up. And as His custom was, He went into the synagogue on the Sabbath day, and stood up to read. **Acts 20:7:** Now on the first *day* of the week, when the disciples came together to break bread, Paul, ready to depart the next day, spoke to them and continued his message until midnight.

[3] **Matt. 12:1-13:** At that time Jesus went through the grainfields on the Sabbath. And His disciples were hungry, and began to pluck heads of grain and to eat. And when the Pharisees saw *it,* they said to Him, "Look, Your disciples are doing what is not lawful to do on the Sabbath!" But He said to

them, "Have you not read what David did when he was hungry, he and those who were with him: how he entered the house of God and ate the showbread which was not lawful for him to eat, nor for those who were with him, but only for the priests? Or have you not read in the law that on the Sabbath the priests in the temple profane the Sabbath, and are blameless? Yet I say to you that in this place there is *One* greater than the temple. But if you had known what *this* means, 'I desire mercy and not sacrifice,' you would not have condemned the guiltless. For the Son of Man is Lord even of the Sabbath." Now when He had departed from there, He went into their synagogue. And behold, there was a man who had a withered hand. And they asked Him, saying, "Is it lawful to heal on the Sabbath?"—that they might accuse Him. Then He said to them, "What man is there among you who has one sheep, and if it falls into a pit on the Sabbath, will not lay hold of it and lift *it* out? Of how much more value then is a man than a sheep? Therefore it is lawful to do good on the Sabbath." Then He said to the man, "Stretch out your hand." And he stretched *it* out, and it was restored as whole as the other.

Q. 74. *What is forbidden in the fourth commandment?*

A. The fourth commandment forbiddeth the omission or careless performance of the duties required, and the profaning the day by idleness, or doing that which is in itself sinful, or by unnecessary thoughts, words or works, about our worldly employments or recreations.[1]

[1] **Neh. 13:15-22 and Isa. 58:13-14, See footnote 1 above. Amos 8:4-6:** Hear this, you who swallow up the needy, And make the poor of the land fail, Saying: "When will the New Moon be past, That we may sell grain? And the Sabbath, That we may trade wheat? Making the ephah small and the shekel large, Falsifying the scales by deceit, That we may buy the poor for silver, And the needy for a pair of sandals— Even sell the bad wheat?"

Q. 75. *What are the reasons annexed to the fourth commandment?*

A. The reasons annexed to the fourth commandment are, God's allowing us six days of the week for our own employments,[1] His challenging a special propriety in the seventh, His own example, and His blessing the Sabbath day.[2]

[1] **Ex. 20:9:** Six days you shall labor and do all your work. **Ex. 31:15:** Work shall be done for six days, but the seventh *is* the Sabbath of rest, holy to the LORD. Whoever does *any* work on the Sabbath day, he shall surely be put to death. **Lev. 23:3:** Six days shall work be done, but the seventh day *is* a Sabbath of solemn rest, a holy convocation. You shall do no work *on it; it is* the Sabbath of the LORD in all your dwellings.

[2] **Gen. 2:2-3:** And on the seventh day God ended His work which He had done, and He rested on the seventh day from all His work which He had done. Then God blessed the seventh day and sanctified it, because in it He rested from all His work which God had created and made. **Ex. 20:11:** For *in* six days the LORD made the heavens and the earth, the sea, and all that *is* in them, and rested the seventh day. Therefore the LORD blessed the Sabbath day and hallowed it. **Ex. 31:17:** It *is* a sign between Me and the children of Israel forever; for *in* six days the LORD made the heavens and the earth, and on the seventh day He rested and was refreshed.

Q. 76. *Which is the fifth commandment?*

A. The fifth commandment is, *Honour thy father and thy mother: that thy days may be long upon the land which the LORD thy God giveth thee.*[1]

[1] **Ex. 20:12:** Honor your father and your mother, that your days may be long upon the land which the LORD your God is giving you. **Cf. Deut. 5:16.**

Q. 77. *What is required in the fifth commandment?*

A. The fifth commandment requireth the preserving the honour, and performing the duties, belonging to every one in their several places and relations, as superiors, inferiors or equals.[1]

[1] **Rom. 13:1, 7:** Let every soul be subject to the governing authorities. For there is no authority except from God, and the authorities that exist are appointed by God.... Render therefore to all their due: taxes to whom taxes *are due,* customs to whom customs, fear to whom fear, honor to whom honor. **Eph. 5:21-22, 24:** submitting to one another in the fear of God. Wives, submit to your own husbands, as to the Lord.... Therefore, just as the church is subject to Christ, so *let* the wives *be* to their own husbands in everything. **Eph. 6:1, 4-5, 9:** Children, obey your parents in the Lord, for this is right.... And you, fathers, do not provoke your children to wrath, but bring them up in the training and admonition of the Lord. Bondservants, be obedient to those who are your masters according to the flesh, with fear and trembling, in sincerity of heart, as to Christ.... And you, masters, do the same things to them, giving up threatening, knowing that your own Master also is in heaven, and there is no partiality with Him. **1 Pet. 2:17:** Honor all *people.* Love the brotherhood. Fear God. Honor the king.

Q. 78. *What is forbidden in the fifth commandment?*

A. The fifth commandment forbiddeth the neglecting of, or doing anything against, the honour and duty which belongeth to every one in their several places and relations.[1]

[1] **Matt. 15:4-6:** For God commanded, saying, 'Honor your father and your mother'; and, 'He who curses father or mother, let him be put to death.' But you say, 'Whoever says to his father or mother, "Whatever profit you might have received from me *is* a gift *to God"*— then he need not honor his father or mother.' Thus you have made the commandment of God of no effect by your tradition. **Rom. 13:8:** Owe no one anything except to love one another, for he who loves another has fulfilled the law.

Q. 79. *What is the reason annexed to the fifth commandment?*

A. The reason annexed to the fifth commandment is a promise of long life and prosperity (as far as it shall serve for God's glory and their own good) to all such as keep this commandment.[1]

[1] **Ex. 20:12:** Honor your father and your mother, that your days may be long upon the land which the LORD your God is giving you. **Deut. 5:16:** Honor your father and your mother, as the LORD your God has commanded you, that your days may be long, and that it may be well with you in the land which the LORD your God is giving you. **Eph. 6:2-3:** "Honor your father and mother," which is the first commandment with promise: "that it may be well with you and you may live long on the earth."

Q. 80. *Which is the sixth commandment?*

A. The sixth commandment is, *Thou shalt not kill.*[1]

[1] **Ex. 20:13:** You shall not murder. **Cf. Deut. 5:17.**

Q. 81. *What is required in the sixth commandment?*

A. The sixth commandment requireth all lawful endeavors to preserve our own life, and the life of others.[1]

[1] **Eph. 5:28-29:** So husbands ought to love their own wives as their own bodies; he who loves his wife loves himself. For no one ever hated his own flesh, but nourishes and cherishes it, just as the Lord *does* the church.

Q. 82. *What is forbidden in the sixth commandment?*

A. The sixth commandment forbiddeth the taking away of our own life, or the life of our neighbour unjustly, or whatsoever tendeth thereunto.[1]

[1] **Gen. 9:6:** Whoever sheds man's blood, By man his blood shall be shed; For in the image of God He made man. **Matt. 5:22:** But I say to you that whoever is angry with his brother without a cause shall be in danger of the judgment. And whoever says to his brother, 'Raca!' shall be in danger of the council. But whoever says, 'You fool!' shall be in danger of hell fire. **1 John 3:15:** Whoever hates his brother is a murderer, and you know that no murderer has eternal life abiding in him.

Q. 83. *Which is the seventh commandment?*

A. The seventh commandment is, *Thou shalt not commit adultery.*[1]

[1] **Ex. 20:14:** You shall not commit adultery. **Cf. Deut. 5:18.**

Q. 84. *What is required in the seventh commandment?*

A. The seventh commandment requireth the preservation of our own and our neighbour's chastity, in heart, speech and behaviour.[1]

[1] **1 Cor. 7:2-3, 5:** Nevertheless, because of sexual immorality, let each man have his own wife, and let each woman have her own husband. Let the husband render to his wife the affection due her, and likewise also the wife to her husband.... Do not deprive one another except with consent for a time, that you may give yourselves to fasting and prayer; and come together again so that Satan does not tempt you because of your lack of self-control. **1 Thess. 4:3-5:** For this is the will of God, your sanctification: that you should abstain from sexual immorality; that each of you should know how to possess his own vessel in sanctification and honor, not in passion of lust, like the Gentiles who do not know God.

Q. 85. *What is forbidden in the seventh commandment?*

A. The seventh commandment forbiddeth all unchaste thoughts, words and actions.[1]

[1] **Matt. 5:28:** But I say to you that whoever looks at a woman to lust for her has already committed adultery with her in his heart. **Eph. 5:3-4:** But fornication and all uncleanness or covetousness, let it not even be named among you, as is fitting for saints; neither filthiness, nor foolish talking, nor coarse jesting, which are not fitting, but rather giving of thanks.

Q. 86. *Which is the eighth commandment?*

A. The eighth commandment is, *Thou shalt not steal.*[1]

[1] **Ex. 20:15:** You shall not steal. **Cf. Deut. 5:19.**

Q. 87. *What is required in the eighth commandment?*

A. The eighth commandment requireth the lawful procuring and furthering the wealth and outward estate of ourselves and others.[1]

[1] **Lev. 25:35:** If one of your brethren becomes poor, and falls into poverty among you, then you shall help him, like a stranger or a sojourner, that he may live with you. **Eph. 4:28:** Let him who stole steal no longer, but rather let him labor, working with *his* hands what is good, that he may have something to give him who has need. **Phil. 2:4:** Let each of you look out not only for his own interests, but also for the interests of others.

Q. 88. *What is forbidden in the eighth commandment?*

A. The eighth commandment forbiddeth whatsoever doth or may unjustly hinder our own or our neighbour's wealth or outward estate.[1]

[1] **Prov. 28:19:** He who tills his land will have plenty of bread, But he who follows frivolity will have poverty enough! **Eph. 4:28:** Let him who stole steal no longer, but rather let him labor, working with *his* hands what is good, that he may have something to give him who has need. **2 Thess. 3:10:** For even when we were with you, we commanded you this: If anyone will not work, neither shall he eat. **1 Tim. 5:8:** But if anyone does not provide for his own, and especially for those of his household, he has denied the faith and is worse than an unbeliever.

Q. 89. *Which is the ninth commandment?*

A. The ninth commandment is, *Thou shalt not bear false witness against thy neighbour.*[1]

[1] **Ex. 20:16:** You shall not bear false witness against your neighbor. **Cf. Deut. 5:20.**

Q. 90. *What is required in the ninth commandment?*

A. The ninth commandment requireth the maintaining and promoting of truth between man and man, and of our own and our neighbour's good name,[1] especially in witness-bearing.[2]

[1] **Zech. 8:16:** These *are* the things you shall do: Speak each man the truth to his neighbor; Give judgment in your gates for truth, justice, and peace. **Acts 25:10:** So Paul said, "I stand at Caesar's judgment seat, where I ought to be judged. To the Jews I have done no wrong, as you very well know. **3 John 12:** Demetrius has a *good* testimony from all, and from the truth itself. And we also bear witness, and you know that our testimony is true.

[2] **Prov. 14:5, 25:** A faithful witness does not lie, But a false witness will utter lies.... A true witness

delivers souls, But a deceitful *witness* speaks lies.

Q. 91. *What is forbidden in the ninth commandment?*

A. The ninth commandment forbiddeth whatsoever is prejudicial to truth, or injurious to our own or our neighbour's good name.[1]

[1] **Lev. 19:16:** You shall not go about *as* a talebearer among your people; nor shall you take a stand against the life of your neighbor: I *am* the LORD. **Ps. 15:3:** He *who* does not backbite with his tongue, Nor does evil to his neighbor, Nor does he take up a reproach against his friend. **Prov. 6:16-19:** These six *things* the LORD hates, Yes, seven *are* an abomination to Him: A proud look, A lying tongue, Hands that shed innocent blood, A heart that devises wicked plans, Feet that are swift in running to evil, A false witness *who* speaks lies, And one who sows discord among brethren. **Luke 3:14:** Likewise the soldiers asked him, saying, "And what shall we do?" So he said to them, "Do not intimidate anyone or accuse falsely, and be content with your wages."

Q. 92. *Which is the tenth commandment?*

A. The tenth commandment is, *Thou shalt not covet thy neighbour's house, thou shalt not covet thy neighbour's wife, nor his manservant, nor his maidservant, nor his ox, nor his ass, nor any thing that is thy neighbour's.*[1]

[1] **Ex. 20:17:** You shall not covet your neighbor's house; you shall not covet your neighbor's wife, nor his male servant, nor his female servant, nor his ox, nor his donkey, nor anything that *is* your neighbor's. **Cf. Deut. 5:21.**

Q. 93. *What is required in the tenth commandment?*

A. The tenth commandment requireth full contentment with our own condition,[1] with a right and charitable frame of spirit toward our neighbour, and all that is his.[2]

[1] **Ps. 34:1:** I will bless the LORD at all times; His praise *shall* continually *be* in my mouth. **Phil. 4:11:** Not that I speak in regard to need, for I have learned in whatever state I am, to be content. **1 Tim. 6:6:** Now godliness with contentment is great gain. **Heb. 13:5:** *Let your* conduct *be* without covetousness; *be* content with such things as you have. For He Himself has said, "I will never leave you nor forsake you."

[2] **Luke 15:6, 9, 11-32:** And when he comes home, he calls together *his* friends and neighbors, saying to them, 'Rejoice with me, for I have found my sheep which was lost!' ... And when she has found *it,* she calls *her* friends and neighbors together, saying, 'Rejoice with me, for I have found the piece which I lost!' ... Then He said: "A certain man had two sons. And the younger of them said to *his* father, 'Father, give me the portion of goods that falls *to me.*' So he divided to them *his* livelihood. And not many days after, the younger son gathered all together, journeyed to a far country, and there wasted his possessions with prodigal living. But when he had spent all, there arose a severe famine in that land, and he began to be in want. Then he went and joined himself to a citizen of that country, and he sent him into his fields to feed swine. And he would gladly have filled his stomach with the pods that the swine ate, and no one gave him *anything.* "But when he came to himself, he said, 'How many of my father's hired servants have bread enough and to spare, and I perish with hunger! I will arise and go to my father, and will say to him, "Father, I have sinned against heaven and before you, and I am no longer worthy to be called your son. Make me like one of your hired servants."' "And he arose and came to his father. But when he was still a great way off, his father saw him and had compassion, and ran and fell on his neck and kissed him. And the son said to him, 'Father, I have sinned against heaven and in your sight, and am no longer worthy to be called your son.' "But the father said to his servants, 'Bring out the best robe and put *it* on him, and put a ring on his hand and sandals on *his* feet. And bring the fatted calf here and kill *it,* and let us eat and be merry; for this my son was dead and is alive again; he was lost and is found.' And they

began to be merry. "Now his older son was in the field. And as he came and drew near to the house, he heard music and dancing. So he called one of the servants and asked what these things meant. And he said to him, 'Your brother has come, and because he has received him safe and sound, your father has killed the fatted calf.' "But he was angry and would not go in. Therefore his father came out and pleaded with him. So he answered and said to *his* father, 'Lo, these many years I have been serving you; I never transgressed your commandment at any time; and yet you never gave me a young goat, that I might make merry with my friends. But as soon as this son of yours came, who has devoured your livelihood with harlots, you killed the fatted calf for him.' "And he said to him, 'Son, you are always with me, and all that I have is yours. It was right that we should make merry and be glad, for your brother was dead and is alive again, and was lost and is found.'" **Rom. 12:15:** Rejoice with those who rejoice, and weep with those who weep. **Phil. 2:4:** Let each of you look out not only for his own interests, but also for the interests of others.

Q. 94. *What is forbidden in the tenth commandment?*

A. The tenth commandment forbiddeth all discontentment with our own estate,[1] envying or grieving at the good of our neighbour, and all inordinate motions and affections to anything that is his.[2]

1 **1 Cor. 10:10:** ... nor complain, as some of them also complained, and were destroyed by the destroyer. **James 3:14-16:** But if you have bitter envy and self-seeking in your hearts, do not boast and lie against the truth. This wisdom does not descend from above, but *is* earthly, sensual, demonic. For where envy and self-seeking *exist,* confusion and every evil thing *are* there.

2 **Gal. 5:26:** Let us not become conceited, provoking one another, envying one another. **Col. 3:5:** Therefore put to death your members which are on the earth: fornication, uncleanness, passion, evil desire, and covetousness, which is idolatry.

Q. 95. *Is any man able perfectly to keep the commandments of God?*

A. No mere man since the fall is able in this life perfectly to keep the commandments of God, but doth daily break them in thought, word and deed.[1]

1 **Gen. 8:21:** And the LORD smelled a soothing aroma. Then the LORD said in His heart, "I will never again curse the ground for man's sake, although the imagination of man's heart *is* evil from his youth; nor will I again destroy every living thing as I have done. **Rom. 3:9, 23:** What then? Are we better *than they?* Not at all. For we have previously charged both Jews and Greeks that they are all under sin.... for all have sinned and fall short of the glory of God.

Q. 96. *Are all transgressions of the law equally heinous?*

A. Some sins in themselves, and by reason of several aggravations, are more heinous in the sight of God than others.[1]

1 **Ezek. 8:6, 13, 15:** Furthermore He said to me, "Son of man, do you see what they are doing, the great abominations that the house of Israel commits here, to make Me go far away from My sanctuary? Now turn again, you will see greater abominations." ... And He said to me, "Turn again, *and* you will see greater abominations that they are doing." ... Then He said to me, "Have you seen *this,* O son of man? Turn again, you will see greater abominations than these." **Matt. 11:20-24:** Then He began to rebuke the cities in which most of His mighty works had been done, because they did not repent: "Woe to you, Chorazin! Woe to you, Bethsaida! For if the mighty works which were done in you had been done in Tyre and Sidon, they would have repented long ago in sackcloth and ashes. But I say to you, it will be more tolerable for Tyre and Sidon in the day of judgment than for you. And you, Capernaum, who are exalted to heaven, will be brought down to Hades; for if the

mighty works which were done in you had been done in Sodom, it would have remained until this day. But I say to you that it shall be more tolerable for the land of Sodom in the day of judgment than for you." **John 19:11:** Jesus answered, "You could have no power at all against Me unless it had been given you from above. Therefore the one who delivered Me to you has the greater sin."

Q. 97. *What doth every sin deserve?*

A. Every sin deserveth God's wrath and curse, both in this life, and that which is to come.[1]

[1] **Matt. 25:41:** "Then He will also say to those on the left hand, 'Depart from Me, you cursed, into the everlasting fire prepared for the devil and his angels.'" **Gal. 3:10:** For as many as are of the works of the law are under the curse; for it is written, "Cursed *is* everyone who does not continue in all things which are written in the book of the law, to do them." **Eph. 5:6:** Let no one deceive you with empty words, for because of these things the wrath of God comes upon the sons of disobedience. **James 2:10:** For whoever shall keep the whole law, and yet stumble in one *point,* he is guilty of all.

Q. 98. *What doth God require of us that we may escape His wrath and curse due to us for sin?*

A. To escape the wrath and curse of God due to us for sin, God requireth of us faith in Jesus Christ, repentance unto life,[1] with the diligent use of all the outward means whereby Christ communicateth to us the benefits of redemption.[2]

[1] **Mark 1:15:** ... and saying, "The time is fulfilled, and the kingdom of God is at hand. Repent, and believe in the gospel."

[2] **Acts 2:38:** Then Peter said to them, "Repent, and let every one of you be baptized in the name of Jesus Christ for the remission of sins; and you shall receive the gift of the Holy Spirit. **1 Cor. 11:24-25:** ... and when He had given thanks, He broke *it* and said, "Take, eat; this is My body which is broken for you; do this in remembrance of Me." In the same manner *He* also *took* the cup after supper, saying, "This cup is the new covenant in My blood. This do, as often as you drink *it,* in remembrance of Me." **Col. 3:16:** Let the word of Christ dwell in you richly in all wisdom, teaching and admonishing one another in psalms and hymns and spiritual songs, singing with grace in your hearts to the Lord.

Q. 99. *What is faith in Jesus Christ?*

A. Faith in Jesus Christ is a saving grace,[1] whereby we receive and rest upon Him alone for salvation, as He is offered to us in the gospel.[2]

[1] **Eph. 2:8-9:** For by grace you have been saved through faith, and that not of yourselves; *it is* the gift of God, not of works, lest anyone should boast. **Cf. Rom. 4:16:** Therefore *it is* of faith that *it might be* according to grace, so that the promise might be sure to all the seed, not only to those who are of the law, but also to those who are of the faith of Abraham, who is the father of us all.

[2] **John 20:30-31:** And truly Jesus did many other signs in the presence of His disciples, which are not written in this book; but these are written that you may believe that Jesus is the Christ, the Son of God, and that believing you may have life in His name. **Gal. 2:15-16:** We *who are* Jews by nature, and not sinners of the Gentiles, knowing that a man is not justified by the works of the law but by faith in Jesus Christ, even we have believed in Christ Jesus, that we might be justified by faith in Christ and not by the works of the law; for by the works of the law no flesh shall be justified. **Phil. 3:3-11:** For we are the circumcision, who worship God in the Spirit, rejoice in Christ Jesus, and have no confidence in the flesh, though I also might have confidence in the flesh. If anyone else

thinks he may have confidence in the flesh, I more so: circumcised the eighth day, of the stock of Israel, *of* the tribe of Benjamin, a Hebrew of the Hebrews; concerning the law, a Pharisee; concerning zeal, persecuting the church; concerning the righteousness which is in the law, blameless. But what things were gain to me, these I have counted loss for Christ. Yet indeed I also count all things loss for the excellence of the knowledge of Christ Jesus my Lord, for whom I have suffered the loss of all things, and count them as rubbish, that I may gain Christ and be found in Him, not having my own righteousness, which *is* from the law, but that which *is* through faith in Christ, the righteousness which is from God by faith; that I may know Him and the power of His resurrection, and the fellowship of His sufferings, being conformed to His death, if, by any means, I may attain to the resurrection from the dead.

Q. 100. *What is repentance unto life?*

A. Repentance unto life is a saving grace,[1] whereby a sinner, out of a true sense of his sin, and apprehension of the mercy of God in Christ,[2] doth, with grief and hatred of his sin, turn from it unto God,[3] with full purpose of, and endeavor after, new obedience.[4]

1 **Acts 11:18:** When they heard these things they became silent; and they glorified God, saying, "Then God has also granted to the Gentiles repentance to life." **2 Tim. 2:25:** ... in humility correcting those who are in opposition, if God perhaps will grant them repentance, so that they may know the truth.

2 **Ps. 51:1-4:** Have mercy upon me, O God, According to Your lovingkindness; According to the multitude of Your tender mercies, Blot out my transgressions. Wash me thoroughly from my iniquity, And cleanse me from my sin. For I acknowledge my transgressions, And my sin *is* always before me. Against You, You only, have I sinned, And done *this* evil in Your sight— That You may be found just when You speak, *And* blameless when You judge. **Joel 2:13:** So rend your heart, and not your garments; Return to the LORD your God, For He *is* gracious and merciful, Slow to anger, and of great kindness; And He relents from doing harm. **Luke 15:7, 10:** I say to you that likewise there will be more joy in heaven over one sinner who repents than over ninety-nine just persons who need no repentance.... Likewise, I say to you, there is joy in the presence of the angels of God over one sinner who repents. **Acts 2:37:** Now when they heard *this,* they were cut to the heart, and said to Peter and the rest of the apostles, "Men *and* brethren, what shall we do?"

3 **Jer. 31:18-19:** I have surely heard Ephraim bemoaning himself: 'You have chastised me, and I was chastised, Like an untrained bull; Restore me, and I will return, For You *are* the LORD my God. Surely, after my turning, I repented; And after I was instructed, I struck myself on the thigh; I was ashamed, yes, even humiliated, Because I bore the reproach of my youth.' **Luke 1:16-17:** And he will turn many of the children of Israel to the Lord their God. He will also go before Him in the spirit and power of Elijah, 'to turn the hearts of the fathers to the children,' and the disobedient to the wisdom of the just, to make ready a people prepared for the Lord. **1 Thess. 1:9:** For they themselves declare concerning us what manner of entry we had to you, and how you turned to God from idols to serve the living and true God.

4 **2 Chron. 7:14:** ... if My people who are called by My name will humble themselves, and pray and seek My face, and turn from their wicked ways, then I will hear from heaven, and will forgive their sin and heal their land. **Ps. 119:57-64:** *You are* my portion, O LORD; I have said that I would keep Your words. I entreated Your favor with *my* whole heart; Be merciful to me according to Your word. I thought about my ways, And turned my feet to Your testimonies. I made haste, and did not delay To keep Your commandments. The cords of the wicked have bound me, *But* I have not forgotten Your law. At midnight I will rise to give thanks to You, Because of Your righteous judgments. I *am* a companion of all who fear You, And of those who keep Your precepts. The earth, O LORD, is full of Your mercy; Teach me Your statutes. **Matt. 3:8:** Therefore bear fruits worthy of repentance. **2 Cor. 7:10:** For godly sorrow produces repentance *leading* to salvation, not to be regretted; but the sorrow of the world produces death.

Q. 101. *What are the outward and ordinary means whereby Christ communicateth to us the benefits of redemption?*

A. The outward and ordinary means whereby Christ

communicateth to us the benefits of redemption, are His ordinances, especially the word, baptism and the Lord's Supper, and prayer; all which are made effectual to the elect for salvation.[1]

1 **Matt. 28:18-20:** And Jesus came and spoke to them, saying, "All authority has been given to Me in heaven and on earth. Go therefore and make disciples of all the nations, baptizing them in the name of the Father and of the Son and of the Holy Spirit, teaching them to observe all things that I have commanded you; and lo, I am with you always, *even* to the end of the age." Amen. **Acts 2:41-42:** Then those who gladly received his word were baptized; and that day about three thousand souls were added *to them.* And they continued steadfastly in the apostles' doctrine and fellowship, in the breaking of bread, and in prayers.

Q. 102. *How is the word made effectual to salvation?*

A. The Spirit of God maketh the reading, but especially the preaching, of the word, an effectual means of convincing and converting sinners, and of building them up in holiness and comfort, through faith, unto salvation.[1]

1 **Neh. 8:8-9:** So they read distinctly from the book, in the Law of God; and they gave the sense, and helped *them* to understand the reading. And Nehemiah, who *was* the governor, Ezra the priest *and* scribe, and the Levites who taught the people said to all the people, "This day *is* holy to the LORD your God; do not mourn nor weep." For all the people wept, when they heard the words of the Law. **Acts 20:32:** So now, brethren, I commend you to God and to the word of His grace, which is able to build you up and give you an inheritance among all those who are sanctified. **Rom. 10:14-17:** How then shall they call on Him in whom they have not believed? And how shall they believe in Him of whom they have not heard? And how shall they hear without a preacher? And how shall they preach unless they are sent? As it is written: "How beautiful are the feet of those who preach the gospel of peace, Who bring glad tidings of good things!" But they have not all obeyed the gospel. For Isaiah says, "LORD, who has believed our report?" So then faith *comes* by hearing, and hearing by the word of God. **2 Tim. 3:15-17:** ... and that from childhood you have known the Holy Scriptures, which are able to make you wise for salvation through faith which is in Christ Jesus. All Scripture *is* given by inspiration of God, and *is* profitable for doctrine, for reproof, for correction, for instruction in righteousness, that the man of God may be complete, thoroughly equipped for every good work. **Acts 9:31:** Then the churches throughout all Judea, Galilee, and Samaria had peace and were edified. And walking in the fear of the Lord and in the comfort of the Holy Spirit, they were multiplied.

Q. 103. *How is the word to be read and heard, that it may become effectual to salvation?*

A. That the word may become effectual to salvation, we must attend thereunto with diligence, preparation and prayer;[1] receive it with faith and love, lay it up in our hearts, and practice it in our lives.[2]

1 **Deut. 6:16:** You shall not tempt the LORD your God as you tempted *Him* in Massah. **Ps. 119:18:** Open my eyes, that I may see Wondrous things from Your law. **1 Pet. 2:1-2:** Therefore, laying aside all malice, all deceit, hypocrisy, envy, and all evil speaking, as newborn babes, desire the pure milk of the word, that you may grow thereby.

2 **Ps. 119:11:** Your word I have hidden in my heart, That I might not sin against You. **2 Thess. 2:10:** ... and with all unrighteous deception among those who perish, because they did not receive the love of the truth, that they might be saved. **Heb. 4:2:** For indeed the gospel was preached to us as well as to them; but the word which they heard did not profit them, not being mixed with faith in those who heard *it.* **James 1:22-25:** But be doers of the word, and not hearers only, deceiving yourselves. For if anyone is a hearer of the word and not a doer, he is like a man observing his natural face in a mirror; for he observes himself, goes away, and immediately forgets what kind of

man he was. But he who looks into the perfect law of liberty and continues *in it,* and is not a forgetful hearer but a doer of the work, this one will be blessed in what he does.

Q. 104. *How does baptism and the Lord's Supper become effectual means of salvation?*

A. Baptism and the Lord's Supper become effectual means of salvation, not from any virtue in them, or in him that doth administer them; but only by the blessing of Christ, and the working of His Spirit in them that by faith receive them.[1]

[1] **1 Cor. 3:7:** So then neither he who plants is anything, nor he who waters, but God who gives the increase. **Cf. 1 Cor. 1:12-17:** Now I say this, that each of you says, "I am of Paul," or "I am of Apollos," or "I am of Cephas," or "I am of Christ." Is Christ divided? Was Paul crucified for you? Or were you baptized in the name of Paul? I thank God that I baptized none of you except Crispus and Gaius, lest anyone should say that I had baptized in my own name. Yes, I also baptized the household of Stephanas. Besides, I do not know whether I baptized any other. For Christ did not send me to baptize, but to preach the gospel, not with wisdom of words, lest the cross of Christ should be made of no effect.

Q. 105. *Wherein do the ordinances of baptism and the Lord's Supper differ from the other ordinances of God?*

A. Baptism and the Lord's Supper differ from the other ordinances of God in that they were specially instituted by Christ[1] to represent and apply to believers the benefits of the New Covenant by visible and outward signs.[2]

[1] **Matt. 28:19-20:** Go therefore and make disciples of all the nations, baptizing them in the name of the Father and of the Son and of the Holy Spirit, teaching them to observe all things that I have commanded you; and lo, I am with you always, *even* to the end of the age." Amen. **1 Cor. 11:23-26:** For I received from the Lord that which I also delivered to you: that the Lord Jesus on the *same* night in which He was betrayed took bread; and when He had given thanks, He broke *it* and said, "Take, eat; this is My body which is broken for you; do this in remembrance of Me." In the same manner *He* also *took* the cup after supper, saying, "This cup is the new covenant in My blood. This do, as often as you drink *it,* in remembrance of Me."

[2] **Acts 22:16:** And now why are you waiting? Arise and be baptized, and wash away your sins, calling on the name of the Lord. **Matt. 26:26-28:** And as they were eating, Jesus took bread, blessed and broke *it,* and gave *it* to the disciples and said, "Take, eat; this is My body." Then He took the cup, and gave thanks, and gave *it* to them, saying, "Drink from it, all of you. For this is My blood of the new covenant, which is shed for many for the remission of sins. **Rom. 6:4:** Therefore we were buried with Him through baptism into death, that just as Christ was raised from the dead by the glory of the Father, even so we also should walk in newness of life.

Q. 106. *What is baptism?*

A. Baptism is a holy ordinance, wherein the washing with water in the name of the Father, and of the Son, and of the Holy Spirit, doth signify our ingrafting into Christ, a covenant transaction unto the party baptized, and our engagement to be the Lord's.[1]

[1] **Matt. 28:19:** Go therefore and make disciples of all the nations, baptizing them in the name of the Father and of the Son and of the Holy Spirit. **Rom. 6:3-5:** Or do you not know that as many of us as

were baptized into Christ Jesus were baptized into His death? Therefore we were buried with Him through baptism into death, that just as Christ was raised from the dead by the glory of the Father, even so we also should walk in newness of life. For if we have been united together in the likeness of His death, certainly we also shall be *in the likeness* of *His* resurrection. **Col. 2:12:** ... buried with Him in baptism, in which you also were raised with *Him* through faith in the working of God, who raised Him from the dead. **Gal. 3:27:** For as many of you as were baptized into Christ have put on Christ.

Q. 107. *To whom is baptism to be administered?*

A. Baptism is to be administered to all those who actually profess repentance towards God, faith in, and obedience to our Lord Jesus Christ; and to none other.[1]

[1] **Acts 2:38:** Then Peter said to them, "Repent, and let every one of you be baptized in the name of Jesus Christ for the remission of sins; and you shall receive the gift of the Holy Spirit. **Matt. 3:6:** ... and were baptized by him in the Jordan, confessing their sins. **Mark 16:16:** He who believes and is baptized will be saved; but he who does not believe will be condemned. **Acts 8:12, 36:** But when they believed Philip as he preached the things concerning the kingdom of God and the name of Jesus Christ, both men and women were baptized.... Now as they went down the road, they came to some water. And the eunuch said, "See, here is water. What hinders me from being baptized?" **Acts 10:47-48:** "Can anyone forbid water, that these should not be baptized who have received the Holy Spirit just as we *have?*" And he commanded them to be baptized in the name of the Lord. Then they asked him to stay a few days.

Q. 108. *What is the Lord's Supper?*

A. The Lord's Supper is a holy ordinance, wherein, by giving and receiving bread and wine according to Christ's appointment, His death is showed forth;[1] and the worthy receivers are, not after a corporal and carnal manner, but by faith, made partakers of His body and blood, with all His benefits, to their spiritual nourishment and growth in grace.[2]

[1] **Luke 22:19-20:** And He took bread, gave thanks and broke *it,* and gave *it* to them, saying, "This is My body which is given for you; do this in remembrance of Me." Likewise He also *took* the cup after supper, saying, "This cup *is* the new covenant in My blood, which is shed for you. **1 Cor. 11:23-26:** For I received from the Lord that which I also delivered to you: that the Lord Jesus on the *same* night in which He was betrayed took bread; and when He had given thanks, He broke *it* and said, "Take, eat; this is My body which is broken for you; do this in remembrance of Me." In the same manner *He* also *took* the cup after supper, saying, "This cup is the new covenant in My blood. This do, as often as you drink *it,* in remembrance of Me." For as often as you eat this bread and drink this cup, you proclaim the Lord's death till He comes.

[2] **1 Cor. 10:16-17:** The cup of blessing which we bless, is it not the communion of the blood of Christ? The bread which we break, is it not the communion of the body of Christ? For we, *though* many, are one bread *and* one body; for we all partake of that one bread.

Q. 109. *What is required to the worthy receiving of the Lord's Supper?*

A. It is required of them that would worthily partake of the Lord's Supper, that they examine themselves of their knowledge to discern the Lord's body, of their faith to feed upon Him, of their repentance, love, and new obedience; lest, coming unworthily, they eat and drink judgment to themselves.[1]

1 **1 Cor. 11:27-32:** Therefore whoever eats this bread or drinks *this* cup of the Lord in an unworthy manner will be guilty of the body and blood of the Lord. But let a man examine himself, and so let him eat of the bread and drink of the cup. For he who eats and drinks in an unworthy manner eats and drinks judgment to himself, not discerning the Lord's body. For this reason many *are* weak and sick among you, and many sleep. For if we would judge ourselves, we would not be judged. But when we are judged, we are chastened by the Lord, that we may not be condemned with the world.

Q. 110. *What is prayer?*

A. Prayer is an offering up of our desires unto God,[1] for things agreeable to His will,[2] in the name of Christ,[3] with confession of our sins,[4] and thankful acknowledgment of His mercies.[5]

1 **Ps. 10:17:** LORD, You have heard the desire of the humble; You will prepare their heart; You will cause Your ear to hear. **Ps. 62:8:** Trust in Him at all times, you people; Pour out your heart before Him; God *is* a refuge for us. *Selah*. **Matt. 7:7-8:** Ask, and it will be given to you; seek, and you will find; knock, and it will be opened to you. For everyone who asks receives, and he who seeks finds, and to him who knocks it will be opened.

2 **1 John 5:14:** Now this is the confidence that we have in Him, that if we ask anything according to His will, He hears us.

3 **John 16:23-24:** And in that day you will ask Me nothing. Most assuredly, I say to you, whatever you ask the Father in My name He will give you. Until now you have asked nothing in My name. Ask, and you will receive, that your joy may be full.

4 **Ps. 32:5-6:** I acknowledged my sin to You, And my iniquity I have not hidden. I said, "I will confess my transgressions to the LORD," And You forgave the iniquity of my sin. *Selah*. For this cause everyone who is godly shall pray to You In a time when You may be found; Surely in a flood of great waters They shall not come near him. **Dan. 9:4-19:** And I prayed to the LORD my God, and made confession, and said, "O Lord, great and awesome God, who keeps His covenant and mercy with those who love Him, and with those who keep His commandments, we have sinned and committed iniquity, we have done wickedly and rebelled, even by departing from Your precepts and Your judgments.... To the Lord our God *belong* mercy and forgiveness, though we have rebelled against Him. We have not obeyed the voice of the LORD our God, to walk in His laws, which He set before us by His servants the prophets.... O my God, incline Your ear and hear; open Your eyes and see our desolations, and the city which is called by Your name; for we do not present our supplications before You because of our righteous deeds, but because of Your great mercies. O Lord, hear! O Lord, forgive! O Lord, listen and act! Do not delay for Your own sake, my God, for Your city and Your people are called by Your name." **1 John 1:9:** If we confess our sins, He is faithful and just to forgive us *our* sins and to cleanse us from all unrighteousness.

5 **Ps. 103:1-5:** Bless the LORD, O my soul; And all that is within me, *bless* His holy name! Bless the LORD, O my soul, And forget not all His benefits: Who forgives all your iniquities, Who heals all your diseases, Who redeems your life from destruction, Who crowns you with lovingkindness and tender mercies, Who satisfies your mouth with good *things*, *So that* your youth is renewed like the eagle's. **Ps. 136:** Oh, give thanks to the LORD, for *He is* good! For His mercy *endures* forever.... Who remembered us in our lowly state, For His mercy *endures* forever; And rescued us from our enemies, For His mercy *endures* forever; Who gives food to all flesh, For His mercy *endures* forever. Oh, give thanks to the God of heaven! For His mercy *endures* forever. **Phil. 4:6:** Be anxious for nothing, but in everything by prayer and supplication, with thanksgiving, let your requests be made known to God.

Q. 111. *What rule hath God given for our direction in prayer?*

A. The whole word of God is of use to direct us in prayer;[1] but the special rule of direction is that form of prayer which Christ taught His disciples, commonly called *The Lord's Prayer.*[2]

[1] **1 John 5:14:** Now this is the confidence that we have in Him, that if we ask anything according to His will, He hears us.

[2] **Matt. 6:9-13:** In this manner, therefore, pray: Our Father in heaven, Hallowed be Your name. Your kingdom come. Your will be done On earth as *it is* in heaven. Give us this day our daily bread. And forgive us our debts, As we forgive our debtors. And do not lead us into temptation, But deliver us from the evil one. For Yours is the kingdom and the power and the glory forever. Amen.

Q. 112. *What doth the preface of the Lord's Prayer teach us?*

A. The preface of the Lord's Prayer (which is, *Our Father which art in heaven)* teacheth us to draw near to God with all holy reverence[1] and confidence,[2] as children to a father[3] able and ready to help us;[4] and that we should pray with and for others.[5]

[1] **Ps. 95:6:** Oh come, let us worship and bow down; Let us kneel before the Lord our Maker.

[2] **Eph. 3:12:** ... in whom we have boldness and access with confidence through faith in Him.

[3] **Matt. 7:9-11:** Or what man is there among you who, if his son asks for bread, will give him a stone? Or if he asks for a fish, will he give him a serpent? If you then, being evil, know how to give good gifts to your children, how much more will your Father who is in heaven give good things to those who ask Him! **Cf. Luke 11:11-13:** If a son asks for bread from any father among you, will he give him a stone? Or if *he asks* for a fish, will he give him a serpent instead of a fish? Or if he asks for an egg, will he offer him a scorpion? If you then, being evil, know how to give good gifts to your children, how much more will *your* heavenly Father give the Holy Spirit to those who ask Him! **Rom. 8:15:** For you did not receive the spirit of bondage again to fear, but you received the Spirit of adoption by whom we cry out, "Abba, Father."

[4] **Eph. 3:20:** Now to Him who is able to do exceedingly abundantly above all that we ask or think, according to the power that works in us.

[5] **Eph. 6:18:** praying always with all prayer and supplication in the Spirit, being watchful to this end with all perseverance and supplication for all the saints. **1 Tim. 2:1-2:** Therefore I exhort first of all that supplications, prayers, intercessions, *and* giving of thanks be made for all men, for kings and all who are in authority, that we may lead a quiet and peaceable life in all godliness and reverence.

Q. 113. *What do we pray for in the first petition?*

A. In the first petition (which is, *Hallowed be thy name*), we pray that God would enable us and others to glorify Him in all that whereby He maketh Himself known;[1] and that He would dispose all things to His own glory.[2]

[1] **Ps. 67:1-3:** God be merciful to us and bless us, *And* cause His face to shine upon us, *Selah*. That Your way may be known on earth, Your salvation among all nations. Let the peoples praise You, O God; Let all the peoples praise You. **Ps. 99:3:** Let them praise Your great and awesome name— He *is* holy. **Ps. 100:3-4:** Know that the Lord, He *is* God; *It is* He *who* has made us, and not we ourselves; *We are* His people and the sheep of His pasture. Enter into His gates with thanksgiving, *And* into His courts with praise. Be thankful to Him, *and* bless His name.

[2] **Rev. 4:11:** You are worthy, O Lord, To receive glory and honor and power; For You created all things, And by Your will they exist and were created.

Q. 114. *What do we pray for in the second petition?*

A. In the second petition (which is, *Thy kingdom come*), we pray that Satan's kingdom may be destroyed;[1] and that the kingdom of grace may be advanced,[2] ourselves and others brought into it, and kept in it;[3] and that the kingdom of glory may be hastened.[4]

1 **Matt. 12:25-28:** But Jesus knew their thoughts, and said to them: "Every kingdom divided against itself is brought to desolation, and every city or house divided against itself will not stand. If Satan casts out Satan, he is divided against himself. How then will his kingdom stand? And if I cast out demons by Beelzebub, by whom do your sons cast *them* out? Therefore they shall be your judges. But if I cast out demons by the Spirit of God, surely the kingdom of God has come upon you. **Rom. 16:20:** And the God of peace will crush Satan under your feet shortly. The grace of our Lord Jesus Christ *be* with you. Amen. **1 John 3:8:** He who sins is of the devil, for the devil has sinned from the beginning. For this purpose the Son of God was manifested, that He might destroy the works of the devil.

2 **Ps. 72:8-11:** He shall have dominion also from sea to sea, And from the River to the ends of the earth. Those who dwell in the wilderness will bow before Him, And His enemies will lick the dust. The kings of Tarshish and of the isles Will bring presents; The kings of Sheba and Seba Will offer gifts. Yes, all kings shall fall down before Him; All nations shall serve Him. **Matt. 24:14:** And this gospel of the kingdom will be preached in all the world as a witness to all the nations, and then the end will come. **1 Cor. 15:24-25:** Then *comes* the end, when He delivers the kingdom to God the Father, when He puts an end to all rule and all authority and power. For He must reign till He has put all enemies under His feet.

3 **Ps. 119:5:** Oh, that my ways were directed To keep Your statutes! **Luke 22:32:** But I have prayed for you, that your faith should not fail; and when you have returned to *Me,* strengthen your brethren. **2 Thess. 3:1-5:** Finally, brethren, pray for us, that the word of the Lord may run *swiftly* and be glorified, just as *it is* with you, and that we may be delivered from unreasonable and wicked men; for not all have faith. But the Lord is faithful, who will establish you and guard *you* from the evil one. And we have confidence in the Lord concerning you, both that you do and will do the things we command you. Now may the Lord direct your hearts into the love of God and into the patience of Christ.

4 **Rev. 22:20:** He who testifies to these things says, "Surely I am coming quickly." Amen. Even so, come, Lord Jesus!

Q. 115. *What do we pray for in the third petition?*

A. In the third petition (which is, *Thy will be done in earth, as it is in heaven*), we pray that God, by His grace, would make us able and willing to know, obey and submit to His will in all things,[1] as the angels do in heaven.[2]

1 **Ps. 19:14:** Let the words of my mouth and the meditation of my heart Be acceptable in Your sight, O LORD, my strength and my Redeemer. **Ps. 119:** Blessed *are* the undefiled in the way, Who walk in the law of the LORD! Blessed *are* those who keep His testimonies, Who seek Him with the whole heart! They also do no iniquity; They walk in His ways. You have commanded *us* To keep Your precepts diligently. Oh, that my ways were directed To keep Your statutes! Then I would not be ashamed, When I look into all Your commandments. I will praise You with uprightness of heart, When I learn Your righteous judgments. I will keep Your statutes; Oh, do not forsake me utterly.... **1 Thess. 5:23:** Now may the God of peace Himself sanctify you completely; and may your whole spirit, soul, and body be preserved blameless at the coming of our Lord Jesus Christ. **Heb. 13:20-21:** Now may the God of peace who brought up our Lord Jesus from the dead, that great Shepherd of the sheep, through the blood of the everlasting covenant, make you complete in every good work to do His will, working in you what is well pleasing in His sight, through Jesus Christ, to whom *be* glory forever and ever. Amen.

2 **Ps. 103:20-21:** Bless the LORD, you His angels, Who excel in strength, who do His word, Heeding the voice of His word. Bless the LORD, all *you* His hosts, *You* ministers of His, who do His pleasure.

Heb. 1:14: Are they not all ministering spirits sent forth to minister for those who will inherit salvation?

Q. 116. *What do we pray for in the fourth petition?*

A. In the fourth petition (which is, *Give us this day our daily bread*), we pray that of God's free gift we may receive a competent portion of the good things of this life, and enjoy His blessing with them.[1]

1 **Prov. 30:8-9:** Remove falsehood and lies far from me; Give me neither poverty nor riches— Feed me with the food allotted to me; Lest I be full and deny *You,* And say, "Who *is* the LORD?" Or lest I be poor and steal, And profane the name of my God. **Matt. 6:31-34:** Therefore do not worry, saying, 'What shall we eat?' or 'What shall we drink?' or 'What shall we wear?' For after all these things the Gentiles seek. For your heavenly Father knows that you need all these things. But seek first the kingdom of God and His righteousness, and all these things shall be added to you. Therefore do not worry about tomorrow, for tomorrow will worry about its own things. Sufficient for the day *is* its own trouble. **Phil. 4:11, 19:** Not that I speak in regard to need, for I have learned in whatever state I am, to be content.... And my God shall supply all your need according to His riches in glory by Christ Jesus. **1 Tim. 6:6-8:** Now godliness with contentment is great gain. For we brought nothing into *this* world, *and it is* certain we can carry nothing out. And having food and clothing, with these we shall be content.

Q. 117. *What do we pray for in the fifth petition?*

A. In the fifth petition (which is, *Forgive us our debts, as we forgive our debtors*), we pray that God, for Christ's sake, would freely pardon all our sins;[1] which we are the rather encouraged to ask, because by His grace we are enabled from the heart to forgive others.[2]

1 **Ps. 51:1-2, 7, 9:** Have mercy upon me, O God, According to Your lovingkindness; According to the multitude of Your tender mercies, Blot out my transgressions. Wash me thoroughly from my iniquity, And cleanse me from my sin.... Purge me with hyssop, and I shall be clean; Wash me, and I shall be whiter than snow.... Hide Your face from my sins, And blot out all my iniquities. **Dan. 9:17-19:** Now therefore, our God, hear the prayer of Your servant, and his supplications, and for the Lord's sake cause Your face to shine on Your sanctuary, which is desolate. O my God, incline Your ear and hear; open Your eyes and see our desolations, and the city which is called by Your name; for we do not present our supplications before You because of our righteous deeds, but because of Your great mercies. O Lord, hear! O Lord, forgive! O Lord, listen and act! Do not delay for Your own sake, my God, for Your city and Your people are called by Your name. **1 John 1:7:** But if we walk in the light as He is in the light, we have fellowship with one another, and the blood of Jesus Christ His Son cleanses us from all sin.

2 **Matt. 18:21-35:** Then Peter came to Him and said, "Lord, how often shall my brother sin against me, and I forgive him? Up to seven times?" Jesus said to him, "I do not say to you, up to seven times, but up to seventy times seven. Therefore the kingdom of heaven is like a certain king who wanted to settle accounts with his servants. And when he had begun to settle accounts, one was brought to him who owed him ten thousand talents. But as he was not able to pay, his master commanded that he be sold, with his wife and children and all that he had, and that payment be made. The servant therefore fell down before him, saying, 'Master, have patience with me, and I will pay you all.' Then the master of that servant was moved with compassion, released him, and forgave him the debt. "But that servant went out and found one of his fellow servants who owed him a hundred denarii; and he laid hands on him and took *him* by the throat, saying, 'Pay me what you owe!' So his fellow servant fell down at his feet and begged him, saying, 'Have patience with me, and I will pay you all.' And he would not, but went and threw him into prison till he should pay the debt. So when his fellow servants saw what had been done, they were very grieved, and came and told their master all that had been done. Then his master, after he had called him, said to him, 'You wicked servant! I forgave you all that debt because you begged me. Should you not also have had compassion on your fellow servant, just as I had pity on you?' And his master was angry, and

delivered him to the torturers until he should pay all that was due to him. "So My heavenly Father also will do to you if each of you, from his heart, does not forgive his brother his trespasses." **Eph. 4:32:** And be kind to one another, tenderhearted, forgiving one another, even as God in Christ forgave you. **Col. 3:13:** ... bearing with one another, and forgiving one another, if anyone has a complaint against another; even as Christ forgave you, so you also *must do.*

Q. 118. *What do we pray for in the sixth petition?*

A. In the sixth petition (which is, *And lead us not into temptation, but deliver us from evil*), we pray that God would either keep us from being tempted to sin, or support and deliver us when we are tempted.[1]

1 **Luke 22:31-32:** And the Lord said, "Simon, Simon! Indeed, Satan has asked for you, that he may sift *you* as wheat. But I have prayed for you, that your faith should not fail; and when you have returned to *Me,* strengthen your brethren." **1 Cor. 10:13:** No temptation has overtaken you except such as is common to man; but God *is* faithful, who will not allow you to be tempted beyond what you are able, but with the temptation will also make the way of escape, that you may be able to bear *it.* **2 Cor. 12:7-9:** And lest I should be exalted above measure by the abundance of the revelations, a thorn in the flesh was given to me, a messenger of Satan to buffet me, lest I be exalted above measure. Concerning this thing I pleaded with the Lord three times that it might depart from me. And He said to me, "My grace is sufficient for you, for My strength is made perfect in weakness." Therefore most gladly I will rather boast in my infirmities, that the power of Christ may rest upon me. **Heb. 2:18:** For in that He Himself has suffered, being tempted, He is able to aid those who are tempted.

Q. 119. *What doth the conclusion of the Lord's Prayer teach us?*

A. The conclusion of the Lord's Prayer (which is, *For thine is the kingdom, and the power, and the glory, forever. Amen.*) teacheth us to take our encouragement in prayer from God only,[1] and in our prayers to praise Him, ascribing kingdom, power and glory to Him.[2] And, in testimony of our desire, and assurance to be heard, we say, *Amen.*[3]

1 **Dan. 9:4, 7-9, 16-19:** And I prayed to the LORD my God, and made confession, and said, "O Lord, great and awesome God, who keeps His covenant and mercy with those who love Him, and with those who keep His commandments ... O Lord, righteousness *belongs* to You, but to us shame of face, as *it is* this day—to the men of Judah, to the inhabitants of Jerusalem and all Israel, those near and those far off in all the countries to which You have driven them, because of the unfaithfulness which they have committed against You. "O Lord, to us *belongs* shame of face, to our kings, our princes, and our fathers, because we have sinned against You. To the Lord our God *belong* mercy and forgiveness, though we have rebelled against Him.... O Lord, according to all Your righteousness, I pray, let Your anger and Your fury be turned away from Your city Jerusalem, Your holy mountain; because for our sins, and for the iniquities of our fathers, Jerusalem and Your people *are* a reproach to all *those* around us. Now therefore, our God, hear the prayer of Your servant, and his supplications, and for the Lord's sake cause Your face to shine on Your sanctuary, which is desolate. O my God, incline Your ear and hear; open Your eyes and see our desolations, and the city which is called by Your name; for we do not present our supplications before You because of our righteous deeds, but because of Your great mercies. O Lord, hear! O Lord, forgive! O Lord, listen and act! Do not delay for Your own sake, my God, for Your city and Your people are called by Your name." **Luke 18:1, 7-8:** Then He spoke a parable to them, that men always ought to pray and not lose heart ... And shall God not avenge His own elect who cry out day and night to Him, though He bears long with them? I tell you that He will avenge them speedily. Nevertheless, when the Son of Man comes, will He really find faith on the earth?

2 **1 Chron. 29:10-13:** Therefore David blessed the LORD before all the assembly; and David said:

"Blessed are You, LORD God of Israel, our Father, forever and ever. Yours, O LORD, *is* the greatness, The power and the glory, The victory and the majesty; For all *that is* in heaven and in earth *is Yours;* Yours *is* the kingdom, O LORD, And You are exalted as head over all. Both riches and honor *come* from You, And You reign over all. In Your hand *is* power and might; In Your hand *it is* to make great And to give strength to all. "Now therefore, our God, We thank You And praise Your glorious name. **1 Tim. 1:17:** Now to the King eternal, immortal, invisible, to God who alone is wise, *be* honor and glory forever and ever. Amen. **Rev. 5:11-13:** Then I looked, and I heard the voice of many angels around the throne, the living creatures, and the elders; and the number of them was ten thousand times ten thousand, and thousands of thousands, saying with a loud voice: "Worthy is the Lamb who was slain To receive power and riches and wisdom, And strength and honor and glory and blessing!" And every creature which is in heaven and on the earth and under the earth and such as are in the sea, and all that are in them, I heard saying: "Blessing and honor and glory and power *Be* to Him who sits on the throne, And to the Lamb, forever and ever!"

[3] **1 Cor. 14:16:** Otherwise, if you bless with the spirit, how will he who occupies the place of the uninformed say "Amen" at your giving of thanks, since he does not understand what you say? **Rev. 22:20:** He who testifies to these things says, "Surely I am coming quickly." Amen. Even so, come, Lord Jesus!

THE

SUM OF SAVING KNOWLEDGE:

OR,

A BRIEF SUM OF CHRISTIAN DOCTRINE,

CONTAINED IN THE HOLY SCRIPTURES, AND HOLDEN FORTH IN THE FORESAID CONFESSION OF FAITH AND CATECHISMS

All that the Father giveth me shall come to me; and him that cometh to me I will in no wise cast out — John 6:37.

THE

SUM OF SAVING KNOWLEDGE

The Sum of Saving Knowledge may be taken up in these four heads: 1. The woeful condition wherein all men are by nature, through breaking the divine pledge, communion, and righteous law of God. 2. The remedy provided for the elect in Jesus Christ by the covenant of grace. 3. The means appointed to make them partakers of this covenant. 4. The blessings which are effectually conveyed unto the elect by these means. — Which four heads are set down each of them in some few propositions.

HEAD 1:

Our Woeful Condition by Nature, Through Breaking the Divine Pledge, Communion, and Righteous Law of God. *O Israel, thou hast destroyed thyself* — Hosea 13:9.

1. The almighty and eternal God, the Father, the Son, and the Holy Spirit, three distinct persons in the one and the same undivided Godhead, equally infinite in all perfections, did, before time, most wisely decree, for His own glory, whatsoever cometh to pass in time: and doth most holily and infallibly execute all His decrees, without being partaker of the sin of any creature.

2. This God, in six days, made all things of nothing, very good in their own kind: in special, He made all the angels holy; and He made our first parents, Adam and Eve, the root of mankind, both upright and able to obey His command not to eat of the tree of knowledge of good and evil and to keep the law written in their heart, all of which they were naturally bound to obey under pain of death; and whilst they kept it, they were happy in their communion with God, and had dominion over the creatures. Yet they, nor their posterity in them, could ever have attained the hope of life and eternal rest, upon condition of perfect personal obedience, but by some voluntary condescension on God's part, which He hath been pleased to express by way of covenant, the solemn promissory oath of God.

3. Both angels and men were subject to the change of their own free will, as experience proved, (God having reserved to Himself the incommunicable property of being naturally unchangeable:)

for many angels of their own accord fell by sin from their first estate, and became devils. Our first parents, being enticed by Satan, one of these devils speaking in a serpent, did break the divine pledge, communion, and righteous law of God, in eating the forbidden fruit; whereby they, and their posterity, being in their loins, as branches in the root, and the guilt of the sin imputed to them, became not only liable to eternal death, but also lost all ability to please God; yea, did become by nature enemies to God, and to all spiritual good, and inclined only to evil continually. This is our original sin, the bitter root of all our actual transgressions, in thought, word, and deed.

HEAD 2:

The Remedy Provided in Jesus Christ for the Elect by the Covenant of Grace. *O Israel, thou hast destroyed thyself; but in me is thine help* — Hosea 13:9.

1. Albeit man, having brought himself into this woeful condition, be neither able to help himself, nor willing to be helped by God out of it, but rather inclined to lie still, insensible of it, till he perish; yet God, for the glory of His rich grace, hath revealed in His word a way to save sinners, *viz.* by faith in Jesus Christ, the eternal Son of God, by virtue of, and according to the tenor of that eternal purpose and secret counsel of redemption, resolved and agreed upon between God the Father, God the Son, and God the Holy Spirit, in the council of the Trinity, before the world began.

2. The sum of the counsel of redemption is this: God having freely chosen unto life a certain number of lost mankind, for the glory of His rich grace, did determine to give them, before the world began, unto God the Son, appointed Redeemer, that He would humble Himself so far as to assume the human nature, of a soul and a body, unto personal union with His divine nature, and submit Himself to the law, as surety for them, and satisfy justice for them, by giving obedience in their name, even unto the suffering of the cursed death of the cross, He should ransom and redeem them all from sin and death, and purchase unto them righteousness and eternal life, with all saving graces leading thereunto; to be effectually, by means of His own appointment, applied in due time to every one of them by God the Holy Spirit, who is the Helper sent from the Father and the Son to convict the world of sin, and of righteousness, and of judgment. This eternal will the Son of God (who is Jesus Christ our Lord) and the Holy Spirit did undertake before the world began, and in the fullness of time the Son came into the world, was born of the Virgin Mary, subjected Himself to the law, and completely paid the ransom on the cross: But by virtue of the foresaid counsel, determined before the world began, He is in all ages, since the fall of Adam, still upon the work of applying actually the purchased benefits unto the elect; and that He doth by way of a covenant of free

grace and reconciliation with them, through faith in Himself; by which covenant, He makes over to every believer a right and interest to Himself, and to all His blessings.

3. For the fulfillment of this determinate counsel of redemption, and making the elect partakers of the benefits thereof in the covenant of grace, Christ Jesus was clad with the threefold office of Prophet, Priest, and King: made a Prophet, to reveal all saving knowledge to His people, and to persuade them to believe and obey the same; made a Priest, to offer up Himself a sacrifice once for them all, and to intercede continually with the Father, for making their persons and services acceptable to Him; and made a King, to subdue them to Himself, to feed and rule them by His own appointed ordinances, and to defend them from their enemies.

HEAD 3:

The Outward Means Appointed to Make the Elect Partakers of This Covenant, and All the Rest That are Called, to be Inexcusable. *Many are called* — Matthew 22:14.

1. The outward means and ordinances, for making men partakers of the covenant of grace, are so wisely dispensed, as that the elect shall be infallibly converted and saved by them; and the reprobate, among whom they are, not to be justly stumbled: The means are especially these four. 1. The word of God. 2. The holy ordinances of baptism and the Lord's Supper. 3. Public worship. 4. Prayer. In the word of God preached by sent messengers, the Lord makes offer of grace to all sinners, upon condition of faith in Jesus Christ and repentance toward God; and whosoever do confess their sin, accept of Christ offered, and submit themselves to His ordinances, He will have them received into the honour and privileges of the covenant of grace. By the holy ordinances of baptism and the Lord's Supper, God will have them be a sign of His fellowship and a pledge of their communion with Him. By public worship, He will have them hedged in, and helped forward unto the keeping of the covenant. And by prayer, He will have His own glorious grace, promised in the covenant, to be daily drawn forth, acknowledged, and employed. All which means are followed either really, or in profession only, according to the quality of the covenanters, as they are true or counterfeit believers.

2. The covenant of grace, set down in the Old Testament before Christ came, and in the New since He came, is one and the same in substance, albeit successively revealed through the divine covenants of promise: For under the law, laid upon the foundation of the Noahic Covenants, it is held forth to the people of the Jews through the Abrahamic Covenant, the Old Covenant, and the Davidic Covenant, all fore-signifying Christ's death to come, and the benefits purchased thereby, under the shadow of bloody sacrifices, and sundry ceremonies: but since Christ came, the covenant of grace doth clearly and fully reveal Christ, already crucified before our eyes, through the New Covenant, victorious

over death and the grave in the visible and outward signs of baptism and the Lord's Supper; and gloriously ruling heaven and earth, for the good of His own people, through the Messianic Covenant where the priesthood is united with the kingship eternally after the order of Melchizedek by virtue of the solemn promissory oath of God.

HEAD 4:

The Blessings which are Effectually Conveyed by these Means to the Lord's Elect, or Chosen Ones. *Many are called, but few are chosen* — Matthew 22:14.

1. By these outward ordinances, as our Lord makes the reprobate inexcusable, so, by the power of His Spirit, He applies unto the elect, effectually, all saving graces purchased and determined to them in the counsel of redemption, and maketh a change in their persons. In particular, 1. He doth regenerate them, by giving spiritual life to them, in opening their understandings, renewing their wills, affections, and faculties, for giving spiritual obedience to His commands. 2. He gives them saving faith, by making them, in the sense of deserved condemnation, to give their consent heartily to the covenant of grace, and to embrace Jesus Christ unfeignedly. 3. He gives them repentance, by making them, with godly sorrow, in the hatred of sin, and love of righteousness, turn from all iniquity to the service of God. And, 4. He sanctifies them, by making them go on and persevere in faith and spiritual obedience to the law of God, manifested by fruitfulness in all duties, and doing good works, as God offereth occasion.

2. Together with this inward change of their persons, God changes also their state: for, so soon as they are brought by faith into the covenant of grace, 1. He justifies them, by imputing unto them that perfect obedience which Christ gave to the law, and the satisfaction also which upon the cross Christ gave unto justice in their name. 2. He reconciles them, and makes them friends to God, who were before enemies to God. 3. He adopts them, that they shall be no more children of Satan, but children of God, enriched with all spiritual privileges of His sons. And, last of all, after their warfare in this life is ended, He perfects the holiness and blessedness, first of their souls at their death, and then both of their souls and their bodies, being joyfully joined together again in the resurrection, at the day of His glorious coming to judgment, when all the wicked shall be sent away to hell, with Satan; whom they have served: but Christ's own

chosen and redeemed ones, true believers, students of holiness, shall remain with Himself forever, in the state of glorification.

INDEX

OF

THE CHIEF SUBJECTS CONTAINED IN THE CONFESSION OF FAITH AND CATECHISMS

LCR: The London Confession of Faith Revised
LLC: The London Larger Catechism
LSC: The London Shorter Catechism

D

E

F

G

H

I

T

www.ingramcontent.com/pod-product-compliance
Lightning Source LLC
Chambersburg PA
CBHW031824090426
42741CB00005B/122

* 9 7 8 0 9 9 7 9 6 8 0 0 2 *